D1231965

*Q and the
History of Early Christianity*

Q and the History of Early Christianity

Studies on Q

CHRISTOPHER M. TUCKETT

HENDRICKSON
PUBLISHERS

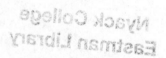

Typeset by Waverley Typesetters, Galashiels
Printed and bound in Great Britain by Bell & Bain Ltd, Glasgow

For

KATE, MARK AND JOHN

Contents

Preface

This book has been a long time in its gestation as well as in its writing. My interests in Q were first aroused during my doctoral studies whilst writing a thesis on the Revival of the Griesbach Hypothesis, with its rejection of the necessity to postulate any Q document at all. Since my thesis was finished in 1979, various aspects of the problems associated with Q have occupied me in different ways. The present volume is an attempt to collect together some of my thoughts on a number of aspects of the study of Q to try to bring various strands together. Inevitably there are several loose ends which critics will no doubt be able to identify very easily. It may be that others can tie them together more neatly than I have been able to do. Nevertheless it seemed worthwhile to try to see if sense can be made of the Q tradition as a unified whole. I remain convinced that Q did exist, and have tried to give my reasons in the first chapter. It then seemed reasonable to try to determine what kind of document Q was, whether it gave a characteristic or distinctive presentation of the Jesus tradition, and who might have preserved the tradition in just this form. The rest of the book is an attempt to begin to answer some of these questions in a preliminary way. Others will no doubt be able either to develop some of the ideas here further, or alternatively demolish them for good.

A number of sections in the book are based on my earlier published work, and are reproduced here with kind permission of the publishers concerned. Chapter 1 is a slightly expanded version of my 'The Existence of Q', in R. A. Piper (ed.), *The Gospel Behind the Gospels. Current Studies on Q* (NovTSupp 75; Leiden: Brill, 1994) 19–47; some of the material in chapter 4 was first published in 'Q, Prayer and the Kingdom', *JTS* 40 (1989) 367–76, and appears here somewhat revised; part of chapter 7 is a revised version of my 'Luke 4, Isaiah and Q', in J. Delobel (ed.), *LOGIA. Les Paroles de Jésus — The Sayings of Jesus* (BETL 59; Leuven: Leuven

University Press & Peeters, 1982) 343–54; a section of chapter 8 appeared in 'The Son of Man in Q', in M. C. de Boer (ed.), *From Jesus of John* (FS M. de Jonge; Sheffield: Sheffield Academic Press, 1993) 196–215; part of chapter 10 also appeared as 'A Cynic Q?', *Biblica* 70 (1989) 349–76.

Research for this book was substantially assisted by some generous grants. The Alexander von Humboldt Stiftung, Bonn, granted me a fellowship to study in Marburg for nine months in 1988, when a great deal of preliminary research and some early drafts were written. The Faculty of Arts Research Committee of the University of Manchester kindly made available money to provide some teaching assistance in 1993 to enable more time to be spent on research. And the British Academy kindly awarded me a Fellowship in 1994, extending a period of sabbatical leave from my own University from one semester to a full academic year, which enabled me to finish the book for publication. To all these bodies I am very grateful.

Throughout my studies I have been enormously helped and stimulated by other scholars working in the same field. Many of them I have never, or only very occasionally and briefly, met in person. The general state of Q studies in the United Kingdom is now such that the vast majority of those engaged in such work are based outside my own home country! I hope that those with whom I have ventured to disagree at times will accept my very sincere appreciation for their work and stimulus. I would especially like to thank Professor James Robinson of Claremont, and Professor John Kloppenborg of Toronto, for kindly corresponding with me and also sending me some of their unpublished material, or sending in advance some of their not yet published work. I would also like to thank my host in Marburg, Professor Dieter Lührmann, who made my stay there especially enjoyable: I am very grateful to him for his kindness and his friendship, both during and after my time in Germany. Finally I owe a great debt to Professor David Catchpole, who has been over the last twenty years variously doctoral supervisor, mentor, friend and helper. It was he who initiated me into the delights — and complexities — of synoptic research, and his own magisterial work on Q has influenced me very considerably (though with no pressure from him to do so), as is no doubt apparent at several points. Needless to say, however, if the inspiration is his, the blemishes in the present work are entirely my responsibility.

My wife and children have borne with the struggles of this project at second hand for many years. In relation to the former, a comment in the present context would be traditional, but totally inadequate. To the latter, for keeping me in the realms of sanity, this book is dedicated with thanks.

Abbreviations

2ST	Two Source Theory
AnB	Analecta Biblica
ANRW	W. Haase & H. Temporini (eds), *Aufstieg und Niedergang der Römischen Welt* (Berlin & New York: de Gruyter)
BAG	W. Bauer, W. F. Arndt, F. W. Gingrich, *A Greek-English Lexicon of the New Testament and Other Early Christian Literature* (ET Chicago: University of Chicago Press, 1957)
BBB	Bonner Biblische Beiträge
BDF	F. Blass, A. Debrunner, R. W. Funk, *A Greek Grammar of the New Testament and Other Early Christian Literature* (ET Chicago & London: University of Chicago Press, 1961)
BETL	Bibliotheca Ephemeridum Theologicarum Lovaniensium
BJRL	Bulletin of the John Rylands Library
BZ	Biblische Zeitschrift
BZNW	Beiheft zur Zeitschrift für die neutesamentliche Wissenschaft
CBQ	Catholic Biblical Quarterly
ET	English Translation
ETL	Ephemerides Theologicae Lovanienses
EvTh	Evangelische Theologie
ExpT	Expository Times
FRLANT	Forschungen zur Religion und Literatur des Alten und Neuen Testaments
FS	Festschrift

FzB	Forschung zur Bibel
FZPT	Freiburger Zeitschrift für Philosophie und Theologie
GH	Griesbach Hypothesis
GTh	Gospel of Thomas
GTA	Göttinger Theologische Arbeiten
HTR	Harvard Theological Review
Int	Interpretation
JAC	Jahrbuch für Antike und Christentum
JBL	Journal of Biblical Literature
JR	Journal of Religion
JSNT	Journal for the Study of the New Testament
JSNTSS	Journal for the Study of the New Testament Supplement Series
JSJ	Journal for the Study of Judaism
JSP	Journal for the Study of the Pseudepigrapha
JTS	Journal of Theological Studies
LkR	Lukan redaction
MA	Minor agreement
MattR	Matthean redaction
MkR	Markan redaction
MP	Markan priority
MThA	Münsteraner Theologische Abhandlungen
NovT	Novum Testamentum
NovTSupp	Novum Testamentum Supplements
NTAbh	Neutestamentliche Abhandlungen
NTOA	Novum Testamentum et Orbis Antiquus
NTS	New Testament Studies
SB	H. L. Strack & P. Billerbeck, *Kommentar zum Neuen Testament aus Talmud und Midrasch* (München: C. H. Beck, 1926)
SBL	Society of Biblical Literature
SBLDS	Society of Biblical Literature Dissertation Series
SBS	Stuttgarter Bibelstudien
SM	Son of Man

SNTU	Studien zum Neuen Testament und seiner Umwelt
SNTSMS	Society of New Testament Studies Monograph Series
StEv	*Studia Evangelica*
TTZ	Trier Theologische Zeitschrift
TU	Texte und Untersuchungen
TWNT	G. Kittel and G. Friedrich (eds), *Theologisches Wörterbuch zum Neuen Testament* (Stuttgart: Kohlhammer, 1933–1979)
TynBull	Tyndale Bulletin
WMANT	Wissenschaftliche Monographien zum Alten und Neuen Testament
WUNT	Wissenschaftliche Untersuchungen zum Neuen Testament
ZNW	Zeitschrift für die neutestamentliche Wissenschaft
ZThK	Zeitschrift für Theologie und Kirche

1

Introduction: The Existence of Q

This study is about 'Q', the 'name' given to the source material believed to lie behind the gospels of Matthew and Luke. The 'standard' solution to the Synoptic Problem, i.e. the problem of the relationship between the three synoptic gospels, is often known as the Two Source Theory (2ST). According to this theory, one of the major sources common to Matthew and Luke is the gospel of Mark. But Mark's gospel cannot account for all the agreements between Matthew and Luke. In order to account for these further, non-Markan, Matthew–Luke agreements, many have resorted to a theory of a lost source, or a lost body of (possibly disparate) source materials. This material is usually known today as 'Q'.[1]

In contemporary gospel studies, 'Q' has aroused considerable interest. Several scholars have tried to identify characteristic and distinctive features of the Q material, some trying to delineate a theology of Q, some seeking to identify a particular group of Christians responsible for the collection and editing of the Q material. Indeed the major part of this study will be devoted to such an approach to Q. For others, such a venture is the height of absurdity. It represents the attempt to determine 'the hypothetical theology of the hypothetical community of the

---

[1] Precisely when the siglum 'Q' was established as the designation of this postulated source has itself been the subject of a mini-debate. Scholars in the early and mid-nineteenth century had tended to refer to a 'Sayings Source' or a 'Logia Source'. (Holtzmann referred to this source as 'Λ': see ch. 2 below.) The credit (or otherwise!) for the change in nomenclature has sometimes been ascribed to P. Wernle (see, for example, S. Schulz, *Q — Die Spruchquelle der Evangelisten* [Zürich: TVZ, 1971] 15; H. H. Stoldt, *History and Criticism of the Marcan Hypothesis* [ET Edinburgh: T. & T. Clark, 1980] 112). But more recent study is probably correct in seeing the origin of the Q siglum in the work of J. Weiss: see F. Neirynck, 'The Symbol Q (= Quelle)', *ETL* 54 (1978) 119–25, repr. in *Evangelica I* (BETL 60; Leuven University Press & Peeters, 1982) 683–90, referring to an article by Weiss of 1890.

hypothetical document Q',[2] being based on a 'text' which many today would deny ever existed at all. Certainly in all discussions about Q, all are agreed that *if* Q ever existed, it is now lost and we possess no manuscript copy of it. Further, it appears to have left little or no influence on any extant documents in early Christianity other than the gospels of Matthew and Luke.[3] Is it then justifiable to talk of 'Q' as a well-defined body of material when the evidence for its existence appears to be so slim?

In general terms one must say initially that the apparent silence elsewhere in the tradition about any evidence of Q is not particularly surprising, and certainly no bar to postulating the existence of a Q source. It is quite clear that our knowledge of primitive Christianity is at best somewhat fragmentary. There are a number of texts whose existence we know of, or can postulate, but which we do not possess. For example, we know of the existence of Jewish Christian gospels such as the Gospel of the Hebrews from citations in the Church fathers, although we have no manuscript copies of these gospels;[4] from Paul's extant letters we can deduce the existence of other letters written by Paul (e.g.

---

[2] See E. E. Ellis, 'Gospel Criticism', in P. Stuhlmacher (ed.), *Das Evangelium und die Evangelien* (WUNT 28; Tübingen: Mohr, 1983) 27–54, p. 35. Cf. also E. P. Sanders & M. Davies, *Studying the Synoptic Gospels* (London: SCM, 1989) 116: 'This work [seeking to discover a theology, or a community, of Q] is mostly of curiosity value, since it shows how far a hypothesis can be pushed despite its lack of fundamental support.' M. D. Hooker, 'In His Own Image', in M. D. Hooker & S. G. Wilson (eds), *What About the New Testament? Essays in Honour of Christopher Evans* (London: SCM, 1975) 28–44, p. 30, also bemoans the attempt to write a theology of Q 'without really considering the question whether Q ever existed' (with reference to R. A. Edwards).

[3] Occasionally attempts have been made to try to find evidence of Q (or something closely related to Q) in other texts, e.g. in 1 Corinthians, or in some of the Nag Hammadi texts, notably the Gospel of Thomas. I have examined some of these claims elsewhere with uniformly negative results: there appears to be no clear evidence for the existence of anything akin to Q lying behind any of these other texts. For 1 Corinthians, see my '1 Corinthians and Q', *JBL* 102 (1983) 607–19. For Thomas, see my 'Thomas and the Synoptics', *NovT* 30 (1988) 132–57, and 'Q and Thomas: Evidence of a Primitive "Wisdom Gospel"?, *ETL* 67 (1991) 346–60. For the other Nag Hammadi texts, see my *Nag Hammadi and the Gospel Tradition* (Edinburgh: T. & T. Clark, 1986). The attempt to see evidence of Q in the tradition behind James by P. J. Hartin, *James and the Q Sayings of Jesus* (JSNTSS 47; Sheffield Academic Press, 1991), suffers somewhat by failing to provide clear criteria for identifying what is Q and by being rather optimistic in locating parallels.

[4] See E. Hennecke (ed.), *New Testament Apocrypha. Volume One* (London: SCM, 1963) 117–65.

to Corinth) which have not been preserved. We know too of areas of primitive Christianity, for example in Egypt or in Rome, that must have developed very quickly but which have left little or no literary deposit. Thus the fact that Q, if it existed, has not left its mark on other preserved elements within primitive Christianity is not necessarily surprising. Such silence may simply indicate the sparse extent of the evidence which has survived.

Further, we may note that, if Q was used by Matthew and Luke, such use would almost certainly have led to a lessening of concern to preserve Q itself.[5] The situation may not have been dissimilar to that involving Mark and the other two synoptic gospels. If Mark was used by Matthew and Luke, then the very fact of (say) Matthew's existence inevitably led to an eclipse in interest in Mark, since Mark must have appeared to many to be somewhat redundant alongside the fuller gospel of Matthew.[6] Certainly we know that in the period after the writing of the gospels, Matthew was the most widely used and interest in Mark's gospel was severely limited.[7] It is easy to conceive of the same happening with Q, if it existed. The appearance of Matthew and Luke's gospels must inevitably have led to Q's being regarded as somewhat redundant and hence its lack of prominence elsewhere in primitive Christianity is not at all surprising. Nevertheless the non-appearance of Q in any explicit manuscript form has always led some to doubt the existence of such a source, and such doubts have continued right up to the present.

One should however note that the question 'Did Q exist?' is not necessarily as straightforward as it appears at first sight, or perhaps better, any alleged straight 'yes' or 'no' answer to the question might need some further clarification. The theory of the existence of a Q source arose as part of the 2ST to explain the agreements between the texts of Matthew and Luke which were not to be explained by common dependence on Mark. These agreements are often so close, amounting at times to almost verbatim agreement in the Greek texts of the gospels (cf. Q 3:7–9;

---

[5] Cf. G. D. Kilpatrick, 'The Disappearance of Q', *JTS* 42 (1941) 182–4.

[6] The same is true even if Mark was written after Matthew.

[7] Cf. E. Massaux, *Influence de l'Evangile de saint Matthieu sur la littérature chrétienne avant saint Irénée* (repr. BETL 75; Leuven: Leuven University Press & Peeters, 1986).

11:9f.),[8] that some form of literary relationship seems to be demanded: either one evangelist has used the work of the other directly, or both are dependent on (a) common source(s).[9]

At one level, the Q hypothesis is simply a negative theory, denying the possibility that one evangelist made direct use of the work of the other.[10] However, within such a denial, a variety of positions can be adopted. One could, for example, argue that Luke and Matthew both had access to a single common source which existed as a self-contained written document. (This is often regarded as 'the' Q hypothesis.) Alternatively, whilst still denying any direct use of Matthew by Luke, one could argue that Matthew and Luke depend at various points in the tradition on a variety of different source materials, and the nature and extent of these materials might have been rather varied: some might have formed smaller written collections, some might have constituted isolated traditions preserved orally.[11] On this view, the whole of the so-called Q material may never have been collected into a single document prior to its use by Matthew and Luke and we should perhaps speak of 'Q material' rather than 'Q' *simpliciter*. Advocates of such a theory might say 'no' to the question 'Did Q exist?', meaning by this that they were denying the existence of a single, well-defined (possibly written) 'source' or document called Q.

[8] In accordance with what is now becoming standard convention, I give the references to verses in Q using the chapter and verse numbers of the Lukan version of the saying(s) in question, prefaced by 'Q'. Thus 'Q 3:7–9' refers to the Q saying which appears in Luke 3:7–9. Such a decision is purely one of convenience and is in no way intended to prejudge the issue of whether Luke's version of the saying is more original or not.

[9] The almost verbatim nature of the verbal agreement between Matthew and Luke in examples such as this makes it almost mandatory to accept that a literary relationship is involved: a theory of common dependence on oral tradition seems insufficient to account for such close agreement.

[10] For various reasons, this is almost always postulated in the form of Luke's dependence on Matthew. Matthean dependence on Luke is hardly ever advocated, though one sometimes wonders why given the tendency of many to believe that Luke's version is very often more original (cf. below). However, Luke 1:1 clearly implies that Luke is aware of the existence of predecessors in writing some account of Jesus' ministry.

[11] Cf. Ellis, 'Gospel Criticism', 37. Cf. too the classic theory of W. Bussmann, *Synoptische Studien* (Halle: Buchhandlung des Waisenhauses, 1929), arguing for two quite separate Q sources, one in Greek, one in Aramaic. Similarly, more recently, C. J. A. Hickling, 'The Plurality of "Q"', in Delobel (ed.), *LOGIA*, 425–9.

But they would not be pleading for any direct dependence of Luke on Matthew. Further, even amongst those who have tended to think in terms of a single well-defined Q, there has been a notable trend in recent years to argue for stages in the development of Q, so that we have Q^1, Q^2, Q^3, etc. and 'Q' itself is by no means a static, monolithic entity.[12] Others again have argued that the 'Q' used by Matthew and Luke may have been available to the two evangelists in different forms, a Q^{mt} and a Q^{lk}.[13]

It is also possible to combine some of these theories. For example, the question of whether Luke used Matthew could be answered differently in relation to different parts of the tradition. Thus Luke may have known Matthew's gospel and used it on some occasions; but at other points Luke may have had access to other sources which provided him with his information about the relevant tradition.[14]

There is not enough space in the course of this chapter to examine every nuance of every theory that has in some way or other denied the existence of Q as a single source. Thus simply in order to keep the discussion within manageable limits I shall confine attention in what follows to those who have tried to deny the existence of 'Q' by arguing explicitly for Luke's knowledge and direct use of Matthew.

The theory that Luke used Matthew has always had a number of defenders and is still advocated strenuously by some today. Within the history of scholarship, the Q hypothesis arose as part of the 2ST, and hence is frequently coupled with the theory of Markan priority (MP). However, the two theories are not inseparable. Thus some today have retained a belief in MP, but have argued that Luke is directly dependent on Matthew as well

[12] See above all J. S. Kloppenborg, *The Formation of Q* (Philadelphia: Fortress Press, 1987), and many essays of H. Schürmann, including 'Das Zeugnis der Redenquelle für die Basileia-Verkündigung Jesu', in Delobel (ed.), *LOGIA*, 121–200, and 'Beobachtungen zum Menschensohn-Titel in der Redequelle', in *Jesus und der Menschensohn* (FS A. Vögtle; Freiburg: Herder, 1975) 124–47.

[13] For a discussion of this, see ch. 3 below.

[14] In recent times the view of R. Morgenthaler, *Statistische Synopse* (Zürich: Gotthelf, 1971), esp. 300ff. Also R. H. Gundry, *Matthew: A Commentary on His Literary and Theological Art* (Grand Rapids: Eerdmans, 1982); and his 'Matthean Foreign Bodies in Agreements of Luke with Matthew against Mark', in Van Segbroek et al (eds), *The Four Gospels 1992*, 1467–95. The view of Farmer and other supporters of the Griesbach Hypothesis often reduces to this: cf. below.

as on Mark (see (1) below).[15] Other scholars have however questioned MP itself and this in turn has led to a rejection of the Q hypothesis in various ways. Thus for some, Mark is directly dependent on Matthew alone, with Luke then dependent on Matthew and Mark (the so-called Augustinian hypothesis: see (2) below).[16] Several recently have argued that Mark's gospel comes last of the three, dependent on Matthew and Luke and representing a conflation of those two gospels, with Luke directly dependent on Matthew alone (the Griesbach hypothesis [GH]: see (3) below).[17] The 'traditional' Q hypothesis is represented by (4):

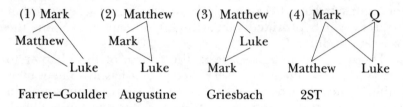

One must however note that, in relation to the agreements between Matthew and Luke, these all represent rather different solutions. For example, (1) above presumes that Luke used Mark as well as Matthew; hence some of the Matthew–Luke agreements are due to common dependence on Mark. (2) also assumes that Mark is the mediator of some of the material common to Matthew and Luke. On the other hand, (3) presupposes that all the agreements between Matthew and Luke are due to Lukan

[15] Cf. A. Farrer, 'On Dispensing with Q', in D. E. Nineham (ed.), *Studies in the Gospels. Essays in Memory of R. H. Lightfoot* (Oxford: Blackwell, 1967) 55–88; H. B. Green, 'The Credibility of Luke's Transformation of Matthew' and 'Matthew 12.22–50 and Parallels: An Alternative to Matthean Conflation', in Tuckett (ed.), *Synoptic Studies*, 131–56, 157–76; and above all the works of M. D. Goulder, especially his 'On Putting Q to the Test', *NTS* 24 (1978) 218–34, and *Luke — A New Paradigm* (JSNTSS 20; Sheffield Academic Press, 1989).

[16] In recent years B. C. Butler, *The Originality of St Matthew* (Cambridge University Press, 1951); J. W. Wenham, *Redating Matthew, Mark & Luke* (London: Hodder & Stoughton, 1991).

[17] See above all the works of W. R. Farmer, *The Synoptic Problem* (London: Macmillan, 1964), and many other works since; also the relevant essays in D. L. Dungan (ed.), *The Interrelations of the Gospels* (BETL 95; Leuven University Press & Peeters, 1990). In recent years, advocates of the Griesbach hypothesis have preferred the description 'Two-Gospel Hypothesis', though without any change in the hypothesis itself. I have kept the earlier term here.

dependence on Matthew alone since Mark had not yet been written. In (1) and (2) the relationship between Matthew and Luke is rather different from that implied by (3), and explanations of Luke's use of Matthew in non-Markan passages cannot *ipso facto* be regarded as explanations of Luke's use of Matthew in the whole tradition without more ado.

There is clearly not enough space here to discuss all the solutions in detail. In terms of contemporary scholarship, the most influential theories which claim to deny the existence of Q by referring to Luke's direct knowledge of, and use of, Matthew are probably (1) and (3) above: the GH ((3) above) has a small but influential body of support today; and (1) above, accepting MP but denying Q, is argued most strongly by M. D. Goulder. It is on these as the main alternatives to the Q theory that I shall focus attention in the rest of this chapter.

1. Traditional Arguments for Q

Before looking at these alternative explanations of the Matthew–Luke agreements themselves, we should perhaps consider the standard arguments used to defend the Q hypothesis and how the evidence to which they refer can be related to these other theories. The arguments are mostly of a negative form, claiming that Luke's use of Matthew seems very improbable. If then one decides that Luke did not know Matthew, the options available within some kind of 'Q' theory are not uniform, as we have already seen. However, at this point I shall consider only the problem of whether Luke can plausibly be seen to have known and used Matthew. The main arguments against this view can be considered under four headings.[18]

1.1. Matthew's Additions to Mark

Luke never appears to know any of Matthew's additions to Mark in Markan material. Sometimes, in using Mark, Matthew makes

[18] For standard defences of the Q hypothesis, see W. G. Kümmel, *Introduction to the New Testament* (ET London: SCM, 1975) 63ff.; J. A. Fitzmyer, 'The Priority of Mark and the "Q" Source in Luke', in *Jesus and Man's Hope I* (Pittsburgh Theological Seminary, 1970) 131–70, repr. in *To Advance the Gospel: New Testament Studies* (New York: Crossroad, 1981) 3–40. Cf. too P. Vassiliadis, 'Did Q Exist?', Ἐκκλησία καὶ Θεολογία 1 (1980) 287–328.

substantial additions to Mark, cf. Matt 12:5–7; 14:28–31; 16:16–19; 27:19, 24.[19] If Luke knew Matthew, why does he never show any knowledge of Matthew's redaction of Mark? It seems easiest to presume that Luke did not know of these Matthean additions to Mark and hence did not know Matthew.[20]

Such an argument clearly presupposes MP and might at first sight appear irrelevant for other hypotheses which deny MP, especially the Augustinian or Griesbach hypotheses.[21] Yet essentially the same problem is still there for both these alternative hypotheses. For the Augustinian hypothesis, the problem is similar though the Matthew–Mark relationship is reversed. The longer Matthean version is now abbreviated by Mark; but why then does Luke consistently ignore the longer Matthean versions? Why too has Mark abbreviated Matthew in the first place?[22] Very similar problems are faced by the GH in these passages, though with different 'actors'. On the GH, Mark comes third and so is irrelevant to the problem of Luke's use of Matthew, but the problems are fundamentally similar: why does Mark consistently ignore the longer Matthean versions? And why has Luke abbreviated Matthew in the first place? No answer in detail in relation to these passages has (as far as I am aware) been offered by contemporary advocates of the GH. Goulder's answer to the problem is to claim that, when using Mark, Luke generally used that gospel as his main source and did not use Matthew at all in Markan passages. In abstract terms this is quite plausible though, as we shall see, it scarcely explains all the required facts satisfactorily (cf. below).

1.2. Order

After the opening pericopes of the Baptism and the Temptation narratives, none of the non-Markan material which Luke shares with Matthew appears in the same context relative to the non-

---

[19] Further examples in J. A. Fitzmyer, *The Gospel according to Luke I–IX* (New York: Doubleday, 1981) 73f.

[20] The situation is quite different in a very few passages, the so-called 'overlap' passages, where Luke seems to know *only* Matthew's additions to Mark and resolutely ignores both Mark and Matthew's use of Mark. These are discussed separately below in section 4.

[21] Cf. W. R. Farmer, 'A Response to Joseph Fitzmyer's Defense of the Two Document Hypothesis', in Farmer (ed.), *New Synoptic Studies* (Macon: Mercer University Press, 1983) 501–523, pp. 517f.

[22] The issue is not discussed by Butler or Wenham.

Markan material in the two gospels. Streeter's (slightly polemical) statement of the facts is often cited in this context:

> If then Luke derived this material from Matthew, he must have gone through both Matthew and Mark so as to discriminate with meticulous precision between Marcan and non-Marcan material; he must then have proceeded with the utmost care to tear every little piece of non-Marcan material he desired to use from the context of Mark in which it appeared in Matthew — in spite of the fact that contexts in Matthew are always exceedingly appropriate — in order to re-insert it into a different context of Mark having no special appropriateness. A theory which would make an author capable of such a proceeding would only be tenable if, on other grounds, we had reason to believe he was a crank.[23]

When Luke's alleged procedure is compared with his use of Mark, the situation becomes even harder to envisage, for Luke generally preserves Mark's order closely. Thus many have concluded that Luke cannot have proceeded in such a radically different way in relation to his two alleged sources. Rather, Luke's use of Mark suggests that he cannot have used Matthew as well in such a completely different way.

As before the same argument could apply to the Augustinian hypothesis: the problem is to try to explain the Lukan text if Luke had both Matthew and Mark before him, and the precise relationship between Matthew and Mark themselves is immaterial at this point. For the GH the problem is again slightly different, since Mark had not appeared when Luke wrote. Yet that hypothesis must still explain why Luke chose to keep some of Matthew's material in its original context (the material which, for the most part, Mark later decided to include) but to change the order of the rest very considerably.[24] There is also the further problem of explaining why Mark decided to include primarily (but not exclusively) only that material whose *order* Luke kept from Matthew. Goulder himself has attempted to meet Streeter's argument head on and give a very detailed explanation of Luke's ordering of the Matthean material: this will be considered in detail later.

[23] B. H. Streeter, *The Four Gospels* (London: Macmillan, 1924) 183.
[24] One attempt to explain this is that of B. Orchard, *Matthew, Luke & Mark* (Manchester: Koinonia, 1976); I have tried to respond to Orchard's argument in my *The Revival of the Griesbach Hypothesis* (SNTSMS 44; Cambridge University Press, 1983) 31–40.

1.3. Greater Originality

It is argued that, in the double tradition (i.e. the material common to Matthew and Luke alone), Matthew has no monopoly on the more original form of the tradition. Sometimes Matthew, sometimes Luke, seems to be more original at different points. This, it is said, tells heavily against any theory of direct dependence of Luke on Matthew since in that case we should expect Luke to have the secondary form of the tradition at every point. Examples of Luke's greater originality which are often cited include the beatitudes (Luke 6:20–23), the Lord's prayer (Luke 11:2–4) and the doom oracle (Luke 11:49–51).

With this argument the problem is the same for all defenders of Lukan dependence on Matthew. The relative position of Mark is immaterial. However, different scholars have adopted different lines of defence. Some have argued that the case for Lukan originality can at every point be countered: Luke is secondary to Matthew everywhere so that where the two gospels differ, Luke's version is due to LkR. This might be termed a 'hard-line' position and is defended most strongly today by Goulder. Others would adopt a more 'soft-line' approach, arguing that, whilst Luke is dependent on Matthew most of the time, there may be occasions where Luke had access to other sources of information which overlapped with Matthew.[25] The last option is of course not far removed from a form of the Q hypothesis (see n. 14 above and pp. 13–14 below).

1.4. Doublets

Finally, appeal is made to the presence of doublets in Matthew and Luke. One half of the doublet evidently comes from Mark (assuming MP) and, it is argued, the other can most naturally be explained as stemming from a second common source, i.e. Q. (See for example the versions of the saying about saving/losing one's life in Matt 16:25/Mark 8:35/Luke 9:24 and also in Matt 10:39/Luke 17:33.)

---

[25] So, for example, Butler, *Originality*, 16, 57, 58, 59, etc.; also Farmer, 'A Fresh Approach to Q', in J. Neusner (ed.), *Christianity, Judaism and Other Greco-Roman Cults. Studies for Morton Smith at Sixty. Part One* (Leiden: Brill, 1975) 39–50, and on several occasions since: cf. his *The Gospel of Jesus: The Pastoral Relevance of the Synoptic Problem* (Louisville: Westminster John Knox, 1994) 140, etc. Cf. too below.

This is perhaps one of the weakest arguments for the existence of a Q source. Certainly the evidence is adequately explained by the Q hypothesis; but the evidence could equally well be explained in other ways. For advocates of Matthean priority, doublets in Matthew could be due to a variety of reasons (e.g. overlapping sources in the pre-Matthean tradition, or Matthew's redactional repetition of material he wished to emphasise). For the Augustinian hypothesis, Mark would then have chosen one half of each doublet and Luke for some reason decided to include a version from Mark and a version from Matthew. (In any case, reasons for Luke's inclusion of a doublet have to be found whether Luke derived the second half of the doublet from Matthew or from Q.) Similarly, on the GH, Luke's doublets simply repeat Matthew's doublets and Mark would then have included only one half of each parallel pair.

These then are some of the main arguments for the existence of Q. As we have seen, they are mostly negative arguments, trying to refute the possibility that Luke knew Matthew. What then are the counter arguments? As already noted, the most influential theories today which advocate Luke's dependence on Matthew are probably the GH and the Goulder–Farrer theory. I consider therefore each of these in turn.

2. The GH

Not a great deal of space will be devoted to the GH in this chapter. The reasons for this are two-fold. First, the GH has been extensively debated in modern discussions since its contemporary revival in the work of W. R. Farmer and others who have followed him. There is therefore no need to rehearse in detail arguments about the GH which can be found elsewhere.[26] Secondly, it is probably fair to say that the problem of Q and the relationship between Matthew and Luke has not been at the top of the agenda in many modern scholarly discussions of the GH. The hypothesis' most controversial claim concerns the position of Mark in relation to the other gospels. Thus a great deal of attention has been focused on the problem of whether Mark should be regarded as the source of Matthew and Luke, or as a conflation of those two gospels. The precise relationship between Matthew and

---

[26] See my *Revival* and the relevant essays in Dungan (ed.), *Interrelations*.

Luke themselves has not received such detailed examination
within discussions of the GH.

This is not surprising, at least at one level. Griesbach himself
never really addressed the problem of the relationship between
Matthew and Luke in detail. Further, it is logically perfectly
possible to maintain a Griesbachian view about Mark and yet
claim that Matthew and Luke are not directly dependent on each
other. This was the view of De Wette and Bleek in the last century,
and is also the view of scholars such as Stoldt and Walker in the
current debate.[27] There is thus disagreement even within the
ranks of those who might call themselves 'Griesbachians' on the
question of the precise relationship between Matthew and Luke.

In the most recent discussions of the GH, the Matthew–Luke
relationship has still not been very much to the fore. In published
discussions in the 1980s from supporters of the GH, most attention has been focused on patristic testimony about the gospels
and on the argument from order. Indeed one recent writer called
these the 'two foundational pillars' on which the hypothesis rests.[28]
However, quite irrespective of the question whether these two
considerations do give positive support to the GH's claims about
Mark,[29] the fact is that neither really says anything about the
Matthew–Luke relationship. It is true that some patristic testimony may support the view that the gospels were written in the
order Matthew–Luke–Mark; but such witness says nothing about
the problem of whether Luke, writing after Matthew, used
Matthew's gospel directly or whether both are dependent on a
common source.[30] And the argument from order referred to
above, alluding to the absence of Matthew–Luke agreements
against Mark in order, relates only to the problem of the relative
position of Mark's gospel: it says nothing about the Matthew–
Luke relationship.

Nevertheless, for many advocates of the GH, Q is an
unnecessary hypothesis and Luke should be seen as directly
dependent on Matthew. Arguments adduced by modern

[27] Stoldt, *History*, 260; W. O. Walker, 'The State of the Synoptic Question',
Perkins Journal 40 (1987) 14–19.

[28] A. J. McNicol, 'The Composition of the Eschatological Discourse', in
Dungan (ed.), *Interrelations*, 157–200, p. 200.

[29] See my 'Response to the Two Gospel Hypothesis', in Dungan, (ed.),
Interrelations, 47–62.

[30] The only exception might be Augustine, but that is very late. The earlier
witnesses simply state the order without any comment about literary
dependence.

Griesbachians against Q very often reduce to a single appeal to 'simplicity', and a general mistrust of appealing to hypothetical sources to explain the synoptic data. Farmer made such an argument basic in his 1964 book, inaugurating the modern revival of the GH: he argued there that priority should be given first and foremost to theories which did not suppose the existence of hypothetical sources.[31] And in various other places the same argument has been alluded to and repeated without much change. Thus to take a recent example, A. J. McNicol writes:

> We believe, in balance, that the simplest solution to a literary problem should be preferred unless there is compelling evidence against it. The simpler solution (i.e. *one that does not need to postulate unnecessary hypothetical source[s]*) is to be preferred to a solution which requires such a postulation.[32]

I have argued elsewhere that such a claim is not convincing.[33] Modern Griesbachians have never denied the existence of other traditions, or even 'sources', available to all three evangelists. Unless one is prepared to argue that Matthew invented his gospel *de novo*, then Matthew according to the GH must have been heavily dependent on earlier sources and traditions. The same applies to Luke in material which is peculiar to his gospel. What is perhaps ironic in the present discussion is that many advocates of the GH today would adopt precisely this view in relation to several passages in Luke where Luke runs closely parallel to Matthew. Such a theory is said to be necessary to account for the fact that Luke's version sometimes seems to be more primitive than Matthew's parallel. Thus Farmer has argued that Luke may have had access to parallel, and more original, traditions in the parables of the lost sheep and the talents/pounds, as well as for parts of the eschatological discourse.[34] Similarly the recent detailed discussion of the eschatological discourse by a team of scholars defending the GH makes extensive appeal to the existence of such traditions available to Luke.[35]

---

[31] Farmer, *Synoptic Problem*, 209. For a discussion, and critique, of the importance of this step in Farmer's overall argumentation, see A. D. Jacobson, 'The Literary Unity of Q', *JBL* 101 (1982) 365–89, esp. pp. 367f.; also his *The First Gospel. An Introduction to Q* (Sonoma: Polebridge, 1992) 17.

[32] McNicol, 'Eschatological Discourse', 167 (stress added). For a similar appeal to 'simplicity', cf. Goulder, *Luke*, 24, and see n. 36 below.

[33] See my 'Response', 61f.

[34] See n. 25 above.

[35] See McNicol, 'Eschatological Discourse', e.g. 161.

The irony is that this is effectively some kind of Q theory. It is perhaps not the Q hypothesis that thinks of a single written 'document', or 'source', called Q. But it is a clear admission that the parallel versions cannot all be satisfactorily explained by Luke's direct use of Matthew without recourse to other (lost) sources or traditions. Further, it is equally ironic that the number of sources that has to be hypothesised is in danger of growing almost without control. For if one does not wish to argue that all these parallel traditions available to Luke were united in any kind of unified Q source prior to Luke, then the number of such 'sources' is greatly increased. To quote my earlier study:

> One could argue that the 2DH [= 2ST] is rather 'simpler' in this respect. If one were to regard the Q material as constituting a unitary source in the tradition, then an enormous amount of material in the gospels can be ascribed to just two major sources, Mark and Q. By appealing to a number of 'earlier traditions' to which Luke had access, the 2GH [= GH] potentially multiplies the number of prior sources behind the gospels to a greater extent than does the 2DH. An appeal to 'economy', or 'simplicity', to support the 2GH is thus unpersuasive. An appeal to such a criterion would appear to work against, rather than for, the hypothesis.[36]

[36] Tuckett, 'Response', 62. Parallel strictures against the alleged 'simplicity' of Goulder's theory are made by F. G. Downing, 'A Paradigm Perplex: Luke, Matthew and Mark', *NTS* 38 (1992) 15–36. Goulder is less ready to postulate extra sources (being more prepared to ascribe a very great deal to MattR), but he has to postulate a large number of other hypotheses to explain the Lukan text. To quote Downing's conclusion:

> The simplicity of an hypothesis cannot be assessed solely on the basis of the number of conjectural sources involved. Goulder's hypothesis has fewer documents than has Streeter's. But to justify it there are innumerable hypotheses about what was going on in Luke's mind. And, more serious still, we find an unquantifiable cluster of surreptitious hypotheses about an apparently fairly ordinary first-century writer's ability and willingness to ignore simple and rational contemporary compositional conventions and scribal techniques and pioneer new, complex, and self-defeating ones all of his own (pp. 34f.).

(For the question of the 'compositional conventions', see pp. 31–4 below. on the so-called 'overlap' texts as they have to be explained by Goulder's theory.) One could also add to Downing's list the hypothesis Goulder has to propose concerning Matthew's creativity; alternatively, he would have to postulate various sources to account for the non-Markan material in Matthew, and this then reduces to the situation noted above in relation to the GH.

One other point in discussions of Q by Griesbachians should also be made here. Clearly attempts to isolate a theology, or characteristic features, of Q are worthless for those who do not think that Q existed. Thus Farmer has claimed that any apparently distinctive features of the Q material arise from the fact that it is Luke who has chosen to include this material in his gospel:

> That 'Q' could have produced an 'intelligible' theology is explained by the fact that Luke selected from Matthew only material that was useful for his Gentile readers. . . . [Q] is generally free of Jewish *Tendenz* which would be offensive to Gentile readers. . . . 'Q' is more representative of Luke's version of the Jesus tradition than it is of Jesus himself.[37]

Once again, to repeat what I have written elsewhere:

> All this would be more convincing if recent studies of the theology of Q had produced a theology that was basically Lukan. But this is scarcely the case. Parts of Q show a markedly strong Jewish *Tendenz* particularly in its attitude to the Jewish Law (cf. Mt 5:18/ Lk 16:17; Mt 23:23d/Lk 11:42d). So too the 'Wisdom Christology', often thought to be one of the most distinctive features of the Q material, can hardly be said to be very characteristic of Luke since it does not recur outside the Q passages concerned (Mt 11:19/Lk 7:35; Mt 23:34/Lk 11:49).[38]

The fact that the material common to Matthew and Luke turns out to be rather un-Lukan at times (and also perhaps un-Matthean) may be a strong indication against the theory that this material is in Luke because of Luke's redactional decision to select precisely this from Matthew's gospel.

Goulder has responded to Downing, claiming that his reference to 'simplicity' only justifies prior consideration of his theory over other theories which postulate lost documents. (See his 'Luke's Compositional Origins', *NTS* 39 (1993) 150–2, p. 151.) But why 'simplicity' should be located at this specific point in the whole web of complex and interrelated hypotheses which any overall explanation of the synoptic tradition demands is not at all clear.

[37] Farmer, 'The Two Gospel Hypothesis', in Dungan (ed.), *Interrelations*, 125– 56, p. 143. Cf. also Farrer, 'On Dispensing', 57: the Q sections of Matthew 'have a special character of a sort, but a character which can be plausibly enough described as Luke-pleasingness. It seems a sufficient account of them to say that they are those parts of St. Matthew's non-Marcan material which were likely to attract St. Luke.'

[38] Tuckett, 'Response', *Interrelations*, 59.

Arguments produced by advocates of the GH against Q are thus unconvincing for many. Even if one wishes to dispute the theory of Q as a unified written 'document', the alternative of direct use by Luke of Matthew is not sustained consistently by modern Griesbachians. As often as not, by appealing to independent parallel traditions available to Luke, advocates of the GH are implicitly supporting some kind of Q theory by admitting that the evidence is better explained by a less direct relationship between Matthew and Luke themselves and by common dependence of both gospels on earlier traditions.

3. M. D. Goulder

Whilst most modern Griesbachians have been unwilling to argue that the Matthew–Luke agreements can in their entirety be explained by Luke's borrowing directly from Matthew, precisely this view has been argued in recent years with great clarity and boldness by Goulder. He has produced probably the most comprehensive series of arguments against the existence of Q (although, unlike advocates of the GH, Goulder accepts the theory of MP — hence his arguments only concern those Matthew–Luke agreements which are not explained by dependence on Mark). He has published a number of important articles on the subject, and has brought this work to a climax in the publication of a massive two-volume commentary on Luke (see n. 15 above) seeking to explain the whole of the text of Luke on the basis of dependence on Mark and Matthew alone. Goulder is by no means unique in questioning the existence of Q, even from within the presuppositions of MP (cf. n. 15 also). However, his discussion of the issue is by far the most wide-ranging and comprehensive in the contemporary debate and I shall therefore restrict my remarks in this section to the views of Goulder himself.[39] Hence in what follows I shall try to indicate where Goulder's case is perhaps weak in order to defend the theory of the existence of Q in some form.

[39] I have tried to respond to some of Goulder's earlier arguments, especially in relation to some of the minor agreements, in my 'On the Relationship between Matthew and Luke', *NTS* 30 (1984) 130–42. For a recent critique of Goulder's theory in relation to a series of sixteen individual passages in the gospels, see the first chapter of D. R. Catchpole, *The Quest for Q* (Edinburgh: T. & T. Clark, 1993) 1–59. In the discussion in this chapter, I have tried to focus on more general, methodological issues, rather than on individual passages.

Not every aspect of Goulder's arguments can be considered in detail here.[40] He starts by arguing that some knowledge of Matthew by Luke is demanded by the presence of 'minor agreements' (MAs) between Matthew and Luke in Markan material where Q presence is never postulated, e.g. in the passion narrative (cf. Mark 14:65 and pars.).[41] Clearly the MAs cause some problems for the theory of MP; yet whether they should be explained by Lukan knowledge of Matthew is not certain. Further, the MAs might show at most a subsidiary use of Matthew by Luke in Markan material; from this one might perhaps deduce a subsidiary use of Matthew in non-Markan material.[42] But the MAs themselves cannot show, even on Goulder's presuppositions, that Luke used Matthew alone where Mark was not available.[43]

---

[40] A full discussion of every point in his two-volume commentary on Luke would require at least two volumes in return!

[41] As is well known, a number of scholars have sought to explain this MA by postulating a primitive corruption in the text of Matthew's gospel, a corruption which has affected all known MSS of Matthew: see F. Neirynck, 'ΤΙΣ ΕΣΤΙΝ Ο ΠΑΙΣΑΣ ΣΕ; Mt 26,68/Lk 22,64 (diff. Mk 14,65)', *ETL* 63 (1987) 5–47, repr. in *Evangelica II* (BETL 99; Leuven University Press & Peeters, 1991) 95–138, with further literature; also my 'On the Relationship', 136f. For a discussion of the more general issue of the legitimacy of invoking a conjectural emendation in the text to solve a source-critical problem, see my 'The Minor Agreements and Textual Criticism', in G. Strecker (ed.), *Minor Agreements* (GTA 50; Göttingen: Vandenhoeck & Ruprecht, 1993) 119–143, esp. pp. 135ff. See too n. 59 below.

[42] See Neirynck, 'Recent Developments in the Study of Q', in Delobel (ed.), *LOGIA*, 29–75 (repr. in *Evangelica II*, 409–63), on p. 34, 'ΤΙΣ ΕΣΤΙΝ', 27, Also T. A. Friedrichsen, 'The Matthew–Luke Agreements against Mark', in Neirynck (ed.), *L'Evangile de Luc*, 335–92, esp. pp. 375f., 384, 391.

[43] Goulder has in the past placed great weight on the value of the MAs in relation to the question of the existence of Q: his earlier (1978) article, discussing twelve significant MAs, was entitled 'On Putting Q to the Test' (n. 15 above). So too, a number of sentences in his *Luke* volume suggest that he thinks that a few agreements, or even a single one, would win the day in the battle against Q. Thus: 'If there were one significant and clear MA in the Passion story, then we should know that Luke was following Matthew; *and Q, and with it the whole structure, would be undermined*' (*Luke*, 6). And having cited the famous MA in Mark 14:65, he says: 'It might seem that we have done it in one: *Q (and with it much of the paradigm) are under threat of ruin*' (*Luke*, 7: italics mine in both instances). Yet, as already noted, such claims about the demise of the whole Q hypothesis are probably premature: as noted above, the MAs can only show at most a limited, subsidiary influence of Matthew on Luke (n. 42 above).

Goulder has sought to respond to this in a recent paper, defending again his appeal to (most of) his MAs which formed the basis of his 1978 'On Putting Q to the Test' article. Thus in response to my own, and Friedrichsen's, comments

One other preliminary point made by Goulder is about the allegedly 'unscientific' argumentation of defenders of the Q hypothesis. He claims that defenders of Q constantly change their theories to meet problems (e.g. the MAs): as a result the theory becomes almost unfalsifiable and hence worthless.[44] By contrast he claims that his own theory is falsifiable: he adopts what might be termed a 'hard-line' position, arguing that at *every* point Luke's version is secondary to Matthew. Hence if just one example could be produced where Luke's version is more original than Matthew's, this would be enough to falsify the theory. Goulder thus claims that his own theory is falsifiable, and hence more scientific than those he is opposing. Whether this is in fact the case remains to be seen.

As well as giving a detailed commentary on the whole of the text of Luke, Goulder offers a number of more general arguments by way of criticisms of the Q hypothesis and in favour of his own theories. These may be divided in two major categories: linguistic arguments, and arguments based on the choice and ordering of the material.

3.1. *Linguistic Arguments*

Within this category Goulder's arguments may be sub-divided further into discussions of Matthew and of Luke respectively.

---

about the title of this article, Goulder says: 'The logic of [the title] has been criticised both by Tuckett . . . and also by Timothy Friedrichsen . . . It is certainly true that no amount of argument on the minor agreements would "automatically undo the Q hypothesis" and I have said that plainly in my *Luke: A New Paradigm*.' (See his 'Luke's Knowledge of Matthew', in G. Strecker (ed.), *Minor Agreements* (GTA 50; Göttingen: Vandenhoeck & Ruprecht, 1993) 143–62, p. 159. The quotation is from Friedrichsen, 'Matthew–Luke Agreements', 384.) However, in a footnote to back this up, Goulder proceeds simply to cite again the sentence quoted above from his *Luke*, 6, apparently suggesting that '*one* significant and clear MA' *would* 'undermine' the whole Q theory. Perhaps it is a semantic quibble, depending on what precise force one gives to words such as 'put to the test', 'undermine' and 'under threat of ruin'. Nevertheless, the fact remains that the MAs cannot on their own determine the truth or falsity of the Q hypothesis. The theory of the existence of Q depends on far more than just one or two isolated (Markan!) texts, and what is at issue is whether the *whole* pattern of Luke's agreements and disagreements with the other two synoptic gospels can be explained without recourse to some kind of Q.

[44] Goulder refers here to the work of Karl Popper in the philosophy of science on the value of any scientific hypothesis being falsifiable. On this see n. 58 below.

3.1.1 Matthew. Goulder argues forcefully that all linguistic arguments in favour of Q are really fallacious. One such argument he dubs the 'Matthean Vocabulary Fallacy'. Many, he claims, argue that if there are instances where Matthew and Luke differ and Matthew's version is Matthean, then Luke's version must be more original. In fact, he suggests, Matthew's version turns out to be extraordinarily like Q, and Matthew and Q are almost indistinguishable.[45]

With regard to the first point, no defender of the Q hypothesis has (as far as I am aware) argued quite as baldly as Goulder suggests and claimed that simply because Matthew's version is MattR, then *ipso facto* Luke's version is more original. Such an argument might be used by some who are presupposing the Q hypothesis, but also with the proviso that Luke's different version is unlikely to be LkR. However, this will be discussed in more detail when we look at what Goulder calls the 'Lucan Priority Fallacy'.

Goulder's other point about Matthew deserves more attention. He claims that repeatedly, in terms of language, style and even theology, Q and Matthew are virtually identical.[46] At the level of style and vocabulary, Goulder's argument is repeated with several examples. He refers to many instances where allegedly Q words or phrases turn out upon examination to be highly characteristic of Matthew's terminology. For example, the use of ὀλιγόπιστος in Matt 6:30/Luke 12:28 is usually taken to be part of Q, assuming some form of Q hypothesis. But the word is distinctively Matthean: it is used by Matthew in 8:26; 16:8; 17:20, all of which are redactional additions to Mark (assuming MP), and in 14:31 which is probably also due to MattR.[47] Thus Matthew's vocabulary and that of Q are indistinguishable. The same applies to the case of the phrase 'there will be weeping and gnashing of teeth'. It is used once in the allegedly Q tradition (Matt 8:12/Luke 13:28) and frequently elsewhere in Matthew alone (Matt 13:42; 22:13; 24:51; 25:30). 'Thus Q shares Matthew's enthusiasm for the pangs of hell.'[48]

The whole argument is however based on a major flaw in logic, part of which Goulder has seen but part of which still remains

---

[45] Goulder, *Luke*, 11ff.

[46] For language and style, see *Luke*, 11–15; for theology, 52ff.

[47] The argument is conducted within the presuppositions of MP; but even without this assumption, the use of the word five times in Matthew (none in Mark, one in Luke) indicates Matthew's distinctiveness here.

[48] *Luke*, 12.

hidden behind his rhetoric. Practically all the examples Goulder gives concern words or phrases which occur once in alleged Q, but several times in Matthew. Goulder's conclusion is that the *style* and *characteristic* vocabulary of Q are thus indistinguishable from that of Matthew. Now no one would dispute that the features indicated by Goulder are characteristic of Matthew and, to a certain extent, distinctive of Matthew in the synoptic tradition. The question is whether they must be judged necessarily unique to Matthew, and also whether a single occurrence of the same phenomenon in alleged Q can be taken as indicative of the *style*, or *Tendenz*, of Q. Goulder is at least alive to the latter problem, though his answer is scarcely convincing. He argues that since there are only c. 1800 words common to Matthew and Luke in Q and c. 18,000 words in Matthew, one occurrence of (say) ὀλιγόπιστος in Q as against five in Matthew is about par for the course.[49] This is however special pleading. Whatever the size of Q in relation to Matthew, we cannot deduce from a single occurrence in alleged Q anything about its style or characteristic features. For matters of style, we need recurring features and it is just this which Goulder's examples do not supply *for Q*.

Another more dangerous hidden assumption within Goulder's argumentation is that all the features isolated as characteristic of Matthew can be ascribed to Matthew's own redactional activity: in other words, everything which is characteristic of Matthew has been *created* by Matthew. Such an assumption is of course a dangerous nonsense,[50] and can be seen to be immediately false on a moment's reflection. Matthew does not write out of a cultural vacuum, even though his cultural milieu may be different from Mark's or Luke's. Thus Matthew typically refers to the 'kingdom of heaven', rather than the 'kingdom of God'. But 'kingdom of heaven' is not a Matthean redactional creation *de novo* — it simply represents a more Jewish terminology which distinguishes Matthew from Mark and Luke but which Matthew shares with many other Jewish contemporaries.

More importantly, it is clear that, on almost any source theory, Matthew collects together teaching material systematically into blocks of thematically related teaching; and he often repeats himself.[51] But is every such doublet then created due entirely, in

[49] Ibid., 13.
[50] See Hooker, 'In His Own Image?', 35.
[51] Cf. W. D. Davies & D. C. Allison, *The Gospel according to Saint Matthew I* (Edinburgh: T. & T. Clark, 1988) 88–93.

both halves of the doublet, to Matthew's creativity? Goulder him-self would agree that this is not the case as Matthew sometimes takes up material from Mark and repeats it.[52] Thus in relation in Mark, Matthew is quite capable of taking up a feature which occurs once in his source and repeating it. The same can equally have happened with the examples from alleged Q cited by Goulder.

Goulder's argument could have been used with different examples to argue for Mark's dependence on Matthew. For example, Matthew is fond of castigating opponents of Jesus as 'hypocrites'; yet at one point Mark has Jesus refer to opponents as hypocrites, in parallel with Matthew (Matt 15:7/Mark 7:6). Similarly, Matthew's fondness for τότε as a connecting particle is well known; yet on a few occasions Mark too has τότε in parallel with Matthew (cf. Matt 24:30/Mark 13:26). These examples are of exactly the same nature as the Q examples adduced by Goulder. Yet they do not necessarily show any dependence of Luke or Mark on Matthew, or any identity between Matthean and Q's/Mark's *style*. They can just as easily be taken as showing Matthew's willing-ness to take over terminology systematically so that it becomes characteristic and distinctive in its repeated use in his gospel, but not necessarily unique to him.

In fact Goulder himself has argued in precisely this way, replying to Farmer's attempt to prove Mark's dependence on Matthew via exactly the same kind of argumentation. Goulder writes:

> [Farmer's argument] is of the form: If document A (Mark) has favourite expressions not found in document B (Matthew), A is unlikely to be known by B; whereas if B has favourite expressions occurring once in A, it is likely that A has carried them over inadvertently. But this is a fallacy. . . . Sometimes later B may copy an expression from earlier A inadvertently; and *sometimes a casual expression of earlier A may appeal strongly to B so that he uses it often.*[53]

Goulder then goes on to excuse Farmer by admitting that he made 'virtually the same error of method' in a paper to an SNTS seminar in 1981, referring to characteristic Matthean phrases re-occurring in Luke, including the 'weeping and gnashing of teeth'. 'They might just be Q phrases that Matthew liked very

---

[52] *Luke*, 34. cf. Matt 3:2 + 4:17; 5:32 + 19:9; 10:22 + 24:9; 9:27ff. + 20:29ff.; 9:32ff. + 12:22ff.

[53] Goulder, 'Some Observations on Professor Farmer's "Certain Results . . ."', in Tuckett (ed.), *Synoptic Studies*, 99–104, p. 100 (my italics).

much; though there are other reasons in fact for preferring the inadvertence explanation, which I offered.' In fact the preface to Goulder's latest book indicates that a 1981 SNTS seminar paper forms the basis of his chapter on Q in his 1989 *Luke* volume. But, as far as I can see, there is no difference in the manner of argumentation from that criticised by Goulder himself in 1984. The argument is still exactly the same, appealing to the Matthean nature of the phrases concerned to argue against Q. No 'other reasons' are offered for these individual cases, even in the later study.

We may conclude that Goulder's reference to the alleged Matthean nature of Q's style is unconvincing. On the 2ST, a consistent picture of Matthew emerges as a writer who is capable of latching on to a word or a phrase in his source material and repeating it frequently. And this happens in the case of both Markan and Q material.

A discussion of Q's theology, and the alleged similarity between Q theology and Matthean theology, would take us too far afield in the present chapter. Indeed part of the present book is an attempt indirectly to isolate some distinctive features in Q which serve to distinguish Q from Matthew (and other NT writers) to some extent (though see also below). As just one possible counter example, I would refer again to the phenomenon of the so-called 'Wisdom Christology' in Q, whereby Jesus appears as the envoy of Wisdom. Matthew regularly 'up-grades' the Christology so as to identify Jesus with the figure of Wisdom itself.[54] Hence Q's theology cannot be identified with Matthean theology completely.[55] However, it is also the case that some level of continuity between Q and Matthew is not unexpected on the Q hypothesis. This applies perhaps more at the level of ideas than of style and vocabulary. But the very fact that Matthew used the Q material (if indeed he did) suggests that Matthew must have found it not uncongenial. He may have wished to modify it in places and perhaps did so; but the very fact that he decided to use the material at all indicates a measure of agreement between the ideas of the source and Matthew's own ideas.[56] A measure of

---

[54] See p. 167 below.

[55] Further examples can be found in a number of Catchpole's examples in his *Quest*, ch. 1: cf. pp. 23 (on poverty), 42f. (on the Law), 45 (the connection of Jesus' kingly status with his miracles, and his messiahship).

[56] See U. Luz, *Matthew 1–7* (ET Edinburgh: T. & T. Clark, 1990) 74–76, 82f. on Matthew as the 'heir' of his predecessors.

agreement between Matthew and Q is thus entirely expected, and Goulder's arguments about the possible overlap between Matthew and Q are thus no bar to the Q hypothesis.

3.1.2 Luke. A second aspect of Goulder's argument concerns Luke's stylistic features. Goulder criticises what he calls the 'Lucan Priority Fallacy', arguing against claims that Luke's version might at some points be more original than Matthew's.[57] He criticises excessive use of appeals to isolated *hapax legomena* in Luke's work, referring to the fact that Luke has a very wide vocabulary and is quite capable of rewriting Mark using hapaxes — hence an odd hapax cannot prove anything. Indeed the whole of his massive two-volume work is an attempt to show that Luke's version is at every point LkR when different from Matthew. Goulder also objects to arguments which appeal to the Matthean nature of Matthew's version as showing the pre-Lukan nature of Luke's version. By itself, of course, such a form of argumentation is quite indecisive, but few would in fact argue in this way quite so baldly today. As noted above, attempts to show that Luke's version is pre-Lukan at any one point would always be coupled with arguments seeking to show that Luke's version is in some way uncharacteristic of Luke.

Now such an attempt will inevitably be a delicate operation. Moreover one will never be able to *prove* such a theory one way or the other. It will be a delicate operation because at one level one is trying to show the impossible. Luke can only be said to be 'un-Lukan' in a rather unusual sense; for what is 'Lukan' is almost by definition what is in Luke. By 'un-Lukan' we therefore have to refer to something that is not impossible for Luke to have written, for if it is in Luke's gospel he patently did write it. What we mean is something which is rather unlike what Luke wrote elsewhere and which Luke probably did not invent *de novo*. But this means that we are in the realms of probabilities and not certainties. At most, we can only say that such and such is improbable, unlikely or whatever; we shall never be able to say that such and such is totally impossible. We are not in the realm of mathematics where a result of $0 = 1$ is a total impossibility, nor in the realm of natural sciences where hypotheses can be tested empirically and the untenability of hypotheses established if expected results do not match up to

[57] *Luke*, 15.

predictions.[58] The same applies to Goulder's theory as well. Despite his own claims, his own theory is no more 'falsifiable' than alternative hypotheses. Goulder can and does produce arguments to show that Luke's version may be LkR. Others may be rather unconvinced. But one cannot be more than unconvinced! One cannot 'prove' that the proposed feature of LkR is not redactional after all and thus 'falsify' the theory with mathematical finality.[59]

To take a concrete example, many would argue that at Q 11:49, Luke's version is more original in having the doom oracle spoken by the 'Wisdom of God' in the past ('Therefore the Wisdom of God said "I will send to them . . ."') by contrast with Matthew's version in which the oracle is spoken by Jesus in the present ('Therefore, behold I am sending to you . . .'). From the side of the Q hypothesis, Luke's version looks decidedly un-Lukan. Nowhere else in Luke (apart from Luke 7:35 which is also a Q passage, or one borrowed from Matthew) does Wisdom appear as an almost personified being. On the other hand, Matthew's replacement of 'Wisdom' with the 'I' of Jesus is part of a consistent pattern whereby Matthew's Jesus takes the place of

---

[58] Hence the application of Popper's principle of the falsifiability of 'scientific' hypotheses by Goulder to what he calls the discipline of 'neutestamentliche Wissenschaft (New Testament *science*)' (Goulder, *Luke*, 3, his italics) is rather questionable. The principle of empirical falsification as a criterion for defining genuinely 'scientific' hypotheses in Popper's work was in part developed explicitly in order to *distinguish* empirical science from other theories (philosophical, metaphysical or whatever) and to escape from the trap of Logical Positivism which sought to restrict meaningfulness only to 'verifiable' statements. See D. Stanesby, *Science, Reason and Religion* (London & New York: Routledge, 1988) 69. Goulder appears to be transferring the words 'science' and 'scientific' from a completely different context. To call New Testament studies a 'science', or 'scientific', may be justified in claiming that such study is carried out with full intellectual rigour, but the discipline has its own rules which are not necessarily those of the empirical sciences.

[59] It is also perhaps ironic in the present context that Popper himself was perfectly ready to agree with the principle of adapting an overall explanatory system to cater for odd apparent 'refutations' at individual points: cf. Stanesby, *Science*, 89, on Popper's 'immunizing strategems', and the possibility of introducing auxiliary hypotheses into an overall theory to account for otherwise unexplained details (cf. the theory of the existence of the planet Neptune, first postulated to explain the otherwise inexplicable perturbations in the orbit of Uranus). The idea of 'elastic' hypotheses is not as alien to a Popperian system as Goulder seems to think. Certainly the theory of a conjectural emendation of the text of one of the gospels to account for a single MA on the 2ST would fit into this category of an auxiliary hypothesis perfectly easily.

Wisdom in such texts (cf. above). Thus Luke's version seems to represent the more original Q version which Matthew then redacts.

Goulder's reply is to argue that the change can be explained as LkR.[60] Luke has just spoken of OT prophets so he takes the reference to the people sent by Matthew's Jesus (prophets, wise men and scribes) as a reference in part to OT figures. He thus has to change Matthew's 'I' (= Jesus) to 'God' and in doing so chooses a periphrasis for 'God' by writing 'the Wisdom of God', prompted perhaps in part by the σοφούς who are sent out by Matthew's Jesus. Now clearly none of this is totally impossible, and if Luke used Matthew he must have made the actual changes involved. At the most a sceptic can say that the proposed reasons seem unconvincing. Why should Luke have interpreted the 'prophets' of Matt 23:34 as OT figures? They are (in Matthew) clearly figures sent out by Jesus and Luke certainly knows of Christian prophets (cf. Acts 11:27; 13:1; 21:10). Further, even if Luke did decide to change things here and make God the subject, why did Luke feel obliged to introduce a periphrasis for God, and why this particular periphrasis? Elsewhere Luke has no compunction about talking of God himself sending prophets;[61] and as already noted, this is a highly unusual periphrasis in Luke's writings. Only once elsewhere (in a passage that Q-proponents and Goulder would agree is due to a source in Luke) does Luke refer to the Wisdom of God in personified terms.[62] Thus Goulder's arguments seem weak and uncompelling (to this particular sceptic, at least!).

But the important thing to note here is that that is all we can say. We cannot prove that Luke did not make these changes, perhaps for the reasons Goulder suggests, perhaps for quite different (as yet undiscovered) reasons. In that sense Goulder's theory is not falsifiable. It could have happened that way. Each critic has then to make up his/her mind whether things did happen in this way or whether the cumulative evidence is such that a theory of Lukan dependence seems less probable than some kind of Q hypothesis. If Goulder thinks that the only respectable hypotheses are those which are falsifiable, then his own theory is no more (or less!) respectable than the one he

---

[60] *Luke*, 523.

[61] For God speaking through, or raising up, prophets: cf. Luke 1:70; Acts 3:13, 21, 22; 7:37.

[62] Cf. above. The other text in Luke 7:35 which is either dependent on Q (according to the 2ST) or on Matthew (according to Goulder).

opposes. No theory about the Synoptic problem is falsifiable in the strict sense. All are at best the result of weighing up likelihoods and making more or less coherent guesses and combinations of hypotheses to try to explain the evidence of the texts themselves. There is not enough space here to give detailed arguments about other specific texts, but cumulative arguments similar to those already given have convinced many that on a significant number of occasions, Luke preserves a more original form of the tradition than Matthew and hence any theory of Luke's dependence on Matthew is unconvincing (cf. Luke 6:20–23; 7:35; 11:2–4; 11:20; 11:30, etc.).

3.2. Choice and Order of Material

Goulder's other main line of argumentation concerns the choice and ordering of material by Luke. A strong part of the argument for the existence of Q has always been the fact that (*a*) Luke never uses any of Matthew's additions to Mark in Markan material, and (*b*) Luke never has the Matthean material in the same context relative to the Markan material (cf. pp. 8–9 above).

Goulder's answer to (*a*) is to appeal to a general policy by Luke of wishing to cut down the length of the preaching discourses in his sources.[63] This is then the reason for Luke's splitting up the material in Mark 4, in Matthew's Great Sermon, etc. Luke wants 'manageable sections',[64] and long discourses in Matthew and Mark are 'too long and indigestible'.[65] Thus Luke 'regularly likes teaching pericopes of about twelve to twenty verses, which he regards as the amount a congregation (or reader) can assimilate at one time'.[66]

Such a policy may sound reasonable in general terms, but it fails to fit all the facts. Luke 12:22–53 (or even 12:22–59)[67] constitutes a sustained piece of teaching with no real break at all (Peter's interjection in v. 41 is scarcely enough to stop the flow of thought). Chapter 15 is a long section with admittedly three well-defined parables, but no clear markers between them supplied by Luke. What too of Luke 21/Mark 13? Here Goulder says that Luke

[63] Goulder, 'The Order of a Crank', in Tuckett (ed.), *Synoptic Studies*, 111–30, p. 112; *Luke*, 39f.
[64] Ibid.
[65] *Luke*, 41.
[66] *Luke*, 40.
[67] The introductory 'and he said to the crowds' in v. 54 scarcely stems the flow of the discourse.

retained Mark's long discourse because it 'cannot be broken up'.[68] This, however, is patently false: Mark 13 can be broken up and was broken up — by Matthew (assuming MP): Matthew uses Mark 13:9–13 by itself in Matt 10 (as well as repeating its substance in Matt 24), possibly because Matthew knows that persecution of Christians is not only a preliminary to the End but also a matter of past experience for Matthew's own Christian community. But Luke too knows of Christian persecution (cf. Acts 8:1–3). He could thus have made the same redactional change to Mark 13 as Matthew did. Luke thus did not have to keep Mark's discourse intact here. Indeed on Goulder's theory he does hive off the (substantively related) material in Matt 24–25 which, *ex hypothesi*, he knew and included earlier in his gospel (in Luke 12 and 17).

The argument about the indigestibility of long discourses is thus very fragile. When one compares too the lengths of some of the 'pericopes' in Acts (cf. Peter's long Pentecost speech, Stephen's 52-verse oration in Acts 7, the story of Cornelius' conversion in Acts 10), any appeal to the short supply of stamina on the part of Luke's audience/readership becomes even harder to conceive. The appeal to Luke's desire for brevity thus seems unconvincing. The problem therefore remains: why does Luke split up all his material in the way he has?

Goulder's second argument is to appeal to what he sees as Luke's overall policy of using his sources in 'blocks'. He envisages Luke as using one source at a time,[69] using first Mark, then Matthew, etc. Thus the reason why Luke never includes any Matthean modifications of Mark is simple:

> When he [Luke] is treating Marcan matter he has Mark in front of him, and he has made it his policy not to keep turning up Matthew to see what he had added. So again the problem disappears on examination: Luke does not include the additions because he had decided on a policy which involved letting them go.[70]

However, although this may explain some of the text of Luke, it cannot explain everything: in particular the Mark 13 material again causes problems.[71] Here Matthew has reworked the Markan discourse, expanding it very considerably with other material in

---

[68] *Luke*, 39.
[69] 'Crank', 113.
[70] *Luke*, 44.
[71] Cf. G. N. Stanton, *A Gospel for a New People. Studies in Matthew* (Edinburgh: T. & T. Clark, 1992) 33.

Matt 24–25. But now Luke evidently decided not to ignore Matthew's additions to Mark. He must have gone through Matthew very carefully,[72] marking off all those extra bits of Matthew which he would include. Moreover, Luke must then have distributed this material in three quite separate places in his gospel: in chs. 12, 17 and 19. Clearly Luke's 'block' policy has been rather different in Mark 13/Matt 24–25 than elsewhere!

One other feature also casts some doubt on Goulder's overall case. Goulder explains the lack of Matthean additions to Mark as due to Luke's policy of not referring to Matthew to see how Matthew redacted Mark. Yet Goulder elsewhere refers to the MAs as evidence that Luke does know Matthew in Markan passages. But the very nature of the MAs is that they are (individually) very minor. One such agreement referred to by Goulder is in Mark 8:31 pars. where Matthew and Luke agree in using ἀπό instead of ὑπό for Jesus' being rejected 'by' the elders, etc., and in having no definite article with the 'chief priests' and 'scribes'. Goulder's theory thus implies a situation where Luke resolutely follows Mark in Markan blocks, using one source only (his copy of Matthew being left 'on the floor'); so resolutely does Luke follow Mark that any substantial changes which Matthew might have made are studiously ignored by Luke. Yet Luke apparently knows Matthew's Greek text well enough to be influenced to the extent of changing a Markan ὑπό to ἀπό, and a Markan 'the elders and the chief priests and the scribes' to 'the elders and chief priests and scribes'. The overall picture does not seem very convincing. The fact that the MAs are so minor makes it hard to believe that Luke has been both influenced positively by Matthew's text in such (substantively) trivial ways, but also totally uninfluenced by any of Matthew's substantive additions to Mark. Undoubtedly the MAs constitute a problem for the 2ST, but precisely their minor nature constitutes a problem for Goulder's theory as well.[73]

The rest of Goulder's case depends in part on a detailed argument about Luke's reasons for producing his order of events from Matthew and Mark. Not all of Goulder's case can be discussed in detail here. However, in one article, Goulder has attempted to face directly the charge of Streeter (see p. 9 above) that Luke's ordering of the material, if derived from Mark and Matthew, seemed so totally lacking in rhyme or reason that Luke

---

[72] Goulder actually suggests that Luke used a pen to do so: *Luke*, 40.
[73] Cf. Friedrichsen, 'Matthew–Luke Agreements', 384.

could on this theory only be regarded as a 'crank'. Goulder boldly sets out to account for the 'order of a crank'.[74] He claims that Luke first went forwards through the texts of Mark and Matthew, taking some of the material he wanted, and by the end of ch. 13 of his gospel had worked his way through to Matt 25; but then, according to Goulder, Luke realised that there was other material from Matthew which he still wanted to include; he therefore decided to go backwards through the text of Matthew picking up non-Markan material from Matthew he had missed out up until now, sometimes using it directly, sometimes providing a 'substitute' of similar material.[75]

In very general terms such a procedure might seem plausible; however, the theory fails to fit the facts in an uncomfortably large number of cases. Part of Goulder's claim is that Luke's version is as often as not a substitute for Matthew's version: e.g. the worthless salt of Luke 14:35 which is 'cast out' is seen as the equivalent of Matthew's appendix to the parable of the Great Supper where the man without the wedding garment is also 'cast out' (Matt 22:13). 'Not one diamond shall be lost from the Matthaean tiara: all must be included'.[76] But however delightful the imagery and language, the application is not clear. What is the Matthean tiara? It is scarcely the whole gospel, since some parts of Matthew have no counterpart at all in Luke. For example, the parable of the Labourers in the Vineyard is 'left out' by Luke,[77] perhaps because it was redundant after the Two Sons, or perhaps because its theme (Matt 20:16) had already been used in Luke 13:30. Evidently some diamonds from the Matthean tiara are not quite as valuable as others for Luke!

Further, the choice and order which Luke follows is scarcely explained, even on Goulder's theory. For example, the two parables of the tower builder and the king who 'sent' an embassy of peace (Luke 14:28–32) are said to be inspired by the parable of the Wicked Husbandmen in Matt 21, these parables being Luke's 'substitute' for Matthew's parable.[78] Yet according to Goulder, Luke has resolutely decided to ignore Matthew's use of Markan material and this is a Markan pericope which Luke himself will include later in Luke 20. This section in Luke thus fails to fit

---

[74] 'Crank', *passim.*
[75] 'Crank', 121; also *Luke,* 581f.
[76] 'Crank', 122; also *Luke,* 582.
[77] 'Crank', 123.
[78] 'Crank', 122f.

Goulder's explanation since (*a*) it is no substitute but a doublet (Luke does include the Markan parable in his gospel later), and (*b*) it is material which, on Goulder's own theory, Luke should be ignoring here.

Working backwards, Luke is now said to come across the parable of the Two Sons (Matt 21:28–32) for which Luke provides a substitute in his own 'Two Sons' parable in Luke 15:11ff.[79] But before that Luke must have skipped back three whole chapters in Matthew to rescue the small parable of the Lost Sheep from Matt 18. This is quite a jump, including leap-frogging over material which (according to Goulder) Luke will include later anyway (at least via substitution: Matt 18:23–35, cf. Luke 16:1–13). Thus again the theory scarcely explains the actual Lukan order.

There is a similar failure for the theory to explain the facts later. According to Goulder, Luke 16:1–13 is inspired by Matt 18:23–35; but then instead of following Matthew backwards through his scroll, Luke now moves forwards — this time into Matt 19 where his attention is allegedly caught by v. 24, the saying about it being easier for a camel to go through the eye of a needle than for a 'rich man' to enter the Kingdom. This is supposedly the inspiration for the story of the rich man and Lazarus in Luke 16:19ff. and the discussion about the Law.[80] Again this seems both difficult to envisage in itself[81] and also contradictory of Luke's alleged general policy. Luke is meant to be working backwards, not forwards, through Matthew, and also ignoring Matthew's treatment of Markan material. Yet Goulder's theory suggests that Luke's eye was caught by a saying 24 verses ahead of the point in Matthew he has reached (and 24 verses is not just one line!); and in any case this is all Markan material in Matthew which Luke is supposedly ignoring!

These are some of the problems that seem to beset Goulder's theory. His discussion of Luke's order still provides no very convincing explanation for why Luke should have selected and divided up the material in Matthew in the way he must have done if he knew it in its Matthean form and order. When one couples this with Luke's very conservative treatment of the order of Mark, the problem becomes even more acute. Why should Luke have

---

[79] 'Crank', 123.

[80] 'Crank', 124f.

[81] The physical difficulties of jumping around a text in scroll form across great distances are rightly pointed out by Downing, 'Paradigm Perplex', 21.

had so much respect for the order of Mark, scarcely changing it at all, and yet change the order of Matthew at almost every point? Streeter's comment that such a procedure seems like that of a 'crank', although expressed somewhat polemically, still has force. Not even Goulder's defence of the 'order of a crank' seems sufficient to meet the problem.

Goulder's theory thus seems to many untenable. Further, the problems encountered by Goulder in seeking to explain the Matthew–Luke agreements whilst still assuming MP are very similar to those faced by the Augustinian hypothesis. For both theories, problems arise in trying to explain Luke's text as the result of Luke's redaction of Matthew and Mark together. Thus many of the objections mentioned above in relation to Goulder could apply, with only slight modification of the argument, to the Augustinian hypothesis.

4. The 'Mark–Q Overlaps'

One further piece of evidence should also be noted at this point as providing a major difficulty faced, in slightly different but very similar ways, by both the GH and by the Goulder–Farrer theory. This concerns the so-called 'overlap' passages in the tradition.

According to most defenders of some form of the 2ST, there are a few passages which seem to have been preserved by both Mark and Q. The exact extent of these passages is disputed, but most defenders of the Q theory would agree that Mark and Q both have versions of the temptation narrative (Mark 1:12–13/Q 4:1–13), the Beelzebul controversy (Mark 3:22–30/Q 11:14–23), the parable of the mustard seed (Mark 4:30–32/Q 13:18–19), the mission charge (Mark 6:7–13/Q 10:1–16), the request for a sign (Mark 8:11–12/Q 11:29–30), as well as parts of the eschatological discourse (Mark 13/Q 17:22–37) and some of the individual isolated sayings noted already as doublets (see p. 10 above).[82] According to the 2ST, Matthew and Luke were then faced with two versions of the same pericope, and each handled the tradition in his own way; broadly speaking, it would appear (again assuming the 2ST) that Luke preferred the non-Markan version, whilst Matthew conflated the two versions.

---

[82] Other passages may also come into this category, e.g. the pericope about the double love command (Matt 22:34–40/Mark 12:28–34/Luke 10:25–28), though this is more disputed: see p. 416 below.

Whatever one makes of the 2ST's explanation here, the fact remains that these texts exist, and that they have to be explained by any global source theory. Moreover, the same facts, which have led many today to postulate at least a duality of basic sources here, create immense problems for both the GH and the Goulder–Farrer theory. In general terms, many of these texts are characterised by a situation where Matthew has a very full text, Mark has parallels to some parts of Matthew, and Luke has parallels to precisely those parts of Matthew which do *not* appear in Mark. On the 2ST, Luke tends to prefer the Q version and to ignore Mark; Matthew conflates the two versions (Mark and Q) together. The GH and Goulder are essentially similar at this point in that both argue that the third evangelist (Mark for the GH, Luke for Goulder) had both his predecessors' gospels in front of him. In either case then the third evangelist must have proceeded in these texts to 'unpick' Matthew's version very carefully in order to preserve precisely those elements from that version which the second evangelist did *not* have. Thus for the GH, Mark must have decided to include precisely and only those parts of Matthew which Luke did *not* use; for Goulder, Luke must have decided to use only those parts of Matthew which Matthew added to Mark and to *ex*clude all the elements where Matthew had used Mark directly.[83]

Such a procedure seems very hard to square with the overall redactional procedure proposed by either hypothesis. On the GH, Mark is generally adopting a procedure of including all the material common to both his alleged sources; yet in these few passages he must have suddenly decided on a deliberate policy of *ex*cluding what was common to both his sources and including only what appeared in Matthew alone. According to the Goulder theory, Luke usually sticks very close to Mark, being considerably more influenced by Mark's ordering of events than by Matthew's so that he preserved the Markan order almost unchanged whilst exercising considerable freedom with the order of Matthew's material; yet in these passages he must have suddenly decided to take a violent aversion to Mark and preserved only those parts of Matthew where Matthew differed substantially from Mark. Such a

---

[83] For more detail, in relation to the Goulder–Farrer position, see F. G. Downing, 'Towards the Rehabilitation of Q', *NTS* 11 (1965) 169–81; in relation to the GH, see my *Revival*, 78–93; more generally, see also Downing, 'Compositional Conventions and the Synoptic Problem', *JBL* 107 (1988) 69–85; also his 'Paradigm Perplex'.

procedure produces a pattern of redactional activity by Mark or Luke that seems considerably at variance with what must have happened elsewhere in the tradition.

Further, Downing has pointed out that such activity by an author using two sources is quite unlike that of any other writer we know about in the ancient world faced with a similar situation.[84] Other writers (such as Josephus, Tacitus, Plutarch) when faced with more than one source of information endeavoured to run their sources together, often in a fairly simplistic way, or alternatively used one source only. There is no real precedent in other literature of this period for a writer, faced with two divergent accounts of the same story, seeking to 'unpick' one source from the other and give only the residue peculiar to one of the sources. All the evidence suggests that common testimony is what a later writer would fasten on, welcome and reproduce. The sudden aversion by a Griesbachian Mark, or a Goulderian Luke, in these few passages of the tradition to the common testimony of their alleged sources thus sets them apart from any other known writer of the period.

By contrast, a more reasonable scenario emerges on the 2ST. Mark and Q overlapped in a few instances. Luke then decided to follow one of these sources (usually Q). Matthew adopted a policy of running the two sources together. But in neither case does one have to postulate a prior process by the later writer of 'unpicking' one source from another, a process which would in any case be inherently extremely complex (without the advantages of a modern printed synopsis) and in any case apparently unprecedented.

It has been claimed by some that the theory of a Mark–Q overlap constitutes an enormous problem for the 2ST, and that other hypotheses can explain these texts without difficulty. Thus D. Dungan asserts:

> The existence of Q has always been essential to the argument for Mark's priority — precisely as the loophole to invoke anytime one finds a pericope that is more primitive in Matthew and/or Luke when they are supposedly using Mark: the blessed overlap.[85]

---

[84] See especially his 'Compositional Conventions'; also, on Josephus, his earlier 'Redaction Criticism: Josephus' Antiquities and the Synoptic Problem', *JSNT* 8 (1980) 46–66; 9 (1980) 29–48.

[85] D. Dungan, 'Mark — The Abridgement of Matthew and Luke', *Jesus and Man's Hope I* (Pittsburgh, 1970) 51–97, p. 73.

And M. Devisch claims:

> Pour ceux qui défendent d'autres solutions du problème
> synoptique, les textes que, dans la théorie des deux sources, on
> appelle généralement 'les passages qui se recouvrent', ne font
> aucun problème. Ils constituent, au contraire, les exemples les plus
> probants pour confirmer ces autres théories.[86]

In fact precisely the opposite is probably the case. Contra Dungan, such an overlap is postulated not to explain cases where a pericope in Matthew/Luke is more primitive than in Mark, but simply where a different version seems to have been used by Matthew and Luke alone. And it is precisely these texts which cause so *much* difficulty for hypotheses other than the 2ST. Consideration of these 'overlap' passages is thus probably one of the strongest arguments in favour of a form of the 2ST and against other hypotheses such as the GH and the Goulder–Farrer theory.

5. Unity and Order of Q

In this chapter I have tried to discuss the major theories currently proposed which claim that the agreements between Matthew and Luke are to be explained by Luke's direct knowledge and use of Matthew. For those who regard these theories as unsatisfactory, the alternative is to accept some sort of Q theory: the agreements between Matthew and Luke in the material which they have in common and which they have not derived from Mark are to be explained by their common dependence on prior source material.

Whether this 'source material' ever existed in a unified form prior to its inclusion by Matthew and Luke is logically a further question, as I tried to show earlier (cf. pp. 4–5 above). It is certainly possible to deny the existence of Q at one level by refusing to accept that the material common to Matthew and Luke ever existed independently in a fixed (written?) form whilst still refusing to accept Luke's dependence on Matthew. In this case 'Q' would be rather more a mass of amorphous unrelated material than a single 'source', or even 'document'. Is it then

---

[86] M. Devisch, 'Le relation entre l'évangile de Marc et le document Q', in M. Sabbe (ed.), *L'Evangile selon Marc. Tradition et Rédaction* (BETL 34; Leuven University Press, 1974) 59–91, p. 60.

justified to think of 'Q' as a more unified body of tradition, rather than as just 'Q material'?[87]

In one way of course such a question is unanswerable with any degree of finality. Unless we discover an actual manuscript of Q, we will never know for certain whether the Q material ever existed as a unified body of tradition prior to its incorporation by Matthew and Luke. Nevertheless, some indication may be shown by considering the possible ordering of the Q material. If it can be shown that the Q material exhibits a common order in both Matthew and Luke, this would suggest that this material did come to the two evangelists in an ordered, and hence unified, form. Further, in this context, a common order combined with proximity would be even more significant, since such a phenomenon would suggest very strongly that the material concerned belonged closely together in the underlying tradition.[88]

At one level, any attempt to show such a common order would seem to be extremely difficult. The lack of agreement in the order of this material in the gospels of Matthew and Luke was a key point in Streeter's argument against any theory of direct dependence between the two gospels, as we have seen. Nevertheless, despite this overall perspective, it is clear that there are a number of smaller groupings of traditions which clearly do exhibit a common order in both Matthew and Luke; and at times these traditions are evidently part of a unit that is considerably larger than the individual sayings and pericopes which constitute it. Thus Q 7:18–35 is a large unit, perhaps composed of three pericopes (7:18–23, 24–28, 31–35) which appear in the same sequence, and combined, in both Matthew and Luke (cf. Matt 11:2–19). The sayings on cares in Q 12:22–31 also come in exactly the same order in both gospels (cf. Matt 6:25–33) and in a form which almost certainly suggests that originally disparate sayings and traditions have already been combined (see pp. 149–52 below). Thus both gospels witness to a common collocation of traditions in their common source(s). The material in common between Matthew's Sermon on the Mount and Luke's Sermon on the Plain also appears in a recognisable common order (even if the presence of extra material, especially in Matthew, does not make all this material fit the criterion of proximity quite so well):

---

[87] On this, and other related questions, see P. Vassiliadis, 'The Nature and Extent of the Q-Document', *NovT* 20 (1978) 49–73, who summarises much of the debate amongst earlier scholars.

[88] Cf. also Catchpole, *Quest*, 5.

Matt	Luke	
5:3–11	6:20–23	Beatitudes
5:39–48	6:27–36	Love of enemies
7:1–5	6:37–42	On judging
7:16–20	6:43–45	Trees and fruits
7:21	6:46	'Lord, Lord'
7:24–27	6:47–49	Hearers and Doers[89]

We have also seen that Q material overlapped with Mark at times and, as often as not, Matthew conflated the two whereas Luke kept the two separate. Given this, the Q material in these overlap passages often seems to exhibit a clear common order, as in for example the mission charge (Q 10:1–16), the Beelzebul controversy (Q 11:14–23) and the eschatological discourse (Q 17:22–37). Again on several occasions the Q material almost certainly represents the coming together of originally separate traditions, and this coming together appears to have already happened in the tradition common to the two evangelists.

At times broader collocations of Q material can be discerned. The blocks of material involving the Beelzebul controversy, the sayings about the return of the evil spirits, the request for a sign, and the double saying about the Queen of the South and Jonah (Q 11:14–23, 24–26, 29–30, 31–32) come in close proximity in both gospels and in all but identical order (the parallels are in Matt 12:22–32, 43–45, 38–40, 41–42 respectively: the main difference is the relative position of the sayings about the return of the evil spirits). So too a fairly clear common order can be discerned in the early parts of Q with the preaching of John the Baptist, the temptation narrative, the Great Sermon, and the healing of the centurion's servant (Q 3:7–9, 16–17; 4:1–13; 6:20–49; 7:1–10).

The failure of the Q material to exhibit such a clear ordering after the opening sections is sometimes felt to be a difficulty for belief in a unified Q. However, one must bear in mind that the Q material is only indirectly available to us as mediated via Matthew and Luke, and that both evangelists had particular agendas when using the material in their sources. In particular, Matthew has a

[89] I realise that grouping the material this way conceals a number of complexities in the detailed ordering within each broad section here: e.g. the beatitudes in Luke 6:20, 21a, 21b, 22f. are parallel to Matt 5:3, 6, 4, 10f. respectively. Similarly the love of enemies material is extremely complex, and within the broad section Matt 5:39–48/Luke 6:27–36 there is some disagreement in the order of the individual sayings.

clear policy of collecting related teaching material into his great teaching discourses (e.g. in Matt 5–7, 10, 13, 18, 24–25).[90] When one takes this fully into account, some of the problems of the apparent differences in order of the Q material in Matthew and Luke may be resolvable. Thus in two important articles, Vincent Taylor has argued that, provided one takes note of Matthew's redactional policy, a clear ordering of the Q material may be discernible.[91] Taylor showed that, if one compares the order of Q material in Luke with that in each Matthean discourse in turn, there is a remarkable correlation in the order. This suggests that the Q material may have existed in a fixed order: Luke then (in line with his general redactional procedure of preserving the order of his sources, as shown by his treatment of Mark) kept the Q order mostly intact; Matthew (in line with his general redactional procedure and again in a way similar to his treatment of Mark) changed the order at times to bring substantively related material together in his teaching discourses. This would then suggest that the Q material existed in a fixed order and hence may have constituted a unified source.

Taylor's arguments are not fool-proof, and not all the evidence quite fits the facts. At times he has to postulate a 'Q–M' overlap (i.e. to deny to Q a saying which does not quite fit his pattern but which seems to be common to both gospels);[92] and he has to postulate on occasions Matthew going through the Q material more than once to pick up in order the material he will use in his large discourses.[93] Nevertheless, many have accepted the general conclusions suggested by Taylor's work in seeing (at least the bulk of) the Q material as forming a unified and ordered whole at some stage in the development of the tradition, with Luke preserving the order of Q more faithfully than Matthew.[94]

In conclusion, we may say that considerations of order do suggest that Q was more of a unity and less of an amorphous mass of unrelated traditions. Certainly the evidence does not suggest

[90] This is almost indisputable whatever source theory one adopts.

[91] V. Taylor, 'The Order of Q', *JTS* 4 (1953) 27–31; and 'The Original Order of Q', in A. J. B. Higgins (ed.), *New Testament Essays. Studies in Memory of T. W. Manson* (Manchester University Press, 1959) 95–118.

[92] E.g. the saying on treasure (Q 12:33–34), or the parable of the lost sheep (Q 15:3–7): see Taylor, 'Original Order', 252, 259.

[93] This applies especially in the case of Matthew's Sermon of the Mount. On this question, see Kloppenborg, *Formation*, 68f.

[94] Cf. Vassiliadis, 'Nature and Extent', 62f.

that Q consisted only of isolated sayings or individual pericopes which were only brought together for the first time by Matthew and Luke independently. The clear common clusterings of material (cf. above on Q 7:18–35, or 12:22–31) which is at times evident indicate otherwise. Also the common ordering of wider sections indicates that a presumption about the unity of the Q material is at least a reasonable working hypothesis for further study. Further, the common ordering of the Q tradition reinforces what was said earlier about the written nature of Q (cf. pp. 3–4 above). Just as the (at times) verbatim verbal agreement between the texts of Matthew and Luke seems to demand common dependence on a written *Vorlage*, so too the common ordering of such extensive parts of the Q tradition is really only explicable if that tradition existed in written form.[95]

The same conclusion about the unity of the Q material may also follow from attempts to determine a 'theology' of Q, or to see Q as reflecting the beliefs and practices of a specific group of Christians in the early church. At first sight, such attempts would appear to be heavily dependent on arguments for the existence of Q. One cannot find a 'theology of Q', or locate a 'Q community', if 'Q' did not exist. However, it may be that attempts to isolate a distinctive Q theology can provide, in a back-handed way, further support for the theory of the existence of Q as a unified source. If it can be shown that the Q material exhibits a distinctive theological profile, then this in turn may show that this material did exist in a unified form at some stage of the developing tradition.[96] The rest of this book is an attempt to do just that, but one example to illustrate the point may be appropriate here. I refer once again to the so-called 'Wisdom Christology' of the Q material, where Jesus is presented as one of the prophets sent by Wisdom, all of whom suffer violence and rejection. I have already tried to show that this Christological schema is neither Matthean nor Lukan (cf. above). And the combination of motifs (the rejected prophets, and rejected Wisdom) is also not evidenced

[95] See Vassiliadis, 'Nature and Extent', 52; Kloppenborg, *Formation*, 47–9.

[96] Cf. too Catchpole, *Quest*, 5: 'If we succeeded in establishing a congruence of concerns and emphases between secondary editorial additions made to a series of individual traditions, then the possibility of literary unity would be enhanced.' As I have tried to argue below (see pp. 76–82), I would urge a broader consideration of the whole Q material as well as focusing on secondary editorial additions, even though the latter (if established) are clearly of great value.

outside these Q texts as far as I am aware.[97] The schema thus seems to be a distinctive feature of the Q tradition in the gospels. As such it may then reflect the beliefs of a specific group of Christians within early Christianity. Others too have sought to identify other features of Q and to build up a Q theology. The measure of distinctiveness will of course vary from case to case; and, as noted earlier (n. 56 above), it is inherently likely that there will be a high degree of continuity between the theology of Q and that of both Matthew and Luke. Still many are convinced that such a theological profile in relation to the Q material can be built up. And in turn, if successful, this can be used to argue more strongly for the existence of Q as a unified source.

It may of course be that, even if 'Q' was more than an amorphous mass of unrelated traditions, 'Q' was not a static entity. Indeed the trend in recent Q studies has been to postulate (at times quite complex) developments in the growth of Q. Nevertheless such theories would still assume that it is indeed sensible to talk of Q as a unified source in some sense. It is precisely this belief in the existence of a Q source, coupled with a realisation that we can no longer think in the static terms that have characterised New Testament studies in the past, that has led to the quickening of interest in Q as an entity worthy of study in its own right and as possible evidence of a distinctive stream, or 'trajectory', within early Christianity. That interest is reflected in the remainder of this book.

[97] See my *Revival*, 164f.; Schulz, *Q*, 340.

2

'Redaction Criticism' and Q

'No man is an island' and the present writer is no exception. All of us work within specific social, literary and cultural contexts and our ideas are constantly shaped in dialogue with these contexts. The present study is consciously set within the stream of studies which has grown over the last forty years or so seeking to apply insights from so-called 'redaction criticism' (in a very broad sense of the term) to Q. It may therefore be worthwhile to glance briefly at the history of scholarship with this issue in mind, both as a useful means of getting one's bearings and also as a way of seeking to clarify some important methodological issues which inevitably arise in studies such as this. No attempt will be made here to give a full history of research on Q. Fuller treatments can be found elsewhere[1] and in any case the aim of the present chapter is not to give a comprehensive *Forschungsbericht* (which would probably need a book-length treatment in its own right). Rather, what is attempted here is a brief survey of past scholarship in order to offer a few critical reflections on the question of method. In passing, too, I shall try to offer some comments about the value of some of the theories which have been proposed in the past about Q's 'theology', etc. However, for the most part, such critical dialogue over the details of the analysis of Q will be reserved for the detailed arguments of subsequent chapters.

---

[1] For surveys, see Neirynck, 'Recent Developments'; U. Luz, 'Die wiederentdeckte Logienquelle', *EvTh* 33 (1973) 527–33; J. S. Kloppenborg, 'Tradition and Redaction in the Synoptic Sayings Source', *CBQ* 46 (1984) 34–62, and *Formation*, 8–40; W. Schmithals, *Einleitung in die drei ersten Evangelien* (Berlin & New York: de Gruyter, 1985); also L. E. Vaage & J. S. Kloppenborg, 'Early Christianity, Q and Jesus: The Sayings Gospel and Method in the Study of Christian Origins', *Semeia* 55 (1991) 1–14.

1. Studies on Q up to 1959

So-called 'redaction-critical' approaches to Q are almost always said to start with H. E. Tödt's dissertation on the Son of Man (henceforth SM) sayings in the synoptic gospels, first published in 1959.[2] However, 'Q' was not a scholarly invention of the late 1950s, and the existence of a 'Sayings Source' had been postulated by scholars for many years before that. The precise origin of the Q hypothesis need not concern us here. The theory of a source common to Matthew and Luke appears in scholarly literature as early as J. G. Eichhorn in 1794[3] (though Eichhorn postulated several sources lying behind our present gospels).[4] However, the most influential figures in establishing the possible existence of a common source underlying Matthew and Luke were C. H. Weisse and H. J. Holtzmann.[5] In particular, Holtzmann's work set the scene for virtually all subsequent gospel study in arguing for a form of the Two Source Theory. The precise details of Holtzmann's theories in relation to Mark's gospel need not concern us here. More relevant is Holtzmann's theory, shared too by Weisse, that behind Matthew and Luke lay a common source of sayings, or logia, which Holtzmann called Λ.

The exact nature of this Logia source was of some concern to both Weisse and Holtzmann. Both adopted the theory (adumbrated by Schleiermacher) that Papias' statement about Matthew having made a collection of λόγια referred not to our Gospel of Matthew but to a collection of sayings;[6] both then

---

[2] H. E. Tödt, *Der Menschensohn in der synoptishen Überlieferung* (Gütersloh: Gerd Mohn, 1959); ET *The Son of Man in the Synoptic Tradition* (London: SCM, 1965).

[3] J. G. Eichhorn, *Über die drey ersten Evangelien. Einige Bemerkungen zu ihrer künftigen kritischen Behandlung* (Leipzig: Weidmann, 1794) 759ff.; also his *Einleitung in das Neue Testament* (5 Bde.; Leipzig: Weidmann, 1804–27) Bd.3, 344–56. Cf. Schulz, *Q*, 13.

[4] See the survey in Schmithals, *Einleitung*, 55f. However, the relevance of Eichhorn for the history of the Q hypothesis is severely questioned by Schmithals, *Einleitung*, 183, who claims that for Eichhorn the postulated source was not a *sayings* source, but a version of a postulated primitive gospel, expanded by sayings.

[5] C. H. Weisse, *Die evangelische Geschichte, kritisch und philosophisch bearbeitet* (Leipzig: Breitkopf und Hartel, 1838); H. J. Holtzmann, *Die synoptischen Evangelien. Ihr Ursprung und geschichtlicher Charakter* (Leipzig: Engelmann, 1863). See Schmithals, *Einleitung*, 182ff.

[6] F. Schleiermacher, 'Über die Zeugnis des Papias von unseren beiden ersten Evangelien', *Theologische Studien und Kritiken* 5 (1832) 735–68. Papias' famous statement about Matthew collecting the λόγια is recorded in Eusebius, *E.H.* 3.39.

identified this sayings collection with a postulated source common to Matthew and Luke. This identification however then led to a certain embarrassment due to the fact that the material common to Matthew and Luke included some narrative as well as just sayings (e.g. Luke 7:1–10 and par.), and Weisse, for example, changed his mind over some details of his overall theory. Thus in 1856 he argued that some passages, especially the narrative sections of his postulated 'Sayings source', should rather be seen as part of his other main postulated source (which was all but Mark's gospel). Weisse thus effectively created an Ur-Marcus which Mark had then abbreviated.[7] Similarly Holtzmann ascribed narrative sections such as Luke 7:1–10 and par. to his other main *Grundschrift* (which he called 'A'), rather than his Logia source (Λ). Whether one should criticise Weisse and Holtzmann in this respect is debatable.[8] In fact the difficulties which both scholars created for themselves are probably due as much as anything to their over-reliance on a specific interpretation of the statement of Papias about Matthew's collection of λόγια. Both assumed that this collection existed, that it was not our Gospel of Matthew, and that it comprised a collection consisting entirely of sayings. All these assumptions are now seen to be highly unlikely. Most today would assume that Papias' statement is intended to refer to our Gospel of Matthew.[9] Its relevance for any Q hypothesis is therefore probably non-existent. Thus the lengths to which Weisse and Holtzmann evidently felt driven in order to make their postulated source fit Papias' description are probably quite unnecessary. The vast majority of scholars today would set no store at all by the evidence of Papias in seeking to establish the existence of Q.

[7] C. H. Weisse, *Die Evangelienfrage in ihrem gegenwärtigen Stadium* (Leipzig Breitkopf und Hartel, 1856) 88f., 156–65.

[8] Cf. the harsh critiques of inconsistency and applying preconceived ideas to the evidence in Stoldt, *History*, 65ff. (on Weisse), and 88f. (on Holtzmann). See too Farmer, *Synoptic Problem*, 23f., 41ff.

[9] See Kümmel, *Introduction*, 120; Kloppenborg, *Formation*, 54; J. Kürzinger, 'Die Aussage des Papias von Hierapolis zur literarischen Form des Markus-evangeliums', *BZ* 21 (1977) 245–64. However, the view that Papias' reference is to a sayings collection which might be Q has always had a number of advocates: cf. T. W. Manson, *The Sayings of Jesus* (London: SCM, 1949) 15f. For the possibility that, although Papias himself had our gospel of Matthew in mind, nevertheless prior to Papias, the statement referred to a sayings collection which might therefore have been related to Q, see Davies & Allison, *Matthew I*, 17, with others cited there; also M. Black, 'The Use of Rhetorical Terminology in Papias on Mark and Matthew', *JSNT* 37 (1989) 31–41. Such a possibility must however remain somewhat speculative.

Arguments for the Q hypothesis must be, and are, found elsewhere — primarily in the analysis of the nature of the agreements
between the texts of Matthew and Luke themselves. Thus the
difficulties of Weisse and Holtzmann about the postulated source
as being exclusively a sayings source are not particularly relevant
today, at least at the level of determining the contents of Q.

The history of scholarship after Holtzmann saw at least one
significant development when the heavy dependence on the
Papias evidence was quietly dropped in the discussion of the
nature and contents of the Sayings source. Indeed, at some stage
the name of the source itself was changed. Holtzmann had called
the source the 'Logia Source' (= Λ) with clear dependence on
Papias. By the end of the century the siglum 'Q' had established
itself, above all in the work of P. Wernle.[10] But Wernle's influential
work on the Synoptic Problem represented a further significant
change of direction in thoughts about Q by breaking with the
theory that Q could only contain sayings material.[11] With regard
to any possible distinctive features in Q, Wernle argued that Q was
put together primarily for the catechetical needs of new
Christians.[12] He argued too that Q did not remain a static entity: it
underwent a later Judaising 'redaction' before being used by
Matthew (so that Matthew's version of Q contained texts like Matt
5:17–20; 10:5f.; 23:3, etc.).[13] However, Q originally was by no
means a Judaising document. 'Aus dem großen Hauptteil der
Sammlung spricht kein Judaismus, sondern das freie, fast revolu-
tionäre Evangelium Jesu selbst.'[14] Hence Q provided an almost
transparent window on to the preaching of the historical Jesus.

This view was even more strongly emphasised by Harnack in his
detailed study of the Q material.[15] After a detailed analysis and

---

[10] P. Wernle, *Die synoptische Frage* (Leipzig & Tübingen: Mohr, 1899). However,
the nomenclature was probably not invented by Wernle himself: see ch. 1 n. 1
above.

[11] See Wernle, *Synoptische Frage*, 228. Wernle is heavily criticised by Stoldt,
History, 112–20, for this, but Stoldt's arguments are really quite beside the point.
Papias' evidence is probably valueless and one does not need Papias to establish
the existence of a source common to Matthew and Luke. The notion that this
source contained sayings, and sayings alone, is solely due to reliance on Papias.
Without this, there is no reason at all why such a common source should be
restricted to sayings alone.

[12] Wernle, *Synoptische Frage*, 228.

[13] *Synoptische Frage*, 229.

[14] *Synoptische Frage*, 230.

[15] A. Harnack, *The Sayings of Jesus* (ET London: Williams & Norgate, 1908).

attempted reconstruction of Q, Harnack compared Mark and Q with each other. Uniformly Harnack claimed that Q was superior in giving the pure gospel teaching of Jesus, unadulterated by later dogma:

> Compared with these gospels [i.e. Matthew, Mark and Luke] the content we have assigned to Q is simply homogeneous. Here a great number of points of view and tendencies which prevail in those other gospels are absolutely wanting ... The author is simply concerned with the commandments of our Lord, and aims at giving a description of His message, in which description he appears to be influenced by no special and particular bias.[16]

> Q is a compilation of discourses and sayings of our Lord, the arrangement of which has no reference to the Passion, with an horizon which is as good as absolutely bound by Galilee, without any clearly discernible bias, whether apologetic, didactic, ecclesiastical, national, or anti-national.[17]

Thus writing explicitly about Mark and Q, Harnack says:

> The portrait of Jesus as given in the sayings of Q has remained in the foreground. The attempts which have been made to replace it by that of St. Mark have met with no success ... The collection of sayings [i.e. Q] and St. Mark must remain in power, but the former takes precedence. Above all, the tendency to exaggerate the apocalyptic and eschatological element in our Lord's message, and to subordinate to this the purely religious and ethical elements, will ever find its refutation in Q.[18]

Despite its many strengths, Harnack's study has not found much support in subsequent scholarly study on Q. His general inclination to prefer the Matthean version as preserving Q more accurately than the Lukan version has not won general assent. Also his high praise for the alleged non-apocalyptic/eschatological nature of the Q material has not stood up well to later scholarly developments, though it could perhaps be seen as having something of a modified revival in recent attempts to regard at least some (possibly earlier) parts of Q as 'sapiential' (see below). Already by 1907, Harnack's views about a pure, non-eschatological teaching of Jesus were considered to be in need of radical modification in the light of the insistence of scholars such

[16] *Sayings*, 167f.
[17] *Sayings*, 171.
[18] *Sayings*, 250f.

as J. Weiss and A. Schweitzer on the centrality of eschatology in the preaching of the historical Jesus.[19] In any case, Harnack's tendency to play down the importance of eschatology in Q itself is very questionable, as we shall see. Further, the allegedly non-dogmatic Q, free from bias, has been radically questioned as more and more scholars have argued that Q has a very specific corner to defend, or case to argue, and that a distinctive theological 'bias', or interest, cannot be ruled out.

Harnack's theories about the historical value of Q had already been implicitly questioned in the work of Wellhausen.[20] In his *Einleitung*, Wellhausen considered the question of the relationship between Mark and Q, looking at the passages where they overlapped. He argued that, on every occasion, Q's version is the more recent and hence must be dependent on Mark.[21] This raised the question of why Q had then omitted so much from Mark. Wellhausen's suggestion has had a great deal of influence: he argued that Q omitted much of Mark's narrative intentionally. Q was intended primarily for catechetical purposes and it could presuppose the Markan passion kerygma.[22] Wellhausen's views about the relationship between Mark and Q have not won widespread support if only because he seems to have ruled out of court, on an almost a priori basis, any possibility of Mark and Q being independent of each other. However, much more significant has been his view that Q is not to be taken by itself, but represents a supplement to the Markan passion-oriented

---

[19] The question of whether eschatology, or apocalyptic, should be seen as central in the preaching of Jesus is once more in the melting pot, in part as a result of more recent Q studies. See, for example, the work of B. Mack, *The Myth of Innocence* (Philadelphia: Fortress, 1988); *The Lost Gospel. The Book of Q and Christian Origins* (San Francisco: HarperCollins, 1993); also J. D. Crossan, *The Historical Jesus. The Life of a Mediterranean Jewish Peasant* (Edinburgh: T. & T. Clark, 1991). In a much more carefully nuanced form, cf. J. M. Robinson, 'The Q Trajectory: Between John and Matthew via Jesus', in B. A. Pearson (ed.), *The Future of Early Christianity* (FS H. Koester; Minneapolis: Fortress, 1991) 173–94. Vaage & Kloppenborg, 'Early Christianity, Q and Jesus', 3f., link Harnack and Mack in this respect.

[20] J. Wellhausen, *Einleitung in die drei ersten Evangelien* (Berlin: Reimer, 1905). In one way it might be considered more appropriate to treat Wellhausen before Harnack, since Wellhausen's work preceded Harnack's chronologically, and Harnack himself was in part reacting against Wellhausen: see Harnack, *Sayings*, 193. However, in many respects Wellhausen belongs more closely with subsequent scholarship than Harnack does.

[21] *Einleitung*, 73–89 (§8) [§6 in the 2nd edn].

[22] *Einleitung*, 2nd edn., 159f. (cited by Kloppenborg, *Formation*, 14).

tradition. One of Q's apparently strangest features, its lack of any account of Jesus' death or resurrection, was thus accounted for at a stroke: the audience for whom Q was intended could be assumed to have had full knowledge of Jesus' passion and (by implication) to have accepted the centrality of the latter in Christian faith.

Such a view was certainly very influential in discussions of Q in the first half of the twentieth century. For example, B. H. Streeter, whose book *The Four Gospels* popularised the theory of Markan priority and the Q hypothesis for the English-speaking world, also considered the question of the relationship between Mark and Q. Although, notoriously, he changed his mind on the details of the subject (arguing in 1911 that Mark knew Q, and in 1924 that Mark and Q were independent),[23] in broad outline his views about the relationship between Q and the cross-centred kerygma of the Church remained the same: Q was essentially a supplement to add to the basic preaching of the cross which could be assumed to be common to all Christians.[24]

T. W. Manson's study *The Sayings of Jesus* took a very similar line. The opening sentences of Manson's book are often cited in this context:

> Historic Christianity is first and foremost a Gospel, the proclamation to the world of Jesus Christ and Him crucified. For the primitive Church the central thing is the Cross on the Hill rather than the Sermon on the Mount, and the characteristic Church act is the Communion rather than the conference.[25]

Again, Q was seen as primarily for use in catechesis.[26] Manson raised the question of why Q then contained nothing explicitly about the 'Cross on the Hill':

> The most probable explanation is that there is no Passion-story because none is required, Q being a book of instructions for people who are already Christians and know the story of the Cross by heart.[27]

One notable feature of Manson's book was his attempt to see the whole of Q as rather more of a structured whole than had

[23] B. H. Streeter, 'St Mark's Knowledge and Use of Q', in Sanday (ed.), *Oxford Studies*, 165–84; and his *Four Gospels*, 186–91.

[24] See his essay 'The Literary Evolution of the Gospels', in Sanday (ed.), *Oxford Studies*, 210–27, p. 215; and his *Four Gospels*, 292.

[25] *Sayings*, 9.

[26] *Sayings*, 15.

[27] *Sayings*, 16.

hitherto been the case. Thus Manson argued that Q could be divided into four major sections:

Q 3:7 – 7:35	John the Baptist and Jesus
9:57 – 11:13	Jesus and His Disciples
11:14 – 12:34	Jesus and His Opponents
12:35 – 17:37	Jesus and the Future.[28]

One conclusion which Manson drew from this was that, since the material started and finished with eschatological teaching, this was probably a deliberate arrangement; further, this constituted 'a strong argument in favour of the view . . . that in Mt. and Lk. we have preserved for us substantially all that Q ever contained'.[29]

Manson's views about the structure of Q partly anticipate later theories of a deliberate compositional activity by the person(s) responsible for Q. However, Manson did not develop his ideas in this respect further and in any case one must say that his grouping of the material under the four headings he gave can only be described as rather 'rough and ready': how does the Great Sermon (Q 6:20ff.) fit into the rubric 'John the Baptist and Jesus', or the section on Cares (Q 12:22ff.) into 'Jesus and his Opponents' (rather than 'Jesus and his Disciples')? Further, it seems clear that Manson was strongly influenced by his overall theory about Q as basically supplementary ethical teaching for Christians when he claimed that the polemical material in Q was minimal:

> A . . . striking feature in Q is the exceedingly small quantity of polemical matter which it contains. It records no disputes with Scribes and Pharisees such as we find in Mk. . . . At the same time, it contains a denunciation of Pharisaism (Lk. 11.[37–41], 42–52). But ninety per cent. of the document is positive religious and moral teaching. This fact again is explicable on the assumption that the work was intended for use within the Christian community as a manual of instruction in the duties of the Christian life.[30]

Subsequent studies of Q have failed to support Manson here since, as we shall see, the aspect of polemic has come to be regarded as one of the most distinctive features of Q.[31]

---

[28] See the detailed textual commentary, arranged under these headings, in *Sayings*, 39–148.

[29] *Sayings*, 16.

[30] *Sayings*, 16.

[31] Tödt, *Son of Man*, 244, points to this weakness in Manson's overall position here.

The idea of Q as a supplement to the cross-centred kerygma of the preaching of the early Church was also adopted in the work of German-speaking form critics. Harnack's positive evaluation of Q's Jesus found little response in German Biblical criticism of the 1920s dominated by dialectical theology with all stress placed on a Pauline-type theology of the cross.[32] Thus for Dibelius, Q was simply 'paranesis', rather than 'preaching'.[33] Further, in line with form criticism's general attitude to the nature of the gospel tradition as primarily oral and un-literary, Dibelius refused to think of Q as a 'document' with an 'author': rather than being a document ('*Schrift*'), Q was simply a stratum, or layer, ('*Schicht*') in the tradition.[34]

R. Bultmann's approach to Q, at least in his *History of the Synoptic Tradition*, is similar. Bultmann treated the individual parts of the Q material separately, but did not have a great deal to say about Q as a whole. He regarded some parts as later accretions to Q, stemming from a Hellenistic origin (Q 4:1–13; 7:1–10; 10:21f.);[35] more generally he saw the Q material, as part of all the sayings material in the gospels, as having been put together in a fairly rudimentary way as in oral tradition, e.g. by catchword connections or by linking units of similar contents.[36] The needs which such collecting met were, as before, primarily those of paranesis, teaching, Church discipline, etc.

Kloppenborg has argued that a slight, but significant, shift occurs in Bultmann's understanding of Q between the writing of his *History of the Synoptic Tradition* and his *Theology of the New Testament*.[37] As is well known, Bultmann claimed that the preaching of the historical Jesus cannot be regarded as part of a genuinely Christian kerygma. Jesus looked forward to an eschatological event in the future, but 'if Jesus' significance to the earliest Church were exhausted in its expecting him as the coming Son of Man, it would still be only a Jewish sect and would not properly be called Christian Church'.[38] Nor did adding in

---

[32] Cf. Tödt, *Son of Man*, 237f.; Schulz, *Q*, 19.

[33] See M. Dibelius, *From Tradition to Gospel* (ET New York: Scribner's, 1935) 233ff.

[34] *Tradition*, 235.

[35] R. Bultmann, *The History of the Synoptic Tradition* (ET Oxford: Blackwell, 1963) 328.

[36] *History*, 322–8.

[37] Kloppenborg, 'Tradition and Redaction', 37; also his *Formation*, 21.

[38] R. Bultmann, *The Theology of the New Testament I* (ET London: SCM, 1952) 37.

reference to the resurrection make any essential difference if the resurrection meant 'no more than proof of the exaltation of the Crucified to Son of Man'. However, although the early Church, in handing on Jesus' teaching, did not achieve the explicit formulation of the Pauline understanding of Jesus' person and death as the eschatological event, nevertheless 'it did implicitly understand him in this sense through the fact that it conceived of itself as the eschatological Congregation'.[39] For Q such an awareness is shown by the presence of the eschatological preaching of John the Baptist, the eschatologically oriented beatitudes, and the Parousia sayings which come at the end. Thus, according to Kloppenborg, Bultmann's Q in his *Theology* is half-way to becoming a representative of genuine Christian kerygma rather than just being a supplement to the kerygmatic preaching of the cross. Kloppenborg also suggests that a not dissimilar ambiguity may be present in Streeter's understanding. For in almost the same breath as claiming that Q's omission of the Passion narrative was due to the fact that it could be presupposed as well known (and hence presumably accepted positively), Streeter suggested another reason: it might have been that in some circles the cross was regarded only negatively, as 'one of those calamities which darken men's understanding of His [God's] purpose, rather than the one act that has unveiled the mystery'.[40] Thus Q might have had an understanding of Jesus' death significantly different from the passion kerygma of Paul and others.[41]

Whether Kloppenborg's claims about a shift in Bultmann's views about Q are valid can remain on one side here since we are concerned primarily with Q itself, rather than exegesis of Bultmann's writings.[42] Nevertheless, the idea that Q had its own version of a Christian kerygma, and that it should not be regarded as simply a supplement to amplify a more fundamental cross-

---

[39] *Theology*, 37.

[40] *Four Gospels*, 292.

[41] Kloppenborg, 'Tradition and Redaction', 38; *Formation*, 21f.

[42] Tödt, in his discussion of Bultmann on Q (*Son of Man*, 240f.), finds no such distinction. In any case it is hard to see how Bultmann's references to preaching about a *future* eschatology preserved in Q really substantiate his claim that Q Christians already understood their existence in the present as part of the 'Eschatological Congregation'. Reference to a text such as Q 11:20 might have been more apposite. But then if, as is widely assumed, Q 11:20 is a saying of Jesus too, can we draw such a firm line between Q and Jesus? Perhaps the problems here say more about Bultmann's claim to be able to separate Jesus from the Christian kerygma.

centred kerygma, has certainly come to the fore very strongly in scholarly discussions over the last forty years or so.

A decisive contribution in the development of the movement to see Q as a self-contained entity, with its own distinctive version of Christian preaching, was undoubtedly Tödt's work on the SM sayings in the gospels. It was really Tödt who finally broke with the idea that Q needed something else (e.g. the preaching of the cross) to make sense of it. Reacting against Bultmann, Tödt pointed out that the very fact that Jesus' preaching was continued by the early Christians had its significance. 'Why did they accept the authority of the words of the one on earth?'[43] Thus Tödt argued that the motive for collecting Jesus material at all required more explanation. Tödt also expressed dissatisfaction with the general view that Q was to be seen as 'paranetic'. He pointed out that several parts of Q failed to fit such a description, e.g. the Beelzebul pericope (11:14–23), the sayings about the Sign of Jonah (11:29–32), the prophecy over Jerusalem (13:34f.), etc.[44]

Tödt then proceeded to take Q on its own terms and to interpret it independently of the passion kerygma so dominant in Mark and Paul. Tödt argued that the very form of Q, representing the teaching of the pre-Easter Jesus in the post-Easter situation, indicated that the Christians who preserved Q were convinced of the contemporary validity of that preaching in their own day. It was this, rather than the passion, which was of decisive importance for them. Further, this activity was not without Christological significance. Almost the only Christological term used in Q is 'SM'. Tödt, following Bultmann, argued that Jesus himself looked forward to the future coming of an SM figure as someone other than himself who would vindicate his cause. The Q Christians, perhaps on the basis of the resurrection experience, became convinced that this coming SM figure was none other than Jesus himself. Thus Q, for the first time in Christian thought, identified Jesus with the SM; hence a 'SM Christology' is one of the most distinctive features of the Q tradition. In Tödt's words, 'Son of Man Christology and Q belong together both in their concepts and in their history of tradition'.[45]

Tödt's work was undoubtedly programmatic in many ways and has been influential in pointing the way for further Q studies,

[43] *Son of Man*, 241.
[44] *Son of Man*, 246.
[45] *Son of Man*, 269.

even if many of the details of his argument have been questioned radically. Tödt's significance was to see that Q could be regarded as making sense on its own and that it could be meaningfully taken as the product of a specific group of Christians, a 'community', which preserved the Q material and handed it on.[46] In this Tödt has very often been hailed as the forerunner and initiator of a 'redaction-critical' approach to Q. In many respects this assessment of Tödt's work seems fully justified, though there have been, and still are, important questions to raise about the proper methodology, as well as the aim, of such an approach. It is with these questions of methodology in mind that the rest of this survey of past studies of Q is undertaken. Thus to reiterate, no comprehensive *Forschungsbericht* of Q is being attempted here. What is in view rather is the question of method: how should we be analysing Q?

2. More Recent Q Studies

'Redaction criticism' (a piece of English translationese for the German '*Redaktionsgeschichte*') is often regarded as a discipline which has influenced gospel studies since the late 1940s as the successor of form criticism. As such it is often taken as starting with the work of G. Bornkamm on Matthew and H. Conzelmann on Luke.[47] Whereas form criticism had tended

---

[46] More recently there has been debate about the propriety of calling this group of Christians a 'community'. For example, P. Hoffmann has insisted on referring to a Q-'Gruppe' (English 'group') as opposed to a Q-'Gemeinde': see his *Studien zur Theologie der Logienquelle* (NTAbh 8; Münster: Aschendorff, 1972) 10. In fact the debate may be more of an issue for German speakers than for English. 'Gemeinde' in German is far more of a theologically loaded word than the English 'community', even though they are often used as translation equivalents. 'Gemeinde' probably implies a much more cohesive set of people (quite often 'Gemeinde' is translated by the English 'Church'). In fact Hoffmann's 'Gruppe' may not be so different from an English 'community', implying by the latter only a group of people who are perhaps more than simply a set of individuals and share some measure of group cohesiveness, but without necessarily any developed organisation. The degree of community awareness on the part of Q Christians is of course something we shall have to return to later (see ch. 13 below). Thus in what follows I shall continue to use the term 'community', though without intending to prejudge any questions by doing so. On the issue, see too C. E. Carlston, 'Wisdom and Eschatology in Q', in Delobel (ed.), *LOGIA*, 101–19, p. 112 n. 63.

[47] Cf. N. Perrin, *What is Redaction Criticism?* (London: SPCK, 1969).

to regard the evangelists simply as editors who did not greatly influence the development of the tradition, redaction criticism sought to redress the balance by focusing on the contribution of the evangelists, seeing them as far more actively involved in the editing process with their own specific theological agendas. Thus redaction criticism sought in general to discover the particular theological aims and outlooks of the evangelists themselves. The method of the early redaction-critical studies was fairly well-defined. Assuming the theory of Markan priority, use of a synopsis shows that at times Matthew and Luke changed ('redacted') their Markan source. An analysis of these redactional changes may then give us an important insight into the thinking of the evangelist who made the changes. Thus in order to find out about the distinctive theological features of Matthew and Luke, attention was focused on their redactional activity in altering their tradition. (The appropriateness of the method will be considered later.) Such an approach has exerted a powerful influence on Q studies from the late 1960s onwards, at least in the very general sense of seeking to identify the distinctive ideas and concerns of Q. In this very general sense, therefore, 'redaction-critical' studies and methods have been applied to Q ever since Tödt's day. However, the precise way in which attempts have been made to find distinctive features in Q has varied.

Tödt's work on the SM tradition made no attempt to isolate any strictly 'redactional' activity by Q. The situation with Q is of course quite different from that of Matthew and Luke, in that we do not have any of Q's source material available to enable us to make any detailed comparisons between Q and its source. We do not even have Q itself directly available! Tödt's approach was thus more 'thematic'. He considered the Q material as a whole and sought to make deductions from the totality of the material about its distinctive features. Such an approach to Q has however gradually changed since Tödt wrote. Today the general tendency has been much more to try to detect stages in the development of Q, to distinguish Q's tradition from Q's redaction, or to postulate a number of stages in the history of the Q tradition. Perhaps the most significant study in this respect has been one of the earliest self-consciously 'redaction'-critical studies of Q, D. Lührmann's *Die Redaktion der Logienqelle*, which was published in 1969 as the first of a number of publications reflecting a remarkable flowering of interest in Q in the late 1960s and early 1970s.[48]

Lührmann's work undoubtedly broke new ground methodologically in Q studies, and has probably had the greatest influence on subsequent research in terms of both method and results despite its relatively short length.[49] Lührmann's approach is to try to refine Tödt's thematic analysis by seeking to identify specifically redactional elements in Q. Taking over the terminology of Bultmann, Lührmann distinguishes between a mere 'collecting' ('*Sammlung*') and a more self-conscious 'redaction' ('*Redaktion*') of the material.[50] By '*Sammlung*', Lührmann means simply the juxtaposition of related materials on the basis of common content or catchword connections, whereas '*Redaktion*' is taken as referring to a much more self-conscious process of amplification, expansion, etc. Lührmann is aware that he is probably going beyond Bultmann himself in making such a distinction,[51] and he also sharply distinguishes his general approach to Q itself from that of Bultmann (and Dibelius). Thus he argues that the process by which Q grew was not just one of gradual evolution, a mere '*Sammlung*' of related materials. Such an evolution might lie behind some of the smaller collections of sayings in Q such as 6:20–49; but Q's '*Redaktion*' is to be regarded as a specific point in the editing process at which a definite viewpoint was expressed. Here Lührmann distances himself from Dibelius's view that Q was only a '*Schicht*' and not a '*Schrift*',[52] as well as from Bultmann's own views about the editing of Q.

[48] D. Lührmann, *Die Redaktion der Logienquelle* (WMANT 33; Neukirchen-Vluyn: Neukirchener, 1969). In the late 1960s, three German doctoral dissertations (by D. Lührmann, P. Hoffmann and A. Polag) were submitted at their respective Universities almost simultaneously. All of these were mutually known as each was subsequently prepared for publication so that, although the publication of the theses followed with varying speeds (Lührmann's dissertation was published in 1969, Hoffmann's in 1972, Polag's only in 1977 and then only in part), each author was able to interact with the views of the others in the published versions. 1972 also saw the publication of the monumental full-scale analysis and commentary of Schulz (Schulz, *Q*).

[49] His analysis of Q itself only occupied 80 pages (*Redaktion*, pp. 24–104), being preceded by an important discussion of methodology (pp. 11–23) and followed by a discussion of a possible post-Q, pre-Matthean development of the Q tradition (pp. 105–21).

[50] *Redaktion*, 15.

[51] Cf. *Redaktion*, 15 n. 1; also Neirynck, 'Recent Developments', 73f. n. 240.

[52] *Redaktion*, 15.

Lührmann proposes various criteria by which Q's redaction can be identified.[53] (i) The putting together of originally isolated units may indicate the interests of the redactor, especially if similar interests can be seen at more than one place within Q. (ii) Comparison of Q with Mark may reveal tendencies within the Q tradition. (iii) The same may also be shown by '*Gemeindebildungen*' (community creations), i.e. sayings created by the community, provided always that it could be shown that such creations took place at the stage of the final redaction of Q.

Lührmann himself in his analysis of Q makes most frequent use of (i) above. In a very influential chapter, he points to the way in which several of the longer discourses in Q have, in the editing process, become vehicles for articulating a polemical attack against 'this generation' (which Lührmann takes to mean all Israel).[54] For example, in 7:18–35 earlier traditions, where perhaps the relationship between Jesus and John the Baptist was an important issue, have been taken up and pressed into the service of a wider unit where Jesus and John appear in parallel, with no rivalry between them, as preachers opposed to 'this generation' which refuses to accept them (7:31–35). Similarly, the series of woes in 11:39ff. has been broadened out at the end by the addition of the final woe in 11:49–51, so that the whole discourse becomes a violent attack on 'this generation', i.e. all Israel. Lührmann finds such polemic at a number of points in Q; he also takes the polemic to be so sharp that he concludes that the Q Christians must have given up all hope for Israel. The Q community was thus open to the Gentiles, and for the non-Christian Jews only judgement remained.[55] Lührmann also argues that the SM material was not so important for Q's redaction. Contra Tödt, he claims that the identification of Jesus with the SM had already taken place in Q's tradition and hence could not be regarded as an integral part of the redaction.[56]

Many of Lührmann's detailed arguments will be considered later and hence will not be discussed here. His claims about the importance of the strand in Q comprising polemic against 'this generation' have certainly been accepted by many, even if its precise interpretation is open to more than one possibility. Above all though, in terms of method, Lührmann has pointed the way

[53] *Redaktion*, 20–2.
[54] *Redaktion*, 24–48.
[55] *Redaktion*, 93.
[56] *Redaktion*, 40f.

forward for many in trying to distinguish between tradition and redaction in Q and his work paves the way for a great deal of subsequent Q study. One must however also say that in practice, Lührmann's '*Redaktion*' is not so different from the '*Sammlung*' from which he would distinguish it. For the '*Redaktion*' is to be seen precisely in the collecting (*Sammlung*), even though Lührmann attributes rather more self-conscious theological interest to the collecting process than, say, Bultmann did: 'Vor allem zeigt sie sich [die Redaktion von Q] in der Zusammenfügung verschiedener ursprünglich isolierter oder bereits in kleinen Sammlungen vereinigter Logien.'[57] Lührmann rarely appeals to the existence of *Gemeindebildungen* as revealing elements of Q's redactional concerns. Such redactional creations are postulated in the cases of Q 10:12; 11:30; 11:51, but mostly these are to be seen as simply transitional elements linking units of the tradition together.[58] So too Lührmann lays little evidential stress on a comparison with Mark, finding here only secondary support for arguments already established.[59] His main stress thus lies as much on the total impact of the larger units in Q in their present form.

Although Lührmann's attempt to isolate Q's redactional activity has been very influential, we should note other approaches which have been less ready to make such distinctions within Q. We have already seen that Tödt's thematic approach made no such attempt to distinguish tradition from redaction within Q. The same may be said of the early brief studies of W. D. Davies and H. C. Kee,[60] both of whom stress the importance of eschatology in Q and both of whom take Q as an undifferentiated whole. The same may also apply to the early dissertation of P. D. Meyer who, whilst at one level discussing the issue of what might be redactional in Q, relies almost exclusively on a criterion of Q's

---

[57] *Redaktion*, 89.

[58] Kloppenborg, 'Tradition and Redaction', 49, refers to the fact that Lührmann designates 10:13–15; 11:31f.; 12:42–46 and 10:21f. as *Gemeindebildungen* (*Redaktion*, 65, 70, 93). However, Lührmann never lays any stress on this as *per se* revealing Q's redactional interests. His references to these verses as *Gemeindebildungen* simply refer to the fact that he regards the sayings as having a post-Easter origin. This does not necessarily imply that they are Q-*redactional* creations.

[59] Cf. Kloppenborg, 'Tradition and Redaction', 49.

[60] See W. D. Davies, *The Setting of the Sermon on the Mount* (Cambridge University Press, 1966) 366–86; H. C. Kee, *Jesus in History* (New York: Harcourt, Brace & World, 1970) 62–103.

choice of material for determining redactional interests.[61] Effectively this reduces to a method of taking the Q material as a whole without distinctions. All these studies were written before Lührmann's work and were uninfluenced by the new 'redaction-critical' approach. But a methodologically very similar approach is offered in the work of P. Hoffmann in his influential 1972 monograph, re-presenting his 1968 dissertation in published form, as well as in the more recent work of G. Theissen.[62]

One striking difference between Hoffmann and Lührmann appears to be over the question of methodology. Hoffmann refuses to try to distinguish too sharply between tradition and redaction. For him, the Q material exhibits a great homogeneity and hence one can in principle work from the Q material as a whole to make deductions about the situation and beliefs of the '*Q-Gruppe*' which preserved it.[63] Hoffmann's monograph does not in fact attempt a detailed analysis of the whole of Q. He deals with the themes of eschatology and SM as well as devoting a very long section to the mission charge. He argues that eschatology was still important for Q and that, despite any delay in the Parousia, the *Q-Gruppe* was imbued with a very vivid expectation of an imminent End to the present world order. He argues too (contra Lührmann) that SM was a very important Christological term for Q. Most importantly his analysis of the mission charge leads him to make some quite specific suggestions about the *Sitz im Leben* of the Q community. He suggests that the Q missionaries followed the instructions of the mission charge to the letter, going

---

[61] Meyer, *The Community of Q* (Ph.D. Dissertation, University of Iowa, 1967).

[62] Hoffmann, *Studien*. The slight delay in publication enabled Hoffmann to interact with Lührmann and others in the published version of his work, above all over the question of method. For Theissen's theories on Q, see *The Gospels in Context: Social and Political History in the Synoptic Tradition* (ET Edinburgh: T. & T. Clark, 1992) (= *Lokalkolorit und Zeitgeschichte in den Evangelien* [NTOA 8; Göttingen & Freiburg: Vandenhoeck & Ruprecht & Universitätsverlag, 1989]) ch. 5. In relation to method, Theissen aligns himself with Tödt and Hoffmann in not attempting too much by way of distinguishing tradition from redaction: see his *Gospels in Context*, 203 n. 3. Unfortunately the English translation of the key sentence in Theissen's note here is badly misleading when it has 'I consider it an advantage of these studies [= Tödt and Hoffmann] that they succeed without excluding redactional elements'. The German original has: 'Daß sie ohne Ausscheidung redaktioneller Bestandteile auskommen, ist m.E. ein Vorzug dieser Studien'. See his *Lokalkolorit*, 212 n. 3. For 'excluding' one should probably have 'separating out' (i.e. in order to focus *on*, not to exclude from consideration).

[63] *Studien*, 3f.

out without any money or protection. All this was a kind of acted parable of a group intent on proclaiming peace and non-violence in the situation in Palestine leading up to the Jewish revolt of 66–70 CE.

Hoffmann's somewhat limited scope in his monograph has been supplemented with detailed articles elsewhere and a full-scale commentary on Q in the EKK series is promised.[64] His specific suggestion about the Sitz im Leben of the Q community has not commanded universal assent and will be discussed later (see pp. 361–3 below). Of more interest here is the methodological question and Hoffmann's general refusal to place too much weight on a distinction between tradition and redaction in Q. Many have criticised Hoffmann for this. For example, Kloppenborg considers Hoffmann together with Tödt, Davies and other representatives of such a thematic approach and says:

> A thematic approach does not . . . sufficiently distinguish tradition from redaction and in M. Devisch's words, runs the risk of accentuating wrongly 'des éléments qui, après tout, ne sont pas typiques de la source Q'.[65]

Whether such a criticism is in principle justified will be considered later, though it should also be noted that Hoffmann himself is by no means averse to trying to identify redactional creations by Q and in effect postulates rather more such creations than Lührmann had. Thus Hoffmann agrees with Lührmann on the redactional nature of 10:12; 11:30; 11:51b[66] but also regards as redactional 3:16; 6:22f.; 7:27, 28b, 33–35; 13:35b,[67] and more recently he has argued for extensive Q-redactional interference in the original tradition (= Jesus' preaching) about Cares.[68] In

[64] See the Bibliography for details of the many articles already published.

[65] Kloppenborg, 'Tradition and Redaction', 46, quoting M. Devisch, 'Le document Q, source de Matthieu, problématique actuelle', in M. Didier (ed.), *L'Evangile selon Matthieu. Rédaction et théologie* (BETL 29; Gembloux: Duculot, 1972) 71–97, 90f. For similar critiques by others, cf. Lührmann, *Redaktion*, 8; Schulz, *Q*, 36; Luz, 'Die wiederentdeckte Logienquelle', 532; Schmithals, *Einleitung*, 390f.

[66] See *Studien*, 28 (for 10:12); 37, 157, 181 (for 11:30); 168 (for 11:51).

[67] *Studien*, 21 (for 3:16), 73 (for 6:22f.), 218–24 (for 7:27, 28b, 33–35), 117 (for 13:35b). Cf. Neirynck, 'Recent Developments', 54.

[68] P. Hoffmann, 'Die Sprüche vom Sorgen in der vorsynoptischen Überlieferung', in H. Hierdeis & H. S. Rosenbusch (eds), *Artikulation der Wirklichkeit* (FS S. Oppolzer; Frankfurt: Peter Lang, 1988) 73–94.

fact, insofar as Hoffmann proceeds by considering the way in which these secondary elements influence and shape the whole tradition, his general approach is not very far removed from that of Lührmann and clearly belongs within the more overtly 'redaction'-critical studies of Q.[69]

A rather different approach was adopted by S. Schulz in his massive volume which remains the fullest detailed 'commentary' on the whole of Q at present available. Schulz, like Lührmann, tries to distinguish different strata within Q. However, his method is quite different from Lührmann's. Indeed he regards Lührmann's attempt to isolate Q's redaction as a failure: 'Es ist Lührmann nicht gelungen, auch nur einen einzigen Vers in Q der Q-Redaktion zuzuweisen.'[70] Schulz's own approach is to proceed inductively, primarily on the basis of Bultmann's original claim that three elements in Q represent later 'Hellenistic' accretions. These are the temptation narrative (Q 4:1–13), the story of the healing of the centurion's servant (Q 7:1–10) and the 'Johannine thunderbolt' in Q 10:21f. On the basis of these three pericopes and others designated as 'late' by Dibelius, Schulz then builds up a list of criteria for distinguishing later from earlier elements in Q, e.g. the apophthegm form, a developed Christology, the use of the LXX, the delay of the Parousia, ideas of personified Wisdom, polemic against Israel, etc.[71] In this way Schulz isolates a large section of Q, Q^2, separated from a (rather smaller) earlier Q^1 stratum with a number of differences between them. The early Q^1 represents the preaching of the earliest phase of the Q community with strong prophetic self-consciousness.

---

[69] Lührmann argued against Hoffmann, defending his own approach, in 'Liebet eure Feinde (Lk 6,27–36/Mt 5,39–48)', *ZThK* 69 (1972) 412–38, 423 n. 46. However, Lührmann himself has now given a more nuanced description of his own approach in his more recent 'The Gospel of Mark and the Sayings Collection Q', *JBL* 108 (1989) 51–71, p. 60 n. 44: 'I myself have emphasised this model [of distinguishing tradition and redaction] very much. Once the possibility of a theology of Q is established one can get more moderate. But even at that time *redaction for me was not so much redactional additions but looking for certain themes which are dominant in the material.*' (My stress.) One should not therefore drive too much of a methodological wedge between Hoffmann and Lührmann!

[70] Schulz, *Q*, 38.

[71] *Q*, 47–53. It should however be noted that, although ostensibly basing himself on Bultmann, Schulz makes a major change from Bultmann: the latter had assigned Q 10:21f. to a Hellenistic milieu, whereas Schulz assigns it to a Hellenistic *Jewish* Christian milieu. See Hoffmann's review of Schulz's book, *BZ* 19 (1975) 104–15, p. 108.

These prophets proclaimed a radicalised Torah in an apocalyptic framework. With Q^2 a decisive shift occurs. Probably the same community is involved but it had moved geographically from a Palestinian milieu to a Hellenistic one (possibly in Syria). With this a shift also occurs in that the words of the *earthly* Jesus are now interpreted kerygmatically:

> Aus enthusiastischen Prophetensprüchen, in denen sich ursprünglich der erhöht-gegenwärtige Menschensohn Jesus meldete, werden jetzt Worte des irdischen Jesus als des Endzeitpropheten vor der nahen Menschensohn-Parusie.[72]

Schulz also occasionally refers to later collections of Q sayings and the final Q redaction,[73] though this aspect of the history of the Q tradition plays virtually no role in Schulz's work as a whole.[74]

Schulz's monumental work remains of value if only because of its comprehensiveness, although his detailed arguments about Q as a whole have convinced few. His discussions of individual sections in Q remain of value (though his source-critical analyses, seeking to determine the more original form of the tradition, are governed by a rather one-sided use of vocabulary statistics alone, applied at times in a rather arbitrary way). He deals with the material of Q in an order which (as far as I am aware) is presented as a *fait accompli* and never defended and Schulz himself never considers the order of the smaller units as a potentially significant factor in interpreting each unit individually.[75]

His theories of two stages in Q has also evoked detailed criticism.[76] For example, his attempt to distinguish between 'Palestinian' and 'Hellenistic' strata as both geographically distinct and chronologically consecutive seems particularly questionable, especially in the light of the work of Hengel and others who have shown that Hellenistic influence cannot be restricted to a non-Palestinian milieu.[77] Further, Schulz's method in building up

---

[72] *Q*, 482.

[73] *Q*, 481, cf. too 484.

[74] Cf. Kloppenborg, 'Tradition and Redaction', 39 n. 24; R. Uro, *Sheep among the Wolves: A Study of the Mission Instructions of Q* (Helsinki: Suomaleinen Tiedeakatemia, 1987) 5.

[75] The order is in part topical, but within each topic, Schulz's order seems quite arbitrary.

[76] See Hoffmann's review; Kloppenborg, 'Tradition and Redaction', 39–45.

[77] Cf. M. Hengel, *Judaism and Hellenism* (ET London: SCM, 1974) passim; Lührmann, 'Erwägungen zur Geschichte des Urchristentums', *EvTh* 32 (1972) 452–67. Cf. also Kloppenborg, 'Tradition and Redaction', 42; Lührmann, *Redaktion*, 16.

criteria for distinguishing later elements from earlier ones is questionable. For example, the fact that two of Bultmann's alleged 'Hellenistic' elements in Q are apophthegms can only be reversed with some difficulty into a claim that an apophthegmatic form itself is a valid criterion for assigning elements in Q to the later stratum.[78] Moreover, it is not at all clear that units which are similar in relation to their tradition history should necessarily be assigned to precisely the same stage in the historical development of Q. As Kloppenborg says, 'Tradition history . . . is not the same as literary history'.[79] Schulz's application of his criteria is also at times problematic.[80] Thus, given Schulz's failure to consider any aspect of the broader structure of Q, his total interpretation of Q remains somewhat idiosyncratic.

Many of the same comments can be made about A. Polag's *Die Christologie der Logienquelle*[81] which also seeks to divide the Q material into various strata. According to Polag, various smaller collections of sayings (*'Kernstücke'*) were brought together by a first redaction in a 'Main collection' (*'Hauptsammlung'*). A 'later redaction' (*'späte Redaktion'*) then added the introductory pericopes (Q 3:7–9, 16f.; 4:1–13) as well as other related material (7:1–10, 27f.; 10:21f., 23f.; 12:10, 49–53; 19:12–27). However, as with Schulz, the reasons for such distinctions seem at best rather arbitrary.[82] The introductory sections are regarded as secondary because they do not consist of sayings of Jesus to the disciples, the crowds or opponents; they are appended simply to undergird the authority of the following collection.[83] Such a criterion for distinguishing strata within Q is in any case scarcely compelling. But then anything else in Q regarded as having linguistic or substantive links with this material is also assigned to this later redactional stage, e.g. the Biblical quotation in 7:27 or the Son Christology in 10:21f.[84] The method is very close to that of Schulz, and exactly the same kind of criticisms which can be levelled against Schulz can be brought to bear here.

The need to have rather more literary controls over the whole process of distinguishing between strata has been recognised in

---

[78] Kloppenborg, 'Tradition and Redaction', 44.

[79] 'Tradition and Redaction', 42.

[80] See Hoffmann's critique in his penetrating review of Schulz's book.

[81] A. Polag, *Die Christologie der Logienquelle* (WMANT 45; Neukirchen-Vluyn: Neukirchener, 1977).

[82] See Kloppenborg, 'Tradition and Redaction', 51.

[83] Polag, *Christologie*, 15.

[84] Polag, *Christologie*, 16.

recent studies. As an example of such an approach we may consider A. D. Jacobson's 1978 Claremont dissertation *Wisdom Christology in Q*, the substance of which is included in his 1992 book *The First Gospel*.[85] Jacobson's method has many affinities with Lührmann's approach. Like Lührmann, Jacobson considers larger units within Q, though he wants to cast his net even wider than Lührmann. Lührmann had mostly restricted attention to sections of c. 20–30 verses in Matthew/Luke, and indeed had not really gone beyond units of tradition whose common order and context were attested in both Matthew and Luke (cf. Q 7:18–35 which is a block of material in the same order in both gospels). Jacobson tries to go further and identify even larger sections in Q with their own inherent unity and structure. Jacobson calls his own approach one of 'composition criticism'[86] and stresses above all the importance and value of working backwards from the 'final' form of the text of Q, i.e. that which is recoverable from the gospels of Matthew and Luke.[87] Thus Jacobson's approach involves an attempt to recover original sequences in Q, to recover larger wholes in the composition of Q, rather than to start from the smallest units of individual sayings or pericopes and work upwards to see how they have been put together. For example, he considers Q 3:1–7:35 as a unit dealing with Jesus and John the Baptist, presenting the preaching of John and Jesus in turn (3:7ff. and 6:20ff. respectively) and culminating in a section dealing with the relationship between them. Within these larger units Jacobson then seeks to identify layers within the text on the basis of what he calls 'literary disunity',[88] indicated by shifts in audience, breaks in the train of thought, changes in ideas, etc. On the basis of these 'seams' it may then be possible to identify points at which earlier material has been reworked, or new material inserted, and hence to identify different 'stages' in the development of Q. Jacobson thus combines an approach which is alert to the aporia in a text which have always been grist to the mill for a 'redaction'-critic with one that is sensitive to the literary *unity* of

---

[85] In his original dissertation Jacobson considered the Q material up to Q 13:35. The 1992 book extends the discussion to the whole of Q as well as including much of the material previously published in Jacobson's earlier articles. Despite the delay in formal publication, Jacobson's work has been widely known since 1978 and has exerted considerable influence.

[86] *First Gospel*, 43.

[87] *First Gospel*, 13, 45.

[88] *First Gospel*, 45.

the Q material, and an awareness that the literary structuring of the material may well be just as significant in any attempt to identify the characteristic features of Q.

On the basis of this methodology, Jacobson argues for at least three levels of redactional activity. A first stage (called by Jacobson the 'compositional stage') evidently had the most influence. Here the material is redacted to show Jesus and John in parallel as messengers of Wisdom in a line of continuity with the suffering prophets before them. It is here that the polemic against 'this generation' (Israel) has its place too. However, this does not end the redactional process. A later 'intermediate' stage attempted to distinguish more clearly between Jesus and John (cf. Q 3:16; 7:18–23, 28); also the motif of polemic against Israel gives way to a calmer belief in divine predestination as the cause of Israel's impenitence (cf. Q 10:21f.) and there is also an increase of positive interest in the miraculous, in secret revelation and enthusiasm (cf. Q 11:2–4, 9–13; 17:5f.). Finally a 'late redaction' added the temptation narrative which in turn reacts against the enthusiasm for the miraculous reflected in the intermediate stage.

Jacobson's approach clearly represents an advance on earlier studies in seeking to bring some kind of control to the process of assigning materials in Q to different strata. Further, as will become clear, I am deeply in sympathy with his general approach which is sensitive to the ordering of the Q material as a whole. However, it is precisely for this reason that I believe that some of the details of his overall reconstruction of the 'stages' in the development of Q are more questionable. His 'compositional' stage is very similar to Lührmann's final redactional stage. In fact the bulk of Jacobson's analysis is taken up with an attempt to demonstrate the unified nature of the material in this compositional stage. Moreover, the extent of the material is very considerable: it covers the vast bulk of the material in Q. This then raises the question of the status of the material which Jacobson believes does not cohere with this and which he assigns to his subsequent 'intermediate' and 'final' stages. I leave aside here the question of whether in fact this material is so dissimilar to the rest of the Q material.[89] But even if it were, should we in fact be assigning it to a *later* stage in the development of Q? Since the

[89] In fact I would question this: cf. pp. 152–5 below on 11:2–4, 9–13 which relates very closely to Q 12:22–31. Q 7:18–23 is also discussed later: see pp. 126–9.

polemic of the 'compositional' stage takes up so much space in 'Q' in its 'present' form (i.e. in the material as apparently used by Matthew and Luke: cf. below), it is hard not to believe that this is the outlook of the final redaction of Q. The logic of a 'compositional' approach would seem to demand then that this be regarded as one of the distinguishing marks of Q itself, not (just) an earlier stage in Q. The very dominance of this stage in the present form of Q suggests that, if there are elements in some tension with it, they are more likely to reflect *earlier* developments in the tradition, not a subsequent redactional stage. As we shall see below, such considerations may affect critically Jacobson's individual analyses, for example on the Baptist material (see ch. 4 below). Jacobson's solution to the phenomenon of apparently different outlooks in different pericopes, by assigning them to different strata (e.g. 7:18–23 is said to be different in its attitude to miracles from 11:14ff.), is also reminiscent of Schulz's approach and is liable to similar criticisms. Without the control of aporia within the text of a single pericope, the attempt to assign whole pericopes to different strata runs the danger of failing to see the unity of the whole which was at least sufficient for the final editor to include all the material of Q in a single text.

So far we have looked at methodological approaches which focus on the possible division of Q into different layers, whether a two-fold division of tradition + redaction, or a more complex model of multi-stage development. A slightly different starting point was provided by a programmatic essay, first published in 1964, by James Robinson which focused on the genre of Q as a whole.[90] The title of Robinson's article, 'LOGOI SOPHON: On the Gattung of Q', states the gist of his thesis in a nutshell. He argues that, on the basis of a comparative study of a number of sayings collections in Judaism and early Christianity, a specific genre of collections known as 'sayings of the wise', or 'logoi sophon', can be isolated. This is not necessarily a fixed and rigid genre: it has its roots in Jewish wisdom collections to be found in Proverbs (e.g. Prov 22:17–24:22; 30; 31), with origins further back still in Near Eastern wisdom collections such as Ahikar and Amenemope, and it stretches forward in time to collections such

---

[90] J. M. Robinson, 'LOGOI SOPHON: On the Gattung of Q', ET in J. M. Robinson & H. Koester, *Trajectories through Early Christianity* (Philadelphia: Fortress, 1971) 71–113. (The original was published in German in 1964 in the Festschrift for R. Bultmann. All references here are to the version in the *Trajectories* volume.)

as the Gospel of Thomas (GTh) and m. Aboth. Within this 'trajectory', Q is to be located and Q is thus a collection of sayings with a basically sapiential orientation.

Robinson's theory about the genre of Q will not be discussed in detail here: we shall consider it more closely when we discuss the question of the extent to which Q can or should be regarded as sapiential (see ch. 10 below). In fact, Robinson's article was as much intended to integrate GTh within a development, or trajectory, which included the canonical gospels and their sources as it was to analyse Q for its own sake.[91] Nevertheless, Robinson's views about the wisdom orientation of Q as a whole have generated a very rich scholarly 'trajectory' of its own; but in addition, this has also merged with the trend to find different strata within Q which we were considering earlier. Thus in a number of more recent studies subsequent to Robinson's article, it has been suggested that Q itself may not be wholly sapiential, but an earlier stage in the development of Q certainly was.[92]

Such a theory has been advocated forcefully in a number of publications over several years by H. Koester. Koester has worked closely with Robinson, and indeed the 1971 *Trajectories* volume, in which the English translation of Robinson's 'LOGOI SOPHON' article was published, was a joint production by both scholars, with a number of important articles from each included. Koester's essays here take up and develop many of the ideas suggested by Robinson.[93] It is probably fair to say that, like

[91] See Robinson's own remarks in his Foreword in Kloppenborg, *Formation*, xiif.; also his 'On Bridging the Gulf from Q to the Gospel of Thomas (or Vice Versa)', in C. W. Hedrick & R. Hodgson (eds), *Nag Hammadi, Gnosticism and Early Christianity* (Peabody, Mass.: Hendrickson, 1986) 127–75, p. 167, reacting in part to the claims of Kümmel, *Introduction*, 75f., that GTh is quite distinct from the canonical gospels, and that the genre of GTh (as a sayings collection with no narrative) is simply due to GTh's secondary deletion of the narrative of the canonical gospels to promote the writer's gnostic views.

[92] In fact Robinson himself may have shifted his position in this respect and would appear now also to support such a view: see the discussion in ch. 10 below.

[93] Important in this respect are his articles 'GNOMAI DIAPHOROI: The Origin and Nature of Diversification in the History of Early Christianity', and 'One Jesus and Four Primitive Gospels', *Trajectories*, 114–57, 158–204 respectively. Recently, Koester has restated his theories in his *Ancient Christian Gospels* (London & Philadelphia: SCM & Trinity, 1990), appealing for support for his general theories to Lührmann and Kloppenborg (see 86ff., 128ff.). For further discussion of Koester's theories, especially in relation to GTh, see my 'Q and Thomas'.

Robinson, Koester is as much interested in other issues as well as Q in and of itself. For Koester, it was (and remains) a key issue of principle that the non-canonical gospels are just as important for rediscovering the history of primitive Christianity as the canonical texts. Hence the apocryphal gospels should not be dismissed as worthless and late.[94] Further, it is vitally important to realise that the earliest period of Christian history to which our sources allow us access reveal a tremendous *diversity*: there is no period of pristine purity from which later developments can be categorised (and dismissed) as 'heretical'. Rather, the very earliest period shows us already a rich diversity of different views.[95]

Like Robinson, Koester sees clear links of some form between Q and GTh. He accepts Robinson's argument that both Q and GTh are characterised by many wisdom sayings, showing the basic sapiential character of both texts.[96] He does not argue that GTh is directly dependent on Q itself: rather, both may depend on earlier smaller collections with GTh and Q representing respectively subsequent eastern and western developments of the tradition in Syrian Christianity.[97] However, the common tradition shared by the two texts is, in Koester's view, sufficiently clear to establish the fundamentally sapiential roots of Q. Thus Koester postulates the existence of a sayings collection underlying both Q and GTh:

> The basis of the *Gospel of Thomas* is a sayings collection which is more primitive than the canonical gospels, even though its basic principle is not related to the creed of the passion and resurrection. Its principle is nonetheless theological. Faith is understood as belief in Jesus' words, a belief which makes what Jesus proclaimed present and real for the believer. The catalyst which has caused the crystallisation of these sayings into a 'gospel' is the view that the kingdom is uniquely present in Jesus' eschatological preaching and that eternal wisdom about man's true self is disclosed in his words. The gnostic proclivity of this concept needs no further elaboration.[98]

[94] See too his 'Apocryphal and Canonical Gospels', *HTR* 73 (1980) 105–30.

[95] Cf. of course also W. Bauer, *Orthodoxy and Heresy in Earliest Christianity* (ET Philadelphia & London: Fortress & SCM, 1971).

[96] 'One Jesus', 166ff.

[97] 'GNOMAI DIAPHOROI', 139.

[98] 'One Jesus', 186. In 'Apocryphal and Canonical Gospels', 113, this sayings collection, or sayings 'gospel', becomes a 'wisdom gospel'.

It is however difficult to fit the apocalyptic expectation, which is a prominent feature of much of Q, into such a model. Most typical of such a genre are wisdom sayings, legal statements, prophetic sayings and parables.[99] Least characteristic are the apocalyptic SM sayings. But precisely these apocalyptic SM sayings are not present in GTh. Thus Koester argues that, in terms of generic development, GTh represents an earlier stage in such development. Thus the apocalyptic SM sayings in Q represent a secondary accretion to Q, in part serving to check any possible gnosticising tendencies in the primitive sayings gospel.[1] Koester also seeks to buttress his argument by referring to Ph. Vielhauer's claim that none of the SM sayings is authentic: all of them are secondary, post-Easter inventions of the early church.[2] For Koester, therefore, the 'sapiential' nature of 'Q' applies primarily to the roots of the tradition visible *behind* Q and GTh. It is thus a pre-Q stage of the tradition which is sapiential, and it is the generic considerations which reveal the different strata within Q.

As with Robinson, we shall defer discussion of whether Q, or a pre-Q stage, is 'sapiential' to a later point. However, some of the methodological problems may perhaps be appropriately raised here, in particular the way in which Koester seeks to make literary critical decisions about the existence of strata within Q on the basis of generic considerations. Certainly Koester's overall approach seems open to a number of objections. His appeal to GTh is in danger of getting the cart before the horse.[3] He appears to assume what perhaps needs to be proved, i.e. that GTh is both independent of the synoptics and is also a pure form of the genre to which Q is supposed to belong, viz. a 'wisdom gospel', before

---

[99] 'GNOMAI DIAPHORAI', 138. The inclusion of both wisdom and prophecy side by side in this context is perhaps rather confusing: see the discussion of what exactly constitutes 'wisdom' in ch. 10 below.

[1] 'One Jesus', 187.

[2] See Ph. Vielhauer, 'Gottesreich und Menschensohn in der Verkündigung Jesu', and 'Jesus und der Menschensohn', in his *Aufsätze zum Neuen Testament* (München: Kaiser, 1965) 55–91, 92–140. In fact it is very dubious how far Koester's later appeal to Lührmann and Kloppenborg (cf. n. 93 above) will support him in this. Although both argue for two or more stages in Q's development (or at least for a redactional overlay of traditional material), they disagree as to where the SM material is to be located. For Kloppenborg, this material is (mostly) part of his Q^2 stage (see later); but for Lührmann, the identification of Jesus with the coming SM was already present in Q's tradition and hence rather peripheral for Q's redaction (*Redaktion*, 40f., 85f.). See my 'Q and Thomas', 347.

[3] See Kloppenborg, *Formation*, 38.

being secondarily adulterated by the apocalyptic SM sayings. For the evidence of GTh is virtually the only criterion used by Koester for distinguishing between early and late elements in Q. In fact, of course, GTh's independence is highly questionable, and several scholars would wish to argue that GTh is in fact 'post-synoptic', i.e. dependent on the finished synoptic gospels:[4] it may therefore be of little value in the present discussion and cannot serve as a criterion for distinguishing between strata within Q without further more detailed justification. Further, Koester's exclusive focus on SM sayings in GTh may not be entirely appropriate, especially if one wants to use the comparison to insist on GTh, and (early) Q, being 'sapiential' and *not* apocalyptic. R. Horsley has pointed out that GTh, at least in its present form, does contain a large number of prophetic and apocalyptic sayings, even if these are not explicitly 'SM' sayings as such.[5]

Koester's appeal to Vielhauer's theories about SM sayings is also of dubious value. Koester is perhaps guilty of confusing two quite different problems: the distinction between authentic and inauthentic Jesus traditions, and the distinction between early and late strata within the literary development of Q. There is, of course, no reason at all why inauthentic material should not have been present in an early stratum of Q, nor why authentic material could not have been brought in at a later stage in the development of Q. Vielhauer's theories about the secondary nature of the SM sayings in the gospels refer to their relative date in relation to Jesus and his claim is that they reflect post-Easter developments. But simply labelling something as post-Easter does not determine its position within the developing Q tradition. A post-Easter tradition is not *ipso facto* to be ascribed to a late stratum in Q. Nor conversely are all traditions in an early stratum within Q necessarily dominical.[6] One must not confuse the issue of authenticity with that of the stratification of Q. Koester's

[4] See for example my 'Thomas' with further literature cited.

[5] R. Horsley, 'Logoi Prophētōn? Reflections on the Genre of Q', in B. A. Pearson (ed.), *The Future of Early Christianity* (FS H. Koester; Minneapolis: Fortress, 1991) 195–209, 200f.

[6] Hence the danger of an approach of scholars such as Mack (cf. too Farmer's recent *Gospel of Jesus*) who tend to identify the historical Jesus with the earliest recoverable stage in just one 'trajectory' of the developing tradition. Sorting out the genuine historical Jesus material is infinitely more complex than seeking to delineate one line of development of the tradition. Cf. too Kloppenborg's comment at n. 79 above.

approach is similar methodologically to that of Schulz and exactly the same criticisms apply. Thus it is very doubtful whether Koester's argument on its own can sustain the view that the apocalyptic SM sayings are latecomers into Q or that at an early stage Q was something like a wisdom gospel.[7]

Nevertheless, despite these caveats, Koester's overall theory of an early, sapiential stage of the Q tradition being overtaken by a later, more apocalyptically oriented layer, has by no means been lost to sight in contemporary Q studies. This is due above all to the full-length study of John Kloppenborg. Kloppenborg's *The Formation of Q* has been rightly acclaimed as one of the most outstanding of the recent attempts to unravel different strata within the Q material, and his solution offered in his book has influenced a large number of Q researchers who have taken up his theories very enthusiastically. Kloppenborg is certainly alive to the dangers of a tradition-historical approach to the problem of stratification in Q and has offered some incisive comments on previous theories.[8] He is aware too of the deficiencies of some of Koester's argumentation.[9] Yet his overall theory is strikingly similar to that of Koester and can be regarded as in some ways one of the most thoroughly grounded attempts to give detailed justi-fication for Koester's (and Robinson's) programmatic insights.

Like Jacobson, Kloppenborg argues for a literary-critical approach, based on a detailed consideration of Q itself, to provide the necessary controls in the whole process of seeking to identify different strata within Q. His own analysis proceeds by arguing that on occasions polemical/judgemental elements in Q seem to be additions to earlier forms of the tradition free from such elements. For example, the theme of the violent fate suffered by the prophets (a theme which is highly characteristic of the polemic in Q) appears in Q 6:23c, apparently appended to a collection of sayings free from such polemic. Similarly, the violent denunciatory language of the woes against the Galilean cities in Q 10:13–15 seems to be a secondary appendage to the mission charge which is directed to the community. Thus Kloppenborg postulates two major stages in Q: an earlier ('sapiential') stage of collections of sayings primarily addressed to the community,

---

[7] For more on the SM sayings in Q, and their appropriate place within any tradition history of Q, see ch. 8 below.

[8] His earlier article, 'Tradition and Redaction', is outstanding, and I have been greatly indebted to it, as the earlier footnotes in this chapter make clear.

[9] Cf. p. 67 n. 3 above.

which was then taken over and used subsequently in the service of polemic against 'this generation' by the addition of various judgemental sayings. Thus Kloppenborg finds sapiential speeches in Q in the bulk of the material in 6:20–49; 9:57–10:16; 10:21–24; 11:2–4, 9–13; 12:2–12, 22–34; 13:24ff. The judgement sayings in part provide glosses on these, e.g. in 6:23c; 10:12, 13–15; 12:8f., 10; 13:25–30; 13:34f.; 14:16–24, etc. as well as being the thrust of longer sections such as 3:7–9, 16f.; 7:1–10, 18–35; 11:14–26, 39–52; 12:39–59; 17:23–37. Finally, as Jacobson and many others have done, Kloppenborg assigns the temptation story, together with some Q texts advocating strict adherence to the Law, to a final stage in the redaction.[10]

A highly significant part of Kloppenborg's work is also to seek to answer the question whether the postulated stages in the development of Q can be placed within appropriate *generic* categories. Indeed it is really the genre question which governs the whole of Kloppenborg's study.[11] Kloppenborg's claim is that his proposed strata can work at this level too. He extends the comparative 'database' of possible parallels to cover more than just Jewish texts (as Robinson had done) and to include a vast range of sayings collections from the ancient world. With this wide range of material, the different layers of Q can take their places alongside many other texts from antiquity: the early sapiential layer is similar to many examples of the 'instruction'; the later judgemental layer moves the genre closer to that of a 'chreia collection'; and the material in the last stage shifts the whole more to the genre of a 'biography'.

Kloppenborg's proposal of three clear stages in the development of Q into a '$Q^1 + Q^2 + Q^3$'[12] has attracted enormous support and has frequently been used as the basis for other studies of Q. Clearly his model of a sapiential Q^1 followed by a prophetic/judgemental Q^2 is very similar in many ways to Koester's proposal, though the argument for it is formulated in a quite different way, by analysing the relevant passages in Q itself

---

[10] The theory about the nomistic parts of Q is particularly developed in his 'Nomos and Ethos in Q', in J. E. Goehring et al. (eds), *Gospel Origins and Christian Beginnings* (FS J. M. Robinson; Sonoma: Polebridge, 1990) 35–48.

[11] Cf. the first chapter of his book, on 'Forms and Genres', which sets out the agenda for the whole study.

[12] Kloppenborg himself does not use this terminology in his book, but it is now widely used by others and (as far as I am aware) Kloppenborg has no objection to it. I therefore use it here for the sake of convenience.

and not by appealing to possible parallels in other texts such as GTh. In view of the immense support Kloppenborg's model now has, it may be worth spending a little time here discussing some details of it. One must say that some aspects of his overall theory are more convincing than others. His proposals about the existence of secondary additions to earlier material are certainly very plausible in principle (though, as with all such proposals, debatable in detail). His isolation of a specific strand stressing the threat of judgement against 'this generation' (i.e. 'Q^2') is well taken: in this he is following lines opened up by Lührmann's programmatic study and followed by many others since. However, Kloppenborg's postulated sapiential strand (i.e. 'Q^1') may be rather less secure.

There is in fact more than one issue involved here, and we should perhaps seek to keep them separate as far as possible. One question concerns the appropriateness of labelling this material as 'sapiential'. This issue I shall leave aside here and discuss in detail in ch. 10 below. Here I am more concerned with the actual division of Q into different strata. In this context, the question arises whether it is justified to regard the 'Q^1' material as a literary unity, existing as a self-contained entity at some stage in the pre-history of Q. This may be problematic at more than one level. First, Kloppenborg's own analysis makes clear that the source material used by any Q^2 redactor is more complex than a monolithic Q^1 and nothing more. Several of the longer sections in Q which are dominated by the polemic characteristic of Q^2 clearly have a pre-history behind them and are not created *de novo* by a Q^2 redactor (e.g. Q 3:7–9, 16f.; 7:18–35). Hence the 'pre-Q^2' material clearly consists of more than the alleged 'sapiential' speeches of Q^1 alone. Second, it is not clear why the Q^1 layer should be considered as a unity at all. Kloppenborg makes a strong case for the existence of some secondary additions modifying earlier traditions, and some of these we shall be considering in the course of our later detailed analyses. But it is a big step to jump from earlier (possibly disparate) material to a unified collection of sapiential speeches in a Q^1. In fact, as we shall see, Kloppenborg's sapiential layer is rather multi-faceted. This applies at the level of the individual alleged 'speeches', or 'blocks', of Q^1 material as well as the whole. Some of the alleged 'collections' postulated turn out to be extremely fragmentary. For example one block of sayings is seen by Kloppenborg in Q 13:24–14:35. Yet a very significant part of this material is assigned to the

Q^2 layer (13:25–30; 13:34–35; 14:16–24). All one is left with is 13:24; 14:26–27; 17:33; 14:34–35. If, as I would argue, 13:24 belongs closely with 13:25–30 (see pp. 189–93 below), then the residue becomes even thinner. All that we have here is then a few sayings (perhaps only two), possibly concerned with discipleship (though 14:34–35 is notoriously difficult to interpret), but hardly evidence of a well-formed 'collection'. Further, there is no evidence that the five alleged collections ever belonged together in a literary whole prior to the use of the materials they contain by 'Q^2'. Can we, for example, know that the mission instructions, without the redactional addition of the woes on the Galilean towns in Q 10:13–15, were *already* joined with the Great Sermon, similarly purged of its reference to the violence suffered by the prophets in Q 6:23c, in an earlier, macro-collection Q^1? The evidence for this just does not seem to be forthcoming. Each collection *may* have its own unity even if this is more obvious in some cases than others; but the collections do not necessarily form a unified whole. One could have different collections (plural) which were never united prior to their use by Q^2.

The distinction between an allegedly sapiential Q^1, addressed to the community, and an allegedly prophetic Q^2, addressed to outsiders, is also not as secure as Kloppenborg's theory sometimes asserts. As we shall see later, a clear insider/outsider distinction may not be fully appropriate for Q (see ch. 13 below), and in any case some of the allegedly Q^2-type material may be addressed to 'insiders' as much as to 'outsiders'.[13] Further, as we shall see, it remains doubtful how far we can really call the 'Q^1' material 'sapiential'. We shall discuss this in more detail later. But, for example, the mission instructions, so specifically related to the followers of Jesus in their concrete situation, can scarcely be called 'sapiential' in any meaningful sense. These instructions can be seen as addressed to 'insiders' (*if* such a distinction is meaningful), and therefore might be distinguishable from the more polemical parts of Q. But that does not of itself make the mission charge very obviously 'sapiential'.

A stronger case for the unity of Q^2's source material could perhaps be made for the more extensive additions made at the Q^2 level itself, their coherence being shown by the fact that these additions all contain Q^2-type material. There is then inevitably more thematic unity here. So too, as noted above, this material

---

[13] Cf. Horsley, 'Logoi Prophētōn', 198f., who refers to Q 7:18–28; also his *Sociology and the Jesus Movement* (New York: Crossroad, 1989) 109.

has its own pre-history and hence was not invented by the Q^2 redactor(s) *de novo*. Could one then make a case for an 'R^1' source alongside 'Q^1' so that Q^2 used *two* 'sources', Q^1 and R^1, Q^1 being the (possibly) sapiential instruction proposed by Kloppenborg, R^1 being the further extensive traditions added by Q^2? R^1 might then exhibit more thematic coherence than Q^1! And if so, which would be the more natural precursor of Q^2: Q^1 or R^1? Since R^1 would be closer in substance to Q^2, would it not be more sensible to see R^1 — not Q^1 — as the literary precursor of Q^2?! I do not propose such a theory very seriously, but simply wish to highlight the methodological problems involved in too optimistic a reconstruction of the earlier history of the 'text' we call Q.

Further problems may arise in relation to the alleged Q^3 stage. Within Kloppenborg's (and others') discussions, the temptation narrative is the prime (and sometimes the only) candidate for inclusion in a postulated 'Q^3'. We shall discuss this story in detail later, and I shall seek to show there that such stratification models are unnecessary. A few nomistic sayings are also assigned by Kloppenborg to the Q^3 stage; again we must defer the detailed discussion to a later stage, but I shall hope to show later that such a strongly nomistic outlook is more widespread in Q than Kloppenborg perhaps allows. (See ch. 12 below.) Further, we have to bear in mind that not *every* saying in a text like Q, nor indeed every pericope in a text such as a gospel, can contain *all* the ideas which are important to the final editor. We cannot therefore excise some parts of Q simply because their concerns are at one level unrelated to other concerns of other parts of Q.[14] I remain therefore unpersuaded that there is any a priori need to separate a Q^3 stage from a Q^2.[15]

In conclusion, Kloppenborg's detailed stratification model may be not quite as securely founded as some have assumed. Certainly his model is perhaps the most detailed and well-argued one that is available in the present debate. However, I remain unpersuaded by certain aspects of it. If, as I have tried to argue, it is unnecessary to postulate a Q^3 subsequent to Q^2, and if the pre-Q^2 material is perhaps rather more disparate, and the alleged 'Q^1' stratum not necessarily capable of being shown to have existed as a literary unity in its own right before Q^2, then we may have a rather simpler

[14] The situation would of, course, be different if the concerns were in tension with each other. But this is not the case in this instance.

[15] I have discussed this further, in relation to other proposals for assigning material to Q^3, in my 'On the Stratification of Q', *Semeia* 55 (1991) 213–22.

model, viz. a Q-editor taking up and using (possibly a variety of) earlier materials.

I have devoted some space here to a more detailed analysis of Kloppenborg's theories because of the wide interest and support they have aroused. In one sense, Kloppenborg's model is quite complex. However, other scholars have proposed even more complex theories of multi-stage development in Q. For example, in a number of articles involving densely argued detail, H. Schürmann has postulated a fairly uniform four-fold development of the tradition in Q.[16] In this postulated development, isolated logia were very soon interpreted with the addition of further sayings, or commentary sayings ('*Kommentarworte*'); these were then put into small clusters ('*Spruchreihen*'); subsequently these were gathered into 'early compositions' ('*frühe Kompositionen*') before finally being compiled into the speech complexes of Q. Schürmann's theories are worked out in impressive detail, and in very general terms they have much to commend them.[17] Nevertheless, one wonders if the scheme is perhaps too rigid.[18] At times the final stage seems to disappear almost completely from the redactional process envisaged.[19] So too it is not at all clear that the schema has arisen from the evidence of the texts themselves and has not been imposed on the text rather arbitrarily. Thus Uro comments: 'We have, indeed, no reason to suggest that traditions include some genetic code driving them to develop through destined successive stages of accretion, e.g., the four compositional stages presented by Schürmann ... Schürmann's description of the Q tradition appears too schematic and deterministic.'[20]

Uro himself is however not averse to postulating a multi-stage development in Q.[21] In his own monograph he develops ideas of

[16] See for example the articles in the Bibliography, notably his 'Zum Komposition der Redenquelle. Beobachtungen an der lukanischen Q-Vorlage', in C. Bussmann & W. Radl (eds), *Der Treue Gottes Trauen* (FS G. Schneider; Freiburg: Herder, 1991) 325–42, for a summary statement, with some nuancing and clarification of terminology, of his earlier views.

[17] Cf. D. Zeller, 'Redaktionsprozesse und wechselnder "Sitz im Leben" beim Q-Material', in Delobel (ed.), *LOGIA*, 395–409, and other writings.

[18] Cf. the comments of M. Sato, *Q und Prophetie* (WUNT 2.29; Tübingen: Mohr, 1988) 30.

[19] Cf. Neirynck, 'Recent Developments', 71, who asks: if the larger complexes are all pre-redactional, 'what is then the *Endredaktion*?'.

[20] Uro, *Sheep*, 12.

[21] Uro, *Sheep, passim.*

D. Zeller who, in a number of studies, has suggested that the Q material went through a series of stages, each with its own *Sitz im Leben*.[22] Uro's main focus of concern is the mission charge. He argues that instructions for itinerant missionaries have been adopted secondarily by sedentary communities giving support to such missionaries (cf. Q 10:2). Further, the negative outlook on Israel, resulting from rejection of the itinerant missionaries by Jews, dominates most of the material, but this gives way to a brighter outlook in one or two later redactional additions as the mission has gone to the Gentiles. Uro's study will have to be discussed later in this study and so will not be dealt with here in detail. (See pp. 185–8 below.) But to anticipate slightly, his theory runs into problems which are not dissimilar to those encountered by Jacobson: how can we conceive of a later redactor leaving so much material from his sources unaltered when (in Uro's case even more than in Jacobson's) a radical change in outlook is brought in by the later redactor? It seems much easier to suppose that the material which dominates in terms of extent and substance coincides, rather than being in antithesis, with the view of the final redactor of Q. Otherwise it is not easy to see why the material has been left as it is in the final redactional process. Uro's study therefore leads on to some critical observations on the whole exercise of 'redaction'-critical approaches to the study of Q.[23]

3. Methodological Observations

What can we say by way of reflection as a result of this survey of recent Q studies? We have seen that the dominant trend over the last thirty-five years or so has been to seek to apply methods from so-called 'redaction criticism' to the study of Q, and that has led to many attempts not only to distinguish between traditional and

[22] See especially Zeller's article 'Redaktionsprozesse' and his earlier *Die weisheitliche Mahnsprüche bei den Synoptikern* (FzB 17; Würzburg: Echter, 1977).

[23] I leave aside here the work of a number of other recent studies which have put forward various other stratification theories concerning the Q material. For example, Sato, *Q und Prophetie*, has also recently argued for a development in the history of Q, pleading for the existence of three separate redactional stages. However, the stages are unrelated, and the theory is somewhat arbitrary. In any case, the main thrust of Sato's book is not primarily to propose a specific theory about the growth of Q in separate stages: rather, it is to question radically the theory that Q is 'sapiential' and not 'prophetic'. As such, therefore, we shall discuss this in more detail when considering the question of how far it is appropriate to regard Q as 'sapiential'. See ch. 10 below.

redactional elements in Q but also to develop a variety of theories
of stages in the development of Q itself so that one should be
thinking of a series of 'editions', or versions, of Q: Q^1, Q^2, Q^3, etc.
Any form of a monolithic 'Q' *simpliciter* seems to have disappeared from sight.

This development in Q studies is not dissimilar to some trends
in Johannine studies, and it may be worth briefly considering
the parallel development in the latter area to see what light it might
throw on Q studies. In recent years, several stages in the development of the Johannine tradition have been suggested as well, with
each stage representing a specific period in the history of the
Johannine community.[24] Even if one might wish to eschew such
attempts to reconstruct the history of the Johannine community
as over-optimistic, there is still a well-established scholarly view,
associated above all with the work of Bultmann, that the text of
the gospel has been expanded by a later redactor who has added
in the references to the sacraments and futurist eschatology (as
well as perhaps adding ch. 21). Thus to interpret 'John', one has
to peel away these later accretions and get back to a stage behind
the present form of the gospel text itself.

A more complicated theory is proposed by D. Seeley in his 'Blessings and
Boundaries: Interpretations of Jesus' Death in Q', *Semeia* 55 (1991) 131–46, to
which I have tried to respond in part in my 'Stratification': Seeley's attempt to
build a theory of five chronological stages of development in the thinking of
the Q community about Jesus' death on the basis of five brief sayings seems
extraordinarily optimistic. See p. 220 below.

F. W. Horn, 'Christentum und Judentum in der Logienquelle', *EvTh* 51
(1991) 344–64, also seeks to delineate a developing situation of increasing
hostility and violence between Q Christians and their Jewish neighbours on the
basis of different strata within Q. But the strata themselves are never clearly
defined (on p. 345f. he refers to the widely differing theories of Schulz,
Lührmann, Polag, Schürmann, Zeller and Kloppenborg, without saying clearly
which model he is using), and it is not always clear whether the stratification is
not in fact determined by the results claimed, so that the reasoning seems
somewhat circular.

B. Mack's book *The Lost Gospel* also proposes a stratification model which
claims to be simply a reproduction of Kloppenborg's with some minor
modifications: in fact the modifications destroy much of the basis on which
Kloppenborg's theory was founded. On this see J. M. Robinson, 'The History-
of-Religions Taxonomy of Q: The Cynic Hypothesis', in T. Schweer & S. Rink
(eds), *Gnosisforschung und Religionsgeschichte* (FS K. Rudolph; Marburg:
Diagonal, 1995) 249–65 (the text of which has kindly been made available to
me in advance of publication by the author). See too ch. 11 below.

[24] See the theories associated above all with the names of J. L. Martyn and
R. Brown.

Such theories are, in principle, perfectly possible and carry varying degrees of plausibility. No one would doubt that the gospel tradition (be it the synoptic or Johannine tradition) underwent a complex history of development before finally culminating in our finished gospels. If nothing else, the work of form criticism has taught us that we ignore that at our peril. Nevertheless there are some important methodological caveats one should perhaps register. In terms of Johannine studies, it has often been pointed out that a Bultmannian approach effectively ignores the present text of John as an appropriate object for interpretation, on the grounds that different viewpoints within the text are almost incapable of harmonisation. However, many would argue that instead we should take the present text as it stands, as an entity having an integrity of its own and thus deserving an attempt on our part to make sense of it on its own terms. Thus theories which involve excising elements of the text as having no real place in the 'true' text of the gospel should perhaps be regarded as only a last resort which should be invoked only if we cannot make sense of the present text as it stands.

Any parallel between John and Q in this respect is not a perfect one.[25] Nevertheless the analogy may not be valueless. John's gospel and Q are not, of course, comparable entities in one way: John's gospel is available to us as an independent text attested in manuscript form, whereas 'Q' is a scholarly construct, postulated on the basis of agreements between the gospels of Matthew and Luke. Nevertheless, for those who agree that the Q tradition should be regarded as a single tradition, the parallel with John is worth consideration.[26] If we are interested in the characteristic features, distinctive elements, or 'theology', of 'Q', then perhaps as with 'John', we should give methodological priority to 'Q' in something like its 'final' form, i.e. that stage in the development of the tradition which Q reached when it was used by Matthew and Luke. (If, as some argue, Q was further expanded/redacted after being used by one evangelist [e.g. Luke] before being used

[25] Some might argue that the analogy should suggest that we should not be undertaking any analysis of an alleged 'theology of Q' at all and stick to the analysis of the written texts we have, viz. the texts of Matthew and Luke!

[26] The situation is, of course, different for those who believe that the Q tradition consists of a number of quite separate traditions which never co-existed prior to their incorporation into Matthew and Luke. This is a quite different model from theories of a Q tradition growing, or being redacted, in successive stages Q[1], Q[2], etc. and it is the latter theory on which I am particularly focusing attention here.

by the other [e.g. Matthew], then the 'final' *common* form would be the stage prior to the use by the earlier evangelist.) No doubt the tradition developed in various ways before reaching this point, and we may be able to identify stages in that development. But it may be worth preserving the siglum 'Q' for this 'final' stage.

With this in mind we may perhaps consider further the whole principle of applying a so-called 'redaction-critical' method to Q, in particular the attempt to sort out Q's material into different strata of 'tradition + redaction', or 'stage 1 + stage 2 + stage 3'.[27]

'Redaction criticism' has dominated gospel studies for nearly fifty years and yet, perhaps surprisingly, it has not developed the same degree of self-criticism with respect to its methodology as has, for example, textual criticism. The early redaction-critical studies of Bornkamm and Conzelmann, as has already been noted, focused on two texts, Matthew and Luke, where the author had used a source (Mark) which was independently available to us. By using a synopsis, one could then observe the way in which one evangelist had introduced changes into his source material and so gain insight into his own interests and ideas.

There are, of course, obvious problems if one seeks to apply the same approach to a 'text' like Q, or indeed to a gospel like Mark or John. For in these cases we do not have the source material used by the final author/redactor independently available to us. We have to try to reconstruct the source material from the text itself and then use the reconstructed source to identify the author's redaction. Such a procedure must obviously be very delicate, though it is not *per se* impossible. We have seen that, for example, Jacobson has attempted to isolate redactional elements in Q on the basis of aporia in the text, and the same approach is used in Markan and Johannine studies. One will however never attain certainty in all this. For example, an aporia in the text, or the presence of a secondary feature (e.g. a 'redactional' comment), by no means guarantees that we have reached something which can be ascribed to the final redactor. We might simply have something which is due to an earlier redactor of a smaller block of material.

However, a more serious problem is raised by the status of any results claimed for a redaction-critical approach. I have considered this problem elsewhere and hopefully may be forgiven if I repeat what I wrote in the earlier context:

[27] For what follows, see also my *Reading the New Testament* (London: SPCK, 1987) 116ff.

Early redaction critics looked at the alterations made by an author to his sources. If all such activity is considered and, hopefully, systematised, the result will be — what? Strictly, the result will be a total picture of the way in which an author altered his sources, *and nothing more*. However, very frequently redaction critics have assumed that there is considerably more: they have assumed that their results give a global picture of the theology of the individual author. There has been an implicit equation made between the theology of an evangelist and the ideas implied in the ways he has altered his sources.

Now it would be quite clearly perverse to deny that [say] Luke's theology has a great deal to do with the way he has altered his sources. The question is whether the two can simply be equated. As soon as one thinks about it, the answer must be No. For there may well be times when an author agrees with his tradition and is content to repeat it unaltered. Indeed, 'quite content' may be an understatement: an author may be passionately convinced of the value of his source material and he makes a thoroughly positive decision to include it without change. Indeed the decision of an author to include the material in the first place must presumably indicate some measure of agreement between the author and his tradition. However, the method of redaction criticism which looks only at the changes which a writer makes to his tradition will ignore such instances completely. Such a method may well end up with a thoroughly distorted picture of an evangelist's theology.[28]

In my earlier work, I referred by way of illustration to the work of Conzelmann in Luke's eschatology: Conzelmann argued that Luke's redactional *changes* to his tradition indicated a tendency to apologise for the delay of the Parousia: elements still in Luke's gospel which still seemed to imply a belief in an imminent End were dismissed by Conzelmann as 'just' vestiges from Luke's tradition. More recent studies of Lukan eschatology have, by contrast, taken much more seriously the combination in Luke's work of his preserved tradition and his redactional changes.[29]

Now, as I noted earlier, the basic aim of redaction criticism has always been to try to discover something about the interests and concerns of the author of the text under consideration. It has never been to try to produce only a summary of the redactional

---

[28] See my *Reading*, 120f.
[29] See, for example, J. T. Carroll, *Responses to the End of History. Eschatology and Situation in Luke–Acts* (SBLDS 92; Atlanta: Scholars, 1988), amongst others.

changes made by an author. Thus, if I may quote my earlier study again:

> With the awareness of the limitations of the older type of redaction
> criticism, there has been a trend to look rather more at the works
> of the evangelists as wholes, as entities in themselves. We have
> therefore seen a move away from the older approach of what has
> been called 'emendation criticism' to what some have called
> 'rhetorical criticism' or even 'literary criticism', using that phrase
> is a sense closer to the way some secular critics use the term. This
> new approach would accept that an author has produced a final
> version of his text, and it is this whole text which is the main evidence
> for discovering something of the author and his concerns. A division
> of the text into 'tradition' and 'redaction' may tell us something,
> but the tradition should not necessarily be discarded when trying
> to discover the author's individual ideas. For this the whole text
> should be used, looking at the ways in which individual parts of the
> text are related to other parts by the author, how the whole presents
> its message, and so on. [30]

Whatever name we care to use,[31] it does seem that such an
approach is perhaps rather different from an older-style redaction
criticism which lays a great deal of emphasis on separating out
tradition and redaction in a text.

All these considerations may have some relevance when
applied to Q in the light of recent studies. If we are really
interested in Q itself (rather than pre-Q stages) then perhaps we
should look to Q in its 'final' form. And if we are interested in the
specific concerns of Q and the Christians who preserved it, we
should perhaps be ready to accept that the whole of the material
in Q potentially has a contribution to make in this respect. Thus,
whilst it may be possible at times to separate out the Q material
into different strata and to write a detailed history of the
development of the growth of the Q tradition, such a separation
may not always be of direct use if our main concern is with the
'theology' and setting of 'Q' itself.

This is not to deride the value of a strictly 'redaction'-critical
approach. There may well be occasions when it is possible to
identify conscious modifications of earlier traditions, and such
instances will be extremely important in assessing the specific
interests of the Christians responsible for Q. However, alongside
this must go an appreciation of the fact that a decision to use a

[30] *Reading*, 122f.
[31] E.g. 'composition criticism', or 'literary criticism'.

tradition may be just as significant as a decision to alter one. Thus, in trying to identify specific concerns of Q, we should perhaps take seriously the whole of Q, no doubt part-tradition part-redaction, as making a contribution to this. The editor's selection of, as well as his changes to, his tradition must not be ignored. In part then this means adopting more the approach of Hoffmann or Theissen than perhaps that of Lührmann in any methodological debate which ostensibly exists between them.[32]

We should also recognise the importance not only of the redactional changes by a later editor and his adoption of tradition: the *way* in which a tradition is used and incorporated into a wider whole may also tell us something important. Traditions were no doubt available to later editors in a variety of forms. But the very fact that traditions are incorporated into wider wholes means that they now do service in a larger composition. This actual composition itself may be revealing. Such an approach (sometimes called 'composition criticism') has often been applied to the synoptic gospels (cf. the various suggestions made about the possible significance of Matthew's arrangement of his teaching material into five great discourses). This kind of analysis has, as we have seen, been used in relation to Q by e.g. Lührmann and Jacobson. Again it is rather different from a strictly 'redaction'-critical approach in that it does not look only at actual changes made to a tradition. In relation to Q its value will always be somewhat limited in view of the uncertainty of being able to reconstruct the wider compositional context in Q when Matthew and Luke do not agree on this. Nevertheless its value should not be underestimated.

By way of conclusion, I would therefore suggest that a balanced approach should be maintained. If the main concern (as is the case in the present study) is to try to find out something of the distinctive features of 'Q', then we should look primarily to Q in its 'final' form. We should also be ready to accept that, although at times redactional changes may have occurred so that traditions may have been modified and corrected in the redactional process, other traditions may have been adopted without change because the final editor agreed wholeheartedly with the ideas expressed. Presumably, the final product (assuming, of course, it existed) made some kind of sense to someone!

[32] However, as we have seen, it would be wrong to drive too much a wedge between Hoffmann and Lührmann themselves in this respect: see n. 69 above.

There is one further methodological point which should perhaps be mentioned at this stage. So far I have talked about the 'editor', or 'author' of Q, and the community of Christians who preserved Q, without any distinction between them. However, with any text, one should perhaps be conscious of the distinction which must always exist between the text's author and the people to whom the text is addressed. In particular we should not assume that the views of the 'author' and the views of the 'community' of Christians to which he/she belongs necessarily coincide. Thus it might well be that, in part at least, the person(s) responsible for producing Q intended the ideas expressed not only to articulate the views *of* the community but also to speak *to* the community, perhaps to change existing ideas. Thus A. Malherbe writes:

> It is at least possible that some documents were rescued from obscurity, not because they represented the viewpoints of communities, but precisely because they challenged them. It is too facile to view literature as the product of communities. The relationship could have been very complex.[33]

Precisely how we should envisage the 'editor' or 'author' of Q is not clear. But insofar as Q represents a unified tradition of Jesus' teaching which is still regarded as valid for some Christians, we should be wary of assuming that it was preserved because it reflected positively all the views of all the Christians for whom it was intended. Presumably the compiler regarded it positively. But it does not seem unreasonable to assume too that it was thought to have relevance for a Christian group who needed to be addressed by it, so that their existing views might undergo some change. We should therefore always be alive to the possibility that the Q editor is speaking *at* the community to which he/she belonged, quite as much as speaking *for* it.

With these preliminary observations in mind we may now turn to our analysis of the Q material itself.

---

[33] A. J. Malherbe, *Social Aspects of Early Christianity* (Philadelphia: Fortress, 1983) 13.

3

━━◦◦◦◦━━

The Nature of Q

In the first chapter, I sought to establish that the agreements between Matthew and Luke, which were not due to common dependence on Mark, could not be explained by the dependence of one gospel on the other. Rather, both must have made use of common source material, Q. Moreover, the close verbal agreement between the two gospels, together with the common order which may be visible in this material (when allowance is made for the redactional activity of the evangelists), suggests that this source material probably existed in a unified, written form. Then in the last chapter, I considered the ways in which so-called 'redaction-critical' studies had been developed in relation to Q, at least in the very general sense of 'redaction-critical' as attempting to isolate distinctive features and characteristics of Q. However, there are a number of other, more 'introductory' questions which we should perhaps consider first about the document, if document it was: for example, in what language was it written? What was its precise extent? When and where was it written? What kind of document was it, what was its genre? It is these questions which we shall try to address in the present chapter, before going on to a discussion of individual features of Q in subsequent chapters.

1. The Language of Q

The question of the original language of Q was a pressing one in the earlier part of the twentieth century.[1] In particular, the question was discussed whether Q was a Greek document or whether it might go back to an Aramaic source. Certainly, as we

---

[1] Cf. the survey in Vassiliadis, 'Nature and Extent', 55–7; also Kloppenborg, *Formation*, 51–64; and in much more detail in relation to the history of scholarship on this issue, H. O. Guenther, 'The Sayings Gospel Q and the Quest for Aramaic Sources: Rethinking Christian Origins', *Semeia* 55 (1992) 41–76.

saw in the last chapter, early proponents of the Q hypothesis in the nineteenth century, basing themselves heavily on the statement of Papias (that 'Matthew collected τὰ λόγια in the Hebrew language')[2] as evidence for the existence of a Sayings Source, assumed that Q may have originally been in Aramaic.[3] We must however be quite clear exactly what we are talking about in any discussion about the original language of Q.

In the present context, we are discussing the 'document' Q. Further, in the previous chapter, I argued that we should reserve the siglum 'Q' for the tradition used by Matthew and Luke in the form in which it was so used.[4] No doubt the Q tradition underwent a process of development prior to its use by the two evangelists. Much of this material may go back to Jesus himself. Moreover, standard critical orthodoxy today would agree that Jesus himself probably spoke (mostly if not exclusively) in Aramaic. Hence some of the individual elements in Q may well stem ultimately from an Aramaic original. However, the question of the original language of 'Q' (as defined above) is *not* the same as the question of the original language of each individual tradition preserved within Q. The individual traditions could well have been translated into Greek by the time they were collected into the relatively stable form of Q itself. Hence the problem of the language of Q cannot be solved by appealing simply to any alleged 'Semitic' flavour in some parts of the Q tradition.

In considering the question of the language of Q, the first point to make is that precisely the evidence which we have already looked at to support the claim that some parts of Q were available to Matthew and Luke in written form also tells strongly in favour of that form being in Greek. The agreement between the Greek texts of Matthew and Luke, which at times is all but verbatim,[5] seems to demand not only a written *Vorlage*, but also a written Greek *Vorlage*. Similarly there are a number of peculiar features in the Greek of Q which seem to point again away from any theory that the Matthew–Luke agreements could be accounted for by common use of oral tradition, and hence also to the fact that the common tradition was not only written, but written in Greek (since otherwise one would have to posit independent translations of an Aramaic Q coinciding in rather unusual Greek

---

[2] Eusebius, *E.H.* 3.39.
[3] See pp. 42–3 above.
[4] See p. 77 above.
[5] Cf. pp. 3–4 above on, for example, Q 3:7–9; 11:9–10.

expressions). J. C. Hawkins points to the presence in the double tradition of 'certain peculiar or very unusual words or phrases, which seem very unlikely to have been preserved in oral tradition'.[6] He refers to the phrase ἐν γεννητοῖς γυναικῶν (Q 7:28), a phrase which occurs nowhere else in the NT and only five times in the LXX, all of which are in the book of Job; moreover, an ordinary term like 'men' or 'sons of men' would have served just as well. Similarly unusual are ἱκανός ἵνα (Q 7:6, never elsewhere in the NT and never in the LXX), εἰπὲ λόγῳ (Q 7:7), φοβεῖσθαι ἀπό (Q 12:4, unique in the NT, though not un-common the LXX), ὁμολογεῖν ἐν (Q 12:8, only here in the NT, not in the LXX). To these examples Kloppenborg adds the use of ἀμφιέννυμι (Q 7:25), διχοτομέω (Q 12:46) and σαρόω (Q 11:25).[7] In these instances, the unusual nature of the vocabulary used seems to be best explained by a written, Greek *Vorlage*.

Nevertheless such evidence will necessarily only apply at the specific points of the tradition concerned. It still remains possible that Q was not so much of a unity as has been assumed so far. It could be, for example, that some parts of the Q material are dependent on a Greek *Vorlage*, whilst other parts are dependent on (an) Aramaic source(s).[8] Perhaps therefore one should be allowing for the possibility of Aramaic sources at some points in the tradition. What then is the evidence for such a view?

Given the complex nature of the tradition, and the over-whelming probability that most of the Q material underwent a development in the history of the tradition before reaching its 'final' stage in Q prior to its incorporation by Matthew and Luke, one must be clear exactly what would count as evidence that Q was (perhaps only in part) at one stage an Aramaic text. Clearly, simply referring to the 'Semitic nature' of Q will not do. As M. Black says, 'the most the Aramaic element can *prove* is an Aramaic origin, not always translation from an Aramaic original'.[9] Thus the evidence adduced by Bussby,[10] referring to many allegedly Semitic stylistic features in Q (parallelism, rhythms,

---

[6] J. C. Hawkins, 'Probabilities as to the so-called Double Tradition of St. Matthew and St. Luke', in Sanday (ed.), *Oxford Studies*, 95–138, p. 99.

[7] Kloppenborg, *Formation*, 47.

[8] Cf. the classic theory of Bussmann: see ch. 1 n. 11 above.

[9] M. Black, *An Aramaic Approach to the Gospels and Acts* (Oxford University Press, 1967³) 191; cf. too N. Turner, *Grammatical Insights into the New Testament* (Edinburgh: T. & T. Clark, 1965) 175.

[10] F. Bussby, 'Is Q an Aramaic Document?', *ExpT* 65 (1954) 272–5.

assonance, etc.) to try to show that Q was an 'Aramaic document', simply indicates that the Q traditions stem from a Semitic milieu. As Turner and Black have correctly indicated, the only evidence of positive value in this discussion is that of possible translation variants, or of mistranslations, which can be shown to have arisen from an Aramaic, not a Greek, original.

However, within the general area of possible translation variants and/or mistranslations, there are a number of different possibilities, each of which may have rather different implications for the question of whether Q was (in part at least) an Aramaic text. For example, one could have a possible mistranslation of an Aramaic original into Greek with Matthew and Luke both having the *same* mistranslation. This *may* have occurred in Q 12:46 where Matthew and Luke, at the end of the parable of the waiting servants, both have Jesus say that the master of the wicked servant will 'cut him in pieces' (διχοτομήσει). Such a punishment seems somewhat out of place in the parable; also the immediate sequel, which talks of placing the man with the unfaithful/hypocrites is distinctly anti-climactic after the mention of such a gruesome punishment. Thus some have suggested that the Greek verb used in Q here represents a mistranslation of an Aramaic word (פלג) which can mean both 'cut in two' and 'divide, apportion'.[11] However, this does not show that Q was an Aramaic text. On the contrary, the very fact that Matthew and Luke both have the difficult διχοτομήσει shows that any alleged mistranslation had already occurred by the time of the formation of Q. This evidence is thus more strongly in favour of the Q tradition being in Greek at this point rather than Aramaic.

Another theoretical possibility is that of translation variants, i.e. instances where Matthew's and Luke's different versions can be plausibly explained as different possible translations of the same Aramaic original. Several scholars have argued in this way, most notably Bussmann who produced 122 examples of possible translation variants.[12] However, such examples rarely necessitate the theory of an Aramaic original. Many of Bussmann's examples turn out to be synonyms in Greek which, whilst they *could* represent different translations of an Aramaic *Vorlage*, could just as easily be due to redactional changes of a Greek text by one of

---

[11] Black, *Aramaic Approach*, 256f.; Turner, *Grammatical Insights*, 175.
[12] Bussmann, *Redenquelle*, 151–5.

the evangelists.[13] Thus, for example, in the cases of differences between αἴρω and λαμβάνω, or between ἐνώπιον and ἔμπροσθεν, the differences can be adequately explained at the level of the Greek texts and there is no need to invoke the theory of an Aramaic Q.

Black is more cautious but still thinks that sometimes the theory of an Aramaic original is well founded. Yet many of Black's examples do not demand that the Q tradition itself must have been written in Aramaic. All they show is that the sayings in question may well have come ultimately from an Aramaic tradition, that one evangelist has preserved the tradition in a form closer to the earlier Aramaic original, and the other has redacted the material. But this in itself says nothing about the precise stage in the history of the tradition at which the saying question was translated from Aramaic into Greek. It could have been at the stage of Q being used by Matthew/Luke; it could equally well have been at a pre-Q stage. Thus when Black appeals to examples such as Matt 6:12 τὰ ὀφειλήματα ἡμῶν (Luke 11:4 τὰς ἁμαρτίας ἡμῶν), or Luke 10:5 λέγετε εἰρήνη τῷ οἴκῳ τούτῳ (Matt 10:12 ἀσπάσασθε αὐτήν), or Luke 12:10 ἐρεῖ λόγον εἰς (Matt 12:32 εἴπῃ λόγον κατά), one can accept quite readily that the usage in question (ὀφείλημα meaning 'sin', the peace greeting, or the use of εἰς in 'speak a word against') may well reflect Semitic, or specifically Aramaic, usage.[14] However, the parallel version in the synoptic gospels can on each occasion be explained quite easily as due to the evangelist's redaction of the more Semitic-looking Greek version reproduced in the other gospel.[15]

The one category of examples which would be much more telling, if such examples could be shown to exist, would be possible instances of variations between Matthew's and Luke's Greek texts which result from slightly different Aramaic versions. If it could be shown that the differences between Matthew and Luke are due to different Aramaic versions, where the differences can only be explained on the basis of Aramaic, e.g. by misreading an Aramaic text, or by supplying an alternative pointing to an

[13] Black, *Aramaic Approach*, 187; Kloppenborg, *Formation*, 55f. Kloppenborg also points out that Bussmann rarely gave any details about which actual Aramaic word underlay the alleged translation variants.

[14] Black, *Aramaic Approach*, 193–5.

[15] See Kloppenborg, *Formation*, 56f., who deals with all of Black's examples in detail.

ambiguous consonantal text, this would be more significant. Not only would it show that Q lay before Matthew and Luke in Aramaic, but it would also show that Q must have been available as an Aramaic *text*.

Unfortunately, possible examples of this kind are very rare in the gospels, and the evidence is often ambiguous. The most famous example concerns the difference in the two versions of Q 11:41: 'give alms' (Luke 11:41)/'cleanse' (Matt 23:26). The suggestion that this difference can be explained on the basis of an Aramaic original is at least as old as Wellhausen. Wellhausen suggested that the two versions reflected two very similar Aramaic words: דכו (= 'cleanse') and זכו (= 'give alms');[16] thus the original דכו had been misread by Luke, and the evidence indicates both the language and the written nature of Luke's source. However, the evidence is not fully compelling. Doubts have been expressed whether the verb זכי can in fact mean 'give alms';[17] others have suggested that, whilst זכי might bear this meaning, it can also have the meaning 'cleanse', so that the different versions in Matthew and Luke could reflect the same Aramaic original.[18] In any case, it is well known that Luke has a particular interest in the importance of alms-giving (cf. Luke 12:33; Acts 9:36; 10:2, 4, 31; 24:17, etc.). There is thus no need to look any further than Luke's redactional interests to account for Luke's difference from Matthew here and any theory of an Aramaic *Vorlage* seems unnecessary.[19]

Another similar suggestion of Wellhausen's concerns the difference at Q 6:23 between Matthew's τοὺς πρὸ ὑμῶν and Luke's οἱ πατέρες αὐτῶν. Again Wellhausen postulated slightly different Aramaic versions to account for the difference here: Matthew read קדמיכן which Luke took as קדמיהון, making it the subject of the verb rather than the object.[20] Black goes even further and suggests that Matthew and Luke each preserved one

---

[16] Wellhausen, *Einleitung*, 36f. The suggestion is enthusiastically approved by Black, *Aramaic Approach*, 2, who claims that the 'brilliant conjecture' of Wellhauen's 'has survived criticism'.

[17] Cf. Turner, *Grammatical Insights*, 57, who also points out that Jastrow's Dictionary does not give this as a possible meaning for the word.

[18] C. F. D. Moule, *An Idiom Book of New Testament Greek* (Cambridge University Press, 1968) 186; Kloppenborg, *Formation*, 58.

[19] M. D. Goulder, *Midrash and Lection in Matthew* (London: SPCK, 1974) 426; Kloppenborg, *Formation*, 58.

[20] Wellhausen, *Einleitung*, 36. According to Black, Wellhausen dropped the suggestion from later editions of his *Einleitung*.

half of an original double statement: 'Blessed are ye when men persecute you, for thus did they persecute the prophets before you. Blessed are ye when men reproach you and revile you, for thus did their fathers do to the prophets.'[21] The latter proposal must however remain very hypothetical and really untestable. In any case Wellhausen's conjecture has been severely criticised by Hare.[22] Hare points out that the difference in any Aramaic *Vorlagen* of Matthew and Luke must have involved more than just one letter in the suffix: for the difference between the projected word being the subject (as in Luke) or an indirect object (as in Matthew) would necessitate an extra ד at the start of the word in Matthew's *Vorlage*. The difference cannot therefore be accounted for by a simple misreading by one evangelist. Once again LkR seems sufficient to account for the difference: Luke is fond of the phrase οἱ πατέρες αὐτῶν/ἡμῶν/ὑμῶν, and also has a predilection for adding subjects to verbs.[23] Thus again the theory of an Aramaic *Vorlage* seems both unnecessary and unconvincing.

A third possible example of a misreading concerns the difference at Q 11:42 between Luke's 'rue' (Luke 11:42 πήγανον) and Matthew's 'dill' (Matt 23:23 ἄνηθον). E. Nestle argued that this could be explained as an original שבתא (= 'dill') being misread by Luke as שברא (= 'rue').[24] Black finds confirmation of this in the fact that dill was liable to tithing (as in Matthew's version) whereas rue was not (as implied by Luke).[25] The evidence is, however, not clear cut. Kloppenborg points out that πήγανον has an exact Aramaic equivalent in פיגם, and others have rejected the identification of שברא with πήγανον.[26] Further, translation variants cannot so easily account for the further differences in these verses, e.g. between Matthew's 'cummin' and Luke's 'every herb'. Black's observation about the details of tithing requirements is also of uncertain value since we do not know the precise practice being addressed here: is it necessarily the case that the Pharisaic practice presupposed consisted only of sticking to the

[21] *Aramaic Approach*, 192.

[22] D. R. A. Hare, *The Theme of Jewish Persecution of Christians in the Gospel according to St Matthew* (SNTSMS 6; Cambridge University Press, 1967) 174f.

[23] See Kloppenborg, *Formation*, 58; also my 'The Beatitudes: A Source-Critical Study', *NovT* 25 (1983) 193–207, p. 204.

[24] E. Nestle, 'Anise and Rue', *ExpT* 15 (1904) 528.

[25] Black, *Aramaic Approach*, 194.

[26] See Kloppenborg, *Formation*, 59.

explicit demands of the Law? Or could it be that what is in the mind is a practice of doing more than is strictly required? Nestle's suggestion must thus remain at a most theoretical possibility.

A final example in this category concerns Luke 11:48 ὑμεῖς δὲ οἰκοδομεῖτε/Matt 23:31 υἱοί ἐστε. Black suggests an 'intentional word play' in an original אתון בנין אתון which could be translated in two ways to produce Matthew's or Luke's version.[27] Whether there is an *intentional* ambiguity is another matter. More relevant here would be simply the possibility of perhaps an unpointed Aramaic text. However, the Matthean and Lukan versions differ drastically, far more than can be accounted for by a theory of translation variants; in addition, Kloppenborg points to the fact that Luke's version has a rather un-Aramaic μέν . . . δέ construction.[28]

The attempt to explain the differences between Matthew and Luke by appeal to slightly different Aramaic versions, the differences being explicable in terms of misreadings, or different pointings of a consonantal text, do not seem to be successful. Further, the differences postulated are all of a rather different nature and depend on a different set of factors involved in accounting for the present versions. The situation in Q 11:41 seems to involve a faulty *hearing* of an Aramaic text *dakku* for *zakku*: there is little evidence that the written letters *daleth* and *zain* would have been confused at this period. Q 6:23 may presuppose a faulty copying of an Aramaic version; Q 11:42 seems to presuppose different pointings. In any instance, we appear to have to postulate quite a complex process in the copying and handing on of the Q material at an Aramaic stage. But in any case, the evidence is very small in extent and often much more easily explained by the redactional activity of the evangelists writing in Greek.

If however the attempt to show that Q was an Aramaic text can be said to suffer from a degree of over-enthusiasm, the same can perhaps be said for attempts to show Q was a Greek document. This applies especially to the short article of N. Turner's which has been enthusiastically supported in general terms recently by Kloppenborg, even though Kloppenborg concedes that there are some deficiencies in Turner's argument.[29]

[27] Black, *Aramaic Approach*, 12f.
[28] Kloppenborg, *Formation*, 59.
[29] N. Turner, 'Q in Recent Thought', *ExpT* 80 (1969) 324–8; Kloppenborg, *Formation*, 59–64.

Turner attempts to isolate features of non-translation Greek which serve to distinguish it from Greek which has been translated from a Semitic language. Having done so, he claims that Q's Greek falls well within the parameters of non-translation Greek and is quite unlike some of the 'translationese' found in many of the more literal Greek translations of the books of the LXX. In itself such methodology is unexceptionable. Unfortunately, when Turner comes to consider the evidence from 'Q' he considers only what he calls 'Matthew's Q' and 'Luke's Q', i.e. the Matthean/Lukan versions of material which derives from Q. But no attempt is made to test whether at any one point 'Matthew's Q' or 'Luke's Q' represents Q itself or MattR/LkR. Given the very detailed nature of the comparisons being made, such precision is really vital to the case being made.

Thus, for example, one of Turner's criteria involves the use of a μέν . . . δέ construction as being uncharacteristic of translation Greek.[30] This, he says, 'occurs relatively often in Q', and he cites as justification for this claim Matt 9:37; 10:13; 16:3; (22:5, 8); 23:27, 28; (25:25). Yet of these instances, only one has a parallel in Luke, viz. Matt 9:37/Luke 10:2.[31] There is thus only *one* clear example of a μέν . . . δέ construction in *Q*, i.e. in the material *common* to Matthew *and* Luke. Similarly Turner suggests that the use of γάϱ in second place in a sentence is a good indicator of non-translation Greek and that again Q's Greek comes out well from this test. But once again Turner has only investigated 'Matthew's Q' and 'Luke's Q'. A quick test of 'Luke's Q' shows that only about half the examples have a parallel in Matthew in this respect and so can safely be regarded as Q's Greek; the remaining examples are peculiar to Luke with no clear indicator that Matthew is secondary at each point: hence they could just as easily be due to LkR.[32] Similarly Turner refers to the use of γέ which, he claims, 'occurs twice in Q (Mt 7:20, Lk 10:6) . . . a good record for Q'.[33] But neither instance is paralleled in the other gospel and so neither can be safely regarded as '*Q*'. This list could

---

[30] 'Q in Recent Thought', 326; cf. too his *Grammatical Insights*, 177.

[31] Kloppenborg, *Formation*, 60, recognises this but still appears to think that Turner's argument has value. He adds Matt 3:11/Luke 3:16 as another possible Q example.

[32] γάϱ is in second place in Q's Greek in Luke 3:8; 4:10; 6:27 (perhaps), 44; 7:8, 33; 10:7, 24; 11:10, 30; 12:12, 30, 34; 17:24; it is peculiar to Luke's version in Luke 6:32, 33, 38, 43, 45; 7:5, 6; 11:4; 12:23, 52, 58; 14:24; 19:21.

[33] 'Q in Recent Thought', 326.

be extended to cover many aspects of Turner's article and so its value must remain doubtful. In fact it is very dubious how far we will ever be able to say very much about the detailed style of Q, given the fact that we have no direct access to Q itself. Certainly in such discussion one should confine evidence to material which *is* clearly part of Q, by being common to both Matthew and Luke; alternatively, if the material concerned is found in only one of Matthew/Luke, then arguments must be given for ascribing this material to Q and not to MattR/LkR.

By way of conclusion in this section, we may say that the theory that Q existed in Aramaic form is hard if not impossible to establish. The evidence of the (at times) verbatim agreement between the Greek texts of Matthew and Luke, and the unusual Greek expressions common to the two gospels, thus retain their value in the present context. Even if we have to register some scepticism about some attempts to prove the Greek nature of Q on the basis of stylistic features, it still seems most likely that the Q material was available to Matthew and Luke in a written, Greek form. Oral and/or Aramaic traditions do not really explain the evidence adequately.

2. The Extent of Q

The question of the extent of Q will be dealt with more briefly here. In the light of the lack of any manuscript copy of Q, the question inevitably arises of precisely what material belonged to Q. Two slightly different problems arise in this context. First, in passages where there is a degree of verbal agreement between Matthew and Luke, how high should the level of verbal agreement be if we are to posit common dependence on Q? Second, are there passages which either Matthew or Luke took from Q and which the other evangelist omitted?

The first question arises because of the (at times considerable) variation in the level of verbal agreement between Matthew and Luke in double tradition passages. As we have seen, some passages exhibit almost verbatim agreement in Greek (e.g. Q 3:7–9). In other passages, however, the level of agreement is considerably less. For example, in the parables of the Great Supper (Q 14:16–24) or the Talents/Pounds (Q 19:12–27), it seems that the same story is being told but the verbal agreement is very much reduced.

The problem may however be more apparent than real. Within the synoptic tradition as a whole, the verbal agreement between the gospels is rarely as close as the verbatim agreement of Q 3:7–9. Within the triple tradition, the agreement between Matthew and Mark, or between Luke and Mark, is rarely verbatim, and hence too the level of Matthew–Luke agreement when both are using Mark is correspondingly lower. In actual fact, the overall level of verbal agreement between Matthew and Luke in Q passages is slightly higher than the level of agreement between them in Markan passages.[34] If then one accepts the literary dependence of Matthew and Luke on Mark, there is no need to doubt literary dependence on a written Q simply because at times Matthew and Luke are not verbally identical.[35] I have therefore taken as a working hypothesis the theory that Q contained at least all the passages where Matthew and Luke agree in substance and (at least some) wording and where their agreement is not due to dependence on Mark.[36]

But did Q include more than this? Are there passages which now appear as Matthean or Lukan *Sondergut* which in fact are derived from Q and which the other evangelist omitted? On a priori grounds, it seems extremely likely that this happened in some cases. A glance at the Markan material in Matthew and Luke should be sufficient to see why. For whilst Mark's gospel is used for the most part in full by Matthew and Luke, there are cases where the later evangelists have omitted passages from Mark (Luke more than Matthew). Hence if we attempted to reconstruct Mark's gospel by using only the Markan passages which appear in

---

[34] See C. E. Carlston & D. Norlin, 'Once More — Statistics and Q', *HTR* 64 (1971) 59–78. The importance of making proper comparison between Matthew–Luke agreements in Mark and in Q material is emphasised by Carlston and Norlin, responding in part to T. Rosché, 'The Words of Jesus and the Future of the "Q" Hypothesis', *JBL* 79 (1960) 210–20: in assessing the level of verbal agreement between Matthew and Luke in Q material, one should compare the agreement between Matthew and Luke in Markan material, not between Matthew and Mark, or between Luke and Mark.

[35] If anything, then, the peculiar feature of the Q material is the quite extraordinary level of agreement in passages like Q 3:7–9, rather than the verbal disagreement elsewhere.

[36] This slightly clumsy expression, i.e. *not* referring simply to 'non-Markan passages where Matthew and Luke agree . . .', is due to the fact that, as we have already seen, Q almost certainly overlapped with Mark at times (see pp. 31–4 above). Q is thus not *just* the non-Markan passages where Matthew and Luke agree.

both Matthew and Luke we would not restore our gospel of Mark. Since there is no reason for thinking that Matthew's and Luke's use of Q was radically different from the way in which they used Mark as a source, it seems highly likely that both the later evangelists will have exercised a degree of editorial freedom by not including every tradition which was available to them from their Q source. Where one evangelist omitted a section of Q which was retained by the other, the material concerned will now appear as a piece of *Sondergut* in the gospel in which it now appears.

The extent to which this has happened is disputed. One estimate is that we in fact have only c. 10–14 per cent of the original Q preserved in our gospels.[37] This is however probably a misleading figure, since it is based on the *verbatim* agreement between Matthew and Luke and their sources; moreover, the only control used by Honoré is between Matthew/Luke and Mark. However, it appears that Matthew's and Luke's use of Q was if anything more conservative than their use of Mark (cf. above), and hence the measure of verbatim agreement between their gospels and Q will be correspondingly higher. If we take a broader look at the tradition, it is clear that, although the level of *verbatim* agreement between Matthew/Luke and Mark is not high, nevertheless, in terms of substance, the amount of material completely omitted is relatively small. Matthew retains c. 90 per cent of all the Markan material. The figure for Luke is certainly lower, though the situation is complicated by uncertainty about whether Luke is actually using Mark on occasions, especially in the passion narrative. However, on other occasions, it seems that Luke quite often omits a Markan pericope precisely in order to retain a parallel version of the same pericope from Q.[38] This suggests that Luke may have had a higher regard for Q than for Mark,[39] and this in turn makes it less likely that Luke has made wholesale omissions from Q.[40]

From very general considerations, therefore, it would appear that the number of actual passages omitted from Q by each evangelist is probably fairly low. Yet if the phenomenon of one (or

[37] See A. T. Honoré, 'A Statistical Study of the Synoptic Problem', *NovT* 10 (1968) 95–147, p. 135f.

[38] See ch. 1 above on the 'Mark–Q Overlaps' (pp. 31–4 above).

[39] Cf. Kloppenborg, *Formation*, 82.

[40] See in general, Vassiliadis, 'Nature and Extent', 65; Kloppenborg, *Formation*, 81f.

even both)[41] evangelist(s) omitting Q material clearly has to be accepted in theory, it is very hard to determine precisely when and where this actually happened. Thus the identification of specific *Sondergut* passages which may have been part of Q has never commanded anything approaching a scholarly consensus. By far the most 'optimistic' scholar in recent years who has sought to identify *Sondergut* material in Matthew or Luke as Q material has been H. Schürmann who, in a variety of publications, has argued for the existence of a large number of such passages.[42] However, very few have followed him in quite such detail.[43] Vassiliadis too has considered the problem and proposed some criteria for determining what could count in this respect: he suggests that passages of *Sondergut* could be ascribed to Q if (*a*) they belong to texts otherwise ascribed to Q, (*b*) they agree theologically with the rest of Q, (*c*) they agree with the 'country life language' of Q, (*d*) they do not show signs of MattR or LkR, (*e*) reasons can be given for why the other evangelist might have omitted them, (*f*) they belong within Luke's 'Great Insertion' (Luke 9:51–18:14).[44] The rationale behind (*c*) and (*f*) seems very dubious,[45] though the rest seem quite reasonable.[46] But a strict application of (*b*) means that in practice little will be added to our understanding of Q by including *Sondergut* passages: if we only

[41] The fact that a few Markan passages are omitted by both Matthew and Luke (cf. Mark 2:27; 7:31–37; 8:22–26, etc.) indicates that the same could, and perhaps did, happen in the case of Q. However, in such instances, we shall never know what has been omitted by both evangelists from Q until we find a version of Q itself!

[42] A convenient list is provided by Neirynck, 'Recent Developments', 38f.

[43] Cf. Neirynck's own comment: 'The excessive expansion he [= Schürmann] gave to Q did not convince ... The main stream of studies on Q remained sceptical of Schürmann's position.' (ibid.).

[44] Vassiliadis, 'Nature and Extent', 67.

[45] Vassiliadis himself does not explain the reasoning behind these criteria. Kloppenborg, *Formation*, 83, suggests that (*c*) is influenced by J. M. C. Crum, *The Original Jerusalem Gospel* (New York: Macmillan, 1927), whose ch. 4 is entitled 'Q and Country Life'. Why possible Q material omitted by Matthew should be confined to Luke's 'Great Insertion' is not at all clear.

[46] Cf. Kloppenborg's endorsement of these as 'sound and responsible criteria' (*Formation*, 84). Vassiliadis himself suggests that a few verses could be ascribed to Q on this basis: Luke 9:60–62; 10:19f.; 11:27f.; 12:32–38 (*sic.* = 12:35–38?); 12:54–56; 13:23–30; 21:34–36; Matt 10:16b; 11:12f. ('Nature and Extent', 70). This is in many ways a strange list: passages such as Luke 12:33–34 and 13:23–30 would appear to be Q material without too much question in the light of the existence of Matthean parallels (cf. Matt 6:19–21; 7:13f.; 25:10; 7:22f.; 8:11f.). The same applies to Matt 11:12f. (cf. Luke 16:16) and perhaps Luke

allow passages into Q that fit with our existing understanding, then that understanding will be simply reinforced and not substantially changed.

Each passage must obviously be considered on its own merits. Later in this study we shall be looking at some particular *Sondergut* passages, including Luke 4:16–30 as well as Matt 18:15–17 and more briefly at one or two others. As will be seen, the possibility of at least one or two of these passages being part of Q will be defended here. But in any such instance, the 'burden of proof' must lie with the person who would argue for such a theory. It is clear that the existence of such passages is both possible and (in view of the nature of Matthew's and Luke's use of Mark) probable, even if it will inevitably remain extremely difficult to identify them precisely.

In conclusion, therefore, we may say that Q probably contained all the material common to Matthew and Luke which was not derived from Mark; it probably also contained more material, some of which may have been preserved by Matthew or Luke alone, but the exact identification of such passages must inevitably remain uncertain. Until we find an actual manuscript of Q, we can only speculate!

3. Different Versions of Recensions of Q?

An apparently slightly different set of problems is raised if we ask the question whether 'Q' was available to Matthew and Luke in exactly the same form. Was Matthew's version of Q exactly the same as Luke's version of Q? Was Q available in slightly different forms to the two evangelists? Or should we even be thinking of two recensions of Q, a Q^{mt} and a Q^{lk}, which may have been rather more different from each other? The two problems are not quite the same and I consider them separately here.

3.1. *Different Versions of Q?*

The question is probably rather more easily answerable in very general terms than in relation to particular texts. In general terms, it is surely extremely difficult to conceive of two identical versions of Q being available to Matthew and Luke respectively.

12:54–56 (cf. Matt 16:2–3, though the text-critical problems of the Matthean text here do make for uncertainty). Luke 21:34–36 does not satisfy Vassiliadis' own (admittedly strange: cf. above) criterion about belonging within Luke's 'Great Insertion'.

The very nature of the writing of texts in the first century, before the days of printing presses and the availability of any sort of technology for producing multiple, identical copies of texts, simply precludes that possibility as a nonsense. Further, it strains credulity to conceive of a single manuscript copy of Q, whether in the form of a scroll or a codex, being used by Matthew and Luke successively (unless we are to think of Matthew and Luke working in far closer geographical proximity to each other than is usually assumed). Any kind of consideration of the physical realities of the situation seems to indicate that there must have been more than one copy of Q. Matthew's copy would not have been the same as Luke's copy, and hence, given the nature of text production at the time, it is highly likely that Matthew's version of Q was not identical to Luke's.

On the other hand, we have to bear in mind the concrete evidence of our texts of Matthew and Luke which we do have. As noted on more than one occasion already, there are instances where Matthew's and Luke's Greek texts agree almost verbatim (cf. Q 3:7–9 yet again!). This surely indicates that, at least at some points in Q, the versions of Q available to Matthew and Luke must have been all but identical. Hence the differences between the wording of Q in the (supposed) two versions of Q cannot have been that great at times. This, of course, does not preclude the possibility that, at other points in the tradition, the differences between Matthew's version of Q and Luke's version of Q might have been rather greater, and hence at these points, the verbal disagreements between the two evangelists might be explicable in this way. In the nature of the case, it is not always possible to determine precisely when this might have happened; and in any case, the present study will generally not be attempting to reconstruct the detailed wording of each Q tradition down to the last preposition or grammatical detail. Here we may simply note the theoretical possibility that some kind of copying or transmission process may well be the reason behind some of the verbal disagreements between Matthew and Luke in Q material, whilst bearing in mind too the striking phenomenon of close verbal agreement in some passages.

3.2. Different Recensions of Q?

A rather different problem in this context has however been raised in some recent works on Q. This concerns the possibility that some *Sondergut* passages may not have been present in the Q material available to both evangelists (and hence omitted by one of them: cf. the phenomenon discussed in the previous section), but may have belonged to expansions of the Q tradition which took place in the 'trajectories' of the tradition history leading to our present texts of Matthew and Luke. Hence Matthew's version of Q, 'Q^{mt}', may have contained Q material of which Luke was unaware. Similarly, Luke's version of Q, 'Q^{lk}', may have undergone a similar, but different, expansion. In this way, some of the *Sondergut* material in Matthew/Luke might have been in a Q^{mt} or a Q^{lk}, but such a theory would not then have to explain at the redactional level why the material was omitted by the other evangelist: the material in question would simply have been present in the version of Q available to one evangelist and not in the version available to the other. We should though note that such a theory about a developing Q is rather different from what we have just considered earlier in this section, viz. the possibility that in the process of copying, different versions of the same material were produced. The present theory presupposes more than simply scribal errors being introduced into the two trajectories of Q.

Such a theory was defended by D. Lührmann, who argued for a substantive expansion of Q in the Matthean tradition.[47] In more recent discussion, such a view has been put forward in the works of M. Sato and D. Kosch.[48] Such theories must however meet some of the criteria outlined in the previous section concerning the possible ascription of *Sondergut* passages to Q. The only difference from the model discussed in the previous section is that the theory being considered here itself precludes any necessity of explaining why the material in question appears in only one of the gospels. That apart, the two models are virtually identical and

---

[47] Lührmann, *Redaktion*, 105–21.

[48] See Sato, *Q und Prophetie*, 47–62; D. Kosch, *Die eschatologische Tora des Menschensohnes. Untersuchungen zur Rezeption der Stellung Jesu zur Tora in Q* (NTOA 12; Freiburg & Göttingen: Universitätsverlag & Vandenhoeck & Ruprecht, 1989); also Kosch, 'Q: Rekonstruktion und Interpretation', *FZPT* 36 (1989) 409–25. See the survey of F. Neirynck, 'Q^{Mt} and Q^{Lk} and the Reconstruction of Q', *ETL* 66 (1990) 385–90 (= *Evangelica II*, 475–80); also his 'Literary Criticism, Old and New', in Focant (ed.), *Synoptic Gospels*, 11–38, p. 28f. Sato's theory is also endorsed by his doctoral supervisor, U. Luz, in his *Matthew 1–7*, 46. See too G. Strecker in several writings, for example his 'Die Makarismen der Bergpredigt', *NTS* 17 (1971) 255–75. Cf. Neirynck, 'Q^{Mt} and Q^{Lk}', 389.

the same comments apply to each. In particular, there is still the obligation to explain how the passages which might belong to the alleged expansions of Q cohere with the rest of the material. This is important, since it is necessary to distinguish between the different possibilities of an expansion of Q into a Q^{mt} or a Q^{lk} at a pre-redactional stage and the possibility that the evangelist himself may have added the relevant material (whether by creating it *de novo* or by incorporating a tradition culled from elsewhere).

This applies especially in the case of Kosch who has argued that a number of passages in Luke (Luke 3:10–14; 6:24–26; 9:61–62; 11:5–8; 12:16–21; 16:19–31; perhaps also Luke 1:51–53) may all belong within an expanded Q^{lk} version as used by Luke.[49] Further, he seeks to outline a 'profile' of this Q^{lk}, seeing it in part, for example, as highlighting the theme of the eschatological reversal of social conditions. However, at this point, one could argue that 'Q^{lk}' looks as if it is becoming rather like Luke himself; or, if not, it is because so much has been ascribed by Kosch to the alleged Q^{lk} and not allowed to contribute to a specifically Lukan profile.[50] There are also rather different nuances emerging from these different texts in Luke. Kosch seeks to make something of a virtue out of necessity of this by arguing that the growth of Q^{lk} itself may have been a progressive one, with different elements entering the growing Q at different stages and from different origins.[51] But this simply raises more acutely the question of how far we should really think of this material as part of an expansion *of Q*, and how far it is simply part of a wide range of material included in his gospel *by Luke*.[52]

---

[49] 'Q: Rekonstruktion', 416–420. Sato agrees at many points with Kosch: thus Sato includes most of these text in his Q^{lk} (though not Luke 16:19–31), and also Luke 10:18–19; 11:36; 12:32; 12:35–38; 12:47–48; 17:28–29; in Q^{mt} he includes Matt 5:5, 7–9; 6:34; 7:6; 10:5b–6; 10:23; 11:28–30; 25:1–12 (all with varying degrees of certainty).

[50] See, however, p. 79 above on the danger of not allowing an author's tradition to contribute to an assessment of his overall ideas.

[51] 'Q: Rekonstruktion', 418.

[52] In the end Kosch's main argument seems to be that Luke uses his Markan and Q material in 'blocks': hence a long sequence of the gospel such as Luke 14–17, which, on the more traditional view of Q, contains a number of scattered, relatively isolated, sayings from Q, may have come to Luke in the form of a more extended block of 'Q' (i.e. Q^{lk}) material (see 'Q: Rekonstruktion', 415). But whether an argument based on such a redactional policy by Luke can really sustain the case seems very doubtful. Perhaps Luke used

Further, it is doubtful how much such theories can, or should, affect study of 'Q' itself. I argued in the previous chapter (in relation to theories of possible earlier, rather than later, stages in the tradition history of Q) that we should reserve the siglum 'Q' for the 'final' form of the tradition as available to *both* Matthew and Luke.[53] Any theory of a subsequent, post-'Q' but pre-Matthean/Lukan expansion of Q would not then really concern 'Q' itself. Rather, it would concern the later development of each evangelist's tradition. In turn this might affect one's view about the redactional activity and contribution of each evangelist (tending probably to ascribe rather less to the evangelists and rather more to the pre-redactional tradition). But in terms of Q studies it would not be relevant to a historical-critical analysis of 'Q', such as this present study, which aims to analyse Q itself. Recensions of Q thus belong to the *Wirkungsgeschichte* of Q, i.e. to the history of the reception and interpretation of Q, not to the tradition history of Q as defined here.

Certainly there is every likelihood that the versions of Q used by Matthew and Luke were not absolutely identical, as we have seen. However, a theory of Q-recensions, insofar as it seeks to explain more than just possible variations in the detailed wording of common pericopes available to Matthew and Luke by including possible *Sondergut* passages in the suggested recension, will not be discussed in detail here. In practical terms the problem in relation to any possible such passage really belongs more to the study of the gospel in which it occurs and not to the study of 'Q', taken as the tradition *common* to both Matthew and Luke.

4. Date and Place of Q

A standard 'introductory' question often raised in relation to any text is the date and place of the writing.[54] In relation to Q we are inevitably in the dark about questions such as this. And indeed to a certain extent, as is the case with all the gospels in the NT, we

---

material in blocks when he could, or when he thought it appropriate. Various other 'L' passages in Luke occur in some isolation: cf. Luke 7:36–50; 8:1–3; 19:39–44; 21:34–36, as does the Q parable in Luke 19:12–27.

[53] See above, p. 77.

[54] For the potential significance of such questions in relation to interpretation, see my *Reading*, ch. 4.

can only postulate answers to such questions on the basis of a consideration of the distinctive features of the text.[55]

4.1. Date

Most would place the date of Q at some point between 40 and 70 CE. There is no clear evidence that Q was composed after the Fall of Jerusalem; and if (as will be argued later; cf. pp. 204–7 below) the lament over Jerusalem in Q 13:34f. is intended by Q in a hopeful sense, with the possibility of the threat implied in the lament being averted, then it seems unlikely that Q was written from a post-70 perspective.[56]

Theissen has sought to be more precise by referring to the way in which the Pharisees are mentioned in Q.[57] He refers to the evidence of the series of woes in Q 11:39ff. and argues that these must reflect a situation of hostility on the part of the Pharisees to the Christian movement. He then claims that such hostility can only be evidenced in the period c. 40–55 CE: after this, the evidence seems to suggest that Pharisees were much more open to the Christian movement and less antagonistic. Hence Q is to be dated to this narrower time band of c. 40–55 CE.

As we shall see, the evidence of the woes in Q 11 and the references to the Pharisees there may well be significant (see ch. 13 below). However, it is not at all clear that Pharisaic attitudes to the Christian movement changed significantly after c. 55 CE. The only evidence adduced by Theissen of Pharisaic sympathy for Christians is from Josephus' account of the death of James (*Ant.* 20.200f.), when some 'who were strict in observance of the Law' (= Pharisees?) protested against the high-priest Ananus' attempt to have James executed, and from the attitude of Pharisees at Paul's appearance before the Jewish authorities in Jerusalem in the late 50's, as recorded by Luke (Acts 23:9). However, the Lukan picture may well owe more to Luke's own *Tendenz* than to

---

[55] The situation is potentially slightly different in the case of the gospels, since we do have a certain amount of external, patristic evidence. However, this is usually regarded as no great help in determining the circumstances of the writing of the gospels. In the case of Q, some external evidence *might* be available if one interpreted the Papias statement about Matthew as a reference to Q: but this is usually discounted now: cf. p. 43 above.

[56] See Kümmel, *Introduction*, 71; I. Havener, *Q: The Sayings of Jesus* (Wilmington: Glazier, 1987) 45. See also p. 362 below for discussion of the view of Hoffmann that Q might be written after 70 CE.

[57] See *Gospels in Context*, 227–34 (= *Lokalkolorit*, 238–45).

historical reality.[58] The evidence of Josephus' account of the death of James is thus somewhat isolated, and it seems therefore precarious to try to generalise from this to make deductions about the attitude of all Pharisees during the whole of the turbulent period from c. 55–70 CE. Thus it may be safer to leave a possible date for Q within a broader time span of c. 40–70 CE, rather than narrow it down further in the way suggested by Theissen.

4.2. Place

As far as the place is concerned, most scholars have located Q somewhere in the area of Northern Galilee or its environs.[59] Apart from the mention of 'Jerusalem' in Q 4:9; 13:34, the only place names mentioned are the Galilean towns of Capernaum (Q 7:1; 10:15), Chorazin (Q 10:13) and Bethsaida (Q 10:13). Q 10:14 also mentions the Gentile cities of Tyre and Sidon in Western Syria, not far from Northern Galilee. The relative obscurity of some of these names (especially Chorazin) has suggested to many that Q may thus emanate from an area near these towns.[60] The evidence is, of course, not conclusive, above all since it is virtually confined to one unit, the woes in Q 10:13–15. Hence the place names there may indicate that only that individual tradition, rather then the whole of Q, stems from such a locale.

However, more circumstantial support for such a placing of Q might be provided by the existence of the gospels of Matthew and Thomas. Matthew's gospel is often taken as emanating from Syria; and GTh may also be Syrian (as is shown by the peculiar name Judas Didymus Thomas which, in view of the same form of the name appearing in other texts associated with Syria, may indicate a Syrian origin for GTh as well).[61] The fact that Matthew used Q, and that GTh *may* have some links with Q or with traditions

---

[58] It is an important theme for Luke to show that Christianity is in a line of positive continuity with at least part of Judaism; and since the debate in Acts 23 is about resurrection, it makes sense for Luke to have Paul supported by the Pharisees who, at least in Luke's schema, also believe in resurrection, unlike the Sadducees who do not.

[59] Havener, *Q*, 42–5.

[60] W. Schenk, 'Die Verwünschung der Küstenorte Q 10,13–15: Zur Funktion der konkreten Ortsangaben und zur Lokalisierung von Q', in Focant (ed.), *Synoptic Gospels*, 477–90, seeks to be even more precise and locates Q to the city of Tiberias, on the basis of the order in which the places are mentioned. Such precision may be a little optimistic.

[61] See Koester, 'GNOMAI DIAPHORAI', 127f., and many others since.

available to Q (cf. above), could then all fit together reasonably well if Q were also to be located in Galilee/Syria. But more than that we cannot say.[62]

5. The Genre of Q

A final question to be considered here — again rather briefly — is that of the genre of Q. What kind of text is Q? To what genre should we assign it? Not much space will be devoted to this question explicitly at this point. This is not because the question of genre is unimportant. Quite the reverse. In one sense the question of genre is the most important question to raise in study of Q. As we have seen, the problem of genre was the key point in the programmatic studies of Robinson, Koester and Kloppenborg; it was also one of the main questions addressed in the book of Sato. The difference between (say) Kloppenborg and Sato is one of the key questions in contemporary Q studies: is Q to be seen (generically) as primarily 'sapiential' (so Kloppenborg, at least for the 'formative layer' of Q), or as 'prophetic' (Sato)?

In one sense, such a question cannot be answered in a small section in an early chapter of a book on Q. How one defines and determines a genre is notoriously difficult. But, at least in one sense, the whole text is constituted as the sum of its parts. We cannot therefore determine the nature of the whole (the 'genre') before determining the nature of the individual parts of Q. We cannot, for example, decide whether Q is 'sapiential' before we decide whether the individual elements are sapiential. I am fully aware that this is not the whole story: a text is more than just the sum of its constituent parts. And insofar as any one element in a text is often ambiguous when considered in isolation, it is precisely one's understanding of the genre of the whole which can determine one's decision about each element.

The importance of genre for understanding any text is accepted by most literary theorists.[63] Thus many would echo

---

[62] And the use of Q by Luke would still need explanation, unless we can locate Luke to a similar location as well.

[63] See R. Wellek & A. Warren, *Theory of Literature* (Harmondsworth: Penguin, 1973) 226–37; E. D. Hirsch, *Validity in Interpretation* (Yale University Press, 1967); A. Fowler, *Kinds of Literature: An Introduction to the Theory of Genres and Modes* (Oxford University Press, 1982). In relation to gospel studies generally, see R. A. Burridge, *What are the Gospels?* (SNTSMS 70; Cambridge University Press, 1992) 26–54; and in relation to Q studies, see also Kloppenborg, *Formation*, ch. 1. More generally, see my *Reading*, ch. 5.

Hirsch's assertion that 'all understanding of verbal meaning is necessarily genre-bound'.[64] In order to understand a sentence in a larger text, we need to have some idea of the nature of that larger text. Thus we distinguish fiction from non-fiction, prose from poetry, novel from history, biography from detective story, and we make the necessary mental adjustments to read any one part of the whole. Without *some* (albeit often vague) idea of the nature of the whole, any understanding is impossible. Hence too, the idea of a totally new genre is not really conceivable if the text concerned is to be intelligible: without some framework of reference which an idea of genre provides, the text could not be understood at all. 'The totally novel form will be unintelligible — is indeed unthinkable.'[65]

There is debate amongst literary critics about whether genre is, or should be, prescriptive or descriptive.[66] Probably neither extreme view is appropriate and it is perhaps more helpful to think in terms of genre as a 'system of expectations'.[67] As such, the genre creates an environment within which understanding a text can start, though also allowing for the possibility that a text may at times create tensions for the initial expectations: genre is not necessarily a rigid set of rules within which a text must operate, but a background against which creative change can, and often does, function.

There is also uncertainty about how to define any one genre. Clearly one can define genre very broadly ('book', 'flysheet', 'story purporting to be the life of a person', 'poem') or more narrowly ('autobiography', 'history', 'novel', 'detective story', 'sonnet'). Clearly too the greater the precision, the greater the interpretative power of the genre classification. If I only know something is a 'book', I know that I should read it. If I know only that it is a 'story about a person', I do not know if I am meant to read it as a historical source, or for light relief. If it is a 'detective story', I know it is *not* usable as a source for history, it is probably *not* to be read as great literature, or for any very deep 'meaning'; it is simply to be read as entertainment. But if the genre is made too precise, then it ceases to provide a genuinely broad context in which the whole can be read.

---

[64] Hirsch, *Validity*, 76.

[65] Wellek & Warren, *Theory*, 235.

[66] See Burridge, *What are the Gospels?*, 32ff.

[67] Hirsch, *Validity*, 83. Cf. too F. Kermode, *The Genesis of Secrecy* (Cambridge, Mass.: Harvard University Press, 1979) 162.

Thus a theorist like Hirsch would distinguish between levels of genre. There is a broad, heuristic genre with which one might start reading a text (that it is a 'book', a 'story about a person'), which is then gradually made more precise and clarified (and also perhaps constantly modified) in the process of reading, so that one has a more narrowly defined 'intrinsic genre' of a text which enables understanding to take place.[68] Perhaps such a distinction may help us in discussing the possible genre of Q.

A claim made by some in the past has been that Q is generically unique. For some this has been a strong argument against the very existence of Q. Thus Farrer asserts: 'There is no independent evidence for anything like Q. To postulate Q is to postulate the unevidenced and the unique.'[69] For others, it is a strong positive assertion: Q, it is claimed, is *sui generis*.[70] Such a claim must, from a literary point of view, be unsustainable. No text can really be *sui generis* and be understood (cf. above). Nevertheless the fact remains that Q is *un*like many other texts often brought into view as possible parallels.

The problem is however probably more apparent than real and can be fairly easily resolved by referring to Hirsch's analysis of the way in which understanding changes. At the level of a very broad genre, Q is quite clearly *not* unique, not *sui generis*. Here the programmatic work of Kloppenborg needs to be taken into account fully. Kloppenborg has shown that, insofar as Q is some kind of 'sayings collection', then it clearly has a large number of parallels in other collections in antiquity. These vary in style, in scope, in content. But at a very broad and general level, Q is by no means *sui generis*. Nor is Q unique if one seeks a little more specificity in taking note of the fact that Q contains not only sayings but also some (though not many) actions of Jesus, narratives about Jesus, etc. Kloppenborg has again shown that collections of chreiae, small stories about the sayings or (at times) actions of an individual, were around in the ancient world. As such, these bear some similarity to Q. So too there were records of the teachings of a famous person, at times preceded by accounts of (for example) that person's trial or test to show the validity of

[68] See Hirsch, *Validity*, ch. 3; Burridge, *What are the Gospels?*, 40f.
[69] Farrer, 'On Dispensing', 58.
[70] See F. Neirynck, art. 'Q', *Interpreters Dictionary of the Bible, Supplementary Volume* (Nashville: Abingdon, 1962) 716. Also Schürmann, 'Zur Kompositionsgeschichte der Redenquelle', 328: Q is 'wohl analogielos'.

their teaching.[71] Thus at this very general level, Q is not unique.

It is perhaps when we seek to go beyond this level of generality that problems may arise. Wellek and Warren claim that genre should be a matter not only of what they call 'outer form' (by which they mean overall structure such as, for example, 'sayings collection') but also 'inner form', by which they refer to 'attitude, tone, purpose — more crudely subject and audience'.[72] It is, of course, here that, if we could firmly establish what the genre of Q was, the generic identification would serve as a vital hermeneutical key to the interpretation of each element of Q. However, we cannot in the end evade the hermeneutical circle which any genre discussion inevitably involves and which we referred to earlier: we understand the whole from the sum of the parts, but we can understand the parts only as part of the whole. If though we are at the level of seeking to find out something about the 'subject and audience' of Q in determining its genre, then we cannot do that in isolation from an analysis of the individual parts themselves. We cannot therefore determine the genre of Q in this more precise sense before considering the contents of Q in much more detail. In this sense, therefore, the determination of the genre can only come at the end of the discussion, not at the beginning. We can start with a 'broad genre': Q is a 'sayings collection'. We can presumably be a little more precise than that. Its 'tone' and 'purpose' are no doubt intended seriously: it is not a series of jokes. One presumes too that the traditions here collected were preserved because they were thought to be (broadly) still relevant for the life of the people who preserved them and for the people to whom they were addressed. But if we wish to have greater precision still, then we have to read Q itself. Just as the determination of the 'intrinsic genre', or 'inner form', of a text only emerges as we read the text and shape, and re-shape, our understanding of the whole, so too with Q. We can only come to understand Q if we are prepared to study it and read it for ourselves.

---

[71] See Kloppenborg, *Formation*, 256–61, on the Q temptation narrative.
[72] Wellek & Warren, *Theory*, 231. Hirsch's distinction of a broad, heuristic genre and intrinsic genre is similar.

4

John the Baptist in Q

The very nature of Q as a collection of Jesus' sayings and teachings which has been preserved and handed on suggests that the Christians responsible for collecting and preserving this body of tradition regarded the teaching which it contained as still valid.[1] This is not to deny that in some respects a more nuanced position may be necessary. We have already noted that one may have to distinguish between an editor/'author' of Q and the community to which (s)he belongs: it may be that the editor thought that the community needed to be convinced of the validity of the preaching of the Jesus of Q and that the community itself did not whole-

[1] The appropriateness of calling Q 'Christian', and hence presumably of calling people in the Q-'group' 'Christians', has been called into question by the claim made by both Jacobson and Mack that Q is not 'Christian': cf. Jacobson, *First Gospel*, 2, 32; Mack, *Lost Gospel*, 4f., 48, 245. Much though depends on the precise definition of 'Christian'. As is recognised now as standard critical orthodoxy, first-century Christianity was characterised by a rich diversity. Precisely what constitutes the essential nature of the unity in that diversity which qualifies one part as clearly 'Christian' is by no means clear. Jacobson gives no definition. Mack implies one negatively by clarifying the assertion that 'the people of Q were not Christians' as follows:

> They did not think of Jesus as a messiah or the Christ. They did not take his teachings as an indictment of Judaism. They did not regard his death as a divine, tragic, or saving event. And they did not imagine that he had been raised from the dead to rule over a transformed world . . . Thus they did not gather to worship in his name, honor him as a god, or cultivate his memory through hymns, prayers, and rituals. They did not form a cult of the Christ such as the one that emerged among the Christian communities familiar to the readers of the letters of Paul. (*Lost Gospel*, 4–5.)

But on this basis, several NT figures might fail the test as well! How far does Matthew think of Jesus as an indictment of Judaism (as opposed to some Jews)? Does Luke regard Jesus' death as a 'saving event'? How many early Christians 'honoured [Jesus] as a god'?

In the present context, I use the term 'Christian' simply to refer to the group of people who regarded Jesus positively. 'Jesus follower' might beg less questions as a term, though it is somewhat clumsy.

heartedly accept this teaching. Even so, it would appear reasonable to assume that, at least for some Christians, the content of
Jesus-tradition in Q was regarded as still valid.

One other possible reservation might concern the question of
how far there is an awareness of a qualitative distinction between
the time of Jesus and the time of Q. At one level there obviously is
a difference. Presumably no one would have dreamt of denying
that Jesus' earthly ministry was to be dated some years in the past.
Q may also be aware that this temporal difference has some
significant consequences. For example, reaction to the preaching
of Jesus seems to be regarded as capable of being evaluated in
different ways depending on when that reaction takes place. Q
12:10 states that speaking against the SM is forgivable whereas
speaking against the Holy Spirit is not. The saying is notoriously
difficult, but one possible interpretation is that a refusal to accept
Jesus' preaching during the earthly ministry of Jesus himself is
forgivable, whereas a refusal to accept Jesus' preaching in Q's
present is not.[2] Thus whilst there is continuity between Jesus and
Q at the level of the contents of the preaching, nevertheless there
is also an awareness of some distinction between the era of Jesus
and that of the Q Christians.

One aspect of Jesus' teaching which Q appears to endorse
concerns eschatology. T. W. Manson noted the way in which
eschatological teaching seems to provide a frame for the whole of
Q, coming at the start (3:7ff.) and finish (17:22ff.) of Q,[3] and
eschatology and warnings about an imminent End have been
claimed by others to dominate large parts of Q.[4] This note is
sounded right at the start with the material on John the Baptist,
and it this material which we shall consider in some detail in the
present chapter.

One of the more surprising features of Q is the amount of space
devoted to John the Baptist. John's preaching is set out in detail

---

[2] The interpretation of this logion is much disputed. For a clear statement
of the problems here and for the above as a possible intepretation, see
Kloppenborg, *Formation*, 212f.; cf. also Tödt, *Son of Man*, 119; Hoffmann,
Studien, 152; Schulz, *Q*, 248 and others.

[3] See p. 48 above. There is, of course, doubt about the precise order, and
hence the identity of the final pericope, of Q. However, seeing Q 19:12ff. or
22:28–30 as the end of Q would not change the statement above significantly.

[4] Cf. Kee and Davies, as in p. 56 n. 60 above. The question of how far this is
justified, in the light of the comments of Kloppenborg, Jacobson and others,
will be considered in the next chapter when we consider the eschatology of Q
more broadly.

in Q 3:7–9 and in 3:16f.,[5] and a long section a little later in Q (7:18–35) discusses the position of John in some detail. So too John's ministry is evidently given a significant place in the saying Q 16:16 (wherever that saying may belong within Q).

The reasons for devoting so much space to John are not clear. Much of this material probably had a complex pre-history behind it before it ever reached Q and, within that history, there may be reflected some concern to ensure that John is not to be evaluated too highly, certainly in relation to Jesus. Whether this in turn implies that the group of people responsible for Q were related in some way to a 'Baptist-"community"' and were trying to play down claims by such a 'community',[6] is not certain. So too the precise significance of John's teaching is at times uncertain because of doubts about the reconstruction of the wording of Q. Nevertheless, despite possible reservations about the status of John at one level, it seems clear that there is also in Q wholehearted support for John's teaching and a willingness to incorporate the tradition of his teaching into Q itself with no hint that John's message had been superseded, or rendered in any way invalid, by the ministry of Jesus himself. It is this that we shall seek to show in the detailed analyses that follow.

1. Q 3:7–9

The reconstruction of the Q wording of John's preaching in this pericope is in one way very easy. The section comprises one of the

---

[5] There is a little doubt as to whether v. 16 should be ascribed to Q at all, since Matthew and Luke are both close to Mark and could have derived the verse from Mark alone. However, v. 17 (which has no Markan parallel and therefore must be from Q) really demands something preceding (cf. the otherwise 'hanging' relative pronoun οὗ at the start of the verse). Further, in v. 16 itself there are a number of agreements between Matthew and Luke against Mark: (i) both Matthew and Luke insert the clause about the 'stronger one' between the two halves of the contrast between John's water baptism and the coming (Spirit + fire) baptism; (ii) both use the present βαπτίζω in relation to John (cf. Mark's aorist ἐβάπτισα); (iii) both place the object ὑμᾶς before the verb when talking of the future baptism; (iv) both use a μέν . . . δέ construction; (v) most importantly, both say that the future baptism will be with 'fire' (καὶ πυρί) as well as with 'Holy Spirit'. Thus most would agree that 3:16 is indeed part of Q. Cf. R. Laufen, *Die Doppelüberlieferungen der Logienquelle und des Markusevangeliums* (BBB 54; Bonn: Hanstein, 1980) 93 ('allgemein anerkannt'); Hoffmann, *Studien*, 16, 18f.; Schulz, *Q*, 368; Kloppenborg, *Q Parallels* (Sonoma: Polebridge, 1988) 12, lists the few who have denied the verse to Q.

[6] Cf. Sato, *Q und Prophetie*, 372, 389.

stock examples of almost verbatim agreement between the Greek texts of Matthew and Luke so that a Greek *Vorlage* is almost demanded (cf. p. 3 above). Within the account of John's preaching itself, the only difference to be noted here concerns John's appeal for 'fruit' (Matthew)/'fruits' (Luke) worthy of repentance. Priority is generally ascribed to Matthew's singular: Luke may well have introduced the plural in view of the specific 'works' referred to in the extra dialogues between John and various people recounted in Luke 3:10–14.[7]

More difficult is the problem of who the addressees are in Q. Matthew has John addressing the 'Pharisees and Sadducees' coming ἐπὶ τὸ βάπτισμα; Luke has 'the crowds' coming to be baptised. Matthew's version is often dismissed as an historically impossible grouping and probably redactional, reflecting his tendency to vilify the Pharisees and to couple them with almost any other group indiscriminately.[8] However, Luke's reference to the 'crowds' is regarded by many as possibly LkR.[9] In part a decision here is tied up with the precise interpretation of John's preaching which follows. In particular, there is the question of exactly what kind of people are being addressed and why precisely they are being accused of failing in some way.

Some have argued that there are two accusations here: one charge is directed at those who have come to be baptised but who think that this alone is sufficient and are unwilling to do anything else (vv. 7, 8a, 9); the other is directed against those who refuse to be baptised at all and who appeal to their national identity (v. 8b). In favour of such a distinction within the text, it is also sometimes claimed that v. 8b interrupts the flow of the speech, breaking the connection between v. 8a and v. 9, both of which focus on the

---

[7] For Luke as secondary here, cf. H. Schürmann, *Das Lukasevangelium I* (Freiburg: Herder, 1969) 165 n. 23 (also referring to Acts 26:20); Schulz, *Q*, 367; Hoffmann, *Studien*, 16; E. Sevenich-Bax, *Israels Konfrontation mit den letzten Boten der Weisheit* (MThA 21; Altenberge: Oros, 1993) 29f., with further literature.

[8] See Schulz, *Q*, 367 n. 288 for a list of those taking Matthew as secondary; also Hoffmann, *Studien*, 17; Sevenich-Bax, *Konfrontation*, 28f. For Matthew's indiscriminate references to Jewish groups, see R. Walker, *Die Heilsgeschichte im ersten Evangelium* (FRLANT 91; Göttingen: Vandenhoeck & Ruprecht, 1967). Pharisees and Sadducees are coupled again in Matt 16:1, 6, 11, 12 — all probably MattR.

[9] Hoffmann, *Studien*, 17; H. Conzelmann, *The Theology of St Luke* (ET London: Faber, 1960) 20f; cf. too J. A. Fitzmyer, *Luke*, 467, who therefore takes Matthew as more original. Goulder, *Luke*, 273, says that 'the Lucan version is quite typical of Luke'.

image of the 'fruit'.[10] Opinions vary, however, about the relative age of the two strands. Davies and Allison take the two elements as simply two separate sayings of John himself. For Schürmann the attack on appeals to national identity is older, the other reflecting later Christian paranesis; according to Jacobson, the attack on national privilege is an addition made at the 'compositional' stage of Q (cf. p. 63 above), modifying earlier material in the rest of the pericope.

Such an interpretation of vv. 7, 8a, 9 is however difficult to maintain in the light of a closer examination of v. 7, where those addressed are called a 'generation of vipers', and the question is put to them 'Who warned you to flee from the wrath that is to come?' The viper imagery is extremely unusual. Fitzmyer comments: 'The imagery is otherwise unknown in the OT, Josephus or rabbinical writings.'[11] It is sometimes suggested that what is in mind is the characteristic of snakes to scurry around in flight in the face of a desert fire.[12] However, it seems unlikely that this is the only image in mind: in a desert fire, *every* living thing would be trying to escape and it is not clear why vipers should be singled out for mention. Thus most agree that what is in mind is the poisonous nature of the viper, implying that those addressed are evil, repugnant and destructive.[13] The language is thus extremely harsh and this suggests that the reference cannot be to people who have come to be baptised (even with only half-hearted conviction).[14] Rather, the whole conduct and nature of those being addressed is under attack; if they are in fact coming for baptism, such a verbal assault would imply rejection of the whole principle of baptism as such, and of this there is no hint anywhere else in the gospel tradition. Elsewhere, baptism (including John's

[10] See variously Schürmann, *Lukasevangelium*, 182; E. Linnemann, 'Jesus und der Täufer', *Festschrift für Ernst Fuchs* (Tübingen: Mohr, 1973) 219–36, p. 228f.; Jacobson, *First Gospel*, 82f. For v. 8b as intrusive, cf. too Hoffmann, *Studien*, 27; Davies & Allison, *Matthew I*, 307.

[11] Fitzmyer, *Luke*, 467.

[12] Cf. C. H. H. Scobie, *John the Baptist* (London: SCM, 1964) 60; also in part Davies & Allison, *Matthew I*, 304; I. H. Marshall, *The Gospel of Luke* (Exeter: Paternoster, 1978) 139.

[13] Cf. W. Foerster, ἔχιδνα, *TWNT* II, 815; Schulz, *Q*, 372; Schürmann, *Lukasevangelium*, 164 n. 15; Davies & Allison, *Matthew I*, 304; Marshall, *Luke*, 139; Fitzmyer, *Luke*, 467. The suggestion that this is an implicit reference to the serpent of the Garden of Eden (cf. J. Ernst, *Johannes der Täufer* [BZNW 53; Berlin: de Gruyter, 1989] 42f. and others cited there) seems rather fanciful.

[14] Rightly pointed out by Goulder, *Luke*, 273; also R. L. Webb, *John the Baptizer and Prophet* (JSNTSS 62; Sheffield: Sheffield Academic Press, 1991) 176.

baptism) is uniformly regarded in positive terms (even if John's baptism is seen as only preparatory for something else).

Part of the problem here might be alleviated if one could ascribe the opening address to the same strand of tradition as the accusation in v. 8b. The reference to 'generation' might then tie up with the appeal of those addressed to be 'sons of' (i.e. the generation of) Abraham.[15] This division of the tradition would mean that those coming for baptism are met with the rhetorical question of v. 7b and the appeal for 'fruit' in vv. 8a, 9; those refusing baptism are met with the invective of v. 7a and the charge of v. 8b. This however meets some problems in the question of v. 7b itself.

For those who see v. 7b as addressed to people coming for baptism and thinking that this is enough, the question is taken as a rhetorical one, setting up an absurd situation. The people think that they can flee from the coming wrath by coming to be baptised; in fact, of course, divine judgement ('wrath') is inescapable, and hence the answer to the question must be 'Certainly not I (John)', since such an attempt to flee is useless.[16] However, Hoffmann rightly questions such an interpretation as reading a great deal into the text: there is nothing explicitly stated about a contrast between an 'external' rite of baptism and an 'internal' attitude of repentance.[17] Hoffmann, following Klostermann, thus takes v. 7b as simply rejecting the idea that judgement will not affect everyone.[18] This may be partly correct. However, it may also involve a slight change in nuance in the interpretation of the question itself. The question asks 'Who warned you to flee?' Yet the sequel seems to make it clear that, although at one level no flight may be possible, at another level it is possible to mitigate some aspects of the coming 'wrath'. Verse 8a exhorts the listeners to produce 'fruit'; and the implication of v. 9 is that every tree which does produce fruit will not be cut down and burnt — it will be preserved alive and well.[19]

---

[15] Cf. Manson, *Sayings*, 40; Marshall, *Luke*, 139; Davies & Allison, *Matthew I*, 304.

[16] Variously Marshall, *Luke*, 139; Davies & Allison, *Matthew I*, 304 (at least at the level of John); Webb, *John the Baptizer*, 177. Cf. too Schürmann, *Lukasevangelium*, 164f., for this as addressed to people relying falsely on baptism.

[17] Hoffmann, *Studien*, 27.

[18] Ibid.; cf. E. Klostermann, *Das Matthäusevangelium* (Tübingen: Mohr, 1927) 23.

[19] Cf. Sato, *Q und Prophetie*, 210: v. 9 is 'eine *bedingte* Unheilsankündigung' (his stress).

Hence it may be better to take the opening question as not a rhetorical *reductio ad absurdum*. In one sense the audience can 'flee' (i.e. escape) from the worst aspects of what is coming, *if* they act decisively now. Thus the implied answer to the question may be '*I* warned you to flee; *therefore* (cf. οὖν in v. 8a) take what I say seriously and produce fruit worthy of repentance if you want to escape the coming destruction'.[20] Escape is thus not an absurd idea entertained by baptism-seeking semi-converts to John; it is an option offered by John himself.[21] The question of v. 7b thus does not appear to be directed at those with a false idea of baptism itself. It is more probably addressed to those who are refusing to accept John's message *in toto*. It would thus seem wrong to drive a wedge between vv. 7b–8a and v. 8b: *both* are directed against those who are not responding to John positively, and John's appeal to such people is that they should take his message with all seriousness.[22]

This in turn makes it unlikely that in Q the people addressed are actually being baptised or even intending to be, at this stage at least. Luke indicates otherwise, but this may well be connected with his later material in Luke 3:10–14 where new baptisands of John are given (appropriately Lukan) ethical teaching.[23] Matthew's language (the Pharisees and Sadducees come ἐπὶ τὸ βάπτισμα) is more ambiguous. Matthew himself presumably took the words as implying that the Jewish groups mentioned came only to look at John, without being baptised themselves,[24] and hence presumably the same is possible for Q, if Matthew is reproducing the Q wording here.[25]

---

[20] The force of the οὖν is occasionally half-recognised by commentators: cf. Davies & Allison, *Matthew*, 305: 'οὖν is not merely transitional, it is allative: if the Pharisees and Sadducees really wish to flee from the wrath to come, then . . .'. Marshall, *Luke*, 139: 'If John's hearers really want to escape, let them show the appropriate fruit.'

[21] Escape from divine wrath is in any case not an impossible idea within Christianity: cf. Rom 5:9, and see G. Stählin, ὀργή, *TWNT* V, 447f.

[22] For the unity of the address in this section, see too Catchpole, *Quest*, 8f.

[23] For this as LkR, cf. Hoffmann, *Studien*, 16; Goulder, *Luke*, 275. However, the origin of the passage is not entirely clear, given the slightly unusual vocabulary: cf. Fitzmyer, *Luke*, 464; Ernst, *Johannes*, 93f.

[24] Goulder, *Luke*, 273; Davies & Allison, *Matthew I*, 304; Webb, *John the Baptizer*, 175.

[25] Matthew's ἐπὶ τὸ βάπτισμα may indicate that those addressed do *not* intend to be baptised (cf. Davies & Allison, *Matthew I*, 304, though they believe that this is MattR). For this as a call *to* baptism in Q, see Catchpole, *Quest*, 8.

If then the whole passage is directed against those who are not accepting baptism from John, then perhaps the easiest interpretation of the 'fruit' which John calls for is that this refers to baptism itself.[26] We have seen that it is not easy to distinguish between baptism (being sought by some) and other 'works' (not being undertaken by the same people) in the passage. If then the prime object of attack is those who are refusing to accept John's preaching *in toto*, the call to them must be to change their ways, to accept the validity of John's call to repentance in the face of a coming potential catastrophe and to undergo the rite that makes visible their commitment to his cause.[27]

The passage is therefore best taken as a unity. It is not to be split up into two different accusations with two different audiences. It is a single tirade directed against those who are refusing to accept the validity of John's preaching and ministry. To such people John responds with strong invective, accusing them of being evil and destructive ('vipers'); he reminds them that he *has* warned them of an imminent event which is potentially disastrous for them if they do not change their ways. Hence they should respond positively to him if they are not to face fiery destruction and they should show their sincerity by undergoing the rite of baptism.

The reason why those addressed have not responded positively is given in v. 8b; and indeed the whole unit requires something like this to explain the audience's negative response. There is thus no need to see v. 8b as a secondary expansion of an earlier tradition. Here, appeal is made to national heritage ('We have Abraham for our father'). John rejects such a plea and implicitly rejects any special exemption from divine judgement which can be claimed by Jews *qua* Jews. Something more is now required and anyone failing to produce that 'more' is threatened with destructive judgement. As we shall see, this is a constantly recurring theme within Q.

[26] H. Merklein, 'Die Umkehrpredigt bei Johannes dem Täufer und Jesus von Nazaret', *BZ* 25 (1981) 29–46, repr. in his *Studien zu Jesus und Paulus* (WUNT 43; Tübingen: Mohr, 1987) 109–26, p. 116.

[27] This seems easier than interpreting the 'fruit' as repentance itself (cf. Schürmann, *Lukasevangelium*, 182; also Hoffmann, *Studien*, 17f.: the reference to 'worthy' then seems difficult), or as radical obedience to a sharpened Mosaic Law (cf. Schulz, *Q*, 374). In one way Hoffmann is quite right to describe the call for repentance here as a 'Leerformel' (*Studien*, 27). No doubt Q sees the behaviour required of those responding as laid out in the teaching of Q's Jesus (ibid.). But whether this is explicitly in mind in 3:8a is less clear.

The basic thrust of John's preaching relates to a belief in an imminent event which may be catastrophic for those who are unprepared. The imminence is stressed in v. 9a ('already the axe is laid to the root of the tree'), and the potentially catastrophic nature of what will happen is spelt out in v. 9b ('every tree not producing fruit will be cut down and thrown into the fire'). Clearly one is in the thought world of Jewish eschatology, with a vivid expectation of an imminent End culminating in some kind of judging process. Further, this message seems to be regarded by Q thoroughly positively: John's message is still in force. 'Die Logienquelle greift *ohne Korrektur* diese Gerichtsankündigung auf. Es ist ein Zeichen dafür, daß auch für sie die johanneische Naherwartung noch Gültigkeit besitzt.'[28] Thus the opening verses of Q stress strongly the belief that divine intervention is imminent, and positive response is demanded.

One final problem which remains unresolved so far concerns the more precise identity of those addressed. As we saw earlier there is uncertainty as to whether Matthew or Luke (or neither) preserves the original Q wording here. Clearly v. 8b implies that John's preaching is directed to Jews alone. So too, an awareness of national identity is not peculiar to 'Jewish leaders' or 'Pharisees' amongst Jews of the period.[29] Should we then see the polemic addressed to 'all Israel'?[30] In one way that is probably correct in that John's appeal is potentially directed to all Jews.[31] On the other hand we should perhaps beware of making the issue too black and white. Despite the harsh language, the section is couched in the form of an appeal. John is pleading with people who so far have failed to respond to his preaching to change their minds and join his cause. John's message is thus directed against the unresponsive within Israel. It is not directed against all Israel indiscriminately. John himself and any followers of John who have accepted his message are also Jews. And even v. 8b does not reject all value in Jewishness completely: it simply says that appeal to Jewish birth alone is in itself insufficient to escape what is coming soon.

---

[28] Hoffmann, *Studien*, 28.

[29] Kloppenborg, *Formation*, 103; contra Jacobson, *Wisdom Christology*, 31f., who ascribes v. 8b to invective against Jewish leaders/Pharisees. In his *First Gospel*, 83, Jacobson appears to have changed his position: it is Israel as a whole that is now addressed.

[30] Cf. Schulz, *Q*, 371; Jacobson, *First Gospel*, 83; Ernst, *Johannes*, 42.

[31] Cf. Hoffmann, *Studien*, 17; Schürmann, *Lukasevangelium*, 163.

Whether we can be more precise about the identity of those addressed is not clear. Luke's 'crowds' may well be LkR, and Matthew's 'Sadducees' look suspiciously like MattR. However, the 'Pharisees' in Matt 3:7 may reflect the Q wording. Even in Matt 16, Matthew does not create a coupling of 'Pharisees and Sadducees' *de novo*: he simply adds 'Sadducees' to the 'Pharisees' who are present in the Markan source already.[32] As we shall see, a significant section of Q may be taken up with polemic against 'Pharisees' and/or lawyers (Q 11:39ff.). Further, a later passage, which is arguably also part of Q (Matt 21:32/Luke 7:29f.), possibly contrasts Pharisees (and others) who do not accept John's baptism with tax-collectors and others who do.[33] Thus it may be that Matthew's opening partly preserves the Q original in having John address 'Pharisees' (and perhaps others) who have come out to see John but who do not respond positively to John's message.

2. Q 3:16f.

The second unit of John's preaching in Q contains his prediction of a coming figure who will 'baptise' people in a way which will in some sense supersede his own water baptism. Sadly any certainty about the interpretation of these verses is almost impossible: the existence of a Markan parallel here as well (cf. n. 5 above) makes it extremely difficult to be sure about the Q wording and at times this is crucial for the interpretation of the passage. For example, will the future figure baptise with fire? or spirit and fire? or spirit? or holy spirit?

[32] Hence I find it hard to follow Webb, *John the Baptizer*, 178, who argues that the reference to Sadducees may be more original (i.e. in Q) and that Matthew has added the reference to the Pharisees.

[33] For this as part of *Q*, see my *Revival*, 148–50; also Catchpole, *Quest*, 66. The verbal agreement between Matthew and Luke is not close, but there is considerable substantive agreement. Luke's use of δικαιόω in v. 30 is unlike Luke's usage elsewhere, yet similar to his v. 35 which is unquestionably Q. Further, Luke's very clumsy πᾶς ὁ λαὸς ἀκούσας καὶ οἱ τελῶναι suggests that a source is being redacted, and the reference to λαός and ἀκούσας looks very Lukan. Matthew's parallel does not mention baptism by John as such, speaking only of 'believing (in) him', but the main thrust is the same: both verses speak of positive and negative responses to John. Matthew also does not explicitly mention 'Pharisees' as refusing to accept John, but this may not be significant given Matthew's tendency to run together all the groups opposed to Jesus and John (cf. n. 8 above). Thus the saying may well have been in Q, contrasting acceptance of John by some (including τελῶναι) with rejection of John by Pharisees and others.

The passage is frequently regarded as non-unitary: John's words in Q 3:16b,[34] expressing his inferiority in some way to the future figure, seem to be extraneous to the contrast between the two baptisms involved and hence are often regarded as due to a secondary addition.[35] At what stage this was added is however not clear. Bultmann simply claims that it was a Christian addition to a Baptist saying. Hoffmann and Catchpole take it as an addition by Q to clarify the position of John in relation to Jesus. Jacobson takes it in similar vein and ascribes it to a later ('intermediate') stage of Q-redaction. Kloppenborg however refers to the parallels in Mark 1:8, John 1:26 and Acts 13:25, claiming that these show that the saying must have originated very early, prior to Q's redaction.[36] Any appeal to the parallels in Mark and John raises important methodological problems. Can we assume that Mark and John are independent of Q? If we make no such assumptions, then the appearance of a Q-redactional element in Mark could be taken as strong evidence that Mark knew Q.[37] Similarly, the presence of a parallel in John says little about the pre-redactional state of the synoptic tradition unless one assumes the independence of John from the synoptics.[38] So too elements in the speeches in Acts may be simply due to Luke's own knowledge

[34] Matthew's version is more likely to be closer to Q in the use of the phrase ὁ ἐρχόμενος, and in speaking of 'carrying', rather than 'undoing', the sandals of the coming figure: Luke seems to follow Mark here. See Schulz, *Q*, 368; Laufen, *Doppelüberlieferungen*, 94f.; Webb, *John the Baptizer*, 265; Sevenich-Bax, *Konfrontation*, 36f.

[35] Cf. Bultmann, *History*, 246: a Christian addition to a pre-Christian Baptist saying. Hoffmann, *Studien*, 31–3; Jacobson, *First Gospel*, 84f.; cf. too Merklein, 'Umkehrpredigt', 112; W. Schenk, *Synopse zur Redenquelle der Evangelien* (Düsseldorf: Patmos, 1981) 19; Kloppenborg, *Formation*, 104; Catchpole, *Quest*, 71f.

[36] Kloppenborg, *Formation*, 104. Kloppenborg claims that 'to credit it [Q 3:16b] to Q-redaction would raise more problems than it would solve'. This is however perhaps rather question-begging. Laufen, *Doppelüberlieferungen*, 98, also refers to the parallel in John as evidence for the independence of the two sayings.

[37] Of those mentioned in n. 35, only Catchpole draws this conclusion explicitly.

[38] The whole question is once more in the melting pot: see the essays in A. Denaux (ed.), *John and the Synoptics* (BETL 101; Leuven University Press & Peeters, 1992). See too F. Neirynck, 'John and the Synoptics', in M. de Jonge (ed.), *L'Evangile de Jean. Sources, rédaction, théologie* (BETL 44; Gembloux & Leuven: Duculot & Leuven University Press) 73–106 (= *Evangelica I*, 365–400), as well as numerous other essays collected in *Evangelica I*, 181–488; also his *Jean et les Synoptiques* (BETL 49; Leuven University Press, 1979).

of Mark's gospel. Kloppenborg's ascription of the saying to a pre-redactional stage in Q's development seems to be almost entirely based on presuppositions about the independence of Q and Mark, of John and the synoptics, and perhaps about the nature of some of the speeches in Acts.[39]

There are here two slightly different questions: (i) whether the saying is secondary to the rest of the unit, (ii) *if* so, whether the saying is to be ascribed to Q's redaction. Now it may well be that the saying about John's unworthiness to undo/carry the sandals of the future figure is secondary to the rest of the saying. Other arguments to the contrary do not always convince. Laufen's plea for the existence of two originally independent sayings[40] seems unconvincing, if only because the 'sandals' saying scarcely makes sense without something additional to say what precisely the figure whose sandals John is unworthy to untie/carry will do. Two recent studies of John the Baptist also seek to trace the saying back to the historical John. Ernst seeks to delete any hint of a 'Christian' interpretation by taking the reference to the 'stronger one' as Yahweh. However he has to delete the μου from the phrase ἰσχυρότερός μου, and take the comparative ἰσχυρότερος as a superlative, to make his case.[41] Webb argues (to my mind convincingly) against this general interpretation, pointing in particular to the problem of the reference to 'sandals' if the figure concerned is God (as well as the lack of evidence for the deletion of the μου).[42] Further, it seems highly unlikely that, at least for Q, the coming figure is regarded as anyone other than Jesus, whatever may have been the case in any pre-Q tradition. The

---

[39] Cf. too Catchpole, *Quest*, 72.

[40] Laufen, *Doppelüberlieferungen*, 116f.

[41] Ernst, *Johannes*, 50; cf. too J. H. Hughes, 'John the Baptist: The Forerunner of God Himself', *NT* 14 (1972) 191–218. Catchpole, *Quest*, 67f., also argues that the original John looked forward to the coming of God, and that Q 3:16 serves to realign that expectation in terms of the coming of a human figure, i.e. Jesus, to whom John is subordinated. But the evidence for the pre-Q expectation of John has to be drawn in part from Luke 1:15–17, i.e. quite outside Q, and there is little control on the hypothesis.

[42] Webb, *John the Baptizer*, 284f. The problem is met only with great difficulty if the image is a completely hypothetical metaphor. Thus Webb says: 'John's statement is *not* simply a descriptive statement concerning what the figure is wearing . . . nor is it a description of what the figure does with his own sandals. . . . Rather, John's words form an evaluative statement of his own unworthiness to perform an action with respect to this figure's sandals. . . . The evaluation of John's unworthiness to perform such an action loses some of its significance if it is an action which it is impossible for him to actually do.'

question of John the Baptist in Q 7:19 clearly picks up the words of John's prediction in 3:16; and Jesus' answer in Q 7:22f. can scarcely be taken as anything other than a positive response to the question whether he himself is the 'coming one', i.e. the one predicted by John. Webb himself simply takes the combined evidence of Mark and Q as sufficient basis for reconstructing the historical Baptist and does not consider the possibility of secondary, pre-Q developments in the tradition, apart from some rather general considerations about the unlikelihood of the existence of secondary creations here at all.[43] However, the clear qualitative distinction drawn between John and the coming figure in the 'sandals' saying does seem rather extraneous in the context of John, and perhaps fits better within a context of later rivalry between (followers of) Jesus and John.[44]

Nevertheless it is very hard to see such rivalry playing any role at the level of Q's redaction. In many respects the saying in Q 3:16b is similar to Q 7:28, with a possible tendency to downgrade John and we shall be considering the latter verse shortly. To anticipate slightly, however, there is little evidence to suggest that Q in its present form has any concern to downgrade John. Rather, the thrust of Q as a whole is to be thoroughly positive about John. Q probably opens with a substantial section giving John's preaching and there is no hint at all that this preaching is in any way to be regarded as second-rate or invalidated. For example, the future activity of Q's 'coming one' includes a baptism with 'fire', and this takes up and affirms John's preaching of a coming threat of fire (Q 3:9, 17). A very similar picture emerges from Q 7:18–35, as we shall see. Thus it may be more appropriate, at least for Q, to take the 'sandals' saying in v. 16b not so much as an attempt to downgrade John, but rather as a statement primarily seeking to underline the importance of the status of Jesus. As we shall see, the intention of Q's composition as a whole is to identify the 'coming one' of John's preaching with Jesus who will 'come' as SM. And in all this John's preaching is emphatically affirmed. Q 3:16b thus reflects the positive Christological concerns of Q quite as much as any worries about rivalry between Jesus and John.

All this suggests that, if Q 3:16b is a secondary addition reflecting an element of reserve about John, this reserve has

---

[43] Webb, *John the Baptizer*, 268.
[44] By 'later' here I mean subsequent to Jesus and John themselves. As will be seen immediately, I believe that this 'later' stage is pre-Q.

nothing to do with Q's redactional concerns. This would then suggest some support for Kloppenborg's view that the saying is a *pre*-redactional element in Q. It seems hard to deny that, taken on its own, the saying does reflect an element of negativity about John. But when the saying is taken up and used by Q, it can only be in a thoroughly positive way, perhaps to highlight the importance and significance of Jesus though without wishing to downgrade John. If this is the case, then the best solution seems to be that the saying is an early addition in the tradition, taken over by Q subsequently. To see it as a later addition seems to create more problems than it solves: if it is a Q addition then it does not correlate with Q's overall presentation and literary structure; and if it is later still (e.g. as in Jacobson's theory, part of a later stage of Q editing subsequent to the 'compositional' stage which has left its mark on the vast bulk of this part of Q), then it is hard to see why reserve about John should be expressed in what is, in literary terms, such an insignificant way, leaving the positive view about John dominating in the rest of the Q material.

What then of John's prediction of a coming 'baptism'? There is first the question of the precise Q wording: does John in Q predict a coming baptism in fire alone?[45] or with spirit/wind and fire?[46] Further, should we be making a distinction between the historical John and Q's John as is done, for example, by Laufen: Laufen argues that John looked forward to a baptism with the Spirit, and καὶ πυρί is a Q-redactional addition.[47] In terms of the wording itself, it seems easiest to assume that Q did contain a reference to πνεῦμα in some shape or form. The alternative involves assuming that the reference to 'Holy Spirit' in both Matthew and Luke at this point is due to influence from the Markan version of the saying on both evangelists independently. This seems rather coincidental and it may be easier to posit a Q version mentioning at least 'spirit and fire', with Markan influence at most leading to both later evangelists qualifying 'spirit' with the adjective 'holy'. There is, however, still a wide variety of possible interpretations of the predicted

---

[45] Manson, *Sayings*, 40f.; Hoffmann, *Studien*, 29ff.; Schulz, *Q*, 370; Catchpole, *Quest*, 9–11; further literature in Laufen, *Doppelüberlieferungen*, n. 51 on p. 413.

[46] Laufen, *Doppelüberlieferungen*, 97; Davies & Allison, *Matthew I*, 316; Webb, *John the Baptizer*, 265. In her otherwise massive detailed reconstruction of the Q wording, Sevenich-Bax does not discuss the issue, but takes it as self-evident that Matthew's and Luke's common reference to 'Holy Spirit' comes from Q.

[47] Laufen, *Doppelüberlieferungen*, 107f.

baptism:[48] is the reference to a single threat of destructive judgement by 'fiery wind'?[49] Or to a purging action by God's Spirit and fire which could be either destructive or purifying?[50] Or are there two 'baptisms' in mind: a Spirit-baptism for the good and a destructive fire-baptism for the wicked?[51]

The discussion is complicated by the different layers in the tradition, so that one answer might be appropriate at one level (e.g. the historical John) and not at another (e.g. Q). For many the meaning at the level of Q is determined by the Q context: here, it is often claimed, the references to 'fire' in vv. 9, 17 clearly have in mind fire as a means of destruction. Hence the prophecy of v. 16 is to be taken as a similar threat of imminent destructive fire alone, or of destructive 'fiery wind'.[52] However, although this line of interpretation may well be appropriate to the 'fire' imagery itself, it does not quite do justice to the whole of the rest of the Q context.[53] In v. 17 the image is of sifting grain from chaff. One part of the saying relates to the destruction of the worthless chaff by fire; but the other part of the process — the positive action of collecting the good wheat — is still present and cannot be ignored, even if more attention is focused on the destruction of the chaff.[54] Thus v. 17 strongly suggests that two possible fates await the listeners. The purpose of John's exhortations is then to

[48] Cf. Laufen, *Doppelüberlieferungen*, 100, for a thorough survey with very full bibliographical details.

[49] So, for example, E. Schweizer, πνεῦμα, *TWNT* VI, 397; C. K. Barrett, *The Holy Spirit in the Gospel Tradition* (London: SPCK, 1947) 126; others in Laufen, *Doppelüberlieferungen*, 412 n. 44.

[50] J. D. G. Dunn, *Baptism in the Holy Spirit* (London: SCM, 1970) 11; Davies & Allison, *Matthew I*, 317; Fitzmyer, *Luke*, 474. The possible parallel in 1 QS 4:20–22 is often noted.

[51] Cf. F. Lang, πῦϱ, *TWNT* VI, 943; Scobie, *John*, 72f.; Webb, *John the Baptizer*, 292.

[52] Cf. Manson, *Sayings*, 41; Schulz, *Q*, 376f.; Hoffmann, *Studien*, 30: 'Das Verständnis des Geistes im Sinne der endzeitlichen Reinigungskraft steht jedoch im Widerspruch zum Gesamttenor der Logien, welche der Gerichtsdrohung Ausdruck geben.'

[53] See Schürmann, *Lukasevangelium*, 171; Laufen, *Doppelüberlieferungen*, 101; Webb, *John the Baptizer*, 294.

[54] Cf. Dunn, *Baptism*, 9; G. B. Caird, *Jesus and the Jewish Nation* (London: Athlone Press, 1965) 7: 'The object of winnowing is not to collect enough chaff to have a glorious bonfire, but to gather wheat into the granary; the bonfire is purely coincidental.' The final clause may be a slight over-reaction, but the rest is surely apposite. See also Webb, *John the Baptizer*, 295–300, for detailed analysis of the exact imagery being used here (winnowing or cleansing), and the possibility that the threshing floor symbolises the new Israel.

try to make them aware of the different possibilities that lie
ahead and, if necessary, to take avoiding action in the present.
Further, there is no indication in the saying that those addressed
will escape the future 'baptism' completely. If that were the case,
we would expect something like 'I baptise you with water so that
he who is coming will *not* baptise you . . .'. Thus it seems unlikely
that the predicted baptism is one which is wholly destructive for
everyone.

Could it be then that the baptism in store is a purgative,
refining process by God's Spirit and fire, a process which all will
undergo but which will result in potentially different results for
different individuals (the righteous will survive but the wicked
will perish)? This would fit the general tenor of the passage; it
would have a close parallel in 1 QS 4 (cf. n. 50 above), and it
would also find a close parallel in the use of the 'fire' imagery to
describe a purgative, testing process elsewhere in the NT (cf. 1
Pet 1:7). However, this option seems to founder on the other
references to 'fire' in the immediate Q context (i.e. in vv. 9, 17).
Here, as we have already noted, the 'fire' is destructive; further, it
is used as part of a simple farming metaphor, not one associated
with metallurgy: the 'fire' is simply the means of burning off what
is no longer useful; it is not the means of sifting pure metal from
base.

One is driven then to consider more seriously the option that
what is in mind (at least at the level of Q) is a two-fold baptism: a
Spirit-baptism for those who respond, and a fire-baptism for those
who do not. Against this interpretation it is often said that the καί
linking 'spirit' and 'fire', as well as the single ὑμᾶς, tells against
the idea of two baptisms here.[55] However, it seems that in general
terms some kind of distinction is clearly in mind. The language
used is *not* that of a simple prediction of what is going to happen
come what may. If the 'fire' of the future baptism is purely destructive (as seems to be demanded by the Q context), then presumably the aim of John's preaching is to try to enable people to
avoid this destruction. Thus although ὑμᾶς occurs as the single
object of the future activity of baptising ('he will baptise "you"'),
and also as the single object of John's baptising activity ('I am
baptising "you"'), the force of the saying as a whole is to seek to
make some distinctions and its main thrust must be 'I baptise you
with water, so that you will be able to survive the coming baptism

[55] Dunn, *Baptism*, 11; Hoffmann, *Studien*, 30.

and not be destroyed by it'. Thus those who are baptised by John
will not undergo the destructive side of the future baptism, i.e.
they will escape the 'fire'. However, the saying gives no hint that
those addressed will escape a future 'baptism' completely. If so we
would have expected something like 'I baptise you with water so
that he who is coming will *not* baptise you with fire'. The most
economical solution seems to be that those who are baptised now
by John will be 'baptised in the Spirit' by the Coming One; those
who are not will be 'baptised in fire', i.e. destroyed. The καί could
then be used to express an element of contrast as well as being a
simple copulative.[56] In support of this interpretation, one can also
point to the fact that, if the predicted future baptism were solely
negative, this would be unprecedented in Jewish 'messianic'
expectation in not giving some positive role to the expected
future figure.[57]

Thus, as with 3:7–9, John's preaching has both a positive and a
negative side. Although at one level it could be thought that the
negative side predominates in stressing the destructive fire which
threatens, the other side is not missing: the coming one will
'baptise' in the 'Spirit' those who respond, and gather the pure
wheat into the granary. Indeed the whole point of the negative
side of the preaching demands the positive side as its
counterpoint. The point of the threat of what is to come is not to
state what is about to happen anyway; rather, it is to warn people
of what will happen *if* they do not change their ways. The 'threat'
is thus part of a clarion call to others to respond to the preaching
in order to ensure that the predicted future event does *not*
happen.

One final point concerns the time reference of John's
preaching as far as the Q Christians are concerned. With regard
to John the future baptism is clearly still to come. But is this so for
Q too? For Mark, who does not mention the 'fire', it is generally

---

[56] BDF § 442.1. Cf. Laufen, *Doppelüberlieferungen*, 106, though Laufen
himself seems to reject this as a possible interpretation at the level of John. He
sees καὶ πυρί as a Q-redactional addition, stressing the judgemental side of
John's message. But he does not clarify how then Q itself understood 'spirit and
fire'.

[57] Schürmann, *Lukasevangelium*, 176: 'Ein Messiaserwartung, die nur den
Richter, nicht primär den Retter gesehen hat, hat es in Israel nie gegeben.' Also
Laufen, *Doppelüberlieferungen*, 102. This might not apply at the level of John if
John expected a divine figure (cf. n. 41 above). But in the context of Q, the
expectation is 'messianic' in some sense at least, referring to the coming of a
divinely appointed agent who is not God.

assumed that the saying about a future 'baptism in the Holy Spirit' is seen as fulfilled in Christian baptism. What though of Q?

If we are right to see the Q version as implying a two-fold baptism, then at least the 'fire' baptism must be still future. The final destruction of the wicked has evidently not yet happened. Matthew and Luke too may also have understood the fire baptism as still future.[58] Is then the Spirit baptism (if this is indeed to be seen as separable from the fire baptism) also to be regarded as future? Most assume that it is.[59] However, it seems difficult to conceive of later Q Christians having a tradition which spoke of a 'baptism' connected with πνεῦμα as having no counterpart in their own present experience. We know of no other Christian group in early Christianity which did not practise baptism in some shape or form and, for example, Paul seems to be able to assume the practice as self-evident, even amongst Roman Christians (cf. Rom 6:3). Further, it is a constant feature in Pauline Christianity that the start of the Christian life is connected with both baptism and the gift of the Spirit. One cannot of course make too sweeping generalisations about the nature of all branches of the early Christian movement solely on the basis of our fragmented evidence. Nevertheless it seems hard to believe that talk of a 'baptism' connected with the 'Spirit' would not ring any bells at all with the experience and practice of a group of Christians. Given too the clear evidence elsewhere in Q of a belief in the activity of the Spirit in the present (cf. 12:10 in relation to the experience of Christians, and possibly Luke 4:16ff. in relation to Jesus),[60] it seems difficult to hold that Q Christians cannot have believed that in some sense at least the predicted 'baptism' by the coming one was in part a matter of experienced fulfilment on their part.

John's preaching is thus accepted by Q as still valid. Despite any hints of a lower status for John (in v. 16b), there is no indication that Q regards John's preaching as invalidated by later events

---

[58] For Matthew, see Luz, *Matthew 1–7*, 171; Davies & Allison, *Matthew I*, 317f. It is often assumed that Luke saw the prophecy fulfilled in the gift of the 'Spirit' in the 'fire' of Pentecost: see Hoffmann, *Studien*, 30; Fitzmyer, *Luke*, 474; Goulder, *Luke*, 277. However it is pointed out by some that when Luke actually cites John's prediction in Acts with clear reference to the Pentecost event, he does so in the Markan form with no reference to Q's 'fire' (Acts 1:5; 11:16): cf. Webb, *John the Baptizer*, 272.

[59] Cf. Laufen, *Doppelüberlieferungen*, 120 n. 162, who dismisses the opposite view as 'nicht wahrscheinlich' without argument.

[60] For this as possibly part of Q, see pp. 226–37 below.

(apart perhaps from its being partly fulfilled). John's imminent expectation of a coming judgement is affirmed. Indeed it may be the very fact that one half of John's prediction is regarded as fulfilled that has given added urgency to the other yet-to-be-fulfilled half of John's prophecy.

One thing remains unclear from Q 3:16f. itself, and that is the identity of the coming one. It is however just this question which is answered in the next section to be considered, viz. Q 7:18–35.

3. Q 7:18–35

The question of the identity of the figure predicted by John is explicitly raised again very shortly in Q in the question put to Jesus in Q 7:18ff., where John, through his messengers, asks Jesus 'Are you ὁ ἐρχόμενος?'. There has been much debate about the problem of whether the participle ὁ ἐρχόμενος could have been a 'messianic' 'title' at the time of Jesus.[61] One must say that any evidence for such a title is very slim and it seems most likely that what is in mind in the use of the term is a more general reference to a coming eschatological figure, but with no greater specificity being ascribed to the figure (e.g. that he might be a judging figure, or a 'messiah' or whatever) than that he is expected to 'come'.[62] But whatever may be the case more generally, within Q it seems clear that John's question refers back to his earlier preaching in Q about a 'coming one' (ὁ ἐρχόμενος) who will baptise with 'spirit and fire'.[63] John is thus asking whether Jesus is to be identified with this coming figure.

The passage in which the question is raised and answered (Q 7:18–23) is part of a longer passage in Q 7:18–35 devoted to the relationship between Jesus and John. Many have seen in the passage a number of different layers of tradition. If our main concern is with 'Q' in its 'final' form (cf. p. 77 above), then the

---

[61] See Laufen, *Doppelüberlieferungen*, 407–9 n. 12, for a full discussion with bibliography.

[62] Cf. W. G. Kümmel, *Promise and Fulfilment* (ET London: SCM, 1957) 110; F. Hahn, *Christologishe Hoheitstitel* (FRLANT 83; Göttingen: Vandenhoeck & Ruprecht, 1963) 393; P. Stuhlmacher, *Das paulinische Evangelium* (FRLANT 95; Göttingen: Vandenhoeck & Ruprecht, 1968) 218; Schulz, *Q*, 194. One must, of course, distinguish between the possibilities of whether the phrase itself was a recognised title, and whether the use of the phrase here refers to another, more specific expectation (e.g. Jesus as the 'messiah', or 'prophet').

[63] See Schulz, *Q*, 194; Hoffmann, *Studien*, 199; Kloppenborg, *Formation*, 107; Catchpole, *Quest*, 239.

primary object of investigation must be the present form of the tradition in Q 7:18–35 as it stands. Nevertheless, the fact that the passage may represent the end-product of a complex tradition-history, with the possible existence of redactional seams and/or additions, means that a traditio-critical analysis may be able to reveal something important about Q's editorial interests. Moreover, the likelihood is that a number of separate traditions have been brought together in this passage, and the common order in this long section in both Matthew and Luke assures us that the collecting process goes back at least as early as Q. Thus the passage as a whole may reveal the compositional activity of the Q editor more clearly than elsewhere.

The first unit of the section comprises John's question to Jesus, Jesus' reply in v. 22 and the final beatitude in v. 23. The history of the development of the tradition here is not clear. According to many, the reply in v. 22, alluding to the implied fulfilment of various Isaianic texts (Isa 29:18f.; 35:5f.; 61:1), can confidently be regarded as an authentic saying of the historical Jesus.[64] However, opinions differ on whether the closing beatitude was an integral part of the saying from the start or whether it was a secondary addition.[65] There is however more agreement about the secondary nature of the conjunction of the Baptist's question with Jesus' answer. The answer, referring to Jesus' credentials as a preacher and miracle worker fulfilling the expectations of the Isaianic prophecies, and the question, referring to John's expectation of an apocalyptic End-time judging figure, seem quite tangential to each other.[66] The best explanation is that the putting together of Jesus' claims with John's question is a secondary composition by a later editor. What though is the effect of this composition?

Many have assumed that in some way the story serves to downgrade the position of John and/or that of possible Baptist disciples.[67] For example, some have seen here a Christian argu-

---

[64] Cf. Bultmann, *History*, 23f.; Kümmel, *Promise*, 111; Schürmann, *Lukasevangelium*, 413f.; Hoffmann, *Studien*, 201 and n. 51.

[65] For example, Bultmann takes it as original. See Hoffmann, *Studien*, 210.

[66] Cf. Bultmann, ibid.; Hoffmann, *Studien*, 201; Catchpole, *Quest*, 239; though cf. J. D. G. Dunn, *Jesus and the Spirit* (London: SCM, 1975) 55ff., for a spirited defence of the originality of the whole unit.

[67] Bultmann, *History*, 23f.; Lührmann, *Redaktion*, 26; Schulz, *Q*, 203; Jacobson, *First Gospel*, 114: 'the pericope emphatically subordinates John to Jesus'; Kloppenborg, *Formation*, 108: 'John's inferiority to Jesus is obvious'; Catchpole, *Quest*, 240.

ment to show that Jesus, rather than John, is the true 'Messiah',[68] or 'prophet'.[69] However, it would seem that any tendency to downgrade John is minimal. Certainly Hoffmann has shown that it is extremely difficult to relate the passage to any rival claims between Jesus and John to be either 'Messiah' or 'prophet', since the actions referred to in v. 22 are for the most part not those associated with expectations of either a messianic or prophetic figure (though the allusion to Isa 61:1 in Q 7:22 may well be intended to allude to Jesus' role as that of 'eschatological prophet': cf. pp. 222–3 below).[70]

Further, it is hard to see the pericope as a whole as clearly negative about John. John's question may indicate doubt on John's part as to whether Jesus fulfils the role predicted of the coming one. Yet, at least within Q, nothing indicates that this prediction is invalid. It does not seem to be the case, for example, that Jesus' reply is regarded as in some way modifying John's prediction, as if the story implied 'John asks whether Jesus is the coming End-time judge, and Jesus says that John's "coming one" will *not* be a spirit-fire baptiser but a healer fulfilling Isaianic prophecies'.[71] In Q itself it is clear that a coming future figure is still expected and indeed that this coming figure is none other than Jesus himself *qua* SM (cf. Q 12:39–46; 13:34f.; 17:22–37). Further, Jesus' reply to John's messengers refers them to the things they have 'seen and heard'. As Catchpole has noted, this relates closely to another Q passage (10:23f.) where Jesus pronounces a blessing on the disciples who have 'seen and heard' the events of Jesus' ministry.[72] John's disciples (and hence, derivatively, John himself) are thus in the category of the 'blessed' who have experienced the eschatological fulfilment of what was only looked for in the future by past prophets. The combination of Q 7:22 with 10:23f. within Q thus implies no downgrading of John at all. Jesus' reply to John must therefore be taken for Q as affirmative in every sense. Jesus *is* the coming one and John's prediction is in no way invalidated.

Nevertheless, the pericope does indicate that the identification of Jesus as John's 'coming one' is a claim which does not give rise

---

[68] Bultmann, ibid.

[69] Cf. Stuhlmacher, *Evangelium*, 219f.

[70] Hoffmann, *Studien*, 198ff.

[71] Though this is not to say that this might have been the case in a *pre*-Q stage of the tradition. Cf. Fitzmyer, *Luke*, 664.

[72] Catchpole, *Quest*, 240f.

to immediate and obvious assent. The credentials which Q's Jesus cites to justify his claim, appealing to healing and preaching, do not obviously relate to the claim to be the figure predicted by John. Hence the recognition that some will be 'scandalised' at such a claim, and the pronouncement of blessing on those who are not so scandalised. It would probably be wrong to suggest that this final saying is directed against John himself.[73] Rather, the saying recognises that Jesus' claims about himself (and hence, for Q, Q's claims about Jesus) are not self-evident and that the evidence which can be adduced for Jesus is at most ambiguous. Such an idea is not foreign to the rest of Q. The ambiguous nature of Jesus' present existence may be hinted at in the Sign of Jonah passage, as we shall see; the idea that the present reality of the presence of the Kingdom of God remains tiny and invisible is presupposed in the twin parables of the mustard seed and the leaven (Q 13:18–21); and if (cf. pp. 256–66 below) Q's answer to such ambiguity is that no unambiguous sign will be given or should even be asked for, the same general idea can be seen to lie behind the second temptation in Q (Q 4:9–12): no clear miracle should be demanded which can dispel the ambiguity of the present. This too is the message of the second temptation in Q (see p. 420 below). Q 7:23 thus fits in well with other parts of Q and there is no need to see this verse as part of any anti-Baptist polemic in Q. Nor is it necessarily any means of trying to bring Baptist disciples over to the Christian fold. Q 7:18–23 thus continues the line of thought from 3:16: John's prediction of a coming one is confirmed with the further clear identification that this figure is none other than Jesus himself, who in his own ministry is already 'fulfilling' the OT dispensation and who in turn will bring the whole to a conclusion soon.

There is moreover no need to ascribe the pericope to a later stratum of Q, as is done by Jacobson.[74] In arguing for such a theory, Jacobson appeals to the use of the LXX in the Isaianic allusion,[75] the unusual interest in miracles in Q, the sub-ordination of John to Jesus, and the link with 3:16b in the reference to the 'coming one' which Jacobson also takes as part of a later strand in Q. None of these arguments is fully convincing.[76]

---

[73] Cf. Kloppenborg, *Formation*, 108; Catchpole, *Quest*, 240.

[74] Jacobson, *First Gospel*, 112f.

[75] τυφλοὶ ἀναβλέπουσιν is usually taken as dependent on the LXX reading of Isa 61, though cf. n. 77 below.

[76] Cf. too Kloppenborg, *Formation*, 115f.

The relationship of John to Jesus both here and in 3:16 is not clearly one of subordination, but simply serves to highlight the positive significance of Jesus; further, the idea that Jesus is the 'coming one' is a strand running through far more of Q than just a few late additions as postulated by Jacobson. The use of the LXX is unconvincing: Q generally does use LXX readings where these can be verified, but this is no surprise in a Greek text such as Q (and in any case it is not certain whether the LXX is presupposed here or not).[77] Further, Q does show some interest in miracles (cf. Q 10:9; 11:14ff.) elsewhere.

Any possible tendency to discount the importance of John in 7:18–23 is surely negated by the start of the next pericope in 7:24–28 where, at least in vv. 24–26, Jesus gives an account of John that accords to the latter a very high status almost without qualification. The precise force of the first two possible (but patently false) answers to the rhetorical question 'What did you go out to see?' is not clear. Why people should have gone to see 'a reed shaken in the wind' or 'a man dressed in soft clothing' is not stated.[78] Clearly though the main point for Q comes in the third possible reply, where an answer is given which Q's Jesus seems to recognise as at least partly true: John is a prophet, and yet more than a prophet.[79] The prophetic category for John is thus both

---

[77] The reference to the 'blind seeing' could derive from Isa 35:5 rather than Isa 61 LXX.

[78] For the possibility that the 'reed shaking in the wind' is a rather specific reference to Herod Antipas (cf. the evidence of coins from Tiberias possibly showing a reed), see Theissen, *Gospels in Context*, 26–42. Others have focused on the reference to 'soft clothing' and seen here a reflection of a typically Cynic critique of those who live in royal palaces: see L. E. Vaage, *Q: The Ethos and Ethics of an Itinerant Radicalism* (Ph.D. Dissertation, Claremont, 1987) 552–66; also his *Galilean Upstarts. Jesus' First Followers according to Q* (Valley Forge: Trinity International Press, 1994) 96–102; R. Cameron, 'What did you come out to see? Characterizations of John and Jesus in the Gospels', *Semeia* 49 (1990) 35–69, pp. 42–4. See however also my 'A Cynic Q?', *Biblica* 70 (1989) 349–76, p. 372: it seems unnecessary to bring in any Cynic background here; the Q pericope is concerned not to highlight John's asceticism in contrast to others' riches — rather John's status is to be seen not as an ideal Cynic wandering preacher but as a prophet. See also the next note.

[79] Cf. the ναὶ λέγω ὑμῖν in v. 26b which 'ensures an unequivocal endorsement of the crowds' views set out in vv. 24b-26a' (Catchpole, *Quest*, 64; cf. also Sato, *Q und Prophetie*, 240, and his whole section [pp. 226–40] on the λέγω ὑμῖν usage). I thus cannot follow Cameron and Vaage who claim that the crowds' view that John is a prophet is as wrong as the previous two possibilities of a shaking reed or one dressed in soft clothing (cf. Cameron, 'What did you come out to see?', 41: 'The descriptions in Q 7:24–26 suggest that the prospect of

correct and also insufficient to express fully his significance. However, such an unqualified positive view of John has seemed to many to be questioned in the verses which follow, especially in v. 28b.

At first sight, vv. 27–28 contain diametrically opposite views of John. Verse 27 ascribes to him, via the use of Mal 3:1 (and perhaps Exod 23:20) the role of Elijah redivivus, and v. 28a seems to continue this high praise of John started in v. 26b: there is no human being greater than John. Verse 28b then appears to give a sharp correction: the smallest (or smaller: μικρότερος) in the Kingdom is greater than John. Many have therefore postulated different layers in the tradition here,[80] and some theory of different strata in the tradition seems almost inevitable at this point. However, one should also bear in mind the obligation to make sense of the present text as a whole. Evidently the apparently contradictory views about John were not felt to be insuperable by either Matthew or Luke who both preserved the same sequence here, and presumably the same must be true for the 'final' form of Q as well. And if we are to envisage a Q editor modifying earlier tradition in order to correct views about John, we must presumably assume that (s)he evidently did not disagree so strongly with the earlier traditional view about John: if that had

---

seeing a prophet in John amounts to a wholly inappropriate expectation'; also Vaage, *Galilean Upstarts*, 97: '7:26 makes clear that such a belief [that John was a prophet] was erroneous'), and hence locate the centre of thought in the alleged Cynic critique of v. 25. Rather, the clear *affirmative* sense of v. 26b indicates that the third possibility (John *is* a prophet) *is* the one which should be the focus of attention.

[80] For v. 28b as a correction to v. 27: see W. Wink, *John the Baptist in the Gospel Tradition* (SNTSMS 7; Cambridge University Press, 1968) 24f. Often such a theory suggests that v. 27 goes back to Jesus, and v. 28b is due to the church: cf. Bultmann, *History*, 165; Lührmann, *Redaktion*, 27; Schulz, *Q*, 233 and n. 376. A useful survey and summary of recent opinion is given in Ernst, *Johannes*, 61f. For others, this is a difference between layers within Q itself: hence, e.g. Jacobson argues that v. 28b is a later secondary comment at his 'intermediate' stage, similar to 3:16 (*First Gospel*, 116, 127). Catchpole, *Quest*, 63–70, sees vv. 27 + 28b as Q-redactional additions. Kloppenborg, *Formation*, 110, 117, argues that vv. 27 + 31–35 constitute the contributions of the final redactional stage here: v. 28 constitutes a first comment on vv. 24–26, which has the effect of slightly mitigating the high estimate of John implied in v. 26b. By contrast, vv. 27 and 31–35 serve to rehabilitate John, to show that he belongs alongside Jesus as a precursor, and friend of the kingdom and — with Jesus — one of the messengers of Wisdom.

been the case, the tradition's high view of John could presumably simply have been omitted.

Further, vv. 24–28 form part of a wider unit in Q comprising Q 7:18–35; and in this larger whole, vv. 31–35 provide, as the concluding section, the literary climax of the wider unit. It is the merit of D. Lührmann to have shown this most clearly.[81] In 7:31–35 in the parable of the playing children, interpreted by the sayings about Jesus and John in v. 33f. and the Wisdom saying in v. 35, John and Jesus appear alongside each other as preachers facing 'this generation'. As such they experience no positive response at all and are rejected, but in their preaching they are occupying their joint role as messengers of Wisdom. We shall return to this passage in a later chapter for more detailed analysis. Here it is sufficient to note that there is no hint at all of any rivalry between Jesus and John. The two are simply placed in parallel and any antithesis is between them jointly on the one hand and 'this generation' which refuses to respond to them on the other. If then we are concerned with the 'final' form of 'Q' (cf. above), we must say that it is this view of the mutually supportive ministries of Jesus and John which forms the literary climax of the section Q 7:18–35 as a whole and hence is the one which must be seen as the dominating view of the Q composition. In any case the 'high' view of John still occupies the lion's share of space in the pericope with the allegedly secondary comment being only a (relatively) short appended note to the rest. Q's compositional technique thus makes it clear that this is the view which is intended to be the key to the whole section.

This general observation must cast some doubts on theories which identify the concern of a relatively late redactional layer in Q as one of downgrading John in any way. Thus, for example, Jacobson's theory that v. 28 (or 28b) is a later editorial modification added at the postulated 'intermediate' stage seems hard to envisage: according to this, a later redactor would be seeking to modify the clear message of the rest of the pericope by making a relatively small insertion in the middle of the unit. Yet the section which presents Jesus and John as partners in parallel (i.e. vv. 31–35) is left unaltered and, in literary terms, still forms the climax of the whole section. This latter consideration in particular makes it very unlikely that the view of a later redactor is different from that of the person responsible for these

---

[81] Lührmann, *Redaktion*, 30f.

verses. On these grounds, therefore, Jacobson's theory seems unconvincing.

Much the same general point can be made in relation to Catchpole's suggestion that vv. 27 and 28b stem from Q's redaction, serving to change the nature of John's expectation from looking forward to the coming of God himself to an expectation of a figure other than God, i.e. Jesus for Q, and to clarify the status of Jesus in relation to John by stressing John's inferiority.[82] Once again there is the problem of why 7:31–35 is left as the climax of the section, since here Jesus and John appear in tandem with no real indication of the inferiority of John.[83] Catchpole may well be right in seeing v. 27 as implying that John's status is only to be seen in relation to that of Jesus (see below). But v. 27 scarcely gives any indication of John's *inferiority*. This is clearer in v. 28b and so it is not quite so easy to see v. 28b as coming from the same stratum as v. 27.[84]

In fact the passage as a whole is not out of line with what has gone before in Q. Here, as we have seen, John's preaching is affirmed: the existence of a figure greater than John is accepted. Thus although John's status is implicitly downgraded slightly, this is precisely within the context of an affirmation of John's message. 7:27f. appears to continue this. Hoffmann points out that v. 27 itself already begins to distinguish between Jesus and John.[85] John's role as an Elijah-figure is emphatically asserted — John *is*

---

[82] See n. 80 above.

[83] Unless it be in the reference to Jesus as SM in v. 34, though this would be a very veiled indication of Jesus' superiority *to John*. The stress is much more on the difference between (John and) Jesus and this generation. Catchpole refers briefly to 7:31–35 and 'its secondary Christological expansion focused on him who "has come", the Son of man' (*Quest*, 69f.). But the 'expansion' involves vv. 33 *and* 34 together (on most reconstructions of the tradition history of the passage) and perhaps v. 35; and in both cases Jesus is clearly associated *with* John.

[84] Catchpole claims that vv. 27 and 28b belong together in 'exhibit[ing] a unity of Christological and future-eschatological concern' (*Quest*, 69). In part this depends on his interpretation of v. 28b as referring to Jesus alone, and moreover to Jesus' role in the future. This is possible (though not easy) for v. 28b, but much harder for v. 27, at least in relation to the alleged future aspect: *is* v. 27 about Jesus' role in the future for Q? It is, of course, future for the scriptural voice quoted; but for Q it is almost certainly regarded as fulfilled in the ministry of Jesus in the present/past (i.e. present in the narrative, past for the readers). John's role is as the forerunner of Jesus' *present* ministry (cf. Q 7:22), not solely of a future role.

[85] Hoffmann, *Studien*, 218f.

the one who fulfils scripture. However, the actual text which is cited and the changes to the text which appear here (whether intentionally or not is impossible to say) mean that John's position is to be seen in relation, and only in relation, to that of someone else. Unlike the MT of Mal 3:1, the text quoted in Q 7:27 has the speaker (presumably God) speaking about a messenger (John) directing his words to someone else (presumably for Q, Jesus).[86] (In Mal 3:1 God says he will send his messenger ahead of himself; in Q God says 'I will send my messenger before *you* to prepare *your* way'.) Thus John is the expected Elijah who will prepare the way for *Jesus*.[87] Hence already in v. 27 there is an emphatically positive statement about John's status, coupled with an implied corollary that John's significance is only to be seen in relation to that of Jesus.

In any case it is hard to see v. 27 as comprising a secondary comment to a tradition containing any part of v. 28 as well as vv. 24–26. The simple fact that v. 27 precedes v. 28 renders it unlikely that v. 27 modifies some or all of v. 28, as one would normally expect a modifying comment to come after the saying it is allegedly commenting on.[88] In fact it is more likely that v. 27 is the earlier comment on vv. 24–26, to which v. 28 is added as a later addition and a strong case could be made out for v. 27 being the original conclusion to vv. 24–26. Verses 24–26 alone seem to be almost a torso and to cry out for some clarification and conclusion.[89] Verse 26 ends with the double claim that it is indeed

---

[86] Unlike all known versions of Mal 3:1 or Exod 23:20.

[87] Though for Catchpole, this marks a definite change by the Q-redactor compared to the historical John: cf. too Crossan, *Historical Jesus*, 235. Jacobson's theory, that Q's John expects Yahweh and this is only modified by the very late Q 7:28 (cf. *First Gospel*, 69), seems unpersuasive: at least for the version of Q which contains v. 27, John is clearly the forerunner of *Jesus*.

[88] This applies especially to the theory of Kloppenborg, that vv. 27 + 31–35 modify vv. 24–26 + 28 (see n. 80 above). Kloppenborg's proposal does avoid the problems of ignoring the dominant compositional force of vv. 31–35 in the section as a whole. But, quite apart from the problems of seeing v. 27 as a secondary comment on a later verse (v. 28), it is hard to see vv. 27 and 31–35 coming from the same redactional stratum. As noted above, v. 27 seeks to establish the position of John by virtue of his distinction from Jesus; vv. 31–35 serve to place John and Jesus alongside each other (despite any differences) and distinguish them jointly from 'this generation'.

[89] Cf. Schürmann, *Lukasevangelium*, 417: 'V. 26b verlangt nach einer eigenen Kommentierung'; also Kloppenborg, *Formation*, 109: 'Q 7:26b invites further explication'; Catchpole, *Quest*, 64: the end of v. 26b 'is forceful but lacks the definition which is necessary to conclude a unit of tradition'.

appropriate to think of John as a prophet, but that John is also more than a prophet. To the question 'Is John a prophet?', the answer seems to be yes and no: he is a prophet, but he is also more. At the very least, one could say that such a claim is enigmatic! What does it mean to say that John is both a prophet and more? At one level Q 7:27 provides a perfect answer. John is described as an Elijah redivivus figure. He is then a prophetic figure in that he is an Elijah-figure; but he is also more than just any prophet: for he is the inaugurator of the new age forecast by Malachi. Thus v. 27 provides a very good conclusion to vv. 24–26 and there is no need to drive too much of a wedge between the two.[90]

There does however seem to be a seam between v. 27 and v. 28. The repeated λέγω ὑμῖν of Q 7:28 (cf. v. 26) makes it unlikely that v. 28 belongs with vv. 24–27 originally.[91] It would appear to be a secondary comment. Whether it is itself a unity, or whether (as some have argued) v. 28b (with its possible implied critique of John) is a secondary addition to a more original v. 28a, is also not entirely certain. However, the tightly structured form of the verse as it now stands, with its clear antithetic parallelism, suggests that the verse may be a unity and should not be split up.[92] Whether the verse implies a down-grading of John is also not clear. This *may* be the case, though equally the verse can be taken rather as saying

[90] For v. 27 as linked to vv. 24–26 very early, cf. Schürmann, *Lukasevangelium*, 417; Zeller, 'Redaktionsprozesse', 403; Ernst, *Johannes*, 61f. Catchpole's claim that form-critically v. 28a 'is the *only* element in vv. 27, 28 which will define and complete v. 26' (*Quest*, 65 — my emphasis) seems too extreme. Verse 27 furnishes at least as good a conclusion as v. 28a (Catchpole's theory) does. If it is indeed the case that v. 27 is not due to Q's redaction, but was already present in Q's tradition, and if (as argued earlier) Q 3:16a is also pre-redactional in Q, then it becomes much harder to argue that Mark (who only has a parallel to Q 3:16a and Q 7:27) must have known Q. *Pace* Catchpole (nn. 35, 37 above), and see my 'Mark and Q', in Focant (ed.), *Synoptic Gospels*, 149–76.

[91] We need not discuss whether Q 7:28 contained an ἀμήν (so Matthew but not Luke) as well. Catchpole, *Quest*, 65, argues that the λέγω ὑμῖν of v. 28a could be a redactional resumption of v. 26, 'so that, although the editor regards v. 27 as important, the remarkable implications of vv. 26b, 28a should not be lost'. This however seems to imply a somewhat ambivalent attitude to v. 27 on the part of the editor: vv. 27 and 28b are added editorially to stress John's inferiority to Jesus, but then v. 28a has to be emphasised to stress the thoroughly positive picture of John emerging from vv. 26 and 28a. I would argue that things are rather simpler if v. 28 is regarded as a unity and secondary to vv. 24–27.

[92] See Schürmann, *Lukasevangelium*, 419; Lührmann, *Redaktion*, 27; U. Luz, *Das Evangelium nach Matthäus II* (Zürich & Neukirchen-Vluyn: Benziger & Neukirchen, 1990) 173.

something supremely positive about the status of those in the kingdom:[93] the latter are greater than even John whose greatness is emphatically affirmed in vv. 24–27 as the prophetic messenger foretold in scripture.[94] There is thus not necessarily any anti-Baptist polemic: the only aim is to clarify the status of John and to use this to say something about the surpassing value of the era which has been inaugurated by him.

Such an interpretation will not necessarily solve all the problems of this passage, and it may be that those scholars are right who see here vestiges of some kind of tendency to down-grade John. Nevertheless, one must say that, if such tendencies are present, they can only be regarded as no more than vestiges and they certainly do not dominate the present arrangement of the passage as a whole, as we have already noted. Our conclusion must therefore be that the passage in Q 7:18–35 in the present form of Q is not intended to downgrade John in any way. Rather it affirms the validity of John's preaching recorded earlier in Q in 3:16, though there are some new features: (i) It is clearly implied that John's 'coming one' is Jesus. (ii) John and Jesus experience rejection at the hands of 'this generation' but do so as envoys of Wisdom: this theme will occupy us later. (iii) It is also implied (in 7:22 and 7:27) that the events of Jesus' ministry (and John's!) are not *just* preparatory for an eschatological future event. They are also in part an era of eschatological fulfilment. John's preaching is thus affirmed and also modified: John's futurist eschatology has a realised element.

This same dual perspective on John, as both the announcer and inaugurator of a new aeon, is also shown by another Q logion on John not considered so far, namely Q 16:16.

4. Q 16:16

The problems of this verse are legion and the debate it has engendered is enormous. The precise Q wording and its Q

---

[93] Or conceivably of Jesus if Jesus is ὁ μιχρότερος (so Hoffmann, *Studien*, 221, Catchpole, *Quest*, 69, and some others).

[94] Cf. D. Zeller, 'Der Zusammenhang der Eschatologie in der Logienquelle', in P. Fiedler & D. Zeller (eds), *Gegenwart und kommendes Reich* (Stuttgart, Katholisches Bibelwerk, 1975) 67–77, p. 70; Davies & Allison, *Matthew II*, 251: 'John's greatness, which is no longer the subject, becomes a foil for the surpassing greatness of the kingdom'; cf. too Sevenich-Bax, *Konfrontation*, 344f.

context are both disputed. Some have argued that Matthew's placing of the saying in Matt 11:12f. represents the more original (i.e. Q) context.[95] Others have argued that Luke's context is more original.[96] Since Matthew and Luke do not agree in their placing of the saying it would probably be unwise to place any weight on arguments based on the alleged Q context.

The wording of the saying is also disputed, though some features of the problem are less contentious. It is, for example, widely agreed that Matthew's πάντες ... οἱ προφῆται καὶ ὁ νόμος ... ἐπροφήτευσαν is secondary to Luke's ὁ νόμος καὶ οἱ προφῆται in (a) inverting the more usual order of 'law and prophets' to 'prophets and law', (b) adding πάντες, and (c) adding ἐπροφήτευσαν: all three differences serve to highlight Matthew's interest in stressing the prophetic nature of the OT and would also be consonant with his general tendency to avoid as far as possible suggestions in his tradition that the validity of the Law has been questioned, a suggestion to which Luke 16:16 is at least open (and which Luke 16:17 seems to guard against).[97] Further, Matthew's version seems to be secondary in having the bi-partite saying in reverse order from Luke's: as Catchpole says, 'the sequence from v 12, describing the post-Johannine period, to v. 13, describing the pre-Johannine period, must be secondary'.[98] More doubt concerns the wording of the other half of the saying, especially the verb which is predicated of the 'kingdom': does the kingdom 'suffer violence' (βιάζεται Matthew) or is it 'evangelised' (εὐαγγελίζεται Luke)? Most have taken Luke's version as LkR, given Luke's fondness for the verb εὐαγγελίζεται,[99] though Catchpole has suggested that Luke's version might preserve the Q wording, appealing to the use of εὐαγγελίζομαι

---

[95] Harnack, *Sayings*, 16; Lührmann, *Redaktion*, 27f.; Jacobson, *First Gospel*, 118f.; Fitzmyer, *Luke*, 662.

[96] Cf. my *Revival*, 152f. and others cited there.

[97] See my *Revival*, 152; Catchpole, 'The Law and Prophets in Q', in *Tradition and Interpretation in the New Testament* (FS E. E. Ellis; Tübingen: Mohr, 1987) 95–109, 95. (The version of this essay reprinted in Catchpole's *Quest*, 229–55, has been heavily revised.) For fuller discussion of this, see pp. 404–9 below.

[98] Catchpole, 'Law and Prophets', 95. Cf. too Schulz, *Q*, 261. Kloppenborg, *Formation*, 114, finds Matthew's order more difficult and hence more original. But Matthew's 'difficult' order is probably due to his concern to stress even more the parallel between John and Elijah in v. 14.

[99] Hoffmann, *Studien*, 51; Schulz, *Q*, 262; G. Barth, 'Matthew's Understanding of the Law', in Bornkamm, Barth & Held, *Tradition and Interpretation in Matthew*, 63.

in Q 7:22 and the 'tautologous' nature of Matthew's, βιάζεται-βιασταί.[1] However, Matthew's version is not so much tautologous as an example of synthetic parallelism, and the Lukan nature of εὐαγγελίζομαι cannot be gainsaid. It still seems more likely, therefore, that Matthew's version is more original. The endless debate about the prepositions used (the law and prophets being 'until' [ἕως/μέχρι] John, and 'from' [ἀπό] then . . .) and the precise nuance they might entail will not be considered in detail here. It is probably true to say that the discussion about whether ἕως, μέχρι, or ἀπό are inclusive or exclusive has been indecisive. Either version could, in terms of semantics, be including or excluding John from the era of the kingdom.

Within the context of Q, however, it would seem that John must definitely be included in the new era. What does seem clear is that the saying implies that with John a new era has started, and it is an era characterised by the phrase 'kingdom of God'; further, this era is one in which the preachers of the kingdom are suffering some kind of 'violence'. The nature of the 'violence' will be considered later. Here we may simply note the way in which, for this Q saying at least, the kingdom is in some sense a present reality. The era inaugurated by John is thus regarded as in some sense an era of eschatological fulfilment. As such the saying coheres well with the outlook of the Q passage in 7:18ff.

Q's eschatology, as evidenced in the material about John the Baptist, thus has a dual element: there is the belief that the final establishment of God's kingdom will be consummated in the near future, and this is coupled with a claim that the present is itself in part an era of eschatological fulfilment.

---

[1] Catchpole, 'Law and Prophets', 96; however, in his revision of this article, in *Quest*, 233, Catchpole appears to have reversed his view.

5

‑‑‑►●◄‑‑‑

Eschatology in Q

Our study of the material about John the Baptist in Q has shown a belief by Q in an imminent eschatological event (the coming of one who will baptise with Spirit and fire) coupled with claims about the eschatological nature of the present era introduced by John. It remains now to be examined how far this dual outlook is reflected in the rest of Q. It may be worth considering these two aspects separately and so we shall look in this chapter at the phenomenon of futurist eschatology in Q. This is an important issue in the light of some recent studies of the apparently eschatological language of Q. Some have argued, for example, that the language often regarded as 'eschatological', e.g. the language about the 'kingdom', should not be read against a background of Jewish eschatology but rather one of Hellenistic philosophical discourse, especially that of Cynicism.[1] Others, working within the paradigm of Jewish eschatology as the broad background of thought, have questioned how far Q's eschatology is appropriately called 'apocalyptic'.[2] As far as the latter point is concerned, I shall consider the question briefly later. In one way it is a matter of semantic quibbling whether one calls the eschatology[3] of Q 'apocalyptic' or 'non-apocalyptic'. In this chapter I am more concerned to establish the more broadly-based eschatological framework of the Q material.

---

[1] See Vaage, *Q: Ethos and Ethics*; *Galilean Upstarts*; also his 'Q and Cynicism: On Comparison and Social Identity', in Piper (ed.), *The Gospel Behind the Gospels*, 199–229, esp. pp. 220ff.; Mack, *Myth of Innocence*, 69–74; *Lost Gospel*, 123–30. However, both Mack and Vaage argue that the Cynic paradigm applies primarily to the *earlier* layer of Q, a 'Q¹', and not to the later parts of Q: cf. explicitly Vaage, 'Q and Cynicism', 200 n. 3. On this see ch. 11 below.

[2] See J. S. Kloppenborg, 'Symbolic Eschatology and the Apocalypticism of Q', *HTR* 80 (1987) 287–306; A. D. Jacobson, 'Apocalyptic and the Synoptic Sayings Source Q', in Van Segbroek et al (eds), *The Four Gospels 1992*, 403–19.

[3] If indeed it is present at all! Cf. above on the Cynic paradigm.

Even within this framework, there is some divergence of opinion about the significance of apparent references to a futurist eschatological expectation in Q. Some, for example, have argued that Q (or some material in Q) is dominated not so much by an imminent eschatology but by an awareness of a delay in the Parousia. At the level of Q as a whole, this has been advocated strongly in the influential (though brief) discussion of D. Lührmann;[4] Schulz too claims that a major characteristic of his alleged later Q^2 stratum was the influence of '*Parusieverzögerung*' and greater eschatological significance being ascribed to the preaching of the earthly Jesus.[5] So too, earlier studies of the material in Q such as the parables of the thief (Q 12:39f.), the watching servants (Q 12:42–46) and the talents/pounds (Q 19:12ff.) have often argued that these have been heavily influenced by the delay in the Parousia.[6]

It is however important not to let any debate become polarised too quickly here. It would, for example, be quite wrong to assume that an awareness of a delay in the Parousia ('*Parusieverzögerung*') and an expectation of imminent eschatological events ('*Naherwartung*') are mutually exclusive options and that one can characterise a strand in the tradition by one or other of these labels. The whole issue of a 'delay in the Parousia' is indeed a complex one and a wide variety of attitudes are possible, even within the broad rubric of an 'awareness of delay'. Such awareness could lead to renewed vigorous expectation of what has been delayed; it could lead to disappointment and to a belief that what has been delayed will be delayed still more in the future; it could lead to a total reorientation of belief so that what had been expected, but has not materialised, is now no longer entertained as a possibility at all. Further, one should remember that the whole Christian idea of a 'parousia' event at all, in the sense of a return of a once present 'salvation figure', is an unusual idea within Jewish eschatological expectations; and hence any alleged doubts about the return of such a figure may just as well be doubts about the validity of the expectation at

---

[4] Lührmann, *Redaktion*, 69–71; cf. too Catchpole, *Quest*, 217.

[5] Schulz, *Q*, 50, and the whole section on pp. 268–322.

[6] J. Jeremias, *The Parables of Jesus* (ET London: SCM, 1963) 48ff.; E. Grässer, *Das Problem der Parusieverzögerung in den synoptischen Evangelien und in der Apostelgeschichte* (BZNW 22; Berlin: de Gruyter, 1969) *passim*.

[7] Hoffmann, *Studien*, 44f.

all.[8] One must also remember the obvious distinction between different sides in any two-way 'conversation'. Thus in relation to Q, it may be that the Q editor, and those to whom the Q material is addressed, did not share exactly the same attitude; indeed the Q material may be seeking to change the views of those being addressed to align them more closely with those of the Q editor. With these preliminary remarks in mind, we turn to an analysis of some of the relevant Q material. The strongest evidence for a powerful eschatological belief in Q is provided by the eschatological teaching in Q 12:39–46 and Q 17:22–37. However, before discussing these passages, I shall consider the evidence from the rest of Q.

1. Evidence of Eschatological Awareness in Q

A great deal of Q seems to be oriented to the eschatological future in general terms. Precisely what time-scale is implied in any one instance is not always entirely clear, since very often nothing is said explicitly on this issue. Nevertheless, the overall thrust seems to be that, fairly consistently, the looked-for future event(s) is (are) expected in the *near* future. However, such temporal precision is by no means always present.

Jesus' explicit teaching in Q starts with the Great Sermon in Q 6:20–49, and the Sermon itself starts with the beatitudes in Q 6:20–23. I would argue that the beatitudes as a whole are all eschatologically oriented: those who are poor, hungry and mourning in the present are promised a reversal of their present suffering state in an eschatological future.[9] So too those who are at present being 'persecuted' in some way are promised in the final beatitude (Q 6:22f.) a reward and a reversal of their present

---

[8] See N. A. Dahl, 'Eschatology and History in Light of the Qumran Texts', in *The Crucified Messiah* (ET Minneapolis: Augsburg, 1974) 129–45, p. 142f.

[9] J. Dupont, *Les Béatitudes II* (Paris: Gabalda, 1969) 115–23; Schulz, *Q,* 84; Catchpole, *Quest,* 86. For the ἐστιν as referring to the future, cf. Davies & Allison, *Matthew I,* 445; Luz, *Matthew 1–7,* 235 and many others. I thus find it hard to accept Vaage's argument (*Q: Ethos and Ethics,* 431–92, more briefly in 'Q and Cynicism', 220ff.; *Galilean Upstarts,* 55–65) that the kingdom of God is a present reality — or rather a potentially present reality for all who follow the Cynic way of life — and who then lets this determine the interpretation of all the other references in Q to the kingdom of God. The first three beatitudes as a whole (if it is legitimate to take them in this way) seem to promise that the present sufferings of hunger, sorrow *and* poverty will be *changed* in the future. For the Cynic, hunger might be alleviated in the present; but a life of poverty,

suffering in an eschatological future. If it is right to take the beatitudes in this way, it is hard to see them as in any way 'sapiential'.[10] As has often been pointed out, the beatitude form itself is multivalent, being usable — and used — in a variety of difference contexts. Thus, whilst clearly at home in a sapiential context to give ethical guidance, it is also used in an eschatological context to give assurance and encouragement to those presently suffering.[11] The Q beatitudes would seem to fit much more readily into the latter category.[12] Thus the opening of Jesus' teaching seems to set a very clear tone of eschatological hope.

So too the end of the Sermon (Q 6:47–49) warns the listeners of the (eschatological) consequences which will result from their attitudes to the teaching of Jesus as just set out: those who hear and obey Jesus' teaching will be secure against the onslaughts of flood and storm; those who do not will perish. The reference is most easily taken as being to the final judgement.[13] The parable

---

and living according to nature, was what was explicitly embraced and welcomed. Further, if, as I shall be arguing later, the language of the Q beatitudes echoes the promises of Isa 61, then again the primary reference is most likely to be the fulfilment of Jewish eschatological hopes for the *relief* of *real* poverty and suffering.

[10] So Kloppenborg, *Formation*, 188f. He includes the beatitudes in his 'sapiential speeches in Q' and refers approvingly to George: the beatitudes 'are not simple moral or religious exhortations of wisdom; they are proclamations of eschatological salvation'. But then Kloppenborg has to undergo some verbal gymnastics: the beatitudes share the 'sapiential form' but are the 'radical wisdom of the kingdom', 'sapiential forms infused with eschatological content'. Cf. too Sevenich-Bax, *Konfrontation*, 402–4. But form alone, especially a beatitude form, is often ambiguous and cannot determine the meaning absolutely: cf. below. The alleged 'sapiential' nature of Q is discussed more fully in ch. 10 below.

[11] See K. Koch, *The Growth of the Biblical Tradition* (London: A. & C. Black, 1969) 6–8; E. Schweizer, 'Formgeschichtliches zu den Seligpreisungen Jesu', *NTS* 19 (1973) 121–6; R. A. Guelich, *The Sermon on the Mount* (Waco: Word, 1982) 64f.

[12] As even Kloppenborg himself seems to admit: cf. n. 10 above.

[13] Jeremias, *Parables*, 194; Schulz, *Q*, 315; Schürmann, *Lukasevangelium*, 383; Fitzmyer, *Luke*, 644; D. Zeller, *Kommentar zur Logienquelle* (Stuttgart: Katholisches Bibelwerk, 1984) 35f.; Davies & Allison, *Matthew I*, 721f.; Kosch, *Tora*, 408f.; Luz, *Matthew 1–7*, 453.

Jacobson and Kloppenborg have appealed to allegedly similar references to a ruined house at the end of wisdom collections (Prov 9:13–18; 15:25; Eccles 12:3; Job 27:13–23) or to more general references to reward and ruin (Prov 1:9–33; 2:20–22; 4:18f.; 5:22f.; 7:24–27; 8:32–36; 24:21f.) to argue for the

and the opening beatitudes thus form a powerful inclusio, setting the whole of the Great Sermon within the context of claims relating to God's eschatological future, promising an overthrow of the existing social order as hope for the poor and downtrodden and also giving severe warnings for those who refuse to respond.[14]

A reference to an eschatological future, though at an unspecified time, also occurs in the parables of the mustard seed and the leaven (Q 13:18–21). In the view of most commentators, the eschatological reference seems clear: the end product of the growth of the mustard seed is a mighty tree, described in terms reminiscent of the great cedar tree of Lebanon (Ezek 17:22f.), itself an image of God's mighty rule. This then is *not* the

---

'sapiential' nature of the parable. (Jacobson, *First Gospel*, 96; 'Apocalyptic and Q', 414; Kloppenborg, *Formation*, 186; 'Symbolic Eschatology', 292f.; cf. too Sevenich-Bax, *Konfrontation*, 434f.). However, the other references to ruined houses are scarcely comparable. The 'house' of Prov 9:13–18 is simply the place where the foolish woman lives and into which she entices others: it is not itself physically ruined; Job 27 is about the ruin of the wicked man himself whose house is simply a part of his accumulated possessions, mentioned in passing; in Eccles 12:3 the house itself is not ruined and the context is about the mortality of human beings in general; in Prov 15:25 (if the 'house' is meant to be the physical building and not the family) the context is of divine judgement. Further, the other references to ruin in the Jewish texts cited are in the context of divine judgement. They are not strictly 'sapiential' in the sense of describing the inevitable outcome of events or actions. The references to ruin in these *Jewish* wisdom texts clearly have *divine* action in mind. Thus the parallels between 6:47–49 and Jewish wisdom traditions are not so much because both are 'sapiential'; rather, the parallels are due to the common *Jewish* belief in divine judgement. The sapiential nature of Q 6:47–49 is also questioned by Zeller, 'Eine weisheitliche Grundschrift in der Logienquelle?', in Van Segbroek et al (eds), *The Four Gospels 1992*, 389–401, p. 399, who also refers to the fact that Prov 15:25 is not a conclusion to a section, and the saying from Cebes' Tablet (cited by Kloppenborg, *Formation*, 187) comes at the start of a series of teachings.

[14] Hoffmann, *Studien*, 38f. Even Koester, who is generally very sympathetic to Kloppenborg's claim about a 'sapiential' formative layer in Q, seems to recognise that the beatitudes and the end of the Great Sermon make the whole burst the limits of any 'sapiential' boundaries: 'A mixture of wisdom sayings and prophetic sayings of Jesus . . . characterises this portion of Q. This is not simply a "sapiential speech", but a prophetic, and thus eschatological, announcement of the presence of the rule of God.' (*Ancient Christian Gospels*, 137f. Within the category of 'prophetic' sayings, Koester includes the beatitudes and the saying in Q 6:46. For some [unexplained] reason Koester does not include the parable in Q 6:47–49 here in the material ascribed to the 'inaugural Sermon' [though it is included later on p. 169]).

description of 'nature', or any natural process.[15] It is rather the image of a divine miracle. So too the parable of the leaven bursts the bounds of any natural process: 'three measures' of flour is an enormous amount.[16] Thus, Jeremias says:

> The features of the parables which transcend the bounds of actuality, δένδρον Matt. 13.32; Luke 13.19 (mustard is not a tree), σάτα τρία (no housewife would bake so vast a quantity of meal), are meant to tell us that we have to do with divine realities.[17]

There is perhaps an implicit claim that the start of the process which will culminate in the final Kingdom is already present in hidden form.[18] However, nothing is stated here about the relative time-scale involved or how soon the whole process will reach its completion.[19]

Further sayings in Q which threaten the listeners with judgement seem to establish the importance of a futurist eschatological expectation in Q, and may also indicate more about the time-scale envisaged. Thus the saying in Q 12:8f., which promises that those who confess/deny Jesus in the present will be correspondingly confessed or denied before the angels of God (i.e. at the divine judgement) could theoretically be taken as independent of the time gap involved between the present and the

---

[15] Thus, contra Kloppenborg, 'Symbolic Eschatology', 297: 'The startling growth of the Kingdom is visualised in the ordinary biological processes of the growth of the mustard and yeast'; Mack, *Lost Gospel*, 124: the kingdom 'is compared to the natural processes of growth'; cf. too Vaage, *Galilean Upstarts*, 63. For the problem of distinguishing the Q version from Mark, see my *Revival*, 84f. The common reference to the 'tree' at the end of the parable in both Matthew and Luke indicates that this is indeed the Q version. The lack of analogy in nature (the mustard seed does not become a 'tree', let alone a cedar tree), and the clear allusion to Jewish eschatological language, makes the Cynic background distinctly less plausible here.

[16] Jeremias, *Parables*, 31f., 147. Possible overtones of meaning in some of the details are explored by R. Funk, 'Beyond Criticism in Quest of Literacy: The Parable of the Leaven', *Int* 25 (1971) 149–70.

[17] Jeremias, *Parables*, 147.

[18] Cf. N. A. Dahl, 'The Parables of Growth', in *Jesus in the Memory of the Early Church* (Minneapolis: Augsburg, 1976) 141–66. Such an interpretation does necessarily entail an implied idea of a 'growth' process.

[19] Hence Weder is probably right to reject theories that find either a vivid *Naherwartung* here (so Schulz, *Q*, 303), or an awareness of a delay in the Parousia (so Grässer, *Parusieverzögerung*, 142) reflected in these parables. See H. Weder, *Die Gleichnisse Jesu als Metaphern* (FRLANT 120; Göttingen: Vandenhoeck & Ruprecht, 1984) 136.

future judgement, though it may make more sense of the urgency implied in the saying to think of the time gap being shorter rather than longer.

Warnings about divine judgement such as Q 11:49–51 seem rather clearer. Here 'this generation' is accused of being guilty of the blood of all the prophets and righteous men shed from the start of creation. We shall return to this passage in more detail later and for the present we shall have to anticipate the analysis of the term 'this generation' in Q: if it is right to interpret γενεά here as indeed meaning a temporal 'generation', rather than 'race' or 'nation' (see pp. 196–201 below), then some kind of temporal limit seems to be built into the saying. This generation is the final generation in the present order of things; it is faced with taking ultimate responsibility for the whole of preceding history and is threatened with divine judgement. Again, whilst it is theoretically possible that a long time gap between the present threat and its future enactment in judgement could ensue (with perhaps other 'generations' intervening?), it seems to make much better sense of the passage if the threatened judgement is regarded as due to be experienced by the audience very soon.

The same is probably implied by the section Q 13:24ff. Again this is a passage which we shall examine in more detail later. Verse 24 says that few will be able to enter into the 'narrow' door. The transition from v. 24 to v. 25 is often said to be very harsh and indicative of disparate traditions being clumsily put together.[20] However, v. 24 really demands a sequel to explain why only few will be able to enter into the door. Such an answer is given in pictorial terms in v. 25: the door will soon be shut! The alleged discrepancy between the 'narrow' door and the 'shut' door is thus by no means insuperable. The reason that people will be unable to enter is because they have refused to accept the opportunity presented by the present, and the 'parable' makes it clear that their failure to respond is disastrous — soon it will be too late. The decisive moment is clearly thought of as coming soon. Thus what is in mind is an imminent event, not simply a future one at an indeterminate time, at which those who have failed to respond to the opportunity of the present will be definitively rejected.

Exactly the same seems to be the case in some of the parables of Q, especially the parable of the Great Supper (Q 14:16–24). There is, of course, always the problem in interpreting a parable

---

[20] Cf. Bultmann, *History*, 130. For a fuller discussion, see pp. 189–95 below.

of how much we can deduce from the details of the parable about the situation being addressed. The era of a patristic type of allegorisation, whereby every detail of a parable was thought to have significance, is clearly long gone. On the other hand, the idea (popularised above all by Jeremias in contemporary scholarship, but reaching back to Jülicher) that a parable has one and only one point to make is probably equally one-sided. We may therefore be justified in looking at the story line in a parable in a little detail to determine how the parable is being interpreted.

In the case of the parable of the Great Supper, the problems of interpretation are heightened by the great verbal dissimilarity between Matthew and Luke (though the general agreement in the outline of the story told does suggest that we are dealing with Q material here).[21] This is particularly important in relation to the versions of the excuses which the guests offer to the host inviting them to the meal, and what these excuses imply.

With regard to the actual wording of the excuses, Luke's version is generally taken as more original: in Matthew's version, where the guests maltreat the servants, the attempt is made to show much more clearly that the refusal of the guests to respond is due to their own perversity.[22] In Luke, however, the situation is not so clear cut. Linnemann has argued forcefully that what is intended is only procrastination: the guests think that they have more time, the call to come to the meal has come earlier than expected and they think that they can come along later. However, she has to cut out the final excuse in Luke 14:20 ('I have married a wife') as not fitting this pattern,[23] though the reference to marriage has no parallel in Matthew's version and hence cannot with confidence be traced back to Q itself.[24] In support of Linnemann's theory, one can argue that the implied negative

---

[21] See Schulz, *Q*, 398; Weder, *Gleichnisse*, 178.

[22] J.Dupont, 'La parabole des invités au festin dans le ministère de Jésus', *Etudes sur les Evangiles Synoptiques* (BETL 70; Leuven University Press & Peeters, 1985) 667–705, p. 687; F. Hahn, 'Das Gleichnis von der Einladung zum Festmahl', in *Verborum Veritas* (FS G. Stählin; Wuppertal: Brockhaus, 1970) 51–82, p. 55; A. Vögtle, 'Die Einladung zum großen Gastmahl und zum königlichen Hochzeitsmahl', *Das Evangelium und die Evangelien* (Düsseldorf: Patmos, 1971) 171–218, p. 180f.; Weder, *Gleichnisse*, 180f.

[23] E. Linnemann, *The Parables of Jesus: Introduction and Exposition* (ET London: SPCK, 1966) 89; cf. too Dupont, *Etudes*, 687. The proposal is however strongly criticised by Fitzmyer, *Luke*, 1056, for thereby destroying the three-fold pattern.

[24] The parallel in GTh is of dubious value in this context if one believes that GTh is post-synoptic.

attitude to marriage here may be due to Luke himself (cf. Luke 14:26 diff Matt 10:37 where the Lukan version alone talks of hating one's 'wife', and Luke 18:29 diff Mark 10:29 talks of leaving one's 'wife' as well as the rest of one's family). It may well be therefore that Linnemann is justified in excluding the third excuse in Luke's version from the earlier (Q) form of the parable. Thus the excuses may originally (i.e. in Q) have represented no intentional ill-will on the part of the guests: they simply represent normal activities of this world where those invited think that there is still plenty of time remaining.[25] In the present context, the important point to note is that the clear message of the parable is that such an attitude is wrong: there is *not* plenty of time left, the crisis is imminent and one cannot procrastinate. The parable thus fits well into the pattern of *Naherwartung* elsewhere in Q which we have already seen.

Exactly the same may be implied by the parable of the talents/pounds in Q 19:12ff., though here the evidence is more ambiguous. Once again the great verbal dissimilarity between Matthew and Luke makes it difficult to be certain about the Q wording (though as with the parable of the Great Supper, the general similarity in the outline of the story in the two gospels makes it highly likely that we do indeed have Q material here).[26] So too clarity is not helped by Luke's apparent attempt to conflate the parable with another story, that of the throne claimant.[27]

The point of the parable is not clear since it is possible to place the audience at different points in the story, and differing placings lead to differing interpretations of the parable. If the listeners are to be placed at a point where the master is going away, then the parable can be an exhortation to the audience to use the period coming to the full. Such a view would fit well with an awareness of some 'delay' by Christians awaiting the return of Jesus.[28] But it is just as possible to place the listeners at the point in the story when the master is about to come back; indeed, given the fact that the bulk of the story concerns what happens when the master does return, this seems more true to

---

[25] Cf. Schenk, *Synopse*, 108; Weder, *Gleichnisse*, 186f.: the excuses are 'durchaus begreiflich', and 'keineswegs etwa gezwungen oder fadenscheinig'; cf. too Dupont, *Etudes*, 687.

[26] Schulz, *Q*, 293; Weder, *Gleichnisse*, 193; Dupont, 'La Parabole des Talents ou des Mines (Mt 25,14–30; Lc 19,12–27)', *Etudes*, 744–760, p. 745.

[27] Weder, *Gleichnisse*, 194f.; Dupont, *Etudes*, 745, and all the commentaries.

[28] So Lührmann, *Redaktion*, 70f.; Schulz, *Q*, 293f.

the parable itself. In this case, the parable functions as a warning to people of what is about to happen to them as a result of what they have done in the past or are doing in the present. It is thus an exhortation to use the opportunity of the present because of the future that is threatening imminently.[29] Thus the parable can function very naturally with an expectation of an imminent End, expressing one aspect of that expectation.

Such a belief in an imminent End may also be indicated by some of the references to the 'kingdom' in Q. Certainly the message which the Q missionaries are exhorted to preach in Q 10:9 is clear: 'The kingdom of God has drawn near!' Insofar as the mission charge is still thought of as applicable in the present in Q, an awareness of, and belief in, an imminent kingdom seems to be clearly attested here.[30]

[29] For a denial of any idea of delay here, cf. Hoffmann, *Studien*, 49; Weder, *Gleichnisse*, 207; contra Lührmann and Schulz (as in previous note).

[30] The (apparent) reference to miracles in the immediate context here in the charge to 'heal the sick' (θεραπεύετε τοὺς ἀσθενεῖς Luke 10:9) would seem to remove this far from any ideas to do with Cynicism, where the idea of a Cynic as a miracle-working (physical) healer is absent (cf. my 'Cynic Q?', 375). However, a quite different interpretation is offered by Vaage ('Q and Cynicism', 214, 221f.). Vaage suggests that the ἀσθενεῖς here could be the spiritually weak, those whose desires are set on the wrong things, and the Q peoples' caring for these, by showing them the true (i.e. Cynic) order of priorities, enables the 'kingdom' to be established. (For the 'weak' in this sense, Vaage refers to A. J. Malherbe, '"Pastoral Care" in the Thessalonian Church', *NTS* 36 (1990) 375–90, p. 379f.).

I find such an interpretation of the charge to 'heal the sick' unconvincing. At the very least, Matthew (one of Q's earliest, perhaps closest, interpreters) did not take it this way as the charge is set in parallel with several injunctions clearly relating to physical miracles (Matt 10:8: raise the dead, cleanse lepers, cast out demons). So too Luke's negative use of the announcement that the kingdom has come (Luke 10:11) hardly fits the suggested interpretation since the Cynic 'kingdom' can scarcely come upon the hearers with the *rejection* of them by the 'missionaries'. Vaage rather ambivalently dismisses my references to other passages in Q (7:1–10; 11:14–20) as showing an interest in miracles, in part because they belong to Kloppenborg's alleged later stratum Q² (though he says in a footnote that he would place at least Q 11:14–20 in Q¹!) However, I have argued above against dividing Q up too much. In any case the saying in Q 11:20 clearly associates the presence of the 'kingdom' with Jesus' *exorcistic* activity. More importantly, the command to 'heal' alongside the announcement of the nearness of the 'kingdom' recalls, at least within the 'final' form of Q, the first beatitude and the claim of Q 7:22 whereby the arrival of the kingdom is good news for the poor which is coupled with genuine healings of the physically disabled (the blind, deaf and lame). Of this there is nothing very comparable in Cynic tradition.

The same may well be implied in the Cares tradition in Q 12:22–31 and in the teaching on prayer in Q 11:2–4, 9–13, both of which refer to the 'kingdom'. Both however need a slightly more extended treatment in the present context, and it is to these I now turn. [31]

2. On Cares (Q 12:22–31) and Prayer (Q 11:2–4, 9–13)

The section on Cares is widely agreed to be non-unitary.[32] Almost certainly an earlier block of teaching has undergone editorial modification at least as early as Q. Thus one may be justified in focusing attention, at least initially, on the editorial modifications, although one cannot ignore completely the whole tradition adopted by Q and indeed we should pay attention to *all* the material which the Q editor has decided to include.

It is widely acknowledged that Q 12:23 (the ψυχή is more than food, and the σῶμα more than clothing) does not fit well after the initial exhortation in v. 22 not to worry about food or clothing.[33] The motives given in v. 23 on the one hand, and in vv. 22, 24, 26–28 on the other, for the general advice not to worry are different: in vv. 24, 26–28 there is no grading of concerns but simply an assurance that God will provide; v. 23 however introduces a contrast between the more important ψυχή-σῶμα and the less important food and clothing. It looks very much as if either v. 23 has been added secondarily to vv. 22, 24 and 26–28, or vice versa. If however, vv. 24 + 26–28 are secondary, then a small original tradition (v. 23) must have been expanded by a relatively enormous secondary overlay. This seems inherently unlikely: why should the original tradition have been preserved at all if it were so small in extent and so heavily redacted? It seems therefore more likely that v. 23 is the secondary comment, added to an earlier tradition in vv. 22 + 24 + 26–28. So too v. 25, interrupting the twin appeals to examples from nature (ravens/birds and

---

[31] For what follows, see my 'Q, Prayer and the Kingdom', *JTS* 40 (1989) 367–76, and the 'Rejoinder' by Catchpole, *JTS* 40 (1989) 377–88 (the substance of which is reprinted in slightly changed form in his *Quest*).

[32] See Catchpole, *Quest*, 31–5; also P. Hoffmann, 'Sprüche'; and his 'Jesu "Verbot des Sorgens" und seine Nachgeschichte in der synoptischen Überlieferung', in D.-A. Koch, G. Sellin, A. Lindemann (eds), *Jesu Rede von Gott und ihre Nachgeschichte* (FS W. Marxsen; Gütersloh: G. Mohn, 1989) 110–41.

[33] Zeller, *Mahnsprüche*, 89; Catchpole, *Quest*, 32; Luz, *Matthew 1–7*, 404f.; Kloppenborg, *Formation*, 217; Hoffmann, 'Sprüche', 84.

lilies) and introducing a quite different kind of argument appealing to human inability to solve the problems of anxiety, is almost universally regarded as a secondary addition to the earlier tradition.[34]

A third addition may occur in vv. 30a, 31, in the references to the Gentiles and the kingdom.[35] The basis for the argument changes quite sharply from appeals to the natural order and to God's care for His creation, to a contrast between the audience and the Gentiles and to an exhortation to 'seek the kingdom of God'. The easiest solution is to see vv. 30a, 31, with their national and eschatological appeals, as secondary additions to an earlier tradition which referred to God's care for the created order.[36]

This stratification of the tradition now has important consequences for the understanding of the whole section at the level of Q. The kernel of the section (which is still retained by Q, even if expanded by secondary additions: hence one must assume that it is still regarded as important for Q) is the twin appeal to consider the ravens and the lilies and to deduce from them that one should not 'worry' (μεριμνάω). Yet what does such worry involve? Is it a reference to anxious thoughts only, or to actions as well?[37] The appeal to the lilies seems to make clear what is in

[34] Bultmann, *History*, 81, 88; Jeremias, *Parables*, 103; Zeller, *Mahnsprüche*, 86; Kloppenborg, *Formation*, 217; R. A. Piper, *Wisdom in the Q-Tradition* (SNTSMS 61; Cambridge University Press, 1989) 28f.; Hoffmann, 'Sprüche', 83f. and many others.

[35] Cf. Catchpole, *Quest*, 34 (reversing his earlier view in 'The Ravens, the Lilies and the Q Hypothesis', *SNTU* A/6–7 [1981–82] 77–87, p. 81f., on which the section in *Quest*, 31–5 is mostly based); Zeller, *Mahnsprüche*, 86f.; Hoffmann, 'Sprüche', 87f., contra Kloppenborg, *Formation*, 218, who sees vv. 29–31 as 'an originally independent admonition attached to 12:22b–24, 26–28 on the basis of catchword and thematic connections'. But the links seem too good to be true if these were really quite independent. A theory of secondary expansion seems more probable.

[36] Hence differing from Piper, *Wisdom*, 24ff., who sees the collection in vv. 22–31 as a structured unity. Piper too recognises that vv. 22, 23 are slightly different appeals (p. 26), yet believes that these are then summed up in the closing exhortations in vv. 30–31 (p. 29): 'It is these sayings in Mt 6:31–3/Lk 12:29–31 that draw together the two lines of argument offered previously', though he concedes that these 'express for the first time the priority of seeking the kingdom of God. It is here therefore that the argument comes to its climax and *its most specific interpretation*' (my stress). The very 'specificity' of the interpretation suggests that perhaps we may have a rather different nuance being introduced and not just simply a summary conclusion. In fact only v. 30b refers to the previous argument. The rest is rather differently oriented.

[37] Cf. the discussion in Guelich, *Sermon*, 335f.

mind. The lilies, who do no work at all, are clothed by God far more resplendently than even Solomon was. The appeal is thus not only not to be mentally anxious, but not to do anything in this direction as well.[38] This meaning for μεριμνάω for Q is emphasised later in the section where it is interpreted by being placed in parallel with 'seeking' (cf. v. 29) which clearly implies activity as well as just thought. Further, if it is right to see the 'seek' clause as a Q-editorial addition, then the force of the addition may be precisely to reinforce this interpretation of μεριμνάω and redirect the listeners' activities.[39]

Such redirection is spelt out explicitly in Q in v. 31 where the object of the 'seeking' as being the 'kingdom'. The force of v. 31, coupled with the (probably editorial) v. 23, is thus to downgrade the value of basic material needs to a very low level on the agenda. The priorities of the Q Christians (as propounded by Q's Jesus) seem clear. They are not to concern themselves with the material needs of life; rather, they are to devote their entire energies to the kingdom of God. Concern for food etc. is a minor concern. They are not to worry, nor even to do anything at that level. God *will* provide them with food (Q 12:31b: 'these things will be added to you') but life is more than food and what is of overriding importance is the kingdom of God.[40]

We may also note that similar ideas may also be not far below the surface in the traditions used by the Q redactor at this point. The appeals to the created order, to the ravens and the lilies, in vv. 24, 26–28, and to God's providential care, are very often held

---

[38] See Catchpole, 'Ravens', 82, thus disagreeing with Guelich, *Sermon*, 338, who claims that there is an *a minori ad maius* argument here: since God provides for birds who do not work, how much more will He provide for human beings who do work.

[39] The force of ζητέω in this respect is stressed by Hoffmann, 'Verbot', 125f.

[40] In his 'Rejoinder' to me (see now also *Quest*, 217f.), Catchpole appeals to the background of the Cares tradition in the Q community, postulating a situation of intense disappointment at the delay of the Parousia and concern about the provision of food and clothing. He uses this to argue that Q is then to be interpreted as a statement that God *will* provide. I am happy to accept much of his analysis of the background situation, and indeed of his analysis of the literary composition of the section. Yet it seems to me that the Q-redactional elements (whose identity we agree on) address the situation in a way rather different from that which Catchpole suggests. The redactional elements seem to be trying to *redirect* Q Christians' energies *away* from concern for food (with a passing reference to the claim that God will provide) and to refocus their efforts in relation to the kingdom. Cf. also Hoffmann, as above.

up as the stock example of sapiential appeals in the Q material.[41] Yet as Catchpole has pointed out, the ethos that is encouraged is quite *un*like the wisdom literature's general expectation that human beings will and should work to sustain themselves. Thus Catchpole says that this section

> involves a resounding clash with the wisdom tradition which lavishly praises the worker and severely chides the non-worker. Only one explanation seems ready at hand for such a clash. That is, the tradition belongs to a situation which is special in character and short in duration. It belongs to that period of time conditioned by the expectation of an imminent eschatological crisis.'[42]

Thus the whole teaching in the Cares tradition is, explicitly or implicitly, thoroughly impregnated with a powerful eschatological awareness and expectation.

This outlook now fits very neatly with the small section in Q 11:2–4, 9–13 which may have constituted a unit in Q devoted to prayer.[43] Here again it is possible to interpret the passage in different ways by focusing on different parts in the tradition as the key to the whole.

Few would doubt that the Lord's Prayer (Q 11:2–4) is essentially dominical (and hence not a Q creation). Within the prayer, the 'bread' petition is notoriously ambiguous (depending

---

[41] Cf. Kloppenborg, *Formation*, 216ff.; Piper, *Wisdom*, 24ff. and others.

[42] *Quest*, 35, with reference to many OT texts such as Prov 6:6–8; 10:21; 12:24, 27, etc. He also refers to Luz, *Matthew 1–7*, 402f., who summarises the problems the passage raises if interpreted very generally. Luz's own answer (at least for Matthew) comes on p. 407f.: The verses make clear that Jesus 'is not concerned with humanity in general but that definite people are addressed. The whole text stands under the sign of the coming kingdom of God . . . Sapiential sayings material is here put in the service of a specific statement about the kingdom of God.'

[43] Following the general 'rule' of accepting Luke's order on Q. On the question of whether Luke 11:5–8 might have been part of Q (so Catchpole, *Quest*, 201–11, originally in 'Q and "The Friend at Midnight"', *JTS* 34 [1983] 407–24), see the critique in my 'Q, Prayer and the Kingdom'. Catchpole himself has responded to me in his 'Rejoinder', the material of which is now included in his unified discussion of this material in ch. 7 of his *Quest*. (As with most of Catchpole's work, I refer to the page numbering in his *Quest* in nearly all instances.) The issue is important as it affects the whole question of what is in mind in the 'answer to prayer' section in 11:9–13. Despite Catchpole's rejoinder, I still remain unconvinced that a strong enough case has been made for including the parable of the friend at midnight in Q. If one does not, then one may be justified in taking the literary unit in Q as Q 11:2–4 + 9–13.

on the meaning of ἐπιούσιος).[44] However, this petition scarcely dominates the Lord's Prayer as it now stands. What seems to be more dominant is the relation implied between the petitioner and God as one of son/daughter to Father, and the opening petitions which pray for the coming of the kingdom and the hallowing of God's name.[45] If then 11:9–13 followed immediately after the Lord's Prayer in Q (see n. 43 above), and since this section is concerned with answer to prayer, the likelihood is that it is seen (by Q) as relating primarily to what has dominated the prayer just given, in this case the prayer for the kingdom.[46]

Q 11:9 exhorts the readers to pray, and the following verse (Q 11:10) states very strongly the assurance that prayer will be answered.[47] What then is it that will be given in answer to prayer? One reply is given in Q 11:13. It is almost universally agreed that

[44] See the discussion in Catchpole, *Quest*, 223f. and all the commentaries. Catchpole argues strongly that the petition refers to ordinary, everyday food, not to eschatological nourishment.

[45] The 'Cynic' interpretation of the reference to the 'kingdom' in the Lord's Prayer relates it almost exclusively to the petition for bread, so that the coming of the kingdom means precisely the supply of bread. Cf. Vaage, 'Q and Cynicism', 222: 'the kingdom of God is here a matter of bodily sustenance' (also *Galilean Upstarts*, 59). But there is more in the prayer than just these two petitions! And the other references to the hallowing of God's name (cf. too the reference to forgiving debts/sins, and the well-known parallels with the Jewish Kaddish prayer) suggest that we are perhaps closer to ideas associated with Jewish eschatology than Cynic ideas. This interpretation of the reference to the kingdom is also somewhat difficult alongside the verse in Q 12:31 which seems to *contrast* concern for daily needs of food etc. with 'seeking' the kingdom.

[46] Cf. G. Schneider, 'Das Vaterunser des Matthäus', in *A Cause de l'Evangile* (FS J. Dupont; Paris: Cerf, 1985) 57–90, p. 73, in relation to the context of the prayer in Q, refers to the 'geradezu rahmenden Funktion der Forderung, vorrangig um die *basileia* zu bitten bzw. diese zu suchen (Lk 11,2; 12,31 par Mt)'. The *inclusio* in the wider section (of Q 11:2–4 + 9–13 with Q 12:22–31) in referring to God as 'Father' (Q 11:2 and 12:31) is also striking. Catchpole interprets the section as explicating only the bread petition, interpreted non-eschatologically as a petition for daily needs.

[47] Catchpole, 'Friend at Midnight', 417, argues that the verse is a secondary addition in Q, being simply a rather redundant repetition of the previous verse. But if so, it must be all the more important for Q (and seems to be recognised as such in Catchpole's rewriting of this section of his article in his *Quest*, 220). Guelich, *Sermon*, 357f., may be justified in seeing a distinction between the command to ask (Q 11:9) and the promise that the request will be answered (Q 11:10). Cf. too Luz, *Matthew 1–7*, 421 (commenting on Matt 7:8): 'In comparison with v. 7 [in Matthew's verse numbering], the accent has shifted; it now lies each time on the second verb.'

Luke's 'Holy Spirit' here is secondary to Matthew's ἀγαθά.[48] What though are the 'good things'? Are they the basic necessities of life, or are they eschatological blessings?[49] The vocabulary is ambiguous and open to a variety of interpretations. Nor is the immediate context of direct help. The argument is of an *a minori ad maius* form, but the precise comparison is not stated: since God the Father is so much greater than any human father, He will ... what? Will He give exactly what a human father would give but with even greater security? Or will He give something far greater than any human father can give?

The sayings here about answer to prayer have always been felt to be difficult in view of their enormous scope. Without a specific context, the sayings become almost embarrassingly absurd in their unconditional promise that prayers will be answered.[50] However, the Q context of the section, whereby the sayings follow immediately after the Lord's Prayer, may provide a rather more precise context for the interpretation of the sayings.[51] Here the dominant (if not exclusive) theme is eschatology and the kingdom of God. The Q Christians pray to God as their Father to bring in the kingdom, and they are given an assurance that their prayer will be answered: if they ask, they will receive; if they seek, that is the kingdom of God, they will find;[52] if they knock, the door will be

---

[48] Schulz, *Q*, 242; Catchpole, *Quest*, 212, and many others. Luke's well-known interest in the Holy Spirit is surely sufficient to account for the difference here.

[49] For the first, see Catchpole, *Quest*, 212; Piper, *Wisdom*, 20; Kloppenborg, *Formation*, 205. For the second, cf. Jeremias, *Parables*, 145; Guelich, *Sermon*, 359, 378f. (though arguing for an inclusive reference); Luz, *Matthew 1–7*, 423 is similar: 'any limitation of the promise would contradict the scope of the text'.

[50] Catchpole, *Quest*, 221; Piper, *Wisdom*, 16.

[51] Catchpole, *Quest*, 221, considers as possible contexts Luke 11:9–13 (which he rejects partly because v. 9 does not fit with vv. 11–13, the Cares tradition (which he rejects partly because the latter is self-contained, partly because the ζητεῖν of Q 12:31 involves more than prayer, partly because there is nothing in the Cares tradition corresponding to the 'knocking' here) and hence Luke 11:5–8 as the only possible alternative. But Luke 11:2–4 is a much more likely alternative as the immediate Q precursor if vv. 5–8 did not belong to Q. Cf. too Jacobson, *First Gospel*, 153, for the connection between Luke 11:2–4 and 11:9–13 in Q. The lack of precise correspondence between some parts of the two units of tradition may simply show that each may have had an independent existence prior to Q: but we are here primarily interested in how the Q editor, in placing these traditions together, interpreted the end product.

[52] For the kingdom of God as the object of ζητεῖν in Q, see Q 12:31. The importance of the theme of reassurance that prayer for the kingdom will be answered may also be shown by the parables of the mustard seed and the leaven

opened (and Q language elsewhere makes it clear that such vocabulary can be understood eschatologically: cf. Q 13:25).[53] On this interpretation the context for Q 11:9 is, for Q, eschatological, and the 'good things' which the Father will give to those who ask Him are the gifts of the Eschaton. Further, this concern for the kingdom is one which overrides concern for material needs. The overriding concern, which must dominate the Christians' lives, is the kingdom of God.

The pattern emerging from the analysis of these sections in Q confirms that already established from other Q sections of the importance of eschatology for Q. The Q Christians are exhorted to work and strive for the establishment of the kingdom of God. Further, although nothing is explicitly stated in the passages on Cares and Prayer about the imminence of the kingdom, the urgency of the appeals only really makes sense if the arrival of the kingdom is thought of as a possibility in the *near* future. To exhort people effectively to forget their worries about the material necessities of life in favour of concern for the coming kingdom would be at best somewhat precious if that coming was thought of as in an indeterminate future with some considerable time still to elapse. However, the most telling evidence for a belief in *Naherwartung* in Q comes in the eschatological sections themselves in Q, in the parables of Q 12:39–46 and the 'little apocalypse' of Q 17:23–37. To these we now turn.

3. The Eschatological Sections (Q 12:39–59 + 17:23–37)

3.1. Q 12:39ff.

The Q parables of the thief and the waiting servants provide the most important evidence for the theories of those who claim that Q is heavily influenced by a delay in the Parousia.[54] However, as

---

which both have the message that, despite the ambiguity of the present, the kingdom *will* come in its fullness and glory.

[53] For this as part of Q, see pp. 188–95 below. Catchpole, *Quest*, 220, objects that this verse itself makes it clear that Q 11:9f. cannot be taken eschatologically, precisely because *not* all those who knock will have the door opened for them. But on any showing, the promises of 11:9f. cannot be meant universally and without any kind of restriction, either in terms of personnel asking, etc. or in terms of what is requested. Cf. at n. 50 above. The promises apply to disciples of Jesus, those who can call God their Father etc. Luz's comment about the limitation which must apply to a passage such as Q 12:22–31 if the words are not to become absurd (see n. 42 above) is just as relevant here.

[54] See above at n. 6.

we have already noted, we must distinguish between a possible situation being addressed in the 'community' and the view being propounded within the text of Q itself. Thus in relation to the present problem, it is quite reasonable to conceive of a situation being addressed in which doubts about a 'Parousia' event are being expressed (whether because such an event has been expected sooner and has not materialised through 'delay', or because such an event is not expected at all) but these doubts are being countered by the Q-editor, re-affirming the belief in an imminent eschatological event.[55]

Such a viewpoint seems to be the major thrust of the two parables in Q 12:39–46. The parable of the thief (12:39f.) may be composite. The parable itself (12:39) has to do with the pre-vention of a theft through foresight and watchfulness. But the application in 12:40 'implies that the coming of the Son of Man cannot be foreseen nor its catastrophic results prevented'.[56] The application in Q thus implies that the coming of the SM will be sudden and unexpected. Further, the warning implied would be faintly ridiculous if the coming were not thought of as, at least possibly, imminent. A warning of a sudden, unexpected event in the far distant future would have no force at all. The urgency of the parable thus derives from a belief in an imminent event. Further, the situation addressed seems to be one 'in which a coming is not expected, rather than being merely postponed'.[57] The parable thus aims to *arouse* a belief in an imminent 'coming'. It *may* reflect a situation where that coming has been thought by some to be 'delayed' and where belief in such a coming has waned or almost disappeared. It *may* also reflect a situation where such belief has never existed at all. But in either case, the aim of the parable and its application in Q is to *urge* such a belief on the listeners.

Exactly the same seems to be implied in the parable of the faithful and unfaithful servants in 12:42–46. A situation of delay is often deduced from the words of the unfaithful servant in the story who says χρονίζει ὁ κύριός μου ἔρχεσθαι (Q 12:45). Once again there is uncertainty whether this refers to a belief in a genuine 'delay' (the coming will come, but much later than expected) or to a belief that the delay is effectively

---

[55] Cf. Hoffmann, *Studien*, to whom this section is much indebted.
[56] Kloppenborg, *Formation*, 149.
[57] Catchpole, *Quest*, 217.

indefinite and all hope for a coming has vanished,[58] or to a belief that no coming was ever envisaged at all. But either way the thrust of the parable itself is clear: the fact of the 'coming' is emphatically asserted; moreover, it will be at an unknown and unexpected hour, and the consequences will be potentially disastrous for those who are not prepared (cf. v. 46). The parable thus serves to emphasise the potentially imminent coming of the SM and to counter the beliefs of those who have cast doubts on such a possibility.[59] In the face of possibly differing views, Q emphatically asserts a belief in the coming of the SM which may occur at any time. John the Baptist's prediction is thus affirmed.

The same is implied in the Q material which follows in Luke 12 (and which, if the Lukan order can be taken as a reliable indicator of the Q order, may well have followed immediately in Q).[60] Many have argued that Luke 12:49 may have been part of Q omitted by Matthew. The case has been propounded in greatest detail recently by März:[61] Luke 12:50 appears to be a Lukan rewriting of Mark 10:38 but there may well be a seam between v. 49 and v. 50 since v. 49 looks forward to the future judgement whereas v. 50 looks forward to Jesus' death. Thus v. 49 may be pre-Lukan, a hypothesis also confirmed by some vocabulary and stylistic considerations.[62] Further, the very similar use of ἦλθον βαλεῖν in Matt 10:34, Matthew's parallel to the Q saying in Luke 12:51, may be a reminiscence of the phrase in Luke 12:49 in Matthew's source.[63] Hence Luke 12:49 may have belonged to Q. Certainty is not possible, but if this verse did belong to Q it would tie in well with John's prediction in 3:16: the 'fire' predicted by John is now seen to be administered by Jesus, and Jesus, as John's

---

[58] Cf. Catchpole, *Quest*, 215f.

[59] Hoffmann, *Studien*, 47f.

[60] For the Lukan order as indeed reflecting the order in Q, see C. P. März, 'Zur Q-Rezeption in Lk 12,35 – 13,35 (14,1–24)', in Focant (ed.), *Synoptic Gospels*, 177–208.

[61] C. P. März, '"Feuer auf die Erde zu werfen, bin ich gekommen . . ." Zum Verständnis und zur Entstehung von Lk 12,49', in *A Cause de l'Evangile* (FS J. Dupont; Paris: Cerf, 1985) 479–511, pp. 480–5; cf. too Kloppenborg, *Formation*, 152, with further literature.

[62] J. Jeremias, *Die Sprache des Lukasevangeliums* (Göttingen: Vandenhoeck & Ruprecht, 1980) 223, referring to the asyndeton, the use of πῦρ βάλλω, ἦλθον + infinitive with Jesus as the subject, θέλω εἰ.

[63] H. Schürmann, 'Protolukanische Spracheigentümlichkeiten?' in *Traditionsgeschichtliche Untersuchungen zu den synoptischen Evangelien* (Düsseldorf: Patmos, 1968) 209–27, p. 213.

'coming one', looks forward here to fulfilment of John's prophecy.[64]

Similar themes are developed in the sayings which follow in Luke 12 (and probably in Q). 12:51–53 evokes the image of the breakdown of social order as part of the End-time events, using in part OT language and imagery.[65] The implicit claim is that the events of the End-time have already started (cf. above on 7:27) and hence the final consummation is not far off. Similar is Q 12:54–56, the saying about the signs of the times and the predictability of the weather from the sight of the clouds (if this was part of Q).[66] The saying points to the present as apparently capable of indicating, for those who have eyes to see, the signs of the End. Once again there is a dual perspective: the significance of the present is highlighted but precisely insofar as it is the prelude to something which is going to happen in the future, and soon. Finally, the saying about the importance of reconciliation before it is too late (12:57–59) again stresses the importance of the present in view of the imminent nature of a future which will overtake those who are unprepared all too quickly.

The main thrust of the whole section is clear. As Kloppenborg says, 'in spite of the apparent acknowledgement of the delay of the parousia, Q repeatedly implies that there is little time left, since the signs of the end are already in evidence'.[67] Whatever delay there may have been, and however much disappointment there is in the hopes of those being addressed by Q, Q itself is emphatic in asserting the imminent coming of the SM as part of the final eschatological events.

The same imminent expectation, which is reflected in the material in Q 12, also reappears in the apocalyptic section in Q 17:23f., 26–30, to which we now turn.

[64] März, 'Feuer', 490f. Note too that if the above analysis is correct, it may give further support to the argument given earlier that the future baptism of 'Spirit and fire' predicted by Q's John refers to two baptisms (see p. 122 above). Q's Jesus here refers to a coming 'fire' alone in a context of warning. The threat of the future is thus a destructive fire — and the more positive counterpart (the possible Spirit baptism) is not mentioned in this context where the dominant note is one of warning.

[65] Cf. Mic 7:6, developed further in texts such as *1 En* 100:1f.; *Jub* 23:19; *4 Ezra* 6:24. See Hoffmann, *Studien*, 72.

[66] So März, 'Feuer', 486f.; also his 'Lk 12,54b–56 par Mt 16,2b.3 und die Akoluthie der Redequelle', *SNTU* 11 (1986) 83–96. Kloppenborg, *Formation*, 152. The problem is of course complicated by the doubt about whether the Matthean version (Matt 16:2–3) is part of the genuine text of Matthew (the verses are omitted by several important manuscripts).

[67] Kloppenborg, *Formation*, 153.

3.2. Q 17:23ff.

The existence of vv. 23f. in Q has occasionally been questioned,[68] though the presence of a doublet in Matthew (Matt 24:23/Mark 13:21, Matt 24:26/Luke 17:23) seems to ensure the presence of the saying in Q.[69] Luke 17:26f., referring to the example of Noah, is unquestionably Q (cf. Matt 24:37–39). The reference to Lot, which accompanies the Noah example in Luke alone (Luke 17:28f.) is also arguably part of Q:[70] Lührmann has shown how the two stories of the flood and the destruction of Sodom were frequently coupled as examples of divine judgement.[71] Given the fact that Luke's own interests seem to focus on the paranetic teaching about not being attached to possessions (vv. 31ff.), the Lot reference (from which Luke himself picks up not Lot but Lot's wife: cf. v. 32) is probably pre-Lukan. Given too Q's allusions already to 'fire' (Q 3:16 and the note about the judgement of Sodom in 10:12; possibly too Luke 12:49 if this were in Q: cf. above) it is easiest to ascribe the verses to Q, rather than to a post-Q pre-Lukan expanded Q^{lk}. Matthew may then have omitted the reference as adding nothing substantively to the reference to Noah.[72]

The main thrust of both sayings in Q is similar: the SM will come without warning suddenly in the midst of everyday activity. It is true that there may be a slight shift of emphasis from vv. 23f. to vv. 26–30, from geographical to temporal concerns,[73] from an assertion of the universal visibility of the events concerned to one of suddenness. However, even if such a shift has occurred, it is still the case that the saying in vv. 23f. (and probably v. 37, the vultures saying, which probably belonged in Q at this point)[74] cohere reasonably well with vv. 26–30. It may be then that vv. 23f. + 37 represent an earlier tradition, taken up by the Q editor and

---

[68] For example, Lührmann, *Redaktion*, 72, regards the verse in Luke as dependent on Mark.

[69] See Laufen, *Doppelüberlieferungen*, 361 and n. 43 with very full bibliography; Schulz, *Q*, 278f.; Kloppenborg, *Formation*, 155.

[70] See my *Revival*, 169; Catchpole, *Quest*, 248; Kloppenborg, *Formation*, 157f.

[71] Lührmann, *Redaktion*, 75–83.

[72] So Kloppenborg, *Formation*, 158.

[73] Catchpole, *Quest*, 254; Piper, *Wisdom*, 141. I would then slightly modify my earlier view which argued that vv. 23f. were also originally to do with suddenness (see my *Revival*, 172).

[74] Catchpole, *Quest*, 252; Kloppenborg, *Formation*, 156; Piper, *Wisdom*, 139f.

pressed into the service of a theme slightly different from the original intention. But this new scheme is to assert emphatically the sudden coming of the SM. And once again, that coming must be conceived of as potentially imminent if the warning is to be a warning at all.

4. Conclusions

Two final points remain to be noted and discussed briefly. The first concerns the place of such eschatological expectation within any possible stratification of Q. We saw in ch. 2 that several scholars have argued that the 'formative' layer in Q, a 'Q¹', was more sapiential, whilst the eschatological and/or prophetic elements only come in the later 'Q²'. So too some have argued, as we have seen, that the formative 'Q¹' is primarily Cynic and not influenced by Jewish eschatology. In relation to the latter point I have tried to argue that the Cynic interpretation at key points is not persuasive. Further, the analysis above has tried to show that the eschatology in Q goes far wider and deeper than just the so-called 'Q²' material. It is of course present in sections such as Q 12:39–46; 17:23–37 which are classic parts of 'Q²' for those who would divide Q in this way.[75] But I have also tried to argue that a futurist eschatology also underlies many other parts of Q, including several passages often assigned to a formative 'Q¹' layer. Thus, for example, the Great Sermon starts and finishes with eschatological promises and warnings respectively. The mission charge (*if* this is indeed 'Q¹')[76] has the 'missionaries' tell their audience that the kingdom has drawn near. And even the apparently more sapiential teaching on cares and prayer, with the appeal to the regularity and order of the created world, turns out

---

[75] Though one must note the danger of circularity here: 'Q²' is taken as encompassing the eschatological parts of Q; hence, almost by definition, parts which are not explicitly eschatological are assigned to the non-eschatological layer Q¹.

[76] Jacobson, 'The Literary Unity of Q. Lc 10,2–16 and Parallels as a Test Case', in Delobel (ed.), *LOGIA*, 419–23, argues that the mission charge as a whole is thoroughly congruent with the deuteronomistic-type polemic evidenced elsewhere in what is usually taken as 'Q²'. However, in his *First Gospel*, 137–49, he appears to have modified his views slightly, arguing that the deuteronomistic perspective comes out primarily in vv. 2, 13–15, which are therefore taken as a later addition to an earlier mission charge.

to be eschatologically determined.[77] Thus, an eschatological outlook pervades large parts of the Q material and one cannot easily ascribe such an outlook to just one stratum within Q (even supposing that such a stratification were both desirable and possible!).

Secondly, I consider very briefly the problem raised by Kloppenborg and Jacobson in two recent articles concerning the appropriateness or otherwise of ascribing the word 'apocalyptic' to Q.[78] So far in this chapter I have sought to avoid the word 'apocalyptic', and have used instead the word 'eschatological'. Both words are of course intensely problematic. I have used 'eschatological' in a rather loose sense of referring to future hopes connected with beliefs about God's future activity conceived within a Jewish ('eschatological') matrix of ideas.

Kloppenborg and Jacobson have focused on what they have called 'apocalyptic' and have claimed that, although Q contains apocalyptic motifs (e.g. references to the 'SM' coming, a future judgement, etc.), Q lacks many other features, and many of the presuppositions, usually associated with 'apocalyptic'; hence they would question how far it is appropriate to ascribe the word 'apocalyptic' to Q. Kloppenborg does agree that 'eschatology' is fundamental to Q's ethical teaching,[79] but questions whether this is really 'apocalyptic'. He sees as essential characteristics of apocalyptic (i) a spatial and a temporal dualism, (ii) a belief that the cosmos is in a state of disorder or anomie, (iii) a forfeiting of all inherited structures with appeals to a new creation, a new earth, etc., (iv) historical determinism, (v) exhortation and consolation as its social function.[80] There is, for example, in Q no apparent feeling of anomie: 'the wrong king is not on the throne and the cosmos is not in revolt or decay'.[81] Q still speaks of the world as carrying on as normal. Absent too from Q is the typically

---

[77] At one level one could argue that this is by virtue of the secondary additions in the cares tradition which bring in the reference to the kingdom in Q 12:31. However, I argued above that even Q's tradition here is probably implicitly just as eschatologically determined. The tradition used in the sequence about prayer includes the Lord's Prayer, which is probably equally eschatologically oriented.

[78] See n. 2 above.

[79] 'Symbolic Eschatology', 292.

[80] 'Symbolic Eschatology', 294f.

[81] 'Symbolic Eschatology', 297, referring to J. Z. Smith, 'A Pearl of Great Price and a Cargo of Yams: A Study in Situational Incongruity', *HR* 16 (1976) 1–19, p. 8.

apocalyptic idea of a timetable of events leading up to the End (cf. Mark 13).[82] So too Q is unusual in painting such a negative picture of the End: there is little on the blessings of the End and much more on the potential disasters which await the impenitent and the unaware.[83] Thus Kloppenborg argues that the primary purpose of the apocalyptic language in Q may be that of 'boundary definition' for the community,[84] and rather than talk of Q as 'apocalyptic' we should perhaps speak of 'symbolic eschatology' in Q. Jacobson too makes many of the same points as Kloppenborg, pointing out too how many of the apocalyptic motifs appear unconnected with each other in Q (e.g. 'SM' and 'kingdom').

Much of what is said here is very appropriate and brings out well some of the salient features of Q. Whether this is appropriately called 'apocalyptic' or not is perhaps almost irrelevant. The word 'apocalyptic' is a modern invention: Q itself makes no claim to be purveying explicitly 'apocalyptic' ideas, still less to be writing an 'apocalypse'. Perhaps the 'definition' with which, for example, Kloppenborg works could be regarded as too narrow and restrictive.[85] We should for example remember that apocalyptic may have had a 'mystical' as well as a more 'historical' element;[86] we should not therefore be too hidebound by the 'timetables' of Mark 13, Revelation or Daniel. So too it is undeniable that Q does contain some elements usually called 'apocalyptic', such as a 'SM' figure coming in a context of judgement.

On the other hand not all of Kloppenborg's comments about Q's 'apocalyptic' language are entirely appropriate. There is a lot about a threatening judgement, set in a highly charged negative tone. But positive counterparts are not lacking: the poor and the suffering *will* be rewarded and recompensed (Q 6:20–23), those

---

[82] See too R. Horsley, 'Q and Jesus: Assumptions, Approaches and Analyses', *Semeia* 55 (1991) 175–209, p. 196: the cluster of sayings in Q 17:23ff. 'is almost anti-apocalyptic in pointedly rejecting any attention to signs and speculations'.

[83] 'Kloppenborg, 'Symbolic Eschatology', 299f.

[84] Ibid., 306.

[85] See R. Uro, 'Apocalyptic Symbolism and Social Identity in Q', *ANRW*, forthcoming. (I am grateful to the author for kindly making the typescript of this article available to me in advance.)

[86] J. J. Collins, *The Apocalyptic Imagination* (New York: Crossroads, 1984); also his 'Apocalyptic Literature', in R. A. Kraft & G. W. E. Nickelsburg (eds), *Early Judaism and Its Modern Interpreters* (Philadelphia: Fortress, 1986) 345–69.

who confess Jesus *will* be confessed by the SM (Q 12:8), and (if this is indeed part of Q) those with Jesus will act as judges over Israel (Q 22:28–30). Nevertheless, Kloppenborg's overall point may stand: Q's 'apocalyptic' language is at times unusual in relation to other contemporary uses of such language in being somewhat negative, and also being generated within a rather more world-affirming ethos than some other apocalyptic language. This in turn might, though, simply reflect the fact that the social alienation, so often thought to be a vital factor in the generation of apocalyptic language, was not quite so deep or intense as the Q Christians themselves appeared to maintain. That question we shall consider in a later chapter.

In conclusion we may say that large parts of Q are dominated by ideas of a futurist eschatology. On an audience which may be doubting the validity of such expectations — whether because an earlier hope has faded, or because no such hope had ever been entertained — the Q editor impresses the importance of the future eschatological events which will probably come sooner rather than later.

6

⇒●◄

Wisdom, Prophets and 'This Generation'

The theme of an imminent eschatology dominates (much of) Q, as we have seen. Yet such a message of an imminent future catastrophe is not issued from the calm of a study. It is put forward both in response to an existing situation and as part of a plea for people to change in order perhaps to avoid the disastrous consequences of what is about to happen. As with all eschatological/apocalyptic language, predictions of future events function quite as much to exhort people to act differently now as to state what is going to happen come what may. Indeed we have already seen a hint of this in Q 3:7-9: John the Baptist's preaching is intended to warn people of what is about to happen precisely in order that they may change their minds/behaviour: they are to produce 'fruit worthy of repentance' so that they will not be regarded as trees which bear no fruit and hence will not be cut down and thrown into the fire.

Within Q it is clear that, in very general terms, the 'behaviour' which Q's Jesus inveighs against can be regarded as in some sense a 'rejection' of the message being put forward. (In one sense this is, of course, virtually tautologous: Q is opposed to those who oppose its message. It is however striking how little Q ever really advances beyond this tautology in terms of ideas. It is sometimes hard to see just why Q's Jesus is so offensive to his contemporaries, and Q often appears simply to assume the offence which its message has produced and to reflect on that.) Further, it also seems clear that Q regards the rejection of its message as some kind of violent rejection. Precisely what form the rejection might have taken, and just what level of 'violence' may have been involved, will be considered in ch. 9 below. For the present we shall be concerned with Q's response to that situation as it is perceived in the Q tradition.

This response draws on a number of ideas and motifs, some of which surface together, some in isolation, in various Q passages.

These motifs include the phrase 'this generation' as the object of Q's preaching, the theme of the violent fate suffered by the prophets, and the theme of Wisdom as the sender of the prophets; in addition positive reference is often made to Gentiles in contrast with the audience addressed. So too in several of the passages concerned, Jesus is referred to as 'SM'. We therefore turn to the relevant passages.

1. Relevant Q Passages

1.1. Q 11:47–51

Several of these motifs come to the fore in the 'doom oracle' of 11:49–51. This oracle occurs towards the end of the series of woes against the Pharisees and/or scribes/lawyers in Q 11:39ff. The order of the woes in Q is very hard to establish with any certainty. Some would refuse any attempt to reconstruct Q's order,[1] and at least one scholar (H. Schürmann) has changed his mind on the subject.[2] For the present purposes, the issue concerns the place of what is in Luke the final woe Matt 23:13/Luke 11:52. Despite a number of defenders of the originality of the Lukan placing of the woe,[3] it would seem more likely that the position of the woe in Luke is due to LkR.[4] The anti-climactic nature of the woe after the powerful invective of 11:49–51, and the fact that the saying fits well into the present Lukan arrangement as a generalising conclusion to the series of woes, suggests that Luke's ordering may well be secondary here.[5] Thus the oracle in Q 11:49–51 may

---

[1] Lührmann, *Redaktion*, 45; Zeller, *Kommentar*, 65f.

[2] Cf. his different positions in his 'Zeugnis' article, 174, over against his view in his 'Die Redekomposition wider "dieses Geschlecht" und seine Führung in der Redenquelle (vgl. Mt 23,1–39 par Lk 11,37–54. Bestand–Akolouthie–Kompositionsformen', *SNTU* A/11 (1986) 33–81, p. 48, on the position of Q 11:52.

[3] Schulz, *Q*, 94f.; D. E. Garland, *The Intention of Matthew 23* (NovTSupp 52; Leiden: Brill, 1979) 17; Kloppenborg, *Formation*, 140; Schürmann, 'Zeugnis', 174.

[4] Lührmann, *Redaktion*, 45; Schürmann, 'Redekomposition', 48; Goulder, *Luke*, 524f.; Catchpole, *Quest*, 260.

[5] There is some dispute as to whether Matthew's position is appropriate (cf. Catchpole, *Quest*, 260: 'In Matthew's presentation it stands formally as the first of the sayings which use the actual word "woe" (Matt 23:13) and as a generalising statement of basic principle it is admirably suited to do so'), or not (cf.

well have formed the conclusion and, in literary terms, the climax of the series of woes preceding it in Q.

Although Matthew and Luke differ somewhat in their wording in Q 11:49–51, there is widespread agreement that Luke's version preserves the Q wording far better and Matthew's version, where it differs from Luke's, is secondary at almost every point.[6] In particular, the ascription of the saying to 'the Wisdom of God' is more easily seen as due to Luke's tradition than to LkR.[7] So too the phrase ἀπὸ τῆς γενεᾶς ταύτης in Luke's v. 50b, creating a very awkward series of three ἀπό phrases, as well as the difficulty of reconciling a statement made apparently by pre-mundane Wisdom addressing 'this generation',[8] is more easily seen as stemming from Q than from LkR. Other details in the oracle will not be considered here.

There is also widespread agreement that the oracle itself in vv. 49–51 should probably be seen as an integral part of the preceding woe in v. 47f. The whole unit in vv. 47–51 has the form of a woe oracle as evidenced in the OT with a reproach introduced by διὰ τοῦτο (or τάδε) λέγει κύριος.[9] There is thus probably no citation formula here, referring to some lost,

---

Kloppenborg, *Formation*, 140: 'Matthew's setting is the more contrived, and in all probablility, secondary'). Jacobson, *First Gospel*, 175f., seems to despair of fitting the woe into the Q sequence at all, calling it a 'floating saying' and not including it in his reconstructed Q sequence.

[6] For the details, see O. H. Steck, *Israel und das gewaltsame Geschick der Propheten* (WMANT 23; Neukirchen-Vluyn: Neukirchener, 1967) 31f.; Schulz, *Q*, 337f.; also my *Revival*, 158–61.

[7] *Pace* Goulder: see p. 25 above. Luke nowhere else introduces a reference to divine Wisdom as a quasi-personified being. Matthew's replacement of Wisdom by Jesus as the speaker is part of a consistent Matthean attempt to identify Jesus with the figure of Wisdom: see M. J. Suggs, *Wisdom, Christology and Law in Matthew's Gospel* (Cambridge: Harvard University Press, 1970); J. D. G. Dunn, *Christology in the Making* (London: SCM, 1980) 201f.

[8] Hence Steck's rather desperate argument that the phrase is a post-Lukan gloss in the textual tradition (*Gechick*, 32): on this see n. 20 below.

[9] Cf. Isa 5:11ff.; Jer 23:1f.; Ezek 34:1ff.; Mic 2:1ff. See Steck, *Geschick*, 51f.; Lührmann, *Redaktion*, 46; Kloppenborg, *Formation*, 143f.; cf. too Schürmann, 'Redekomposition', 55; Jacobson, *First Gospel*, 178; Sato, *Q und Prophetie*, 152. There is however more debate about whether this connection is original, or due to a secondary expansion (in vv. 49–51) of a more original woe (in vv. 47f.). Kloppenborg, for example, has argued that the connection is secondary on the grounds that the addressees change (from scribes/Pharisees to 'this generation'); it is unusual to find a saying of Wisdom in a speech of Jesus; and the saying is not a reproach but a threat of retribution: hence the construction

apocryphal Wisdom book as has sometimes been supposed.[10] However, as many have observed, the oracle does not fit the OT pattern exactly, above all in the fact that the speaker is not Yahweh but 'the Wisdom of God'.[11]

The content of the reproach in v. 49 is unusual in more than just this respect. Alongside the mention of Wisdom is the reference to the prophets (and others)[12] who have suffered death and persecution. This motif of the violence suffered by the prophets has been exhaustively analysed in the monograph of O. H. Steck, who has convincingly shown how this motif developed within Judaism.[13] Although there were some indications in the stories of the classical prophets that they had suffered violence and persecution (e.g. Jeremiah), this idea became a standard motif within what Steck calls a deuteronomistic sketch of history. The earliest example of this motif is to be found in Neh 9:26 (cf. also 1 Ki 18:4, 13; 19:10, 14; 2 Chr 36:14–16; Jer 2:30). Originally the idea was developed as part of a broader explanation for the disasters which befell Israel in 722 BCE and 587 BCE. In this view of history, four stages may be seen:

(A) The whole of the pre-exilic period of Israel is regarded as one of constant disobedience.

(B) In his mercy, Yahweh continually sent prophets to the people, urging them to repent.

(C) However, Israel remained stubborn and rejected the prophets, sometimes killing them.

---

of the form is due to Q's redaction (*Formation*, 143). However Catchpole, *Quest*, 273, has pointed out that this makes it difficult to plead (as Kloppenborg does) for strata within vv. 49–51 themselves. In any case the addressees have not necessarily changed (vv. 47f. are not directed to scribes or Pharisees in Luke's version, and anyway it is not clear how broad the referent of 'this generation' is: see below); further, it is also not clear if the polemic in vv. 49–51 is any more negative than elsewhere. In the light of the clear form-critical parallels in prophetic woe oracles and the evidence of different strata within vv. 49–51, it seems better to treat these verses as connected with vv. 47f. prior to Q's redaction, with some elements then redactionally expanded subsequently (cf. below).

[10] Cf. Bultmann, *History*, 114.

[11] Sato, *Q und Prophetie*, 152.

[12] Whether Q mentioned 'apostles' (Luke) or 'wise men and scribes' (Matthew) is uncertain. (In my *Revival*, I argued that Luke's version may preserve Q.) However, the issue does not affect the discussion here.

[13] Steck, *Geschick*, *passim*.

(D) Thus Yahweh punished (in the destructions of 722 and 587), or will punish, Israel.[14]

In the post-exilic period, when the events of 587 were no longer regarded as Yahweh's final definitive judgement on Israel, the scheme was expanded further with:

(E) further calls for repentance, with the promise of

(F1) restoration for Israel if she repents, and

(F2) judgement for Israel's enemies.[15]

The theme of the violence suffered by the prophets is thus part of a broader schema expressing Israel's continual disobedience to God's will and appealing to the nation to change its ways. It is clear that the saying in Q 11:49–51 takes up this motif, applying it in part to the present experience of Q Christians. The rejection which the Q Christians are experiencing is being placed within the broader context of the rejection experienced by all God's prophets; yet, as in the past, the result will be divine punishment for Israel who rejects the prophetic messengers sent to her.

However, we have already seen that 11:49 contains another motif which is related, but not identical: the one who sends the prophets is not God himself but Wisdom. Probably underlying this is an idea of Wisdom as an almost personified being who seeks to find a home in Israel but is rejected. Several texts in Jewish literature (notably Prov 1, 8; Sir 24; Job 28; *1 En* 42) appear to speak of σοφία not just as an attribute of God (God is wise, therefore God has wisdom) but almost as a being in her own right.[16] The precise force of the language used has been much debated and it is unclear whether Jews who spoke or wrote in this way ever really thought that σοφία was a being having ontological existence alongside God. Nevertheless, language which was at least open to such interpretation was sometimes used (and, notoriously, was heavily exploited in early Christianity where the texts concerned were applied to Jesus). The Jewish texts ascribe a number of functions to Wisdom, including the motif of Wisdom as God's companion in the creation of the world.[17] Now a

---

[14] See the basic outline in Steck, *Geschick*, 63f. The letters A–D are used consistently by Steck to refer to these items in his schema and are often used by later writers dependent on Steck.

[15] Cf. Steck, *Geschick*, 184–9, for a summary.

[16] See the general survey in Dunn, *Christology*, 168ff.

[17] For the variety in Jewish ideas about Wisdom, cf. Piper, *Wisdom*, 162f., and the literature cited there.

significant strand of this tradition speaks of Wisdom calling
people to obedience but meeting refusal and rejection (cf. Prov
1:20ff.). In Sir 24, Wisdom is portrayed as seeking to find a home
in Israel (and indeed finding a home: the identification is made
between Wisdom and Torah); in *1 En* 42, Wisdom also seeks a
home but finds none, and so withdraws. There seems then to have
been a strand in Jewish thought which could talk of Wisdom
appealing to men and women to follow the ways of Yahweh, but
experiencing only rejection and rebuttal.

The two themes we have considered, that of rejected Wisdom
and that of the prophets suffering violence, are evidently closely
related in terms of substance: both concern the idea of Yahweh,
directly or indirectly, appealing to His people to change their
ways and the people refusing to obey. What appears to have
happened in the Q saying Q 11:49 is that these two streams of
tradition have been amalgamated in a highly distinctive way so
that Wisdom herself becomes the agent who sends out the
prophets, all of whom suffer rejection and persecution (if not
death).[18] Q thus seems to have introduced a new combination of
traditions in interpreting the rejection of its own messengers
as in a line of continuity with the rejected prophets of the
deuteronomistic tradition and with the figure of rejected
Wisdom.

The other feature of the oracle to be noted here is the
reference to 'this generation' as the object of the polemic and as
the party which will be required to answer for all the prophetic
blood which has been shed.[19] What exactly the phrase 'this
generation' means will be discussed later. The evident importance of this idea for Q is shown by its repetition in v. 51b with the

---

[18] This is not to deny that the theme ɔɪ the rejected prophets, or prophecy,
had already been joined in a loose way with (general) 'wisdom traditions' prior
to Q: cf. texts such as Wisd 7:27 which speaks of Wisdom 'passing into holy
souls and making them friends of God and prophets'. Nevertheless, there
seems to have been no precedent in pre-Christian Judaism for this peculiar
idea whereby the prophets who suffer violence are directly sent by
(personified) Wisdom. See Steck, *Geschick*, 107, 224f.; Schulz, *Q*, 340; and my
Revival, 164. Uro, *Sheep*, 183, says that Wisd 7:27 'is a kindred but not exactly
the same idea'.

[19] The arguments of Steck, *Geschick*, 32 n. 1, that ἀπὸ τῆς γενεᾶς ταύτης in v.
50 is a post-Lukan gloss has found no support (cf. Lührmann, *Redaktion*, 47;
Hoffmann, *Studien*, 167; Kloppenborg, *Formation*, 145). As Hoffmann says, the
verse demands some object for whom the 'blood' will be 'required'; and
Matthew's ἐφ᾽ ὑμᾶς implies that some such object was already in Q.

ναὶ λέγω ὑμῖν phrase, and the repetition suggests that this may be a Q-redactional addition. At the very least, the repeated reference to the responsibility of this generation shows how important this was regarded by the Q editor. Moreover, the introductory ναὶ λέγω ὑμῖν in v. 51b also serves to make the final comment a saying of Jesus himself rather than of Wisdom, and so may indicate its secondary origin in relation to the rest of the saying. Verse 51a is also somewhat repetitive, with its ἀπὸ αἵματος Ἅβελ ... phrase which adds little to the earlier ἀπὸ καταβολῆς κόσμου phrase of v. 50. Thus many have argued that v. 51 as a whole is a secondary, Q-redactional addition to an earlier tradition.[20]

Kloppenborg, whilst agreeing that v. 51b is Q-redactional, disputes whether 51a is to be ascribed to the same redactional stratum as 51b. His reason is that the mention of Zachariah as the *terminus ad quem* of the prophetic deaths 'would seem strange for the redactor of Q who sees the persecution and killing of the prophets as extending into his own day (Q 6:23; 13:34–35). If v. 51a were due to Q-redaction ... one might expect the *terminus ad quem* to be John the Baptist (cf. Q 16:16).'[21] However, as we shall see, the evidence for actual deaths in the experience of the Q community is rather thin; Kloppenborg's argument is in danger of becoming circular on this point, and we shall consider it again when we discuss the nature of the 'persecution' faced by the Q community (see ch. 9 below). The fact that John the Baptist's death is not mentioned may be due to a similar reason that Jesus' death is not mentioned. However much the Q Christians may have believed that Jesus' words could be used, re-used and adapted in the post-Easter situation, the genre of presenting the message in the form of the preaching of Jesus himself does exert some constraint: one can hardly have a pre-Easter Jesus referring to his own death in the past! Given that Q

---

[20] Lührmann, *Redaktion*, 47; Hoffmann, *Studien*, 168; Neirynck, 'Recent Developments', 66; Schenk, *Synopse*, 79.

[21] Kloppenborg, *Formation*, 146. It is universally agreed that, whatever the problems of the reference to Zachariah as 'son of Barachiah' in Matthew's text, (*a*) Q mentioned Zachariah *simpliciter*, and (*b*) the reference is to the prophet whose death is recorded in 2 Chr 24. See the full discussion in Steck, 33–40, cf. also Hoffmann, *Studien*, 165; Schulz, *Q*, 344. The identity of the figure in Matthew is disputed: see Garland, *Matthew 23*, 182f., for a strong argument in favour of the theory that the same Zachariah is in mind in Matthew as well (contra Steck, *Geschick*, 39f., who argues that the person referred to is the Zachariah whose murder took place just before the fall of Jerusalem: cf. Josephus, *War*, 4.334f.).

does not separate Jesus and John chronologically in the same way as Mark and Luke (variously) do (as we have seen Jesus and John work in parallel in Q), it may be that the Q editor felt that the pre-Easter Jesus cannot yet refer to the death of John.

A Q-redactional origin for v. 51a seems likely (though not absolutely certain); the redactional origin of v. 51b seems more probable. Further, in literary terms, it seems quite plausible to see the final element of the woe as the Q editor's comment: as the final element it provides the literary climax of the saying, and its repetitive nature indicates which part of the previous tradition is being emphasised for the listeners/readers. Further, the fact that the words are now explicitly attributed to Jesus himself (cf. the ναὶ λέγω ὑμῖν) gives the saying added authority. Here it is clear that the stress is placed firmly on the threat of judgement against 'this generation'.[22] Moreover, it may be that this climaxing nature of v. 51b serves to focus (and in part mould) the interpretation of the whole series of woes in Q. Lührmann has argued strongly that the final woe (in vv. 47–51) is different from the preceding woes in that the addressees are no longer the scribes/lawyers and/or Pharisees: rather the polemic has broadened out to apply to all of 'this generation'. Certainly the woe in v. 47 is striking in not being addressed to Pharisees and/or scribes,[23] and if it is right to see vv. 49–51 as closely connected with vv. 47f., the same applies here too. Whether this involves a significant extension of the polemic, as Lührmann and many others following him have argued, is not certain. Lührmann argued strongly that 'this generation' is all Israel, and hence the polemic has broadened from attacking small groups within Israel (Pharisees, scribes) to an attack on Israel as a whole.[24] How much of an 'extension' is involved here must be considered when we look at the problem of the meaning of the phrase 'this generation' in Q. What we can say is that the language here is distinctive. If it is right to see vv. 49–51 as the last, and hence the literary climax, of the whole series of woes, then the position of the woe, its wording and its redactionally emphasised conclusion all point to the importance

[22] Kloppenborg, *Formation*, 147.

[23] It is generally assumed that Matthew's addressing of the woe to 'scribes and Pharisees, hypocrites' is MattR: cf. Schulz, *Q*, 105, and many others, though opinion differs on the 'original' (i.e. Q) addressees: e.g. Schulz claims it is 'Pharisees'; Garland, *Matthew 23*, 164, thinks 'scribes'; Kloppenborg, *Formation*, 144, seems to think of either. See Catchpole, *Quest*, 273.

[24] Lührmann, *Redaktion*, 47; Schürmann, 'Redekomposition', 73.

of the threat of judgement against 'this generation' for the Q editor.

Q 11:49–51 is thus characterised by a distinctive combination of the themes of rejected Wisdom and the violent fate suffered by the prophets, placed in a context of powerful polemic against 'this generation'. These themes occur in various forms in a number of other Q sayings, as we shall now try to show.

1.2. Q 13:34f.

One passage which is widely recognised as having very close affinities with the doom oracle of Q 11:49–51 is the lament over Jerusalem in Q 13:34f. The reconstruction of the Q wording is relatively straightforward since Matthew and Luke agree almost verbatim in Greek. Rather less certain is the original context of the saying in Q. In Matthew the saying follows immediately after the doom oracle (Matt 23:37–39 after Matt 23:34–36), whereas Luke places it rather earlier in his gospel (Luke 13:34f.). Many have argued that Matthew's positioning of the saying is more original. The Wisdom motifs in the saying (see below) and the common theme of the violence suffered by the prophets serve to unite the lament very closely in terms of substance with the doom oracle of Q 11:49–51, so that it would make very good sense if Q 13:34f. followed immediately in Q and hence was also presented as a saying of Wisdom.[25] Luke would then have moved the saying, partly perhaps because of its inappropriateness in his (redactional) context of a meal scene (Luke 11:37), partly because of a catchword link ('Jerusalem') with his (redactional) insertion of 13:31–33 with its interest in Jerusalem as the goal of Jesus' journey and the alleged place where prophets must die. However, others have pointed to the difficulties with the theory of associating the lament too closely with the doom oracle. The connection between the threat of Matt 23:39 and its apparent fulfilment in Matt 24:2 suggests that the connection between the two sayings may be due to MattR.[26] Further, in general terms, Luke is thought to have preserved the order of his sources more faithfully than

---

[25] Cf. Bultmann, *History*, 115; Lührmann, 45, 48; Suggs, *Wisdom*, 64–6; Robinson, 'LOGOI SOPHON', 104; S. Légasse, 'L'oracle contre "cette génération" (Mt 23,34–36 par. Lk 11,49–51) et la polémique judéo-chrétienne dans la Source des Logia', in Delobel (ed.), *LOGIA*, 236–56, pp. 238f.; Catchpole, *Quest*, 257f.

[26] Cf. Steck, *Geschick*, 48; Garland, *Matthew 23*, 26f.

Matthew. Above all, however, there is the problem of apparent dissimilarities, despite common features, between the lament and the doom oracle. Haenchen's comment is frequently referred to in this context: in the doom oracle Wisdom stands at the creation of the world looking forward; in the lament, the speaker looks back in time to the rejection of the prophets in the past.[27] Thus some would argue that the Lukan context should be taken as the original Q context, with Q 13:34f. being the continuation in Q of the Q material coming just before in Luke, viz. Q 13:24–30. Luke 13:31–33 would then be a LkR insertion into a Q sequence comprising 13:24–30 + 13:34f.[28]

It may be that the issue is unimportant in the long run. As we shall see, the lament may introduce a certain corrective to the harsh polemic of Q 11:49–51. But equally, Q 13:28f. presents at first sight an equally negative, polemical view (see below). Q 13:34f. may thus be providing some kind of qualification to such negative language; but whether it does so by being appended directly to Q 11:49–51, or to Q 13:28f. and hence (in terms of the literary structure of Q as a whole, if one is allowed to think in such terms) slightly less immediately in relation to Q 11:49–51, makes not a great deal of difference. But whatever the precise Q context, the thematic connections with the doom oracle are clear. Q 13:34f. makes the motif of the violent fate suffered by the prophets a central theme in the lament, and the deuteronomistic schema is plain: 'Jerusalem' has constantly rejected the prophetic messengers sent to her ('How often would I have gathered you ... but you would not'); as a result, divine punishment is threatened ('your house is left to you').

Further links with the doom oracle have been seen by many in the fact that, although the lament may not have followed immediately after Q 11:49–51 in Q, there are still significant Wisdom

[27] E. Haenchen, 'Matthäus 23', *ZTK* 48 (1951) 38–63, pp. 56f.; cf. Steck, *Geschick*, 47; Hare, *Jewish Persecution*, 94; D. Zeller, 'Entrückung zur Ankunft als Menschensohn (Lk 13,34f.; 11,29f.)', *A Cause de l'Evangile* (FS J. Dupont; Paris: Cerf, 1985) 513–530, p. 514; Jacobson, *First Gospel*, 209. Catchpole, *Quest*, 258, seeks to respond by pointing out that both the lament and the doom oracle contain prospective and retrospective elements. Nevertheless, it is difficult to see the *same* element as prospective and retrospective in what would effectively be a single saying if Q 13:34f followed Q 11:49–51. Hence I am inclined to modify my earlier view (cf. *Revival*, 162f.) and accept the separation of the two sayings in Luke as reflecting a separation of the sayings in Q.
[28] Cf. Garland, *Matthew 23*, 193f.; Uro, *Sheep*, 186f., 236; Kloppenborg, *Formation*, 228, treats it as such.

motifs in the saying, suggesting that Q may have regarded the lament as a Wisdom saying as well: the lament seems to presuppose a supra-historical figure as the speaker (cf. 'how often would I have gathered you') who is however probably not God (cf. the divine passive ἀφίεται in v. 35a). The image of the hen gathering its brood has a parallel in a saying about Wisdom in Sir 1:15 (Gk.). Further, the motif of the withdrawal of the speaker (v. 35a) has a parallel in the idea of Wisdom withdrawing (to heaven) when she cannot find a dwelling place on earth (*1 En* 42).[29]

More problematic is the status and meaning of the final λέγω δὲ ὑμῖν clause in v. 35b. Especially if vv. 34–35a is taken as a Wisdom saying, the idea of Wisdom returning is hard to parallel in Jewish thought. However, it may be that the λέγω δὲ ὑμῖν again indicates a change in speaker, whereby Jesus himself now takes over as the direct spokesman; the half-verse thus looks very much like a secondary addition to the original saying.[30] Even if no change of speaker is intended, the (then unnecessary) introductory formula seems to indicate a seam in the tradition and hence probably the existence of a secondary addition appended to an earlier saying. Either way, therefore, it seems appropriate to regard v. 35b as a secondary comment. It seems clear too that this conclusion to the lament, with its allusion to Ps 118:26, whatever may have been the original reference, refers now to Jesus as ὁ ἐρχόμενος, coming as SM, and picks up the previous references in Q to Jesus as ὁ ἐρχόμενος (cf. 3:16; 7:19).[31] Thus, as with 11:49–51, a saying receives a powerful redactional addendum in Q, looking forward to the future. In this case it is in terms of the coming of the SM, and elsewhere in Q such coming is clearly associated with judgement (cf. already Q 12:39ff.; 17:23ff.). In general terms Q 13:35b thus coheres with Q 11:51. Whether there are still some differences in outlook will be discussed below.

1.3. Q 7:31–35

Several of the motifs already discussed recur in the parable of the playing children (Q 7:31–35) which concludes the long section

[29] Haenchen, 'Matthäus 23', 57; Schulz, *Q*, 349; Piper, *Wisdom*, 164; and my *Revival*, 162.

[30] So many: cf. Hoffmann, *Studien*, 176f.; Neirynck, 'Recent Developments', 66, with further bibliography; Kloppenborg, *Formation*, 228; Catchpole, *Quest*, 273.

[31] Schulz, *Q*, 359; Hoffmann, *Studien*, 177; Zeller, 'Entrückung', 577; Uro, *Sheep*, 236; Kloppenborg, *Formation*, 228.

in Q on the relationship between Jesus and John the Baptist. This concluding section, comprising the mini-parable itself (vv. 31f.), the interpretative saying about John and the SM (= Jesus) (vv. 33f.) and the summary conclusion in the Wisdom saying (v. 35), is almost universally regarded as composite.[32] In particular the interpretative saying in vv. 33f. has been seen by many as an allegorising addition to the parable, its secondary nature being shown by the fact that it is about Jesus and John the Baptist rather than (as in the parable) about 'this generation', and by the fact that the order of the double saying, with John followed by Jesus, does not correspond with the order of the verbs in vv. 31f. (piping followed by wailing). One must, however, say that this particular part of the argument for the composite nature of vv. 31–35 is not fully convincing. It may be that any interpretative, allegorical explanation attached to parabolic sayings is to be regarded as secondary. On the other hand, one should perhaps be cautious here in view of the fact that the alleged allegorisation is said to have failed to allegorise 'properly', putting John and Jesus in the wrong order. Further, the claim that the parable is about 'this generation' whereas the interpretation is about Jesus and John, is perhaps too black-and-white. The parable is clearly about children *responding* and the interpretation is not just about Jesus and John as such, but also about the responses they evoke. There is thus a significant measure of overlap between the parable and its interpretation.

The precise point of the parable has been much discussed.[33] In part the situation is confused by uncertainty about the detailed wording: do the children in the market place call to others within their own group (ἀλλήλοις: so Luke) or to another group of children from whom they are separate (ἑτέροις: so Matthew)? A reasonably coherent picture emerges if we accept the Matthean reading,[34] provided we do not expect a detailed, allegorical interpretation. The initial comparison, likening this generation

[32] Bultmann, *History*, 172; Lührmann, *Redaktion*, 29; Schürmann, *Lukasevangelium*, 425f.; Schulz, *Q,* 381; Hoffmann, *Studien*, 224f.; Kloppenborg, *Formation*, 110.

[33] See the survery in D. Zeller, 'Die Bildlogik des Gleichnisses Mt 11:16/Lk 7:31', *ZNW* 68 (1977) 252–7; Fitzmyer, *Luke*, 678f.; Jeremias, *Parables*, 161f.; also W. J. Cotter, 'The Parable of the Children in the Market Place, Q (Lk) 7:31–35: An Examination of the Parable's Image and Significance', *NovT* 29 (1987) 289–304.

[34] So Cotter, 'Parable', 291; also Sevenich-Bax, *Konfrontation*, 216–8.

to the children in the market place, need not necessarily imply that the people of this generation are to be equated with the children in the parable who call to others. The comparison may be a much more general one, equating the situation of this generation with (aspects of) the whole picture painted in the parable.[35] Thus the people of this generation are not necessarily to be identified with the calling children, but rather with the other, non-responding children. 'This generation' is thus accused of failing to respond to the different messengers and messages given to it by Jesus and John.[36] (There is no need either necessarily to identify John's message with the 'wailing' or Jesus' with the 'piping'. The point is simply that the two are, at one level, different, just as John and Jesus themselves are, at the level of personal habits, different.) There thus appears to be a close and firm connection between the parable and its interpretation in vv. 33f. Whether this unit can be traced back to Jesus without more ado[37] is uncertain: the ἐλήλυθεν formulation may represent a later standpoint, looking back at Jesus' ministry as in the past,[38] and the use of 'SM' here presents its own peculiar problems for interpretation at the level of Jesus. Nevertheless one can say that it would perhaps be dangerous to drive too great a traditio-historical wedge between vv. 31f. and vv. 33f.

A stronger case can be made for regarding v. 35 as a secondary comment. The Wisdom saying appears at first sight to be 'not integrally related' to vv. 31–34,[39] and certainly uses rather different imagery.[40] At one level it picks up the 'children' motif

---

[35] Cf. Jeremias, *Parables*, 100f., on the Semitic ל. Hence contra Cotter who places much weight on the formal parallel between the children and this generation in the parable's introduction in her interpretation.

[36] Cf. Schürmann, *Lukasevangelium*, 426f.; Hoffmann, *Studien*, 226; Zeller, 'Bildlogik', 255; Kloppenborg, *Formation*, 111. Contra Jeremias, *Parables*, 161f., who takes John and Jesus as the responding children and this generation as the calling children. (Cf. also Cotter, 'Parable', 295, 302f.) But he seems right to take the ἑτέροις as original. Strangely, Hoffmann, *Studien*, 197, takes Luke's ἀλλήλοις as original.

[37] So, for example, Jeremias.

[38] Bultmann, *History*, 155f.

[39] Kloppenborg, *Formation*, 110; cf. too Hoffmann, *Studien*, 228.

[40] Hence I find Jacobson's view (*First Gospel*, 124) that v. 35 was added at the same time as vv. 33f. because v. 35 'is not really in tension with' vv. 33f., rather difficult. There is no *tension* in that both can coexist — as indeed they do at present in both Matthew and Luke and hence presumably in Q. But the different outlooks and imagery do seem to betray a different origin and a seam in the tradition.

from the parable,[41] but the reference has altered somewhat. It is not quite clear who exactly the children of Wisdom are intended to be. Again there is doubt about the exact Q wording: is Wisdom justified by 'all' her children (so Luke), or simply by 'her children' *simpliciter*? The latter could be interpreted as Jesus and John; the former possibility would suggest a larger group. However, even if πάντων is regarded as LkR, it still seems most probable that Q has in mind a wider group of Wisdom's children: it is hard to see how John and Jesus alone as 'acknowledging Wisdom to be in the right'[42] really fits the context. Much better is the idea of Wisdom's children as those responding to Wisdom's call (cf. Prov 8:32; Sir 4:11; 15:2)[43] so that Wisdom's children provide the antithetic parallel to the people of this generation who have not responded.[44]

The saying in v. 35 thus provides a polemical thrust at the end of the pericope, implying that 'this generation' do not comprise the true children of Wisdom by their rejection of the calls of Jesus and John. Implicit here is the idea that Jesus and John are messengers of Wisdom, and hence acceptance of their message is acceptance of Wisdom. Thus this saying fits well with the other Q sayings examined so far: Jesus and John constitute part of the series of Wisdom's messengers, though their specifically 'prophetic' status is not spelt out here.[45]

We have also seen that the section 7:31–35 also has considerable importance at the level of Q's compositional structure within the literary unit Q 7:18–35 (see p. 131 above). The section

[41] Many agree that Luke's τέκνων is more original than Matthew's ἔργων. The latter creates an inclusio with Matt 11:2 (τὰ ἔργα τοῦ Χριστοῦ) and is part of Matthew's attempt to identify Jesus with the figure of Wisdom: see n. 8 above.

[42] For this forensic meaning of δικαιόω, cf. Schrenk, art. δικαιόω *TWNT* II, 218; and my *Revival*, 149. Cf. *Ps Sol* 2:16; 3:3, 5; 4:9; 8:7, 27.

[43] See Lührmann, *Redaktion*, 29; and my *Revival*, 151, with further references.

[44] This interpretation would be considerably strengthened if it could be shown that Luke 7:29f. formed part of Q at this point. We have already seen that such a theory is quite plausible, given the presence of some un-Lukan features in the verses, suggesting a pre-Lukan origin, and the similar saying in Matt 21:32, suggesting an origin in Q (see p. 116 n. 33 above). If so, then the very similar (and slightly unusual: cf. n. 42 above) use of δικαιόω in v. 29 may imply a definite link between vv. 29f. and v. 35: the tax-collectors and others who have responded to Jesus and ackowledge God to be in the right have thereby shown themselves to be the true children of Wisdom.

[45] But note 7:26, 28: the prophetic category *is* brought into the discussion and both affirmed and also superseded: John *is* a prophet, but also *more* than a prophet. Cf. p. 134 above.

acts as the literary climax, and serves to provide the interpretative key, for the passage as a whole. The thrust of the small
section in 7:31–35, and derivatively of the wider unit in 7:18–35, is
thus that Jesus and John appear in parallel as messengers of
Wisdom but shunned by this generation. Any possible rivalry
between John and Jesus (as possibly reflected in e.g. 7:28b: cf.
above) is now, in literary terms, superseded by the view that John
and Jesus are to be seen in parallel as Wisdom's envoys. It may
well be that Q does not regard the two as exactly parallel; indeed
the reference to Jesus as 'SM' in 7:34 may in part be serving to
distinguish Jesus' status from that of John.[46] Nevertheless the
main thrust is clear: what is now important is not any concern to
upgrade Jesus at the expense of John, but rather to show Jesus
and John as opposed to this generation. The object of any
'polemic' is clearly 'this generation' and *not* John.

The direction of Q's redactional and compositional activity is
thus clear: it is to stress the opposition and hostility experienced
by Jesus (and John) by highlighting their position as envoys of
Wisdom. Further, the (probably) redactional nature of v. 35
means that it is the Wisdom motif that is stressed by the final
editor.[47] No doubt there are other motifs present, but in this case
it is the Wisdom motif which is made to dominate.

1.4. Q 6:22f.

A slightly different nuance appears in the final beatitude in Q
6:22f. The beatitude itself is widely regarded as separate in origin
from the other three with which it is now joined in Luke/Q,
being a secondary expansion of them.[48] However, even within the
beatitude itself, there may be different strata visible. Many have
followed Steck in seeing the final phrase in 6:23c, referring to the

---

[46] Cf. J. M. Robinson, 'Jesus as Sophos and Sophia', in R. L. Wilken (ed.),
Aspects of Wisdom in Judaism and Early Christianity (University of Notre Dame
Press, 1975) 1–16, pp. 5f.

[47] Hence contra Hoffmann, *Studien*, 230, 232, who takes the Wisdom
prophets theme as traditional and the SM reference as redactional,
corresponding to the Christological interpretation in 7:27, 28b. But in v. 27 the
Christological point is at best hidden and in v. 28b ὁ μιχρότερος is only with
difficulty to be identified with Jesus. In any case, v. 34, unlike v. 35, does not act
as the literary climax of the passage: it is v. 35 which has the 'last word' on the
subject.

[48] Hoffmann, *Studien*, 73; Schulz, *Q*, 454f.; Catchpole, *Quest*, 91 (with further
literature) and many others.

fate of the prophets in the past, as a secondary addition to an earlier form of the beatitude.[49] It is somewhat redundant alongside v. 23b which provides sufficient motive for the exhortation to rejoice in v. 23a and for the claim that those being presently persecuted are blessed. In any case these need no supplement with an additional reference to specifically prophetic suffering. There is thus a seam between v. 23b and v. 23c, and the position of v. 23c at the very end of the beatitude makes it probable that this is a secondary comment appended to an earlier form of the beatitude.

Once again there is a close link with part of the nexus of themes which we have been considering in this chapter: the suffering and hostility experienced by those addressed in the beatitude is said to be similar in kind to the hostility experienced by the rejected prophets of the past. The experience of the Q Christians is thus equated with the experience of rejected prophets and their 'suffering' is interpreted as specifically prophetic suffering. It is true that there is nothing specific here about Wisdom; nor is there any reference to 'this generation'. However, it may be noteworthy that in the context there is a reference to the 'SM' (in v. 22),[50] just as in 7:31–35 the (redactional) Wisdom note in v. 35 follows immediately after as reference to Jesus as 'SM'. Similarly the (redactional) addition to the lament over Jerusalem in 13:35b contains a reference to ὁ ἐρχόμενος, and by implication to Jesus as 'SM' (cf. above).

1.5. *Q 9:58*

Similar ideas may also be reflected in the saying in Q 9:58 'The SM has nowhere to lay his head'. Here there is no explicit reference to 'prophets' as such, nor to 'this generation'. However, many have seen here an allusion to Wisdom ideas, and in

---

[49] Steck, *Geschick*, 257–60; Schulz, *Q*, 456; Kloppenborg, *Formation*, 173, 190, and 'Blessing and Marginality. The "Persecution Beatitude" in Q, Thomas and Early Christianity', *Foundations & Facets Forum 2* (1986) 36–56, pp. 44f.; Sato, *Q und Prophetie*, 258; Jacobson, *First Gospel*, 100.

[50] It is widely agreed that Luke's 'for the sake of the SM' is more original than Matthew's 'for the sake of me'. Luke does not have a tendency to add references to 'SM' with no basis in his tradition, whereas Matthew does sometimes changes a 'SM' reference to a first person pronoun (cf. Matt 10:32 par. Luke 12:8; Matt 16:21 par. Mark 8:31). See Schürmann, *Lukasevangelium*, 334; Schulz, *Q*, 453; Kloppenborg, 'Persecution Beatitude', 41; Luz, *Matthew 1–7*, 229 and many others.

particular to the motif of Wisdom being unable to find a place to dwell (cf. *1 En* 42).[51] Kloppenborg objects to such an idea as 'far-fetched: Q 9:57–58 says nothing of rejection . . . Instead the saying describes the vagrant existence of the Son of Man'.[52] However, the motif of rejection and hostility is hard to banish from the saying, as we shall see.

The saying has sometimes been taken as a popular, general proverb,[53] applying to humankind in general. This is however difficult to accept. The criticism frequently made of such a view is that the saying is manifestly untrue when applied generally, since most people do have homes and beds.[54] We must therefore look elsewhere for the meaning. The logion provides both a parallelism and a contrast between the SM and the 'foxes and birds': the saying as such seems to presume that the 'foxes and birds' are similar to the SM; but an unexpected contrast comes in their having/not having homes.[55] Yet in what way are the foxes and birds parallel to the SM? It is highly unlikely that they can be regarded as friendly creatures. Frequently in the OT, 'foxes' are animals which are regarded as wholly destructive and repugnant.[56] But equally 'birds of the air' are often regarded as very different from modern ideas of 'feathered friends' — rather they are frequently referred to as predators, and presented as destructive and carnivorous in highly negative terms.[57] The first

---

[51] Hoffmann, *Studien*, 181f.; R. G. Hamerton-Kelly, *Pre-Existence, Wisdom and the Son of Man* (SNTSMS 21; Cambridge University Press, 1973) 29; Piper, *Wisdom*, 167; Jacobson, *First Gospel*, 136.

[52] Kloppenborg, *Formation*, 192.

[53] Bultmann, *History*, 102. Cf. too P. M. Casey, *Son of Man* (London: SPCK, 1979) 229; though see his more nuanced view in 'The Jackals and the Son of Man (Matt. 8.20 / Luke 9.58)', *JSNT* 23 (1985) 3–22; and more generally in 'General, Generic and Indefinite: the Use of the Term "Son of Man" in Aramaic Sources and in the Teaching of Jesus', *JSNT* 29 (1987) 21–56: a general statement referring to a particular situation.

[54] Cf. C. Colpe, ὁ υἱὸς τοῦ ἀνθρώπου, *TWNT* VIII, 435; J. D. G. Dunn, *Unity and Diversity in the New Testament* (London: SCM, 1977) 39; B. Lindars, *Jesus Son of Man* (London: SPCK, 1983) 30; Hoffmann, *Studien*, 90f.

[55] See especially R. Tannehill, *The Sword of His Mouth* (Missoula: Scholars, 1975) 161f. I am also indebted to some private correspondence from Professor Catchpole here.

[56] See H. W. Hoehner, *Herod Antipas* (SNTSMS 17; Cambridge University Press, 1972) 343–7. Cf. Judg 1:35 LXX; 3 Kgdms 21:10 LXX; Neh 4:3; Can 2:15; Ps 62:10; Lam 5:18; Ezek 13:4.

[57] Cf. 1 Sam 17:44, 46; 1 Ki 12:24; 14:11; 16:4; 21:24; Ps 79:2; Isa 18:6; Jer 7:33; 15:3; 16:4; 19:7; Hos 2:14; Ezek 19:5; 34:5; 39:4.

half of the saying thus states that even the most destructive and dangerous of animals, generally regarded with loathing, have homes provided for them (presumably by God). The striking mixture of parallelism and contrast then comes in the second half of the saying, where it is said that the SM has no home. The implication overall seems to be that the SM is comparable in one way to the despised foxes and birds. The 'SM' thus seems to be a figure regarded by others with contempt and loathing.[58] Yet in another way the SM is different from the foxes/birds, for he has no home at all: his rejection is even more comprehensive than that of the animals mentioned. It would appear then that homelessness is not something expected or chosen; rather, the saying implies that the end result for the SM is even more drastic than the fate experienced by the universally rejected foxes and birds: they at least have homes, while the SM has nowhere to lay his head. Why the term 'SM' itself is used here will be discussed later, but the analysis above does give support to the view that the homelessness motif is a symbol of rejection.[59] Hence the idea of rejected Wisdom, who also can find no home in texts such as *1 En* 42, is quite in line with the Q saying here.

The verse may also have considerable significance at the level of Q's composition. Some have seen v. 58 as a '*Kommentarwort*', prefixed to the radical summons of Jesus to the would-be disciple to 'let the dead bury the dead' in vv. 59f.[60] Most would agree that vv. 59f., especially v. 60, stem from the earliest stage of the tradition with very strong claims to authenticity.[61] If so, it may well be correct to see vv. 57f. as a secondary comment added to an earlier vv. 59f.[62] However, the present order of the sayings — with vv. 57f. preceding vv. 59f. (an order attested in both Matthew and Luke) — suggests that this is not just a case of a *Kommentarwort*

---

[58] In addition to those who stress the Wisdom idea here, see Tödt, *Son of Man*, 122; Schulz, *Q*, 439.

[59] For a possible distinction between itinerancy and homelessness, see ch. 11 below. Jesus may have chosen to be itinerant and expected a home to be provided en route; but an itinerant existence coupled with rejection can then lead to homelessness in the sense of unwillingly having nowhere to lay one's head.

[60] Cf. Schürmann, 'Beobachtungen', 132f.; cf. too J. Wanke, 'Kommentar-worte: Älteste Kommentierungen von Herrenworte', *BZ* 24 (1980) 208–233, p. 216; Kloppenborg, *Formation*, 192.

[61] See M. Hengel, *The Charismatic Leader and His Followers* (ET Edinburgh: T. & T. Clark, 1981).

[62] Schulz, *Q*, 435f. It is difficult to see the two as originally separate items in the tradition. It looks very much as if one has been modelled on the other.

interpreting a single saying. Most likely the present order serves to make the SM saying function as an introduction to the whole mission discourse which follows in 10.2ff.[63] The homeless SM with nowhere to lay his head functions as the exemplary paradigm for the disciples who are called by Jesus to go out without provisions, dependent on the hospitality of others and open to hostility and rejection.[64] Thus the ideas of rejection in homelessness contribute significantly to the motifs stressed by the Q compiler in placing this saying at the head of the mission discourse.

1.6. Q 10:2–16

We may perhaps appropriately consider certain aspects of the mission charge itself (Q 10:2–16) at this point. This pericope is probably one of the most complex in the whole of the Q tradition and it has certainly been extensively analysed in recent studies.[65] There are almost certainly various strata present in the tradition. At the very least, the existence of a parallel version in Mark suggests that Q (and Mark) are reworking an older tradition.[66]

---

[63] Cf. Wanke, 'Kommentarworte', 216; Sato, *Q und Prophetie*, 37, assuming that Luke preserves the Q order: Matthew's ordering of Matt 8:18–22 is usually regarded as MattR, following G. Bornkamm, *Tradition and Interpretation in Matthew* (ET London: SCM, 1963) 52–7. Cf. Uro, *Sheep*, 88, and others.

[64] Cf. Kloppenborg, *Formation*, 192: 9:58 was attached to 9:59–62 'to provide a structural homologue between the Son of Man and his followers, and thus to motivate and legitimate their radical pattern of discipleship' (though without so clear a reference to the mission discourse and less stress on the rejection theme in the latter). Herein too lies the strength of the interpretations of, e.g. Lindars and Casey on the saying (though both are operating at the level of the historical Jesus): the saying is about homelessness (and rejection?) of *both* Jesus *and* the disciples (Lindars, *Jesus Son of Man*, 30f.; for Casey, see n. 53 above); though whether this is to be read into the term 'SM' itself (so both Lindars and Casey) is quite another matter! For Q at least, 'SM' would appear to be Jesus and Jesus alone. The broader implications of the saying come from its wider literary context within Q, not from the phrase itself.

[65] See, for example, the studies of Hoffmann, *Studien*, 235–311; Laufen, *Doppelüberlieferungen*, 201–301; Uro, *Sheep, passim*.

[66] Unless, of course, one posits Markan dependence on Q. (So, recently, Catchpole, *Quest*, ch. 5.) See the arguments against this by Uro, *Sheep*, 36; Laufen, *Doppelüberlieferungen*, 298: why should Mark omit the explicit command to the disciples to preach and heal when this is stressed in the narrative framework? Why should Mark omit the explicit command to proclaim the nearness of the kingdom? Catchpole, *Quest*, 155f. has sought to counter these by appealing in part to Mark 1:15 as 'in turn defin[ing] the proclamation of the disciples': but this is by no means explicit in Mark!

Uro has shown that, underlying Mark and Q, there was probably a basic mission charge with instructions about equipment (which Mark probably alleviates by allowing staff and sandals) and about appropriate behaviour in the cases of the Christian mission being accepted or rejected. (The problems of the different versions at this point, and whether they are envisaging a 'house mission' or a 'town mission' or both, will not be discussed here.)

As far as one can tell, in the earlier tradition, the emphasis appears to have been roughly equally balanced between positive and negative reactions to the mission itself. In Q, however, the negative reaction is very strongly emphasised. This is shown especially by the presence of the woes against the Galilean cities in Q 10:13–15. The intrusive nature of these woes in the mission charge is also shown by the fact that the speech shifts suddenly from an address to disciples being sent out on mission to an attack on those who are rejecting the Christians' message; then in Q 10:16, the 'you' shifts back again to the disciples.[67] These woes thus constitute a secondary addition, added to the earlier tradition at the point where that tradition mentioned unresponsive cities.[68] The connection between the mission charge proper and the woes is provided by Q 10:12, a verse which many (following Lührmann) have regarded as a Q-redactional creation designed specifically to make the transition.[69] The close parallelism between v. 12 and v. 14, and the fact that v. 12 with its reference to 'that city' can scarcely have existed as an isolated saying in the tradition independent of its present context, makes this highly likely. Thus the mission charge has been modified to highlight the way in which the mission has been rejected by several of the cities in Galilee to which it has (presumably) gone.

The same motif of rejection is probably to be seen in the saying about 'lambs in the midst of wolves' (Q 10:3) which may well have stood at the start of Q's mission charge.[70] The saying again clearly implies that the missionaries will be in a dangerous position, presumably because of the rejection of their message. Probably

[67] Again assuming (with most) that the Lukan order is original.

[68] See Uro, *Sheep*, 100; Kloppenborg, *Formation*, 194; Jacobson, *First Gospel*, 145.

[69] Lührmann, *Redaktion*, 62; Hoffmann, *Studien*, 288, 303; Schenk, *Synopse*, 55; Neirynck, 'Recent Developments', 65; Laufen, *Doppelüberlieferungen*, 275; Uro, *Sheep*, 100; Kloppenborg, *Formation*, 195f.

[70] Matthew has it at the end of the mission charge. For Luke's order as original here, see Hoffmann, *Studien*, 257; Laufen, *Doppelüberlieferungen*, 206; Uro, *Sheep*, 75 and others cited there.

too there is an element of sarcastic inversion in the imagery used: the imagery of lambs and wolves is attested in some Jewish texts to characterise the position of Israel in the midst of the hostile Gentile world. This Q saying thus appears to be taking up this idea and inverting the terms of reference. The woes in Q 10:13–15 make it clear that non-responsive Israelite cities are in mind, and Q 10:3 now ascribes to these Jewish groups the derogatory image (of wolves threatening lambs) previously applied to Gentiles.[71] The saying is thus ostensibly a warning of the danger which is to face the disciples, but presumably also to a certain extent a *vaticinium ex eventu*, i.e. a rationalisation of what is already happening, or has happened, in the experience of the Q missionaries.[72] The function of these two elements in 10:3 and 10:13–15 is thus to provide a significant slant to the mission charge, highlighting the opposition which the disciples are to face from Jewish audiences who in a sense are belying their own heritage (by behaving like 'wolves' rather than as God's 'lambs').

The negative slant which this material gives to the pericope as a whole has been recognised by several scholars.[73] Many have assumed that this is characteristic of the 'final' Q-editor (so Lührmann, Hoffmann, Laufen and others). However, the case has recently been argued by R. Uro that this stratum in the tradition represents only a penultimate stage in the development of Q: the negative, polemical stage has been superseded in Q by a more optimistic stage, represented above all by the saying about 'the harvest is great but the labourers are few' (Q 10:2), as well as possibly Q 10:21f. where the language of polemic has given way to quiet serenity and Israel's disbelief is not the object of bitter reproaches but accepted as part of God's plan. Thus Uro argues that the polemical version of the mission charge was taken up and adapted in a new situation where the opportunities for mission were regarded in a more optimistic way (the image of the great harvest seems to presuppose positive opportunities for success, not uniformly negative rejection). Further, the pre-

---

[71] See Hoffmann, *Studien*, 294f.; Laufen, *Doppelüberlieferungen*, 272f.; Uro, *Sheep*, 111f.

[72] It seems much more likely that the stress is on the danger being faced rather than on the protection offered (so Laufen, *Doppelüberlieferungen*, 273, who sees this as entirely optimistic!).

[73] See Hoffmann, *Studien*, 288; Lührmann, *Redaktion*, 59–64; Laufen, *Doppelüberlieferungen*, 270, 285ff.; Uro, *Sheep*, 111f.; Kloppenborg, *Formation*, 196f.; Jacobson, *First Gospel*, 133–40.

suppositions of the saying in 10:2 differ from what follows. Those addressed are not so much the actual wandering missionaries but perhaps settled communities who are acting as 'support bases' for the missionaries themselves (the 'workers' to be sent out) and who will provide support and prayers. (The model of Acts 13:1ff. may be similar.)[74] Thus Uro attributes the saying to a later stage in the history of the Q community, one in which the earlier practice of wandering missionaries has been in part 'institutionalised' to a certain extent by the existence of back-up groups in the settled communities.[75] Given the fact that such a 'church mission' (cf. Acts 13) may underlie Paul's missionary practice in undertaking the Gentile mission, the positive attitude reflected in 10:2 may have a similar *Sitz im Leben*: after the failure of the Jewish mission, the Q community has turned to the Gentiles with some success and can look forward with optimism to the future. Such an optimistic view Uro finds elsewhere, e.g. in Q 10:21f. and 13:35b.[76]

The question of the Gentile mission in Q is a large issue and will have to be treated later (see ch. 12 below). The slightly awkward nature of v. 2 has been noted by several other scholars[77] in that it is addressed not to the missionaries themselves but to other supporters; also as a saying of Jesus it seems to imply that some one other than Jesus ('the Lord of the harvest' — presumably God) will send the missionaries, whereas v. 3 has Jesus say 'I am sending you'. There are thus good grounds for seeing some kind of a seam in the tradition between v. 2 and v. 3.

Nevertheless, whilst one may concede that the situation presupposed may be slightly different in v. 2 as compared with vv. 3ff., it seems to stretch the evidence to breaking point to argue (as Uro does) that a quite different missionary experience, indeed even a different mission, is in mind. It seems very odd in literary terms that this one verse alone is meant to reflect the current view of the Q Christians regarding their positive attitude

---

[74] Uro, *Sheep*, 113f., 200ff.

[75] Uro, *Sheep*, 204f., referring to the work of W. H. Ollrog, *Paulus und seine Mitarbeiter. Untersuchungen zu Theorie und Praxis der paulinischen Mission* (WMANT 50; Neukirchen-Vluyn: Neukirchener, 1979).

[76] Uro, *Sheep*, 208f.

[77] Jacobson ascribes the saying to a later redactional stage (*First Gospel*, 147), the same stage as vv. 13–15. Zeller, 'Redaktionsprozesse', 404f., agrees with Uro on the changed social situation implied. Hoffmann, Laufen and others had also noted the way in which the saying does not quite fit the context.

to their (Gentile) mission. Simply in terms of the amount of space devoted to the various sections, one must say that the sections concerned with the negative experience of the Jewish mission dominate the whole. Further, the same negative attitude to the Jewish mission is, as we have seen, reflected in the section which comes at the end of the mission charge in 10:13–15, 16, and which therefore by its position provides the literary climax to the whole. In literary terms, therefore, it is this aspect of the Christian mission which is clearly of most importance for Q in its present form. Further there is nothing in the mission charge as it stands to indicate that two missions are in mind — there is, for example, nothing akin to the programmatic statements of Luke's Paul in Acts 13:46; 18:6; 28:28 saying after the Jews' rejection of the Christian mission, 'Behold we go to the Gentiles!' Q 10:2 seems to imply that the harvest is great in the mission about to be outlined in what immediately follows. Thus the structure of the whole discourse strongly suggests that it is a single mission which is in mind. Possibly the verse does reflect a changed social situation, with more settled communities now providing for the missionaries; but it is the same mission of 'lambs' amongst 'wolves'.

This raises the question of how positive and optimistic Q 10:2 really is. Does it present the prospect of a successful mission awaiting only more workers to reap the harvest? Or does it have in view the rejection of the mission? Many refer to the use of the 'harvest' imagery in the OT and in Jewish tradition to refer to judgement.[78] In the wider context of Q's mission charge, it would seem that the negative overtones in the saying are intended to predominate. The idea may be more of eschatological judgement which is imminent, or even taking place in the present;[79] and there is little idea of a hopeful mission separate from the rejected mission about to be described in vv. 3–16.[80] How optimistic Q is about the Jewish

---

[78] Cf. Lührmann, *Redaktion*, 60; Schulz, *Q*, 410; Hoffmann, *Studien*, 289f. Cf. Joel 4:13; Isa 27:13; Jer 51:33; Mic 4:12f.; *4 Ezra* 4:28ff.; *2 Bar* 70:2; SB I, 672.

[79] Cf. Hoffmann, *Studien*, 291f.; Jacobson, *First Gospel*, 147.

[80] See too Piper, *Wisdom*, 134. The Q editor who compiled vv. 2–16 evidently thought it meaningful to to consider vv. 2–16 as a unit, and to regard v. 2 as part of the same discourse as the remainder. It thus seems methodologically more appropriate to consider the verse within its immediate literary context, rather than in isolation, if one is interested in understanding the material at the level of Q itself.

mission in general terms is another issue to which we shall return.

1.7. Q 11:31f.

Many of the same ideas which we have been considering surface again in the double saying about the Ninevites and the Queen of the South (Q 11:31f.).[81] This double saying in Q forms part of the slightly wider unit containing the request for a sign and the answer by Q's Jesus referring to the 'Sign of Jonah' and the SM saying in Q 11:30 (Q 11:16, 29–32). The latter will be considered in more detail when we look at the use of the term 'SM' itself in Q. The unit about the request for a sign may also have been part of a much wider unit in Q containing the Beelzebul controversy and the sayings about the unclean spirits.

The problems raised by the Sign of Jonah passage are enormous and will be discussed later. Here we may simply note the way in which the double saying in Q 11:31f. again threatens 'this generation' with judgement for failing to respond to something which is greater than both the preaching of Jonah and the wisdom of Solomon. By almost universal consent the 'something' is the presence of Jesus' preaching (which is all but the same — but not quite — as the presence of Jesus himself: cf. the neuter πλεῖον, not the masculine). Further, the comparison with Jonah and Solomon are presumably assumed to be, at least in some sense, meaningful comparisons: hence the message rejected by this generation is in one way similar to that of the preaching of the prophet Jonah and the wisdom of Solomon, even though there is also a sense in which the present experience is qualitatively greater than the prophecy and wisdom of the past. The element of similarity suggests that we are once again within the nexus of ideas of rejected wisdom and rejected prophecy, the rejection of both leading to the threat of judgement. Further, the object of the attack is again 'this generation'.

We may also note in passing the presence here of one element which does not surface in any of the passages which we have looked at so far in this chapter. This is the positive reference to non-Jews. The people of 'this generation' are compared unfavourably with Gentile Ninevites and the Gentile Queen of the South: the latter responded positively to Jonah and Solomon in

---

[81] Hoffmann, *Studien*, 181; Jacobson, *First Gospel*, 167f.; Kloppenborg, *Formation*, 133f.; Piper, *Wisdom*, 166f.

contrast to 'this generation' which has not responded to the 'something greater' which is here. This is however not an isolated reference to Gentiles in such a context in Q and may have some significance in determining the attitude of Q to Gentiles, as we shall see.

1.8. Q 13:24–30

A final section to be considered in this chapter is the section in Luke 13:(23), 24–30. Opinions are sharply divided over the question of whether these verses constituted a unified section in Q or whether their present sequence is due to LkR.[82] Certainly the Matthean parallels to Luke are scattered at various points in Matthew's gospel (vv. 24, 25, 26f., 28f., 30 in Luke are paralleled in Matt 7:13f.; 25:10–12; 7:22f.; 8:11f.; 19:30/20:16 respectively). On the other hand the relatively close contexts in Matthew of the parallels in 7:13f., 22f., 8:11f. may suggest an original Q sequence involving these saying.[83] Further, most of those who accept the Q hypothesis at all have tended to assume that the order of Q is generally best preserved by Luke. Hence it may be not inappropriate to start with the presupposition that these verses may have constituted a sequence already united in Q.

The first saying (Luke 13:24/Matt 7:13f.) differs considerably in the two versions in Matthew and Luke. Matthew talks of two gates and ways, with many going along/through the broad way/gate leading to destruction and few finding the narrow gate which leads to life. Luke refers only to a narrow door which few will be able to enter. However, both versions agree in broad terms by presenting a contrast between the 'many' (πολλοί) who wish to 'enter' (εἰσελθεῖν) and the 'few' (ὀλίγοι) who will succeed. In many respects Matthew's version is probably secondary. Matthew's reference to two 'ways' as well as two 'doors/gates' seems to overload the imagery and in any case the language of 'entering' presupposes a gate or a door through which to enter rather than a road leading up to an entrance. Thus it is most

---

[82] For Q, see A. Denaux, 'Der Spruch von den zwei Wegen im Rahmen des Epilogs der Bergpredigt', in Delobel (ed.), *LOGIA*, 305–35, p. 328; Marshall, *Luke*, 564; Luz, *Matthew 1–7*, 433; März, 'Q-Rezeption', 186, 195f. For LkR, see P. Hoffmann, 'Πάντες ἐργάται ἀδικίας. Redaktion und Tradition in Lk 13,22–30', *ZNW* 58 (1967) 188–214; Schulz, *Q*, 310; B. D. Chilton, *God in Strength: Jesus' Announcement of the Kingdom* (Freistadt: Plöchl, 1979) 184–6. Fitzmyer, *Luke*, 1021f., is undecided. See Uro, *Sheep*, 211f., for a summary of the debate.

[83] Cf. Piper, *Wisdom*, 108f.; Uro, *Sheep*, 212.

probable that Matthew has expanded an earlier reference to a gate or a door by adding the motif of the 'way'; moreover he may well have expanded a simpler reference to a single narrow door to make a contrasting pair of wide and narrow gates and ways under the influence of the widespread imagery of the two ways.[84]

More difficult to decide is the question of the original (i.e. Q) wording. Did Q have 'enter' (Matthew εἰσέλθατε) or 'strive to enter' (Luke ἀγωνίζεσθε εἰσελθεῖν)? And will the 'few' who succeed 'find' the narrow way (Matthew), or will the many who fail 'not be able' to enter (Luke)? P. Hoffmann has argued for extensive LkR here, claiming in particular that Luke has ethicised the tradition to stress the moral effort required of the audience, so that the language of 'striving' and not succeeding is due to LkR.[85] However, Matthew's simpler straight imperative εἰσέλθατε is no less demanding in its context. As Piper says, in both versions 'the ethical significance of the call is equally clear . . . Even if the original imperative was simply "Enter by the narrow gate", the requirement for effort or commitment is implied in the command.'[86]

At the end of the saying, Luke's καὶ οὐκ ἰσχύσουσιν is often taken as LkR, given Luke's fondness for the verb ἰσχύειν.[87] However, Matthew's reference to the fact that few will 'find' the narrow gate/way seems equally difficult if it is original. Denaux argues that Matthew's 'find' does not fit easily with Matthew's opening 'enter by the narrow gate': the difficulty presupposed by the opening is not the finding of the gate but the entry itself.[88] The difficulty, he argues, arises from Matthew's imposing of the two ways scheme on an earlier tradition which spoke of 'seeking to enter' a single door. He thus takes the 'finding' reference as original in Q. However, the 'finding' motif scarcely fits into the alleged Q original any better. Nowhere is it suggested that the narrow door is hard to *find*. It may be hard or tight to get through, and great moral endeavour may be required. But just because it is

---

[84] Cf. Denaux, 'Spruch', 322; Luz, *Matthew 1–7*, 434f.; Hoffmann, 'Πάντες', 195.

[85] See especially 'Πάντες', 197.

[86] Piper, *Wisdom*, 238 n. 50. Cf. too Marshall, *Luke*, 565. Denaux, 'Spruch', 324, also points out that much of Hoffmann's argument for the Lukan significance of ἀγωνίζεσθε does not exclude the possibility of the verb being in Q as well.

[87] Jeremias, *Sprache*, 150, 232; Schulz, *Q*, 310; Denaux, 'Spruch', 324.

[88] Denaux, 'Spruch', 322.

narrow does not imply that it is invisible! In fact Matthew's 'find'
really only seems to fit in the Matthean version where there is a
choice of two gates/ways: one may not 'find' the right gate/way if
one has been tempted or seduced to go along/through the
wrong one. Hence it is much more likely that the 'finding' in
Matt 7:14 is due to MattR.

Thus even if Luke's ἰσχύειν is LkR, it is hard to see anything
other than a synonym being present in Q originally. In fact it is
hard to see precisely how Luke's ἰσχύειν fits with Luke's alleged
redactional interest in stressing the ethical endeavour required
of the audience. One might expect something to the effect that
although many strive to enter, few are successful; but the claim
that few are 'able' to enter really demands a further statement
spelling out precisely why only few people are able to enter. This
suggests that Luke's οὐκ ἰσχύσουσιν may thus be original and
also that the saying was not originally an isolated one but had a
continuation.

This is connected too with the meaning of the original saying.
According to Hoffmann, the saying on the lips of Jesus was an
isolated saying and was a call to repent, to make use of the
opportunities of the present. The 'narrow' door is then an image
of the difficulties which the decision demands. The appended
warning about the many who will fail would then be intended to
indicate that soon it may be too late.[89] This may be the case, but
one must say that it reads a very great deal into one sentence and
succeeds in making an enormous amount of the implied warning
in a very indirect way (viz. by the change in tense from present to
future). It is, in fact, hard to believe that the saying ever existed in
isolation. To extract the meaning Hoffmann does, one would
surely expect more: e.g. '(strive to) enter through the narrow
door *now*, because *on that day* many . . .'. There is, in fact, nothing
in the saying as it now stands to suggest that the future tenses are
eschatological. The logion really demands a further continuation
to clarify how and why the 'many' will not be able to get through
the door.

Now a continuation of v. 24, which in one way is perfect, is
provided by Luke 13:25: many will not be able to get through the
door because the door will be shut! However, a sequence of v. 24
to v. 25 in Q has been regarded with some suspicion by many. For

---

[89] 'Πάντες', 197. Denaux, 'Spruch', 328, cites Hoffmann but applies
Hoffmann's interpretation to the Q-redaction rather than to Jesus.

example, the fact that the Matthean parallels appear in different contexts in Matthew (Matt 7:13f.; 25:10–12) is often held to be problematic, as is also the allegedly awkward change in metaphor from a 'narrow' door to a 'shut' door.[90] However, Matthew is quite capable of splitting material originally connected in his tradition; and Matthew's parallel to Luke 13:25 in Matt 25:10–12 forms part of his parable of the ten virgins which may well be in large part a redactional creation.[91]

The alleged discrepancy between the 'narrow' door and the 'shut' door is at first sight more problematic. However, the discrepancy may have arisen not so much from the juxtaposition of independent sayings as from some secondary interference in one of the sayings. In fact the motif of the 'shut' door fits very well: it explains perfectly why others will not 'be able' to enter in the future (and the continuation makes it clear that the eschatological future is in mind). It is rather the 'narrow' door which does not fit very well in v. 24. In v. 24 the main point seems to be a temporal distinction: use the time now because in the future it will be too late. Thus to call the door 'narrow' seems to overload the imagery somewhat. It may therefore be a Q-redactional addition imposed on an earlier sequence of sayings. Its exact force is not clear but it is worth taking seriously the possibility that στενός may have a metaphorical meaning here, referring to affliction and suffering.[92] It may therefore be part of Q's conviction, which we shall see is prominent elsewhere in Q, that the Christian life is one which entails suffering and persecution.

Could the original sequence have ended at v. 25? This seems improbable since v. 25 simply states that others will try to enter the door and will find it shut. Nothing so far has indicated who is being excluded or why. Precisely this is answered in vv. 26f.

In vv. 26f. it is widely agreed that Luke 13:26 is more original than Matt 7:22 in referring to Jewish contemporaries of Jesus rather than charismatics and prophets acting in Jesus' name.[93]

---

[90] Bultmann, *History*, 130; Kloppenborg, *Formation*, 224.

[91] See K. P. Donfried, 'The Allegory of the Ten Virgins (Matt 25:1–13) as a Summary of Matthean Theology', *JBL* 93 (1974) 415–28.

[92] See Luz, *Matthew 1–7*, 436; cf. Isa 30:20 LXX; Job 18:11 LXX; Jer 37:7; 1 Ki 24:14. G. Bertram, στενός, *TWNT* VII, 605. Cf. Piper, *Wisdom*, 109: 'the difficult way of commitment'.

[93] Schulz, *Q*, 424–6; Hoffmann, *Studien*, 200; Marshall, *Luke*, 503; Luz, *Matthew 1–7*, 441 and others.

Those who stand accused here then are Jesus' contemporaries who presumably have witnessed Jesus' preaching but have not responded positively.[94] Verse 27 then paints the picture of the final rejection of these people by Jesus using the words of Ps 6:9. Hoffmann argues strongly that this is the climax of the sequence for Luke: those rejected are guilty of ἀδικία. However, the reference to ἀδικία[95] looks much more like a passing comment than the climactic clarification of the reason for the rejection of the people concerned. It seems inherently unlikely that such a climax should come in a subordinate clause in this way. It seems more probable that the ἀδικία reference is simply filling out and summarising in Biblical language what has already been implied in v. 26. Those rejected here are being refused entry because of their attitude to Jesus: they have not bothered to make any attempt to respond positively in the present, they thought that they had time in hand, and they have only just discovered, too late, that their decisions at that time were crucial. Verse 27 is thus still about positive responses to the present, not about any ethical problems of lawlessness or wickedness in general. The stress is much more on the ἀπόστητε/ἀποχωρεῖτε: the decision is now final and there is no hope of restitution.

We have seen that vv. 24–27 constitute a coherent sequence of sayings which need each other to make sense. It thus seems difficult to see the sequence as only coming together at the stage of Luke's redaction, and it seems much more likely that the sequence was already present in Q (or the pre-Q tradition).

Verses 28f. do break the train of thought slightly at one level, though at another level the connection is good. The imagery shifts from many who will be unable to enter to many Gentiles taking the place of Jews. On the other hand, the idea is continued of Jesus' Jewish contemporaries faced with final exclusion from the eschatological banquet; and indeed the saying only now clarifies for the first time that the rejection involved is that of the final judgement, and that the exclusion is from participation in the eschatological banquet. Q 13:28f. is a bi-partite saying with the two halves appearing in different order in Matthew and Luke.

---

[94] Kloppenborg, *Formation*, 224, sees a problem in the connection of vv. 26f. with vv. 24f. as it implies an 'awkward shift in Bildlogik . . . the exclusion of latecomers gives way to the rejection of evil doers'. But perhaps for Q 'latecoming', or doing nothing, *is* equated with 'doing evil'! See ch. 9 below.

[95] Whether Luke's ἀδικία or Matthew's ἀνομία is the Q reading probably does not make much difference here.

The Lukan ordering, with the polemical charge that 'you' will weep and gnash teeth on seeing Abraham and others in the kingdom preceding the claim that many will come from the East and the West, is probably not original. Its secondary nature is indicated by the opening ἐκεῖ which is highly awkward in the Lukan version but fits perfectly in Matthew's ordering of the material (the 'sons of the Kingdom' will be cast into the outer darkness and 'there' people will weep and gnash teeth). Thus most would argue that Matthew's version is more original in this respect;[96] Luke may have changed the order to lessen the contrast between Jews and Gentiles so as to be able to use the saying to warn his own Gentile readers against complacency.[97]

The saying clearly contrasts the future fate of Jews with that of Gentiles in the kingdom of God and claims that Gentiles will not only come into the kingdom but will actually replace Jews. As such the saying fits well with other sayings we have considered in Q where Gentiles are compared favourably with Jews, and where Jews are warned about the terrible consequences of their present conduct in relation to Gentiles who will be better treated than they (10:13–15), judge them (11:31f.), or even replace them entirely (as here in 13:28f.). This replacement certainly goes beyond what is said elsewhere in Q and indeed in other places where the motif of the eschatological journey of the Gentiles into the kingdom is attested.[98] It has thus been taken by many as an indication of a clear break between the Q community and the Jewish community.[99] That we shall consider later.

The conclusion here must be that 13:24–29 may constitute a coherent collection of sayings in Q, though the slight change in imagery and terms of reference may indicate a seam between v. 27 and v. 28. Again a number of familiar themes recur: although there is no reference to Wisdom or prophets as such, or even to 'this generation', there is strong polemic and warning to those who are contemporaries of Jesus (and presumably of Q) not to waste the opportunities of the present. And the warning takes the

---

[96] See D. Zeller, 'Das Logion Mt 8,11f/Lk 13,28f und das Motif der Völkerwallfahrt', *BZ* 15 (1971) 222–37; 16 (1972) 84–93, pp. 223f.; Kloppenborg, *Formation*, 226f.

[97] Hoffmann, 'Πάντες', 210.

[98] On this see Zeller, 'Völkerwallfahrt'. Zeller calls it a 'schockierendes Novum' (p. 87).

[99] Cf. Zeller, 'Völkerwallfahrt', 93; Uro, *Sheep*, 213f.

form of dire threats about how Gentiles will replace Jews in the final eschatological banquet.

2. Some Implications

We have seen that a significant part of Q is comprised of polemical attacks against 'this generation', accusing the latter of rejecting the overtures which have been made; moreover, such rejection is regarded as part of a standard pattern of rejection and violence which afflicts all God's prophets. The Q tradition also, as we have seen, is highly distinctive in combining this idea, embedded within a deuteronomistic view of history, with the motif of rejected Wisdom so that in this combination Wisdom becomes the agent who sends out the prophets, all of whom suffer violence and rejection. Further, in many of the texts dealing with these themes, it is noteworthy that there is a reference to the 'SM'. It is striking too that no one of these ideas has any monopoly in Q's redactional activity insofar as this can be discovered. Steck argues that the prophetic theme is dominant in Q.[1] Lührmann argues that the theme of the violence suffered by the prophets is only one theme amongst others and that what is characteristic of Q's redaction is the stress on Wisdom. Similarly Lührmann argues against the idea that 'SM' is of central significance for Q's redaction.[2] Hoffmann claims *per contra* that the Wisdom/prophet ideas are traditional in Q and that it is SM which is important for Q's redaction.[3]

The fact is that all views can claim some support from Q. As we have seen, the Wisdom theme is probably emphasised redactionally in Q 7:35; the threat against 'this generation' as responsible for the blood of the prophets is highlighted redactionally in Q 11:51; the continuity of the present suffering of Q Christians with that of the prophets is also stressed redactionally in Q 6:23c. Redactional reference is made to Jesus as the 'coming one' in Q 13:35b, and considerable compositional significance is probably invested in the SM saying in Q 9:58. All in all it seems impossible to isolate one of the strands in the whole complex as clearly redactional and dismiss the others as 'only' traditional and less important for Q. The whole complex seems to be taken as an

---

[1] Steck, *Geschick, passim.*
[2] Lührmann, *Redaktion*, 87f., 97f.
[3] Hoffmann, *Studien*, 185–7, 232.

integral whole with different aspects of it, and different terminology, stressed redactionally at various points.

Two further questions remain to be considered here. First, who is the object of the polemic? I.e. who is 'this generation'? Second, how negative is the polemic? Has the Q community given up all hope for 'this generation'? I consider first the problem of the meaning of the term 'this generation' in Q.

2.1. *'This Generation'*

One very influential view has been that of Lührmann. Taking up the work of Meinertz, Lührmann argues that 'this generation' is virtually a technical term for all Israel. The polemic is thus directed against the Jewish nation as a whole.[4] Further, the polemic is so sharp and pointed that it appears that the Q community has given up all hope of winning Jews to the Christian cause. Israel as a whole is thus threatened with judgement and the Q community is warmly embracing the Gentile mission. Such a picture of the situation of the Q community has been accepted by several scholars in recent years.[5] Yet whilst the analysis may be justified in parts, Lührmann's overall theory may need some modifications.

It is certainly clear that the polemic against 'this generation' is directed not against Gentiles but against Jews who do not support the Christian cause. The deuteronomistic pattern of history which the Q tradition adopts for its own purposes focuses on the rejection which God's prophets have experienced at the hands of Israel herself. The Jewish object of the polemic is also clear from a number of passages in Q which contrast the rejection of the Christian cause by Q's audience with the positive attitude of Gentiles. Such passages vary in the intensity of the polemic. Q 3:8, for example, simply raises the possibility that God can replace the present audience by raising up 'children of Abraham' from stones. Clearly the language implies that Jews are being addressed. Q 7:1–10 contrasts the 'faith' of the Gentile centurion[6] with the widespread lack of faith in Israel encountered by Q's

[4] Lührmann, *Redaktion*, 30f., 93. Cf. M. Meinertz, '"Dieses Geschlecht" im Neuen Testament', *BZ* 1 (1957) 283–9.

[5] Cf. Schulz, *Q*, 340 (though cf. also p. 381 and see below); Schürmann, 'Redekomposition', 73 (on the final woe); Kloppenborg, *Formation*, 148, 167; also Zeller and Uro, as in n. 99 above; Horn, 'Christentum', 362.

[6] Though see now Catchpole, *Quest*, 280–308, for the case that the centurion here might be Jewish. On this see pp. 395–7 below.

Jesus. Q 10:13–15 states that it will be more tolerable for the Gentile cities of Sodom and Gomorrah than for the Galilean cities which have not accepted the Q mission. Q 11:31f. threatens 'this generation' with accusation by the Gentile Ninevites and Queen of the South at the final judgement, the reason being that the latter responded to prophecy and wisdom in the past whereas 'this generation' has not. And finally Q 13:28f. paints the picture of Gentiles replacing the audience at the seats in the eschatological banquet alongside the patriarchs (and perhaps the prophets). It seems quite clear that this language is all Israel-oriented.

Is this however directed to all Israel, or only to a part of Israel? And what is the significance of the use of the word 'generation' (γενεά) in this polemic? The word γενεά itself is notoriously ambiguous. It can mean the sum total of those born at the same time (as in the popular English usage of 'generation'); it can also mean the totality of people born from a common ancestor, hence a 'clan' or 'race' or 'kind'.[7] Although the former meaning is perhaps the usual one,[8] the alternative meaning can be paralleled both inside and outside the NT. Outside the NT reference is often made to Deut 32:5 (γενεά σκολιὰ καὶ διεστραμμένη) to refer to the rebellious Israelites. Here the force of γενεά seems to be primarily to refer to a type of people (cf. too Ps 24:6; 78:8; 95:10: Deut 32:20).[9] Meinertz also refers to the relatively large number of occurrences of the phrase 'this generation' in the synoptic gospels, several of which occur in Q.[10] He refers to the negative overtones which almost always attach to the phrase in the gospels and speaks of it as a '*terminus technicus*', arguing that the phrase in the gospels reflects the OT usage. In Deut 32:5f., the fact that γενεά and λαός appear in parallel indicates that γενεά refers not to a temporal generation but to the 'people of Israel in their sinfulness'.[11] The term is thus not a temporal one but a moral one, and Meinertz applies the same interpretation to the NT occurrences. 'Die ntl Worte mit αὕτη ἡ γενεά haben ebenso durchweg einen moralischen Charakter,

[7] See BAG ad loc.

[8] For the OT, see Exod 12:14, 17, 42; Ps 77:4. In the NT Matt 1:17; Luke 1:48, 50; Acts 13:36; 14:16; 15:21.

[9] See Meinertz, 'Dieses Geschlecht', 283f.

[10] Q 7:31; 11:31, 32; 11:50, 51. Also Mark 8:12, 38; 9:19; 13:30; Luke 17:25; cf. too 16:8.

[11] Meinertz, 'Dieses Geschlecht', 285.

während der chronologische sekundär ist. In keinem Fall ist
verlangt, αὕτη in Gegensatz oder Unterschied zu früheren oder
späteren Geschlechtern zu setzen.'[12]

Meinertz may however have overstated the evidence. It is true
that in some instances in the OT, phrases with γενεά have
primarily a moral aim in view, labelling the addressees as pious or
rebellious or whatever. Yet usually this is done by the addition of
extra adjectives or phrases which make the moral lesson clear. In
Deut 32:5, the generation is 'perverse and crooked'; in 32:20 they
are 'children in whom is no faith'; in Ps 95:10 they are 'a people
that do err in their hearts for they have not known my ways'.
Further, it is clear that in several passages the temporal overtones
of γενεά have not been lost entirely. In Deut 32 and in Ps 95 it is
the people of Israel *in the wilderness wanderings* who are said to be
perverse, erring, etc. At one level it is thus the people as a whole
who are in view, but the wider context makes it clear that it is the
people as a whole at a specific moment in Israel's history during
the forty-year period (approximately one 'generation'!) of
sojourn in the wilderness. This is also the case in Ps 78 where in v.
8 the 'fathers' are referred to as a 'stubborn and rebellious
generation'; but the wider context is that of the Psalmist telling
Israel's history 'to a generation that is to come' (vv. 4, 6). Here
the temporal sense of γενεά is quite clear. Hence it is likely that
temporal overtones are not lacking in v. 8 as well: the fathers are
not just a stubborn and rebellious 'class'; they are a group of
people at one period in the past who were stubborn and
rebellious, whose behaviour is now recounted for future
descendants, i.e. generations. The temporal overtones in γενεά
thus cannot be ignored.

The situation is not dissimilar in the NT. Mark 13:30 presents
its own peculiar problems and will not be discussed here in the
analysis of the Q material.[13] It is striking that most of the Q
passages refer to 'this generation' *simpliciter* without any qualifying adjective (such as 'evil', or 'perverse'), though the context
makes it clear that this generation is being viewed negatively
as failing to respond to John and Jesus (7:31ff.), failing to
repent (11:31f.) and guilty of the blood of all the prophets
(11:51). Yet whilst the 'moral' (or religious) overtones dominate

[12] Ibid., 286.
[13] Légasse, 'L'oracle', 247 n. 63, suggests that it is this verse in Mark which is
the basic reason for the atemporal interpretation of the phrase 'this
generation'.

in the Q usage, it is hard to deny that temporal overtones have vanished completely. In 7:31f. this generation is accused of failing to respond to Jesus and John, despite their different life-styles. Clearly at one level the main point is the (morally culpable) refusal to respond; yet it is clear too that those refusing are those who have heard Jesus and John. They are thus contemporaries of Jesus and John and thus 'this generation' cannot be extended to cover the whole people of Israel in their entirety, past and present. It is only present Israelites who are in view. Further it is clear that those in mind are the Jews who are grumbling about Jesus and John. But this cannot mean all Jews. The conclusion of the pericope talks of Wisdom being justified by her children and, as we have seen, the 'children' are probably those who have responded positively to Wisdom's envoys Jesus and John (rather than being Jesus and John themselves: see p. 178 above). Thus 'this generation' stands over against 'Wisdom's children'. But there is nothing to indicate that Wisdom's children are exclusively Gentile. At the very least Jesus and John themselves, if not to be included in the 'children' of v. 35 as such, are clearly on the side of Wisdom and opposed to 'this generation', so that 'this generation', in its opposition to Wisdom's envoys, does not include Jesus and John. If we are right in our interpretation of the 'children' reference, 'this generation' does not include other Jews who have responded to Wisdom's message. As we shall see, the Q Christians themselves seem to have been strongly Jewish, e.g. in their attitude to the Law. Thus 'this generation' must simply refer to the unresponsive Jews at the time of Jesus and John (and perhaps in Q's own day). It cannot refer to all Israel as a whole.

Some temporal reference also seems demanded in Q 11:31f. 'This generation' is contrasted with the Ninevites and the Queen of the South. The latter responded to Jonah and Solomon respectively 'but something greater than both is here'. There seems to be a clear temporal contrast between the Ninevites and the Queen of the South, responding to Jonah's prophecy and Solomon's wisdom in the past, and 'this generation' failing to respond to the 'something greater' which is 'here' in the present. 'This generation' must then be the present audience, not the whole nation past and present, so that the temporal overtones must be allowed their sway in the phrase itself. We thus cannot necessarily ignore the temporal nuance and interpret the phrase in purely ethnic terms as if the phrase meant 'all Israel'.

Similarly in Q 11:49–51, temporal ideas cannot be dismissed. The saying alone seems to suggest that the collective sin of Israel in murdering the prophets is about to reach its culmination in divine punishment to be exacted on 'this generation'. At one level one could take this as simply 'this people', but the context makes it clear that the people concerned are those who are being addressed in the present and who will be the direct recipients of the threatened judgement. (If not, the saying loses all its force.) This is even stronger if we may take the oracle in vv. 49–51 as closely connected with the preceding woe against the tomb-builders (see p. 167 n. 9 above). Here a clear contrast is drawn between the activity of the 'fathers' in the past and the immediate audience ('you') in the present who try to distance themselves from the fathers. Whatever the logic implied (cf. below), there is a clear distinction drawn between past and present at one level. Verses 49–51 are then a threat to the present audience of imminent divine judgement.

It is thus very hard to get rid of temporal ideas from the phrase 'this generation' *in toto*.[14] Rather, the phrase seems to refer exclusively to the present audience, at times in clear contrast to earlier 'generations'. Given this temporal nuance, it seems illegitimate to read too much of an ethnic meaning into it. Certainly it has moral overtones: 'this generation' is uniformly regarded as bad and failing to do what Q thinks it should have done. (Precisely what it has done, or failed to do, we shall look at in a later chapter.) In this sense then the phrase as used in Q does have 'moral' overtones. But it does not have a clear ethnic meaning. Contra Lührmann, the phrase does not appear to mean Israel as a whole. In the broad context of Q it cannot mean that, since some 'children of Wisdom' evidently exist within the Jewish people and yet are not the object of the polemic directed against 'this generation'.[15] Clearly the contexts in which the phrase is used imply that Jews are in mind. But it is hard to see the term as being other than a broad general reference to those Jews who refuse to respond to the Christian message.

It is thus hard to accept Lührmann's argument that the polemic in Q against 'this generation' broadens the attack from specific groups within Israel to Israel as a whole.[16] Lührmann

---

[14] For similar views, see Steck, *Geschick*, 32; Hoffmann, *Studien*, 64, 169, 184; Schulz, *Q*, 381; Légasse, 'L'oracle', 247.

[15] Hoffmann, *Studien*, 169.

[16] Lührmann, *Redaktion*, 24–48, esp. pp. 30f.

deduces this from the way in which the concern about the relative status of Jesus and John the Baptist gives way to broader polemic against 'this generation' in Q 7:31–35; the series of woes in Q 11 is allegedly broadened in the final woe from an attack on the scribes and Pharisees to an attack on 'this generation'; and the Beelzebul controversy is, unlike the Markan version, directed not against the scribes from Jerusalem but more generally against 'this generation' in Q 11:29–32. Lührmann has certainly identified a clear characteristic of Q's language. But it is questionable precisely how far the use of the phrase 'this generation' actually broadens the polemic. In Q 7 the focus does shift from dealing with possible rivalry between Jesus and John to opposition of John and Jesus to 'this generation'. But this does not imply that the 'opposition' has also broadened out to become all Israel. The phrase simply signifies the sum total of non-responders with no clear indication of how widespread they are. The same applies in Q 11:14ff. and 11:39ff. 'This generation' is simply the non-responsive part of the Jewish people; and the γενεά vocabulary is used primarily to indicate that it is the *present* audience which is in mind.

The conclusion must be that the object of Q's polemic is primarily Jewish, but that one cannot extend this to 'all Israel' *simpliciter.*

2.2. Nature of the Polemic

This leads on to the second major question we raised earlier (p. 196): how negative is the polemic intended to be? At one level the language is very sharp and bitter — hence the claim that Q has effectively given up all hope for Israel.[17] Yet one should perhaps be wary of taking all that is said in Q purely at face value. For there are hints in a few Q passages that the wholly negative view about 'this generation' is not the last word on the subject as far as Q is concerned.

At the very general level, the theory that the Q Christians entertained only condemnation for Israel as a whole seems to create problems concerning the whole existence of Q at all. What would then be the purpose of the polemic in Q? We shall consider the question of Q's attitude to the Gentiles and the Gentile mission later, but it is striking that, for whatever reason and however it is to be interpreted, there is very little reference

---

[17] See those mentioned in p. 196 n. 5 above.

to the Gentile mission as such. Q is almost exclusively concerned with the negative side of the polemic against 'this generation'. Yet such polemic seems almost pointless if Q has indeed given up all hope for the people ostensibly addressed by Q's Jesus in these polemical passages. If, as Lührmann argues, there is now no hope for Israel and only judgement remains,[18] why is it that the anti-Israel tirades dominate so much of Q? Most have assumed that the presentation of the material in Q is due to the fact that the Q Christians believed that the material preserved had some contemporary relevance for them in their own situation. But the model of a Q community which has surrendered all hope for the 'conversion' of 'this generation' is then a curious one: we seem to have to imagine a group of Christians ghoulishly rejoicing in threats of divine judgement against outsiders who cannot now escape what is in store for them, or alternatively we have a community preserving (and perhaps at times redactionally creating) traditions which have no direct contemporary relevance at all if it has turned its back on Judaism and is now embracing the Gentile mission.

Kloppenborg has seen part of the problem here and argues that the conflict with outsiders serves 'a positive and constructive purpose' in social terms 'as a means to define more clearly group boundaries, to enhance internal cohesion and to reinforce group identity.'[19] This is possible, yet it is striking that on two occasions when Q does seem to address internal problems for its own community and uses an outside group as a foil to contrast the behaviour which is expected of Christians, it is Gentiles, not Jews, who occupy this role (cf. Q 12:30; Matt 5:47).[20] Thus in terms of social boundaries, Q's consciousness seems much more determined by the distinctiveness of Q Christians from Gentiles than from Jews. This may suggest that the force of the polemic against this generation does not lie solely, or even primarily, in the strengthening of group boundaries around the Q community against Jewish neighbours.

[18] Lührmann, *Redaktion*, 93.

[19] Kloppenborg, *Formation*, 167f., referring to L. Coser, *The Functions of Social Conflict* (London: Routledge & Kegan Paul, 1956), and J. H. Elliott, *A Home for the Homeless. A Sociological Exegesis of 1 Peter* (London: SCM, 1981).

[20] Matthew's wording here is almost universally recognised as more original than Luke's more general 'sinners': see Davies & Allison, *Matthew I*, 559f.; Marshall, *Luke*, 263; Luz, *Matthew 1–7*, 339, and many others.

We should note that the use of eschatological language and prediction in Judaism never has the function solely of predicting the future for its own sake. Statements which appear on the surface as predictions of what is going to happen in the future are as often as not in fact warnings of what *may* come if people do not change their ways. The bare predictions of judgement are thus implicit exhortations to those addressed to modify their behaviour/beliefs in order to avoid some of the disasters threatened. (Cf. p. 165 above.) Thus any 'eschatological' language about the imminence and certainty of future judgement does not necessarily mean that those addressed are regarded as having no hope. The very imminence and certainty of the future is itself one way of increasing the pressure on the audience to respond positively.

We have already seen that there is a hint of the positive side of polemical threats in John the Baptist's preaching in Q 3:9 (cf. p. 123 above). Those addressed are exhorted to produce 'fruit' in order *not* to be trees that are cut down and burnt; and (if the interpretation given earlier is correct) they are to undergo John's baptism in order to *avoid* the destructive (fiery) nature of the 'baptism' which threatens. The thrust of the passage in Q 7:31–35 may be similar. 'This generation' is compared with grumbling children, but Wisdom is justified by her children: hence the message to the audience is not a statement about a judicial decision already made — rather, it is a call to the audience to stop behaving like the grumbling children of the parable and to become one of Wisdom's children, by responding positively to Wisdom's envoys John and Jesus.

Even the apparently violent polemic in Q 13:24–29 may be taken in a similar way. The picture of vv. 28f. is of Jews excluded from the eschatological banquet. Yet if we are right to see the whole section in vv. 24–29 as a Q unit (see above), this image is not to be seen in isolation. It is the climax of the section beginning with a call to enter by the narrow door now, i.e. (in Q's terms) to respond positively to the call of the Q Christians, because soon it will be too late. Verses 25–29 then spell out the consequences of what will happen if people procrastinate: they will find that the door has been shut, that they are refused entry and that others have taken their place. But all this is for Q in the realm of the future, and functions as a threat to underline the seriousness of the call for action in the present in v. 24. The picture of vv. 28f. is thus not necessarily a statement about what is

going to happen come what may, still less a picture of the
present situation; rather, it is a warning of what may happen if
people do not respond. The violent imagery thus serves to
highlight the importance of the present call and makes that call
all the more urgent. Thus the eschatological polemic in Q may
not be due to 'this generation' having been written off entirely,
nor to the Q community strengthening its own group boundaries
with a rigid 'us/them' sect mentality — rather, it is simply a way of
reinforcing the seriousness of the call to 'this generation' to
respond to the Christian message, a call which may still be
continuing.

This may be hinted at in the very difficult SM saying in Q 12:10,
where speaking against the SM is said to be forgivable, in contrast
to speaking against the Holy Spirit which is not. We have already
noted the difficulties of the logion, and suggested that the least
problematic interpretation may be that the contrast intended is
one between the pre-Easter situation, where rejection of the
Christian cause (= speaking against the SM) is forgivable, and the
post-Easter situation, where such rejection (= speaking against
the Holy Spirit) is culpable.[21] At the very least, this seems to imply
a belief that the Jewish recipients of the Christian message,
although they have not responded to the message of the
historical Jesus himself, are nevertheless being offered another
chance to respond in the post-Easter situation. But since the
whole genre of Q means that it is the pre-Easter Jesus who is, at
least ostensibly, articulating the violent polemic against 'this
generation', this must mean that the Q Christians evidently
believe that those to whom such polemic was/is addressed still
have a chance to repent and to respond positively to the
preaching of the Q Christians.

A hint of a more positive outlook may also be seen in the
Lament over Jerusalem in 13:34f. The early part of the Lament is
clearly of a piece with many other parts of Q in referring to the
rejection of the prophets by Israel in terms which may be
reminiscent of Wisdom (cf. above). What is very striking is the
final clause in v. 35b which, it was argued above, may have been
added at the Q-redactional stage. Earlier we pointed to the
reference to the 'coming one' who in Q is almost certainly the SM
coming in judgement. However, what is so striking here is the
positive way this is referred to at this point. The language used is

---

[21] See p. 108 above.

that of Ps 117:26 LXX, and as Uro says, 'it is difficult to see how the Psalm quotation . . . can be understood in any other way than as an expression of joyful praise.'[22] Similarly, D. C. Allison comments:

> in the LXX ... and in the New Testament, εὐλογεῖν and εὐλογημένος (like the Hebrew ברך) are usually expressions of joy, and they consistently have a very positive connotation: 'to praise', 'to extol', 'to bless', 'to greet'. For this reason it is not easy to envision the words of Ps.118 [117]:26 as coming, begrudgingly or otherwise, from the lips of those for whom the messianic advent must mean only destruction.[23]

Thus, in apparently striking contrast to the earlier polemic in Q threatening judgement on the present generation in line with general deuteronomistic ideas, this saying apparently opens up a chink of light and seems to envisage the prospect of future salvation for those addressed.[24] How can one account for such an apparent volte-face within Q?

R. Uro has argued that the positive outlook reflected in 13:35b is so unlike the earlier polemical passages in Q that it cannot really be reconciled with the rest: rather, it belongs to a later stage in the development of Q, reflecting a positive and optimistic attitude to Q's mission. Thus Uro assigns 13:34f. to the same stratum within Q as Q 10:2 which also (he argues) has a much more optimistic view of the mission and may reflect a later situation of a successful Gentile mission following on from the failure of the Jewish mission. In this Uro appeals to the work of G. N. Stanton who argues for a rather different Jewish background model: rather than the Deuteronomic pattern of sin–prophetic appeals rejected–judgement, as isolated by Steck, there was a pattern, especially evident in the *Testaments of the Twelve Patriarchs*, of Sin–Exile–Return, viewing the exile as

---

[22] Uro, *Sheep*, 237.

[23] D. C. Allison, 'Matt. 23:39 = Luke 13:35b as a Conditional Prophecy', *JSNT* 18 (1983) 75–84, p. 75. Hence contra Hoffmann, *Studien*, 178: 'Dann werden sie Jesus als den Menschensohn erkennen und anerkennen müssen. Doch für ihre Rettung wird es zu spät sein.' Similarly Manson, *Sayings*, 128; Schulz, *Q*, 358; Zeller, *Kommentar*, 86.

[24] *Pace* Horn, 'Christentum', 362; cf. Catchpole, Quest, 274: '13.35b expresses the conviction that a mission calling for repentance in Israel must continue and will achieve good success. It is this mission in which the Q community is occupied.'

punishment for sin but ultimately looking forward to the restoration and rehabilitation of Israel.[25]

It may however be questioned whether the Sin–Exile–Return pattern is fundamentally so different from the deuteronomistic pattern identified by Steck. It is agreed that both patterns of preaching are 'deuteronomistic'. Further, in many examples of the deuteronomistic pattern involving the rejection of the prophets, there are further appeals to Israel to repent, with promises of reward if those appeals receive a positive response (see above). Thus an idea of hope for future Israel is not alien to the pattern of preaching referring to the violence suffered by the prophets. In fact the Sin–Exile–Return pattern in the *Testaments* should probably be regarded as simply one particular aspect of the general deuteronomistic pattern of preaching. The 'sin' part covers Israel's initial sin and the refusal to listen to the prophets; the 'exile' is one particular interpretation of the punishment inflicted by God because of the sin; and the 'return' is again one aspect (set here in positive terms) of the future of which final judgement is an alternative possibility. The Sin–Exile–Return pattern in the *Testaments* may therefore be seen as part of the same pattern of preaching based on a deuteronomistic view of history, as indeed Steck himself argued.[26]

Q 13:35b is thus not an alien element in the general polemical preaching against non-Christian Jews in Q. Its 'optimism' is not necessarily indicative of a later stratum in a developing Q tradition.[27] It is rather an integral part of the strong language used earlier in Q to speak against 'this generation' — but this language is not an indication that those addressed have been written off completely as having no hope: rather, the function of the language is precisely to arouse a positive response, to warn of the terrible consequences if no response is forthcoming, but to look for a bright future in the end. Thus Steck seems justified in

[25] Uro, *Sheep*, 237–40; cf. G. N. Stanton, 'Aspects of Early Christian-Jewish Polemic and Apologetic', *NTS* 31 (1985) 377–92, with reference to M. de Jonge's work on the *Testaments of the Twelve Patriarchs*; see p. 386 for the discussion of Q 13:35.

[26] Steck, *Geschick*, 149–53.

[27] Note too that Uro's link between 10:2 and 13:35b produces some difficulties since 10:2 is meant to refer to an optimistic view of a successful *Gentile* mission following a failed Jewish mission, whereas 13:35b clearly has in mind an optimistic view in relation to the *same* people addressed in vv. 34–35a, i.e. 'Jerusalem' who has killed all the prophets, and these can only be Jews!

his claim that the Q sayings against this generation, like the general pattern of deuteronomistic preaching, is aimed at the '*Erweckung*' of Israel.[28] Such language reflects throughout a mission with at least some hope of a positive response. It has not written off Israel entirely. It is convinced of the seriousness of the decisions being made in the present and may well be faced with rather negative responses now — and in the face of such negativity issues threats with dire warnings of the consequences. But the aim is to convince others — *not* to write them off completely.

---

[28] Steck, *Geschick*, 286–8, contra Lührmann. Cf. too Sevenich-Bax, *Konfrontation*, 190: 'Jedoch wird an keiner Stelle ein definitives Verwerfungsurteil gegenüber Israel ausgesprochen. Vielmehr macht die apokalyptische Ausrichtung der Droh- und Unheilsworte die Dringlichkeit *angesichts* des kommenden Gerichts um so deutlicher.'

7

Q's Christology

In ch. 5 above, we considered the way in which the Q material as a whole coheres well with the futurist eschatology which dominates Q's account of the preaching of John the Baptist. However, another aspect of John's preaching in Q was seen to be the conviction that the present was also a time of eschatological fulfilment (cf. Q 7:27; 16:16). This too finds strong support elsewhere in Q,[1] as can be seen in a number of Q passages:

(i) We have already noted Jesus' reply to the Baptist in Q 7:22 where Jesus' reply alludes to various Isaianic prophecies (Isa 29:18f.; 35:5; 61:1f.). What is implied here is that the events predicted in Isaiah as due to take place in the eschatological future are actually taking place in Jesus' ministry itself.[2] Jesus' words and actions thus constitute eschatological fulfilment.

(ii) Within the same extended Q context, a similar motif is implied in 7:27 where Jesus asserts that OT scripture has been 'fulfilled' in the person of John the Baptist (though the 'scripture' cited is an admixture of Mal 3:1 and Exod 23:20): John is the forerunner predicted in the OT to come prior to the End.

(iii) Q 10:23f. is similar, though couched in more general terms: the longed-for future, looked forward to by prophets and others in the past,[3] is now being experienced in the present.

---

[1] See especially G. N. Stanton, 'On the Christology of Q', in B. Lindars & S. S. Smalley (eds), *Christ and Spirit in the New Testament* (FS C. F. D. Moule; Cambridge: Cambridge University Press, 1973) 27–42, pp. 29–34.

[2] For the eschatological interpretation of Isa 29, 35 and 61 in Judaism, see Stuhlmacher, *Evangelium*, 219; Hoffmann, *Studien*, 204f.

[3] For present purposes, it does not matter whether Matthew's δίκαιοι or Luke's βασιλεῖς is more original.

(iv) So too Q 11:20 asserts that, in some respects at least, the eschatological Kingdom of God is present in Jesus' exorcistic activity.[4]

(v) Similarly the seed parables in Q 13:18–21 imply that, although the final stage of the process leading to the fully established eschatological Kingdom of God lies in the future, it is also already present, albeit in 'seed' and hidden form, in the ministry of Jesus.[5]

(vi) The sayings in 11:31f. also fit in with this general picture. Although, as we have seen, the primary stress is in one sense directed towards a judgement which is threatening in the future, the assertion is made that something greater than Jonah and Solomon is here in the present. Again we seem to have an idea of eschatological fulfilment (albeit stated in very general terms).

(vii) As we have also seen, Q 16:16 also implies that the kingdom is in some sense present, although it (i.e. presumably its messengers) is suffering some kind of 'violence'.

(viii) A similar picture of eschatological turbulence is described in 12:51–53:[6] using the language of Mic 7:6, Q's Jesus refers to the idea, widespread in Jewish apocalyptic, of internecine fighting as part of the events leading up to the End.[7] Thus Q 12:51–53 appears to see the time inaugurated by Jesus as the time of the eschatological events themselves.

This era of eschatological fulfilment is clearly seen in Q as inextricably linked with the person of Jesus. It is Jesus' actions which fulfil the Isaianic prophecies; it is Jesus' exorcisms which constitute the arrival of the kingdom in 11:20 (even though, notoriously, Q seems fully aware that exorcisms as such are not the unique prerogative of Jesus, or even of Jesus' supporters: cf. Q 11:19). And in Q 12:51–53, it is Jesus himself who brings the eschatological division within families.

---

[4] The meaning of 'has arrived' (rather than just 'has drawn near') for ἔφθασεν here is generally accepted as well-established. See Kümmel, *Promise*, 105–7, for a classic statement of the case.

[5] See Dahl, 'Parables of Growth'. One can still hold to the idea of the parables as implying the twin idea of the Kingdom being both present and future, without adopting the by now discredited interpretation of the parables as having an idea of the Kingdom 'growing in the hearts of men'.

[6] See Hoffmann, *Studien*, 63, 72f.; Kloppenborg, *Formation*, 152.

[7] Cf. *1 En* 100:1f.; *Jub* 23:12; *4 Ezra* 6:24; SB I, 586; IV, 977–86. Mic 7:6 is cited in *m.Sotah* 9:15 in relation to the prelude to the coming of the Messiah.

One exception to this general picture might be Q 16:16, where one can interpret the logion as implying that the new era, following that descibed as 'the law and the prophets' which was 'until John', starts with John himself. However, this is no less 'Christological' for Q, as Q 7:27f. clarifies. Here, as we have seen, John's status is at one level emphatically asserted as one which fulfils scripture; but the text cited makes it clear that John, as the one who fulfils this particular scripture (the mixed, and modified, citation of Mal 3 and Exod 23) is the forerunner of someone else, i.e. (for Q) Jesus. John's high status as the inaugurator of the era of eschatological fulfilment is precisely, and only, in relation to the person of Jesus himself. Q's 'realised eschatology' is thus firmly tied to its Christological awareness. We should also note in this context the way in which the significance of Jesus for Q is shown by the nature of Q itself. Q puts forward its message precisely as a re-presentation of the teaching of the earthly Jesus. Further it is made quite clear that that teaching is expected to be heard and obeyed. The end of the Great Sermon in 6:47–49, with the parable of the two houses on the rock/sand, spells out the (eschatological: cf. p. 142 above) significance of responses to the teaching of Jesus. So too the famous SM saying in Q 12:8f. states that reaction to Jesus' preaching in the form of either 'confessing' or 'denying' will have precisely equivalent consequences for the hearers at the final judgement. Jesus for Q is thus a teacher whose teaching has eschatological significance, whose teaching is to be obeyed, and thus a figure whom one ignores at one's peril.

This is, of course, not the whole story. As the whole of ch. 5 has indicated, much of Q is dominated by the idea of a future eschatological event (or series of events) which it is anxious to warn people about. So too, much of the material referred to above, indicating an element of eschatological fulfilment, makes it clear that such fulfilment is by no means final. The kingdom is present only as a tiny, hidden mustard seed or piece of leaven, and the fullness of the kingdom is yet to come. The signs of the kingdom in Jesus' ministry alluded to in Isaianic terms in Q 7:22 are not unambiguous, as the immediately following beatitude in Q 7:23 makes clear: it is still possible to be 'scandalised' at Jesus. Similarly, although the teaching of Jesus may have ultimate significance for Q and reaction to that teaching will be decisive for Q's audience (cf. Q 6:47–49), the saying in Q 12:10 about speaking a word against the SM as being forgivable seems to imply that reaction to the earthly Jesus is not quite so decisive: those who have spoken against the earthly Jesus can and will be forgiven in that they are given another chance by being confronted by the preaching of the Q Christians.[8] Similarly, the eschatological turmoil inaugurated by Jesus in 12:51–53 constitutes only the start of a longer process culminating (presumably for Q) in the coming of the SM in judgement. In this sense, therefore, Zeller is probably correct to say 'Jesus propagiert nach Q freilich keine in ihm "realisierte Eschatologie"'.[9] Nevertheless one cannot deny an element of qualified 'realised eschatology' in Q, and moreover it is an eschatology which is inextricably tied to the person of Jesus. For Q, then, Jesus has central significance.

Such a claim is however trite to the point of being almost vacuous without further clarification. Presumably any group of 'Christians' would ascribe central significance to Jesus: such is presumably almost the self-definition of 'Christian'. And one presumes that the Q 'Christians' will have been no different.[10] However, claims about Jesus' 'central significance' can of course be filled out in a whole variety of ways. In this chapter then I wish to consider the ways in which Q may have tried to give further meaning to the broad conviction of Jesus' importance in God's plan of salvation. In short, I wish to look at the Christology of Q.

1. Christological 'Titles'

The problem of how one should approach the subject of the Christological beliefs of any part of the Christian tradition is one that is fraught with methodological difficulties. One (perhaps traditional) approach to the whole subject of Christology is to examine the Christological titles used by the document or person under consideration.[11] Such an approach has come under fire recently for a number of reasons.[12] It runs the danger of assuming that titles have well-defined ranges of meaning, and of ignoring

---

[8] For this interpretation, see p. 108 above.

[9] Zeller, 'Zusammenhang', 70.

[10] For the use of 'Christian' in this context, see p. 107 above. I am using the term in a very loose sense here.

[11] This is broadly the approach of, for example, O. Cullmann, *The Christology of the New Testament* (ET London: SCM, 1959), or R. H. Fuller, *The Formation of New Testament Christology* (London: Lutterworth, 1965).

[12] See especially L. E. Keck, 'Toward the Renewal of New Testament Christology' *NTS* 32 (1986) 362–77.

the possibility that Christian applications of a title to Jesus may introduce a shift in the range of the meaning of the title itself. More important perhaps is the fact that in many parts of the NT, the significance of Jesus may be expressed in ways other than that of ascribing a specific title to him.[13] Further, the non-appearance of a title in one particular text does not necessarily indicate that that title or category had no significance, or was even rejected, by the writer concerned. 'Given the occasional character of the NT texts, as well as their several genres and functions, a text's christology is but a partial expression of what a writer thought about Jesus' identity and significance.'[14]

Much of this is potentially highly relevant to study of the Christology of Q. The relative sparsity of specific Christological titles in Q may suggest that Jesus' significance was being expressed in ways other than a directly titular one. The phenomenon of the non-appearance of titles or themes in a text is rather harder to assess. It is perhaps all too easy to assume what a writer 'must have' known, *and* regarded as important. As we saw when looking at earlier studies of Q, many earlier scholars took just this line: Q 'must have' presupposed *and* accepted the fuller passion-oriented kerygma of Markan and Pauline Christianity, so that Q was (just) a paranetic supplement to a cross-centred kerygma (see p. 47 above). Nevertheless, such an attitude is clearly reading quite a lot between quite a lot of lines. It remains the case that Q does not explicitly recount a version of the passion narrative, despite its chosen 'genre' of presenting (in some sense) aspects of the 'life' of the earthly Jesus which include some narrative elements. Further, although it is hard to believe that Q is not in some way influenced by Christian claims of the 'resurrection' of Jesus, it remains the case that these are not the things which Q

---

[13] Ibid., 369f.

[14] Ibid., 371. In relation to Q, see too M. Hengel, 'Christology and NT Chronology', in *Between Jesus and Paul* (ET London: SCM, 1983) 37: 'Q in no way contains the whole christology of the community, but only its collection of logia of Jesus.' Similarly P. Pokorny, *The Genesis of Christology* (ET Edinburgh: T. & T. Clark, 1987) 90. It must also be said that Keck himself is rather negative about the whole enterprise of investigating a stratum like Q in relation to Christology since Q was overtaken by Matthew and Luke: he refers to Wrede's insistence that 'the historian must distinguish what was influential from what was of but passing importance' (see Keck, 'Renewal', 367). Nevertheless Q was evidently sufficiently important to be used by both Matthew and Luke! There is perhaps an element of confessional bias in Keck's assertion here in apparently privileging the NT canon.

has chosen to re-present.[15] And this cannot be totally devoid of significance.

1.1. Christ/Messiah

There is a similar silence at the level of Christology. The Jewish term Χριστός/Messiah is never used in Q. This is rather surprising given the evidently very early use of the term to refer to Jesus (e.g. in the pre-Pauline 'credal' statement in 1 Cor 15:3) and the way in which the term then apparently became so firmly attached to Jesus, both inside and outside Jewish Christianity, that it became almost just another proper name (as in 'Jesus Christ' or 'Christ Jesus', or even as in 1 Cor 15:3 just 'Christ'). There is also the fact that 'Messiah' is a very Jewish term, and, as we shall see, Q represents a very 'Jewish' stratum of the tradition, so that the absence of the term from Q is all the more striking. Q's non-use of the term may be purely coincidental. It would perhaps be rather bold to deduce from the non-use of the term in Q that the idea of Jesus' 'Messiahship' was actually problematic for the Q Christians. Nevertheless, the non-appearance of the term serves to distinguish Q from Paul and all the evangelists and makes Q's profile rather distinctive in terms of Christology.

1.2. Lord

Another Christological title common elsewhere in primitive Christianity is κύριος, 'Lord'. This seems to have been used occasionally in Q, though not frequently. In Q 6:46, Matthew and Luke both agree in having Jesus lament those who call him κύριε κύριε but who do not 'do' what they evidently should. The object of the verb 'do' is different in the two gospels: in Luke those accused do not do 'what I say'; in Matthew calling Jesus 'Lord, Lord' is contrasted with doing 'the will of my heavenly Father'. Given Matthew's fondness for the phrase 'my heavenly Father', and his concern for the theme of doing the will of God, it seems most likely that Luke's version is more original at this point.[16]

---

[15] See the discussion in J. S. Kloppenborg, '"Easter Faith" and the Sayings Gospel Q', *Semeia* 49 (1990) 71–99.

[16] Schürmann, *Lukasevangelium*, 361; G. Strecker, *Der Weg der Gerechtigkeit* (FRLANT 82; Göttingen: Vandenhoeck & Ruprecht, 1962) 160; Schulz, *Q*, 428; Guelich, *Sermon*, 398; Catchpole, *Quest*, 97, and many others. For references to 'heavenly Father' in Matthew, cf. Matt 6:1, 14; 12:50; 15:13 (MattR of Mark);

Jesus *qua* κύριος for Q is here someone whose words should be obeyed (though evidently they are not by some): he is thus the authoritative teacher. There seem to be no overtones, in this saying at least, that Jesus *qua* κύριος is the eschatological judge.[17]

Some have seen significance in the apparent conjunction in Q of the Great Sermon, ending as it does with a reference to Jesus as κύριος, and the healing of the servant of the centurion who also addresses Jesus as κύριε (Q 7:6).[18] According to Jacobson, 'the centurion's faith answers directly to the relation of hearing to doing demanded in Q 6:46. The centurion is portrayed as a paradigm for belief in Jesus' words.'[19] This may however read too much into the story. The ἐξουσία of Jesus in the miracle story, and the active power of his healing word, are rather different from the authority of Jesus *qua* teacher and the obedience demanded to his taught word; further, the common use of κύριε in 6:46 and 7:6 is not stressed in literary terms and the usage in 7:6 need be no more than a polite form of address.[20] It would therefore probably be dangerous to see too much significance in the use of κύριε in 7:6 itself. Certainly the story as a whole presents Jesus as a powerful healer; and the story has further significance for Q in highlighting the positive response of the centurion in contrast with the lack of faith

---

16:17; 18:10, 19, 35. For Matthew's stress on the importance of ethical actions, cf. W. Schrage, *The Ethics of the New Testament* (ET Edinburgh: T. & T. Clark, 1988) 146f., and many others.

[17] See Bultmann, *History*, 116; Piper, *Wisdom*, 248 and n. 169; H. D. Betz, 'An Episode in the Last Judgement (Matt 7:21–23)', in *Essays on the Sermon on the Mount* (ET Philadelphia: Fortress, 1985) 132f. (though Betz does not believe that there is a direct relationship between Luke 6:46 and Matt 7:21–23). Catchpole, *Quest*, 99f., links κύριος here with the κύριος of the parable of the waiting servants in Q 12:42–46 so that the κύριος is the eschatological SM. This may read too much into the word κύριος itself. Undoubtedly there is a threat of eschatological judgement in the contexts in Q 6:47–49 (cf. p. 142 above). Also for Q Jesus *qua* SM is intimately concerned with that judgement (cf. 12:8f. and below). But there is no need to read all this into the κύριος reference itself at this point.

[18] Lührmann, *Redaktion*, 58; Jacobson, *First Gospel*, 99f.; cf. too Catchpole, *Quest*, 99.

[19] Jacobson, ibid.

[20] See Kloppenborg, *Formation*, 117. For the ambiguous nature of the vocative use of κύριε, being potentially no more than a polite form of address, see C. F. D. Moule, *The Origin of Christology* (Cambridge University Press, 1977) 35.

shown by (the rest of) Israel.[21] But the use of the vocative κύριε in the middle of the narrative does not appear to have a great deal of Christological significance in itself.

Catchpole seeks to enhance the Christological significance of the centurion's addressing Jesus as κύριος by his interpretation of the notorious crux in Q 7:8, where the centurion appears to imply that Jesus is a person 'under authority', and also by referring to the man's claim that he is not ἱκανός to come to Jesus.[22] Catchpole argues that the ἔχων clause in v. 8b may be just concessive ('I am under authority, *although* I too have . . .'): in v. 8a the words καὶ γὰρ ἐγὼ ἄνθρωπός εἰμι may be intended to associate the centurion not with Jesus, but with others who as men (cf. the explicit ἄνθρωπός) are qualitatively different from Jesus (cf. Acts 10:26 for a similar phrase in relation to Peter). In relation to the 'unworthiness' of the centurion, Catchpole claims that a number of references associate God with ἱκανός (cf. Ruth 1:20–21; Job 21:15; 31:2; 39:32 [= 40:2 MT]). Thus:

> Human expressions of lack of ἱκανότης are provoked, or remedied, by their being set against the overwhelming reality of God [Catchpole refers to Exod 4:10; Joel 2:11; 1 Cor 15:9; 2 Cor 2:6, 16; 3:5, 6]. Therefore a ἱκανός statement such as Q 7:6b necessarily resonates with a sense of the great gulf fixed between the human and the divine. Absolutely no encouragement can be found here for a subordinationist christology.[23]

If I understand Catchpole's argument correctly, he seems to be suggesting that Jesus *qua* κύριος is almost divine. Such a theory is not however entirely persuasive. In relation to Q 7:8, Acts 10:26 is not clearly a real parallel (ἄνθρωπός in Acts 10 is clearly the sole predicate, unlike Q 7:8 where it is in apposition to either ἐγώ or ὑπὸ ἐξουσίας). In Acts there is a clear contrast between a human and a non- (or more than) human figure; in Q 7 any such contrast is not clear, and it is not even certain that a contrast is being drawn at all, rather than a parallel being asserted. Further, the parallels Catchpole cites for a concessive participle[24] are not extensive and in any case are

---

[21] For the question of whether the centurion is thought of as being a Gentile, see pp. 395–7 below.

[22] Catchpole, *Quest*, 299–304.

[23] Catchpole, *Quest*, 302.

[24] He cites in turn the examples from Moule, *Idiom Book*, 102: 1 Cor 9:19; 2 Cor 10:3; Gal 2:3; Phlm 8.

not clearly concessive.[25] The more traditional interpretation — that the centurion implies that Jesus, like he himself, is *under* authority (for Jesus, under God), but thereby in a position to give orders to others, seems more persuasive.[26]

The argument about ἱκανός is also a little forced. Texts such as Ruth 1:20f.; Job 21:15, etc. simply use ἱκανός (as the 'translation' of the Hebrew שַׁדַּי) as virtually a proper name for God. Such a usage is scarcely comparable to Q 7:6.[27] Lack of worthiness in the presence of God is certainly a standard Jewish theme,[28] but lack of worthiness itself need not imply a divine co-referent (cf. Luke 15:19; Matt 10:37f., perhaps too Q 3:16, though as this refers to Jesus, the argument here may be somewhat circular!) Given the ambiguous nature of the vocative κύριε, and of the reference to ἱκανός, it would seem precarious to try to get quite as much Christological mileage out of this as Catchpole does.

Other references to Jesus as κύριος in Q are uncertain. It might be that in the account of the two would-be disciples (Q 9:57–60), the second addresses Jesus as κύριε. Matt 8:21 has the man say this; Luke's immediate parallel (Luke 9:59) does not, but Luke's third claimant (in Luke 9:61, peculiar to Luke) also addresses Jesus as κύριε, possibly in reminiscence of the κύριε in Matt 8:21 = Q. On the other hand, Matthew's use of κύριε is explicable as MattR, given Matthew's tendency to have disciples in his story use this address of Jesus.[29] Further, Luke's usage in 9:61 is fully in line with Luke's tendency to multiply references to Jesus as κύριος, and is closely followed by Luke 9:54, so that a LkR origin is just as likely. Given the lack of a clear parallel between Matthew and Luke here it would probably be precarious

[25] For example, Gal 2:3, and perhaps 1 Cor 9:19, could be causal: e.g. does Gal 2:3 say that 'although Titus was a Greek, he was not compelled to be circumcised', or 'precisely because he was a Greek . . .'?

[26] Cf. Manson, *Sayings*, 64f.; Tödt, *Son of Man*, 257; Schulz, *Q*, 243. Such an interpretation would also mesh well with the Q temptation narrative, where, as we shall see, a prime feature of the story is to show Jesus as supremely *obedient* (see pp. 420–2 below).

[27] The man's saying 'I am not ἱκανός' is in no sense saying 'I am not God Almighty'!

[28] Joel 2:11 LXX. Exod 4:10 is scarcely comparable (*pace* also Davies & Allison, *Matthew II*, 23): there Moses says simply οὐκ ἱκανός εἰμι in a context which seems to imply only that Moses is not *able* to do what he has been told to do, not that he is not worthy to do so. This is at least what the MT here implies, and the LXX Greek *can* be taken in this way.

[29] Strecker, *Weg*, 124; Bornkamm, *Tradition*, 41.

to place any weight on a possible use of κύριος at this point in Q.[30]

Q also contains references to ὁ κύριος in the parable of the waiting servants (Q 12:43 ὁ κύριος αὐτοῦ) and possibly also in the parable of the talents/pounds (cf. Q 19:16, 18, 20 — in both Matthew and Luke). The κύριος of the parable of Q 12:42–46 is probably seen by Q as the returning Jesus; and the master of the parable of the pounds is seen as equivalent to an eschatological judging figure who could well be identified by Q as Jesus (cf. below). Nevertheless it would probably be pressing the imagery and wording of the parables too far to claim that the precise verbal representation in a fictional story of a master (κύριος) of a slave is being transferred directly to Jesus so that Jesus becomes ὁ κύριος in a religiously and Christologically significant sense.[31] It seems much more likely that the κύριος references in the parables are simply parts of the stories. It is true that aspects of the story are seen by Q as Christologically significant: the master of each story will 'return' and will reward/punish servants who have been faithful/idle. Yet, as we shall see, the primary 'title' by which Q refers to Jesus acting in this capacity is 'SM', not κύριος. Thus κύριος for Q does not appear to be a term of great Christological significance.

2. Wisdom's Envoy

Far more important for Q seem to be the passages where Jesus is connected in some way with the figure of Wisdom. Some of the relevant passages have been considered already so there is no need to repeat the detailed analyses here. In Q 9:58, for example, it is possible the saying about Jesus' homelessness is intended to reflect the motif of the rejection and consequent homelessness of Wisdom (cf. p. 182 above). Texts such as these have led some scholars in the past to speak of a 'Wisdom Christology' whereby Jesus is identified with the person of Wisdom.[32] More recent studies have tended to be rather more cautious; for example, in the light of tendencies to identify different strata in Q, some have seen a full-blown Wisdom Christology only in the saying often

---

[30] And in any case we must remember the potentially insignificant nature of the vocative address: see n. 20 above.

[31] *Pace* Catchpole, *Quest*, 99.

[32] Cf. especially F. Christ, *Jesus Sophia: die Sophia Christologie bei den Synoptikern* (Zürich: TVZ, 1970).

regarded as a relative late-comer into Q, viz. Q 10:21f.[33] Elsewhere in Q, Jesus' position is seen rather as one of Wisdom's messengers, and it is primarily Matthew who 'upgrades' the Christology to identify Jesus with Wisdom.[34] For example, the saying in Q 7:35 'Wisdom is justified by (all) her children'[35] provides the climax of the parable of the playing children and indeed probably the climax of the whole section in Q 7:18–35 about Jesus and John (cf. p. 131 above). We saw earlier that probably the 'children' of Wisdom are those who respond to Wisdom's message, rather than the messengers themselves, and that this reflects language used elsewhere in the Wisdom tradition (cf. Prov 8:32; Sir 4:11; 15:2). John and Jesus appear in tandem; hence Jesus can scarcely be identified with Wisdom itself in any Christologically significant way which distinguishes him from John. Rather, Jesus and John are messengers of Wisdom, rejected by 'this generation', but acknowledged to be in the right by Wisdom's true children.[36]

The same idea is probably in mind, though with a significant extra degree of specificity, in the doom oracle in Q 11:49–51. As we saw earlier, this oracle is for Q cast mostly in the form of a saying of Wisdom in the past,[37] so that any identification of Jesus with Wisdom seems impossible at the level of Q. Here Wisdom appears as the agent who sends out the prophets, all of whom suffer rejection and violence. We saw earlier too that this saying represents a highly distinctive coming together of two themes in Judaism, that of rejected Wisdom and that of the violent fate suffered by the prophets. There is nothing explicitly Christological in the saying in Q: the oracle gives the prediction of Wisdom of the future rejection of (all) her prophetic messengers with no one messenger explicitly singled out for mention. Nevertheless, if we are right to see some temporal reference in the use of the phrase 'this generation' (cf. above), then there is an

---

[33] In view of the complexity of these verses, this text is discussed separately at the end of the next chapter: see pp. 276–81 below.

[34] Cf. Suggs, *Wisdom*; Dunn, *Christology*, 197ff., and see p. 167 n. 8, p. 178 n. 42 above.

[35] Matthew's ἔργων for τέκνων serves to create an inclusio between Matt 11:2 ('the works of Christ') and 11:19 ('the works of Wisdom'). See Suggs, *Wisdom*, 37; Lührmann, *Redaktion*, 29f.; Schürmann, *Lukasevangelium*, 428.

[36] See also my *Revival*, 150f., with further references.

[37] Matthew again identifies Jesus with Wisdom and makes the oracle into a saying of Jesus in the present. Within Q, v. 51b may be intended to be a saying of Jesus in the present: see p. 171 above.

implied focusing of attention here. The oracle threatens 'this generation' with the consequences of the rejection of all Wisdom's messengers up to the present. 'This generation' thus represents the climax of the whole series of those who have rejected Wisdom's envoys; by implication the series of Wisdom's envoys itself is now reaching its climax. Thus, by implication, Jesus himself probably represents the climax of this series so that Jesus is being seen as the culmination of the succession of Wisdom's messengers and, as such, one of the suffering prophets.[38] The oracle thus implies less of a 'Wisdom Christology' and more of a 'prophetic Christology'.

The same is probably true of the lament in Q 13:34f. Here it is not certain whether Q regards the speaker as Wisdom (perhaps continuing the doom oracle) or as Jesus (see p. 173 above). However, the substance of the saying is so closely related to that of the doom oracle that it is unlikely that there is any great difference in terms of the basic Christological scheme being proposed: Wisdom is still the one who sends out the prophets; Jesus is the final envoy of Wisdom, and indeed that finality is shown by the fact that 'Jerusalem' is now about to be forsaken — the appeal of Wisdom through her envoys is coming to an end. Thus once again Jesus appears as one of Wisdom's envoys, the last in the line of prophetic messengers who (by implication) suffers the fate of all such messengers, viz. rejection and violence.

In this context it may then be worth noting that Q does implicitly take some note of Jesus' death. Jesus' death seems to be on a par with the violence and death suffered by all the prophetic messengers sent by Wisdom down the ages.[39] Thus Q does seem

---

[38] Cf. Hamerton-Kelly, *Pre-Existence*, 32; Dunn, *Christology*, 201f.

[39] Cf. Hoffmann, *Studien*, 187–90; Schulz, *Q*, 343; Lührmann, 'The Gospel of Mark and the Sayings Collection Q', 64; Jacobson, 'Literary Unity', 386; Kloppenborg, *Formation*, 111f., 201, 228f.

The attempt by Seeley, 'Blessings', to delineate up to five different stages in 'Q's' thinking about the death of Jesus via the sayings in Q 14:27; 6:22ab, 23ab; 6:22c + 23c; 7:31–35; 11:49–51; 13:34f. seems to me to be unpersuasive. The question of whether Q 14:27 can be interpreted as the willingness to follow in the steps of a philosopher-teacher to death, as in the Cynic and/or Stoic tradition, is considered briefly later (see p. 321 below). I am also sceptical about separating Q 6:22c from the rest of the beatitude (cf. pp. 246–7 below): hence I am not persuaded that a 'Cynic' interpretation of an earlier form of the beatitude is appropriate. Besides these problems of detail, there is the methodological problem of trying to distinguish different views on the basis of such a small amount of data, and of taking the silence of a (very) small isolated logion (e.g. the absence of any explicit reference to the prophets in Q 14:27) as significant: see my 'Stratification', 217f.

to have an awareness of Jesus' death and to have provided that death with an interpretative category. This is not to say that Q presupposes a passion narrative. Nor does Q's interpretative scheme ascribe any strictly 'redemptive' significance to Jesus' death (in the manner of Paul or Mark 10:45). It is thus a relatively 'low' view of Jesus' suffering and death. It is unclear too how far Q views Jesus' sufferings as unique.[40] In one way they are qualitatively the same as the sufferings of the prophets in the past, and their uniqueness seems to lie more in the fact that the rejection of Jesus and his message is being presented as the final definitive rejection of God.[41] Still one is probably justified in saying that Q has taken at least some note of Jesus' death and has sought to find meaning in it.

We have seen that the Wisdom passages in Q imply that Jesus is seen as the final messenger of Wisdom, the last in the line of Wisdom's envoys, these envoys being regarded as prophets who experience rejection and violence. In terms of 'titles', it might then be more appropriate to think in terms of Jesus as 'eschatological prophet' quite as much as in Wisdom categories. This can be supported from elsewhere in Q by the use made of Isa 61:1f. to refer to the ministry of Jesus. This text is referred to in the reply of Jesus to the messengers of John the Baptist (Q 7:22), arguably in Q's version of the beatitudes (Q 6:20f.) and in the rejection scene in Nazareth in Luke 4:16ff., which *may* also in part stem from Q. It is to these passages which we now turn.

3. Isa 61 and Q

The potential significance of Isa 61 for the development of NT Christology is now widely acknowledged. In particular, the evidence from Qumran, especially the 11QMelch text, has shown that Isa 61:1f. was being interpreted in the first century as referring to an eschatological prophetic figure.[42] In the 11QMelch fragment, the text of Isa 61 is applied to the prophetic figure of Isa 52:7, the 'evangeliser' who brings good news to

---

[40] The corporate, non-unique, aspect of the schema is stressed by Kloppenborg, 'Easter Faith', 76–82.

[41] With of course the proviso that Jesus' message is now being *re*-presented by Q Christians and giving 'this generation' a last chance to repent.

[42] See Stuhlmacher, *Evangelium*, 142–7; cf. too 1QH 18:14. Stanton, 'Christology', 30f.; A. S. van der Woude & M. de Jonge, '11QMelchizedek and the New Testament', *NTS* 12 (1966) 301–26, pp. 306f.

Israel. Thus the one who is described as 'anointed' with the holy spirit is being seen as a prophetic figure (rather than, for example, a royal figure).

3.1. Q 7:22

There is clear evidence that, at least at one point in Q, the language of Isa 61:1 was predicated of Jesus. This occurs in Jesus' reply to the Baptist, where the climax of the reply is the claim that with Jesus 'the poor are being evangelised' (Q 7:22).[43] Thus in Jesus' ministry, the activity of the figure described in Isa 61:1 as anointed to 'evangelise the poor' is finding its fulfilment.[44] Q's Jesus is thus here presenting himself primarily in prophetic terms: Jesus' ministry is to be seen as the fulfilment of various Isaianic texts (cf. p. 126 above), but above all of the text in Isa 61 referring to the final End-time prophet.

The prophetic category implied at the end of the saying may also make sense of one or two odd features in the rest of the verse. Very often Jesus' reply is taken as a pastiche of OT references, taken from Isaianic prophecies of the End-time, notably Isa 29:18f. and 35:5f. However, at least one clause in Q 7:22 finds no parallel in the Isaianic prophecies, viz. the reference to 'cleansing lepers'. So too the reference to 'raising the dead' is hard (though not quite impossible) to derive from the Isaianic prophecies (cf. Isa 26:19).[45] It is however possible that both references are influenced by the prophetic tradition: the one who raised the dead in the OT is the prophet Elijah (1 Ki 17), and the one who healed leprosy was the prophet Elisha (2 Ki 5). Thus the allusions here to raising the dead and healing leprosy, whilst no doubt heavily influenced by traditions of the historical Jesus' own

[43] For this as the climax of the reply, see Hoffmann, *Studien*, 205; Schulz, *Q*, 199; Schürmann, *Lukasevangelium*, 411; Dunn, *Jesus and the Spirit*, 60. *Pace* Sevenich-Bax, *Konfrontation*, 328f., though her appeal to, for example, Hoffmann to support her is surely misguided. Hoffmann's claim that the idea of an end-time prophetic messenger lies 'in the background' ('im Hintergrund') here is not intended as a denial that such an idea is in the foreground. Rather, it is an assertion that such an idea *is* the appropriate background to interpret the Q text here. Cf. his earlier comment: 'Durch die ungewöhnliche Stellung am Ende der Reihe (nach der Totenerweckung) bekommt die Botschaft an die Armen einen besonderen Akzent.'

[44] See Stanton, 'Christology', 30. The reference to Isa 61 here is universally acknowledged.

[45] Cf. Schürmann, *Lukasevangelium*, 412; Hoffmann, *Studien*, 208f.; Polag, *Christologie*, 30.

activity,[46] may also have been explicitly mentioned here to show Jesus, as the eschatological prophet, continuing in the line of the prophets Elijah and Elisha. The text here thus provides a significant link with another part of the story in Luke 4:16–30, viz. vv. 25–27 where Jesus' activity is also compared with that of Elijah and Elisha.

3.2. Q 6:20f.

The evidence of the beatitudes (Q 6:20f.) is not quite so unambiguous. Few would deny that Isa 61:1f. has influenced the wording of the beatitudes at some stage in the development of the tradition. For example, the blessing on the 'poor' in the first beatitude reflects Isa 61:1; and the language of Matthew's second beatitude ('Blessed are those who mourn for they will be comforted') echoes the wording of Isa 61:2 ('comfort all those who mourn'). There is however dispute about whether this similarity is already present at the level of Q, or whether it is MattR which has significantly enhanced the allusions to Isa 61.[47]

In the first beatitude, most would agree that the object of the beatitude in Q is the 'poor', and that Matthew's 'poor in spirit' is due to his redactional change, 'spiritualising' the beatitude in the same way as he has modified the 'hungry' of Matt 5:6 to refer to those who 'hunger and thirst after righteousness'.[48] The promise of the 'kingdom' to the 'poor' may be seen as, in general terms, an actualisation of the prophecy of Isa 61:1, where the prophetic figure brings good news (evangelises) the poor. However, one must say that apart from the common reference to the 'poor' and the very general idea of eschatological promise, the verbal overlap between the first beatitude and Isa 61:1 is not strong.

The beatitude about the mourners/weepers is more significant for the present enquiry. It is in the Matthean version (οἱ πενθοῦντες . . . παρακληθήσονται) that the allusion to Isa 61:2

---

[46] Cf. Hoffmann, *Studien*, 208f.

[47] For what follows, see my 'The Beatitudes: A Source-Critical Study', *NovT* 25 (1983) 193–207, with further detail at times. For the allusions to Isa 61 as due to MattR, see Guelich, *Sermon*, 74 and *passim*; H. Frankemölle, 'Die Makarismen (Mt 5,1–12, Lk 6,20–23). Motive und Umfang der redaktionellen Komposition', *BZ* 15 (1971) 52–75; for Q, see Dunn, *Jesus*, 55; Schürmann, *Lukasevangelium*, 326f.; Dupont, *Béatitudes II*, 92–9; Davies & Allison, *Matthew I*, 437f.

[48] Schulz, *Q*, 77; Strecker, *Weg*, 150f.; Luz, *Matthew 1–7*, 227; Davies & Allison, *Matthew I*, 442, 451; Catchpole, *Quest*, 84, and many others.

(παρακαλέσαι πάντας τοὺς πενθοῦντας) is clearest. Luke's version (οἱ κλαίοντες νῦν . . . γελάσετε) is not so close verbally to the OT text. A decision about whether Matthew or Luke is closer to the Q version here is thus critical and we must examine the possible Q wording here in more detail. The situation is complicated by the presence in Luke of four woes (Luke 6:24–26) which correspond closely to the beatitudes. The origin of the woes is disputed, though it is uniformly agreed that the woes had no independent existence apart from the beatitudes with which they now form antitheses. Woes without beatitudes do indeed occur elsewhere (cf. Isa 5:8ff.; Hab 2:9ff.; Q 11:42ff.), but the very close parallelism between the detailed wording of the woes in Luke 6 and the corresponding beatitudes suggests that the former have been constructed only in the light of the latter.[49] This suggests either that the woes are a LkR creation in the light of the beatitudes, or a pre-Lukan (?Q) expansion of them. Thus in looking at the beatitude of the mourners/weepers we have to consider the corresponding woe as well.

One feature of potential significance here is the reference to 'laughing' in both Luke's version of the beatitude and in the corresponding woe. These are the only occurrences of the word γελάω in Luke–Acts and hence it seems unlikely that the usage here is due to LkR in the beatitude *and* to a redactional creation imitating it in the woe.[50] Either both are pre-Lukan, or one is pre-Lukan and the other due to redactional assimilation. In either case it seems that Luke's tradition has supplied the word at least once.[51]

The use of γελάω elsewhere leads further. Rengstorf has shown how γελάω/שָׂחַק has a somewhat pejorative use in the OT.[52] Here 'laughing' is an act of scorn, or an expression of superiority (cf. 2 Ki 19:21; Job 9:23; 22:19; Neh 2:19; Ps 22:7; 80:6; Isa 37:32), or of

---

[49] Schürmann, *Lukasevangelium*, 341; Marshall, *Luke*, 247.

[50] For the un-Lukan nature of the word, see Schürmann, *Lukasevangelium*, 332; Schulz, *Q*, 78.

[51] This incidentally provides difficulty for Goulder's view that Luke's beatitude, and the woe, are both due to LkR. Cf. my 'Beatitudes', 197. Goulder's reply does not address the unusual 'laughing' reference. In his *Luke*, 350, he simply appeals to a 'rather crude opposition' of 'weep and laugh'. But still the un-Lukan nature of the reference to laughing is unexplained.

[52] K. H. Rengstorf, γελάω, *TWNT* I, 656–60. One exception may be the use of שָׂחַק in Ps 126:2; but the LXX uses χάρα here so that if γελάω is explained as due to LkR under the influence of Ps 126 (so Harnack, *Sayings*, 50), one must still explain why Luke uses the (for him) unusual word.

mocking disbelief (Gen 17:17; 18:12, 13, 15). It rarely has any connotations of joy. The use of γελάω in the woe in Luke 6:25 fits this background well. Those who laugh are *not* those who will be ultimately rewarded: rather, 'laughing' seems to be regarded as reprehensible. On the other hand, the use of γελάω in Luke 6:21, to denote the promised state of those presently in distress, does not seem to fit the OT linguistic background so well. It seems most likely that, of the two, the usage in the woe is more original and that in the beatitude is due to LkR, Luke being perhaps unaware of the slightly specialised use of the verb in Jewish tradition. Hence if γελάω in Luke 6:21 is LkR, Matthew's παρακληθήσονται is more likely to be original.[53]

The other main difference between Matthew and Luke here concerns the description of those addressed as οἱ πενθοῦντες (Matthew)/οἱ κλαίοντες (Luke). πενθέω could be due to MattR, though the evidence is not strong. The word occurs elsewhere in Matthew only in Matt 9:15 (diff Mk 2:19 — hence clearly MattR assuming Markan priority, but this is the only other occurrence in Matthew). On the other hand, κλαίω is used frequently by Luke (2–4–10 + 3) and hence may well be due to LkR. Further, Luke's πενθήσετε καὶ κλαύσετε in the woe in v. 25 looks overloaded, and if κλαίω is redactional, this would confirm the use of πενθέω in Luke's tradition here. Hence Matthew's use of πενθέω most probably preserves his tradition's wording (i.e. Q) and Luke's version can be adequately explained as LkR. The result of this discussion is that Matthew's wording of the beatitude is probably more original and hence the allusion to Isa 61:2 ('comfort' for those who 'mourn') is part of Matthew's tradition already in Q. It is not due to MattR.[54]

The third beatitude, about the hungry, might just reflect Isa 61 too in that the motif of the hungry being fed is similar (though no more) to the general promise of well-being in Isa 61:6f. which includes the reference to 'eating the wealth of nations'.[55]

---

[53] Contra Schürmann, Schulz, as in n. 50 above, who take both uses in Luke as traditional. This ignores the possibility of redactional assimilation.

[54] The evidence above may also give some support to the theory that the woes also formed part of Q since the woe considered here is in part pre-Lukan and yet intimately connected to the beatitude. However, not a lot of weight will be placed on such a theory here for the study of Q as a whole. For further argument about the possible presence of the woes in Q, see my 'Beatitudes', 199.

[55] Cf. Schürmann, *Lukasevangelium*, 331, with other references.

However, the verbal agreement is not at all close and one should probably not lay any great value on such a possible parallel.

Nevertheless, whatever one decides about the third beatitude, the evidence of the first two beatitudes is not to be gainsaid. Probably all three beatitudes should be seen together, so that the 'poor', the 'mourners' and the 'hungry' are not three separate groups but a single group described in three ways with the promise to them couched in the language of Isa 61:1f.[56] Further, these beatitudes occur at a vitally important point in Q. They form the start of the Great Sermon which inaugurates Q's account of Jesus' teaching. They can therefore justifiably be seen as outlining the terms in which the whole of what follows is to be seen.[57] It could be argued that the opening three beatitudes are 'only' part of Q's tradition: these three beatitudes are widely regarded as stemming from the historical Jesus, and the fourth beatitude is more probably of post-Easter origin containing at least one secondary, probably Q-redactional, gloss in 6:23c (cf. p. 180 above). Nevertheless, it would probably be misleading to 'write off' elements of Q's tradition as contributing nothing to Q's interests (cf. p. 80 above). The important place which the opening beatitudes occupy within Q's structure and composition suggests that Q regards them as extremely important. Q's Jesus thus starts with the programmatic claim that the promises of Isa 61:1f. are now being articulated afresh in his own preaching. Jesus himself is thereby implicitly being presented as the eschatological fulfilment of that text: he is the one anointed by the Spirit to evangelise the poor, i.e. the eschatological prophet.

3.3. Luke 4:16ff.

Neither of the passages considered so far explicitly cites Isa 61: they simply use the language of that text in describing and re-presenting Jesus' words. The one place in the NT where Isa 61 is explicitly cited is the rejection scene in Nazareth in Luke 4:16ff. The importance of Isa 61 for Q's Christology would be significantly increased if it could be shown that this passage in Luke 4 also stemmed from Q (although the importance of Isa 61 in Q is still strongly evidenced by the passages already considered,

---

[56] Dupont, *Béatitudes II*, 13; Catchpole, *Quest*, 86.

[57] Catchpole, *Quest*, 80: 'The Q editor signals his conscious concern with design, his intention to place all that follows under the control of Q 6:20b–23.'

viz. Q 6:20f. and 7:22). Any theory that a piece of Matthean or Lucan *Sondergut* formed part of Q must be tested critically, as we have seen already.[58] The 'burden of proof' must inevitably lie with those who would claim that M or L traditions did belong to Q. However, in the case of Luke 4:16ff. I believe a strong case can be mounted for arguing that a significant part of the passage belongs within Q. I have given detailed reasons elsewhere,[59] and I remain persuaded, despite the counter-arguments which have been produced.[60]

It is widely recognised that this pericope in Luke is extremely important for Luke's overall literary plan, functioning as a programmatic summary of the story that is to follow in his two-volume work: the rejection of Jesus in his home town prefigures the rejection of Jesus in the passion, and that of the gospel by the Jewish nation, the Gentile mission being alluded to in the notes about Elijah and Elisha (Luke 4:25–27).[61] However, there is wide divergence of opinion about the nature of Luke's sources here with various possibilities proposed, e.g. that Luke redacted the

---

[58] For the problem in general, see pp. 92–6 above.

[59] See my 'Luke 4, Isaiah and Q', in Delobel (ed.), *LOGIA*, 343–354, following in part H. Schürmann, 'Der "Bericht vom Anfang". Ein Rekonstruktionsversuch auf Grund von Lk 4,14–16' in *StEv* 2 (*TU* 87; Berlin, 1964) 242–58; also his 'Zur Traditionsgeschichte der Nazareth-Perikope Lk 4,16–30', in *Mélanges Bibliques* (FS B. Rigaux; Gembloux: Duculot, 1970) 187–205, on which see also Stanton, 'Christology', 32f.

[60] See J. Delobel, 'La rédaction de Lc IV,14–16a et le Bericht vom Anfang', in Neirynck (ed.), *L'Evangile de Luc*, 113–33, and his 'Notes Additionelles' on p. 310f.; F.Neirynck, 'Ac 10,36–43 et l'Evangile', *ETL* 60 (1984) 109–17 (= *Evengelica II*, 227–36). Goulder, *Luke*, 308 notes the possibility briefly; Schmithals, *Einleitung*, 217, dismisses it as a 'Verletzung'. See the survey in C. J. Schreck, 'The Nazareth Pericope: Luke 4,16–30 in Recent Study', in Neirynck (ed.), *L'Evangile de Luc*, 399–471, pp. 414–24. Most recently, D. R. Catchpole, 'The Anointed One in Nazareth', in M. C. de Boer (ed.), *From Jesus to John* (FS M. de Jonge; Sheffield Academic Press, 1993) 231–51.

[61] See Conzelmann, *Theology*, 31–8; Fitzmyer, *Luke*, 526; R. C. Tannehill, 'The Mission of Jesus according to Luke iv 16–30', in W. Eltester (ed.), *Jesus in Nazareth* (BZNW 40; Berlin: de Gruyter, 1972) 51–75; also his *The Narrative Unity of Luke–Acts* (Philadelphia: Fortress, 1986) 61. Further references in Schreck, 'Nazareth Pericope', 399f. The general programmatic nature of the pericope is widely accepted, though some recent doubts have been expressed about whether there is really any allusion to the Gentile mission in the references to Elijah and Elisha: see B. J. Koet, *Five Studies on Interpretation of Scripture in Luke–Acts* (Leuven University Press & Peeters, 1989) 42–52; Catchpole, 'Anointed One', 245–50.

rejection story of Mark 6 alone, or that Luke had access to an independent source here.[62] The theory that Luke used a source here, and that that source was in part Q, has been argued by H. Schürmann, developing in part earlier studies about the existence of Q in Luke 4:14–16.[63]

For the present purposes, I shall bypass the problem of Luke 4:14–16 here apart from one feature in v. 16. This concerns the common reference to Ναζαρά in Matt 4:13/Luke 4:16. In Matthew the name is probably traditional, since elsewhere Matthew uses the more usual forms Ναζαρέτ (2:23) or Ναζαρέθ (21:11).[64] The unusual spelling suggests that Matthew is using a source here, and the same form of the name in Luke 4:16 (which is equally singular in Luke) suggests that Luke has used the same source. Hence this feature constitutes strong evidence for the existence of Q material at this point.[65]

If there was an account reaching as far as v. 16a in Luke 4, it would seem inherently unlikely that it stopped there; rather, it seems more probable that it gave some account of what actually happened in Nazareth. Further, the Isaiah quotation is

---

[62] See the very full survey in Schreck, 'Nazareth Pericope', 403–27; for older literature, see M. Dömer, *Das Heil Gottes. Studien zur Theologie des lukanischen Doppelwerkes* (BBB 51; Köln-Bonn: P. Hanstein, 1978) 50f.

[63] See n. 59 above.

[64] These are the readings of the 26th edition of the Nestle-Aland text. There are variants in all the texts concerned, but there is virtually no support for reading Ναζαρά apart from Matt 4:13 and Luke 4:16. At both the latter places, Ναζαρά is generally reckoned to be the harder reading and therefore more likely to be original. For a full discussion of the evidence, see G. M. Soarez Prabhu, *The Formula Quotations in the Infancy Narrative of Matthew* (AnB 63; Rome: Biblical Institute Press, 1976) 130f.; Chilton, *God in Strength*, 105f., 129, 311–3. Goulder, *Luke*, 307, argues that Ναζαρά may be Matthew's own redactional creation, based on Mark 1:24 where Jesus is said to be Ναζαρηνός, Matthew then creating Ναζαρά on the analogy of Γαδαρηνός/Γαδαρα and Μαγδαληνός/Μαγδαλα. (See also his 'Luke's Knowledge', 147f.) But Matthew seems to have avoided *any* reference to Jesus as Ναζαρηνός. Mark 1:24 is part of a whole pericope omitted by Matthew; and in Mark 10:47; 14:67; 16:6, Matthew appears deliberately to avoid just this adjective. Further, it is not clear why Matthew should have changed the form of the place name to an -αρα ending here but never elsewhere.

[65] For the existence of Q here on the basis of this evidence, see too Streeter, *Four Gospels*, 206; W. O. Walker, 'Nazareth: A Clue to Synoptic Relationships?' in E. P. Sanders (ed.), *Jesus, the Gospel and the Church* (FS W. R. Farmer; Macon: Mercer University Press, 1987) 105–18, pp. 111–3; Catchpole, 'Anointed One', 235f.

integral to the sequel, and without it the whole section collapses to nothing.[66] This suggests that the reference to Ναζαρά in v. 16a and the Isaiah quotation belong together.[67] Thus if Ναζαρά derives from Q, the Isa 61 citation may also derive from Q. The alternative would be that Luke has joined the two together. However, if the use of Isa 61 here can be shown to be, at least in part, un-Lukan (and hence pre-Lukan) in significant ways, this possibility is rendered less likely.[68] Despite several features of LkR,[69] there are indications that Luke is using source material here. For example, the use of τρέφω, rather than Luke's usual ἀνατρέφω, to mean 'to bring up',[70] and the use of βιβλίον, rather than βίβλος, both seem to be non-Lukan and hence pre-Lukan.[71]

This leads on to a consideration of the use of Isa 61 itself, where Jesus is said to be anointed by the Spirit. Elsewhere in Luke–Acts, the supreme task of the Spirit is 'prophetic' and, as we have seen, Isa 61 was being interpreted by some Jews in the first century as referring to a prophetic figure. Thus what is being propounded here is a prophetic Christology, and such a theme is

---

[66] Tannehill, 'Mission', 64, for at least vv. 16b–21; cf. too U. Busse, *Das Nazareth-Manifest Jesu* (SBS 91; Stuttgart: Katholisches Bibelwerk, 1978) 32, for vv. 17–20.

[67] This is denied by Tannehill and Catchpole who think that the Ναζαρά reference is the one traditional element here. Both take the use of Isa 61 here to be LkR, but I shall argue later that it may be pre-Lukan.

[68] The quotation is, of course, un-Lukan in the sense that the words are a quotation of Isaiah, and are not due to Luke's writing freely. Hence some parts can be accepted as un-Lukan even though Luke may have added the citation. What is more important here is if significant parts of the editing process which produced the present text can be shown to be uncharacteristic of Luke.

[69] See Tannehill, 'Mission', 64f.; Busse, *Nazareth-Manifest*, 32.

[70] Cf. Schürmann, 'Nazarethperikope', 196. Delobel, 'Rédaction', 128 (cf. too his additional note on p. 311), argues that the two verbs are interchangeable, referring to W. C. van Unnik, 'Tarsus or Jerusalem', in *Sparsa Collecta Part One* (NovTSupp 29; Leiden: Brill, 1973) 307. So also Goulder, *Luke*, 308. But the issue here is *Luke's* preferred usage, not the usage in other writers. Luke's usage elsewhere appears to be to use ἀνατρέφω for this meaning (cf. Acts 7:20, 21; 22:3), with τρέφω used for 'feed, provide with food' (cf. Luke 12:24; 23:39; Acts 12:20). Thus the usage here, whilst not impossible as Greek, does appear to be uncharacteristic of Luke. Goulder concedes that this is unlike Luke's normal usage and has to appeal to 1 Maccabees and Josephus for parallels.

[71] For βιβλίον/βίβλος, see Schürmann, 'Nazarethperikope', 192; Jeremias, *Sprache*, 121; Dömer, *Heil*, 54.

by no means uncongenial to Luke.[72] Nevertheless, there seem to be a number of un-Lukan features in the use of the Isa 61 quotation here.

Outside the present passage in Luke–Acts, the supreme task of the Spirit seems to be that of inspiring (verbal) preaching. The Spirit guides the church's mission (Acts 8:39; 10:19; 13:2; 16:7; 19:11); it inspires Christian preaching and witness (Luke 12:12; Acts 1:8; 2:4; 6:10) and it inspires prophets to prophesy (Luke 1:41, 67; 2:27; Acts 2:18). On the other hand, in Luke–Acts the Spirit is never the agent by which miracles occur.[73] Luke can refer to many 'agencies' by which miracles occur: they can occur by the 'finger' (Luke 11:20) or 'hand' (Acts 4:30; 7:35; 13:11) of God, by 'power' (Luke 4:36; 5:17; 6:19; 9:1; Acts 6:8; 10:38), or by the 'name' of Jesus (Acts 3:16; 4:18; 16:18), by 'faith' (Luke 8:48; Acts 3:16), by prayer (Acts 16:25; 18:8) or

---

[72] G. W. H. Lampe, 'The Lucan Portrait of Christ', *NTS* 2 (1956) 160–175. Cf. Luke 7:16, 39; 9:35; 24:19; Acts 3:22f.; 7:37. See too Fitzmyer, *Luke*, 213ff.; U. Busse, *Die Wunder des Propheten Jesus. Die Rezeption, Komposition und Interpretation der Wundertradition im Evangelium des Lukas* (FzB 24; Stuttgart: Katholisches Bibelwerk, 1977) esp. pp. 372f.

[73] See E. Schweizer, πνεῦμα, *TWNT* VI, 405. Also M. Rese, *Alttestamentliche Motive in der Christologie des Lukas* (Gütersloh: Mohn, 1969) 143–5; R. P. Menzies, *The Development of Early Christian Pneumatology with Special Reference to Luke–Acts* (JSNTSS 54; Sheffield Academic Press, 1991) 166ff. Busse, *Wunder*, 59f., has objected to the theory on the grounds that, if it were so, the Isaiah quotation in Luke 4 would then only apply to part of Jesus' activity, and this is contradicted by the importance which the quotation has in Luke's redaction. Further, the Spirit in Luke is synonymous with 'power', cf. 4:14. However, the question of whether the reference to the activity of the Spirit in Luke 4:18 is due to LkR, and is meant to include the whole of Jesus' ministry, is precisely the point at issue: Busse's argument is therefore circular. On Spirit and 'power' see below.

The theory has also been searchingly examined by M. Turner, 'The Spirit and the Power of Jesus' Miracles in the Lucan Conception', *NovT* 33 (1991) 124–52. Turner (rightly in my view) questions whether one can make a neat equation between Luke's view of the Spirit as a 'typically Jewish' idea of the Spirit as the 'Spirit of prophecy' (so Menzies). He shows clearly that Jewish ideas associated with the Spirit, even ideas associated with 'prophetic' activity, are quite variegated; and they do not correspond so clearly to Luke's idea of the Spirit as the agency of 'preaching' or proclamation. (See the further detail in his 'The Spirit of Prophecy and the Power of Authoritative Preaching in Luke–Acts: A Question of Origins', *NTS* 38 [1992] 66–88.) But Turner too argues that πνεῦμα for Luke can be the agency by which miracles occur. In part like Busse, Turner's argument is based on the occurrences where πνεῦμα and δύναμις occur together, or possibly interchangeably. On this see below.

even by physical contact (Luke 8:44; Acts 19:12). But miracles
do not generally seem to be the work of the Spirit. Some have
argued that δύναμις and πνεῦμα are virtually synonymous in
Luke–Acts on the basis of instances where the two appear
together or in parallel (Luke 1:35; 4:14; Acts 1:8; cf. too Luke
1:17; 24:49).[74] However, the context in which such parallelism is
used usually refers to verbal preaching and witnessing: in 4:14
Jesus comes to Galilee 'in the power of the Spirit' and teaches
(v. 15);[75] in Acts 1:8 the disciples will receive the 'power of the
Holy Spirit' and will be witnesses. So too in Acts 6:8, 10 Stephen
full of 'power' performs miracles (v. 8), but his irresistible verbal
speech is related to the work of the Spirit (v. 10).[76] On the other
hand it remains the case that, apart possibly from Luke 4 (and
perhaps Luke 1:35) the Spirit is never explicitly related to
miracles.[77] With this in mind we may now turn to the use of Isa 61
in Luke 4 itself.

It is not difficult to see why this text was congenial to Luke. The
references to 'the Spirit', 'evangelising' and 'the poor' are all

[74] See, for example, Conzelmann, *Theology*, 182f. and Busse as above. Also
Neirynck, 'Ac 10,36–43', 116. The point is strongly emphasised by Turner, 'The
Spirit and the Power', esp. pp. 138–42 (to which see also the reply by R. P.
Menzies, 'Spirit and Power in Luke–Acts: A Response to Max Turner', *JSNT* 49
[1993] 11–20).

[75] Turner, 'The Spirit and the Power', 139, argues that 'contextually the φήμη
(4:14b) of Jesus empowered by the Spirit (4:14a) appears to be based in the
miracles he performed (4:23)'. But 'contextually', the immediate context in v.
15 speaks exclusively of Jesus' 'teaching' only.

[76] Schweizer, *TWNT* VI, 405. Neirynck, 'Ac 10,36–43', 116, runs the two
together and allows each phrase to interpret the other. I would interpret the
parallel phrases as not quite so synonymous.

[77] I would not wish to argue for a rigid distinction in Luke's mind whereby
πνεῦμα always generates speech, and δύναμις always generates miracles.
δύναμις for Luke is clearly broader than that, as texts like Luke 4:14 show.
Similarly the gift of the Spirit is referred to as the bestowal of δύναμις in Luke
24:49, though again explicitly in the context of an empowerment to witness (v.
48). Luke 1:17 is also set in a context implying verbal activity.

Luke 1:35 perhaps comes closest to providing a counter-example to the
thesis I am trying to maintain (though on any showing, the 'miracle' concerned
is qualitatively quite different from the other miracles in the gospel story).
Menzies argues that the reference to the Spirit here alludes to the agency
enabling Mary to utter the Magnificat (*Development*, 127). This is not entirely
convincing, as Turner rightly says ('The Spirit and the Power', 141f.). Perhaps
though one is pressing Luke for too much precision. The reference to the *Holy*
Spirit is clearly important to enable the child Jesus to be called 'holy' (v. 35, cf.
too v. 49), and it is still the case that Luke's tendency is always to use δύναμις
language when referring to miracles.

clearly of a piece with Luke's interests.[78] However, the citation here is unusual in (*a*) omitting a clause from Isa 61:1 ('healing the broken hearted') and (*b*) adding a clause from Isa 58:6 ('setting free the oppressed'). There is no other example of a similarly mixed citation in Luke–Acts.[79] The link appears to have been made via the Greek word ἄφεσις in both Isaianic texts and hence seems to depend on the LXX version of the two texts concerned (the MT has חפשים in Isa 58:6 and דרור in Isa 61:1). It is hard to see why Luke himself should have omitted the healing clause from Isa 61.[80] Further, it is not easy to see the clauses in the composite citation which come after the clause about 'evangelising the poor' as being particularly appropriate as a Lukan summary of Jesus' or the early church's, life and work. The quotation speaks of 'sight for the blind' and 'release for the prisoners and the oppressed'. But curing blindness is not prominent among Luke's miracle stories;[81] nor is a metaphor of

[78] In Luke Jesus is the Spirit-filled man (Luke 3:21; 4:1, 14), who 'evangelises' (Luke 4:43; 7:22; 8:1; 20:1) and has a keen interest in the poor (Luke 6:20; 14:13, 21; 16:20; 18:22; 19:9; 21:3). See Tannehill, 'Mission', 69f.

[79] For Chilton, *God in Strength*, 143–7, this is decisive in assigning the quotation here to the pre-Lukan tradition. See too Dömer, *Heil*, 55f. Catchpole, 'Anointed One', 239, has to argue that 'every writer must be allowed the freedom to do something once and only once'. But as the point is precisely whether Luke has himself done this here or not, the lack of any other comparable example elsewhere in Luke's writings must be a significant factor in the decision of who was responsible for this mixed citation.

[80] I find it hard to accept the theory that Luke deliberately omitted the clause specifically to avoid any idea of Jesus performing miracles by the Spirit (so Rese, *Alttestamentliche Motive*, 145, 214; Menzies, *Development*, 166f.). Turner, 'The Spirit and the Power', 147, rightly points out that the 'healings' referred to in Isa 61 are of the 'broken hearted', and hence the reference is clearly not to physical healing at all.

[81] Luke uses Mark's story of blind Bartimaeus, but he omits the story of the blind man at Bethsaida (Mark 8:22–26). If the Q story about the cure of the possessed man referred to him as deaf and blind (Matt 12:22), Luke has omitted the reference to his blindness (Luke 11:14). There are no cases of the blind being cured in Acts apart from Paul's temporary blindness after his conversion. Turner, 'The Spirit and the Power', 149f., refers to Luke's redactional additions in 7:21 (καὶ πολλοῖς ἐχαρίσατο βλέπειν) and 18:42f. (ἀνάβλεψον) as evidence to the contrary of Luke's redactionally highlighting the allusions to Isa 61. But the clause in 7:21 prepares for 7:22 which is more likely to be an allusion to Isa 35:5 (and in any case this is already in Q, not LkR); and ἀνάβλεψον in 18:42 is more likely simply a case of Luke making Jesus respond directly to the blind man's request ἵνα ἀναβλέψω (v. 41 = Mark). The fact remains that healing blindness is scarcely a prominent feature in the activity of the Lukan Jesus.

'spiritual' 'blindness' particularly Lukan.[82] Prisoners are rarely released in Luke–Acts (only Barabbas in Luke 23 and this is simply taken over from Mark; in Acts 16, 27 prisoners do not take the opportunity to go free). If 'oppression' has any political meaning, as a reference to freedom from Roman domination, this too would be uncharacteristic of Luke since it is a feature of Luke's writings to present Christianity as not politically subversive.[83] In any case such a literal meaning of ἄφεσις would be unique in Luke–Acts since everywhere else ἄφεσις is used in the stereotyped phrase ἄφεσις ἁμαρτιῶν with the meaning 'forgiveness (of sins)'. As such this clearly represents an important Lukan theme,[84] but if that is the meaning of the word here too, then 'prisoners' and 'oppressed' would have to be metaphors for 'sinners' and this would be unique in Luke–Acts.[85]

It may be that the 'oppressed' of Isa 58:6 in Luke 4:18 is seen by Luke as referring to oppression by Satan. Acts 10:38, which is probably referring explicitly to Luke 4:18f., speaks of Jesus as anointed with the Spirit 'doing good and healing all those who were oppressed by the devil'. But if this is Luke's own understanding of Isa 58:6, it is not easy to see both this and the original reference in Luke 4:18 as Luke's own summary of the ministry of Jesus. First, it involves giving ἄφεσις in Luke 4:18 a

---

[82] Such an idea might be more characteristic of Matthew: see Matt 23:16, 17, 19, 24, 26 and also 15:14, but this is by no means so clear in the Lukan parallel in Luke 6:39.

[83] See Conzelmann, *Theology*, 138–44.

[84] Cf. Luke 1:71; 3:3; 24:47; Acts 2:38; 5:31; 10:43; 13:38; 26:18. The fact that this frequently occurs at the climax of the speeches in Acts also shows its importance for Luke. See Tannehill, 'Mission', 70.

[85] Tannehill, 'Mission', 71, implicitly recognises the difficulty, but in the end begs the question. He writes: 'The Isaiah quotation in iv. 18 speaks, of course, of release for "prisoners" and the "oppressed", and does not refer to release of sins. However, when these phrases are no longer applied to physical imprisonment, they leave considerable room for interpretation. Luke may well have included Jesus' work of healing in this release of prisoners. However, in the light of the importance to Luke of the "release of sins", this must have been an important aspect of what he had in mind when he chose to emphasise the word ἄφεσις in Luke iv. 18.' But the point at issue is whether it is indeed Luke who has chosen to emphasise ἄφεσις here. Tannehill's argument is circular if it is seeking to show that the form of the citation here is due to LkR. The reference is almost certainly to the much broader idea of release associated with the Jubilee: cf. Schürmann, *Lukasevangelium*, 230. The association of Isa 61 and Jubilee ideas is shown by the 11QMelch text: see van der Woude & De Jonge, '11QMelchizedek', 308. For Busse's theory, that 'release' here means release from the power of Satan, see below.

meaning ('healing') which the word has nowhere else in Luke–Acts. Such an uncharacteristic interpretation of the word in Luke 4:18 suggests that the latter comes to Luke as part of his tradition and the context has forbidden him from ascribing his usual meaning of 'forgiveness' to the word.[86] Secondly, it is noteworthy that Acts 10:38 appears to avoid attributing this aspect of Jesus' work to the Spirit. Luke here says that Jesus was anointed with the Spirit 'and power' (δύναμις being often used by Luke to describe the agency by which miracles occur: cf. above), and that Jesus heals 'because God was with him'. Luke's interpretation of the earlier passage seems to involve a slight modification and this again suggests that the original passage is pre-Lukan.[87] Thirdly, 'healing those oppressed by the devil' cannot easily be seen as a Lukan summary of the life of Jesus or of the early church. Certainly Luke does not see the struggle against demonic powers as negligible.[88]

[86] *Pace* Catchpole, 'Anointed One', 238 (also Turner, 'The Power and the Spirit', 147), I am *not* ascribing the meaning 'forgiveness' to ἄφεσις here for Luke. I am simply saying that the meaning which seems to be demanded for the word here is unlike Luke's usage anywhere else in Luke–Acts, and that elsewhere the usage is rather stereotyped. And since the form of the mixed citation revolves around the use of the word in precisely this sense, which is *un*characteristic for Luke, this suggests that the citation here may be due to one of Luke's source, not LkR. The stress on *this* kind of ἄφεσις as being uncharacteristic of Luke is also noted by Dömer, *Heil*, 56. Similar comments apply to the critique of Neirynck, 'Ac 10,36–43', 115, who says that I have ignored the complement ἁμαρτιῶν in referring to Luke's 'usual' meaning. My point is simply that the usage of ἄφεσις alone makes it highly unusual in Luke, and hence it is correspondingly harder to see Luke as the person responsible for the mixed citation, given the centrality of ἄφεσις in the present form of the citation. Nor is it enough to argue that this reference to 'liberation' can be a 'fitting' Lukan summary for the whole of Jesus' ministry in the light of the fact that 'liberation' is an aspect of the typically Lukan 'salvation' (so Turner, 'The Spirit and the Power', 150). In one sense this is right, since Luke has allowed the citation to have the position it does in his gospel. But the mixed form of the citation suggests more of a free composition on the part of the person responsible for it, and the stress specifically on the ἄφεσις motif, rather than σωτηρία, suggests that this is not Luke.

[87] It is of course pre-Lukan in the sense of being words from Isaiah, not freely created *de novo* by Luke, but still the use of the passage in Acts 10 suggests that that the use of the Isaiah citation in Luke 4 itself may be pre-Lukan.

[88] Jesus withstands the Devil in the Temptation (Luke 4:1ff.). In the miracles which follow the Nazareth scene in Luke 4, Luke also stresses this: the next story (4:31–37) is an exorcism; Jesus 'rebukes' Peter's mother-in-law's fever as one rebukes a demon (4:38f.); and he heals many possessed by devils (4:40f.). However the arrangement is Markan, and only the rebuking of the fever is peculiar to Luke.

He takes over the exorcism stories from Mark and Q, and he sometimes adds references to exorcisms in his generalising summaries (cf. Luke 7:21; Acts 5:16; 8:7). However, there are no extra exorcism stories in the gospel, and few explicit exorcisms in Acts.[89] Further, other diseases are only once attributed to demonic influence (Luke 13:16), so that it is doubtful how far the general healing ministry of Jesus and the early church would have been seen by Luke as part of a battle against Satan.[90]

[89] Schweizer, *TWNT* VI, 405.

[90] A quite different view is taken by Busse, who claims that all the miracles of Jesus are seen by Luke as acts of liberation from demonic powers (*Wunder*, passim, esp. pp. 428ff.). He regards the ἄφεσις motif in Luke 4:18f. as redactional; this is interpreted in 4:31–44 as release from demonic powers and this is confirmed by Acts 10:38 (p. 62). Further, he claims that Luke does not distinguish between illness and demon possession, so that all the healing miracles can be seen as similar acts of liberation. This, he claims, is shown by the use of ἀσθενοῦν to refer to a case of demon-possession (13:11) and so its link with νόσος in the summaries in 6:18; 7:21; 9:1 shows that νόσος too includes the idea that the demons are the origin of illness (p. 80); Luke 11:14; 13:16 show the same tendency to ascribe illness to Satan (p. 302), and the connection of θεραπεύω with ἀπὸ πνευμάτων νόσων in 7:21 shows that 'aus dämonischer Knechtschaft werden die Kranken errettet' (pp. 181f.). So too the normal verb for healing ἰάομαι is used in 9:42 to refer to an exorcism (p. 355). Thus, Busse, concludes 'Demnach unterscheidet Lukas nicht eindeutig zwischen Heilungen und Exorzismen' (pp. 355f.). Much of the same evidence is referred to by Neirynck, 'Ac 10,36–43', 115f.

However, much of this evidence is very weak. The link between illness and demonic possession is hard to establish. The use of neutral words like ἰάομαι and ἀσθενοῦν to apply to both healings and exorcisms is certainly not a strong enough argument on which to build such a case. (Cf. in English one speaks of 'curing' 'illness', referring to both physical and mental disorders without necessarily confusing the two.) Busse appears to misread Luke 7:21, which reads ἀπὸ νόσων καὶ μαστίγων καὶ πνευμάτων πονηρῶν, where the two categories of 'diseases' and 'evil spirits' are clearly distinguished. Similarly, Luke 4:41 ('devils came out from many') by no means requires that *all* those who were healed (v. 40) were thought of as possessed. Similarly 6:18 does not demand that *all* the sick of 6:17 were thought of as possessed. Luke 11:14 is probably Q material (cf. Matt 12:22); Luke may have agreed with his source here, but in 9:38 he does not use the note from Mark which says that the demon was 'dumb'. Luke 13:16 is the only case where physical illness is attributed to demonic power, and even here the main interest of the story lies elsewhere, i.e. in the debates about the Law (cf. P. J. Achtemeier, 'The Lucan Perspective in the Miracles of Jesus', *JBL* 94 (1975) 547–62, p. 558). Thus Busse's case that Luke regards all healings as acts of liberation from demonic powers is very uncertain. Achtemeier's comment seems appropriate when he says that it is 'clear that Luke is by no means preoccupied with Jesus' battle with the demonic' (p. 558, commenting on the similar thesis of J. M. Hull, *Hellenistic*

It is thus very unlikely that the mixed citation of Isa 61 and 58 in Luke 4 is due to LkR. It seems most probable that Luke is using a source here which he interprets, and characteristically modifies, in Acts 10. In particular, there appears to be a difference between the views of Luke and his source about the precise work of the Spirit. Luke elsewhere sees the work of the Spirit primarily in inspiring verbal preaching, whereas the source has a wider view. For the latter, the work of Jesus *qua* Spirit-anointed may also be seen in the miracles. This corresponds with what is implied in Q 7:22 where 'evangelising the poor' is closely correlated with the activity of healing the sick.[91]

The use of Isa 61 thus appears to be an important and distinctive feature of Q's Christology. Via the use of this text Jesus is shown to be a prophetic figure, possibly 'the eschatological prophet' (though one should probably be wary of tying any aspect of Jewish eschatological expectation down too closely, as if even some Jews had a definite fixed idea, e.g. of the eschatological prophet). As a prophetic figure Jesus is thus in a line of continuity with all the prophets (possibly including Elijah and Elisha: cf. Luke 4:25–27 and see p. 223 above on Q 7:22). In Q's understanding this however has further implications. For the prophets according to Q are those who suffer rejection, hostility and violence; as such they are the messengers sent out by Wisdom. Thus Jesus *qua* prophet is a rejected figure, and it may

---

Magic and the Synoptic Tradition [London: SCM, 1974]). With this in mind it becomes very doubtful if one can place too much stress on Luke 4:31–44 and Acts 10:38 as providing the key to the interpretation of the rest of Luke–Acts. Rather, these verses may show how Luke interpreted what was given to him in his tradition in Luke 4:18f., but this was not necessarily seen as governing the whole of the account in the way Busse suggests.

[91] This is by no means an obvious connection. Although it is sometimes said that miracles were associated with the eschatological prophet (cf. Hahn, *Hoheitstitel*, 393), this needs greater precision. In fact, the miracles associated with the messianic prophets mentioned by Josephus are of a quite different character: they were attempts to repeat the miracles of the Exodus and Conquest periods (cf. Hoffmann, *Studien*, 206; Dunn, *Jesus*, 58). There were hopes that the new age would see the end of all illness and a restoration of the paradisal Sinai conditions, often with reference to Isa 29, 35, but there is never any idea that these works of healing would be performed by the eschatological prophet (Stuhlmacher, *Evangelium*, 219; Hoffmann, *Studien*, 208). This conjunction, bringing together the motifs of Jesus as healer and Jesus as eschatological prophet, is thus a highly distinctive feature in the tradition, probably determined by Jesus' own ministry which included both proclamation and miracles (cf. Hoffmann, *Studien*, 208).

be no coincidence that, if indeed the Isa 61 quotation in Luke 4 comes to Luke from Q, the presentation of Jesus as the fulfilment of Isa 61 is in a scene of rejection.

One feature noted briefly earlier is that in many of the Q passages dealing with the combined ideas of rejected Wisdom and the violence suffered by the prophets, there is a mention of Jesus as 'SM'. (Cf. Q 6:22f.; 7:34f.; 9:58; 11:30.) What then is the significance of this appellation for Jesus in Q? Is it just coincidence that Jesus is often called 'SM' in these contexts? Is the 'SM' designation a way of upgrading the Christology, for example by seeking to distinguish Jesus from John the Baptist? Or is there some integral relationship between the 'SM' idea and the Wisdom–prophecy strand of the tradition? It is to this that we now turn in our further discussion of the Christology of Q.

8

━━━━◆◆◆◆━━━━

The Son of Man in Q

The problem of the use of the phrase 'SM' in the gospels is perhaps one of the most intractable in contemporary gospel studies and the secondary literature on the subject is enormous. It is, however, probably fair to say that the prime interest in the topic for many today is at the level of what the term may have meant within the preaching of the historical Jesus. Thus for many, the burning questions are whether Jesus used the term and what he may have meant by it (when probably speaking in Aramaic). For the present purposes, such problems will be shelved. We shall be primarily concerned with the meaning of the term in Q which I am taking to be a Greek 'text' (cf. pp. 83–92 above). Thus the meaning of 'SM' in any Aramaic form of the tradition will not be considered here.

However, even within Q studies, the problem of the use of 'SM' is a highly controversial one with a variety of different theories and a mushrooming secondary literature. We have already noted in passing at a number of points, especially in ch. 2, that discussions of Q's use of the term 'SM' have played a key role in many recent theories about Q's 'theology'. At times the use of the term in Q has been regarded as a key factor in distinguishing layers within Q. But in any case, the SM sayings in Q have been assigned to different postulated strata within Q in a bewildering variety of ways.[1] And especially for those who regard the distinction between 'tradition' and 'redaction' (or more complicated stratification theories) as important for isolating the Q editor's own views (e.g. by focusing on Q's 'redactional' activity), this variety has led to a corresponding variety in the assessment of the significance of 'SM' for Q's Christology.

---

[1] Some of these are surveyed in P. Hoffmann, 'QR und der Menschensohn. Eine vorläufige Skizze', in Van Segbroek et al (eds), *The Four Gospels 1992*, 421–56. ET 'The Redaction of Q and the Son of Man: A Preliminary Sketch', in Piper (ed.), *The Gospel Behind the Gospels*, 159–98.

As we saw earlier, 'SM' was the point of access for one of the earliest 'redaction'-critical studies of Q, viz. the work of Tödt. According to Tödt, Q identified Jesus with the coming SM, a figure whom Jesus himself envisaged as someone other than himself who would appear at the End-time to vindicate his cause. Thus the identification of the SM with Jesus was first made by the Q community and a 'SM Christology' (by which Tödt meant primarily an idea of Jesus returning as SM at an eschatological future event) was an extremely important aspect of the ideology of the Q Christians. In Tödt's words, 'Son of Man Christology and Q belong together both in their concepts and in their history of tradition.'[2]

However, we noted in ch. 2 the ever-increasing tendency since Tödt wrote to postulate more and more strata within Q; and such studies have sometimes suggested that SM sayings do not characterise Q's redaction but only Q's tradition. Thus SM ideas have been quietly relegated by some from the forefront of discussions about Q. Those such as Tödt, and more recently Hoffmann, who have not made much of possible distinctions between tradition and redaction within Q, have ascribed great significance to 'SM' for Q's Christology. By contrast, Lührmann's more strictly 'redaction'-critical study comes to a different conclusion.[3] Lührmann argues that the identification of the SM as Jesus had already taken place prior to the redactional stratum of Q which he identifies, i.e. that concerned above all with polemic against 'this generation'. In this polemic, use of SM sayings was only one means amongst several employed by the Q redaction and hence these sayings are not necessarily of great significance in isolating the distinctive features of that redaction.[4]

The view that the SM sayings are all pre-redactional within Q has however been argued in great detail in an influential article by H. Schürmann.[5] As we have seen, Schürmann postulates a fairly uniform four-fold development of the tradition whereby individual sayings (stage I) are interpreted by the addition of

[2] Tödt, *Son of Man*, 269.
[3] Lührmann, *Redaktion*, 40f.
[4] It should however be noted that Lührmann himself does not argue that all the SM sayings were present in Q's tradition: at least one saying (Q 11:30) is ascribed by Lührmann to Q-redaction: cf. *Redaktion*, 41f. All Lührmann claimed was that *the identification of the coming SM as Jesus* had already occurred in the pre-Q tradition. Lührmann's own use of the distinction between tradition and redaction is in fact much more flexible, as noted already: see p. 59 n. 69 above.
[5] Schürmann, 'Beobachtungen'.

further sayings, '*Kommentarworte*' (II) before being incorporated into slightly larger collections of sayings (III) and then finally into the larger speech complexes of Q (IV). Schürmann argues in detail that the SM sayings all belong at stage II: they act as *Kommentarworte* to individual sayings but not as comments to the larger collections of sayings in Q.

We have also noted earlier, and already discussed in a little detail, the views of H. Koester, whose theories about different strata within Q are closely connected with his theories about the SM sayings in Q (see p. 67 above). The fact that there are no eschatological SM sayings in GTh, despite the large number of other parallels between GTh and Q, is a key factor for Koester in arguing that the eschatological SM sayings in Q must be secondary accretions to Q. The earlier form of the tradition had no eschatological SM.

In the theory of Q's development proposed by Jacobson in his earlier work, the major compositional stage characterised by the themes of Wisdom and the rejection of the prophets comes after the stage at which the eschatological SM sayings entered the tradition. Thus 'SM' characterises only the tradition *prior* to the three compositional stages proposed. Jacobson is thus very similar to Lührmann in this respect.[6] Kloppenborg's theories, although similar in many respects to Jacobson's earlier views, differ significantly in relation to the SM sayings: for Kloppenborg implies that the eschatological SM sayings are often part of the same stratum in Q ('Q^2') concerned with polemical threats of judgement against 'this generation'. Amongst the whole corpus of SM sayings in Q, only Q 6:22 and 7:34 seem to be assigned to the earlier 'Q^1' level; the rest are all assigned to the later 'Q^2' stage. Vaage's analysis is similar, though not identical:[7] for Vaage, Q 7:34 and 9:58 are to be assigned to the Q^1 level; most of the rest of the SM sayings are assigned to Q^2, but the saying in Q 12:10 creates so many difficulties for Vaage if it belongs with Q 12:8f. (cf. below) that he assigns it to a later stage still, his 'Q^3'.[8] Not dissimilar is the overall stratification theory of Sato (although this is not explicitly related to SM sayings): for Sato most of the SM

---

[6] See his 'Literary Unity', 388f. In his later *First Gospel* he seems to have changed his mind, ascribing the eschatological SM sayings to the same compositional stage as that of the deuteronomistic/wisdom material (*First Gospel*, 238, 249).

[7] L. E. Vaage, 'The Son of Man Sayings in Q', *Semeia* 55 (1991) 103–29.

[8] For a critique of some of Vaage's proposals, see my 'Stratification'.

sayings seem to come in his 'redaction C' which takes up the earlier blocks of material in Q 3:2–7:28 and 9:57–10:24.[9]

The net effect of the arguments of Lührmann, Schürmann and others had been to shift attention away from SM in studies of Q's Christology. The view that SM belonged only to Q's tradition was said by Neirynck in 1981 to be the 'prevailing view'.[10] More recently the trend seems to have been to ascribe the SM sayings to the later strata of Q, though perhaps not to the latest. Within more recent stratification theories of Q, interest has often been focused on the 'formative layers' of Q (with conclusions sometimes drawn about Jesus himself: cf. p. 46 above), so that again the SM sayings have been slightly sidelined. Thus Kloppenborg has written (apparently with approval in relation to the implied critique of Tödt):

> Independently of each other, and using strikingly different methods, Helmut Koester and Heinz Schürmann both concluded that Son of Man sayings did not belong to the earliest strata of Q. Schürmann, in addition, argued that the Son of Man sayings were not added as late as the final assembling of Q. Hence, these sayings characterise neither the formative layers of Q nor the perspective of the final redaction. This conclusion effectively overturned Heinz E. Tödt's assertion that 'Son of Man Christology and Q belong together both in their concepts and in their history of tradition'.[11]

It may however be worth registering a few caveats before we relegate 'SM' to oblivion as far as Q's Christology is concerned. I argued earlier that we should reserve the siglum 'Q' for the 'final' form of the common tradition before being used by Matthew and Luke. Stages in the 'pre-Q' tradition should be regarded as clearly pre-Q, and not Q itself. In that case then any coupling of Koester and Schürmann in this context is perhaps slightly misleading. For Koester is effectively arguing that SM is thoroughly characteristic of the 'final' stage of the editing of Q (and hence supports Tödt's view). Koester presupposes a relatively simple two-stage process in the development of Q, with an earlier 'sapiential' layer (with all the parallels in GTh) being overtaken later by an eschatological layer (with the eschatological SM sayings). This is of course similar to Kloppenborg's theory of the development of Q

---

[9] Sato, *Q und Prophetie*, 28–47.
[10] Neirynck, 'Recent Developments', 70.
[11] Kloppenborg, 'Symbolic Eschatology', 291.

as we have seen; but it is quite different from Schürmann's theories about the place of the SM sayings in that development. For Schürmann, the SM sayings all come in at an early stage in the development of the tradition. For Koester they are effectively 'redactional' (though he does not use the term); they are dismissed by Koester not because they are unimportant for Q, but because Koester himself is not really concerned with Q as such: his primary concern is with the pre-Q tradition.

I have also argued earlier that we should not drive too much of a wedge between Q's tradition and redaction in seeking to determine the elements which Q might have regarded as important. Assigning one part of Q to 'tradition' does not mean that the Q editor(s) did not regard it as significant. The decision to include a tradition must be seen as potentially just as important as a decision to alter a tradition. Hence in assessing the significance of SM for Q's Christology, a division of the tradition into different strata may have only limited importance or relevance.

In the next section of this chapter I consider some of the SM sayings to see if they support a theory that these sayings are less significant for Q's redaction than was claimed by, for example, Tödt. Further, I shall look at a cross-section of *all* the SM sayings and not confine attention only to the so-called 'eschatological' SM sayings. The precise relation between the eschatological and the non-eschatological sayings will be considered later. As with the distinction between tradition and redaction in Q, one should perhaps not drive too much of a wedge between the eschatological and non-eschatological sayings. If one is considering the problem of the SM in Q, and if one defines 'Q' as the 'final' stage in any development of the Q tradition, then it is clear that the 'SM' in Q is Jesus and Jesus alone. (Whether this was also the case in the pre-Q tradition is of course debated.) Further, if one may assume that, for Q, the phrase 'SM' meant something and was not a wholly meaningless cipher,[12] then presumably the fact that

---

[12] So apparently Vaage, 'Son of Man Sayings', 124: 'the figure's contribution to the saying itself is quite abstract: we would even say mathematical ... Logically, in every case we could replace the "son of man" with an x and still grasp whatever is at stake. The only thing added by the actual words "son of man" in the text of Q's redaction is semantic contact with a certain intertextual (apocalyptic) field of play. The name allows a set of associations to be made, giving the interested imagination (e.g. that of New Testament scholars) a range to fill in the blank.' Cf. too the similar thesis of D. R. A. Hare, *The Son of Man Tradition* (Minneapolis: Fortress, 1990) 224: 'in each [of the SM sayings alleged

some SM sayings, which do not explicitly refer to eschatological activity as such, still refer to Jesus as SM indicates that it is the same figure, who will be involved in eschatological activity.[13] Whether this is the only point of the usage of the term 'SM' (so Hoffmann) is quite another matter. But it would be foolish to try to deny that, for Q, the 'earthly SM' is not also the same as the figure described in the eschatological SM sayings and that the common use of the same phrase to refer to Jesus makes it meaningful to consider the SM sayings together.

1. SM in Q: Tradition or Redaction?[14]

I consider first the question of whether the presence of the SM sayings in Q can legitimately be taken as telling us something significant about Q's own concerns.[15] Some of the detailed argumentation has in fact already been given in earlier chapters and hence will not be repeated here. However, before dealing with this, two preliminary points should be made. First, in discussing whether a SM saying in Q is 'traditional' or 'redactional', I am not necessarily seeking to determine the ultimate origin of the saying. Just as important as any possible redactional creation of a saying *de novo* is the possibility that an editor has positioned a saying at a strategic point in his arrangement of the material, even though the saying may have originated elsewhere. Hence what is important is whether a saying appears to be an integral part of the rhetorical strategy of the text, i.e. whether its presence is regarded by the Q editor as significant. Whether any individual saying is dominical or not is a quite separate issue. Second, I shall

---

to be authentic by Tödt and others], "your Lord" could be substituted without changing the force of the saying.' However, given the unusual nature of the phrase ὁ υἱὸς τοῦ ἀνθρώπου in Greek, such a theory seems unpersuasive for a text such as Q. (The situation might be very different in Aramaic: but I argued earlier that Q was to be taken as a Greek text.)

[13] Cf. Hoffmann's critique (*Studien*, 143ff.) of Tödt's theories about the significance of the present SM sayings in the tradition.

[14] My approach is here very close to that of A. Yarbro Collins in her article 'The Son of Man Sayings in the Sayings Source', in M. P. Horgan & P. J. Kopelski (eds), *To Touch the Text* (FS J. A. Fitzmyer; New York: Crossroad, 1989) 369–89. My results are in many respects very similar to hers, though at times the details of the arguments I offer are slightly different.

[15] A fuller form of the argumentation here can be found in my 'The Son of Man in Q', in M. C. de Boer (ed.), *From Jesus to John* (FS M. de Jonge; Sheffield Academic Press, 1993) 196–215.

not in this section discuss every SM saying. One saying (Q 11:30) will be discussed in detail in the next section. Q 7:34 will also be left on one side here. But even if we decide that a saying such as Q 7:34 is 'traditional' (cf. p. 179 above for Q 7:35 as the final 'redactional' element in the section Q 7:31–35, so that 7:34 was probably part of the Q editor's tradition), one must not forget the fact that one cannot simply write off all tradition as worthless in assessing a writer's/editor's theology (cf. p. 81 above).

1.1. Q 6:22

The fourth beatitude, Q 6:22–23, has been discussed in some detail already (see pp. 179–80 above). I argued there that the beatitude in Q probably did contain a reference to Jesus as SM, Matthew's 'I' version being redactional. The beatitude has undergone one redactional addition in 6:23c (the reference to the violence suffered by the prophets) and hence the SM reference may have been part of the tradition used by the Q editor. Does this mean though that the bulk of the beatitude, including the SM reference, has little significance for Q?

Schürmann sees no hiatus between vv. 22–23ab and 23c; instead he sees the whole beatitude as a secondary *Kommentarwort* added to the primary tradition of vv. 20–21. Further, since 'SM' does not occur in the rest of the Q complex (i.e. the section 6:20–23 + 27–35 or even 27–49) it must be part of a pre-formed unit, later adopted without change.[16] Such a theory is not altogether convincing. The lack of any explicit reference to 'SM' later in the Sermon is not decisive. If we are right to allow some interplay between the eschatological and non-eschatological SM sayings, then the fact that Jesus is referred to here as SM implies to the reader/listener that he is also the one who will come in the future at the final judgement (cf. Q 12:40; 17:23ff.).[17] All four beatitudes

---

[16] 'Beobachtungen', 130f. So too Collins, 'Son of Man Sayings', 376f., takes the beatitude as a unity. She refers to the motif of the violence suffered by the prophets as part of the argument for seeing the whole beatitude, and hence the SM reference, as important for Q. However, the clear seam visible between v. 23b and v. 23c may mean that one must proceed a little more cautiously.

[17] This is not to say necessarily that Q 6:22 should be regarded as an 'eschatological SM saying' *in toto*. Insofar as the traditional three-fold division of SM sayings (into present, suffering and eschatological sayings) is valid, I would argue that 6:22 has primary reference to the present and hence should be taken as a 'present SM' saying. However the saying defies neat categorisation. The 'present' of the saying refers to the time of the suffering of the

are concerned with the promise of the eschatological reversal of fortunes which is promised by Jesus. This in turn correlates closely with the more negative warnings about judgement at the end of the Sermon in 6:47–49. Thus the whole Sermon may be seen as dominated by a grand inclusio, setting the whole under the rubric of eschatological promises and warnings, part of which is for Q related to Jesus' role as the coming SM.[18] In any case Schürmann himself has argued that there is an integral relationship between the wording of the final beatitude in 6:22–23b and the section which probably follows in Q, i.e. the section on love-of-enemies.[19] All this suggests that the beatitude as a whole, with the SM reference, plays an important role within the much wider Q context. As such it is hard to see it as simply a traditional vestige with no significance for Q's final composition.

Kloppenborg has argued that the SM clause may also be secondary to the rest of the beatitude,[20] and (following Colpe) he assigns the SM phrase in v. 22 to a secondary development

---

disciples, probably in the *post*-Easter (but pre-eschatological) situation. Still, the fact that the same phrase is used in all three sets of sayings makes it not unreasonable to assume that, at least for Q which contains both present and future sayings, there is an element of overlap between the sayings. The recent discussion of Hare, *Son of Man Tradition*, seems to me to suffer from seeing the issue in too black-and-white terms and not to allow for any interplay between the various interpretative possibilities, or to allow for the possibility that allusions to eschatological activity might be carried by the phrase 'SM' itself in some sayings, at least in the Christian gospel tradition.

[18] I would prefer this more general idea to Catchpole's suggestion of a very specifically *Christological* inclusio, whereby the SM reference in 6:22 correlates with the reference to Jesus as κύριος in 6:46 which in turn is to be related to the references in Q 12:42–46 and 19:12–27 where the κύριος figure of the parables is defined as the SM (cf. Q 12:39f.): cf. p. 218 above. There is certainly eschatological warning at the end of the Great Sermon in 6:47–49; but the reference in 6:46 is more plausibly seen to Jesus as the authoritative *present* speaker who demands obedience now. However, the existence of such an inclusio may answer the criticism of Hare, *Son of Man*, 219f, who argues that the eschatological SM cannot have been that important for Q if no such reference appears in the eschatological section of the great programmatic discourse in Q, viz. Q 6:46–49. The answer must be that 6:46–49 is not to be seen in isolation within the discourse, but precisely by the literary arrangement of the redactor, is related strongly to the opening beatitudes, *with* the reference to Jesus as SM!

[19] For the verbal and conceptual links here, see his *Lukasevangelium*, 346; also Lührmann, 'Liebet eure Feinde', 414f.

[20] Kloppenborg, 'Persecution Beatitude'. He is followed by Seeley, 'Blessings', 134f. In his *Formation*, 173, in discussing the beatitude, Kloppenborg implies that only v. 23c is secondary (no other possibility is mentioned).

(though whether this is at the same stage as v. 23c is not clarified); the rest of the beatitude Kloppenborg sees as plausible within the context of the pre-Easter Jesus.[21] Colpe however argues that 'because of me' was the earlier form of the tradition, which was then later changed to a 'because of the SM'. But the 'I' form is more naturally explained as MattR and there is no other example of a 'for the sake of the SM' being added to a tradition secondarily.[22] In any case the ἕνεκεν phrase is in some respects essential to the beatitude in order to specify that those addressed are being persecuted and ostracised because of their commitment to Jesus.[23] Thus some equivalent to the ἕνεκεν phrase seems essential to make this clear (unless, of course, it is implied in the second person address: Jesus' disciples, not any who suffer social ostracism, are called blessed). Thus Kloppenborg's suggestion of an original beatitude lacking such a clause seems unconvincing.

Standard critical opinion is that the beatitude is a post-Easter formulation, reflecting the situation of Christians suffering in some way for their faith. However, the beatitude has undergone one gloss in v. 23c and hence must pre-date the gloss itself. Verse 23c is most plausibly to be assigned to a Q-editorial stage in the light of the prominence of the theme of prophetic suffering elsewhere in Q. Hence the tradition must have included the SM saying. However, the structural importance which the beatitude

---

[21] 'Persecution Beatitude', 45f. Cf. Colpe, ὁ υἱὸς τοῦ ἀνθρώπου, *TWNT* VIII, 446 n. 308.

[22] Colpe's argument is based on the assumption that versions of another saying with a ἕνεκεν phrase are secondary to those without (Matt 10:39; Mark 8:35; cf. Luke 17:33; John 12:25). However, it seems somewhat dangerous to generalise from here to claim that *all* such ἕνεκεν phrases in *other* sayings are secondary additions.

[23] See Sato, *Q und Prophetie*, 258. Kloppenborg and Seeley argue that the beatitude, without the 'Christological' reference, can be read appropriately against a Cynic-type background. However, I remain persuaded that the primary reference in the apodoses of the beatitudes is an eschatological future (cf. p. 141 above on the first three beatitudes with their reference to Isa 61; and the fourth beatitude is clearly linked with the first three on any showing): hence the phrase in v. 23 about a reward in heaven is more likely taken as a reference to a future reward (despite the lack of an explicit verb), rather than to 'the persecuted addressees' participation in a divinely established and sanctioned [i.e.Cynic] mode of life' (so Seeley, 'Blessings', 136). In any case, if the 'persecution' here is because of the behaviour of the addressees which broke conventional norms (so Seeley, 'Blessings', 135), this is nowhere alluded in the beatitude itself.

now has in the wider Q context shows that SM is clearly still of central importance at the stage when much larger units in Q were being formed — and that stage cannot be easily distinguished from the stage of the final editing of Q.

1.2. Q 9:58

The SM saying in Q 9:58 has also been considered in detail earlier (see pp. 180–3 above). Against Schürmann's view that the saying is simply a *Kommentarwort* prefixed to the saying in Q 9:59f. (with perhaps Luke 9:61f. as well), we may note the widely held view that the saying acts as the introduction to the whole mission discourse which follows.[24] The SM saying may well be secondary, at least at the level of its time of entry into the wider context. However, contra Schürmann, this secondary position seems to be of great significance in the structuring of the 'final' form of Q and hence of great importance for Q's composition.

1.3. Q 12:8f. + 12:10

The problems raised by these verses are legion and cannot all be dealt with in full here. Most agree that Luke's form of 12:8, with 'SM', is more likely to preserve the Q wording than Matthew's 'I' form;[25] also Luke's order probably best represents the order of

[24] See pp. 182–3 nn. 61, 64, 65 above.

[25] Schulz. *Q*, 68 n. 66, and many others. Goulder (*Luke*, 530) thinks that Luke changed Matthew's wording under the influence of Matt 16:27, thereby introducing the 'SM' and the 'angels'. This seems very unlikely. Matt 16:27 appears to exercise no influence on Luke when Luke deals with Mark 8:38 (the Markan parallel to Matt 16:27), so it is difficult to envisage why Matthean influence should take place here. Why too should any change of Matt 10:32 be regarded by Luke as necessary at all? Goulder refers to SM as the more 'numinous' term — but does Luke elsewhere prefer more 'numinous' Christological terminology? And does Luke regard SM as 'numinous'?

Another recent attempt to defend the originality of the Matthean wording is that of P. Hoffmann, 'Jesus versus Menschensohn', in L. Oberlinner & P. Fiedler (eds), *Salz der Erde — Licht der Welt* (FS A. Vögtle; Stuttgart: Katholisches Bibelwerk, 1991) 165–202. Hoffmann argues that 'SM' would have fitted Matthew's purposes well if it were in his source, and that Luke's change can be explained as due to Luke's adapting the tradition in line with his belief that the SM is constantly ready to be witnessing on behalf of Christians being martyred (cf. Acts 7:58). Hoffmann makes a powerful case. Yet his theory has to assume coincidental, but independent, redaction of the saying by Mark (cf. Mark 8:38) and Luke into a 'SM' form; further, Luke uses the Markan *SM* form of the saying with clear reference to the Parousia in Luke 9:26, from which it is most natural to assume that Luke interprets Luke 12:8 in the same way.

the sayings in Q. Many too have argued that 12:4–7 may have constituted a primitive unit (with its own history of development)[26] which has been expanded by the sayings in 12:8f. at one stage. The well-known aporia between 12:8f. (where present attitudes to Jesus appear to have decisive, eschatological significance) and 12:10 (where opposition to the SM [who presumably is Jesus] is forgivable)[27] may be explicable (at one level anyway) if 12:10 is a later secondary comment appended to 12:4–9 partly on the basis of a *Stichwort* connection with 12:8. So far then this would support Schürmann's theory whereby the SM saying in 12:8 is a *Kommentarwort*, added secondarily to an earlier tradition but prior to the final editing.[28]

But can one then deny that 12:10 is part of the final compositional stage in Q? Schürmann denies any connection between v. 10 and vv. 2f. which introduce the unit. But it is just as plausible to see v. 10 as connected with vv. 2f. in order to make the whole unit relate more specifically to Christian preaching.[29] If (as many assume) the contrast implied in v. 10 between speaking against the SM and speaking against the Holy Spirit is a contrast between the pre- and post-Easter situations of the disciples,[30] then this would correlate well with the concerns of vv. 2f. which stress the contrast between the present (in context, pre-Easter) situation of hiddenness, secrecy, darkness and whispering, and the future (i.e. post-Easter) situation of clear, unambiguous proclamation.[31]

I find it hard too, to accept Kloppenborg's claim that vv. 8f. and v. 10 constitute secondary expansions of a community-directed speech, added in the same stratum of the tradition and making prophetic threats against outsiders.[32] Those addressed

---

[26] Cf. Zeller, *Mahnsprüche*, 94ff.; Piper, *Wisdom*, 52ff. See also pp. 315–9 below.

[27] See Kloppenborg, *Formation*, 211–4, for a clear statement of the problems.

[28] Cf. too Vaage, 'Son of Man Sayings', 118, who also 'solves' the problems of the aporia by the source-critical gambit of assigning 12:10 to a later stratum of the tradition. But whether this really solves anything is rather dubious (cf. my 'Stratification', 215): the Q^3 editor must have countenanced having both sayings together, and hence the problem is simply shifted away from Q^2 to Q^3.

[29] See Collins, 'Son of Man Sayings', 379.

[30] So e.g. Tödt, *Son of Man*, 119; Schulz, *Q*, 248; Hoffmann, *Studien*, 152, and many others.

[31] The close connection of v. 10 with vv. 2f. seems to me to make it more sensible to take the unit in Q as vv. 2–10, rather than to try to relate vv. 2f. to vv. 8f. as Piper, *Wisdom*, 58f., does.

[32] *Formation*, 208ff.

in v. 9 are not necessarily 'opponents', but people who are facing the same opposition as the Christian confessors of v. 8 but who do not have the necessary boldness: the language of 'denying' seems to presuppose a prior commitment on the part of those addressed.[33] Verse 10 seems to be directed to more active opponents of the Christian movement. Thus Kloppenborg may be making the 'polemical' stratum of Q too uniform. The polemic of Q is directed quite as much against waverers and those who would claim to be disinterested and neutral as against any active opponents of the Christian cause.

Many would see 12:10 as exercising some interpretative role on 12:8f., perhaps qualifying and correcting it to assert that, whilst rejection of the earthly Jesus by Jewish opponents in the past was not decisive, rejection of the disciples' preaching in the post-Easter situation is.[34] This would cohere well with other parts of Q which stress the importance of the disciples' preaching: cf. Q 10:16 and indeed the whole of the mission discourse in Q 10:2–12, where the disciples are bidden to continue Jesus' preaching of the imminence of the kingdom.[35] Given the close correlation between v. 10 and vv. 2f., there is thus little to stand in the way of the theory that v. 10 has been added in Q at a final stage of the development of the tradition, exercising a significant role in the composition of the wider unit and correlating with other important parts of Q. By contrast Q 12:8f. may be present already in the pre-Q tradition though its concerns cohere well with other parts of Q: the implied attack on the neutral, the wavering and the uncommitted can be paralleled from a number of other Q passages, as we shall see in the next chapter. Thus 'SM' is part of both the pre-redactional stage (vv. 8f.) and the compositional stage (v. 10). And for those who would see the distinction as significant, it is the eschatological SM which is the earlier of the two.

1.4. Q 12:40

We have already seen that the parable of the thief in the night together with its interpretation may be composite and that v. 40

---

[33] Cf. H. Schlier, art. ἀρνέομαι, *TWNT* I, 469: 'Verleugnung kann nur dort stattfinden, wo vorher Anerkennung und Verpflichtung bestanden hat', and see the discussion in ch. 9 below.

[34] Cf. Hoffmann, *Studien*, 152; Schürmann, 'Beobachtungen', 137 and others.

[35] Indeed one could say that the very existence of Q itself is a witness to the crucial importance for the Q Christians of the continuation of Jesus' preaching in the post-Easter situation by the later disciples.

represents an application of the parable which is not entirely apposite. It may well thus be a secondary comment added to the parable (see p. 156 above). Schürmann argues that the verse functions as a conclusion only to the smaller unit comprising Luke 12:35–39 which he takes as Q.[36]

The question whether Luke 12:35–38 belonged (perhaps in part) to Q should probably be answered affirmatively. In view of the reminiscences of this parable in Matthew's version of the parable of the thief with the note about the 'watch' in which the thief is coming (Matt 24:43; cf. Luke 12:38) and the note about staying awake (Matt 24:43; cf. Luke 12:37), it is indeed quite plausible that Luke 12:35–38 did (at least in part) belong to Q.[37] On the other hand, part of the argument for such a theory is that the parable coheres so well with other Q material: hence, at one level, not a great deal is gained in understanding Q by including the parable: it simply confirms the picture already established.

However, the presence of the parable in Q may imply the existence of a rather more extended section of parabolic teaching here in Q on a single subject, and this in turn must imply that the subject is of some importance for the editor responsible for the present form of Q. Schürmann claims that Luke 12:35–39 + 12:40 was subsequently expanded by the parable in 12:42–46 at a later stage in the development of Q. This is however simply asserted by Schürmann and there seems to be little direct evidence. In fact 12:40 coheres extremely closely with 12:42–46 in terms of subject-matter: both concern the unexpected return of the 'SM' (12:40) / the master (κύριος) of the story (12:42–46) which will involve potential disaster for those who are unprepared.[38] It seems there-

---

[36] 'Beobachtungen', 138.

[37] See my *Revival*, 181f.; also B. Kollmann, 'Lk 12,35–38 — Ein Gleichnis der Logienquelle', *ZNW* 81 (1990) 254–61, with further literature. However, I am less persuaded by his appeal to *Did* 16:1 as evidence of this since *Did* 16 may be dependent on our synoptic gospels. See my 'Synoptic Tradition in the Didache', in J. M. Sevrin (ed.), *The New Testament in Early Christianity* (BETL 86; Leuven: Leuven University Press & Peeters, 1989) 197–230, pp. 213f.: *Did* 16:1 has a parallel in Luke 12:35, and it might be that this verse is a LkR introduction to the parable which Luke, apart from this, derives from Q.

[38] This is simply noted as just one possibility by Collins, 'Son of Man Sayings', 381, who would then see this as an 'allegorizing interpretation'. The other possibility she mentions is that the unit appears here via a catchword association (via 'thief') with the preceding saying about treasure in Q 12:33–34, and she is uneasy about ascribing Luke 12:35–38 to Q. But if one does take this as Q, then the whole section comprising Luke 12:35–46 becomes a unit of appreciable length

fore much more economical to see 12:40 as added at the same time as 12:42–46 and, given the way in which the theme covered here runs through the whole of this substantial section in Q, to assign this to the stage of Q's 'final' composition. The SM saying in 12:40 is thus important for Q's redaction and cannot be dismissed as only of significance at a pre-redactional stage.

1.5. Q 17:23f. + 26–30

Once again I refer to my earlier discussion of the passage (p. 159 above). The 'SM' is referred to both in vv. 23f. and in vv. 26–30. I argued in the earlier chapter that the SM saying in vv. 23f. may have been part of the tradition available to the Q editor (although almost certainly 'secondary' in the sense of being undominical). This is shown by the slight shift in emphasis, from one of the universal visibility of the SM's coming to the sudden-ness and unexpected nature of the event. Thus 'SM' seems to be present both in the tradition and in the redactional elements of the section. Moreover the concerns of the wider composition cohere very closely with other parts of Q, notably Q 12:39–46 (or perhaps Luke 12:35–38 + Q 12:39–46), which also stress the sudden unexpected nature of the SM's coming.[39] These thematic links make it hard to deny that it is this concern which is of primary importance for the Q-editor(s), i.e. those responsible for the editing and composition of the final form of Q.

1.6. Conclusion

The results emerging from Q 17:23ff. are typical for the whole of Q. SM sayings appear embedded in Q at all stages of the tradition insofar as these are visible to us. SM *is* a feature of Q's redaction/composition (cf. Q 17:26–30; the composition of the Sermon on the Mount; the programmatic use of Q 9:58 in relation to the mission charge). SM is also present in the traditions used by the Q-editor(s) (cf. Q 6:22; 17:23f.). Contra Koester one cannot ascribe all the SM sayings, nor even just the eschatological SM sayings (cf. Q 17:23f.!) to a later strand within Q. Contra

---

with its own internal coherence and unity of theme, viz. the coming of the master (= Jesus as SM) in a scene which will involve judgement. With this in mind, Q 12:40 is an integral part of the whole sequence which, by virtue of its size, must have considerable significance for the composition of Q in its present form.

[39] See my *Revival*, 182.

Schürmann, one cannot write off SM from the '*Endredaktion*' of Q (unless one can identify such a stage much more precisely and distinguish it more clearly from earlier stages in the composition of Q).[40] 'SM' *is* important for Q and hence Tödt's claim of long ago about the importance (in general terms) of a SM Christology for Q may still be justified (even if his more precise suggestions about the identification between Jesus and the SM being first made by the Q Christians is more debatable).

The establishment of the importance of the term SM for Q does not, of course, determine its meaning or its significance for Q. The standard classification of the SM sayings in the gospels divides those sayings into three, almost mutually exclusive groups: 'A' sayings, referring to the present activity of the SM; 'B' sayings, referring to the suffering (and sometimes the resurrection) of the SM; and 'C' sayings, referring to the eschatological activity of the SM.[41] In relation to Q, it is widely recognised that the 'C' sayings are strongly represented (cf. Q 12:40; 17:23f.; 17:26–30) and are often thought to be the most distinctive features of Q.

What though of the other SM sayings in Q? It is often said that Q contains no suffering ('B') SM sayings.[42] At one level this is of course correct: there is nothing in Q corresponding to the detailed predictions of the suffering and resurrection of Jesus *qua* SM as in Mark 8:31, etc. However, the assertion that Q knows of no suffering SM may need some modification, as we shall see if we examine the so-called 'present SM' sayings in Q. To this we now turn.

2. The Present SM Sayings in Q

In his influential discussion of the sayings referring to Jesus' present activity *qua* SM, Tödt separates these from the eschatological sayings entirely. He claims that 'SM' is used in these 'A' sayings simply to refer to the authority of Jesus.[43] Hoffmann rightly questions such a sharp distinction between the 'A' and 'C' SM sayings in Q, but he agrees with Tödt that a fundamental aspect of the Q sayings is that of authority. It is, however, not an

---

[40] Cf. p. 74 n. 19 above.

[41] Cf. Bultmann, *Theology*, 30; Tödt, *Son of Man*, *passim*.

[42] Bultmann, *Theology*, 30; Vielhauer, 'Gottesreich', 57f.; A. J. B. Higgins, *Jesus and the Son of Man* (Philadelphia: Fortress, 1964) 132f.

[43] Tödt, *Son of Man*, 114–25.

authority which is independent of, and unrelated to, that of the eschatological SM:

> Nicht der Menschensohntitel wird neu interpretiert, sondern die Exusia Jesu ... Zweifellos beanspruchte schon der irdische Jesus eine besondere Vollmacht, aber nun eben die Exusia des Irdischen, der den Menschensohn ankündigte und für seine Vollmacht in Anspruch nahm, wahrgenommen als die Exusia dieses Menschensohnes selbst.[44]

This has the merit of linking the Q sayings about the SM more closely together but it still remains questionable how far the motif of authority should be read into the term at all, at least in the present SM sayings. I therefore consider each of these in turn.

2.1. Q 7:34

With regard to Q 7:34, Tödt rightly says: 'This generation's objection to the Son of Man's mode of behaviour is the dominant point in this section.'[45] Tödt then goes on to refer to the allusion made to Jesus' associating with tax-collectors and sinners, and claims that this bestowing of table-fellowship on outcasts is an act of supreme authority:

> That action of the Son of Man for which this generation reproaches him here is a specific act of sovereignty superior to the restraints of the Law by virtue of the authority of a direct mission. It is action which befits only an authorized person. It is this distinctive action which is emphasized by the name Son of Man.[46]

However, this appears to read quite a lot into the text. The primary action ascribed to the SM here is 'eating and drinking', i.e. not adopting John's ascetic life-style. The fundamental point seems not to be any prior claims to authority in befriending tax-collectors, but the rather simpler one that Jesus is arousing opposition. Jesus is here said to be claiming that, whatever one does (eat or not eat), he and John are being rejected by this generation. Thus 'SM' here is primarily a figure who arouses hostility and rejection.

---

[44] Hoffmann, *Studien*, 145f., followed by Schulz, *Q*, 382f.; Schürmann, 'Beobachtungen', 131f.

[45] *Son of Man*, 115.

[46] *Son of Man*, 116. Cf. too Hoffmann, *Studien*, 149; Schulz, *Q*, 382f.; Schürmann, 'Beobachtungen', 131.

2.2. *Q 9:58*

The same is true of the saying in Q 9:58. Tödt rightly points to the context as being one of a call to discipleship and a warning of the consequences for those who respond: 'The same will happen to the one who follows as to the one who leads the way.'[47] However, Tödt continues:

> The very one who summons men to follow with full authority is the same whom this generation refuses to receive, thus depriving him of a home . . . The name Son of Man is thus used to designate his [Jesus'] sovereignty, his supreme authority.[48]

But this seems to go too far. All that is said about the SM is that he is homeless. Tödt rightly says that this results from the hostility of other people, so that the saying cannot easily be interpreted in a generic sense.[49] Rather, it is a statement about Jesus' own life-style and the consequences which a commitment to Jesus' cause will bring. It is not really a statement about the (logically prior) claims to authority of the one who calls to discipleship; it is about the cost of discipleship itself, to be shared by Jesus and the would-be disciple.[50] Thus again 'SM' is used in a saying which refers to Jesus as one who arouses opposition and hostility.

2.3. *Q 12:10*

The same can be seen in the saying Q 12:10. Again Tödt seems justified in saying that 'SM' here 'designates Jesus acting on earth and being attacked by his opponents'.[51] But he concludes by claiming that the term itself signifies 'the claim to full authority uttered by Jesus on earth which the opponents resist'.[52] However, such 'full authority' is by no means explicit here. Indeed the authority must be considered by Q to be somewhat relative since rejection of it is said here to be

---

[47] *Son of Man*, 122.

[48] *Son of Man*, 122f.

[49] *Son of Man*, 122, and see above p. 181.

[50] By implication, therefore, it suggests that the life-style ascribed here to the 'SM' will be shared by others; but this is very far from saying that the term 'SM' itself *refers* to others besides Jesus (*pace* Lindars, Casey and others). The saying only refers to others by virtue of its context.

[51] *Son of Man*, 119.

[52] *Son of Man*, 120.

forgivable.[53] Tödt's other observation seems more relevant: it is Jesus 'being attacked by his opponents'. Once again this fits well with the pattern I have tried to delineate so far: sayings about the present activity of Jesus *qua* SM occur in contexts where Jesus is seen as one who arouses opposition, hostility and rejection.

2.4. Q 6:22

The same may also be implied in Q 6:22 which refers to persecution 'for the sake of the SM'.[54] Tödt says:

> Attachment to him [the SM] exposes his followers to men's hostility. Thus here, too, the name Son of Man is used to designate Jesus' acting in a certain way. For his sake the disciples are subject to persecution. This sovereignty and this uncompromising claim are emphasized by the name Son of Man. In this way the name is here a title designating the specific unique authority of the one who bears the title.[55]

But again this seems to read too much into the text. The beatitude is about the cost of discipleship, not primarily about the one who calls to discipleship. As in Q 9:58, the primary concern is with the consequences of following the SM as involving suffering and persecution. Hence this saying too binds together the motif of suffering and the term 'SM', even though it is not explicitly stated here that the SM himself is a suffering figure.

2.5. The Sign of Jonah (Q 11:30).

The final SM saying to be considered in this section will have to have a more extended treatment in view of the complexity of the problems it raises. This is the saying about the Sign of Jonah in Q 11:30, where is great debate and lack of agreement even about which category of SM sayings the logion should be placed in.

The SM saying itself (Q 11:30) occurs in the middle of a pericope in Q containing a request for a sign from Jesus by some

---

[53] Cf. too Hamerton-Kelly, *Pre-existence*, 44f.: 'If a blasphemy against the risen Lord, revealed by the Spirit, is unforgivable, the implication is that there is some mitigating circumstance included in the title "Son of Man". It is difficult to see any such circumstance on Tödt's view of the earthly Jesus, as one exercising sovereignty so clearly.' Whether, however, the term SM carries ideas of hiddenness, as Hamerton-Kelly goes on to claim, is more doubtful: 'SM' could simply refer to Jesus as a rejected figure.

[54] See p. 180 n. 50 above for this as the Q version.

[55] *Son of Man*, 123.

Jews (Q 11:16), Jesus' refusal to give a sign 'except the sign of Jonah' (Q 11:29), and the appended double saying about the Queen of the South and the men of Nineveh condemning this generation at the final judgement (Q 11:31–32). One of the least controversial aspects of the pericope is the reconstruction of the Q wording of the SM saying. Almost all agree that Matthew's interpretation of the 'sign of Jonah' in Matt 12:40, interpreting the reference in terms of the time of Jonah's sojourn in the belly of the fish, is secondary in relation to Luke's shorter and more enigmatic version ('for just as Jonah was a sign to the Ninevites, so will the SM be to this generation').[56] Thus Luke 11:30 is widely accepted as probably preserving the Q version most accurately. Further, the close connection between the Sign of Jonah saying and the double logion in Q 11:31f. is attested in both Matthew and Luke and may thus confidently be traced back to Q. The order of the double logion is disputed (Matthew and Luke have the two halves in reverse order). However, the likelihood is that Luke's order (Solomon–Jonah) is more original, corresponding to the canonical order, and that Matthew has reversed the two halves to bring the references to Jonah together.[57]

Not surprisingly, an enormous amount of attention has been focused on the occurrence of the term 'SM' in v. 30, with all the usual questions raised about whether the saying can be traced back to Jesus and what the term might signify at that level. However, one should note that 'SM' itself is only one of a network of problematic terms in vv. 29f. These include the nature of the 'sign' requested, and of the 'sign' offered (in v. 29 *and* by implication in v. 30), the precise force of the ἔσται in v. 30, etc. The existence of the intense scholarly debate on this pericope, and the lack of scholarly unanimity, indicates at the very least the variety of possible solutions to the various conundrums posed by such problems.

For some, analysis of the tradition history of the passage is the key to its interpretation. Certainly it would seem that the passage is not a traditio-historical unity, in that there appears to be a clear distinction between the request for a sign + reply in vv. 29f. and

---

[56] See A. Vögtle, 'Der Spruch vom Jonaszeichen', in *Synoptische Studien* (FS A. Wikenhauser; München: Karl Zink, 1953) 230–77, p. 249; Hoffmann, *Studien*, 181; Schulz, *Q*, 151f.; H. F. Bayer, *Jesus' Predictions of Vindication and Resurrection* (WUNT 2.20; Tübingen: Mohr, 1986) 120, and most others.

[57] Vögtle, 'Spruch', 249f.; Schulz, *Q*, 252; Catchpole, 'Law and Prophets', 99; *pace* Lührmann, *Redaktion*, 38.

the double logion about Solomon and Jonah in vv. 31f.:[58] above all it is hard to explain the presence of the reference to Solomon's wisdom and the Queen of the South in a unit which is otherwise dominated by Jonah and the themes of 'preaching' and 'repentance' if the whole section in vv. 29–32 is conceived as a unit. The tangential note struck by the references to Solomon thus suggests that the passage represents the end-point of a development of the tradition.

Some have argued that the double logion is the last unit to be added in the growth of the tradition.[59] Thus, on this theory, the SM saying in v. 30 had been added to the request for a sign *before* the double logion has been appended. Jacobson even argues that the double logion has been *created* by the Q community.[60] This latter theory seems unlikely if only because it is once again hard to explain the presence of the saying about Solomon in v. 31. It is true that Q is fond of double sayings (cf. Q 11:11f.; 12:26–30; 13:18–21) and Q also has a special interest in the theme of wisdom.[61] Yet it is still the case that v. 31 strikes a rather tangential note in the present context. Other arguments that vv. 31f. is the latest element in the development of the tradition are also not entirely convincing. Schürmann argues for this on the basis of an analysis of the SM saying in v. 30. He claims that the ἔσται of v. 30 must be a real, and eschatological, future; hence v. 30 must refer to the Son of Man at the parousia. But vv. 31f. clearly refer to Jonah as a preacher of repentance. According to Schürmann, if v. 30 had been added after vv. 31f., it would have been made clearer that v. 30 referred to the present activity of Jesus' pre-Easter preaching (as indeed, Schürmann argues, must be the interpretation of the verse in the present Lukan context). [62]

Such an argument does however make a number of presumptions about v. 30 itself. The ἔσται, as many have noted, is not necessarily a real, let alone eschatological, future: it could be non-eschatological; it could equally well be a logical, gnomic future

---

[58] *Pace* Bayer, *Predictions*; also A. J. B. Higgins, *The Son of Man in the Teaching of Jesus* (SNTSMS 39; Cambridge University Press, 1980) 90ff. See Catchpole, *Quest*, 244, for a clear statement of the differences between the two traditions; also Kloppenborg, *Formation*, 128; Sato, *Q und Prophetie*, 150f.

[59] Schürmann, 'Beobachtungen', 133f.; Zeller, 'Entrückung', 526f.; Kloppenborg, *Formation*, 130f.; Jacobson, *First Gospel*, 166f.

[60] See *First Gospel*, 71: 'a *product* of the Q community' (my stress).

[61] Cf. Jacobson, *First Gospel*, *passim*; Hoffmann, *Studien*, 158ff.; and see ch. 10 below.

[62] 'Beobachtungen', 134.

corresponding to the previous δοθήσεται.[63] So too 'SM' for Q, and also for pre-Q traditions, can refer to either the present or future (eschatological) activity of Jesus.[64] Indeed a different answer to the traditio-historical problem would imply that the interpretation of these key terms in v. 30 should be altered. Schürmann's suggestion also makes it unclear exactly what the interpretation of 'Q' should be. In Schürmann's reconstruction there is in fact very little, if any, difference between the 'final' form of Q and Luke's version: Luke 11:29–32, according to Schürmann, preserves the Q version accurately. Thus the proposed interpretation of v. 30 can only apply at an earlier *pre*-Q stage. Schürmann's theory thus reduces to a claim that Q understood v. 30 in one way, and the pre-Q tradition understood the same words in the same saying in another way. But given the fact that it is precisely the same wording which is involved in v. 30, it seems difficult to be so confident about driving a wedge between the alleged meanings of the same verse in two proposed strata of the tradition.[65] And since the separation of the strata on this theory is defended precisely on the basis of such a distinction of meaning, the whole theory becomes questionable.[66]

Some have claimed that vv. 31f. could only have been appended to vv. 29f. when v. 30 was present, since it is linked via the catchwords 'Jonah', 'Ninevites', and 'this generation'.[67] But this does not exclude the possibility that vv. 31f. could have been appended at the same time as v. 30 was added. And in any case vv. 31f. are still closely related to v. 29 in being a powerful negative statement directed against 'this generation'.[68]

The other main alternative to the solution of the traditio-historical problem of the passage is to take either v. 30 alone,

---

[63] Vielhauer, 'Jesus', 112, is frequently cited in this respect.

[64] See the earlier part of this chapter. If this is pre-Q, then Q 7:34 and 17:24 provide examples of each category respectively. At the level of Q, one may refer to Q 9:58 and 17:26–30 respectively.

[65] Cf. the similar critique (of the views of A. Polag) by A. Vögtle, 'Bezeugt die Logienquelle die authentische Redeweise Jesu vom "Menschensohn"?', in Delobel (ed.), *LOGIA*, 77–99.

[66] Schürmann's reconstruction of the history of the tradition is adopted by Kloppenborg, *Formation*, 130f., almost as an a priori assumption; but he argues for a quite different interpretation of 'SM' here (cf. below). However, since Schürmann's reconstruction is virtually exclusively dependent on the meaning he ascribes to 'SM' here, this seems an illegitimate procedure.

[67] Cf. Zeller, 'Entrückung', 526; Kloppenborg, *Formation*, 130.

[68] See Schulz, *Q*, 253.

or the whole exceptive clause ('except the sign of Jonah') in v. 29c together with v. 30, as the latest expansion of the tradition.[69] Of these two alternatives, perhaps the second is more attractive, if only because the exceptive clause in v. 29c without any explanation is enigmatic to the point of being almost incomprehensible.[70] The precise relation of the Q saying to the Markan version of what appears (ultimately) to be the same tradition in Mark 8:12 is also unclear. Trying to establish any direct *literary* relationship between the two sayings is difficult; and the Markan version, with its well-known Semitic features, may well reflect a pre-Markan *Vorlage*.[71] Certainly a coherent picture of the tradition history emerges if one postulates an early (dominical?) version of the saying giving a blanket refusal of a sign, one version of this being preserved in Mark. Q then perhaps glossed this by adding the reference to Jonah in vv. 29c and 30, and perhaps also appended the double logion in vv. 31f. (if this had not already been appended in the earlier tradition). Such a reconstruction is certainly possible (though of course, in the nature of the case, one cannot say more).[72]

It may be though that any fine distinctions between tradition and redaction are otiose. I have already noted on more than one occasion that the use of a tradition is potentially just as significant in assessing an author's ideas as any strictly redactional activity we may be able to identify. We must therefore look at the way in which any tradition has been used in Q and certainly not dismiss it completely simply because it is 'tradition'. It is thus not inappropriate to look at the context in Q in which the saying is placed, whether we judge the saying itself to be a traditional element in Q or a redactional creation. However, the 'context' in question can be taken in different ways: we could consider the

---

[69] For v. 30 as redactional, see Hoffmann, *Studien*, 181. For vv. 29c + 30 as redactional, see Lührmann, *Redaktion*, 41f.; R. A. Edwards, *The Sign of Jonah in the Teaching of the Evangelists and Q* (London: SCM, 1971) 84f.; Schenk, *Synopse*, 71.

[70] Cf. Catchpole, *Quest*, 246.

[71] Cf. the Semitic oath formula with εἰ. See Edwards, *Sign*, 75. On the relationship between Q and Mark here, see my 'Mark and Q', 158–62: Mark seems to show no awareness of any Q-redactional or editorial features.

[72] Bayer, *Predictions*, 122f., dismisses such a reconstruction as lacking any concrete evidence, though there is equally little direct evidence for his own view of the whole as a traditio-historical unity from the start. The shifts in emphasis, and the existence of the Markan parallel, seem to demand some kind of reconstruction of the tradition history as outlined above.

immediate 'literary' context in Q, or we could look at the wider context of the whole of the Q tradition.

For some, the broader context within Q as a whole is decisive for interpreting the SM saying here. In particular, it has been suggested that the form of the SM saying here is similar to that of other sayings found elsewhere in Q, viz. in Q 17:24, 26–30, a so-called 'eschatological correlative'.[73] Here a close comparison is made between an event/person in the past and a future, escha-tological event concerning the SM. Edwards argues that this is an unusual, and highly distinctive form, used in both Q contexts to speak of the 'SM'. Since in Q 17 the reference is to the SM as one returning at the parousia, the same must apply in Q 11: the saying in Q 11:30, that 'the SM will be a sign to this generation', must therefore refer to the SM returning at the parousia.

However, the precise nature of the parallel with Q 17, and the alleged distinctiveness of the form, are debatable. D. Schmidt has shown that the form occurs frequently in the LXX and elsewhere.[74] Further, it is not clear that the saying in Q 11:30 and the sayings in Q 17 are quite as closely parallel as Edwards maintains. There is, it is true, a formal parallel at one level: all the sayings concerned have a structure using καθώς/ὥσπερ . . . verb in the past . . . οὕτως . . . ἔσται . . . reference to the SM. Yet there are also formal differences. The precise syntax of the apodosis, and the force of the ἔσται, vary. In Q 17, the verb ἔσται simply describes the state of affairs with a reference to the 'day/days': 'as it was . . . so it will be'. In Q 11:30 the ἔσται has a subject ('SM') and an implied predicate ('sign'): 'The SM will be (a sign) to this generation.' The comparison is thus not between a general state of affairs in the past and the SM in the future (as in Q 17); rather, it is between a specific sign in the past and a (similar) sign in the present/future.[75]

Further, it is not at all clear that the contents of the two contexts should necessarily be equated. Form and content can never be neatly separated;[76] indeed Edwards himself reads a great deal of 'content' into the 'form' by calling it an 'eschatological' correla-

---

[73] See Lührmann, *Redaktion*, 40; Edwards, *Sign*, esp. 47ff., and also his 'The Eschatological Correlative as a Gattung in the New Testament', *ZNW* 60 (1969) 9–20.

[74] D. Schmidt, 'The LXX Gattung "Prophetic Correlative"', *JBL* 96 (1977) 517–22.

[75] Kloppenborg, *Formation*, 132.

[76] See my *Reading*, 100.

tive.[77] *Is* Q 11:30b referring to an eschatological event? To assume so is to prejudge many of the crucial issues involved. Others have pointed to important differences between the two contexts. Vielhauer refers to the fact that the presumed audiences are rather different: Q 17 is aimed at people who are eschatologically unaware, warning them of the impending catastrophe; there is nothing of that in Q 11.[78] Bayer too points to several differences: e.g. in the case of the examples of Noah and Lot, judgement came; in the case of Jonah, the whole point was that judgement was averted. Thus Bayer asserts that one 'should distinguish between an "eschatological correlative of *finality*" (Noah and Lot) and an "eschatological correlative of *urgency*" (Jonah)'.[79] Edwards recognises the distinction in part: he says that the Jonah saying has moved beyond the 'admonitory' use of the form in Q 17 and hence is rather different.[80] But if that is the case, how far is it still legitimate to speak of a single form here? Since one cannot divorce form from content completely (cf. above), and if the contents of Q 11:30 and Q 17 differ significantly, how legitimate is it to use Q 17 as the key to interpret the enigmatic language of Q 11:30?

There are further difficulties raised by the theory that v. 30b refers to the Son of Man returning at the parousia in judgement,[81] and these arise from the structure of v. 30 itself. Verse 30 asserts that there is a very precise parallel between the way in which Jonah was a sign[82] to the Ninevites and the way the SM will be to this generation. Many are content to refer to a fairly general comparison between Jonah and the SM, the prime reference being the themes of preaching and repentance. Jonah preached and the Ninevites repented; Jesus preaches and 'this generation' has not repented. Jonah threatened judgement; the SM will bring judgement. The 'sign of Jonah' in v. 29 is then often taken as a reference to Jonah's activity as a preacher, and hence to Jesus' activity as a preacher. 'No sign will be given except the sign of

---

[77] Schmidt also points out that many of the examples of the form in the LXX use the future to refer to an event in the imminent (non-eschatological) future, or in a gnomic way. Cf. Kloppenborg, *Formation*, 132.

[78] Vielhauer, 'Jesus', 112.

[79] Bayer, *Predictions*, 123.

[80] Edwards, *Sign*, 56, 85.

[81] So Tödt, *Son of Man*, 53, as well as Lührmann, Edwards and others. Full bibliographies in Schulz, *Q*, 256 n. 546; Bayer, *Predictions*, 139 n. 193.

[82] The genitive is probably exegetic: cf. Lührmann, *Redaktion*, 40; Zeller, 'Entrückung', 520; *pace* Schulz, *Q*, 256.

Jonah' (v. 29) then means that 'no sign will be given beyond the preaching of Jesus'.[83] Yet whilst this makes good sense of v. 29, it runs into difficulties with an eschatological interpretation of v. 30b. Verse 30 is intended to explain v. 29 (cf. γάϱ) and hence v. 30a, which repeats the references to 'Jonah' and the 'sign' from v. 29, must refer to the same sign as v. 29. But the structure of v. 30 as a whole asserts that there is a close parallel between the way in which Jonah was a sign to the Ninevites and the way in which the SM will be (a sign) to this generation. If the latter is a reference to the SM coming in judgement at the Eschaton, there is no real comparison. Jonah's preaching was intended to avert judgement; the SM will bring judgement. One sometimes reads comments to the effect that this generation will see the SM as the sign but then it will be too late.[84] But this 'too late' only serves to destroy the close parallelism that v. 30 is so carefully asserting.[85] Thus the interpretation which would see the Son of man as a parousiac figure and Jonah as primarily a preacher of repentance cannot really do justice to the wording of v. 30.[86]

[83] Cf. Tödt, *Son of Man*, 53.

[84] Tödt, *Son of Man*, 53.

[85] See Vögtle, 'Spruch', 267; Schulz, *Q*, 256; Bayer, *Predictions*, 139; Kloppenborg, *Formation*, 132f.

[86] Edwards offers a slight variant of this view. He argues that the exceptive clause, 'except the sign of Jonah' (v. 29c), is not just a reference to Jesus' pre-Easter preaching. For the Q community living after Easter, Jonah must have had a two-fold significance as both a preacher of repentance *and* one who had been rescued from death. The 'sign of Jonah' is thus an indication to the Q community that Jesus is the one who has been rescued from death and whose preaching continues in the post-Easter community. (*Sign*, 57f., 85f.). However, this only complicates matters even further. It fails to explain how Jonah was a sign 'to the Ninevites' (cf. below); it also fails to explain the precise comparison asserted by v. 30, since Edwards maintains the view that 'SM' in v. 30b is a reference to the eschatological SM. Hence the difficulties mentioned above still apply.

Similar problems arise with the suggestion of Zeller ('Entrückung'), who refers to the idea, evidenced in some Jewish texts, of a famous person being taken off to heaven, either before or after death, in order to reappear as Judge at the End-time. In the light of this, Zeller interprets Q 11:29f. as referring to the eschatological SM returning at judgement after having been assumed to heaven/rescued from death in a similar way to Jonah who was rescued from the great fish. However, whilst such a background might well be fruitful in interpreting some of the eschatological SM sayings in Q, its relevance for Q 11:30 seems less certain. There is above all the problem of why Jonah is the other correlate in the comparison given here, since he is scarcely an obvious candidate for this role. Zeller produces plenty of evidence for why a figure like Enoch, or even possibly Moses, might be a suitable person (cf. too the link with

In the light of these difficulties, one should perhaps look again at the more immediate Q context in order to interpret the passage at the level of Q. In this context we have three references to Jonah. This surely cannot be coincidental (Jonah is not mentioned elsewhere in the gospels), and hence the likelihood is that the references can be taken as interpreting each other (at least for Q, where the references lie side by side).[87] Verse 32 is quite unambiguous: Jonah is presented as the person who preached to the Ninevites and who evoked a positive response of repentance from them. This correlates with v. 30a, where again Jonah and the Ninevites are mentioned. Indeed in the present Q arrangement, v. 32 looks as if it provides the clarification of the more cryptic v. 30. Thus for Q, Jonah was a sign to the Ninevites

---

the eschatological SM idea in *1 En* 71). Zeller himself tries to answer this by referring to a version of *Midr.Ps* 26 §7 (110b) ('Entrückung', 524f.), but the text refers only to Jonah being translated to Paradise; it has no reference to Jonah returning as Judge. So too it is not clear why this sign of Jonah should be a sign 'to the Ninevites' (v. 30a). The Ninevites were *not* witnesses to Jonah's rescue from the fish (cf. below); and they were not the recipients of eschatological judgement itself from Jonah (cf. above).

Others have argued that the sign must be something other than Jonah's preaching. The only real alternative is the miraculous delivery from the great fish. It is this part of the Jonah story which attracts attention in other Jewish literature and hence, it is argued, it is this which is in mind here. Jonah is thus a sign to the Ninevites as one who has been miraculously preserved from death. (Cf. J. Jeremias, art. Ἰωνᾶς, *TWNT* III, 412f.; Vögtle, 'Spruch', 272f.; Marshall, *Luke*, 485; Bayer, *Predictions*, 141f.) But this interpretation is also unconvincing. First, the non-Christian parallels which are often adduced (3 Macc 6:8; *PRE* 1:10 are always cited) are scarcely very extensive. Further *PRE* is a ninth-century text and hence can only be used here with caution. Kloppenborg has also shown that other Jewish texts fastened on Jonah's preaching to the Ninevites as the key part of the story. (*Formation*, 133.) In any case, there is no evidence connecting the Ninevites with the story of the fish. Both 3 Maccabees and *PRE* refer to the attitude of the sailors to the miracle of Jonah's rescue. Thus if the 'sign of Jonah' is primarily a reference to Jonah as one rescued from death, it remains unexplained how Jonah was a sign 'to the Ninevites'.

[87] Vielhauer criticises Tödt for using v. 31 to interpret v. 30 at the level of Jesus when the verses probably have different origins. But such a procedure is perfectly in order for the interpretation of Q! It is perhaps ironic that Vielhauer in fact reaches an interpretation of v. 30 which coheres perfectly with v. 31: see below. It is Tödt who seeks to drive a wedge between the 'sign of Jonah' (= preacher of repentance) and 'SM' (= eschatological judge). Bayer's argument is curious: he pleads strenuously for an original (i.e. dominical) link between vv. 29f. and vv. 31f., but then refuses to allow v. 32 to play any role in the interpretation of v. 30 (*Predictions*, 129f.).

in the sense that he preached and they responded in time to avoid the catastrophe of divine judgement which threatened them. This must be the interpretation of v. 30a when v. 30 is juxtaposed with vv. 31f.; and hence it must also be the interpretation of v. 29c since v. 30a largely repeats v. 29c.[88]

The precise comparison which v. 30 as a whole asserts must now mean that the SM is a sign to this generation in precisely the same way as Jonah was a sign to the Ninevites. Hence 'SM' must be a preacher prior to the End, i.e. 'SM' must refer to the present, preaching Jesus, not to an eschatological judging figure.[89]

The stock objections to this view are easily met: e.g. the future tense of ἔσται could be gnomic future (see above); and the term 'SM' is certainly a polyvalent term for Q. So too the argument which says that such a 'sign' is totally unlike the sign requested is unconvincing. In fact the Q context, both immediate and wider, really demands that any 'sign' given must be different in kind from the one requested.[90] It is clear that for Q (as indeed for Mark) the request for a sign is regarded as evil. Although the πειράζω references in the tradition are all probably due to influence from the Markan tradition,[91] it is still clear from Jesus' response in Q that the request has found no favour: it is the request of 'this evil generation', and we have seen how significant a feature of Q is the polemic against 'this generation'.[92] The introduction to the pericope is thus cast in totally negative terms. It would therefore be extremely unlikely if the request were taken by Q's Jesus and responded to positively on its own terms. Far more in keeping with the structure of the pericope as a whole, and with Q as a whole, is the interpretation given above: the request is from evil people; the only 'sign' which is available is the presence of Jesus himself whom 'this generation' has already

---

[88] Zeller, 'Zusammenhang', 71, argues that the context of vv. 29–32 demands a future reference for v. 30, since vv. 31f. is all about future judgement. But whilst there is a future reference in v. 32, it has nothing to do with Jonah himself. Jonah is the one who warns about the future; he is not himself the future judge (and none of the examples in Zeller's later 'Entrückung' article seem to establish that).

[89] Thus agreeing with Vielhauer, 'Jesus', 112; Schulz, *Q*, 256 and others mentioned there; also Kloppenborg, *Formation*, 133f.

[90] Cf. Zeller, 'Entrückung', 521; Kloppenborg, *Formation*, 131f.

[91] They occur in Matt 16, Mark 8 and Luke 11, but not in Matt 12 where Matthew is probably primarily dependent on Q; thus the use of the verb in Luke 11 may be due to Markan influence on Luke.

[92] See ch. 6 above.

rejected/is currently rejecting and refusing to acknowledge in the very act of asking for further accreditation.

Finally, this may explain why the term 'SM' is used here. Earlier in this section I tried to show that all the other 'A' SM sayings in Q occur in contexts which imply hostility and rejection. Insofar as such hostility is the cause of Jesus' sufferings, these 'present SM' sayings function as crypto-suffering SM sayings. Q 11:30 turns out to fit this pattern remarkably neatly. Here too Q's Jesus refers to his own role as that of SM. Here too the context is one of opposition, of hostility and a refusal by others to accept his own message without further proof or validation from outside. The 'present SM' sayings in Q thus exhibit a remarkable homogeneity.

3. SM in Q: Background

I have argued that the present SM sayings in Q are primarily concerned with hostility, suffering and rejection. At one level this brings us back to our starting-point for this chapter in that the SM sayings occur regularly in the same Q contexts as those to do with Wisdom and the prophets. At another level however it raises just as acutely as before the problem faced by Tödt's interpretation of these SM sayings: how is one to relate the 'A' (or possible crypto-'B') sayings to the eschatological 'C' sayings? Hoffmann's interpretation has the merit of linking the two together, though I have argued that he has to force the meaning of the 'A' sayings themselves. Has the interpretation of these sayings offered here simply surrendered the possibility of linking the two groups of sayings together? I believe not, but in order to show this we must investigate the possible background of the term 'SM' itself a little further.

The possible background of the term 'SM' is an enormous topic, deserving perhaps a monograph in its own right. At the risk of gross generalisation, one might say that German scholars have tended to be far readier than English scholars to see the SM sayings in the gospels as reflecting an already existent 'SM concept' in the sense that the term 'SM' itself is thought to refer to a well-established belief in an eschatological judging figure.[93] By contrast, English speaking scholarship has been far readier to

---

[93] So, for example, Bultmann, *Theology*; Colpe, ὁ υἱὸς τοῦ ἀνθρώπου, *TWNT* VIII; Tödt, *Son of Man*, and others.

see more direct influence from Dan 7:13 on the gospel sayings at all levels of the tradition.[94] Alternatively, there has recently been a strong upsurge of opinion for the view that the term 'SM' was originally never a title at all; it was simply a normal Aramaic phrase (though the range of possible meanings of the idiom in Aramaic is disputed) which, when it was (in part mis-) translated into the Greek ὁ υἱὸς τοῦ ἀνθρώπου, started to take on overtones of meaning from Dan 7.[95]

It may be, however, that exclusive concentration on Dan 7 alone is misleading and unhelpful. The Q SM sayings cluster around two fundamental ideas: the SM is one who experiences hostility and rejection in the present; and the SM is the one who will exercise a key role in the final judgement (Q 12:8f.; 12:40; 17:24; 17:26–30).[96] Both these aspects can find roots in Dan 7, or at least can find parallels in roughly contemporary texts which are indebted or related in some way to Dan 7. We need therefore to consider not only Dan 7 but also other texts related to it. I start with the eschatological activity of the SM.

The idea that in the final judgement God would be assisted by another figure is by no means unparalleled in Jewish thinking of this period, A number of texts indicate this.[97] The figure of Melchizedek in the 11QMelch scroll appears to be a person alongside God, playing a decisive role in the divine judgement. In the *Testament of Abraham* (Rec. A) 13:2f., Abel, the first victim of murder, administers judgements on behalf of God.[98] Above all, there is the evidence of *4 Ezra* and *1 Enoch*. In *4 Ezra* 13, a figure is described who will execute divine judgement. And in *1 Enoch*, especially in the Similitudes (*1 En* 37–71), Enoch is shown a figure who will be the one to administer

---

[94] So Moule, *Origin*, 11–22; M. D. Hooker, *The Son of Man in Mark* (London: SPCK, 1967) and others.

[95] Cf. G. Vermes, *Jesus the Jew* (London: Collins, 1973) 160–91; Casey, *Son of Man*; Lindars, *Jesus Son of Man*.

[96] The precise role is not clear. In Q 17 it seems to be left open and undefined; in Q 12:8f. it is to be a witness speaking on behalf of, or against, other human beings. Q 12:40 (as also the sayings in Q 17) seem to imply that the coming of the SM will have negative effects on those who are unprepared.

[97] Cf. B. Lindars, 'The Apocalyptic Myth and the Death of Christ', *BJRL* 57 (1975) 366–87, pp. 376f; also Zeller, 'Entrückung', 516f., with further literature cited.

[98] Here it seems to be the first stage of a three-fold judgement.

the judgement, only to be told at the end that he himself is this figure (*1 En* 71:14).[99]

We may note here too that in some of these texts, the figure concerned is not a completely new figure in history, but rather a figure from the past, evidently held in reserve for precisely this function. Thus in *TestAbr* 13, it is the first victim of violence from past history, Abel, who is the one who administers judgement. In *1 Enoch*, it is Enoch the antediluvian figure who is finally identified as the agent of judgement. So too it is likely (though the fragmentary nature of the text makes it not possible to be certain) that the Melchizedek of the 11QMelch scroll is the same figure as the king who appears mysteriously in Gen 14. Indeed this idea of a figure of the past being kept in heaven to reappear at the End-time in some capacity is a widespread one, even if the 'capacity' concerned cannot always be clearly identified as being God's agent in judgement. Thus in addition to the examples already cited, we may refer to what is implied by Mark 6:15 (where it is assumed that Jesus could be one of the prophets from of old returned), and also texts such as Sir 48:9ff. (Elijah will return), *Ezekiel the Tragedian* 68ff. (Moses placed on a throne), *Sib. Or.* 5.256–259 (a man from heaven will appear, who seems to be Joshua).[1] In sum, therefore, there seems to have been a widespread belief that a figure of the past could be taken away to reappear at the Eschaton.

---

[99] There is the ever-present problem of the date of this material and the legitimacy of using it to compare NT texts. *4 Ezra* is to be dated towards the end of the first-century CE, though with no clear Christian influence. *1 Enoch* has been dated to a wide variety of possible dates: see the survey in M. A. Knibb, 'The Date of the Parables of Enoch: A Critical Review', *NTS* 25 (1979) 345–59. Knibb himself inclines to a date towards the end of the first-century CE, partly on the grounds that no fragment of the Similitudes has yet been discovered at Qumran. However, arguments from silence in this context are not compelling. In any case, even if *1 Enoch* in its present form is later than the NT texts, it may well still preserve earlier traditions and therefore provide evidence of developments of traditions which are earlier. It is almost universally agreed that *1 Enoch* does not show any influence of Christian tradition.

[1] On this see J. C. O'Neill, 'The Man from Heaven: *Sib. Or.* 5.256–259', *JSP* 9 (1991) 87–102. One line of the oracle may be a Christian interpolation (the reference to the man stretching out his hand on the fruitful wood): see J. J. Collins, in J. H. Charlesworth (ed.), *Old Testament Pseudepigrapha I* (London: Darton, Longman & Todd, 1983) 390, 399. I remain persuaded, *pace* O'Neill, who argues the case for seeing the oracle as a unity and referring to a Jewish victim of crucifixion.

It is notable that several of these examples use the language and imagery of Dan 7 in relation to the figure concerned. In a way this is of course not at all unexpected. Insofar as the figure is concerned with the final judgement, and Dan 7 is itself a scene involving judgement, it is scarcely surprising that Danielic language is used in such a context. On the other hand, the link is not inevitable, if only because the SM figure in Dan 7 is one who primarily receives judgement (from the Ancient of Days) rather than being one who dispenses judgement and judges others. However, it is clear that a link was made — at times more clearly, at times less so. The clearest example is *1 Enoch* where the Danielic allusion is quite unmistakable. In *1 En* 46, the figure is introduced with clear allusion to the language of Dan 7, and thereafter the figure is spoken of as 'that SM', evidently referring back to the initial mention and description of the figure. Many have thus argued that *1 Enoch* gives no evidence that the phrase 'SM' itself was ever a 'title': rather the literary allusion is spelt out on the first occasion it is used, and thereafter the demonstrative 'that' consistently refers back to the earlier context.[2] We shall return to the question of how far 'SM' is a 'title' later, but here we may simply note the clear use of Dan 7 to refer to the figure described in *1 Enoch*.

Very much the same happens in *4 Ezra*. In the vision in ch. 13, where the seer describes the man coming from the sea ('I looked, and behold, this wind made something like the figure of a man come up from the heart of the sea. And I looked, and behold, that man flew with the clouds of heaven', *4 Ezra* 13:3), the language is clearly Danielic even though it is not quite clear if the term 'SM' itself was used in the (now lost) original.[3] The further allusions made about this figure (e.g. the fact that he is referred to as God's 'son' in 13:37, 52, and therefore perhaps to be identified as the Messiah, as also in 12:32, cf. 7:28) will be left on one side here. What is important for the present purposes is the Danielic allusion. Thus whatever we may make of the possibility of any possible 'SM concept' in any possible background, the use of Daniel is clear. Thus Collins says: 'It can hardly be doubted . . .

---

[2] Cf. Casey, *Son of Man*, 99–112; Lindars, *Jesus Son of Man*, 9f.

[3] See C. Caragounis, *The Son of Man* (WUNT 2.38; Tübingen: Mohr, 1986) 127f.; J. J. Collins, 'The Son of Man in First Century Judaism', *NTS* 38 (1992) 448–66, pp. 459f.

that an allusion to Dan 7:13 was readily recognisable both to the author of the interpretation and his readers.'[4]

Danielic imagery and language is not quite so clear in some of the other examples cited; but there may be an allusion to Dan 7 in the language of *Sib. Or.* 5.256 ('There will come again one exceptional man from the sky').[5] Similarly the language of *Ezekiel the Tragedian*, describing the appearance of a 'man' (φώς) who hands over his crown and sceptre to Moses, is very close to the picture of the Ancient of Days and the SM in Dan 7,[6] though again there is no explicit use of the phrase SM as such.

This evidence has been recently reviewed by J. J. Collins who concludes that, whilst there may not have been a fixed 'SM title' in first-century Judaism, nevertheless there may well have been a developed exegetical tradition based on Dan 7, interpreting the Danielic figure as the agent in the divine judgement. Thus, after considering the evidence of *1 Enoch* and *4 Ezra*, Collins states:

> We may at least conclude that anyone in the late first century who spoke of one in human form riding on the clouds, or appearing with an Ancient of Days, or in any way reminiscent of Daniel 7, would evoke a figure with distinct traits which go beyond what was explicit in the text of Daniel's vision.[7]

Alongside this we need to note another development — partly overlapping, partly independent: this concerns the use made of motifs from the fourth servant song in Isa 53 in parts of *1 Enoch* and in Wisd 2–5.[8] Dan 7 is of course not a text that can be treated in isolation. The vision of the chapter is one attempt to provide an answer to the problem of theodicy in the face of the existence of righteous, but apparently unredeemed, suffering. As is well known, Judaism at the end of the OT era gradually began to

[4] Collins, 'Son of Man', 463.

[5] Translation in Charlesworth (ed.), *OT Pseudepigrapha I*, 399. Dan 7 is noted as a parallel here in the margin by the editor, J. J. Collins; also J. Jeremias, *New Testament Theology* (ET London: SCM, 1971) 270f. Cf. the reference to a 'man' coming 'from the sky' (ἀπ' αἰθέρος).

[6] See the note in Charlesworth (ed.), *OT Pseudepigrapha II*, 819. Cf. also A. Y. Collins, 'The Origin of the Designation of Jesus as "Son of Man"', *HTR* 80 (1987) 391–407, p. 405.

[7] Collins, 'Son of Man', 466. He also rightly refers to W. Horbury, 'The Messianic Associations of "the Son of Man"', *JTS* 36 (1985) 34–55.

[8] On this see especially G. W. E. Nickelsburg, *Resurrection, Immortality and Eternal Life in Intertestamental Judaism* (London: Oxford University Press, 1972) 62–78. This is explicitly related to the SM problem in his article 'Son of Man', *Anchor Bible Dictionary* 6 (New York: Doubleday, 1992) 137–50.

develop ideas of an afterlife to try to 'explain' how belief in a righteous God and apparently unredeemed human suffering could be reconciled. The answer was to transfer the 'reward' for the righteous to a *post mortem* existence when the righteous would be rewarded. Thus the vision of Dan 7 serves to bring assurance to the loyal Jews who are being violently persecuted for their loyalty and commitment during the time of Antiochus Epiphanes: and it does so by promising a future reward and vindication through the person of the 'SM' figure being given the favourable verdict in the divine court. Yet as often as not, the 'suffering' endured by Jews involved active persecution by others. The theodicy problem therefore involved not only the reward which the righteous appeared to be failing to receive on earth, but also the punishment which the wicked persecutors seemed to be escaping. In some texts, therefore, both these 'problems' were met by a 'story-line', or 'myth', in which the righteous were exalted to heaven and given a position of power whereby they then became the agents through whom divine judgement fell on the wicked.

In some of these texts, the fourth servant song of Isa 52:13–53 played a significant role. Nickelsburg has shown that Isa 53 may have influenced Daniel itself. Thus the vision of the 'wise' (מַשְׂכִּילִים) and those who bring many to righteousness (מַצְדִּיקֵי הָרַבִּים) in Dan 12:3 seems to be an echo of the language used of the servant in Isa 52:13 (יַשְׂכִּיל עַבְדִּי) and 53:11 (יַצְדִּיק צַדִּיק עַבְדִּי לָרַבִּים),[9] so that the vindication promised to the singular servant of Isaiah has now been extended to a wider group of people. However, the Isaianic influence is considerably extended in two further texts, in *1 En* 62 and Wisd 2–5. In both the influence of Isa 53 seems clear. In both too the story-line is similar (though not identical). In both, the righteous is/are persecuted by human figures; but in a *post mortem* scene the erstwhile persecutors are confronted by their one time victim(s) and are then condemned.[10] Thus in both texts, the Isaianic poem has been reinterpreted so that those who are amazed and aghast

---

[9] Nickelsburg, *Resurrection*, 24.

[10] Again the situation is not quite identical in the two texts in that while in Wisdom the persecutors see the man himself, in *1 Enoch* they see the 'SM' figure who may be the heavenly counterpart of the suffering righteous: hence the ambiguity about whether the persecutors can or cannot recognise the figure they now see: cf. Nickelsburg, *Resurrection*, 72, on *1 En* 62:1 ('Open your eyes and lift up your horns if *you are able* to recognise the Elect One').

at the new appearance and status of the once despised figure are the active persecutors themselves who have led to the figure's (temporary) demise. Nickelsburg also points to the way in which in both texts the language and imagery of the account of the fall of king of Babylon in Isa 14 is used to refer to the downfall of the persecutors.[11] Thus Nickelsburg argues persuasively for the existence of a common exegetical tradition, based on Isa 53 and surfacing in different forms in Wisd 2–5 and *1 En* 62, whereby the righteous sufferer(s) confront(s) his/their opponents in a *post mortem* judgement scene.

Now it is clear of course that Wisd 2–5 and *1 En* 62 are not identical. We have already noted the fact that in Wisdom, the persecutors see the righteous man himself, whilst in *1 Enoch* they see the Elect One in whom they are bidden to recognise the persecuted victims. And, as has already been alluded to, *1 Enoch* here uses the term 'SM'. Wisd 2–5 does not: there is barely a reference to Dan 7 in the whole section.[12] Thus *1 Enoch* works into the story-line an implicit allusion to Dan 7 and the SM terminology which is lacking in the Wisdom version. Nevertheless, the SM tradition of Dan 7 and the whole theme of the story line based on Isa 53 are clearly not unrelated, as Nickelsburg points out.[13] The developed version of Isa 53 is about suffering, and vindication after suffering. Dan 7 too is focused on the same twin ideas. The SM figure in Daniel is the one who receives vindication in the heavenly court. Whether the SM in Dan 7 is himself a suffering figure has been the subject of much heated discussion. But on any showing, it is clear that the SM represents the persecuted Jews and as such is clearly closely connected with their suffering.

In the light of this background material, the Q sayings about the SM in the gospels take on a new significance. Much discussion has taken place over whether 'SM' is a 'title' in the non-Christian texts, and whether the Q sayings refer to Dan 7 or not.[14] The

[11] Nickelsburg, *Resurrection*, 69 (on Wisdom: cf. Wisd 4:18–19), 75 (on *1 Enoch*, cf. *1 En* 46:6f.).

[12] Possibly Wisd 3:8 may echo Dan 7:14, 27: cf. Nickelsburg, 'Son of Man', 140.

[13] Nickelsburg, *Resurrection*, 76.

[14] Cf. the contrasting views on Q 12:8f. of Caragounis, *Son of Man*, 203 ('The connections with Dan 7:13f. are so obvious that it is unnecessary to belabour the point', and Casey, *Son of Man*, 194 ('It cannot be seen as a deliberate reference to this text [= Dan 7:13]').

question of whether 'SM' is a 'title' or not is perhaps a slight red herring. The older view that there was a fixed 'SM concept' in pre-Christian Judaism has now been shown to be, if not wrong, at least unproven.[15] But we must take care what we are saying, or what we are denying, by such a claim.[16] If by 'title' we mean a fixed idea of an eschatological judging figure, associated with the phrase 'SM' alone and in complete isolation, then it is probably right to reject the idea that such a title existed. On the other hand, we have to note the gospel evidence itself which suggests that the 'SM' *was* a well-known figure with apparently assumed functions.[17] We should also note here that we are dealing with Q, not with Jesus' own preaching; hence we are dealing with the tradition in a Greek form, not Aramaic. Thus all the problems of whether the Aramaic phrase (א)שׁנ(א) בר would have been distinctive enough to evoke a clear set of ideas (i.e. be in some sense 'titular'),[18] may be left on one side here.

Certainly it is very striking how many affinities there are between the Q SM sayings and the tradition of Dan 7 itself together with the exegetical developments which that text both generated and with which it was associated. The idea of Jesus as a figure present on earth, but to be active in some way in the future judgement, is one that links the eschatological Q SM sayings closely with the tradition as evidenced in *1 Enoch, 4 Ezra,* etc. The common phrase 'SM' in both Q and Dan 7 is striking. Moreover, the use of the phrase in Greek in the gospels is highly unusual,[19] as many have pointed out. The coincidence in terminology is thus almost unbearable if it is only coincidence.[20] It seems much easier to assume that the phrase itself *is* an intentional allusion to the Danielic context. As such, the articles might then be the equivalent of the demonstratives in the

---

[15] 'Wrong' and 'unproven' are of course not identical! For a strong statement on the non-existence of such an idea, see Lindars, *Jesus Son of Man*, ch. 1; also Casey, *Son of Man, passim.*

[16] Cf. too A. Y. Collins, 'Origin', 404: 'This argument [that SM was not a title in pre-Christian Judaism] is basically sound but should not be pressed too far.'

[17] Cf. Tödt, *Son of Man*, 224.

[18] This is consistently denied by Casey in all his publications.

[19] Especially in the use of the definite articles. Dan 7:13 does not use the definite articles.

[20] This is one of the weaknesses of the theory of those such as Lindars who has to argue that the gospel tradition of the SM sayings (and only the SM sayings!) draws on the *ideas* implicit in Dan 7 but not on the phrase 'SM' itself (cf. his *Jesus Son of Man*, 15).

Ethiopic text of *1 Enoch*, an indication that reference is being made to a figure in the specific text of Dan 7.[21] Certainly the highly unusual nature of the phrase in Greek makes the theory of a direct allusion to Dan 7 via the phrase alone quite possible.[22] Thus the lack of any explicit allusion to the actual wording of Dan 7 in many, if not all, of the Q eschatological sayings need be no bar. Casey and others have argued that we need some indication, beyond the use of the phrase 'SM' itself, in the wider context of the saying before we can postulate an allusion to Dan 7.[23] But such a demand is usually operated at the level of the individual saying taken in isolation (so that, for example, the *verse* Mark 14:62 could be seen as referring to Dan 7 because of the presence of the clouds, etc. whereas Mark 2:10 cannot). Such an approach may be still too atomistic. We need to look not only at the use of the phrase within the wider literary unit of the sentence in which it is placed. We also need to look at it in the broader stratum of the tradition in which it occurs.[24] Thus, in Q, the whole stratum of the tradition presupposes that, as SM, Jesus will act as agent in the final judgement in a way not dissimilar to the figure described in *1 Enoch* or *4 Ezra*,[25] and given the fact that the latter texts clearly develop Dan 7, it seems reasonable to conclude that Q's use of 'SM' does the same.

If that is the case, then the remaining SM sayings may also fit here if we recall the other strand of the tradition to which I referred. The so-called 'present' SM sayings are, I argued, all implicitly to do with suffering and persecution: they present Jesus as a figure who is under attack, suffering hostility and rejected by those with whom he has contact. Thus the SM references taken as a whole in Q, i.e. the 'present' and the 'eschatological' sayings

[21] So recently A. Y. Collins, 'Origin', 404 (though she thinks this might be the case even in Aramaic); also Moule, *Origin*, 16f.

[22] So also Lindars, *Jesus Son of Man*, 24–6, following Hengel, *Between Jesus and Paul*, 27f.: the choice of this peculiar Greek phrase for the (idiomatic?) Aramaic phrase was a deliberate allusion to Dan 7 on the part of the first translators of the tradition. This does not of course solve the problem of the meaning of the phrase in any underlying Aramaic stratum.

[23] See Casey, *Son of Man*, *passim*. Also Vermes, *Jesus the Jew*, 178.

[24] Just as 'that SM' in *1 Enoch* only makes sense in relation to the *whole* text of the Similitudes of Enoch and thus as a reference back to *1 En* 46 and the clear Danielic allusion there.

[25] The roles are similar but of course not identical: the SM in Q is (only) a witness (at least in Q 12:8), whereas he is more of a judge figure in *4 Ezra* and *1 Enoch*.

together, show a pattern of hostility and suffering followed by vindication and retribution in the divine court. All this is remarkably similar (though again not identical) to the story-line as evidenced in Wisd 2–5 and *1 En* 62. All three portray a story-line of suffering, followed by a judgement scene (explicit or implicit) at which the one presently experiencing hostility and rejection will play a key role in deciding the fate of his erstwhile 'opponents'.

There are, it is true, variations. Wisd 2–5 and *1 En* 62 build on Isa 53; Q apparently does not (though it does portray Jesus as fulfilling the role of Isa 61, a text often associated with the Servant songs).[26] There is no 'SM' in Wisd 2–5, whilst 'SM' is present in *1 Enoch* and Q. Moreover, the SM figure is slightly different in the two texts: in Q the SM is Jesus, whereas in *1 Enoch* the SM is the heavenly counterpart of the righteous. In this then Q is perhaps closer to the version in Wisd 2–5 where there is a clear identity between the persecuted figure of Wisd 2 and the vindicated figure who becomes the agent in judgement in Wisd 5. Further, there is in Q no 'recognition' scene comparable to both *1 Enoch* and Wisdom. Yet despite these differences, the similarities remain. Thus, although neither Wisdom nor *1 Enoch* explicitly state that the 'SM' figure is an individual who both suffers and is vindicated, the seeds are clearly present for such a development in the tradition. We may note in passing too that the common use of the language of Isa 14 to describe the fate of the opponents may also have a parallel in Q, since Q 10:15 uses the language of Isa 14 to refer to the fate of Capernaum in not accepting Jesus.

1 En 62 shows that this complex of ideas had, in one strand of Jewish tradition, already linked with the Dan 7 context. It does not seem inconceivable that the Q tradition represents a third form of the development of this complex of ideas. In this the Isa 53 roots of the tradition have been lost. Rather, the suffering and hostility experienced (by Jesus) is now cast in terms of the 'language game' of Dan 7, i.e. by using the phrase 'SM', rather than by using the language and imagery of Isa 53. Perhaps as part of the same process, the motif of the recognition of erstwhile persecutors, based also on the Isaianic servant song (cf. Isa

---

[26] See above. Even if the argument about Luke 4:16ff. being part of Q is not accepted, the presence of Q 6:20f. and 7:22 show the importance of Isa 61 for Q.

52:13), has also disappeared. Further, unlike *1 Enoch*, the 'SM' language is applied to an earthly figure as well as a heavenly one. In this then Q is closer to Wisd 2–5. But the same underlying pattern is visible, whereby a figure at present suffering will be vindicated in the future and will himself exercise a key role in judging others.

In conclusion, the SM sayings in Q *in toto* represent a remarkable homogeneity and consistency. If 'SM' refers to the persecuted righteous sufferer, then this fits the evidence of Q admirably; it finds parallel evidence in Wisd 2–5 and *1 En* 62 shows that a very similar set of ideas *was* linked with the phrase 'SM' (*with* clear Danielic overtones) as well. 'SM' for Q therefore both is and is not a 'title'. If by 'title' we mean an independent set of meanings, associated solely with the phrase 'SM' alone, then SM in Q is clearly not a title. But if we allow that 'SM' alone (at least in Greek!) *could* be a reference to Dan 7, then a consideration of the ways in which Dan 7 and related texts were used in first century Judaism shows that the Q SM sayings can be placed thoroughly appropriately within such a setting. Further, if this is indeed the significance of the term, then it would also explain why the phrase is used so frequently in contexts dominated by ideas of hostility and rejection and is so often connected with the motifs we considered in earlier chapters, viz. the rejection of the prophets who are sent out by Wisdom. Both the prophetic/wisdom category and the SM terminology are rooted in the idea of suffering and hence it is no coincidence that both appear together in Q.

4. Q 10:21f.

Finally, in any discussion of the Christology of Q, some attempt should be made to say something about the notoriously difficult and complex two verses Q 10:21f., the so-called 'cry of exaltation' where, as we shall see, 'SM' ideas may also be lurking not far below the surface.[27] We have already noted in passing that a number of scholars have ascribed the verses to a very late stage in the development of Q,[28] partly because the ideas they contain

---

[27] For a thorough survey of the verses, with very full bibliographical information, see A. Denaux, 'The Q-Logion Mt 11,27/Lk 10,22 and the Gospel of John', in Denaux (ed.), *John and the Synoptics*, 163–99.
[28] Cf. above on Bultmann, Schulz, Jacobson, Uro and others.

and the explicit 'Son' Christology which they apparently imply, seem to be unlike, and more developed than, anything else in Q.

It is widely agreed that the two verses are almost certainly not an original unity. Verse 21 has the form of a thanksgiving prayer,[29] whereas v. 22 shifts from being an address to God to being a self-recommendation of the revealer and discusses the mediation of revelation.[30] There is debate about whether the two verses originally existed separately as independent sayings; however, the verbal links between the two make it more likely that v. 22 was added as an expansion of v. 21 to act as a commentary on it.[31] The stage within Q at which this happened is also debated. As we have seen, many have argued that the double saying is a relative late-comer into Q. However, a number of the arguments for the allegedly unusual nature of Q 10:21f. within Q have now been answered by Piper.[32] For example, Jacobson has argued that, unlike the deuteronomistic perspective dominating much of the polemical passages in Q, Q 10:21f. seems to suggest that Israel is no longer culpable for her failure to respond, and the verses imply an almost predestinarian view in the suggestion that revelation has been hidden from her.[33] However, as Piper observes, the criticism of the 'wise and understanding' is probably an inversion of the claims made by others, and therefore almost certainly contains an implicit rebuke. Moreover, other parallels to the idea of the withdrawal of Wisdom (cf. *1 En* 42; *4 Ezra* 5:9–10) suggest that this occurs in the context of the prelude to eschatological judgement: it is not a means of excusing others.

However, the verses have often been felt to be somewhat anomalous within Q by virtue of the Christological ideas implied. Not only is the absolute use of the term 'Son' felt to be unusual, but also the very close association suggested between Jesus and the person of Wisdom in these verses has been regarded by many as unlike the rest of Q.

[29] See J. M. Robinson, 'Die Hodayot Formel in Gebet und Hymnus des Früh-christentums', in *Apophoreta* (FS E. Haenchen, BZNW 30; Berlin: Töpelmann, 1964) 194–235.

[30] See Bultmann, *History*, 159f.; Robinson, 'Hodayot Formel', 228; Lühr-mann, *Redaktion*, 65; Hoffmann, *Studien*, 109; Schulz, *Q*, 215; J. S. Kloppenborg, Wisdom Christology in Q', *LTP* 34 (1978) 129–47, p. 137; also his *Formation*, 198; Jacobson, *First Gospel*, 150; Denaux, 'Q-Logion', 170.

[31] So Kloppenborg, Hoffmann, Schulz. It is however taken as an independent saying by Bultmann, Lührmann (references as in previous note).

[32] See Piper, *Wisdom*, 171f.

[33] See Jacobson, *First Gospel*, 149; also Uro, *Sheep*, 230ff.

The Wisdom background of these verses is widely acknowledged. Perhaps such a background is even clearer in the
Matthean context, where the Q verses are linked with the
invitation of Jesus to the weary and the heavy-laden (Matt 11:28–
30 following Matt 11:25–27, which is the Matthean parallel to
Luke 10:21f.). Here the parallels between the invitation of Jesus
and the invitation of Wisdom in Sir 51 have long been noted, and
it is generally agreed that Matthew at least is presenting Jesus in
the form of Wisdom.[34] The situation regarding Q 10:21f. is more
debated. At one time it was popular to argue that Matt 11:25–30
might have constituted an original unity which Luke then
abbreviated.[35] However, the alleged parallels in Sir 51, upon
which such a theory was in part based, have now been shown to
be rather weak. Subsequent finds have shown that Sir 51 itself
may not be an original unity,[36] and in any case reasons why Luke
might have omitted Matt 11:28–30 from Q are not easy to
envisage.[37] Hence one cannot interpret Q 10:21f. in its Q context
by reference to Matt 11:28–30.

Nevertheless, several scholars have argued that the
identification of Jesus with Wisdom has already taken place by
the time of Q 10:22, as well as in Matt 11:28–30. The exclusive
mutual knowledge of the Father and the Son is seen by some to
be similar to what is said elsewhere of God and Wisdom: God
knows Wisdom (Job 28:1–27; Sir 1:6, 8; Bar 3:15–32), and only
Wisdom knows God (Prov 8:12; Wisd 7:25ff.; 8:3f., 8f.; 9:4, 9, 11),[38]
and Wisdom is the one who reveals God to other men (Wisd 7:21
9:17; Sir 4:18).[39] However, Dunn has pointed out that some these
alleged parallels are not equally persuasive.[40] Some of the texts
adduced for the motif that God knows Wisdom need only imply

[34] See all the commentaries, though a dissenting note is sounded by Stanton
Gospel for a New People, 364–77.

[35] Cf. E. Norden, *Agnostos Theos* (Berlin: Teubner, 1913) 276–308; Dibelius
Tradition, 279–83.

[36] See Lührmann, *Redaktion*, 67; Suggs, *Wisdom*, 77ff.; Kloppenborg, 'Wisdom
Christology', 134; Stanton, *Gospel for a New People*, 368. Cf. the version of Si
51:13ff. found in 11QPs[a], i.e. lacking Sir 51:1–12 which is the substantive
parallel to Q 10:21.

[37] Kloppenborg, ibid.

[38] Cf. Christ, *Jesus Sophia*, 88f.; also Schulz, *Q*, 224f.; Robinson, 'Jesus a
Sophos', 9f.; Kloppenborg, 'Wisdom Christology', 144; Denaux, 'Q-Logion'
175f.

[39] So Kloppenborg, 'Wisdom Christology', 144; Christ, *Jesus Sophia*, 88f., cite
Wisd 7:28.

[40] See Dunn, *Christology*, 198f.

that God knows the source, or locus, of Wisdom.[41] So too the idea of Wisdom as the agent of revelation is not easy to parallel in Wisdom texts. Sir 4:18 ('I will reveal to him my secrets') is perhaps closest in the texts cited above, though it is not explicitly knowledge of God that is referred to here. Other texts from the book of Wisdom seem far less close.[42] In addition to this is the fact that any reference to σοφία/wisdom is at best implicit: the one 'title' used here is not σοφία but υἱός.[43] Further, the first part of v. 22 ('All things have been delivered to me by my Father') is hard to parallel from the Wisdom tradition and has far closer links with apocalyptic thought, especially the SM tradition (cf. Dan 7:14).[44]

All this may suggest that it is wrong to look for a single Christological schema reflected in Q 10:21f., or even in v. 22 alone: rather, the verses may reflect 'a mixture of different motifs and materials'.[45] As we have seen, v. 22a may reflect SM ideas and terminology. The reference to Jesus as 'son' may be closer to the sonship language of Wisd 2–5 (itself not unconnected with SM as we have seen), where it is the righteous sufferer, and perhaps the *follower* of Wisdom, who is the 'son' of God (Wisd 2:16; also Sir 4:10) and, perhaps significantly, who is also thought to be claiming to have knowledge of God (cf. the taunt in Wisd 2:13: 'he claims to have knowledge of God').[46] It may therefore be easier to see Q 10:21f. as very similar to the other Q passages we

[41] Dunn, *Christology*, 199, refers to Job 28:20, 23; Sir 1:6; Bar 3:27, 29–31, 36. Job 28 talks of the 'way' of Wisdom being known by God; similarly Sir 1:6 talks of the 'root' of Wisdom.

[42] Wisd 7:21 talks only of Wisdom 'learning' secret things. Wisd 7:28 ('For God loves nothing so much as the man who lives with wisdom') seems scarcely comparable, and Wisd 9:17 ('Who has learned thy counsel unless thou hast given wisdom?') really seems to make God himself the mediator of revelation, and 'wisdom' the content of the revelation itself. Perhaps Wisd 10:10 (Wisdom 'gave him knowledge of holy things') would be closer to the idea of Q 10:22d: cf. Uro, *Sheep*, 225.

[43] Any 'title' predicated of Wisdom in this context is usually 'daughter', not 'son', of God: cf. Philo, *Fuga* 52; *Leg.All.* 2.49.

[44] See Hoffmann, *Studien*, 121f.; Schulz, *Q*, 222; Kloppenborg, 'Wisdom Christology', 141f.; Dunn, *Christology*, 199; Uro, *Sheep*, 226; Denaux, 'Q-Logion', 174.

[45] Uro, *Sheep*, 226.

[46] See Dunn, *Christology*, 199; Suggs, *Wisdom*, 91f.; also Dunn's remark in his *Christology*, 200: 'Q is merging apocalyptic and wisdom motifs (as in Luke 7.35) to present Jesus as Wisdom's eschatological envoy rather than as Wisdom, as the righteous man par excellence who knows God as Father and has the task of bringing God's final wisdom to men.'

have reviewed where Jesus is presented as the envoy of Wisdom. Language associated with speculations about Wisdom are certainly present here; but it still remains doubtful how far an *equation* between Jesus and Wisdom has already taken place here. Certainly the sonship language is not unparalleled elsewhere in Q (cf. Q 4:1–13; 6:35; cf. too 11:2, 13; 12:30 — significantly in the latter passages it is applied, explicitly or implicitly, to disciples of Jesus as well as Jesus himself) where it refers to the one who is obedient to God.[47]

One might speculate further and ask whether the final reference to the Son as the unique medium of revelation is really intended by Q in quite such an exclusive Christological way as is usually assumed.[48] If the Q followers of Jesus are indeed continuing the preaching of Jesus in their own day, then they are in a sense themselves acting as the mediators of the 'knowledge' of God which is regarded as so critical for their hearers. Hence the Q Christian, as the one who can address God as Father (cf. Q 11:2, 13; 12:30), is in a sense also a 'son' of God, a person who can claim knowledge of God, and to be known by God, and hence charged with the task of making known to others what that knowledge involves. Such an interpretation is proposed here somewhat tentatively, though it might claim some support from the Q context in which Q 10:21f. is probably placed. If (as most assume) Luke's ordering of the Q material reflects the Q order,[49] then Q 10:21f. must have come in Q between Q 10:16 and Q 10:23f. Both the latter passages are not necessarily primarily Christological but are to do with Jesus' followers: Q 10:16 speaks of the Q missionaries re-presenting Jesus himself (so that rejection of them is rejection of him and of God); and Q 10:23f. talks of the disciples as the recipients of a 'revelation' denied to earlier 'prophets' and others.[50] So too the change from the first person of v. 22a ('*my* father') to the third person

---

[47] For this as the force of the references to Jesus as Son of God in the temptation narrative, see my 'The Temptation Narrative in Q', in Van Segbroek et al (eds), *The Four Gospels 1992*, 479–507, p. 495, and see pp. 420–2 below for further discussion of the temptation narrative in Q.

[48] It is this which, according to Kloppenborg, 'Wisdom Christology', 145, tells against the theory that the background of the saying is to be found in traditions such as Wisd 2 (arguing against Suggs).

[49] Cf Denaux, 'Q-Logion', 169, in relation to this saying.

[50] On the other hand, it is equally arguable that what the disciples have seen and heard according to Q 10:23f. are the events of Jesus' own ministry, so that the reference is implicitly Christological.

of v. 22b–d (the Son) might support the above interpretation.[51]

However, whatever the precise reference in v. 22b–d, the wisdom background proposed here would fit extremely well with the probable Q context of the saying. If the saying did indeed follow immediately after Q 10:16 in Q, then the context is surely significant. Q 10:16 comes at the end of the mission charge, following on from Q 10:13–15 where the rejection of the mission is clearly in mind. Similarly, the second half of Q 10:16 itself (where arguably the stress of the antithetically parallel saying lies)[52] refers to rejection, not acceptance. So too we have seen that Q prefaces the mission instructions with the SM saying in Q 9:58 which also alludes to the idea of hostility and rejection (cf. above). Thus the whole of the preceding section is dominated by the motifs of hostility and rejection, and we have seen that such ideas are endemic in all the Q traditions about Jesus as SM and envoy of Wisdom. Q 10:21f. may then reflect much of the same flavour. Jesus alludes to himself as SM in v. 22a; and if v. 22b–d also reflects the language and ideas of Wisd 2 (cf. above), whether seen as referring to Jesus alone or to Jesus and others, the latter passage too is set in a context of hostility and antagonism. Thus the whole saying in its Q setting may be thoroughly integrated with other Christological material in Q. There is therefore no need necessarily to hive the saying off and see it as a later addition to Q. It coheres well with the rest of the Q material we have considered.

Conclusion

In all the Christological material we have considered, there is an underlying unity, despite the at times bewildering variety of ideas and terminology used. In one sense the variety may be due to the peculiar choice and combination of traditions which Q has produced, including ideas associated with Wisdom, the prophets, SM, the persecuted Israelite as Son, etc. But underlying much if not all of the Christological language is the idea of rejection, hostility, suffering and violence experienced by Jesus and/or his followers. Thus Jesus is presented as the envoy of Wisdom,

---

[51] This is then not quite the same as the interpretation of Jeremias, *Theology*, 58, who argues that the saying about Father and Son is about any father and any son: I am suggesting that it is about God as Father and others (plural!) who might be called 'sons' of God the Father.

[52] See Jeremias, *Theology*, 18.

identified as one of the prophets, all of whom are seen as suffering rejection and violence; similarly, he is 'SM', which also evokes ideas of suffering, as well as the further idea of vindication and judgement after suffering; and the sonship language of Q 10:21f. may recall the similar (and perhaps related) idea of the righteous sufferer. Q undoubtedly produces what is at times a somewhat idiosyncratic 'blend' of the various traditions. For example, as we have seen, the particular combination whereby Wisdom becomes the agent who sends out the prophets, all of whom suffer rejection and violence, seems to be peculiar to Q. So too Q's use of the SM terminology is peculiar, even if (as I tried to argue above) closely linked with similar uses of related ideas in texts like *1 En* and Wisd 2–5. But common to all this is the idea of conflict leading to rejection and suffering. What then has given rise to such an outlook? This will be the topic of our next chapter.

9

Polemic and Persecution

Much of what we have considered so far indicates that the Q Christians believed themselves to be in a situation of conflict. We have seen (cf. ch. 6 above) that there is a great deal of polemic in Q directed against 'this generation', and at times this is connected — at least in Q's view — with 'violence' being suffered by the Christian side, a violence which is placed by Q in a line of continuity with the violence suffered by the prophets (cf. 6:23; 11:49–51; 13:34f.). So too, much of the Christological awareness in Q focuses on the hostility and rejection experienced by Jesus, as we have just seen (see ch. 8 above); and the same experiences will come to his followers. It seems clear that the Q editor sees his/her Christian community as facing some kind of 'persecution' situation and a lot of the polemic is directed against the perpetrators of this 'persecution'. Jacobson even suggests that it may have been the onset of persecution which led to the redaction of Q which has provided the deuteronomistic-prophetic stratum which he postulates as a major stage in the compositional history of Q.[1]

We should however perhaps be wary of concluding too prematurely that Q's polemic and Q's experience of 'persecution' are two sides of precisely the same coin. As we shall see, there is a great deal of polemical language in Q which is not apparently directed against who are actively 'persecuting' the Christian movement. Further, the nature of any alleged 'persecution' may need some precision. The aim of this chapter will be to explore the phenomena of polemic and persecution in the Q material to see if we can gain any further insight into the situation in which the Q Christians found themselves in relation to their neighbours.

In discussing the possible persecution faced by the Q Christians, sayings like Q 6:22f.; 11:49–51 and 13:34f. must play a

---

[1] Jacobson, 'Literary Unity', 389.

crucial role. Yet it may not be appropriate to make these sayings provide the hermeneutical key, and the social and ideological background, for the interpretation of all the other references to possible persecution in Q; nor may it be appropriate to let the persecution background dominate the interpretation of the other polemical passages in Q. We have seen that much of the polemical material is linked from the side of Q by the common use of the themes of Wisdom, the fate of the prophets, references to 'this generation', references to Jesus as 'SM', and possible allusions to Gentiles in contrast with the present audience. Yet when we seek to press the evidence a little further and ask what kind of situations are presupposed, there is a considerable amount of material in Q which suggests that it is not really 'persecution' (in any normal sense of that word in English, though cf. below) which is the object and reason for Q's polemic. It is these 'polemic' passages which we shall consider first, before going on to look at those parts of Q which do appear to reflect a 'persecution' situation.

1. Polemic

1.1. Q 3:7–9, 16–17

The preaching of John the Baptist in Q (3:7–9, 16–17) is full of polemic. We have examined this pericope in some detail in an earlier chapter and need not reproduce the same analysis again here. We saw earlier that it is unclear precisely who is being addressed by Q's John: Matthew has 'Pharisees and Sadducees', Luke has the 'crowds', though I argued that a case could be made for at least the 'Pharisees' of Matthew being present in Q. John addresses the people in very harsh tones, calling them 'vipers' and challenging them to produce 'fruit(s) worthy of repentance'. In the earlier analysis, I argued that the section in 3:7–9 can quite easily be taken as a traditio-historical unity, there being no need for example to separate off the saying about raising up children for Abraham (Q 3:8b) as a secondary addition to an earlier tradition. Further, I argued that the passage is best taken as an attack not on people who were coming to be baptised but without the proper 'inner' attitude; rather, the polemical language makes best sense if the attack is directed against those who have not accepted baptism by John at all. (See pp. 109–16 above.)

But this raises all the more acutely the question of why they have come to see John in the first place and what kind of setting is presupposed here. For what is so striking is the fact that the people concerned are portrayed as so *in*active. Nothing suggests that they have come out to spy on John, to try to report something to the authorities which would incriminate John; there is no indication that they have come with the aim of physically disrupting John's baptising ministry in any way. As the tradition is reported in Q, they have come apparently only to watch, but to remain uncommitted. They have come, it would seem, to do *nothing*. John remains entirely free to rant against them in the strongest possible language and to exhort them to take note of his warnings. The listeners are thus simply the uncommitted. They are not active persecutors of John or his movement. And this picture is by no means unique in Q. As we shall see, there is a large amount of material in Q which propounds a similarly polemical attitude to what appears to be simply a passive neutrality and merely an unwillingness to respond positively to the Christian movement.

1.2. Q 7:1–10

The material in the Great Sermon will be considered later when we look at the material in Q which possibly reflects more explicitly a persecution situation. However, probably immediately following the Sermon in Q was the story of the healing of the centurion's servant (Q 7:1–10). At the end of the story, the centurion is held up by Jesus as an exemplary figure exhibiting πίστις, the like of which has not been found by Jesus in all Israel (Q 7:9). The precise nature or object of the πίστις need not be discussed here in detail: the 'faith' could perhaps be faith in Jesus, but is more likely to be faith in the power of God as mediated through Jesus.[2] Further, the unusual nature of the story within Q (it is the only 'miracle' story with any detail in Q) will not be discussed here. What is important for our present purposes is simply to note that all that is implied by way of criticism against the Jewish listeners by Q's Jesus is that they have not shown πίστις. Nothing is said, or implied, that such lack of faith has resulted in any physical violence or active opposition against Jesus or his followers. It is simply that, unlike the centurion who has come to Jesus and asked for help, the rest of Jesus' contemporaries have not. They have simply failed to

---

[2] On 'faith' and miracles generally in the synoptics, see Held, in Bornkamm, Barth and Held, *Tradition and Interpretation in Matthew*, 276ff.

respond positively. Once again, as in 3:7–9, the people have failed to commit themselves in any way to the Jesus movement — but that is all.

1.3. Q 7:31–35

We have looked at Q 7:18–35 in some detail in an earlier chapter. To recapitulate that earlier discussion briefly, I argued that the section in 7:31–35 with the parable of the playing children and its accompanying interpretative sayings (in vv. 33–35) represents the climax of the wider section whereby the Q editor may have moulded earlier traditions which dealt with the relationship between Jesus and John the Baptist so that now the whole concerns the opposition between Jesus and John together on one side against 'this generation' on the other. (See p. 131 above.)

There is still however the question of the nature of that opposition. The situation is evidently illustrated by means of the parable in vv. 31f. As we have already noted, it is difficult to know precisely how far one may transfer details from the story of a parable to the reality it is meant to be illuminating in a quasi-'allegorical' way. Much of the discussion about the place of allegory in the parables has taken place at the level of the meaning of the parables on the lips of Jesus; but few would deny that a tendency towards allegorisation of the parables can be seen already amongst the early Christians of the NT period (cf. Mark 4:14–20; Matt 13:36–43). And, as we saw earlier, many have regarded Q 7:33f. itself as a secondary allegorisation of the parable of the playing children in vv. 31f. It may therefore be not inappropriate to press the details of the parable just a little to see what they might imply about the situation being illustrated and addressed, at least at the level of Q.

What is striking is that neither in the parable itself nor in the appended interpretation is there any mention of violence. The parable tells of children refusing to respond to invitations to play. But in the story the children concerned do not get up and start beating their friends or seeking to have them arrested and tried for breach of the peace! They simply sulk and do nothing. So too, the interpretation of the parable (where one is probably more justified in seeing a reasonably close approximation to the situation in mind) does not imply any violence. Those addressed, it is true, have apparently rejected the claims of John and Jesus: they accuse John of being an ascetic and Jesus of being a glutton. But the rejection seems to be purely verbal. There is no hint that the charges against John or Jesus have resulted in any judicial action against the two preachers. There is thus strong polemic by Q's Jesus against people who have failed to respond positively to the appeals made to them. But there is no hint here that such failure to respond has involved anything more than a verbal rejection with at most a slightly aggressive edge to it.

1.4. Q 10:2–16

The mission charge in Q 10:2ff. also shows many features of a polemical attitude towards those who do not accept the Christian message and mission. At one point there is a hint of possible danger facing the missionaries. This occurs at Q 10:3 where the missionaries are told that they are being sent out like lambs in the midst of wolves. We have already noted the possibly polemical nature of the imagery used: Jewish tradition had spoken of Israelite 'lambs' living in the midst of hostile Gentile 'wolves', and this Q saying seems to take up, and invert, the same image so that it is now the Christian missionaries who are the 'lambs' and the Jewish non-Christians who are the 'wolves' (see p. 185 above). Some kind of dangerous situation is thus envisaged. Yet precisely what danger is involved is not spelt out here. The saying remains at the level of a very high degree of generality. At the very least one might expect the form of the hostility involved to become clearer in the mission instructions which follow.[3]

In the mission charge itself, we are told of possible negative reactions to the missionaries with instructions given for the cases when a house/city does not welcome the mission.[4] Yet even here, the situation presupposed seems relatively mild in terms of the opposition being faced. The missionaries are warned that they may find no welcome in some places. In such a situation the missionaries are to leave the place concerned. (It is implied that this is a voluntary act on the part of the missionaries, though it is conceivable that the other side would have seen it as more of a forcible removal: the missionaries might have been expelled from the place.) But then they are to come out and fling the dust of their feet against the city. The meaning of the gesture is

---

[3] Assuming (as with most) that Luke preserves the Q position of the saying in relation to the rest of the mission charge. Cf. Lührmann, *Redaktion*, 59; Hoffmann, *Studien*, 263; Uro, *Sheep*, 75; and most others.

[4] I leave aside here the problems of whether there are two missions implied here.

uncertain,[5] but it seems clear that the action is one which is undertaken in some freedom from the Christian side. The missionaries are evidently free to show their feelings — and do so! There is no suggestion that the lack of acceptance of the mission has led to any violence against the Christians. At most it has led to hospitality failing to be offered to, or accepted by, the mission. Once again, negative reactions against the Christian movement seems to have been purely verbal.

The woes against the Galilean cities (Q 10:13–15) were probably connected with the mission charge in Q (cf. p. 184 above). Again the language is strong and the polemic harsh. (The words used against Capernaum echo the taunt song against the king of Babylon in Isa 14.) But once again there is no direct indication of any violence having been inflicted on the Christians. Chorazin and Bethsaida are charged with failing to 'repent' (the accusation is thus very similar to what is implied in 3:7–9) despite the mighty works done there. It seems that again the 'trouble' is simply that the Jewish cities have failed to respond positively but nothing indicates that this failure has taken the form of any violent counter-response.

It may be that the logion of Q 9:58 about the homeless SM should be interpreted in a very similar way. I have argued above that the position of the saying in Q may be deliberate: the homeless SM acts as a paradigm for the Christian disciple whose task is about to be outlined in the mission charge which follows — and hence the homeless SM acts as a model for the rejection which is to be experienced by the Christian disciples. (See p. 183 above.) As such then the homelessness of the SM is brought about by rejection. But if the SM's life-style is to be seen as paradigmatic of that of the missionaries, then it seems that homelessness is also a way of life that is partly chosen: the missionaries choose to leave their homes and travel around without possessions. Their itinerant life-style is thus voluntary at one level. Yet it is undertaken in the hope and/ or assumption that they will receive board and lodging from those who accept their message as they go. Their itinerancy is thus not intended to lead to a life of poverty and material hardship. The latter only comes when the missionaries find no

---

[5] H. J. Cadbury, 'Dust and Garments', in F. J. Foakes Jackson & K. Lake (eds), *The Beginnings of Christianity. The Acts of the Apostles V* (London: Macmillan, 1933) 269–77; SB I, 571; Hoffmann, *Studien*, 302.

welcome.[6] One can perhaps begin here to talk of 'persecution'. However, it is probably the case that others would have regarded any deprivation suffered by the Christians as entirely self-inflicted.

1.5. Q 11:14–32

Further polemic can be seen in the Beelzebul controversy in Q 11:14ff. which in Q evidently led on to the story involving the request for a sign and the reply about the Sign of Jonah. Again the pattern we have observed so far is repeated. Jesus' cause is opposed: after performing an exorcism he is charged with using demonic power. Clearly the Jewish audience fail to perceive the true nature of his exorcistic activity and they show their lack of perceptiveness by asking for a sign. Had they been aware of the 'true' nature of Jesus' exorcisms, i.e. as part of the inauguration of the kingdom of God (cf. Q 11:20), they would have had no need of an extra sign. Yet once again there is nothing to indicate that the opposition is anything more than verbal. The Beelzebul charge does not lead to Jesus' being arrested or charged. There is no 'persecution'.

Similarly, in the polemic against 'this generation' which characterises the double saying in Q 11:31f. at the end of the Sign of Jonah pericope, the implied charge against the listeners is again simply that of failing to respond positively (by 'repenting'). 'This generation' is compared unfavourably with both the Queen of the South and the Ninevites, and in each case the point of comparison is the issue of 'repentance': they 'repented' on encountering the wisdom of Solomon and the preaching of Jonah. By implication, 'this generation' has not, even though something greater than both Solomon and Jonah is here now. As in 3:7–9 and 10:13–15, the audience is accused of failing to 'repent'; but there is nothing to indicate that this has involved inflicting any physical violence upon Jesus or the Jesus-movement. Once again it seems that the besetting sin of 'this generation' is simply that of failing to accept the Christian message.

This may also be confirmed by a consideration of the other traditions which were evidently closely associated in Q with the Beelzebul story and the Sign of Jonah tradition, viz. the mini-

[6] On the question of whether the homelessness involved here is voluntary or involuntary, see ch. 11 below.

'parable' about the unclean spirits in Q 11:24–26 and the saying in 11:23: 'He who is not with me is against me.' Both Matthew and Luke agree in having all these traditions in the same literary context, thus indicating their collocation in Q, even if the precise order of the sayings is slightly different in the two gospels: in Luke the parable about the unclean spirits follows immediately after the 'He who is not with me . . .' logion, before being followed by the Sign of Jonah pericope; in Matthew the relative order of the Sign of Jonah and the Unclean Spirits is reversed (Luke 11:24–26 + 29–32 par Matt 12:43–45 + 38–42). Matthew's ordering is probably to be regarded as secondary, with the parable of the unclean spirits then functioning as a summary of the whole of Matthew's ch. 12.[7] If this is correct, then the parable of Q 11:24–26 followed immediately after the saying in Q 11:23 which concluded the Beelzebul story.

This in turn may give us some clue as to the interpretation of the parable of the unclean spirits in Q. The unit is very obscure and has been interpreted in a number of ways, e.g. as polemic against Jewish exorcists or as providing rules for the practice of Christian exorcists.[8] However, neither possibility seems very convincing: Q 11:19 seems to accept quite openly the activity of Jewish exorcists; and nothing in 11:24–26 really indicates that any 'rules' about exorcistic practice are being prescribed. Much more convincing is the interpretation which links 11:24–26 with the saying in 11:23 as indeed the (probable) Q context suggests.

Q 11:23 is the Q counterpart of the saying which also appears in Mark 9:40. Yet compared with the Markan version the Q saying is far more exclusive.[9] In Mark those who are rejected are those who actively oppose Jesus: the neutral are accepted as implicitly on Jesus' side ('He who is not against me is for me'). In Q the situation is reversed: neutrality is taken as opposition ('He who is not with me is against me'). What is opposed in the Q version of the saying is thus neutrality.[10] This line of thought may then be continued in the parable of the unclean spirits.[11] In the context

---

[7] Schulz, *Q*, 476 n. 562; Kloppenborg, *Formation*, 126; *pace* Laufen, *Doppelüberlieferungen*, 140; Piper, *Wisdom*, 123; Jacobson, *First Gospel*, 154f.

[8] See the survey in Laufen, *Doppelüberlieferungen*, 141–7. For the first, cf. Schulz, *Q*, 478f.; for the second, cf. Hoffmann, *Studien*, 37, 299.

[9] D. Lührmann, *Das Markusevangelium* (Tübingen: Mohr, 1987) 167.

[10] Kloppenborg, *Formation*, 126; Piper, *Wisdom*, 123f.

[11] See especially Laufen, *Doppelüberlieferungen*, 144–7, followed by Kloppenborg, *Formation*, 126f.; Piper, *Wisdom*, 123f.

of 11:23, the parable may be saying again that neutrality is impossible. It is not enough to drive out an unclean spirit and leave the house empty — otherwise the spirit will return with seven others and make things even worse. There must then be continued active opposition to the forces of evil. In terms of Q's context, one must be actively engaged on the side of Jesus, rather than remaining passively dormant (i.e., in the imagery of the parable, 'empty'). The saying and parable thus inveigh heavily against neutrality as the besetting sin and danger.

Whether this constitutes a significant shift from the earlier Beelzebul controversy is questionable. Laufen and Piper argue that there is such a shift, the focus of attention moving from an attack on Jewish opponents to a paraenetic address to vacillating Christians.[12] However, as we shall see, this may be presupposing too much of a 'Christian community' consciousness on the part of Q. In fact the polemic here fits well with what we have discovered so far. What Q's Jesus opposes is neutrality by the members of this generation, not just by weaker Q-Christians. The Jewish audience here have simply done nothing. They have remained neutral. They have not necessarily been violently opposed to Jesus' cause. But their very inaction is what is condemned in the strongest possible terms.

1.6. Q 12:8–10

The sayings about confessing/denying the SM, and speaking a word against the SM/Holy Spirit (12:8f. + 12:10) may also be relevant. Once again there is harsh polemic and threats. But for whom? The *Sitz im Leben* of 12:8f. is often assumed to be one of Christians on trial,[13] though Catchpole has shown that the language of 'confessing'/'denying' and ἔμπροσθεν cannot really sustain such a theory.[14] Although a forensic situation is not impossible, the language used is much more general, emerging often in a context of an already existing relationship.[15] This probably applies also to the second half of the saying where those who

---

[12] Laufen, *Doppelüberlieferungen*, 146; Piper, *Wisdom*, 124. Laufen explicitly opposes Lührmann, *Redaktion*, 42f., who sees the whole as directed against 'this generation'.

[13] See Vielhauer, 'Gottesreich', 77–9; Hoffmann, *Studien*, 155; Schulz, *Q*, 72.

[14] D. R. Catchpole, 'The Angelic Son of Man in Luke 12:8', *NovT* 24 (1982) 255–65, pp. 257–9; Fitzmyer, *Luke*, 960.

[15] Catchpole, ibid., and Tödt, *Son of Man*, 55f.

'deny' Jesus are sharply warned of the consequences of their actions. 'Denying' too seems to presuppose a previous situation of commitment.[16] Thus the strong language of 12:9, threatening those who deny Jesus with corresponding denial (probably by the SM) at the final judgement, is reserved not necessarily for outright opponents of the Christian movement, let alone for any potential 'persecutors'.[17] The addressee of v. 9 is not an opponent, but one who is unprepared to accept and acknowledge the full commitment to the Christian cause. The saying is as much to do with those who would remain neutral as it is to do with those who actively persecute the Christian movement.[18] Verses 8 and 9 thus concern Christians and wavering 'Christians', not Christians and opponents.[19] The sharp polemic and warnings are thus reserved for the waverers and the neutral as much as for any persecuting opponents of the Christian cause.

It is worth noting that a very similar kind of audience seems to be presupposed in the saying in Q 6:46 where Q's Jesus somewhat plaintively asks 'Why do you call me "Lord, Lord", but do not do what I say?'.[20] Those addressed are those who call Jesus 'Lord', and hence presumably acknowledge his authority in some sense, but who are not 'doing' what he teaches. These then seem to be people who have some commitment to the Christian cause but whose commitment is regarded as incomplete.

Q 12:10 may be similar. The precise connection between 12:8f. and 12:10 is problematic. I argued earlier (see p. 108 above) that 12:10 is perhaps best taken as implying a distinction between the time of Jesus and the time of the Q Christians' preaching: rejection of Jesus himself (= speaking against the SM) is

---

[16] See p. 250 n. 33 above.

[17] Cf. too Piper, *Wisdom*, 60f.

[18] Cf. too Tödt, *Son of Man*, 55.

[19] The interpretation offered above differs then somewhat from that of, for example, Lührmann, *Redaktion*, 52, followed by Hoffmann, *Studien*, 156; Kloppenborg, *Formation*, 211, who argue that the discourse shifts in direction from vv. 4–7 to vv. 8f., from being addressed to Christians (vv. 4–7) to an address to those who hear the Christian preaching (vv. 8f.). There is no hint of such a change of address, and in any case the presuppositions of the 'confessing/ denying' vocabulary would seem to necessitate some kind of positive commitment on the part of the addressees. Hence Kloppenborg's claim that 12:8f. effects 'a similar shift [similar to e.g. 10:12, 13–15] from community to outsiders' is hard to accept. On the relationship of vv. 4–7 to vv. 8f., see below.

[20] For the reconstruction of the Q version, cf. p. 214 above.

forgivable in the light of the renewed presentation of Jesus' message in the preaching of the Q Christians, rejection of which will not be forgiven. Here however we may simply note the mildness of the language. The Q version of the saying refers only to 'saying a word against'.[21] At most it would seem that the 'opposition' presupposed is purely verbal. There is no hint of any physical violence being threatened against the Q Christians. (This is not, of course, to deny the seriousness of the situation, as seen from the side of Q: the 'speaking a word against' is threatened with eternal punishment! Q offers no mildness at all! Nevertheless, in the present context we are simply concerned with trying to discover what it is that has provoked this stern reaction from Q's Jesus in the situation of the Q Christians.)

1.7. Q 12:51–53

A harsh situation may be reflected in Q 12:51–53. However, the language is very general and in any case heavily influenced by OT texts such as Mic 7:6. A situation of divisions across traditional family boundaries seems to be presupposed, though the OT background and the stereotyped nature of the description makes it difficult to be certain exactly what historical and social conditions are presupposed here. Certainly it would seem precarious to deduce that physical violence is in mind from the reference to the 'sword' here.

1.8. Q 13:24–29

Further support for the general pattern we have seen so far is provided by the section in Q 13:24ff. Earlier I argued that Q 13:24–29 may well have been a unified section in Q (cf. pp. 189–95 above). Here some people are warned of the terrible consequences which will follow their failure to enter the narrow door: they will find the door shut and their places at the banquet taken by others. But who are the people and why are they excluded? What is it that they have done, or failed to do, that has

---

[21] So Luke 12:10a/Matt 12:32. The reference to 'blasphemies' in Luke 12:10b and Matt 12:31 is probably due to influence from the Markan version of the saying: see Schulz, *Q*, 246; Tödt, *Son of Man*, 285f.; M. E. Boring, 'The Unforgivable Sin Logion Mk III 28–29/Matt XII 31–32/Lk XII 10. Formal Analysis and History of the Tradition', *NovT* 18 (1976) 258–79, p. 267; also my *Revival*, 88.

led to their being excluded with such finality? We have seen that vv. 28f. shows clearly that Jews are in mind. Further, their pleas articulated in v. 26 ('we ate before you and you taught in our streets')[22] shows that they have been contemporaries of Jesus. However, nothing in the text implies that they have actively opposed the Christian movement. They have simply been non-committal, they have failed to respond positively, but as a result they now find themselves excluded and rejected.[23] Thus once again it is neutrality which is being forcefully condemned here (cf. 11:23–26).[24]

1.9. Q 14:16–23 + 19:12–29

A very similar picture emerges from the two parables of the Great Supper and the talents/pounds (Q 14:16ff. and 19:12ff.). As before, one cannot be entirely certain how far the precise details of the stories are meant to correspond to the realities which the stories are intended to illuminate. But it is striking that once again what is condemned is a failure to respond positively, rather than any violent negative reaction. In the parable of the Great Supper, the excuses which the guests offer are all probably morally neutral at worst, simply asking for more time. It is Matthew who makes the guests react in a way which is explicitly morally reprehensible by having them inflict violence on the servants, and this is probably due to MattR.[25] Thus in Q there is no clear antagonism to the invitations by the original guests. All that is implied is that the invitation to the supper is not very high on their list of priorities and they think that the time is not very pressing. So too in the parable of the pounds, the third servant is condemned by his master simply because he has not used what he has been given. He has not beaten up the first two servants or even mocked them in any way.

---

[22] Matthew's version in Matt 7:22f., making the people into Christian charismatic miracle workers, is almost certainly MattR. See above p. 192.

[23] It is probably wrong to stress the ἀδικία/ἀνομία in the actual words of rejection in Q 13:27 (contra Hoffmann: see p. 193 above). Their ἀδικία/ἀνομία may consist for Q precisely in their lack of positive response.

[24] Cf. too Piper, *Wisdom*, 124, for the connection between the two passages, though he sees it as concerning 'not just outsiders, but also lukewarm insiders'. My point is that perhaps 'lukewarm outsiders' are also in view; or rather, maybe we are not yet at the stage of an 'insider/outsider' mentality.

[25] See p. 147 above

He has simply done nothing and it is this which the parable condemns.

Q 16:16 should perhaps be mentioned briefly here since some kind of violent opposition may be alluded to in this verse. However, the saying is so general that it is quite unclear who the 'men of violence' (βιασταί) are and what is the nature of the 'violence' which they are in some way inflicting on the kingdom. Physical persecution of the Christian supporters *might* be in mind; so too might the death of John the Baptist.[26] But the saying is probably too general for us to be able to build much, if anything, on it for the present purposes.

1.10. Q 17:22–37

The attitude of the guests in the parable of the Great Supper is very similar to the attitudes of the people referred to in Q 17:23ff., especially in vv. 26ff. Clearly this is a passage which is not quite so overtly 'polemical' as others, and yet warnings are clearly implied. People are being warned of the imminent coming of the SM, whose arrival will be sudden, universally visible and who will confront those who are unprepared with terrifying speed. The future event is compared with the coming of the flood in Noah's day and the destruction of Sodom in Lot's. But equally a comparison is suggested between the situation just before these terrible events in the past and the present situation which (by implication) is immediately prior to the coming of the SM. It is at this level that the parallel with the parable of the Great Supper is so striking. For 17:26ff. describes a situation of people going about their ordinary, everyday business of eating, drinking and getting married.[27] These then are people who are simply ignoring any possible warnings about the future. Thus the disaster which is imminent is being seen as a threat *not* to those who are violently persecuting the Christian movement; rather, it will be disastrous primarily for those who take no notice, who are unaware of the

---

[26] See P. S. Cameron, *Violence and the Kingdom. The Interpretation of Matthew 11:12* (Frankfurt: P. Lang, 1984), who argues that Herod is in mind (though this is at the level of Jesus, not Q).

[27] See my *Revival*, 170; D. R. Catchpole, 'The Son of Man's Search for Faith (Luke xviii 8b)', *NovT* 19 (1977) 81–104, p. 85. For a connection between the parable of the Great Supper and Q 17, see also Schenk, *Synopse*, 108.

importance of the hour, who disregard and ignore the appeals of others made to them — in short, for those who do *nothing*.[28]

In summary, there is a great deal of material in Q which is concerned above all to fight *neutrality*. Large amounts of Q seem concerned to meet a situation where those addressed are simply doing *nothing* in response to the Christian message. Such people have not necessarily opposed the Christian cause. They have not necessarily inflicted any physical violence upon Christians. They have simply refused to listen; they have turned away and done nothing. Some indeed may have 'turned away' from a position of some support for the Christian movement (cf. 12:9 above; also 6:46). Thus much of Q seems to be a response to a situation of possibly wavering commitment, but principally one of *apathy*.

This is however not the whole story. There are other parts of Q which do seem to suggest a situation of more open hostility to the Christian movement. It is to these 'persecution' texts that we must now turn.

2. Persecution

A number of texts in Q are often adduced as reflecting a situation of direct physical persecution being experienced by the Q Christians. The prime examples here are the final beatitude (Q 6:22f.), the doom oracle in Q 11:49–51 together with the preceding woe against tomb-builders in Q 11:47f., and the lament over Jerusalem in Q 13:34f. These passages have, of course, been considered in some detail in ch. 6 above, since they provide the main examples in Q of the use of the theme of the violence suffered by the prophets. The very fact that reference is made to such violence in the past has led many to infer that similar violence and persecution is part of the present experience of the Q Christians.

Before examining the texts themselves, some preliminary observations must be borne in mind. First, at the semantic level, the Greek word διώκω, like the English 'persecute' which is often used to translate it, is a very general one. The claim that Christians are being 'persecuted' can cover a wide variety of

---

[28] Cf. Jacobson, *First Gospel*, 238: the SM sayings in Q 17 'reflect a deep frustration with contemporaries who seem immune to warning, who move through the daily round indifferent to the gravity of the moment. We have seen this frustration again and again in Q. It is a leitmotiv in Q.'

experiences, ranging from judicial execution at one extreme down to less severe actions of mob violence, or more general phenomena such as social ostracism, verbal abuse, mistrust, or even just polite ignoring. All these can be covered by the term 'persecution'.[29] Secondly, one must remember that 'persecution' is a rather loaded word and may reflect only one side's description of the events concerned. The word is often used in relation to sufferings endured by Christians solely on the grounds of their confession of their Christian faith. Yet it is probable that individual Christians may well have suffered in many ways for reasons which others would have judged differently.[30] Certainly all the evidence we have suggests at most sporadic persecution of Christians; and this renders it unlikely that any systematic persecution by the judicial authorities was directed against Christians simply because they were Christians.[31] Nevertheless, there cannot be any doubt that the early Christian movement did provoke some hostility from its non-Christian neighbours, especially within Judaism, and at times this spilled over into varying degrees of violence. Our problem is to try to determine what degree of violence and hostility is reflected in the Q tradition.

2.1. Q 6:22f.

I consider first the final beatitude in Q 6:22f. with its clear reference to a situation reflecting some kind of hostility and its claim that such hostility is similar in kind to the violence suffered by the prophets. This beatitude is almost universally recognised as separate from the preceding three beatitudes in terms of tradition-history. As we have already seen, it is much longer and more detailed than its predecessors and seems to presuppose a

[29] See A. J. Hultgren, 'Paul's Pre-Christian Persecutions of the Church. Their Purpose, Locale and Nature', *JBL* 95 (1976) 97–111. The very varied nature of 'persecution' is also shown by Hare, *Jewish Persecution*, 20ff. (looking primarily at more formal kinds of persecution involving official punishments imposed on Christians).

[30] Cf. E. P. Sanders, *Jesus and Judaism* (London: SCM, 1985) 284.

[31] See Sanders, *Jesus*, 281–7. Hence the view that Christians caused offence by their preaching of a crucified Messiah, a claim which was then seen as blasphemous in the light of Deut 21:23, seems most implausible: see my 'Deuteronomy 21,23 and Paul's Conversion', in A. Vanhoye (ed.), *L'Apôtre Paul. Personnalité, Style et Conception du Ministère* (BETL 73; Leuven University Press & Peeters, 1986) 345–50, with further literature cited.

rather different situation. (See p. 179 above.) We have already considered some aspects of the wording of the beatitude in Q. Here however I wish to focus on the treatment which is predicted as being in store for the followers of Jesus.[32]

Matthew has Jesus warn the disciples that others 'will revile you, persecute you and say all manner of evil against you falsely'; Luke's version speaks of people who 'will hate you, separate you, revile you and cast out your name as evil'. It seems most likely that Matthew's 'persecute' (διώκω) is MattR, whereas μισέω in Luke is probably not LkR and may have stood in Q.[33] 'Reviling' (ὀνειδίζω) is common to both Matthew and Luke and may therefore be confidently assigned to Q. The question of whether Matthew's 'say all manner of evil against you falsely' or Luke's 'cast out your name as evil' is more original is not certain, but the theory that Matthew is more original and Luke redacts is quite possible.[34] On the other hand, Luke's ἀφορίζω may be original

---

[32] For what follows, see my 'Beatitudes' for more detail, especially pp. 202f.

[33] Matthew has διώκω 7 times; Luke uses the word 3 + 9 times, so there is no clear reason why he should omit it if he had read it in Q (cf. Dupont, *Béatitudes I*, 229f.; Hare, *Jewish Persecution*, 114f.; Schulz, *Q*, 452f. For Luke's μισέω as pre-Lukan, see Steck, *Geschick*, 22; Schürmann, *Lukasevangelium*, 333 n. 48; Schulz, *Q*, 452. Horn, 'Christentum', 348, postulates an original wording consisting at this point of only ὀνειδίσωσιν ὑμᾶς ὡς πονηρόν; but this seems ungrammatical (why not πονηρούς?) and also simply appears to take the common words from the two gospels rather literally, without considering the possiblity of MattR or LkR.

[34] Several have argued that the difference here is to be traced back to a Semitic Vorlage: Luke's version may provide a literal translation of the Hebraism הוֹצִיא שֵׁם רַע, with Matthew interpreting it with slightly more freedom. See Dupont, *Béatitudes I*, 235; Black, *Aramaic Approach*, 135f.; Davies & Allison, *Matthew I*, 462. The Lukan version is taken as a Semitism by Steck, *Geschick*, 23; Kloppenborg, *Formation*, 56. (Steck argues that Luke's version must be pre-Lukan but post-Q since Luke 6:26 implies that a version like Matthew's was in Q: hence Luke used a Q[lk] edition of Q. This seems unnecessary if one can explain Luke's version as LkR.)
The theory is however not very convincing (see my 'Beatitudes', 202; also Hare, *Jewish Persecution*, 115): ἐκβάλλω is never used with this idiom in the LXX; and in any case the alleged literal translation by Luke has to postulate as well a slight misunderstanding of the meaning by the addition of ὡς and ὑμῶν to the phrase: rather than 'giving an evil report (lit. name)', the Lukan version speaks of 'giving out *your* name *as* evil'. Matthew's εἴπωσιν phrase corresponds with the καλῶς εἴπωσιν in Luke's corresponding woe in Luke 6:26 (wherever the woe came from), and this may suggest that Matthew's version of the beatitude is more original at this point. Luke's ἐκβάλωσιν could then be a redactional improvement of the Greek.

(i.e. Q).[35] However, one should probably not read too much into this word. This is not necessarily a reference to the Birkath-ha-Minim.[36] The exact date and force of the (in)famous Blessing on the heretics is much disputed,[37] but it is not at all clear that the language of 'separation' in Luke 6:22 is to be interpreted in relation to this. Prior to the Birkath-ha-Minim, probably the only 'ban' in operation in Jewish law was the *niddui* ban, imposed by Jews to maintain discipline.[38] But Hare has argued that in the earlier (i.e. pre-70) period, the ban was unlikely to be used as a threat against ordinary members of the community: rather, it was a means of trying to maintain uniformity amongst the leading teachers. Thus Hare argues strongly that Luke 6:22 reflects no formal synagogue ban at all:

> A more likely frame of reference for Luke 6:22 is the informal ban employed by every community, ancient and modern, towards individuals it despises. Social ostracism is a kind of excommunication which could well inspire the words of the Lukan beatitude.[39]

There is thus nothing in the wording of the Q beatitude which suggests either experience of physical violence or official judicial actions directed against the followers of Jesus. ὀνειδίζω only implies verbal abuse.[40] μισέω is quite general and need refer to no more than the general feeling of mistrust and dislike which Christians aroused in others. 'Speaking all manner of evil against you' (or indeed Luke's 'casting out your name as evil' if that is more original) refers only to verbal abuse: 'both versions speak of defamation of character by slander'.[41] Hence Hare concludes: 'Both the malediction [i.e. Luke 6:26] and the beatitude are concerned primarily with oral persecution, that is, name-calling,

---

[35] The use of the word in Acts 13:2; 19:9 is quite different. Hence Schulz's appeal (*Q*, 452) to these texts to argue that the word here is due to LkR is unconvincing.

[36] So Goulder, *Luke*, 352; cf. also Fitzmyer, *Luke*, 635; Horn, 'Christentum', 349.

[37] Cf. Hare, *Jewish Persecution*, 48–56; W. Horbury, 'The Benediction on the *Minim* and Early Jewish–Christian Controversy', *JTS* 33 (1982) 19–61.

[38] Hare, *Jewish Persecution*, 49. See also SB IV.1, 293–333.

[39] Hare, *Jewish Persecution*, 53.

[40] Hare, *Jewish Persecution*, 118: 'The reference is not to the use of insulting language when describing Christians to a third party but rather face-to-face insults.' Cf. too Kloppenborg, 'Persecution Beatitude', 48: 'In Q the focus is upon social ostracism and verbal abuse.'

[41] Hare, *Jewish Persecution*, 118.

ridicule, public insults and the like.'[42] ἀφορίζω too, if original, need refer to no more than social ostracism. The 'persecution' presupposed here thus seems at most to involve verbal abuse, perhaps social ostracism, but not necessarily any physical violence.

What though of the final phrase of the beatitude where the parallel is drawn between the reception of the disciples and the treatment experienced by the prophets? It is, however, clear that the claim that all the prophets suffered violence is in part a standard topos in a pattern of preaching which does not necessarily reflect historical fact accurately. Actual instances of violence being suffered by prophets in the OT are relatively rare, and the claim that 'all' the prophets experienced violence and death cannot be taken literally. The fact that it is hard to document actual instances of violence should then perhaps warn us against taking this language too literally. What was primary in the Deuteronomic pattern of preaching was that the people had refused to listen to the prophets. It is primarily in that context that the theme of the rejection of the prophets is referred to, and only in some cases is that rejection referred to in terms of physical violence and even death. Perhaps then the same is the case in Q 6:22f. The Christian followers of Jesus are warned that they will experience hostility and rejection. Their message will not be accepted, they will be 'reviled' verbally and not be accepted socially, and in this their non-acceptance is akin to that experienced by the prophets. But no more by way of hostility needs to be read into the beatitude than this.

What though of the continuation of the Sermon? Many have plausibly argued that the beatitudes were immediately followed in Q by the section on love-of-enemies (Q 6:27ff.).[43] This would imply that the 'enemies' concerned were probably very closely associated with the 'opponents' envisaged by the final beatitude. Does then the Q section on love-of-enemies throw any further light on the situation presupposed?

2.2. *Q 6:27–35*

Once again there is uncertainty about the precise Q wording of the section and about the order of the material in Q. The passage is notoriously complex and has been analysed by several scholars

[42] Hare, *Jewish Persecution*, 118.
[43] Schürmann, *Lukasevangelium*, 346; Lührmann, 'Liebet eure Feinde', 414f.

in great detail in recent years.[44] No attempt will be made here to provide a full reconstruction of the tradition-history of the passage, but it is clear that diverse traditions are being combined in this section. For example, the command to love one's enemies (Q 6:27f.) seems to have been originally separate from the teaching about non-retaliation (Q 6:29f.): there is a change from second person plural to second person singular (in both Matthew and Luke); further, the sayings in Q 6:32ff. which follow the exhortations about non-retaliation seem to pick up the love-of-enemies material in vv. 27f. again. Thus the sayings about non-retaliation (and perhaps the Golden Rule in Q 6:31) are probably secondary insertions into the sayings about love-of-enemies. The problem is to determine at what stage of the tradition this insertion occurred. Since Matthew keeps the two sets of sayings separate in two different antitheses (Matt 5:39–42, 44–48), it has been argued that the insertion is due to LkR.[45] Others have argued the insertion was already present in Q.[46]

Almost every conceivable variation in the possible history of the tradition has been proposed. However, one of the more striking pieces of evidence concerns the references to 'lending' (δανίζω) in both Luke 6:34 and Matt 5:42. The verb is rare in the synoptics and so the common occurrence of the word in two very closely related, but not identical, Q contexts in Matthew and Luke is unlikely to be coincidental. In Luke the exhortation to 'lend' comes as the third of the series of rhetorical questions that refers back to the preceding imperatives about

---

[44] See in addition to the standard studies on Q, Lührmann, 'Liebet eure Feinde'; Zeller, *Mahnsprüche*; H. Merklein, *Die Gottesherrschaft als Handlungsprinzip. Untersuchung zur Ethik Jesu* (Würzburg: Echter, 1978); G. Strecker, 'Die Antithesen der Bergpredigt', *ZNW* 69 (1978) 36–72; J. Piper, *Love Your Enemies, Jesus' Love Command in the Synoptic Tradition and the Early Christian Paraenesis* (SNTSMS 38; Cambridge University Press, 1979); Guelich, *Sermon*; P. Hoffmann, 'Tradition und Situation. Zur "Verbindlichkeit" des Gebots der Feindesliebe in der synoptischen Überlieferung und in der gegenwärtigen Friedensdiskussion', in K. Kertelge (ed.), *Ethik im Neuen Testament* (Freiburg: Herder, 1984) 50–118; J. Sauer, 'Traditionsgeschichtliche Erwägungen zu den synoptischen und paulinischen Aussagen über Feindesliebe und Wiedervergeltungsverzicht', *ZNW* 76 (1985) 1–28, and several others.

[45] So Bultmann, *History*, 79, 96; Schulz, *Q*, 120f.; Zeller, *Mahnsprüche*, 101–3, and his *Kommentar*, 30; Merklein, *Gottesherrschaft*, 222f.

[46] Cf. Schürmann, *Lukasevangelium*, 345f., 357f.; Lührmann, 'Liebet eure Feinde', 417f.; Guelich, *Sermon*, 223; Luz, *Matthew 1–7*, 323.

loving enemies.[47] But the love-of-enemies material itself contains no reference to lending in either the Matthean or Lukan versions. Rather, the 'lending' reference in Matthew is in the middle of the section about non-retaliation. The references to 'lending' in Luke 6:34 may be secondary and due in part to LkR: they overload the balance of the speech unit as a whole, and also reflect Luke's own redactional concerns.[48] However, the fact that the other two rhetorical questions (in Luke 6:32f.) pick up the sayings earlier in the section suggests strongly that the same is true of Luke 6:34f. This implies that Luke's tradition already included a command to 'lend'. Thus Luke 6:34f. may be a reminiscence of Matt 5:42/Luke 6:30b. If so, this implies that (*a*) Matthew's wording here is more original in speaking of giving to those who would 'borrow' ($\delta\alpha\nu\iota\zeta\omega$) rather than those who 'take', and (*b*) Q 6:30 did belong within the love-of-enemies material in Luke's tradition.[49] Thus we may conclude that the combination of the love-of-enemies complex with the material on non-retaliation was already present in Q.

Whether the combination of the traditions was the work of the Q editor or was already present in the pre-Q tradition is impossible to say. The secondary nature of the composition makes it implausible to regard the whole unit being originally composed/spoken (i.e. by Jesus himself) in just this form. The combination may well be the work of Q. However, even if it is a pre-Q composition, we may presumably still assume that the effect of the conjunction of the traditions is acceptable to Q (if not created by Q) (cf. p. 81 above).

It is quite possible that Q 6:29f. is itself composite, and indeed this forms the basis of P. Hoffmann's analysis of the passage.[50] Hoffmann argues that the Golden Rule and the command to be merciful (Luke 6:36) fit well with the exhortation to give and to lend to those in need (Luke 6:30), whereas the exhortation to

---

[47] The exhortation to 'love' in Luke 6:32 echoes the command to love one's enemies in 6:27a and the exhortation to 'do good' in 6:33 echoes the command to do good to those who hate you in 6:27b.

[48] See especially W. Stegemann, in L. Schottroff & W. Stegemann, *Jesus von Nazareth. Hoffnung der Armen* (Stuttgart: Kohlhammer, 1978) 144ff.

[49] See especially Schürmann, *Lukasevangelium*, 345–7; Lührmann, 'Liebet eure Feinde', 417f.; Guelich, *Sermon*, 223; Davies & Allison, *Matthew I*, 548. Schürmann however complicates the case by arguing that Luke 6:34f. is pre-Lukan; this seems unnecessary and the argument still has force if Luke 6:34 is LkR.

[50] Hoffmann, 'Tradition', 64ff.

endure violence (Luke 6:29) fits with the command to love one's enemies. Hoffmann thus argues that Q contained two quite separate series of exhortations, one on enemies (vv. 27f., 29, 32f., 35) and one on helping those in need (vv. 30, 31, 36).[51] Hoffmann makes some incisive points about possible layers in the tradition here and he may well be right in seeing 6:29 and 6:30 as originally separate. However, it is not so clear that this was also the case in Q itself. The common conjunction of the exhortations in Q 6:29 and Q 6:30 in both Matthew and Luke (Luke 6:29 = Matt 5:39f.; Luke 6:30 = Matt 5:42, separated in Matthew only by Matt 5:41 but clearly seen by Matthew as part of a unit in a single antithesis) suggests that the two verses were already combined in Q. Hoffmann may well be right in terms of a pre-Q stage in the tradition. But at the level of Q itself, we should perhaps allow the common contexts of the verses in Matthew and Luke to be determinative for decisions about the context in Q. As with Q 6:29f. as a whole in relation to the wider context, it may be the case that the bringing together of 6:29 and 6:30 is the work of the Q editor. But as before, we may still see some significance for Q in the conjunction of the two verses, even if they belonged together prior to Q. I shall therefore assume that the examples given in the teaching about non-retaliation in Q 6:29f. provide what Q regards as appropriate illustrations of the command to love one's 'enemies' in Q 6:27. and it seems entirely appropriate to use the material in 6:29f. as well as 6:32ff. to try to gain insight into the nature of the 'enmity' experienced by the Q Christians.

With this in mind, we may take the unit in Q 6:27–35 as a whole within Q. The section starts with the general command to love one's enemies. Again the precise Q wording is uncertain: Matthew's shorter two-fold form of the saying ('love your enemies and pray for those who persecute you') is paralleled by Luke's longer four-fold form ('love your enemies, do good to those who hate you, bless those who persecute you, pray for those who abuse you').[52] It may however be the case that in the last

---

[51] See especially his summary on pp. 72f.

[52] The longer four-part saying is taken as more original by Schürmann, *Lukasevangelium*, 346; Merklein, *Gottesherrschaft*, 225; Luz, *Matthew 1–7*, 306; Davies & Allison, *Matthew I*, 553; Catchpole, *Quest*, 103. The shorter two-part saying is taken as more original by Lührmann, 'Liebet eure Feinde', 416; Zeller, *Mahnsprüche*, 102; Hoffmann, 'Tradition', 52f.; Fitzmyer, *Luke*, 637. I myself would incline to the view that the second and third clause in Luke's longer version are due to LkR: the second clause reflects the ideas associated

phrase, Luke's version is more original in using the rather
uncommon verb ἐπηρεάζω. Matthew's διώκω may well be MattR
and Luke shows no clear dislike of the word (cf. n. 33 above);
nor is Luke unaware of Christian 'persecution'. Hence Luke's
wording may preserve Q more accurately.[53] If so this might be an
indication of how the 'enmity' of the 'enemies' is actually
experienced: it is primarily a matter of verbal abuse, rather than
any physical violence.[54]

The examples which follow in 6:29f. are more specific. Q 6:29
speaks of striking a blow on the cheek and taking a cloak (or
being sued for a cloak); then follows (Q 6:30) the exhortations
to give to those who ask and not to demand back from/refuse
those who wish to borrow.[55] In the first pair of sayings (Luke
6:29 = Matt 5:39f.) it is probable that Matthew's judicial
terminology in Matt 5:40 is secondary.[56] Matthew's version
seems to switch rather abruptly from addressing one who is
offended (v. 39) to one who is apparently an offender and
being sued for a debt (v. 40). So too the apparent link between
Matthew's v. 40 and v. 42 in that both concern debtors (cf.
Exod 22:25–27; Deut 24:10–12, dealing with debts, pledges
and the rule about not taking a poor man's cloak as a pledge)[57]
is rather artificial: v. 40 is addressed to one who owes a pledge,
v. 42 is directed at those who will lend to others. Hence in view of
Matthew's propensity for legal language in this section, it seems

---

with a Hellenistic reciprocity ethic (see below), and the third has parallels with
other early Christian paraenesis (cf. Rom 12:14; 1 Pet 3:9). However, certainty
is simply impossible.

[53] So Schürmann, *Lukasevangelium*, 333; Schulz, *Q*, 128; Hare, *Jewish
Persecution*, 122f.; Hoffmann, 'Tradition', 52.

[54] The extra clauses in Luke's version would not affect this general picture
even if they were taken as part of Q.

[55] See above for the reference to borrowing (as in Matthew) being part of the
Q version here. Between Q 6:29 and 6:30, Matthew alone has the reference to
being press-ganged for service (Matt 5:41). It is however very doubtful whether
this verse belonged to Q. It overloads the number of examples (Luke's version
has two pairs of double sayings, Matt 5:41 makes a fifth) and seems somewhat
extraneous. Hoffmann, 'Tradition', 61, defends a Q origin here, but this is
connected with his thesis of the Q Christians as closely involved in the period
leading up to the outbreak of the Jewish War, and his argument here is in
danger of becoming circular.

[56] Cf. Guelich, *Sermon*, 222; Catchpole, *Quest*, 306. *Pace* Schürmann,
Lukasevangelium, 351; Schulz, *Q*, 123; Hoffmann, 'Tradition', 60, who argue
that Luke is generalising Matthew's more technical language.

[57] Luz, *Matthew 1–7*, 324, refers to the common contexts in the OT.

best to assume that Luke's version is more original, so that the Q version probably referred to striking on the cheek and taking one's cloak.

Luke himself evidently understands the second half of the saying as a reference to a situation of robbery. However, this is by no means certain for the meaning at the level of Q. The first part of the saying refers to blows on the cheek. In Matt 5:39 the blow is by the 'right' hand. Commentators have frequently referred to the mishnaic ruling in *Baba Kamma* 8:6 which lists slapping someone with the back of the hand among the most serious forms of insult. This may well indicate that Matthew's reference to the 'right' hand is more original (although Matthew could have added the detail himself being aware of the nuance involved.)[58] What is not so often observed is that in this list in the Mishnah of insults requiring double recompense is the act of pulling a person's cloak off him.[59] If this is the proper background of the verse then the two halves cohere very closely together. (Luke then misunderstands the second half and interprets it as a reference to a robbery.) The situation is thus not necessarily one of any extreme physical violence. It is one of personal animosity, perhaps of jeering and insulting gestures[60] — but that seems to be all.

Even less violence, or even enmity, is involved in the second pair of sayings in Luke 6:30/Matt 5:42. I argued above that Matt 5:42b is probably more original in referring to requests to lend (δανίζω) in comparison with Luke 6:30b which seems to be continuing the robbery idea in referring to one who 'takes' your possessions.[61] Here the situation becomes even less antagonistic to the Christians being addressed.[62] The situation is now simply that of Christians being exhorted to lend money and/or give to

---

[58] Opinions are divided: for an origin in Q, see Schulz, *Q*, 122; Merklein, *Gottesherrschaft*, 269; Catchpole, *Quest*, 111. For MattR, see Schürmann, *Lukasevangelium*, 347; Guelich, *Sermon*, 221f.; Fitzmyer, *Luke*, 638; Hoffmann, 'Tradition', 59f.

[59] See Catchpole, *Quest*, 111.

[60] Cf. Catchpole, *Quest*, 110: 'the theme is insult'.

[61] Luke's conclusion is extraordinarily weak in having Jesus exhort people not to demand their possessions back. If one has been robbed, simply demanding one's property back is unlikely to be very successful! The confusion has probably resulted from Luke trying to weld together two originally disparate sayings (i.e. v. 29b on robbery, and v. 30b on lending).

[62] So much so that Hoffmann separates v. 30 from v. 29 in terms of tradition history: cf. above.

those who ask.[63] It *may* be that those begging are doing so with hostile intent to the Christians. But nothing indicates this directly. The behaviour demanded is thus the much more positive one of building community relationships rather than allowing them to be severed by hostility and bitterness. But there is no hint at all of any physical 'persecution' or violence.

The same is reflected by the rhetorical questions which follow in Q 6:32f. Here those addressed are exhorted to 'love' not only those who 'love' them and to 'greet' (Matthew)/'do good to' (Luke) not only those who do the same to them. Many have followed van Unnik here in regarding Luke's reference to 'doing good' as LkR, modifying Q to address a typically Hellenistic reciprocity ethic and using language frequently used in discussions of ethical behaviour in a Hellenistic context.[64] Hence Matthew's reference to greetings, or withholding greetings, may have been in Q. Catchpole has objected to this on the grounds that the language here is part of an argument intended 'to negate a reciprocity ethic in a setting of persecution. But the withholding of greetings is scarcely persecution'.[65] This however may presuppose too much about the actual situation involved. Luke's ἀγαθοποιεῖν may indeed be LkR, in which case one should take all the more seriously the allusions to greetings (or lack of them) which may have been in Q as a positive indication of Q's situation. Thus all that is in mind is at one level simply the withholding of greetings. In other words, the 'persecution' implied is much less extreme, and certainly much less physical, than any kind of judicial persecution. It may have been more at the level of ostracism, personal insults, jibes, polite ignoring, but not necessarily involving any great physical violence.

The picture that emerges from the Great Sermon in Q is reasonably consistent. Insofar as the warnings by Q's Jesus to the disciples reflect the actual situation of the Q Christians, there does not seem to be any very systematic 'persecution'. There may well have been a number of insults being flung at the Christians, involving perhaps symbolic gestures. But for the most part the 'enemies' seem at most to be abusing the Christians verbally, possibly excluding them from social groups and hence possibly

---

[63] If, as Catchpole, argues, ἀπαίτει was in Q, the saying is effectively an exhortation to give when simply asked to lend.

[64] See W. C. van Unnik, 'Die Motivierung der Feindesliebe in Lukas VI 32–35', *NovT* 8 (1966) 288–300, esp. pp. 288f.

[65] Catchpole, *Quest*, 104.

marginalising them socially. But no great physical harassment seems to be involved.

What then of the other passages in Q where many have deduced that violence is presupposed? In particular many have appealed to the doom oracle in Q 11:49–51 and the lament over Jerusalem in Q 13:34f. as clear evidence of persecution. It is to these passages that we must now turn.

2.3. *Q 11:47–48 + 49–51*

The doom oracle (Q 11:49–51) has already been analysed in some detail above (see pp. 166–73). The oracle comes at the end of a long series of woes in Q 11:39ff. which in itself may represent the end of a complex tradition-history.[66] Yet whatever one makes of the nature of the polemic implied in the earlier woes, by the time one gets to the end of the series, the polemic seems to become considerably sharper. The 'opposition' is accused not only of various nit-picking practices but, according to many, of more open — and violent — opposition to the Christian movement.

The doom oracle itself (Q 11:49–51) was probably already connected in Q with the woe against the tomb-builders (11:47f.): the link between the two units is attested in both Matthew and Luke and hence, almost certainly in Q as well, and in many respects 11:49f, with its διὰ τοῦτο καὶ ἡ σοφία τοῦ θεοῦ εἶπεν corresponding to לכן כה אמר יהוה, provides the reproach forming the threat following an accusation in a prophetic woe-oracle.[67] Thus we cannot consider the doom oracle of 11:49–51 in isolation from the woe in 11:47f.

The woe in Q 11:47f. is however one of the most difficult in the whole series to interpret. The variation in wording between Matthew and Luke is considerable and thus the precise Q wording is almost impossible to recover. Most would agree that Matthew's opening 'scribes and Pharisees, hypocrites!' is (almost) entirely redactional, as is the phrase about decorating the memorials of the righteous.[68] Beyond this, there is little clarity or certainty. It is not even certain to whom the charge is addressed

---

[66] See, for example, Schürmann, 'Redekomposition'; Catchpole, *Quest*, ch. 9, pp. 256–79.

[67] See p. 167 n. 9 above.

[68] See Haenchen, 'Matthäus 23', 58; Steck, *Geschick*, 28; Schulz, *Q*, 108; Garland, *Matthew 23*, 95.

in Q, whether to scribes alone, or to Pharisees alone, or whether the polemic has broadened out in the mention in vv. 49–51 of 'this generation'.[69] The precise interpretation of the woe is also much disputed and the logic of the charge is, to say the least, somewhat defective.[70] Reference is made to ancestors of those addressed as people who murdered the prophets; the fact is then noted that the addressees build tombs for the prophets. From this, somehow or other, a deduction is made that the present audience is just as bad as the original murderers. The problem is to know precisely what the present audience is being accused of.

Two competing main lines of interpretation of the woe have been proposed in recent years. One view has been argued by Steck[71] who starts from Matt 23:30 which he takes as part of Q. In this verse the audience seek to distance themselves from the actions of their ancestors by saying, 'If we had been living in the days of our fathers, we would not have taken part with them in shedding the blood of the prophets'. Steck argues that what the audience stands accused of is a failure to acknowledge the continuing guilt of their fathers' actions: instead of trying to distance themselves from their ancestors' behaviour, they should have acknowledged their collective sin and repented. The woe is thus directed against their refusal to repent, rather than against any specific actions of murder or violence of their own.

Steck's interpretation has been strongly questioned by Hoffmann who argues that the continuity between the audience and their ancestors is not only one of guilt but also of action.[72] He claims that Steck's interpretation is only possible on the basis of Matthew's v. 30 which, he argues, is due to MattR and does not stem from Q.[73] Thus he claims that the original woe consisted

---

[69] See above, pp. 196–201.

[70] Cf. Hare, *Jewish Persecution*, 83: 'It is the logic of polemic, not of reasoned argument'. Garland, *Matthew 23*, 163: 'The meaning of the . . . woe is clouded by what seems to be tortuous logic.' Similar statements are made by many others.

[71] See Steck, *Geschick*, 28f., for the reconstruction of the text; his interpretation is on pp. 280f. Steck is followed by Schulz, *Q*, 109, and others listed there.

[72] Hoffmann, *Studien*, 163f.; cf. too Légasse, 'L'oracle', 249ff.; Kloppenborg, *Formation*, 141f. Also Miller, as discussed below.

[73] Hoffmann argues that Matthew has formed the verse to highlight the charge of hypocrisy. Steck had referred to the phrase 'the blood of the prophets' in v. 30 as providing a link with the next woe, though Hoffmann argues that this could be a Matthean anticipation. Steck also appeals to the phenomenon of a 'Gegnerzitat' as a standard part of such oracles (cf. Isa 5:19; Jer 22:13f.; *1 En* 97:8f.) and to the absence of any clear Matthean characteristics of style or vocabulary.

only of something close to Luke's v. 47b (the reference to the fathers killing the prophets) with Matthew's v. 31 ('You are witnesses against yourselves that you are the sons of those who murdered the prophets'): the woe thus speaks only of the murder of the prophets and any idea of continuing guilt alone, rather than continuing activity as well, has to be read in. The audience is thus accused of being at one with their murderous ancestors: they too are murdering the prophets.

Yet despite Hoffmann's argument, it seems difficult to deny that something similar to Matthew's v. 30 must have been present in Q.[74] Matthew's v. 30 has the audience explicitly distancing themselves from the past murders. However, Luke's version is similar, though the differentiation of actions involved is a statement by Jesus rather than by the audience: in Luke it is acknowledged (by Jesus) that the activity of tomb-building distinguishes the listeners from their predecessors: cf. v. 48b 'they (μέν) killed, you (δέ) build' (repeating the substance of v. 47). Thus in both versions there is a claim (Matthew) or acknowledgement (Luke) that tomb-building represents a distancing of the present audience from their past. Hence it is hard to deny that some such attempt at distancing was present in Q. Without some kind of parallel to Matt 23:30 in Q, the saying asserts that the act of tomb-building itself is the very action which identifies the present audience with their ancestors: you build the tombs and *thereby* show yourselves to be at one with your predecessors. It is precisely this logic which is so tortuous and causes all the difficulty in the interpretation of the woe, especially if the continuity in question is that of violent murder: how does the action of honouring victims of murder condone, or even continue, the activity of the initial murderers?

Recently R. J. Miller has argued that the logic of the woe only makes sense under the presupposition that the audience is actively persecuting the Christian movement:

> Only in this way does tomb-building become an act of hypocrisy: they honor the prophets whom their fathers killed (attempting to dissociate themselves from their ancestors), while themselves persecuting the prophets of the present (showing that they are truly the sons of those who murdered the prophets).[75]

[74] Cf. Schürmann, 'Redekomposition', 54: 'Ohne V.30 wäre V.31 nicht mehr verständlich'. Also Catchpole, *Quest*, 269.

[75] R. J. Miller, 'The Rejection of the Prophets in Q', *JBL* 107 (1988) 225–40, p. 230.

However, it is by no means certain that Q understood the main charge of the woe as one of hypocrisy. Matthew's ὑποκριταί in v. 29 is almost certainly MattR and it is clear too that Matthew wishes to bring out the continuity in actions between past and present by the (ironical) command in v. 32 by Matthew's Jesus to 'fill up the measure of your fathers!'.[76] Thus the contrast between past and present remains in Q, and it is only in Matthew's version that the distinction becomes blurred.

Hoffmann's (and Miller's) interpretation thus fails to explain adequately the logic of the charge without reading a certain amount into the text of Q insofar as we can reconstruct the latter. Q does seem to presuppose a difference at the level of activity between past and present: murders happened in the past, tomb-building is taking place in the present and it is precisely the latter which is condemned. The audience are thus not necessarily murderers themselves: on the contrary they honour the victims of past violence. And yet the woe fiercely attacks them for apparently thinking that such action is enough. Thus Steck's interpretation seems preferable: what the present generation have failed to do is *repent*. They have tried to distance themselves from their ancestors, but perhaps they too have rejected the present prophetic preaching. They have failed to show solidarity with their forefathers, but precisely in so doing, they have failed to see the need to repent and thus show themselves to be in the same underlying situation. Thus what is in view is not so much any actual physical violence being inflicted by the present audience on the Christian community, but simply a refusal to respond positively, to repent and to acknowledge their common guilt with their ancestors.

The doom oracle in vv. 49–51 presents at first sight rather fewer problems than the preceding charge against the tomb-builders. The wording differs in Matthew and Luke, but in almost all cases of difference, Luke's version is more likely to represent the Q version.[77] (The only major doubt concerns the group alongside the 'prophets' sent by Wisdom: cf. Matthew's 'scribes and wise men'/Luke's 'apostles', but the issue is immaterial here.)

Steck argues that vv. 49f. represent a pre-Christian saying, which has been taken up and adapted by Christian preachers who added v. 51 ('from Abel to Zachariah') to stress that the violence

---

[76] Garland, *Matthew 23*, 166f.
[77] See p. 167 n. 6 above.

mentioned in vv. 49f. is restricted to the OT era. He also, as we have seen, excludes v. 50c as a post-Lukan scribal gloss (to avoid the problem of Wisdom speaking at the start of creation and then referring to 'this generation').[78] Thus, as in the previous woe, the violence involved belongs to the past. Once again Hoffmann has taken issue with Steck over his interpretation.[79] Hoffmann disputes the claim the v. 50c is a post-Lukan gloss, though this probably does not affect the present discussion very much, and in any case Hoffmann agrees with Steck in regarding v. 51 as Q-redactional (cf. p. 171 above). More important for the present purposes is whether the violence mentioned in a feature of the present as well as the past. Hoffmann argues again that violence is being experienced in the present, appealing to Q 6:22f.[80] Yet we have seen that the latter need only imply a situation of possible verbal abuse at most, and does not necessarily imply a situation of physical violence.

Hoffmann's theory also seems to encounter some problems in the interpretation of the limits mentioned in v. 51 which describe the 'blood of the prophets' to be required of this generation as stretching 'from the blood of Abel to the blood of Zachariah'. Whatever the problems associated with Matthew's reference to Zachariah as the 'son of Barachiah', it seems probable that (*a*) the reference to Barachiah was not in Q, and (*b*) the Zachariah implied by Q is the prophet whose murder is recorded in 2 Chron 24:20–22.[81] The limits thus confine the 'blood' to the era covered by the writings of the OT. They do not apparently reach up to the present! Lührmann claims that the references to Abel and Zachariah are intended to stress the fact that it is Israelite blood which has been shed and which requires vengeance.[82] But if so, it seems a strange way to emphasise what is then an ethnic distinction by means of these temporal limits. Hoffmann too seeks to avoid the slight problem.

---

[78] Steck, *Geschick*, 29–33, 222–7, 281f. Miller, 'Rejection', 231f., gets round the problem by suggesting that Wisdom's statement is thought of as being made in the *recent* past: hence the prophets sent by Wisdom (v. 49) are the present prophets, whereas vv. 50f. refers to all prophetic deaths from the creation of the world, many of which may have occurred before the time of the oracle. This however seems rather artificial in driving such a wedge between v. 49 and v. 50.

[79] Hoffmann, *Studien*, 166–71.

[80] Hoffmann, *Studien*, 166.

[81] See above p. 171.

[82] Lührmann, *Redaktion*, 47.

He argues that the addition in v. 51 serves to 'illustrate' (*veran-schaulichen*) the charge of murdering the prophets, and the details which are given of Zachariah's murder serve to provide a concrete example of the charge.[83] However, the reference to Zachariah in v. 51 does not provide simply a graphic example of a more general charge: it is rather the end-point of an apparently closed time-interval.

Kloppenborg also sees the problem but tries to avoid it by ascribing v. 51a to a pre-Q form of the saying:[84] since, according to Kloppenborg, Q regarded prophetic murders as still continuing in the present (including the death of Jesus and John the Baptist),[85] the choice of Zachariah (rather than say John the Baptist) as the *terminus ad quem* cannot represent the viewpoint of Q and hence must be part of the pre-Q tradition. This is however almost a counsel of despair. For we then have to imagine Q taking over and repeating a saying which represented a viewpoint considerably different from its own. This might be conceivable if some redactional addition by Q served to alter the relevant viewpoint. But the only redactional addition postulated here by Kloppenborg is v. 51b and this simply repeats (though perhaps in words intended to be spoken directly by Jesus rather than by Jesus quoting Wisdom: cf. p. 171 above) the claim in v. 50 that responsibility for all prophetic blood will be laid at the feet of this generation. Thus Kloppenborg's solution also fails to satisfy. Given then that Q does not modify the limits in v. 51a in any way, we must assume that Q agreed with the sentiments expressed (cf. p. 81 above).

None of the arguments which seek to avoid the difficulty of the limits in v. 51a for any theory that Q believed that prophetic blood was still being shed is fully convincing. The conclusion must be that v. 51a implies — and Q seems to accept — that the murderous activity for which this generation is responsible belongs to the past. The saying does not imply that prophetic murders are a feature of the present.[86]

---

[83] Hoffmann, *Studien*, 168f.

[84] Kloppenborg, *Formation*, 146, and see p. 171 above.

[85] Kloppenborg appeals to Q 6:23 and 13:34f. 6:23 is considered above; for 13:34f., see below.

[86] Does this then affect the claim made earlier (p. 221 above) that Q regarded the death of Jesus as in a line of continuity with that of the prophets? If the 'blood' belongs to the past and stops with the murder of Zachariah, why is there no mention of Jesus? However, part of the reason why Jesus' death (like that of John the Baptist) is not mentioned here may be due to the 'genre' of Q:

If then the murders are thought of as primarily in the past, this may also account for the somewhat strange order of the verbs in v. 49. It is uniformly agreed that Matthew has expanded Q's 'kill and persecute' with the references to 'scourging in your synagogues' and persecuting 'from city to city', to make the saying correspond with the fate of Christian missionaries in his own community (cf. Matt 10:17, 23).[87] Q then just refers to 'killing and persecuting'. The order is rather anti-climactic,[88] but this might be explained if the 'killing' is thought of as in the past, and what is being experienced in the present is (in Q's terms anyway) 'persecution'. So too there is the admission that only 'some' (ἐξ αὐτῶν) of the missionaries will be at the receiving end of the antagonism.[89] The Q wording thus does seem to indicate that the experiences of the present are somewhat variable, to say the least.

This picture of the situation of the Q Christians fits well with all the other evidence considered so far: it is a situation where there is not necessarily any physical violence, but rather a more general

---

Q chooses to present its message in the form of the preaching of Jesus himself and one cannot have a pre-Easter Jesus referring to his own death in the past. (See p. 171 above.)

[87] Cf. my *Revival*, 158, and others noted there. The reference to 'crucify' in Matthew is universally regarded as problematic. In the absence of any clear evidence of Christians in Matthew's community being crucified, the easiest solution is probably to see this as a reference to the death of Jesus himself. So Hare, *Jewish Persecution*, 92; Garland, *Matthew 23*, 176f. and others. Perhaps the fact that Matthew felt the need to supply a reference to the death of Jesus implies that Matthew at least took his Q tradition as referring to a series of deaths which did *not* include Jesus' own death!

[88] The anti-climactic nature of the sequence in Matthew (kill–crucify–scourge–persecute) is often noted: cf. Hare, *Jewish Persecution*, 92; Garland, *Matthew 23*, 176; Légasse, 'L'oracle', 242. But the 'kill–persecute' sequence is attested in Luke as well and therefore may be justifiably traced back to Q. Légasse, 'L'oracle', 242 n. 31, thinks the sequence is unusual enough to ascribe the reference to persecution to a secondary expansion of an earlier form of the saying, although apparently already there in Q: 'Quoique mentionnées déjà dans la source . . . les persécutions relèvent ici d'une seconde main, car elles surviennent maladroitement à la suite du meutre.'

[89] Hoffmann, *Studien*, 169, may be right to protest (against Steck, *Geschick*, 227 n. 1) that some Christians are experiencing hostility in the present (Steck argues that it is all past). But not all are being '*killed* and persecuted', and perhaps the ἐξ αὐτῶν is another indication that physical violence has not affected everyone.

situation of at most hostility and animosity.[90] This is perhaps a less direct form of hostility than physical violence, but it is nevertheless one which the Q Christians regard as 'persecution', and their failure to evoke a positive response from the present generation is seen as on a par with the rejection and hostility which, according to the Deuteronomic pattern, has been experienced by all God's prophets down the ages and which has in the past led to prophetic deaths.

2.4. Q 13:34f.

The same situation may be presupposed in the lament over Jerusalem (Q 13:34f.), though here the evidence is more ambiguous. The saying speaks of the prophets and other messengers being killed and stoned. There is, however, no need to assume that the killings and stonings reflect the present experience of Q Christians.[91] We know of no other evidence that Christians were stoned to death (apart from Stephen). Given the nature of the audience elsewhere in Q, which all seems to indicate that any physical violence related to the past and the present is characterised by a situation of at most verbal animosity and insulting gestures, it would seem best to interpret 13:34f. in the same way. The speaker is looking back at the past, and sees past examples of prophetic deaths (or perhaps better, refers to such as a standard topos). But this does not necessarily say anything about the present.

So far we have seen that the polemical parts of Q reflect a 'persecution' situation only in a rather mundane sense. The 'persecution' implied seems to be rather muted, and there does not

---

[90] Indeed the wording of the woe in Q 11:47f. indicates only a failure to respond positively: it is thus similar to the general picture of apathy which we uncovered in the first part of this chapter.

[91] Contra Hoffmann, *Studien*, 179. Miller, 'Rejection', 238, refers to the ποσάκις ('how often') in the saying and claims that this only makes sense if it is the *risen* Jesus speaking with reference to repeated attempts to gather Israel through the preaching of the Q prophets. Miller has to admit that there is no other reference to an extended Jerusalem ministry by Q Christians (indeed texts like Q 10:13–15 would suggest *per contra* that Q Christians, and their preaching, are primarily located in Galilee: see p. 102 above). It seems easier to see the ποσάκις as a reference to Israel's *past* history. Miller also refers to the *present* participles ἀποκτείνουσα and λιθοβολοῦσα as indicating present experiences — but the tense of the participles need only indicate habitual protracted activity in the past.

seem to be any great physical violence being rained down upon the Christian community. Polemic is certainly present in Q. But the polemic is reserved primarily for those who are doing nothing in response to the Christian preaching (failing to 'repent'), or who are wavering in their commitment. However, besides the polemical parts of Q, there remain a few sayings within Q where persecution of a more extreme, and/or judicial, nature might be implied. These are the texts in Q 12:4f.; 12:11f. and 14:27. One striking feature of these passages is the lack of polemic against any would-be 'persecutors'. There is strong language used but the sayings are all paraenetic: they are directed to those possibly facing persecution. They are not directed against those inflicting persecution. What then of the sayings themselves?

2.5. Q 12:4f.

I consider first the saying in Q 12:4f., where the audience is told not to fear those who kill the body, but rather to fear those who can destroy both body and soul in Gehenna. (With most, I take the Matthean version as probably preserving the Q wording more accurately. Luke's introductory λέγω δὲ ὑμῖν τοῖς φίλοις μου may well be redactional.[92] Further, the absence of any mention of destroying the soul in Luke may be due to Luke's concern to make the saying more intelligible for his Hellenistic readers for whom the destruction of the soul would have been unthinkable.)[93] It is often assumed that Q 12:4–7 formed a small unit of tradition prior to Q and was subsequently incorporated at a later stage into a wider Q context containing the SM saying in 12:8f.[94] Further, it is often assumed that vv. 4f. presuppose a situation where Christians are being threatened with death. The exhortation not to fear those who kill the body is taken as an indication that those addressed are facing the threat of violent physical death through martyrdom.[95] Both these assumptions are however questionable.

[92] See Schulz, *Q*, 157f.; Piper, *Wisdom*, 52; J. Schlosser, 'Le Logion de Mt 10,28 Par. Lc 12,4–5', in Van Segbroek et al (eds), *The Four Gospels 1992*, 621–31, p. 623. Matthew is fond of λέγω ὑμῖν so it is not clear why he should omit the phrase if it stood in Q; φιλός is a Lukan word.

[93] Schulz, *Q*, 158; Zeller, *Mahnsprüche*, 94; Piper, *Wisdom*, 52f.; Schlosser, 'Logion', 624.

[94] Cf. Schulz, *Q*, 157ff., who treats 12:4–7 as a separate unit. See too Zeller, *Mahnsprüche*, 96; Kloppenborg, *Formation*, 207ff.; Piper, *Wisdom*, 52ff.

[95] Schulz, *Q*, 161: 'Furchtlosigkeit angesichts der konkreten Märtyrersituation'; similarly Zeller, *Mahnsprüche*, 101; Kloppenborg, *Formation*, 209f.; Piper, *Wisdom*, 53.

Q 12:4–7 is itself clearly a composite collection. This is universally acknowledged in the case of vv. 6–7, where the appeal to the sparrows (v. 6) is interrupted by the reference to the hairs of one's head (v. 7a) before the example of the sparrows is concluded (v. 7b).[96] The thrust of the two examples is, however, clear and summed up in the concluding μὴ φοβεῖσθε. The listeners are not to be afraid because God in His providence will care for them in the same way as He cares for sparrows and knows all about even the hairs of one's head. Verses 6f. are thus a call to put all one's trust and confidence in the God who is here presented as a caring, trustworthy person who banishes 'fear'.

Verses 4f. seem to breathe a rather different atmosphere. It is true that at one level there is a link with vv. 6f. in the common use of the word 'fear'. However, the thrust of the saying in vv. 4f. is not the same as vv. 6f. Verses 4f. do not advocate an absence of 'fear'. Rather they say that one *should* 'fear' — but fear God rather than men.[97] The double saying in vv. 4f. is a unit and, as with much parallelism in the gospels, the stress seems to fall on the second half of the saying.[98] The main thrust of the saying is thus to instil fear (with some feelings of dread) at the prospect of God in the light of future judgement. 'Fear' here is thus something which *is* appropriate in relation to God, whereas in vv. 6f. the tradition is seeking to banish 'fear' by referring to God. Clearly the 'fears' are of a rather different nature, suggesting that the sayings have a different origin.

If though the thrust of vv. 4f. is to instil fear in the face of divine punishment, it becomes questionable how far this is intended to be taken as reflecting a realistic possibility for the audience. At one level, v. 4 links with vv. 6f. in that both advocate the

---

[96] See Zeller, *Mahnsprüche*, 95; Sato, *Q und Prophetie*, 174; Schlosser, 'Logion', 622. Piper, *Wisdom*, 55, sees this as evidence of some forcing of a pattern involving two questions introducing a small block of teaching, a pattern which he finds at a number of places within the Q tradition. Yet he has to admit that v. 7a does not quite fit the pattern: it is a statement not a rhetorical question, in which case the pattern may not be present at all and the section in vv. 4–7 rather less of a traditio-historical unit than Piper allows.

[97] The one who can destroy both body and soul in Gehenna is almost certainly God, not the Devil. See Schulz, *Q*, 160f.; Fitzmyer, *Luke*, 959; Schlosser, *Logion*, 626f. Pace Lührmann, *Redaktion*, 50; Schenk, *Synopse*, 85.

[98] Cf. Jeremias, *Theology*, 18. Piper, *Wisdom*, 53, argues that as the command not to fear is repeated in v. 7, the positive command to fear in v. 5 is 'part of the argumentation rather than the basic exhortation'. This however presupposes that vv. 4–7 are intended as a unit, and it is just this which I would question.

banishment of one kind of fear, viz. fear of other human beings. But v. 4 in its immediate context (i.e. with v. 5) is simply a hyperbolic way of referring to the very worst that any human being could theoretically do; and the example is only adduced to provide a contrast with something portrayed as far worse, namely the power of God to destroy the soul as well as the body. It is this latter possibility that the saying is primarily concerned with and not necessarily with any real situation presupposed by v. 4. The saying is thus primarily intended to evoke fear before God. If this is the case, there is then no need to see v. 4 as accurately reflecting a situation being faced by the audience. The listeners are not necessarily facing the possibility that someone will actually kill their bodies. It may be that they are facing a situation producing some 'fear' of what other human beings might do. But the point of the saying is that whatever other people may do, God can do even worse.

The saying in vv. 4f. is thus rather unlike the paraenetic sayings about possible martyrdom situations often adduced as parallels to this saying (e.g. 2 Macc 6:30; 7:29; 4 Macc 13:13–15 and various texts from the *Epistle of Enoch*, e.g. *1 En* 95:3; 96:1, 3; 102:4; 103:4).[99] In such texts, very often the martyrs (or would-be martyrs) claim that other people are not to be 'feared'; however the corollary is usually that God is to be trusted, relied upon and to be looked to with confidence. Any 'fear' of God in such contexts is regarded thoroughly positively as simply the fear which is virtually synonymous with 'reverence' and 'worship'. It may be that non-Christian Jewish texts urging reluctant martyrs to face death are simply lacking. But Q 12:5 is rather different in tone from 2 Maccabees or 4 Maccabees: the 'fear' of God mentioned here is not a reverencing in joyful confidence, but a terrified awareness of the power of God to turn against the listeners with destruction.[1]

This in turn means that vv. 4f. have little in common with vv. 6f. beyond the common use of the verb 'to fear'. Verses 4f. do however connect very well with vv. 8f.. As we have seen, the double saying in vv. 8f. is concerned with commitment to the cause of Jesus which, it is asserted, will have consequences of ultimate significance: whoever confesses Jesus now will be confessed at the

---

[99] Cf. Zeller, *Mahnsprüche*, 96f.; Kloppenborg, *Formation*, 208.

[1] Cf. too Sato, *Q und Prophetie*, 174, on the difference between 12:4–7 and any *Heilsorakel.*

final judgement; whoever denies Jesus now will be denied. I argued earlier that v. 9 is probably to be referred to people who are wavering in their commitment to the Christian cause, rather than to any possible 'persecutors'. But then it is to just such people that vv. 4f. apply even more forcefully. Those who are in danger of 'denying' Jesus are just those who have some 'fear' of other men.[2] The answer of vv. 6f. is to plead with people that 'fear' is inappropriate in the light of the all-caring activity of a loving God. Verses 4f. and v. 9 take a quite different view: fear of men may be inappropriate but only because God is to be feared all the more in the light of the future judgement, described in terms of the destruction of body and soul in Gehenna in v. 5, and of denial by the SM in v. 9. Thus vv. 4f. and 8f. correlate well in terms of their eschatological outlook and contrast rather strongly with the somewhat uneschatological (possible 'sapiential') and more optimistic outlook of vv. 6f.

The situation here is very similar to that which I tried to outline in relation to the Cares tradition in Q 12:22ff. There an earlier tradition expressing confidence in God's care for His creation had been overlaid by a secondary layer of tradition placing concern for the material needs of life very low on any agenda of priorities and placing all weight on the eschatological future kingdom of God. Here too in Q 12:4ff., a similar shift seems to have taken place. An earlier 'optimistic' outlook advocating fear-free trust in God has been incorporated into a wider unit dominated by concern for a future judgement. In terms of tradition and redaction, it seems easiest to see the Q-redactional layer as concerned above all with the eschatological outlook (as in the Cares tradition).[3] Q is thus concerned to stress the dangers of wavering in the present and it expresses this concern by pointing to the fearful aspects of what the future will bring. If this is correct, then there is no need to see any 'persecution' situation being envisaged here. The aim of the saying is to banish all 'fear' of men and the way this is done is by contrasting human beings with God. But the logic of the argument does not demand that

[2] But it is not at all clear that those in v. 9 who are 'denying' Jesus are doing so because of threats to their life, whether judicial execution or not.

[3] In this sense I agree with Kloppenborg that a 'sapiential' layer has been overlaid by a 'polemical' layer. However, unlike Kloppenborg, I would see vv. 4f. as part of the polemical stage; and the polemic is not necessarily addressed to 'outsiders'. There is perhaps rather less of an insider/outsider mentality in Q than Kloppenborg presupposes.

the 'fear' in question relates to concrete fears of real death by the audience.

2.6. Q 12:11f.

The situation is not necessarily any different in Q 12:11f. Here uncertainty is even greater than usual. It seems likely that a saying like this was part of Q,[4] but there is also a Markan version of the tradition (in Mark 13:11), and Matthew at least appears to have conflated the Markan and Q versions of the saying. The existence of the Markan version thus creates enormous problems in trying to recover the exact wording of the Q version. This becomes quite crucial in the present context where we are interested in the precise situation presupposed.

The saying functions as encouragement to Christians facing some kind of hostile situation where they will be required to say something in 'defence' of themselves, the assurance being given that Christians will be helped, or inspired, by the Holy Spirit in such situations. The problem is to know just what situations are in mind. Luke talks of Christians being brought before 'synagogues, rulers and authorities'. The reference to 'rulers and authorities' is probably due to LkR, Luke clarifying what he understands the situation to be (i.e. one of judicial hearings) for his Gentile readers.[5] So too it may be that Luke's ἀπολογήσεσθε, with its overtones of formal defence at a formal trial, may be LkR.[6] On the other hand, Matthew's λαλήσετε may have come from Mark 13:11, so we cannot be sure of the Q wording. Nor is it clear whom it is that the Christians will be addressing. Luke speaks of 'synagogues'; Matthew mentions no specific forum in Matt 10:19, though in vv. 17f., Matthew (in dependence partly on Mark) speaks of Christians being handed over to 'Sanhedrins' and being beaten in 'your synagogues'. Doubtless Matthew and Luke are thinking of some kind of formal judicial hearings. But whether this is the case for Q[7] is not quite so clear. *If* Q referred to

---

[4] Cf. the agreements between Matthew and Luke alone: μὴ μεριμνήσητε, πῶς ἢ τί.

[5] Cf. Schulz, *Q*, 442, and others cited there; also R. Kühschelm, *Jüngerverfolgung und Geschick Jesu* (Klosterneuburg: Österreichisches Katholisches Bibelwerk, 1983) 141f.

[6] Schulz, *Q*, 443; Goulder, *Luke*, 531; Kühschelm, *Jüngerverfolgung*, 141f. Cf. Luke's parallel to Mark 13:11 in Luke 21:14, where Luke changes Mark's λαλήσητε to ἀπολογηθῆναι.

[7] So, for example, Schulz, *Q*, 443f.; Kühschelm, *Jüngerverfolgung*, 227; Kloppenborg, *Formation*, 214f.

'synagogues' here,[8] we cannot be sure if any formally constituted law court is in mind. The word συναγωγή itself is ambiguous and might refer to a separate building and institution, but might only refer to an assembly of people, formal or otherwise.[9] Thus we cannot be certain that the language in Q clearly reflects a *Sitz im Leben* of formal Jewish trials against Christians. All that is in mind may be simply informal gatherings at which Christians may be asked to give some account of themselves. From the Christian side, such a situation might be perceived as threatening, and the result might have been some abusive ridicule with an occasional act of violence. But there is no need to read the saying as implying a situation of a formally constituted court of law in which Christians have to defend themselves.

2.7. Q 14:27

The final saying to be considered here is the very difficult logion about taking up one's cross in Q 14:27. Once again the situation is partly complicated by the existence of a Markan parallel to the saying (Mark 8:34), though the reconstruction of the substance of Q's version is not greatly affected. Q's Jesus states that 'taking

---

[8] However, 'synagogues' are also mentioned in this context in Mark 13:9 as the object(s) to which Christians will be handed over. The word in Matthew and Luke may therefore derive from Mark.

[9] Cf. the debate about the rise of the 'synagogue' in Judaism of this period. H. C. Kee has argued forcefully that the 'synagogue' as a separate building can hardly be traced back to the pre-70 period in Palestine: see his 'The Transformation of the Synagogue after 70 C.E.: Its Import for Early Christianity', *NTS* 36 (1990) 1–24. Kee's theories have been strongly attacked by R. E. Oster, 'Supposed Anachronism in Luke–Acts's Use of συναγωγή: A Rejoinder to H. C. Kee', *NTS* 39 (1993) 178–208, and E. P. Sanders, *Jewish Law from Jesus to the Mishnah* (London: SCM, 1990) 341–3, though most of the argument focuses on whether there were separate *buildings* at this period. Much of this critique remains appropriate: cf. the descriptions of what are clearly buildings in Josephus, *Life* 276ff. (a synagogue at Tiberias) and *War* 2.285ff. (a synagogue at Caesarea). However, it still remains the case that the Greek *word* συναγωγή is ambiguous (cf. Kee's counter-response 'The Changing Meaning of Synagogue: A Response to Richard Oster', *NTS* 40 (1994) 281–3), and that a 'synagogue' building was as often as not referred to as a προσευχή, (cf. M. Hengel, 'Proseuche und Synagoge: Jüdische Gemeinde, Gotteshaus und Gottesdienst in der Diaspora und in Palestina' in G. Jeremias, H. W. Kuhn, H. Stegemann (eds), *Tradition und Glaube* (FS K. G. Kuhn; Göttingen: Vandenhoeck & Ruprecht, 1971) 157–84; E. Meyers, 'Synagogue', *Anchor Bible Dictionary* 6 (New York: Doubleday, 1992) 251–60.

up one's cross' is a *sine qua non* of being a follower of Jesus.[10] (Mark's version is slightly less harsh: taking up the cross is not an absolute precondition for being a disciple, but an exhortation to the would-be disciple: 'let him take up his cross . . .')

The problem is to know exactly what is intended. A great variety of interpretations have been offered.[11] It seems, however, very improbable that the saying can be taken as implying that death by crucifixion is a *sine qua non* for Christian disciple- ship. The very fact of the finality of death really precludes the idea that the Christian disciple must 'take up his cross' to be executed.[12] Otherwise there would no longer be any Christian disciples alive! So too, crucifixion is hard to imagine as a real threat posed for the Christian community in or near Palestine at any stage in the first century. Crucifixion was primarily, if not exclusively, a Roman punishment reserved for political rebels. Trying to explain how and why Jesus ended up on a Roman cross is difficult enough. There is no other evidence that other Christians were crucified in the early period (unless it be in the Neronian persecutions in Rome: but few would place Q in a Roman *Sitz im Leben*). It thus seems highly unlikely that the saying has real crucifixion in mind in exhorting the listeners to 'take up the cross'.

What is probably intended is a stark and powerful metaphor to impress upon the audience the hardness of the Christian calling, the harsh life to which the Christian may be summoned. In this the Christian is called upon to 'suffer' in various ways.[13] However, the metaphorical nature of the language used means that we cannot deduce very much in concrete terms about the suffering which is envisaged.[14] The disciple must be prepared to follow his

---

[10] The precise wording of the ending of the saying in Q (Matthew: 'is not worthy of me'; Luke: 'cannot be my disciple') is uncertain but probably does not matter too much here. Both Matthew and Luke have similar differences at the end of the saying about one's attitude to one's family which immediately precedes the cross saying in both gospels (and hence probably in Q as well).

[11] See the survey in Laufen, *Doppelüberlieferungen*, 309ff.

[12] Cf. Seeley, 'Blessings', 132.

[13] Cf. Schulz, Q, 432f.; Laufen, *Doppelüberlieferungen*, 313f.; Kloppenborg, *Formation*, 231f.; H. Fleddermann, 'The Cross and Discipleship in Q', *SBL 1988 Seminar Papers* (Atlanta: Scholars, 1988) 472–82, p. 482, who also refers to Q 6:40.

[14] Seeley interprets the saying against a background of Cynic and Stoic attitudes to death, as 'a call to be willing to follow a teacher or model in suffering and even death'. (See his 'Blessings', 132–4; also his 'Jesus' Death in

master — if necessary to death. But that does not imply that Q Christians were experiencing such sufferings already.

Conclusion

This chapter has had to cover a wide spectrum of the material in Q. However, the analysis does show a fairly consistent pattern in the material. Undoubtedly Q reflects a situation of some antagonism and hostility. The Q Christians are not receiving a positive response! And from the Christian side, such negative reactions are being interpreted as 'persecutions', the rejection and hostility being put on a par with the rejection and hostility suffered by the prophets according to the schematic outline in the Deuteronomic pattern of preaching. Yet when we press the details, it seems hard to see the persecution as involving anything very systematic. There may have been hostility, taunts, verbal abuse, social ostracism. But there is no direct evidence of sustained physical attacks, nor of any deaths. The hostility may have become violent at times, but so much of the polemic in Q seems to presuppose a situation of silent ignoring. What seems to have provoked the strongest language in Q is simply the refusal of the audience to respond positively. They have failed to 'repent'. They have done nothing. It is possible that violence occurred on occasions — but if so it is notable how little polemic there is in the relevant Q material (cf. Q 12:4f., 11f.; 14:27): language that might imply that Christians were facing death seems to provoke only positive encouragement to the Christians. By contrast it is to the neutral, or the waverers, that Q's harshest polemic is directed.

Q', *NTS* 38 [1992] 222–34. The quotation is from 'Jesus' Death', 227.) The difficulty with this is that the saying is then interpreted as implying a *readiness* to follow in the footsteps of the model by dying a similar death, whereas the saying says that 'taking up the cross' itself is an essential and inescapable part of Christian discipleship. It is this that really demands that the saying cannot refer to death by physical crucifixion, but must be in some sense metaphorical.

The apparent parallel from Epictetus (2.2.20: 'if you wish to be crucified, wait and the cross will come'), cited by Downing on several occasions (cf. his 'Quite Like Q. A Genre for "Q": The "Lives" of Cynic Philosophers', *Biblica* 69 [1988] 196–225, p. 217; *Cynics and Christian Origins* [Edinburgh: T. & T. Clark, 1992] 139) is not very apt. The broader context in Epictetus is one of exhorting the listener *not* to provoke any possible suffering: if it is coming, it will do so anyway. This is really quite *un*like the Q saying which says that 'taking up one's cross' is essential and unavoidable for the Christian disciple.

It could be then that Q is not facing any great 'persecution' in any sense of that word as would be used by those outside the Christian camp. Q Christians are perhaps facing the archetypal modern response to Christian preaching: apathy!

10

Wisdom in Q

In an earlier chapter (ch. 6 above) we discussed the importance of several texts in Q which deal with the figure of personified Wisdom, directly or indirectly. In that context I argued that there was a very close connection between ideas of Wisdom and prophetic ideas, in particular ideas associated with the motif of the violence suffered by the prophets. I argued that the motif of the prophets was an important one for the Q community in explaining its own experiences of hostility and rejection as well as the hostility and rejection experienced by Jesus himself (even if the level of physical violence experienced by the Q Christians themselves was relatively low: cf. ch. 9 above). So too, the 'prophetic' category is, I suggested above, an important one by implication in Q's presentation of Jesus as the one who fulfils the role of Isa 61:1. It has however been a feature of a great deal of Q research in recent years to see 'wisdom', or 'sapiential' influences, as exercising a far more significant role in Q than only in the (perhaps relatively few) 'wisdom' texts which we discussed earlier. In this chapter, therefore, we shall look at the claims made about the alleged wisdom influences on Q, or parts of Q, to see how useful it may be to regard Q as in some way 'sapiential'.

The list of scholars who have supported the view that Q, or part of Q, is in some sense 'sapiential' is an impressively long one, and the list of verses in Q displaying possible wisdom influence can be equally impressive in its scope. Thus, for example, C. E. Carlston gives a long list of texts in Q displaying influence from either ideas about speculative Wisdom, or wisdom maxims, or other wisdom material, and concludes:

> The sheer bulk and variety of wisdom-materials in Q shows that wisdom is a basic, not an adventitious, element in the theological outlook of the Q community.[1]

[1] Carlston, 'Wisdom and Eschatology', 112.

Similarly, H. von Lips lists 106 units of tradition in Q which have been categorised by various scholars in form-critical terms as similar to wisdom materials in some way or other.[2] It must, however be noted that behind such claims about the importance of 'wisdom' in Q, there is a very great variety of different ideas about the nature of the 'wisdom' influence involved, the stage of Q at which such influence is to be posited, and the opposite pole with which wisdom is being contrasted. Thus, before discussing the view that 'wisdom' is integral to 'Q', we must try to clarify terminology, if only to see what is being claimed and what is being implicitly rejected, in order to come to some assessment of the value of the assertion being made. But first, a brief survey of some of the key works in recent years which have argued for the importance of wisdom in Q is in order.

1. Q and Wisdom: Some Recent Discussions

One of the earlier attempts to document the importance of sapiential influence on Q was J. M. Robinson's essay 'LOGOI SOPHON — On the Gattung of Q', which first appeared in 1964 and which we have already noted in our discussion of 'redaction-critical' approaches to Q.[3] As we have seen, Robinson's prime concern is with the *genre* of Q as a collection of sayings, the roots of which are to be found in the genre 'sayings of the wise', or λόγοι σοφῶν. The details of Robinson's argument we shall consider later in this chapter, but it is certainly the case that his suggestions about the essentially *wisdom* nature of the origin of the genre have been very influential.[4]

Robinson's theories are developed further by H. Koester, whose views we have also already noted in part (see pp. 65–7 above). Koester sees Q and GTh as closely related, although not

[2] H. von Lips, *Weisheitliche Traditionen im Neuen Testament* (WMANT 64; Neukirchen-Vluyn: Neukirchener, 1990) 198–203, referring to Bultmann, *History*; M. Küchler, *Frühjüdische Weisheitstraditionen* (Freiburg and Göttingen: Universitätsverlag and Vandenhoeck & Ruprecht, 1979); K. Berger, *Formgeschichte des Neuen Testaments* (Heidelberg: Quelle und Meyer, 1984); Kloppenborg, *Formation*; Sato, *Q und Prophetie*; J. D. Crossan, *In Fragments: The Aphorisms of Jesus* (San Francisco: Harper & Row, 1983). See also Sevenich-Bax, *Konfrontation, passim.*

[3] Robinson, 'LOGOI SOPHON'.

[4] Cf. Lührmann, *Redaktion*, 91; Küchler, *Weisheitstraditionen*, 562f.; Carlston, 'Wisdom and Eschatology', 111f., and others cited in Kloppenborg, *Formation*, 30.

in a direct relationship with each other: rather, both represent develoments of an underlying 'wisdom gospel'. However, as we have also noted already, the present form of Q has been fairly radically changed by the incorporation of the futurist 'apocalyptic' expectation of the coming of the SM. Thus for Koester, 'Q' is only really 'sapiential' if 'Q' is seen as an earlier stage in the development of the Q tradition. We have already noted some difficulties with Koester's overall thesis, especially his reference to GTh in this context. Further, we have seen that futurist SM sayings are not all necessarily late-comers into the Q tradition but are already present early on (see ch. 8 above). Still, for Koester, 'sapiential' and 'apocalyptic' seem to be mutually exclusive terms (though not 'sapiential' and 'eschatological': see below). Thus for Koester, the introduction of the futurist 'apocalyptic' SM sayings into Q produces something of a change in the basic orientation of the alleged original 'wisdom gospel'.

Robinson's and Koester's views have been considerably developed and refined in the work of Kloppenborg. The literary controls lacking in Koester's attempt to stratify the Q material are now supplied in full measure as Kloppenborg seeks to show that a distinction can be made between different strata within Q. For Kloppenborg, the earlier layer of Q (Q^1) can be called 'sapiential'. Here the bulk of the sayings are hortatory, addressed to the Christian community from within, and display many parallels with material in other wisdom literature. By contrast, the later layer within Q (Q^2), which often expands the earlier 'sapiential' speeches with additions which can be separated on literary-critical grounds, is termed by Kloppenborg as more 'prophetic': it is directed against outside opponents rather than Christian adherents, and is characterised much more by themes of prophetic judgement and warnings.[5] Thus Kloppenborg agrees with Koester in categorising an earlier stratum within Q as sapiential. Further, for Kloppenborg, 'sapiential' is taken as contrasting with 'prophetic'. And in a recent article, Robinson too, has expressed whole-hearted support for Kloppenborg's theory that it is an earlier stage of Q that is to be seen primarily as sapiential, and the later stage as prophetic, so that the genre of Q is to be seen not as static but as developing

---

[5] For Kloppenborg's summaries of these different strata, see his *Formation*, 238–44, 166–70 respectively.

and changing during the course of Q's own tradition history.[6]

The work of Piper is broadly similar in seeing wisdom influence in many parts of the Q tradition.[7] But his concern is primarily with the smaller units of the tradition contained in Q, and Piper deliberately eschews any attempt to produce a theology of Q as a whole. Thus he deals with small collections of aphorisms such a Q 11:9–13, or Q 12:22–31. So too, the contrast is frequently drawn between wisdom and 'prophetic' or 'eschatological' ideas, especially as proposed in Schulz's work on Q. Thus again 'wisdom' is seen as the antithesis of 'prophetic' and 'eschatological'.[8]

There are, however, others who have stressed the importance of wisdom for Q but who have seen no contrast between 'wisdom' and 'prophecy' or 'eschatology', at least in Q. For these scholars, any contrast between these complexes of ideas has to reckon with their simultaneous presence in Q. Thus, R. A. Edwards sees the theology of Q as characterised by the three poles of prophecy, eschatology *and* wisdom, so that any tension between them has been overcome at least to some extent by Q itself which unites all three into some kind of synthesis.[9] W. Grundmann regards 'wisdom' as an essential feature of Q but sees such wisdom as receiving something of a decisive shift under the influence of eschatology so that Q's 'wisdom' is a 'Weisheit im Horizont des Reiches Gottes'.[10] So too, Carlston sees clearly some of the problems and acknowledges that however important wisdom may be for Q, the theme of eschatology is just as pervasive in Q and hence the two must be combined in some sense.[11]

[6] See his 'Die Logienquelle: Weisheit oder Prophetie?', *EvTh* 53 (1993) 367–89, esp. pp. 385, 388. Robinson's article is primarily a critique of Sato's *Q und Prophetie*.

[7] Piper, *Wisdom, passim.*

[8] In a later part of the book, however, Piper does attempt to correlate 'wisdom' and 'eschatology' and to see how the two might relate to each other within Q: see his *Wisdom*, 178–84, and also the discussion below (pp. 351–4).

[9] R. A. Edwards, *A Theology of Q. Eschatology, Prophecy and Wisdom* (Philadelphia: Fortress, 1976). Cf. too B. Witherington, *Jesus the Sage. The Pilgrimage of Wisdom* (Edinburgh: T. & T. Clark, 1994) 211–36, and his claim that Q presents Jesus as a 'prophetic sage' (pp. 217, 233).

[10] W. Grundmann, 'Weisheit im Horizont des Reiches Gottes' in R. Schnackenburg, J. Ernst, J. Wanke (eds.), *Die Kirche des Anfangs* (FS H. Schürmann; Freiburg: Herder, 1978) 175–99.

[11] Carlston, 'Wisdom and Eschatology', *passim.*

For other scholars, on the other hand, the 'prophetic' nature of Q is much more important. For some, there is no great problem here since 'wisdom' and 'prophecy' are not seen as mutual rivals.[12] For others, however, the claim that Q is 'prophetic' is definitely intended to be more antithetical to the claim about any 'wisdom' influences on Q. Thus claims that (perhaps only part of) Q is sapiential and not prophetic are mirrored by the assertion of Boring that Q is primarily prophetic and *not* sapiential.[13] Boring's views on the 'prophetic' nature of Q are similar to those of Kelber (though Kelber's concern is not so much to set up an antithesis between 'prophetic' and 'sapiential', but rather between the 'prophetic' Q as contemporising and oral in contrast with the historicising and written nature of Mark).[14] Perhaps the most detailed case for the theory that Q is 'prophetic' and not 'sapiential' has been developed by Sato who has sought to show how *un*like the wisdom literature Q is, and how many parallels there are between Q and the prophetic writings of Judaism.[15]

There is thus a wide variety of views adopted in relation to the problem of possible 'wisdom' influence in 'Q': is Q as a whole to be seen as sapiential? Or is only an earlier stage in the development of Q sapiential? There is also some difference of opinion about what the opposite of 'sapiential' is, and what it is to be contrasted with: is sapiential to be seen over against 'prophetic'? Are 'sapiential' and 'apocalyptic' mutually exclusive? Are 'sapiential' and 'eschatological' binary opposites of each other? Or can some, or all, of these terms be seen as possibly complementary to each other? There is then a fundamental problem of how we define 'wisdom' or 'sapiential' in this context: what exactly do we mean when we claim, or deny, that there is 'wisdom' influence in Q, or that Q is 'sapiential'?

[12] Cf. Schulz, *Q*, 153, who otherwise stresses the prophetic and apocalyptic nature of Q and does not discuss any possible tensions between these aspects and the possible sapiential outlook of Q.

[13] M. E. Boring, *Sayings of the Risen Jesus. Christian Prophecy in the Synoptic Tradition* (SNTSMS 46; Cambridge University Press, 1982) 180f.

[14] Cf. W. Kelber, *The Oral and Written Gospel* (Philadelphia: Fortress, 1983).

[15] Sato, *Q und Prophetie, passim.* See too his response to Robinson's critique (n. 6 above) 'Q: Prophetie oder Weisheit? Ein Gespräch mit J. M. Robinson', *EvTh* 53 (1993) 389–404; also his 'Wisdom Statements in the Sphere of Prophecy', in Piper (ed.), *The Gospel Behind the Gospels*, 139–58.

2. What is wisdom/sapiential?

The problem of defining 'wisdom' is occasionally raised in Q
studies, but rarely discussed in detail. Kloppenborg raises the
issue,[16] but in the end evades the question by proposing what
amounts to a hermeneutical closed circle which ultimately
provides little help. He rightly notes that individual sayings are
ambiguous and can often appear to be either sapiential or
prophetic.[17] He appears to argue at one point that the two are
virtually self-evident: 'No one would confuse Proverbs with
prophecy, or Isaiah with wisdom — this despite the facts that Prov
8 contains prophetic motifs, and 1 Isaiah has absorbed sapiential
elements.'[18] Sayings, however, generally become clearer when
placed in a wider context of a known genre: for example, a saying
is seen to be sapiential if it is part of a wisdom book, prophetic if
part of a prophetic book.[19] The problem is to know precisely
whether a given context *is* sapiential or prophetic, and in the case
of Q that is precisely the problem! In any case, a vital part of the
way one determines the genre of the whole is on the basis of an
interpretation of its individual parts. Kloppenborg claims that
many of the individual sayings of his Q[1] have parallels with
wisdom sayings; but then his point about the ambiguity of any
individual saying in isolation becomes all the more pressing. Just
because one saying has parallels with other wisdom traditions
does not make that saying 'sapiential' without more ado. Whether

[16] Kloppenborg, *Formation*, 37f. Cf. also n. 38 below.

[17] And hence it seems clear from his discussion here, as well as from his
general discussion and characterisation of his two proposed main strata in Q,
that 'sapiential' and 'prophetic' are somewhat antithetical. On the other hand,
he notes that some attempts to distinguish the two on material grounds (e.g.
sapiential = 'eudaemonistic, anthropocentric and fundamentally debatable',
prophetic = 'theological, theocentric and categorical') are 'too schematic':
'The sage's counsel presupposes an appeal to divine authority no less than the
prophet's oracle.' But whether these are the only, or even the most appropriate,
antitheses with which to distinguish wisdom and prophecy is of course debatable.

[18] Kloppenborg, *Formation*, 37.

[19] 'Sirach's statement [that the prayer of a poor man is heard immediately:
Sir 21:5] is identified as sapiential because it occurs in the context of a wisdom
instruction. Were it to occur in the middle of a prophetic indictment of the
rapacity of the rich and powerful, it would doubtless be read differently. This
illustrates the importance of framing devices and formulae for determining
the overall genre. Content is not enough, because it is too often ambiguous.'
(Kloppenborg, *Formation*, 38.) But the 'framing devices' and 'formulae' are so
often lacking, especially in sayings collections!

Kloppenborg's claim at the end of his analysis of Q to have established the sapiential nature of his Q^1 is justified remains to be seen.

The great merit of Piper's book in the present context is that it sets up a clear definition of what is to be discussed under the heading of 'wisdom'. For Piper, the main focus of attention is what he calls 'aphoristic wisdom' which is then closely defined as referring to general, short pithy statements ('aphorisms') which are self-contained, hermeneutically open, appealing generally to collective experience and not tied to any particular situation.[20] There is then here a clear and explicit contrast drawn between aphoristic wisdom and prophetic insight, and Piper's contrast between 'sapiential' and 'prophetic', and between 'sapiential' and 'eschatological', is both meaningful and justified in terms of his definitions. How far though 'Q' is really then 'sapiential' remains to be seen.

The problem of the definition of what might constitute 'wisdom' or 'sapiential' traditions is not confined to Q studies. It is also a standing problem for OT research, and one scholar has written, almost in despair, 'an adequate definition of wisdom eludes interpreters of the OT'.[21] One must however be aware of what one is trying to do in defining 'wisdom' or 'sapiential'. Clearly part of any claim being made about Q in any assertion that Q (or part of Q) is 'sapiential' is that it is sufficiently similar to the wisdom literature of the OT, which in turn is universally accepted as having links with a very wide range of ideas and writings in the ancient world, to make the description meaningful.[22] But what is to count as 'wisdom literature' in this context? Are we to take any reference, or any 'significant' (however defined) reference to the *word* 'wisdom' as relevant here? Does any indication that someone is spoken of as 'wise', or displaying 'wisdom', mean that we are in the realm of wisdom thought or ideas or writings or whatever? The trouble is that the word 'wisdom' itself is a very general one. Thus Crenshaw writes:

> Wisdom shares a common vocabulary with prophecy, priestly discourse, and historiography. Certain words are universal, hence cannot be used to establish wisdom influence. Into this category of

---

[20] Piper, *Wisdom*, 4f.
[21] J. L. Crenshaw, 'Wisdom in the OT', *Interpreters Dictionary of the Bible* Supplementary Volume (Nashville: Abingdon, 1976) 952.
[22] The international nature of wisdom is universally acknowledged.

common linguistic stock fall such words as knowledge and intelligence, good and bad, *wisdom and* folly, obedience and disobedience. Impoverished indeed is the language of any group without such words. Even when an Israelite is called a wise man or woman, it does not necessarily imply a technical use of the adjective.[23]

Similarly, formal parallels may be misleading as we have already seen.[24] Thus we cannot simply undertake a word study of occurrences of the words 'wisdom/wise' in ancient texts to isolate what is meant by wisdom ideas. Nor can we be goverened solely by formal similarities. Rather, for most people, 'wisdom' is a *modern* category, seeking to *abstract* from within the whole range of Jewish thinking and writing a more limited set of ideas and texts. Indeed the word 'wisdom' itself will not always be present.[25] Conversely, references to the 'wise' or 'wisdom' do not necessarily mean that we are in the realm of wisdom thought. One could, of course, decide that this should not be so and define 'wisdom' accordingly. However, we may well find that, in that case, the category of 'wisdom' would then become so all-embracing that it potentially includes almost everything and excludes nothing: as an interpretative category it therefore becomes virtually useless.[26] On the other hand, one must be alive to the fact that 'wisdom' ideas may well have changed and developed over the course of time. Thus, most would include the books of Job and Ecclesiastes within the realm of 'wisdom literature'; and yet their questioning and pessimism are radically different from the outlook of a book such as Proverbs. Similarly, within a book such as Proverbs itself, the idea of Wisdom as a personified being in her own right is clearly a significant development which shifts the very use of the word 'wisdom' itself in a new direction. (And, of course, it is this use of 'Wisdom'

---

[23] Crenshaw, 'Wisdom in the OT', 953. (My italics.)

[24] Cf. above on the ambiguity of sayings taken in isolation, and earlier on the beatitude form (p. 142 above).

[25] It is, in fact, relatively rare in Q: σοφία occurs in Q 7:35 (personified wisdom) and probably 11:49 (ditto), as well as 11:31 (the wisdom of Solomon); σοφός occurs in Q 10:21 in a rather negative sense: 'these things' have been *hidden* from the 'wise'. There are no other uses of the Greek root in Q.

[26] Cf. too von Lips, *Weisheitliche Traditionen*, 185; Sato, 'Prophetie oder Weisheit?', 392, 397. Witherington's study, *Jesus the Sage*, suffers perhaps from a tendency not to discriminate and to include a vast amount of material under the category of 'wisdom': cf. n. 31 below.

terminology that becomes so important in Q, as we have seen.)[27]

Crenshaw has argued in a number of places that one should make finer distinctions within the broad category of 'wisdom': one should perhaps think of wisdom literature, wisdom traditions, and wisdom thought as three obviously overlapping, but not necessarily identical, areas, all encompassing different kinds of wisdom such as juridical wisdom, natural wisdom, practical wisdom and theological wisdom, all with different *Sitze im Leben* of family, courtly and scribal wisdom.[28] Crenshaw's suggestions are certainly apposite in warning against too simplistic and facile an attempt to produce a single definition of 'wisdom' which can cover all the many facets of what is usually subsumed under the term. On the other hand, without some attempt to provide a single description of what might be appropriately called 'wisdom', there is the danger, noted already, that the term 'wisdom' becomes so wide-ranging that as a descriptive category it becomes virtually worthless. Thus, with all the dangers of over-specifying in mind, it may still be worth trying to find some, albeit very general, description of 'wisdom' in order to make a contemporary use of the category meaningful.

When a unifying definition is attempted, reference is often made to G. von Rad's classification of wisdom as referring to 'a practical knowledge of the laws of life and of the world based upon experience'.[29] Above all there is a belief in the regularity and order of the created world and that the task of wisdom is to discover that order, even if it is not immediately discernible to the human mind. Nevertheless, the basis for understanding is human

---

[27] The fact that the alleged 'wisdom' of Q is significantly different from the older, 'classical' types of wisdom is stressed by Robinson, 'Weisheit oder Prophetie?', 369; cf. too n. 34 below on 'mantic' wisdom. It may be justified to retain the word 'wisdom' to describe the phenomenon being discussed; however, I wonder if the further that the category of wisdom is extended, and the more it is conceived as incorporating, the less useful it becomes as a hermeneutical key for actually interpreting Q.

[28] As well as his 'Wisdom in the OT' article, see his 'Method in Determining Wisdom Influence upon "Historical" Literature', *JBL* 88 (1969) 129–42, pp. 130f.; 'Prolegomena', in J. L. Crenshaw (ed.), *Studies in Ancient Israelite Wisdom* (New York: KTAV, 1976) 1–45.

[29] G. von Rad, *Old Testament Theology Volume One* (ET Edinburgh: Oliver & Boyd, 1962) 418. For similar views, often appealing to von Rad, see J. McKenzie, 'Reflections on Wisdom', *JBL* 86 (1967) 1–9, pp. 5f., 8; R. B. Y. Scott, 'The Study of the Wisdom Literature', *Int* 24 (1970) 20–45, p. 29; Crenshaw, 'Prolegomena', 3; Zeller, *Mahnsprüche*, 16; von Lips, *Weisheitliche Traditionen*, 11.

experience, to be communicated and taught to others.[30] For present purposes, I shall adopt this as a working definition, simply in order to try to clarify what exactly we are talking about when we speak of 'wisdom'. Such a definition does however suggest a firm (if somewhat rough-and-ready) contrast between wisdom and prophecy: wisdom is an attempt to 'explain' things on the basis of collective experience; prophecy is the claim to 'announce' on the basis of direct revelation.[31] A number of scholars have argued that wisdom and prophecy are not necessarily so antithetical and that there are various wisdom influences in several of the 'prophetic' and historical writings of the OT.[32] So too, many would see no antithesis between wisdom and apocalyptic.[33] One should however perhaps take note at this

---

[30] Cf. von Rad, *Old Testament Theology*, 428; Edwards, *Theology*, 73; von Lips, *Weisheitliche Traditionen*, 15.

[31] Cf. Edwards, *Theology*, 45: 'The wise man explains what he has learned from the past while the prophet announces that which YHWH has revealed.' Also Crenshaw, 'Wisdom in the OT', 953: 'Prophet and sage inevitably come to blows, for each represents a world view wholly alien to the other. Stated crassly, the extremes are revelation and reason.' See too Sato, *Q und Prophetie*, 106; also the implied recognition of some distinction between the two by Kloppenborg, *Formation*, 37; G. von Rad, *Wisdom in Israel* (ET London: SCM, 1972) 309. A full list of antitheses between wisdom and prophecy is set out by von Lips, *Weisheitliche Traditionen*, 76: prophecy accuses, wisdom warns; prophecy addresses groups of people (using 2nd person plural), wisdom generalises (using 2nd person singular); prophecy appeals to the authority of God, wisdom to experience; prophecy holds out the sanction of God's intervention and activity, wisdom refers to an almost automatic pattern of action and result (*Tun-Ergehen*). No doubt some of these could be disputed, but the general outline seems justifiable in distinguishing two patterns of thought.

Witherington's discussion of what is to be treated as wisdom effectively blurs such a distinction. By distinguishing between a 'proverb', taken as a deduction from general experience, and an 'aphorism', taken as a unique insight from an individual, and by including both in the general category of 'wisdom' (cf. his *Jesus and Sage*, 9–11), Witherington effectively incorporates what others would call 'prophetic' into his 'aphoristic wisdom'.

[32] Cf. Crenshaw, 'Method', 129f. See also Kloppenborg, as above; Sato, 'Prophetie oder Weisheit?', 391. The situation in relation to prophecy is complicated by the possibility that some of the prophets may have been consciously reacting against 'wisdom' influences (e.g. Isaiah, Amos): see von Lips, *Weisheitliche Traditionen*, 70–3.

[33] See M. Hengel, *Judaism and Hellenism*, 202ff.; G. Nickelsburg, 'The Apocalyptic Message of 1 En 92–105', *CBQ* 39 (1977) 309–28, p. 327; also Sevenich-Bax, *Konfrontation*, who frequently refers to 'apocalyptic wisdom', or wisdom in an apocalyptic context. Cf. also the so-called 'mantic wisdom' of, for example, Daniel as the wise man who shows his wisdom by interpreting dreams, etc. See von Lips, *Weisheitliche Traditionen*, 168–70.

point about Crenshaw's proposed distinction between wisdom thought and wisdom literature: the presence of wisdom thought at some points in literature that is not usually classified as wisdom does not mean that the literature itself is, in fact, to be regarded as 'wisdom'. Thus a qualitative distinction between wisdom and prophecy does not preclude the possibility of some wisdom elements appearing in prophetic literature. But any attempt to broaden the category of 'wisdom', for example to include prophecy and apocalyptic, runs the danger of extending the category so far and making it so elastic that it almost excludes nothing and hence becomes correspondingly less useful.[34] The distinction between wisdom thought and wisdom literature must also alert us to the danger of deducing too much too quickly from verbal or formal parallels with wisdom traditions, as if the existence of a parallel necessarily means that the tradition under review is therefore 'sapiential'. The fact that the same words can mean different things in different contexts, and that wisdom elements can appear quite appropriately in literature that is not in itself sapiential, should warn us here.[35]

[34] One wonders if the inclusion of, for example, the so-called mantic wisdom within the broader category of 'wisdom' may not be confusing a word-study approach with the attempt to provide a modern taxonomy. The dangers of running together a whole range of ideas associated in different places with a single word should be too well known after the strictures of J. Barr, *The Semantics of Biblical Language* (London: SCM, 1961), against such an approach in some of the earlier articles in the Kittel *Wörterbuch*. For a strong statement on the difference between wisdom and apocalyptic, see von Lips, *Weisheitliche Traditionen*, 88.

[35] In relation to Q studies, this warning applies especially to Kloppenborg, who is fully alive to the dangers of such an approach (*Formation*, 37), but who in the end appears to reach conclusions about the 'sapiential' nature of large parts of Q rather quickly on the basis of parallels between aspects of the individual elements of Q and parts of the wisdom literature. Similarly Sevenich-Bax, *Konfrontation*, seems to me to deduce too quickly the 'weisheitlich' nature of individual passages on the basis of formal parallels and/or a comparison of individual elements. For example, her claim (pp. 286–313) that John the Baptist's preaching in Q 3:7–9 is to be seen as sapiential, partly because it is formally close to the complaint of Wisdom in Prov 1 (as well as because of the presence of themes such as repentance not found in the classical prophets), seems unconvincing: any formal parallels scarcely place John in the category of a wisdom teacher, and not even the category of 'apocalyptic wisdom' (p. 313) really changes that. The complaint of Wisdom in Prov 1 might be seen as sapiential in the light of other sapiential teaching of Wisdom; but this is just what is not there in the case of John.

Insofar as wisdom is a reflection of collective experience, Jewish wisdom may well be qualitatively different from other, non-Jewish, wisdom. Clearly the collective experience of the Jewish people contained many elements which were peculiar to Israel, including her claimed experience of God, and of God's actions in the world on behalf of His chosen people, as well as more mundane observations about the world.[36] Jewish wisdom was then ineradicably theocentric. However, it still remains rather questionable whether eschatology and eschatological warnings can very easily be fitted in to the category of 'wisdom'. Certainly some have wanted to speak of an 'eschatological wisdom' in Q.[37] However, it seems that in such a process, the category of 'wisdom' has been stretched almost to breaking-point. If it is indeed right to think of wisdom as based on experience of the past, then eschatology must to a certain extent be the antithesis of wisdom: for eschatology looks to the future; it announces the *end* of the present order, and looks to a *new* order being inaugurated which will signify a break with the past. At one level there is, of course, some continuity: insofar as eschatology is concerned with a new intervention of *God*, and God is the same God who is both Creator and Sustainer of the world in the past and present as well as the radical new Innovator, then the identity of God as God serves to provide continuity with the past. And, of course, that continuity is reflected in several strands of Jewish eschatological hope, where Jews looked forward to a new era in which the great acts of God in the past would be 'recapitulated' in, for example, a new Exodus, the appearance of a new David, a new temple, etc. In this sense therefore there could be said to be a real continuity between past experience and future expectations and hope. But little then seems to be served by using the category of 'wisdom' as such to describe a part of this continuity. The continuity is provided by the Judaeo-Christian monotheistic faith as such and is a reflection of 'theology' (strictly speaking). Thus, when Kloppenborg, for

[36] Even though it is of course well known that Jewish wisdom literature rarely appeals to the saving history of Israel's faith claims as such: Cf. von Lips, *Weisheitliche Traditionen*, 40–5. One does of course start to get appeals to figures of past history in books like Sirach and Wisdom; but even in the section in praise of the fathers in Sir 44–50, the focus is on the fathers themselves and their virtues, not on the activity of God as such.

[37] Edwards, *Theology*, 78, 148; Carlston, 'Wisdom and Eschatology', 113 ('wisdom materials are shaped in an eschatological direction'); Kloppenborg, 'Symbolic Eschatology', 291f. ('eschatological tenor of these [i.e. Q] wisdom elements').

example, is forced to say that 'the Q beatitudes, while not typically sapiential in content, could well be characterised as the "radical wisdom of the Kingdom"', one wonders if the term 'wisdom' itself here is in danger of stretching its meaning too far to be useful.[38]

With these general points in mind we may turn to a more detailed discussion of claims made in recent years to the effect that Q betrays a significant degree of 'wisdom' influence.

3. Q and 'Wisdom'

I start with a consideration of J. M. Robinson's thesis that, in terms of its genre, Q is to be seen as part of a developing *Gattung* which has its roots in Jewish (and other) wisdom traditions and hence can justly be called '*logoi sophon*', 'sayings of the wise'. Robinson himself makes it clear that his proposal is not about the genre of Q as a static entity existing in a number of documents independently. Rather, over a period of time, the genre could and did change. The (or perhaps better, a) tendency in the genre was to associate the speaker of the 'wise words' with the figure of Wisdom herself. When this was coordinated with the trajectory leading from Sophia to the gnostic redeemer, then the '*logoi sophon*' became the 'hidden sayings' of Gnosticism;[39] and even within the tradition history of Q itself, the genre may have developed significantly by incorporating more prophetic elements.[40]

---

[38] Kloppenborg, *Formation*, 189. Cf. the comment of Sato, 'Prophetie oder Weisheit?', 398: 'Damit wird die Kategorie "Weisheit" zu sehr gedehnt.' On the beatitudes, see also p. 142 above. In more general terms, Kloppenborg refers to the way in which sayings in Q serve to question the whole basis of the present world order and the everyday presuppositions of the hearers: 'The intensified wisdom of Q plays a negative function of "deconstructing" the former world view of the hearer. . . . It not only disorients the hearer with respect to ordinary existence . . . , but it also reorients towards the new reality of the kingdom and God' (*Formation*, 320, referring too, to W. A. Beardslee, 'Uses of the Proverb in the Synoptic Gospels', *Int* 24 [1970] 61–73). I would agree whole-heartedly with this assessment of the function of the Q sayings, and also with the description of them as 'intensified'. My only question would be how far this should be called 'intensified *wisdom*'. Yet again, we can call this 'wisdom' if we wish, but this is only at some cost to precision. It is certainly unlike the older form of wisdom with which I started (cf. too n. 27 above). Such differences are also highlighted by Horsley, 'Logoi Prophētōn', 199.

[39] Robinson, 'LOGOI SOPHON', 112f.

[40] 'Wir haben es bei der Spruchquelle eben nicht nur mit den einfachen Frage nach der Gattung zu tun, sondern mit der viel komplizierten Frage nach einer innerhalb der sukzessiven Schichten der Spruchquelle selbst sich

In past discussions of Robinson's thesis, a great deal of attention has been focused on the more recent end of the proposed trajectory, i.e. the culmination in Gnosticism, and on the question of whether the genre necessarily includes any gnosticising tendencies.[41] However, for the present purposes we shall focus attention on the other end of the proposed trajectory and ask if it is indeed sensible to see a generic relationship between Q and earlier wisdom collections. Robinson proceeds by identifying several collections of sayings in early Christian and Gnostic literature, all of which appear to have the 'title' λόγοι ('words'). These collections are to be found in the NT itself, in some of the Nag Hammadi texts, in Justin, *1 Clement* and elsewhere. Thus Robinson postulates a common genre, or *Gattung*, of λόγοι, sayings. The *Gattung* comes into view in Christian sayings as the 'hidden sayings' of texts like GTh. However, Robinson locates the roots of the genre elsewhere, as we have seen. Taking his cue from Bultmann's suggestion that the introduction to the Q saying in Q 11:49 ('Therefore the Wisdom of God said . . .') may indicate a citation from a lost wisdom text, and also from *1 Clem* 57:3ff. where a similar introduction leads into a reference to λόγοι and quotations of wisdom sayings from Prov 1, Robinson argues that the roots of the *Gattung* lie in the wisdom tradition. Thus he finds confirmation of his thesis in *m.Aboth*, in some of the titles of the *Testaments of the Twelve Patriarchs*, in the *Apocalypse of Adam*, and in parts of *1 Enoch*.[42] Earlier still there are collections in Jewish wisdom texts such as Prov 22:17–24:22, (cf. v. 17 LXX λόγοις

---

vollziehenden Gattungs*geschichte*' ('Weisheit oder Prophetie?', 385, my stress). Similarly on p. 388: 'Wenn auch die späte Schicht der Spruchquelle nicht mehr ausschließlich als Λόγοι Σοφῶν bezeichnet werden kann. . . . Wir haben es in Q mit einer gattungsgeschichtlichen Entwicklung zu tun'. Thus Robinson speculates that Q as a whole could perhaps be designated Λόγοι Σοφῶν καὶ Προφητῶν τῆς Σοφίας, or οἱ Λόγοι τῆς Προφητείας τῆς Σοφίας, though in the end he inclines to the description 'Sayings Gospel' (Spruchevangelium) as the best description (ibid., 388f., cf. too his 'The Sayings Gospel Q', in Van Segbroek et al. (eds), *The Four Gospels 1992*, 361–88).

[41] Cf. the reservations expressed by Lührmann, *Redaktion*, 91; Küchler, *Weisheitstraditionen*, 562f.; Kloppenborg, *Formation*, 31, points out that the trajectory leading into gnosticism was only one possible development of the genre.

[42] All these are considered by Robinson in his section entitled 'Jewish Wisdom Literature and the Gattung LOGOI SOPHON': see 'LOGOI SOPHON', 105–9.

σοφῶν παράβαλλε) and similar collections in Prov 30 and Prov 31, and further back still in Near Eastern collections such as Ahikar and Amen-em-Opet. It is the phrase used in Prov 22:17 (and implied elsewhere) — λόγοι σοφῶν — that gives Robinson both the title and the characteristic feature of the genre or *Gattung* he seeks to identify: such sayings collections are 'sayings of the wise', i.e. they are fundamentally wisdom collections whose basic orientation is sapiential.

It is, however, doubtful whether Robinson's argument can be fully sustained. There is in fact more than one issue here. There is first the question whether, *if* such a *Gattung* entitled λόγοι (σοφῶν) existed, Q actually belongs to it. The question is by no means trite, since Q does *not* contain any introductory title at all as far as our evidence goes: it does *not* call itself λόγοι Ἰησοῦ or λόγοι σοφῶν.[43] So much of Robinson's article is devoted to collecting references to sayings collections via the word λόγοι. Yet Q does not have such a title (at least extant).

Now in one way this may be immaterial. Robinson has successfully shown the (possible) existence of a number of sayings collections, at least in general terms. Hence it is indeed right to put Q, as another sayings collection, alongside all these collections. And in a very real sense too, the very nature of such collections as *sayings* collections is distinctive enough to warrant the ascription of a genre, or *Gattung*, to it in its own right. A collection of sayings is not the same as a narrative, or a poem, or a play or a romance. Thus in terms of a relatively 'broad' genre,[44] Robinson has, in my view, successfully shown that Q is generically similar to other collections. However, a second, more serious problem with Robinson's overall theory arises at this point. For it

---

[43] Though this has not stopped some speculation to this effect: see Kloppenborg, *Q Parallels*, 2, who tentatively suggests that Q may have started with an incipit οὗτοι οἱ λόγοι οὓς ἐλάλησεν Ἰησοῦς (καὶ Ἰωάννης) (cf. GTh 1), or κυριακὰ λόγια (cf. Papias in Eusebius, *E.H.* 3.39.1), or possibly Λόγοι (τοῦ κυρίου) Ἰησοῦ (so also A. Polag, *Fragmenta Q* [Neukirchen: Neukirchener, 1982] 28: cf. Acts 20:35; *1 Clem* 13:1f.).
Robinson too is clearly sympathetic to the idea of an incipit containing the term λόγοι (with debate about what follows: cf. his 'Sayings Gospel', 379f., 388). Perhaps the nearest Q itself (i.e. as we have access to it from Matthew and Luke) gets to this is the saying in Q 6:47–49, where Q's Jesus refers to the importance of hearing and obeying his λόγοι: cf. Robinson, 'LOGOI SOPHON', 95, though he takes this as referring to a possible earlier collection of Jesus' words in the Great Sermon.

[44] For this idea, see p. 105 above in the discussion of genre.

seems to me questionable whether we can be more precise and say that such sayings collections are inherently sapiential. Of course wisdom ideas do often find expression in sayings collections, and indeed such collections are often the prime locus for articulating wisdom concepts. But one cannot necessarily reverse this and say that all such sayings collections, including Q, are inherently sapiential.

Thus, Robinson's argument is open to question from two different angles. First, when we consider his own examples, it is not at all clear that these necessarily belong together generically, despite their common self-description (at times, at least!) as λόγοι. As we have already noted, Robinson ranges very widely referring, for example, to the incipits in several of the *Testaments of the Twelve Patriarchs*, references in *ApocAdam*, in *1 Enoch*, as well as collections in Proverbs, Ecclesiastes, etc. But it is questionable how much generic similarity these collections reflect, despite the fact that they call themselves (or are called by others) λόγοι.[45] The word λόγοι itself is a very general one, and the referents in these cases are texts, or parts of texts, which many would regard as rather dissimilar generically. *ApocAdam* is a narrative presenting a survey of history, sliding over into an apocalyptic preview of the future. *1 Enoch* is, of course, composite though most would put its various constituent parts into the genre of apocalyptic rather than sapiential sayings collections.[46] The *Testaments of the Twelve Patriarchs* undoubtedly include much sapiential-type teaching, though the genre of the whole is usually regarded as that of a 'testament' which is distinct from that of a wisdom collection of sayings.[47] We could, of course, decide to label all

---

[45] See Sato, *Q und Prophetie*, 4; also A. Y. Collins, 'Son of Man Sayings', 371–3.

[46] Cf. above for a difference between wisdom and apocalyptic. I am well aware that such a radical distinction is questioned by some. And Robinson himself refers to a number of references to 'wisdom' in *1 Enoch*. Nevertheless, as Collins points out ('Son of Man Sayings', 372), this wisdom is similar to the mantic wisdom of Daniel and the Joseph cycle, and quite unlike the proverbial wisdom of Proverbs, Ecclesiastes, etc. Cf. n. 34 above.

[47] Cf. Robinson's own explicit rejection of the theory that Q is a 'testament' (so E. Bammel, 'Das Ende von Q', in *Verborum Veritas* [FS G. Stählin; Wuppertal: Brockhaus, 1970] 39–50): see his 'Bridging the Gulf', 164. Part of the problem with Bammel's thesis is whether the decisive 'testamentary' idea in Luke 22:29 belongs to Q, since there is no Matthean parallel to just this element. But Robinson does seem to work with a clear distinction between the genre of a testament and that of a sayings collection (though in 'LOGOI SOPHON', 107, he talks of 'some overlapping' between the genres).

these heterogeneous types as 'wisdom': but then we are back to the problem of making the category of so-called 'wisdom' too broad to be really useful.

Second, we may note that Robinson has chosen his examples of collections of λόγοι somewhat selectively. Not all collections of sayings, even with a 'title' λόγοι, are clearly sapiential. As we have already noted the word λόγοι itself is a very general one. Thus it is scarcely surprising to find that there are collections with some sort of heading as 'words' which one would barely describe as sapiential. There are for example instances where *prophetic* oracles are introduced by the heading 'words'. Thus Amos 1:1 introduces Amos' prophecies as 'the words of Amos' (LXX λόγοι Αμως). Hag 1:12 speaks of 'the words of Haggai the prophet' (τῶν λόγων Αγγαιου τοῦ προφήτου), referring to the totality of Haggai's prophetic message. So too the 'title' of the book of Jeremiah in the Hebrew MT is 'The words of Jeremiah' (דברי ירמיהו: LXX is different).[48] On the other hand, the historical account of Nehemiah is introduced as λόγοι Νεεμια, 'the words of Nehemiah' (2 Esd 11:1 LXX). One could again argue that 'wisdom' and 'prophecy' are not to be separated; but once again there is then the problem that 'wisdom' becomes too wide-ranging a term to have any usefulness at all. The fact that such a general word as λόγοι is used to introduce such a wide variety of literary texts thus suggests that the word itself is insufficient as a clear indicator about the generic nature of such texts at a more precise level than simply indicating that they are collections of 'utterances' of some sort (though in the case of Nehemiah they are barely that!). Thus it is doubtful if it can be shown that sayings collections as such, or collections called λόγοι, are intrinsically sapiential. In terms of the original 'roots' of the genre, it seems impossible to specify these with any precision simply on the basis of any characterisation of a collection as a sayings collection (with or without the term λόγοι to refer to it).

Robinson may well be right to identify one possible 'sub-genre' of the broad category of sayings collections in wisdom collections as evidenced in Prov 22–24, etc, the λόγοι σοφῶν. There are however further problems in identifying Q (or even part of Q) with this more precise sub-genre. Robinson, as we saw, took an

---

[48] Cf. too Jer 36:4, 10, 16, etc., referring to Jeremiah's prophecies. There are also many instances in the OT where 'words' refers to a more general collection of prophetic oracles (cf. 1 Sam 15:1), or to legal collections (cf. Exod 19:6; 20:1, etc.).

important cue from Bultmann's suggestion that one Q saying (Q 11:49–51) may have been a quotation from a lost wisdom document (cf. above). However, such a theory is now widely discarded: the oracle in Q 11:49–51 is seen as closely linked with the preceding woe in 11:47f., and the introductory 'therefore the Wisdom of God said' is seen as more likely to be an equivalent to 'therefore thus saith the Lord' in *prophetic* oracles.[49] Without such a starting point, it becomes rather harder to make the link between Q and specifically *sapiential* sayings collections. Robinson himself notes, quickly and in passing, that some of the references to collections of sayings which he has identified associate the collection in question with prophetic oracles.[50] The prophetic nature of so much of Q would seem to make it easier to link Q with a *prophetic* sayings collection.[51]

There are too a number of differences between Q and wisdom collections, as noted by Sato and others.[52] For example, the ascription of the Q sayings to particular 'charismatic' figures such as John the Baptist and Jesus is unlike the more general, experience-based sayings of wisdom collections which are effectively mostly anonymous;[53] similarly the Q sayings are directed to particular individuals in a specific situation, rather than being general observations about life in general. Connected with this too is the fact that the imperatives in exhortations in Q

[49] Cf. Sato, *Q und Prophetie* 152, and others: see p. 167 above. For the qualitative distinction between this kind of 'wisdom' material and the aphoristic wisdom sayings in Q, see Piper, *Wisdom*, 174, and also the discussion below.

[50] 'LOGOI SOPHON', 99f. on Justin, cf. *1 Apol* 63:14. *Dial* 139:5; 18:1 associate sayings of Jesus with sayings of the prophets.

[51] Cf. too Horsley, 'Logoi Prophētōn', esp. p. 201f. Horsley says: 'Robinson made it quite clear that the literary label or self-designation *logoi* was used far more broadly than for collections of wisdom sayings' (p. 201). I wonder whether Robinson's essay is quite so clear. He moves very quickly, and without explanation, from a variety of different collections called *logoi* ('LOGOI SOPHON', 95–100) to '*the* gattung (sing.) of sayings collections' (101–3), and the 'the Gattung itself' (103), which then becomes 'the' Gattung of the logoi sophon (111, after comparison with other wisdom collections). The possibility of different *Gattungen* within the broad *Gattung* of sayings collection is not really considered.

[52] Sato, *Q und Prophetie*, 4f., 106f.

[53] However, Kloppenborg, *Formation*, 256f., refers to the importance of a *named* sage as the source of many wisdom collections in Egyptian and other Near Eastern 'instructions'. Nevertheless, the appeals to personal authority, rather than to a common experience of life, as the ultimate ground in sayings such as Q 6:46 + 47–49; 10:16, as well as Q's overriding interest in the person of Jesus, distinguishes much of Q from the general tenor of the wisdom tradition.

regularly use the second person plural, whereas the wisdom tradition almost without exception uses the second person singular.[54] The eschatological nature of much of Q also shifts the contents of what is said in a decisively new direction, away from an experience-based look to the past and present to a revelation-based look to the future. And finally, the chronological, even 'biographical', nature of at least the start of Q (with the sequence of John's appearance, his preaching, perhaps Jesus' baptism, Jesus' temptations) is unlike the exclusive concentration on sayings alone, divorced from any concrete situation, which characterises so many of the wisdom sayings collections.[55]

Some of this critique relates less to the actual genre of the collection as such and more to the contents of the sayings themselves. However, any distinction between genre/form and content cannot be maintained with any rigidity.[56] I turn therefore to a consideration of the work of others who have claimed that Q is in some sense 'sapiential' by focusing on the contents of Q, looking first at the work of H. Koester.

Although clearly similar in one way to Robinson's theories about the genre of Q, Koester's theories about Q are in fact related rather more to the individual *contents* of Q at one level, though Koester then seeks to make deductions at the level of genre.[57] Koester accepts Robinson's view about the generic similarity between Q and GTh, provided that Q is purged of all futurist apocalyptic elements, especially the apocalyptic SM sayings. As we have seen, Koester argues that GTh and the earlier stage of Q represent a form of 'wisdom gospel', by which Koester appears to mean a document which is sapiential and kerygmatic, intelligible on its own and unrelated to the passion kerygma. Thus, Koester speaks of

> the authority of the word of wisdom as such, which rests in the assumption that the teacher is present in the word which he has spoken. If there is any 'Easter experience' to provide a Christology

---

[54] The point is made forcefully again by Zeller, 'Weisheitliche Grundschrift?', 397, repeating the results of his earlier discussion in his *Mahnsprüche*, esp. his second part and the conclusion on p. 142. Cf. also n. 31 above for this distinction as one of von Lips' features distinguishing wisdom from prophecy.

[55] Though Kloppenborg has shown that a 'testing story', similar in some ways to the temptation narrative, is not alien to wisdom sayings collections: see *Formation*, 256–62.

[56] See my *Reading*, 100.

[57] Koester himself makes clear his debt to Robinson in 'GNOMAI DIAPHORAI', 135; 'One Jesus', 186.

congenial to this concept of the *logoi*, it is here the belief in 'Jesus, the Living One' (incipit of the *Gospel of Thomas*).[58]

And in relation to the alleged early form of Q, Koester writes:

> Faith is understood as belief in Jesus' words, a belief which makes what Jesus proclaimed present and real for the believer. The catalyst which has caused the crystallisation of these sayings into a 'gospel' is the view that the kingdom is uniquely present in Jesus' eschatological preaching and that eternal wisdom about man's true self is disclosed in his words. The gnostic proclivity of this concept needs no further elaboration.[59]

Now such a description may well be apt when applied to GTh. It *may* also be apt if applied to the alleged early form of Q, if such a form of Q existed. And the 'gnostic proclivity' of the idea would not be disputed by many (even if there is endless debate about what should be termed 'gnostic'!). The problem here is whether such a view can really be called 'sapiential' in any meaningful sense of the word. Koester certainly excludes any kind of apocalyptic eschatology from such a view and hence, perhaps rather arbitrarily, excludes all the futurist eschatological parts of Q from the early pre-Q which he posits as lying behind Q and GTh. In this sense there is then no danger of trying to subsume futurist eschatology within the category of 'wisdom'. But simply because something is not futurist does not make it *ipso facto* 'sapiential'! The historical books of the OT are not wisdom writings simply by virtue of the fact that they display no overt interest in 'apocalyptic' eschatology. There seems to be an equally large qualitative difference between the 'gnostic proclivity' of faith in the secret sayings of a 'gnostic' redeemer such as the Jesus of GTh and the sapiential orientation of wisdom collections.[60] In the latter there is no 'revelatory' sense of the sayings. The teaching is based on experience of the world and open to all those who take the trouble to see and attempt to understand. Precisely the point which distinguishes wisdom from prophecy, namely that prophecy is based on divine revelation given to a

---

[58] 'GNOMAI DIAPHORAI', 135f.

[59] 'One Jesus', 186.

[60] I leave aside here the vexed question of how justified it is to describe GTh as 'gnostic'. Certainly the incipit makes it clear that GTh contains 'secret sayings' known to the chosen few and demanding interpretation. As such they represent at the very least a significant development from the wisdom tradition, as Robinson's own 'LOGOI SOPHON' essay makes clear, even if it is a development along a single trajectory.

specific individual whereas wisdom is based on common shared experiences of the world, must surely also distinguish 'wisdom' from 'gnosticism' (or at least the 'gnostic proclivity' outlined by Koester). Once again we could include such ideas within a broader category of 'wisdom' but, as before, the category would probably then cease to be meaningful since then almost anything could be regarded as 'sapiential'. The whole basis of Koester's 'gnostic proclivity' in GTh and in the alleged early stage of Q is that revelation is uniquely available in, and only in, the teaching of the revealer Jesus. The integral connection of the teaching with the person of Jesus, and the effective divorce of the teaching from what can be known by collective experience, thus effectively aligns such a proclivity with a 'prophetic' model and against a 'sapiential' model.

Koester's theories about the origins of Q are suggestive, though (as we argued above on pp. 67–8) in need of further support from a literary-critical point of view. His stress on the importance and value placed by Q on the teaching of Jesus, and the importance of Jesus himself as *the* teacher for Q, is fully justified (cf. above). But precisely this concentration on the figure of Jesus himself renders questionable his view that Q can then be regarded as 'sapiential' in some meaningful sense. Calling Q 'gnostic' may well be more confusing than helpful, though the parallels and similarities between Q and GTh are important. But little seems to be gained in the present discussion by describing them both as related in some way to a '*wisdom* gospel'.

We have already seen that an extremely important attempt to fill in some of the gaps of Koester's argumentation about the stratification of Q is provided in the work of Kloppenborg, seeking to identify strata within Q on literary-critical grounds. When such a division of the material has been made, with secondary additions to some of the speech complexes in Q identified and stripped away, the residue is, according to Kloppenborg, most appropriately labelled 'sapiential', as we have seen. Kloppenborg's analysis is undoubtedly one of the most well-argued and thoroughly grounded in contemporary Q studies. As such we have already had occasion to discuss many aspects of his overall theory, as well as his many detailed analyses. Thus I have already discussed, and offered some critique of, his theory that if we strip away secondary additions to some of the speech complexes in Q, we can recover an earlier stage in the history of the Q-*document* consisting of these five discourses, all belonging together in a single 'Ur-Q', or 'Q¹' (see pp. 71–3 above). Here however I wish to focus on the question of how far it is appropriate to label this material as in some sense 'sapiential'.

Kloppenborg bases this description of Q¹ on the large number of sapiential forms (rhetorical questions, apodoses expressing symmetry between act and consequence, appeals to nature, beatitudes, proverbs and wisdom sayings, τίς ἐξ ὑμῶν sayings, parables, etc.).[61] And by contrast with the other speech units and the Q² secondary additions which are (effectively) directed as prophetic threats against outsiders, the Q¹ strand is directed towards insiders within the Christian community.[62] Kloppenborg concedes that

> proverbs and wisdom sayings are also found in the judgment speeches (e.g., 7:35; 11:17b–18, 21–22; 11:33, 34a; 12:54–55; 17:37). But there is an important difference in their usage: these function not to reinforce ethical imperatives, but to undergird the pronouncements of judgment.[63]

This, however, begins to concede rather too much. For it tacitly admits that the 'sapiential' nature of individual sayings is not solely to do with their formal structure and individual contents considered in isolation, but also with their 'function' and their context, and hence, since meaning is so integrally related to context, their meaning within their given context. With this in mind it becomes highly debatable how far it really makes sense to describe the Q¹ layer as 'sapiential' and set it in antithesis to the 'prophetic' Q². In one sense of course there is a difference between the more polemical and the less polemical parts of Q, though whether this is best described as due to a difference in audience as 'outsiders' and 'insiders' respectively will be considered later.[64] But, for example, it is hard to describe the mission instructions of 9:58–10:16, even if purged of the polemical woes in 10:13–15, as 'sapiential', as opposed to 'prophetic'.[65] This section is certainly extremely specific in its

---

[61] Kloppenborg, *Formation*, 239.

[62] Kloppenborg, *Formation*, 238.

[63] Kloppenborg, *Formation*, 239.

[64] Horsley has criticised this aspect of Kloppenborg's overall theory on a number of occasions: see p. 72 above.

[65] See p. 72 above. Jacobson has shown the strong judgemental nature of the mission instructions and their implied threat to the recipients of the mission: cf. his *First Gospel*, 68f., summarising his earlier article 'Lc 10,2–16'. However, in

details and addressed to a very specific situation: it is thus not really a piece of general wisdom. Although it could be classed under the very general rubric of 'instruction',[66] and although it undoubtedly includes some sayings which, *if* isolated, could be regarded as wisdom maxims (e.g. 10:2, 7: see below), nevertheless it seems as a whole too specific to be regarded as 'sapiential' in any meaningful sense of the word.[67] Similarly in the Great Sermon in Q 6:20–49, the neat distinction between a 'sapiential', community-directed Q^1, contrasted with a 'prophetic', opponent-directed Q^2, seems to break down. Kloppenborg himself has to admit that the beatitudes, although using a sapiential form, break through the limits of the 'sapiential' in terms of their content.[68] Thus, in their context and with their present wording, they use a sapiential form to say something which is rather un-sapiential. So too the warnings at the end of the Sermon in 6:47–49 have probably far greater affinities with the warnings and threats of future judgement in Kloppenborg's Q^2 than Kloppenborg himself seems to allow.[69] Thus the warnings about the future are directed not only at outsiders but at insiders as well.

The content of several other alleged Q^1 sections is also rather un-sapiential. I have argued above that the whole section in Q 11:2–4, 9–13 is determined by a futurist eschatology,[70] as is also the section on Cares in Q 12:22–31, at least in its form as redacted by Q. The latter theory could of course be accommodated within Kloppenborg's thesis if some elements in Q 12:22–31 (e.g. the reference to the 'kingdom' in v. 31) could be assigned to Q^2 and

---

First Gospel, 140–9, he appears to have modified his view somewhat (cf. p. 160 n. 76 above). Nevertheless, his earlier argument shows that such ideas really dominate the whole of the mission charge.

[66] Kloppenborg's own term of the genre of Q^1, referring to various Jewish and non-Jewish parallels: *Formation*, 265–89.

[67] So also Zeller, 'Weisheitliche Grundscrift', 391; Sato, 'Prophetie oder Weisheit?', 399f. Sato also points to the broad parallel between Q's Jesus sending out his disciples and prophets sending others out with particular tasks in view (Amos 3:9; Jer 36:5f.; 51:59–64; cf. too 2 Ki 4:29–31). Also the instructions not to take money, staff or sandals have closer links with the symbolic actions of the prophets than with the wisdom tradition.

[68] Kloppenborg, *Formation*, 188f. cited above (p. 142 n. 10). Cf. too Sevenich-Bax, *Konfrontation*, 402, 404; Sato as in n. 38 above.

[69] See above, pp. 142–3; also Zeller, 'Weisheitliche Grundschrift', 399f.; Sato, 'Prophetie oder Weisheit?', 399; 'Wisdom Statements', 145.

[70] See pp. 152–5 above; cf. too Sato, 'Prophetie oder Weisheit?', 400.

stripped away to reach a Q^1.[71] And indeed several of the earlier, pre-redactional elements here do appear to be more sapiential at one level (cf. the appeals to nature in vv. 24, 26–28). Yet even here one must take note of how 'un-sapiential' the actual teaching is: the exhortations *not* to work, and *not* to make provisions for the future, contrast very violently with so much of the Jewish wisdom tradition which generally praises the conscientious worker and encourages wise and sensible provision for the future.[72]

Thus, from the alleged 'sapiential speeches in Q', several turn out to be rather un-sapiential in their content. It is no doubt right to draw some kind of distinction between the polemical and less polemical parts of Q; so too there is no doubt that some sapiential images and traditions are used here. But so often the sapiential, pre-redactional speeches turn out to be highly fragmentary, and/ or not clearly sapiential in their outlook. Kloppenborg's great merit is to have drawn attention to a wider body of comparable material in assessing the genre of Q, and he is right to point to the model of the 'instruction' as having important generic affinities with Q, at least at the level of a relatively broad genre.[73] However, this should not hide the great differences which still exist between the actual contents of Q and the contents of what I have chosen here to call 'wisdom' or 'sapiential'. It may therefore be misleading to speak of Q as 'sapiential', even in its formative stages.[74] Although there may be similarities between the structure and form of Q and that of other 'instructions' or other sayings collections, the actual *contents* of the specific instructions given seem to differ significantly and it is only at a high level of abstraction that Q can be called 'sapiential'.

In the works we have considered so far, there has been a tendency to leave the category of 'wisdom' a little fluid. This cannot be said of the work of Piper who, as we have seen, focuses on the category of 'aphoristic wisdom' in the Q-tradition and provides a very clear definition of what is under review. Piper sees

[71] Though Kloppenborg himself does not follow such a route: he treats the passage as a unity (*Formation*, 216–21). The significance of how the reference to the kingdom might affect the alleged 'sapiential' nature of the whole passage is recognised by von Lips, *Weisheitliche Traditionen*, 211f.

[72] Cf. Catchpole, *Quest*, 35, as cited above, p. 152.

[73] Though Zeller, 'Weisheitliche Grundschrift', disputes how close some of the parallels really are.

[74] I am however aware that such a negative conclusion may simply reflect the excessive narrowness of my own definition of 'wisdom' in this context: cf. the earlier discussion of what should count as 'wisdom' or 'sapiential'.

the essential nature of aphoristic wisdom as being an appeal to experience, to the regularity of the created order, with a view to trying to persuade the listeners of the correctness of what is proposed. This is by way of contrast with prophecy or eschatology which refer to radical innovation in the present order of things to make their point. Piper then finds a number of 'clusters' of aphoristic wisdom (e.g. in Q 11:9–13; 12:22–31; 6:37–41; 6:43–45; 12:2–9) with a similar structuring arrangement, suggesting a strong interest in aphoristic wisdom on the part of the editor(s) of this stage of the developing Q tradition and suggesting too that the function of the admonitions here is to persuade and not to coerce.[75] Piper also finds a number of isolated wisdom admonitions in Q.

Many of the comments made above in relation to Kloppenborg's work apply however to Piper's theories as well. We have had occasion already to refer to some of his analyses in some of the discussions of individual sections of Q treated earlier in this study. I have argued above, contra Piper (see pp. 149–55 above), that the sections in Q 11:9–13 and 12:22–31 are, at least in their redacted form, heavily eschatologically oriented. It is true that the tone of these sections is not as polemical as other parts of Q. In this sense Piper is right to call them 'persuasive' rather than polemical. And appeal *is* made to the regularity of the created order (e.g. in Q 12:24, 26–28 and Q 11:11f.). But still the main thrust is primarily eschatological: the reference to the certainty of receiving when asking, etc. (Q 11:9f.) does *not* reflect everyday experience, and seems to be more of a prophetic assertion than a sapiential insight; and the exhortation in Q 11:13 is (I argued earlier) primarily eschatologically oriented, as is the demand to seek the kingdom in Q 12:31, which in turn shifts the section as a whole away from the sapiential (see n. 71 above). So too the section in Q 12:2–9 is clearly eschatologically oriented (Q 12:8f. + 4f.). As with Kloppenborg, it might be possible to isolate a non-eschatological section in the pre-Q tradition, and indeed Piper makes no pretence to be delineating Q-redactional features.[76]

---

[75] Though Sato, 'Wisdom Statements', 151, has pointed out that a similar structuring of argumentation can be found in a wide range of literature, including prophetic texts. Hence he asks: 'Is this not a general rhetorical pattern more or less common elsewhere?'

[76] In Kloppenborg's theory, Q 12:2–12 is a unit which has undergone a secondary expansion in vv. 8–9 + 10: hence the earlier section is to be found in vv. 2–7 + 11f., and this, according to Kloppenborg, can be seen to be of a piece

Nevertheless, Piper does claim that these whole sections (e.g. in Q 12:22–31 and Q 12:2–9) are primarily concerned with themes of aphoristic wisdom rather than being eschatological, prophetic exhortations, and my own analysis offered here would suggest otherwise.

With regard to the isolated aphorisms, and indeed to some of the alleged clusters, it must also remain doubtful whether it is right to regard them in isolation from their present contexts. Several of them *can* be so isolated in the sense that they can be abstracted from their contexts and they seem to be able to stand on their own and make sense as some kind of 'proverb' or relatively banal statement about the way the world is. For example, Q 3:9, when taken in isolation, could be just saying that useless trees are cut down and burnt; Q 6:43–45 says that good trees produce good fruit, and bad trees bad fruit; Q 17:37 says that vultures gather round a corpse; Q 10:2 says that there are always too few helpers at harvest-time. However, one suspects that, in several instances, these allegedly independent sayings are closely tied to their contexts in Q. For example, the saying about the narrow door in Q 13:24[77] is probably integrally related in Q to the succeeding verses giving stern warnings of what is to come in the imminent future (see p. 191 above). Similarly, the statements in 3:9 and 17:37, referred to above, occur in the midst of eschatological warnings: the sayings are not necessarily general aphoristic proverbs seeking to persuade by their innate clarity and sweet reasonableness;[78] rather, they are more probably attempts to make even more vivid and threatening the dire warnings which the immediate context (i.e. 3:7–9 and 17:23–37) is trying to get across. It is thus difficult to believe that just a simple observation about life has been incorporated into a

---

with his 'Q¹'. But I argued earlier that vv. 8f. relate closely with vv. 4f., and v. 10 with vv. 2f. (See pp. 315–9 above.) Thus the alleged earlier cluster reduces to very little indeed. Piper makes no such attempt to distinguish between earlier and later elements in 12:2–9 but seeks to interpret the whole as a rhetorical unit. I have no objection at all to such an attempt; my point is simply that the material as a whole, with the strongly eschatological orientation of vv. 8f., *and* vv. 4f., is hardly that of aphoristic wisdom!

[77] Cf. Piper, *Wisdom*, 107ff.

[78] Pace Piper, *Wisdom*, 138ff. Cf. the challenge and the pressure inherent in the *uses* of such 'proverbs', as well set out by Beardslee, 'Uses'; cf. also Kloppenborg's description of the intensified nature of such 'wisdom' (see n. 38 above).

(rather alien) context to 'persuade' the listeners gently about the truth of what is being proposed. The language, in its context, is rather more violent.

Similarly, although other sayings can in theory be isolated from their context, and can be seen to make reasonable sense on their own (e.g. Q 6:40; 10:2; 10:7; 14:34f.), the question remains whether in fact it is right to isolate them in this way. The simple fact that they can be so abstracted does not constitute any proof that they were so abstracted before being put into their present context. Further, the Q context often changes the 'aphoristic' nature of the admonitions very considerably. For example, Q 6:43–45, when placed just before 6:46 and 6:47–49 ceases to be a piece of quiet gentle persuasion and becomes a warning backed up by the threat of fierce eschatological sanction! (Cf. p. 142 above.)[79] Piper can justifiably refer to several wisdom-type elements in Q. But it seems doubtful if one can see more than isolated elements. Again and again the Q context forces such wisdom features into a strongly eschatological mould, breaking out of the wisdom tradition and referring *not* to experience and the regularity of the world, but to the radical new order that is coming.

It is, of course, clear that in one way Q is extremely 'sapiential' in stressing the person of Wisdom, as we noted at the start of this chapter. Nevertheless, we must again take care with our own language. At one level this makes Q very positive about the figure of Wisdom; but that does not make Q sapiential as I have tried to define the term earlier. Rather, Q's use of Wisdom is to stress the *prophetic* aspect much more: Wisdom is for Q the agent who has sent out the *prophets* whose prophetic message has been rejected; Wisdom's messengers are *not* the sages bringing timeless wisdom in aphoristic proverbs. Solomon, the archetypal sage of the Jewish tradition, is indeed mentioned once in Q, but only once (Q 11:31); far more important is the prophetic nature of Q's envoys.[80] It is perhaps slightly ironic that for Kloppenborg, the

---

[79] Sato, 'Wisdom Statements', also seeks to show that a large number of allegedly 'wisdom' sayings occur in a context of prophetic warnings and admonitions. They are thus 'propheticised' in their present Q contexts.

[80] Robinson casts doubts on how far the Q Christians regarded their own activity, or that of Jesus or John the Baptist, as prophetic (see his 'Weisheit oder Prophetie?', 388). He refers to Q 7:26 which claims that John is *more* than a prophet, and 7:28 which implies that even the smallest in the kingdom is greater still; Q 11:49f. implies that the series of persecuted prophets only reaches up to Zachariah; Q 16:16 implies that the Law and the prophets only

Wisdom texts (Q 7:35; 11:49, etc.) are assigned to the 'prophetic' Q^2 stage, and not to the 'sapiential' Q^1 stage.[81]

Piper is one of the few scholars to have seen the problem of the distinction between the allegedly 'sapiential' material and the material which actually mentions 'Wisdom', and to have struggled with it. He refers to 'an epistemological difference between the emphasis on experiential knowledge in the aphoristic material and the implication of a "revelation" to be presented by those who represent divine Sophia'.[82] This is effectively not far from my earlier distinction between wisdom and prophecy. Later Piper does try to argue that this 'epistemological tension ... is one which can be easily over-stated',[83] as he seeks to integrate the two modes of argumentation together. In the end, however, it is notable to what extent the aphoristic wisdom has to be subordinated to a rather different, i.e. eschatological, outlook as the underlying one: 'The persuasive power of sapiential insight must not be underrated, even though experience of the world alone may not be sufficient to originate the line of argument, and even though the argument may be logically dependent on the authority of a more funda-mental interpretation of reality.'[84] But if the sapiential insight is

---

go as far as John; and Q 10:24 suggests a clear distinction between the addressees and the prophets of the past. 'Die Q-Gemeinde sah sich also wohl bereits in der Erfüllungszeit, wo es keiner Propheten mehr bedurfte.'

However, I argued earlier that Q 7:26 should not be taken as denying that John was a prophet: he *is* a prophet *and* more than a prophet (see p. 129 above). Q 11:49f. may only imply that physical violence and death is a feature of the past (as well as being under the constraints of being spoken by the pre-Easter Jesus: see pp. 308–14 above). As we shall see in ch. 12 below, Q retains a belief in the validity of the Law, so that Q 16:16 cannot mean that the Law has come to an end (cf. Q 16:17!): hence it is unlikely that the verse should be taken in Q as implying that 'the prophets' are also a thing of the past alone. And Q 10:24 need only refer to a distinction between the prophets of the past and the addressees. Robinson is quite right to refer to a belief in Q that the present is an 'Erfüllungszeit' (cf. pp. 209–10 above), but that need not mean that Q thought that the era of 'prophets' was now over. As we saw earlier, Q probably regarded John and Jesus as in the line of Wisdom's prophetic envoys, and to a certain extent the Q Christians continue the work of Jesus (cf. Q 10:16).

[81] The point is noted by Jacobson, *First Gospel*, 57. However, the terminological link is stressed by Robinson, 'Weisheit oder Prophetie?', 388.

[82] *Wisdom*, 174.

[83] *Wisdom*, 178.

[84] *Wisdom*, 181.

'logically dependent' on 'a more fundamental interpretation of reality', is this not an admission that Q, or even the smaller parts of Q analysed by Piper, are *not* basically sapiential at all?

What then can we say by way of conclusion on the question of the theme of wisdom motifs in Q? There is no doubt that Q does contain elements which most would regard as 'sapiential' in some sense, i.e. appealing to experience, to the regularity of the created world, etc. and without reference to any new situation brought by prophetic revelation and/or eschatology. Thus, for example, the saying about the blind leading the blind (Q 6:39) or salt losing its taste (Q 14:34) seem clearly to fall into this category.[85] Many other possible examples of 'wisdom' in Q (e.g. as listed by Carlston or Edwards) are rather more dubiously 'sapiential'. Several such sayings are clearly placed in an eschatological, or other specific, context (cf. Q 11:9; 11:13; 12:33; 12:34); others are clearly somewhat 'anti-sapiential' in what they say (cf. above on the beatitudes, also 9:60; 6:32a; 14:26).[86]

Insofar as the analysis offered here is valid, then it would seem that any sapiential elements in the tradition have been overlaid by a powerful eschatological/prophetic element which uses any sapiential traditional elements to build up a powerful critique against the present world order and against all those who wish to cling to that order. In one sense this might support Kloppenborg's thesis of a prophetic Q[2] succeeding a sapiential Q[1]. I am however sceptical about how successfully we can reconstruct layers of the tradition behind our Q with such accuracy. I am also more sceptical than Kloppenborg about the extent of such 'sapiential' traditions: on several occasions they seem to be far less extensive than Kloppenborg argues, and many seem to be 'prophetic', rather than 'sapiential'.

It would seem therefore that most of the sapiential elements in Q lie in the background for Q. The interest of Q (i.e. the 'final' form of Q) seems to have left behind the wisdom category and focuses more on prophetic warnings and eschatology. One can call this the 'radical wisdom of the kingdom' if one wishes, but I suspect that in so doing the term 'wisdom' itself is in danger of losing its meaning and becoming such an inclusive catch-all term that it encompasses almost anything. If we keep to a stricter

---

[85] Perhaps too the Golden Rule in Q 6:31; also Q 6:38, 40; 11:34; 12:25.

[86] For the stark difference between the ethos encouraged in Q 9:60 and 14:26 and the wisdom tradition in relation to the family, see von Lips, *Weisheitliche Traditionen*, 224.

definition of wisdom then perhaps Q is rather less 'sapiential' than many in the recent past have supposed. In terms of genre, Q is undoubtedly to be seen as some kind of sayings collection; and there are sapiential sayings collections. But there are also other kinds of sayings collections as well, such as prophetic collections. And in many respects Q shows greater affinity with prophetic collections than sapiential ones.[87]

---

[87] I am not however arguing that Q is to be seen as some kind of resurrection of 'the' genre of an OT prophetic book (so Sato: see the powerful critique of Robinson, 'Weisheit oder Prophetie?'; also the review of Sato's book by Downing in *Bib* 72 [1991] 127–32.) But such precise generic parallels may not be possible. All I am arguing is that, on the basis of the (admittedly somewhat crude) distinctions outlined above between 'wisdom' and 'prophecy', large parts of Q are to be aligned more with the latter than the former, and not even appeals to stratification models necessarily change this view very much. Certainly in terms of 'inner form' as opposed to 'outer form' (cf. the discussion of Wellek and Warren noted above on p. 106 in the discussion of genre), i.e. in terms of 'attitude, tone and purpose', Q seems to have closer affinities with prophetic writings than sapiential ones.

11

Discipleship in Q

In the course of the discussion of Q's eschatology (ch. 5 above), I considered briefly the sections on prayer in Q 11:2–4, 9–13 and on cares in Q 12:22–31. I argued there that a prime concern of the Q editor(s) was to try to direct the attention of the readers/ audience to the overriding importance of the work of proclaiming the imminence of the kingdom. In the course of that exhortation, one prominent feature is a tendency to downgrade the importance of material concerns such as food and clothing: the body is more than food (cf. Q 12:22) and God knows His children's needs in this respect before they even ask so that (by implication) prayer should be directed to other ends than simply asking for the basic necessities of life (Q 12:30f.). This attitude is also closely related to the first temptation (Q 4:3f.), where Q's Jesus refuses to change stones into bread and asserts 'Man shall not live by bread alone'. This positive lack of concern about material needs is clearly also related to the Q mission charge (Q 10:2–11) where the disciples are sent out with virtually nothing by way of material support: they are to take no food, no staff, no sandals. This extraordinary set of instructions is interpreted by some as casting direct light on the life-style of (some) Christians who may have obeyed these instructions to the letter. This is above all the case in the macro-thesis of G. Theissen concerning the existence of 'wandering charismatics' in the early church, and in the theories of P. Hoffmann.[1] It is these which we shall

[1] In relation to Q studies, Theissen's most important essays are his articles 'Wanderradikalismus. Literatursoziologische Aspekte der Überlieferung von Worten Jesu im Urchristentum', *ZThK* 70 (1973) 245–71; '"Wir haben alles verlassen" (Mc. X.28). Nachfolge und soziale Entwurzelung in der jüdisch-palästinischen Gesellschaft des 1. Jahrhunderts n. Ch.', *NovT* 19 (1977) 161–96, both reprinted in his *Studien zur Soziologie des Urchristentums* (WUNT 19; Tübingen: Mohr, 1979) 79–105, 106–41. Also important is his 'Gewaltverzicht und Feindesliebe (Mt 5,38–48/Lk 6,27–38) und deren sozialgeschichtlicher Hintergrund', *Studien*, 160–97. All three essays are now available in English

consider in this chapter, together with an attempt to discern what
may lie behind the activity which is presupposed. I consider first
the phenomenon itself.

1. The Phenomenon

Theissen's approach is more general than Hoffmann's. Theissen
does not make quite such specific suggestions as Hoffmann about
the social and political *Sitz im Leben* presupposed by these gospel
traditions; moreover, Theissen includes a rather wider body of
material in his discussion than just Q. However, a fundamental
point of agreement between Theissen and Hoffmann is that the
instructions of the Q mission charge, and other related sayings,
reflect the life-style of a group of Christians who obeyed them
literally. For Theissen, these 'wandering charismatics' formed the
nucleus of a very powerful and influential group within early
Christianity. Theissen adduces a very large number of texts in
early Christian literature, seeking to show that the phenomenon
of '*Wanderradikalismus*' was extremely widespread. Theissen sees
these wandering charismatics reflected in the sayings about the
mobile prophets in *Did* 11, in Markan sayings such as Mark 1:16–
20; 2:14; 3:13ff.; 6:7–13; 9:41; 10:28–30, in Matthean traditions
such as Matt 10:23; 10:40f. as well as in Q sayings such as Q 6:22f.;
9:57–60; 10:2ff.; 11:47–51; 12:22–31; 14:26, etc.[2] These Christians,
whom Theissen sees as the bearers of the '*Logienüberlieferung*'
(which is clearly considerably wider than the '*Logienquelle*'!),
obeyed the commands quite literally, leaving their families and
their possessions to preach the Christian message; and it is
precisely because of this that the sayings in the gospel tradition
have been preserved. Theissen has also referred to a large
number of similar patterns of behaviour (involving uprooting
from established social patterns of behaviour) amongst several
other groups within first-century Palestine suffering under a
variety of severe social and economic pressures.[3] Whether

---

translation in his *Social Reality and the Early Christians* (Edinburgh: T. & T. Clark,
1993). His overall theories are presented in more compact form in his *The First
Followers of Jesus. A Sociological Analysis of the Earliest Christianity* (ET London:
SCM, 1978). For Hoffmann, see his *Studien*, 312ff.; also his 'Tradition' and his
'Redaction of Q and the Son of Man'.

[2] See especially his *Social Reality*, 145f. n. 62 (= *Studien*, 187f., n. 62).

[3] Theissen, 'Wir haben alles verlassen', = *Social Reality*, 60–93.

these parallels drawn by Theissen help in the discussion of Q remains to be seen.

A more specific *Sitz im Leben* of the Q Christians is suggested by Hoffmann. According to Hoffmann, the life-style of home-lessness adopted by the Q Christians was intended as an acted 'sign' of their message: their lack of equipment implied a total trust in God and a complete lack of defence. Their message was one of the imminent arrival of the kingdom, and of 'peace' (Q 10:5). According to Hoffmann, this message of 'peace' is to be interpreted against the concrete political realities of the events in Palestine leading up to, or during, the Jewish revolt of 66–70.[4] In this period of increasing violence and social unrest, the Q-'group' advocated its message of peace, of non-violence, and of love of enemies (i.e. the Romans), in part through its life-style by practising what it preached and displaying visibly what it was seeking to advocate. Hoffmann's suggestions about such a specific *Sitz im Leben* for Q have been welcomed by many,[5] even if criticised by others (cf. below).

A rather different approach has been suggested by others who have argued that the life-style described in the mission charge (and possibly implied elsewhere) is extremely close to that of Cynics in this period. Those who adopted a Cynic way of life led

[4] Hoffmann's views about the precise relation of Q's redaction to the Jewish revolt have varied over time. In his earlier *Studien*, he dates Q in the period *before* the revolt: cf. 'die Boten treten in den Jahren vor dem jüdischen Aufstand gegen Rom auf' (p. 326), and he follows Hengel in interpreting the command to love one's enemies (Q 6:27ff.) as part of an anti-'Zealot' *Tendenz* (p. 75). I have tried to show earlier that the 'enmity' envisaged and experienced by Q may be rather less tangible, and less violent. In his later 'Tradition' article, Hoffmann has broadened out the proposed *Sitz im Leben* to include social and economic pressures faced by the mass of the Jewish population: he speaks of the 'wirtschaftliche Not' and 'die Konflikte im Volk selbst' (p. 80) and 'die Unterpriviligierte in der damaligen Gesellschaft' (p. 75) suffering in the increasingly severe economic climate. Thus, Hoffmann rightly asserts that the political and social factors cannot be divorced from each other. However, his most recent 'Redaction of Q and the Son of Man' article represents a further significant shift: Hoffmann now suggests that Q's redaction could be dated to the time of the revolt itself, possibly even after the fall of Jerusalem (cf. p. 192: 'The saying [Q 11:49–51] looks back to the vain efforts on Israel's behalf and reflects the imminently expected, and perhaps already completed (?), destruction of Jerusalem in the framework of the deuteronomistic view of history as the consequence of the rejection of the envoys' [the question mark is Hoffmann's own]).

[5] Lührmann, 'Liebet eure Feinde', 437; Sato, *Q und Prophetie*, 312; cf. Kosch, *Tora*, 294, 423, with further references.

an itinerant existence, having no money and begging from others. Further, some have argued that a significant part of the sayings of Q show a remarkable similarity to sayings attributed to Cynic teachers. A discussion of this proposal will occupy us in the later part of this chapter.

Theissen's overall thesis of the presence and influence of 'wandering charismatics' within early Christianity has been much debated with a certain amount of criticism levelled against various aspects of his general theory.[6] As already noted, Theissen goes far wider than the limits of the Q tradition to find his supporting evidence, and he explicitly denies that his reconstruction of the social situation of this early Christian phenomenon is to be limited to Q.[7] For the present purposes, I shall however confine attention primarily to the Q tradition. Thus the question of whether, for example, Theissen is right to interpret traditions such as Mark 10:28–30 in terms of *Wanderradikalismus* is not directly relevant to our purposes in seeking to illuminate the possible *Sitz im Leben* of the Q material;[8] so too I shall not consider in detail the question of whether Theissen is correct in seeing virtually all the leaders of the earliest Christian comunities (the Twelve, Stephen and the Hellenists, etc.) as wandering charismatics.[9] Such a reconstruction is probably too one-sided and pushing the evidence further than it will go.[10] Rather more relevant here is the fact that Theissen, as often as not, fails to provide any tradition-critical or redaction-critical discussion of the relevant materials.[11] Theissen generally refers to the 'oldest traditions' of the '*Logienüberlieferung*'; and yet in his *First Followers*, the only criterion given for distinguishing earlier from later

---

[6] Cf. Schottroff & Stegemann, *Jesus von Nazareth*; W. Stegemann, 'Wanderradikalismus im Urchristentum? Historische und theologische Auseinandersetzung mit einer interessanten These', in W. Schottroff & W. Stegemann, *Der Gott der kleinen Leute* (München: Chr. Kaiser, 1979) 94–120; H.-W. Kuhn, 'Nachfolge nach Ostern', in D. Lührmann & G. Strecker (eds), *Kirche* (FS G. Bornkamm; Tübingen: Mohr, 1980) 105–32. For a critique from the side of sociological studies, see Elliott, 'Social-Scientific Criticism'; and for a strong critique of the sociological theory (i.e. functionalism) implicit in Theissen's work, see Horsley, *Sociology*, esp. ch. 3. See too Uro, *Sheep*, 18f.

[7] See n. 2 above.

[8] See n. 14 below, p. 359.

[9] See his *First Followers*, 8–10.

[10] Uro, *Sheep*, 127f.; Horsley, *Sociology*, 46.

[11] Kuhn, 'Nachfolge', 122; Stegemann, 'Wanderradikalismus', 100; Uro, *Sheep*, 19.

traditions is that of excluding material which is of 'Hellenistic origin'.[12] Clearly more care is needed to distinguish earlier from later, pre-redactional from redactional, even within material that is not clearly of 'Hellenistic' origin.

Despite these caveats, it is still the case that the strongest evidence for Theissen's reconstruction is provided by passages from Q. Q's version of discipleship is very radical, extremely harsh and painted in very black-and-white terms. Certainly in comparison with Mark, the picture in Q is far more extreme. We have already noted the existence of the mission instructions in Q where the missionaries are told to take nothing at all for their journey: in Mark at least they are allowed a staff (Mark 6:8). So too the sayings about leaving family and home behind are rather different in Mark and in Q. In Q the break seems to be total and extreme: 'If anyone does not hate his father and mother . . . he cannot be my disciple' (Q 14:26).[13] In Mark 10:28–30 the break seems to be one that leads to another form of settled existence: giving up one 'house' will lead to incorporation into another social structure.[14] In Q such a settled existence is not mentioned. In many other respects, Q's vision of discipleship seems to brook no mediating middle road: the disciples *must* take up the cross (Q 14:27: in Mark 8:34 the exhortation is more concessive — 'Let him take up his cross').[15] We have already seen that in Q the saying about being for or against Jesus (Q 11:23) is formulated differently from Mark (Mark 9:40): in Mark the version of the

[12] *First Followers*, 3. Cf. Stegemann, ibid. Horsley also refers to the somewhat ironical situation whereby Theissen excludes 'Hellenistic' material from the earliest strata of the gospel tradition, and yet finds alleged examples of 'wandering radicals' from Hellenistic texts about Paul and Barnabas operating in Hellenistic churches, as well as possible analogies to the itinerant radicals in Hellenistic philosophers such as Cynics (*Sociology*, 45, 47).

[13] The Lukan form is very widely accepted as more original in this respect: see Fitzmyer, *Luke*, 1063; Schulz, *Q*, 446; Uro, *Sheep*, 129 and many others.

[14] See Stegemann, 'Wanderradikalismus', 107–10. Theissen's reply (*Social Reality*, 147 [= *Studien*, 189]) is to argue that Mark 10:29 is not to be taken literally (because of the reference to a hundred-fold). The reference to a hundred-fold mothers clearly indicates that the language cannot be completely literal (cf. Kuhn, 'Nachfolge', 125). But the reference to 'lands' in Mark 10:30 is less clearly metaphorical; and hence the metaphorical nature of the language may be confined to the description of the new 'relatives'. The Markan disciple does appear to be offered a new settled existence in a way which the Q disciple is not. See Lührmann, *Markusevangelium*, 176; and his 'Gospel of Mark', 70.

[15] Cf. Lührmann, *Markusevangelium*, 152.

saying given accepts neutrality as really support for Jesus' cause; in Q neutrality is condemned (cf. p. 290 above).

Thus the model outlined by Theissen of wandering charismatics who have left everything behind, including possessions, family and livelihoods, can find considerable support from the Q tradition in the gospels (if perhaps slightly less support from elsewhere in Christian literature, for example, in Mark). It does therefore seem reasonable to assume that, given the fact that these traditions were preserved in Q, at least some Christians may have taken them literally, so that it is appropriate to think of the presence of such itinerant disciples in any Q 'community'.[16] On the other hand, one must also say that this extreme view of discipleship evidently did not apply to all the followers in any Q 'community' or 'group'.[17] Even within the Q mission discourse itself, some of the instructions evidently have in mind other people supporting wandering missionaries: cf. Q 10:2, where the exhortation seems to be directed at those with*in* a community who are sending *others* out from their midst.[18] Similarly, the instructions about receiving hospitality clearly presuppose the existence of groups with*in* the population supporting the Christian preachers. A number of other passages in Q imply that the people addressed are, if not well-to-do, at least not destitute. Warnings about storing up treasure on earth (Q 12:33f.) or against serving mammon (Q 16:13), only make sense if directed against those who have a certain amount of money and/or possessions.[19] Similarly the exhortation to lend to those who ask without expecting any return (which reduces to an exhortation to give freely: see pp. 305–6 above) presupposes an audience who have the wherewithal to give money away. One must not therefore make the situation presupposed too uniform.

What though lies behind this proposed (and, one presumes, partly practised) ascetic life-style in Q? What is the ethos, the underlying ethical principle of a life of *Wanderradikalismus*? Or is it right to think of any 'ethos' at all (in the sense of an ethical

---

[16] I use the word 'community' very loosely here since it is clear that itinerancy at one level excludes belonging to any community, at least in any geographically fixed sense, almost by self-definition.

[17] For this, see Kuhn, 'Nachfolge', *passim*. So too in Theissen's global reconstruction, the 'wandering charismatics' are supplemented by 'sympathisers in local communities': see *First Followers*, 17–23.

[18] See Zeller, 'Redaktionsprozesse', 404; Uro, *Sheep*, 113.

[19] Zeller, 'Redaktionsprozesse', 407f.

decision freely chosen) in this connection? In other words, is the life-style recommended a voluntary one? Or is it simply a matter of adjusting one's attitude to what is the case already? I consider first Hoffmann's view that the behaviour of the Christians is related to the activities of nationalists associated with the outbreak of the Jewish revolt in 66–70 CE.

2. Opposition to 'Zealotism'?

It is rather doubtful if Hoffmann's suggestion of Christians supporting an anti-'Zealot' 'peace' movement in the period before the Jewish revolt can be sustained.[20] The interpretation of the 'peace' greeting (Q 10:5) to refer to political peace by contrast with violence and war is probably too restricted and narrow. The parallel greetings in Q 10:5 and 10:9 suggest that the exhortation that 'peace' be in/on a certain house is to be seen as equivalent to the announcement of the imminence of the Kingdom.[21] Thus the 'peace' greeting should probably be interpreted in terms of a much broader set of ideas than simply the cessation of violence.[22] Hoffmann refers to a passage in Josephus *War* 4.128–134, describing some who were suing for peace in the turbulent conditions of the Jewish revolt, to illustrate the situation of the Q Christians.[23] It may not be appropriate to say that Josephus is talking here of relatively well-to-do elements within Jewish society who are scarcely comparable to the Q Christians;[24] but it is still the case that Josephus is talking about the time during the revolt itself, and if one dates Q to a period prior to the war, such a parallel has little force.[25] There are now also well-known criticisms about the existence of any kind of 'Zealot' 'party' prior to the time of the revolt,[26] and it thus

[20] For critiques, see Kloppenborg, *Formation*, 183, 254–6; Uro, *Sheep*, 139f.
[21] Laufen, *Doppelüberlieferungen*, 540, n. 546.
[22] Uro, *Sheep*, 139; Theissen, *Social Reality*, 48 (= *Studien*, 94 = 'Wanderradikalismus', 260).
[23] *Studien*, 74; 'Tradition', 77.
[24] So Schottroff, *Jesus*, 80f.; see the response by Theissen, *Social Reality*, 153, n. 75 (= *Studien*, 194f.), and Hoffmann, 'Tradition', 79: the statement of Josephus need only be taken as evidence of *one* party campaigning for peace.
[25] Uro, *Sheep*, 139f. It then clearly becomes quite critical what precise period Hoffmann has in mind: cf. n. 4 above.
[26] See S. Zeitlin, 'Zealots and Sicarii', *JBL* 82 (1961) 395–399; M. Smith, 'Zealots and Sicarii: Their Origin and Relations', *HTR* 64 (1971) 1–19; R. A. Horsley, 'Josephus and the Bandits', *JSJ* 10 (1979) 37–63; 'The Sicarii. Ancient

becomes correspondingly more difficult to conceive of a corresponding 'peace' party prior to the outbreak of the revolt in 66 CE.

This critique would be lessened if one were to accept Hoffmann's latest suggestion of Q's final redaction being dated to the time of the revolt itself, possibly even after 70 CE (cf. above). Such a late dating does however seem extremely improbable. I have argued earlier that Q's eschatological statements, including 11:49–51 and 13:34f., are not to be interpreted as a fatalist reflection on Israel's final and definitive rejection with no hope for the future: rather, they are a desperate plea to the Jewish people to change their ways before it is too late (see ch. 6 above). This certainly seems to exclude the possibility that, for example, Q 13:34f. is looking back on the fall of Jerusalem as an event in the past and interpreting it as God's final and definitive judgement. The whole point of Q 13:35b seems to be to offer a ray of hope for the future. But even a date only slightly earlier than 70 CE seems improbable. For example, the imagery used in the eschatological warnings of Q 17:23ff. does not paint a picture of an ever-worsening crisis situation in political terms. Rather, the picture is one of supreme *normality* (cf. p. 295 above) and what the section seems to want to do is to *arouse* an awareness of the potentially critical nature of the present. Thus, despite Hoffmann's arguments, a date for Q some time before the Jewish revolt still seems preferable.

Other facets of Hoffmann's theory are also unconvincing. Hoffmann finds anti-Zealot ideas in the warning against 'blind guides' (Q 6:39) and in the criticism of those who do not produce fruits worthy of repentance (Q 6:43f.), viz. love of enemies and rejection of violence. However, as Kloppenborg says, if this is anti-Zealot polemic it is 'highly oblique: nothing in the speech touches on the principal political tenets of the Zealot movement'.[27] The other main passage appealed to by Hoffmann is the third temptation (Q 4:6–8) where Q's Jesus refuses to try to seize political power. However, as others have pointed out, Jesus'

Jewish Terrorists', *JR* 59 (1979) 435–58; 'The Zealots: Their Origin, Relationships and Importance in the Jewish Revolt', *NovT* 28 (1986) 159–92; Horsley and J. S. Hanson, *Bandits, Prophets and Messiahs. Popular Movements in the Time of Jesus* (Minneapolis: Winson, 1985). See the summary of the debate in Horsley, *Sociology*, 51f.

[27] Kloppenborg, *Formation*, 183.

reply here ('You shall worship the Lord your God and Him only shall you serve') is in fact thoroughly in line with 'Zealot' ideology: cf. the slogan of Judas the Galilean in Josephus *Ant.* 18.23 'God alone is our ruler and master'.[28] Thus, the theory that the Q Christians were consciously proposing a peaceful alternative to the warring aims of Jewish nationalism in a 'Zealot' party seems unconvincing.

Theissen does not discuss the principles underlying the ethos of *Wanderradikalismus* in great detail, and certainly does not make such specific suggestions as Hoffmann does. The closest parallel to the behaviour presupposed Theissen finds in that of the Cynic wandering preachers.[29] In his 'Wir haben alles verlassen' essay, Theissen refers to parallels amongst several different groups in first-century Jewish Palestinian society who display comparable life-styles,[30] though it seems to be the Cynic model which Theissen finds to be the closest, at least at the sociological level.[31] Thus, as with the Cynics, Christian *Wanderradikalismus* is to be seen as an expression of freedom from the cares of the world: the renunciation involved is an essentially voluntary act.[32] Yet is such an assumption justified? I consider now

[28] Zeller, 'Die Versuchung Jesu in der Logienquelle', *TTZ* 89 (1980) 61–73, p. 69; Kloppenborg, *Formation*, 256.

[29] *Social Reality*, 44 (= *Studien*, 90 = 'Wanderradikalismus', 256) 146–8 (= *Studien*, 188–190), drawing heavily on the picture of the ideal Cynic in Epictetus 3.22. Cf. too *First Followers*, 14f.

[30] See n. 3 above. However, the value of many of these as genuine parallels to the phenomenon of Christian itinerant radicalism in other groups within Jewish society as sketched out by Theissen in this essay is rather doubtful. As Horsley points out (*Sociology*, 53f.), Theissen often confuses the phenomenon to be explained and the explanation in terms of socio-economic factors. For the Christian group, the social rootlessness is the result of a freely chosen decision; for others (e.g. beggars, emigrants), it is the result of other pressures. The true parallel to the Christian group should be any who have *chosen* to adopt such a way of life. One parallel might then be the members of the Qumran community, although they did not become homeless: rather they gave up their old homes to join a new settled community.

[31] 'Since the ethic of the Cynics was spread by itinerant philosophers, it will be permissible to conclude, by analogy, that the people who passed on the Jesus tradition belonged to a comparable sociological group' (*Social Reality*, 44), though he immediately goes on to say: 'This conclusion by analogy is based on structural similarities, not on historical links between the two movements'. See also n. 44 below. The possible links with Cynics are discussed later in this chapter.

[32] *Social Reality*, 148 (= *Studien*, 190): 'Their very way they live is a sign of liberty'. Cf. too Stegemann, 'Wanderradikalismus', 103.

the question of the voluntary nature of the life-style apparently adopted.

3. A voluntary and distinctive life-style?

Both L. Schottroff and W. Stegemann have questioned the interpretation of Theissen, Hoffmann and others in relation to just this point. Stegemann (perhaps misleadingly) calls Theissen's view the 'Cynic' interpretation (meaning apparently only that the renunciation concerned is voluntary). More significantly, he and Schottroff have argued that, rather than being voluntary, the poverty of the missionaries simply reflects the general poverty of the population as a whole and the fact that the Q missionaries share this lot with others.[33] Thus, the message of the Q Christians shows them not to be speaking at the people, but at one with the people — in their common poverty. The exhortations not to worry about food, etc. are not to be seen as exhortations to become poor: the missionaries and their audience are poor already; rather, the point is to be free from cares, and in this way to find a way to overcome the grinding poverty that besets everyday life. Stegemann, in fact, argues that the 'Cynic' type model (i.e. voluntary renunciation of wealth) is only a feature of Luke's literary production.[34] It appears, he claims, in Luke's redaction of Q and is a highly stylised picture, confined in Luke's story to the pre-Easter period and serving to act as a critique of well-to-do Christians in the radically changed social conditions of Luke's day when Christians were no longer so poverty-stricken. Thus, for Stegemann, it is wrong to look for an 'ethos' of *Wanderradikalismus* in Q: there is 'kein Ethos der Heimatlosigkeit',[35] since the life-style is not chosen voluntarily by a free ethical choice but is endured with the vast majority of the poor peasant population of Palestine.

Such a view must again be regarded as somewhat one-sided and not applicable to the whole of Q. At times the details of Stegemann's argumentation are questionable. For example, he has to ascribe the Lukan version of the saying about 'hating' one's father and mother, etc. in Luke 14:26 to LkR and to take the milder version in Matt 10:37 (which speaks of loving parents

---

[33] Schottroff, *Jesus*, 66f.; Stegemann, 'Wanderradikalismus', 111ff.
[34] Stegemann, 'Wanderradikalismus', 115f., developed more in his contribution to ch. 3 of Schottroff & Stegemann, *Jesus*.
[35] Stegemann, 'Wanderradikalismus', 115.

more than Jesus) as more original. This is, however, improbable: the Lukan version is almost certainly more original and hence the element of active renunciation seems hard to avoid.[36] Similarly the instructions given to the Q missionaries clearly suggest that the latter are to be in a state very different from that of the ordinary person. If indeed they were not, it remains unclear why specific instructions are given at all! So too it is assumed in the mission instructions that the itinerant missionaries will find a welcome in some places and be given shelter and food: at the very least this implies that shelter and food among the rest of the population is available to be given. It is debatable how destitute the 'ordinary people' of this period were (though it is likely that economic and political pressures were such as to make 'normal' life quite oppressive for many).[37] Nevertheless it is not clear that the ordinary people were as totally destitute as Schottroff and Stegemann imply. Hoffmann has shown that the ban on equipment in the Q mission charge is quite unlike anything else at this period in forbidding staff and sandals.[38] Thus there seems to be more involved than simply assuming an attitude of mind (care-free-ness) that will 'overcome' the stark realities of present existence.

Other elements within Q also suggest that this life-style of homelessness, etc. is unlike that of the rest of society, and indeed that of the people to whom the exhortations are addressed. We have already noted the Q warnings about storing up treasure on earth (Q 12:33f.), about serving mammon (Q 16:13), as well as the exhortation to lend, which all suggest an audience which is not destitute. It is thus hard to see the life-style commended to,

[36] See n. 13 above; also Kosch, *Tora*, 354, for a strong critique of Stegemann here.

[37] Theissen, *Social Reality*, 60–93 (= 'Wir haben alles verlassen'); also Horsley's work on banditry, etc. (cf. his *Bandits*). However, such a view is not unanimously shared: see, for example, T. E. Schmidt, *Hostility to Wealth in the Synoptic Gospels* (JSNTSS 15; Sheffield: JSOT Press, 1987) esp. ch. 1.

[38] Hoffmann, *Studien*, 312–8. This is recognised by Stegemann, 'Wander-radikalismus', 112f. But Stegemann then seems to imply that one can forget about the command to take no staff or sandals almost entirely. He sees that these distinguish the Q Christians from others — they are part of the way in which the message of trust in God is put into practice. But then later he says: 'Doch in Wahrheit unterscheidet sich die Existenzweise der Wanderpropheten *nur um Nuancen* von der der Armen und Bettler. Sie haben wohl den Schritt in der Nicht-Seßhaftigkeit freiwillig vollzogen. Doch nicht im Zuge eines hehren Besitzverzichtes . . .' (pp. 113f. My italics). But how can one distinguish in this way?!

and apparently practised by, some Christians as exactly the same as that of their contemporaries in the surrounding society.

The same conclusion probably also emerges from some of the references to 'persecution' in Q. We have considered some of these already (see ch. 9 above) in another context. Here we may simply note that the life-style of the Q Christians as homeless, without protection or family ties, is connected in some way with what Q at least regards as 'persecution'.[39] The homelessness of Jesus alluded to in Q 9:58, which then acts as a paradigm for the Q missionaries in their activity, is probably to be seen in this light (cf. the discussion earlier, p. 182). Even the opening beatitudes, promising blessing on 'the poor, the hungry and the mourners', are interpreted by Q in relation to those being persecuted for their allegiance to Jesus (Q 6:22f. after 6:20f.). Yet at this point it is clear that the existence of the Q Christians cannot be considered as on a par with that of the 'kleine Leute', the poor and exploited masses. One may wish to argue that the masses were exploited, and were suffering economic hardship as a result of social factors and social policies inflicted on them. But this is in no way similar to the 'persecution for the sake of the SM' which the Q Christians evidently believed they were suffering. I argued above that such 'suffering' may have been considerably less severe, and certainly less 'physical', than other forms of 'persecution'. But nevertheless what is involved is social rejection of the Christian group by others outside the group. Similarly the break with family, which seems to be presupposed in Q 14:26, cannot be seen as a feature affecting the population as a whole.[40] Whatever the social and economic pressures afflicting the mass of the population at this period, a break with one's family was not a necessity for everyone!

The conclusion of this discussion is that Schottroff and Stegemann's critique of Theissen's (and Hoffmann's) views about the voluntary, and a-typical, nature of the renunciation which some of the Q sayings demand cannot be sustained. If then such renunciation is in some sense voluntary, then it does seem

---

[39] Both Hoffmann, *Studien*, 328, and Schottroff, *Jesus*, 59f., connect the homelessness motif to persecution.

[40] Stegemann, 'Wanderradikalismus', 111, refers to the break with family as being for Q an 'unabdingbare und bittere Notwendigkeit, nicht aber als ein a-familiäres Ethos'. But *why* is it a 'bitter necessity'? Presumably, whatever the social and economic problems facing the mass of the population, a break with the family was not a *necessity* for everyone.

appropriate (*pace* Stegemann) to enquire about its ethos. What then lies behind the demands, and what message is such a life-style intended to express?

At this point we may note two separable strands in the traditions of Q which imply that (at least some) Q Christians may have been homeless and without material support. On the one hand there are those traditions which appear to welcome such a life-style positively: the calls to discipleship (Q 9:57–60) demand a radical break with family ties, freely undertaken by the would-be disciple. The call to abandon cares about material goods (Q 12:22ff.) similarly implies a voluntary break with old life-styles. On the other hand, there are parts of Q which suggest that the phenomenon of homelessness results from hostility and rejection experienced by the Q Christians from their contemporaries. I have already argued (cf. p. 182 above) that the saying about the Son of Man having nowhere to lay his head is probably to be connected with the rejection that Jesus experiences: and the position of the saying at the head of the mission charge probably implies that the Q Christians too, are expected to experience the same rejection. In the mission charge itself, the missionaries go out without any possessions; yet it is clear that they are not expected to follow a monastic life-style extolling poverty for its own sake. Rather, they are to expect hospitality from friendly houses/towns where they go and these will provide them with shelter, food and all the material necessities of life. The converse is of course that there will be rejection, and in those situations the missionaries will find themselves with nowhere to lay their heads.

In trying then to identify the ethos of the wandering charismatics in Q, it may be worthwhile to distinguish between itinerancy and homelessness. What seems to be reflected in Q is that (some of) the Q Christians have chosen itinerancy, but not necessarily homelessness. Discipleship is seen as involving a break with previous family ties and going around preaching the Christian message in a partly itinerant life-style. But homelessness and poverty only result when the mission and the missionaries are rejected. Thus it is itinerancy that is chosen and welcomed; homelessness and other associated deprivations are not.

This, however, as we shall see, raises some difficulties for those who would claim that there is a significant analogy between Q and the Cynic tradition, and it is this problem that I shall try to discuss in the rest of this chapter.

4. A Cynic Q?

A few scholars have argued very strongly in recent years that Cynic
traditions do provide a very close analogy to (some of) the
traditions in Q, especially the Q mission charge: this is above all
the case in the work of Downing, Vaage and Mack.[41] I have
examined some of these alleged parallels elsewhere and will not
repeat the whole of that analysis in detail here.[42] However, since
the publication of my article in 1989 on the subject, others
(notably Downing and Vaage) have responded to my arguments,
often in quite strong language.[43] In view of the interest in the

[41] For Downing, see a whole series of publications in recent years: 'Cynics
and Christians', *NTS* 30 (1984) 584–93; 'The Social Contexts of Jesus the
Teacher: Construction or Reconstruction', *NTS* 33 (1987) 439–51; *Jesus and the
Threat of Freedom* (London: SCM, 1987); *Christ and the Cynics: Jesus and Other
Radical Preachers in First-Century Tradition* (Sheffield Academic Press, 1988);
'Quite Like Q'; *Cynics and Christian Origins*; 'A Genre for Q and a Socio-Cultural
Context for Q: Comparing Sets of Similarities with Sets of Differences', *JSNT* 55
(1994) 3–26. For Vaage, see his *Ethos and Ethics*, much of which is now published
in his *Galilean Upstarts*, and the summary of this in his article 'Q and Cynicism'.
For Mack, see his *Myth*, and *Lost Gospel*.

[42] See my 'Cynic Q?'. For other critiques of the Cynic hypothesis, see H. D.
Betz, 'Jesus and the Cynics: Survey and Analysis of a Hypothesis', *JR* 74 (1994)
453–75; J. M. Robinson, 'Cynic Hypothesis'. For a critique of the possible Cynic
background for Q 7:25, see above p. 129; and for a discussion of some attempts
to interpret the references to the 'kingdom' in Q in a Cynic fashion, see ch. 5
above.

[After the present chapter had been written, and the typescript about to be
sent to the publishers, I became aware of two further forthcoming studies by
Professor J. M. Robinson: 'Building Blocks in the Social History of Q', in
H. Taussig & E. Castelli (eds.), *Rethinking Christian Origins: A Festschrift in Honor
of Burton L. Mack* (Philadelphia: Trinity Press International, 1996), and
'Galilean Upstarts: A Sot's Cynical Disciples' in a forthcoming Festschrift for
Robert Funk, in *Forum*. (Both essays were kindly made available to me by the
author in typescript form in advance of publication.) The first essay develops
and takes further some of the comments on Mack's work, strengthening some
of the critical points made in Robinson's 'Cynic Hypothesis' essay. The second
is a detailed critique of Vaage's book which in some respects parallels, though
also sharpens and significantly deepens, my own comments below, especially
on Vaage's division of the material in Q into different strata. I have left the
present form of the chapter unaltered, though Robinson's essays here clearly
add considerable further weight to the critique of the whole 'Cynic hypothesis'
in relation to study of Q, and will have to be considered in all debates about the
hypothesis in future.]

[43] See Vaage, *Galilean Upstarts*, and 'Q and Cynicism' *passim*. (The latter
article is set in the form of an explicit response to my article.) Downing, *Cynics
and Christian Origins*; also his 'Genre for Q', esp. pp. 22–5.

topic, it may therefore be worth devoting some space here to considering the problem in a little more detail, looking in particular at some of the arguments and counter-arguments which have been proposed.

As we have seen already, a possible parallel at the level of the life-style adopted by (perhaps some of) the Q Christians is advocated by Theissen. But Theissen simply leaves this at the level of a parallel — and no more than a parallel — between the practices and apparent life-style adopted. Theissen himself makes clear that as well as similarities, there are also important differences between Q Christians and Cynics.[44] But the debate between Theissen and Stegemann on the 'Cynic' theory (as adopted by Theissen and opposed by Stegemann) only uses the word 'Cynic' to refer to the voluntary nature of the life-style, as we have seen. Downing, Vaage and others would claim that there is a far closer substantive link between the 'ideas', or the ethos, of the Q Christians and those of the Cynics. However, the nature of such a link is developed in significantly different ways by different scholars.

4.1. Q or part of Q?

One important area of divergence concerns the question of how much of Q is to be seen as similar to Cynicism. Vaage and Mack base themselves ostensibly on the stratification model of Kloppenborg, and claim that only the early layer of Q, Q^1 (or in Mack's case, a slightly smaller corpus of material), is to be seen as Cynic.[45] Downing would claim that the whole of Q is to be seen as Cynic and he never (to my knowledge) discusses possible stratification theories in relation to Q: thus he finds Cynic parallels to the whole of the Q tradition.

Robinson has however pointed out that, in the overall theory of Mack (and by implication of Vaage too), the stratification model as proposed by Kloppenborg has been so radically altered that the whole basis for the model has almost been effectively undermined, and this then creates great difficulties for assuming the existence of a 'Q^1' at all.[46] Thus, for example, the most

---

[44] See also n. 31 above; also Theissen, *Social Reality*, 148 n. 65 (= *Studien*, 190), where Theissen refers to criticism of any who compromised, and the way in which the Cynic adopted the (superior) role of father.

[45] Vaage, 'Q and Cynicism', 200 n. 3; also *Galilean Upstarts*, 7. Mack, *Lost Gospel*, 105–30.

[46] For what follows, see Robinson, 'Cynic Hypothesis', 261–5.

powerful argument of Kloppenborg's for making the case for separable strata within Q depends on the identification of seams in the tradition and the isolation of secondary additions to an earlier form of the tradition on literary grounds.[47] A (logically secondary) further move is made by Kloppenborg in claiming that these secondary additions all cohered together, both with each other and with other whole speech complexes in Q, in exhibiting a unitary focus on prophetic warnings of judgement directed at outsiders and dominated by a deuteronomistic view of history; by contrast, the speech units where secondary elements were isolated, once these elements were removed, were all allegedly unitary in showing a quite different, 'sapiential' outlook with non-polemical teaching addressed to outsiders.

Both Vaage and Mack profess to be following the basic theory of Kloppenborg, yet in some ways they 'modify' it to the point of changing it out of all recognition. For example, one of the strongest pieces of evidence for the existence of a secondary ('Q²') expansion is the note in Q 6:23c, the reference to the violence suffered by the prophets, which is probably an extraneous addition to an earlier form of the beatitude (see p. 180 above). Yet both Vaage and Mack assign the beatitude as a whole to their 'Q²', not 'Q¹'.[48] But then part of the whole basis for separating a Q² layer from Q¹ has vanished![49]

Vaage also adds to Kloppenborg's Q¹ a significantly large amount of material: thus some of the John the Baptist material (Q 7:24–26, 28a, 33–34), the Beelzebul controversy and some of the appended sayings (Q 11:14–20, 24–26, 33–34), as well as most (but not all) of the woes (Q 11:39b-48, 52) are all now assigned to Q¹, not Q². Again this tends to undermine the whole basis of the claim that 'Q¹' existed in a unified form prior to 'Q²': Kloppenborg had argued that the Q¹ material showed a unitary

[47] *Formation, passim.* The argument is clearer in his earlier 'The Formation of Q and Antique Instructional Genres', *JBL* 105 (1986) 443–62.

[48] Vaage, *Galilean Upstarts*, 10, lists all the passages he assigns to his Q¹. He argues the case in relation to this text in his 'Son of Man Sayings', 107–9. Cf. too Mack, *Lost Gospel*, 73.

[49] Robinson also refers to Mack's assignment of Q 13:34f. to a Q³ stage, not Q², despite the very close thematic links binding Q 13:34f. to the almost quintessentially Q² passages like Q 11:49–51 with their clear deuteronomistic ideas and terminology. This however does not affect the Cynic theory as such. Since Robinson's article is entirely focused on Mack's book and offers some detailed critique of Mack's adoption of the Cynic theory, I shall focus more on Vaage's and Downing's work here.

outlook by being unpolemical and directed at insiders. The inclusion of the woes in 'Q¹' significantly alters this. Vaage may well be right to question whether one should subsume all the woes under a general rubric of an undifferentiated 'polemic'.[50] So too it is almost certainly the case that the series of woes in Q 11:39–52 represents the end point of a long and complex tradition history.[51] Nevertheless, those woes which one decides may be earlier can only be ascribed specifically to Q¹ (rather than to other traditions used by a later Q editor(s)) by radically altering the nature of Q¹ almost out of all recognition. Similarly, Q 7:24–26, 28b, 33–34 is ascribed to Q¹ by Vaage on the grounds that it must pre-date the editorial elements in Q 7:18–35 since there are tensions or even contradictions in the present form of the text.[52] But this simply ignores the possibility of diverse traditions being available to the 'Q²' editor.[53]

The net result is that Vaage's Q¹ is quite unlike Kloppenborg's Q¹: the basis for separating out a Q¹ from a Q² has been in part dismantled; and since the rather specific nature of the Q¹ material was an integral part of Kloppenborg's argument for the very existence of Q¹ as a unified body of the tradition, the claim that (a rather differently constructed) 'Q¹' exhibits a quite different profile cannot really claim Kloppenborg's support for its very existence. Yet the existence of an earlier stratum of Q is essential for Vaage and Mack's overall case. Both acknowledge that the allegedly later material in Q, 'Q²', is decidedly different in its outlook, with its heavy indebtedness to the Jewish deuteronomistic view of history. Similarly, Vaage argues that the 'kingdom' references in Q¹ are all in line with Cynic views;[54] but this then needs the clearly eschatological reference to the kingdom in Q 13:29 excluded from consideration of Q¹ and assigned to a separate Q².[55]

I have already indicated my disagreement at points with Kloppenborg's stratification model; and some of my disagree-

---

[50] See his chapter on the woes in *Galilean Upstarts*, 66–86.

[51] See below (pp. 409–13).

[52] *Galilean Upstarts*, 108.

[53] Vaage rejects very forcefully the view that later texts might represent the coming together of smaller isolated form-critical units from oral tradition (cf. his *Galilean Upstarts*, 6f.). But his extreme reaction to what may have been an over-simplified schema seems equally untenable in arguing that virtually all earlier forms of the Q tradition must be assigned to a unified stratum.

[54] *Galilean Upstarts*, 55–65.

[55] It is, of course, also assigned to the later stratum by Kloppenborg as well.

ments correlate with Vaage's modifications of the model in that Kloppenborg's 'Q¹' may not be so unitary — or at least not so unitary in the way described by Kloppenborg. But I am not so convinced that one can rescue the model simply by radically altering the nature of the proposed 'Q¹', by making wholesale changes to its contents, and by removing part of the basis for deducing its existence in the first place!

These caveats apply only to Vaage and Mack who espouse a Q^1 + Q^2 (+ Q^3) model,[56] and not to Downing who, as we have already noted, takes the Q material as an undifferentiated whole in this respect. However, there are other problems involved here, some of which I tried to outline in my earlier article. These concern some more fundamental issues of the date and provenance of the Cynic material adduced as parallels to the Q material, as well as the problem of how far it is to be seen as 'Cynic'. One can, of course, put any two bodies of material side by side and compare them;[57] and the comparison may or may not be illuminating. But if we are to put two such sets of material alongside each other and claim that the similarity is so great that one term appropriate to one set can and should be applied to the other, so that in this case we should talk about a 'Cynic Q',[58] then one must be able to show that the Cynic background is a feasible one in terms of time and space to postulate as the appropriate background for interpreting the Q tradition.[59] Without this the existence of possible parallels remains uninteresting and hermeneutically insignificant. Yet it is at this level that considerable problems arise in relation to the

[56] In fact, Mack has more than three stages, postulating other intermediate stages as well: see Robinson, 'Cynic Hypothesis'.

[57] Vaage, *Galilean Upstarts*, 10, = 'Q and Cynicism', 198f., refers to J. Z. Smith, *Drudgery Divine: On the Comparison of Early Christianity and the Religions of Late Antiquity* (London & Chicago: School of Oriental and African Studies & Chicago University Press, 1990), for the legitimacy of such an approach as justification for this, and also in part as a criticism of my own earlier critique about some aspects of the legitimacy of such a comparison, by claiming that some (such as myself) confuse parallels with a statement about origins or genealogical derivation. On this, see n. 59 below.

[58] So Vaage, 'Q and Cynicism', 198: 'The present article is, in large measure, a response to Christopher Tuckett's recent enquiry, "A Cynic Q?". Tuckett's negative reply is answered here with a reciprocal: Yes.'

[59] This then does not assume that the existence of a parallel implies genealogical derivation. But if anything is to be made of the parallel, so that the similarity between two sayings in two separate bodies of tradition is to be taken as indicating a common background of thought, and hence providing a hermeneutical advance in the understanding of the text involved, then one

possibility that Cynic traditions might provide a significant parallel to the Q sayings of Jesus. There are in particular problems regarding the date and provence of the Cynic evidence, as well as problems concerning what is to count as 'Cynic' in this context. It is to these areas that I now turn.

4.2. Date

I have elsewhere discussed the problem of the relevant dates of Cynic traditions in relation to Q.[60] Cynics are evidenced over a long period of time from the fourth century BCE to the fourth century CE. Yet there are considerable doubts about whether Cynics were at all active during the first half of the first century CE. Cynicism seems to have faded away quite considerably in the second and first centuries BCE, but to have revived in importance in the second half of the first century CE with figures such as Demetrius and Epictetus writing about the ideal Cynic. Whether Cynics were active though in the earlier period is much debated. Downing argues that the dating of texts such as some of the Cynic epistles to the first century, as well as some negative comments in other writers such as Cicero, shows that Cynic traditions, and probably Cynics, were alive and active in the earlier period too.[61] Nevertheless, the fact remains that there is an awkward gap in our extant evidence about the actual *activity* of Cynics in the first half of the first century CE.[62]

---

must be able to show that the alleged common background is a possible one in historical terms for the saying in question. Smith's plea (cf. n. 57 above) is for a genuinely comparative exercise, highlighting differences as well as similarities. Vaage's approach argues not just for similarity but virtual identity: Q *is* Cynic!

[60] See my 'Cynic Q?', 355f., with further literature.

[61] Downing, *Cynics and Christian Origins*, 58ff. Cf. too M.-O. Goulet-Cazé, 'Le cynisme à l'époque impériale', *ANRW* II.36.4, 2720–2823, esp. p. 2724. However, Downing's argument that much of Paul's argumentation shows an awareness of Cynic ideas seems rather weak: much of the evidence (e.g. the language of riches, the kingdom, etc.) is not exclusively Cynic; however, in this case the question of provenance would also be a pressing problem: can Paul and Q be placed in the same, or comparable, geographical milieus? See below on the question of the provenance of Cynics.

[62] According to Vaage, such concerns do not matter if we rid ourselves of the idea that parallels imply genealogical derivation (*Galilean Upstarts*, 12f.). But it would be decidedly odd if the Q Christians appeared and behaved as, and sought to be understood as, Cynics in a society where no Cynics were otherwise present or where Cynicism was not known.

4.3. Provenance

More problematic may be the question of the provenance of Cynicism and of Q.[63] I have argued (and Vaage and Downing both seem happy to agree) that Q is to be linked with Galilee (see p. 102 above). Yet there are real problems of seeing Cynicism as a phenomenon which would have existed in Galilee at this period.[64] The fact remains that we know of no Cynics in Galilee at this period. There is a little evidence of a Cynic presence in the cities of Gadara and possibly Tyre,[65] though nothing dating from the period of Q (i.e. the first century CE). Thus, Betz says:

> The presumed presence of Cynics in the Galilean society in which Jesus lived is mostly a fanciful conjecture. The evidence for Cynicism is limited to Gadara and Tyre, Hellenistic cities outside Galilee, though smaller cities existed in Galilee itself, especially Sepphoris. It is, therefore, wrong to make up for our lack of evidence by projecting a sophisticated urban culture replete with Cynics into every part of Galilee and then to place a Cynic-inspired sayings source Q together with the Jesus movement in this Galilee.[66]

Similarly, all our other evidence suggests that Cynicism was primarily an urban phenomenon, with Cynics addressing crowds in the great centres of population. Yet Sepphoris in Galilee is notorious by its absence from Q (as indeed from the whole gospel tradition); and the place names which are mentioned in Q (Chorazin, Bethsaida, Capernaum) seem to be the smaller rural towns or villages.

[63] See further my 'Cynic Q?', 356–8.

[64] Vaage appears (or chooses) to misunderstand my argument at this point in my earlier article by asserting that I simply deduce the impossibility of correlating Q and Cynicism because of the alleged opposition between 'Judaism' and the 'Hellenistic' world (*Galilean Upstarts*, 13; 'Q and Cynicism', 205f.). To this Vaage responds with the obvious counter of the Hellenisation of Judaism, or better Judaisms: 'Early "Judaisms" in their multiple forms belonged as much to the Hellenistic world as did "Cynicism" in its various guises' (ibid.). In fact, my argument in my article was intended to be the whole of the discussion on pp. 356–8, not just the opening paragraph of the section on p. 356 (to which Vaage refers). Here it is a question not of how far (all) Judaisms were influenced by 'the' Hellenistic world, but how far *Galilean* Judaisms may have been affected by specifically *Cynic* ideas and/or people.

[65] Menippus, Meleager and Oenomaeus are from Gadara: Cf. Theissen, *Social Reality*, 44 (= *Studien*, 90 = 'Wanderradikalismus', 256); Betz, 'Jesus and the Cynics', 471. For Tyre, see Betz, *ibid.*

[66] Betz, 'Jesus and the Cynics', 471f.

Downing has tried to answer this point by arguing that the ideal was in fact to live in the country, living off the land as the animals do, and many Cynics may well have put their ideals into practice: we only hear of Cynics in cities because that is where literate commentators met them.[67] But this really proves too much: such Cynics being true to their ideals would live totally isolated from the rest of society! They would not be in the smaller population centres of rural Galilee. Notable too in this context must be the complete silence about any Galilean Cynics on the part of Josephus: as one who describes much of the situation in Galilee in the first century, it is surely striking that he never mentions the presence of Cynics there.[68] The fact remains that Cynics appear to have been active in the larger cities of the Empire, and not in the smaller villages and rural centres. As such it may not be surprising to see Paul, and the Pauline mission, possibly encountering Cynic ideas in cities such as Thessalonica or Corinth.[69] But this is very far from establishing Cynicism as a living phenomenon in the less populated parts of first century Galilee.

4.4. What/Who is 'Cynic'?

What though are we talking about when we speak of 'Cynicism'? Who were 'Cynics'? And what should we count as 'Cynic'? The problem of defining 'Cynic', or 'Cynicism', is by no means an easy one.[70] The problem arises acutely in the work of

[67] Downing, *Cynics and Christian Origins*, 82f.

[68] I remain totally unpersuaded that Josephus' reference to the followers of Judas as a 'fourth philosophy' (cf. *Ant.* 18.4–10, 23; *War* 2.118) is intended to portray these people as Cynics. (Cf. my 'Cynic Q?', 258 n. 34 with references to Downing's earlier work; the view is repeated again in his *Cynics and Christian Origins*, 153. See also Betz, 'Jesus and the Cynics', 457.) There is no support at all for any link between the two groups beyond the most superficial one of a common concern for 'freedom'. Precisely this kind of link shows clearly the importance of putting isolated words into a context before deducing similarities and parallels.

The problem of the spread of Cynicism is dealt with in very general terms by Vaage, *Galilean Upstarts*, 145 n. 49, who simply refers to the broad area covered by Cynics. The problem of whether Cynics were to be found outside the big cities, and whether they might be found in small towns/villages of Galilee, is not addressed.

[69] See above. But it is still striking that Luke in Acts never mentions the mission coming into contact with Cynics, despite mentioning, e.g. Stoics and Epicureans at Athens: cf. Betz, 'Jesus and the Cynics', 460.

[70] See further, my 'Cynic Q?', 351–5.

Downing who adduces a very wide range of evidence, and a large number of authors, as evidence of 'Cynic' views. Nobody would dispute that some of this evidence is clearly 'Cynic' in some sense at least: for example, Epictetus writing about the (ideal) Cynic (3.22), Diogenes Laertius writing his Lives of Cynics such as Diogenes (in Book 6 of his *Lives*), Lucian's *Life of Demonax*, some of Dio Chrysostom's *Orations*, and the Cynic epistles. However, other authors not usually regarded as Cynics are also often cited by Downing. These include the Stoics Musonius Rufus and Seneca, the life of Socrates in Diogenes Laertius 2, Epictetus outside his description of the Cynic in 3.22. Also all of Dio's writings are sometimes referred to very freely.

The relationship between Cynicism and Stoicism is a complex one. The earliest Cynics (Antisthenes, Diogenes, Crates) pre-date the rise of Stoicism (founded by Zeno, the pupil of Crates). To a certain extent Stoicism grew out of Cynicism, so that many Stoics appealed to Cynic figures of the past quite positively at times. However, the two movements cannot and should not be identified.[71] What was important for Cynics was, above all, practice of the simple life, life according to nature, with philosophising given a fairly low priority. Stoicism on the other hand added a theoretical superstructure to Cynic practices and in many instances modified those practices considerably (in a less ascetic direction). The Cynic stress on the importance of practice is reflected in the often-made claim that the Cynic way of life was a short cut to happiness (i.e. by by-passing philosophy: cf. *Ps.Crates* 13, 16) and in Diogenes Laertius' observation that many regarded Cynicism as not so much a philosophy and more a way of life (6.103). Cynics could thus be quite eclectic in their comments and 'teachings': 'what made a Cynic was his dress and conduct, self-sufficiency, harsh behaviour towards what appeared as

---

[71] See A. J. Malherbe, 'Pseudo-Heraclitus Epistle 4: The Divinisation of the Wise Man', *JAC* 21 (1978) 42–64. See too Vaage, 'Q and Cynicism', 202f. = *Galilean Upstarts*, 11f., referring to Seneca, *Ep. Mor.* 5.4f. for the difference between the two (and Seneca's own clear position on the side of Stoicism); also M. Billerbeck, 'Greek Cynicism in Imperial Rome', in *Die Kyniker in der modernen Forschung* (Amsterdam: B. R. Grüner, 1991) 147–66, p. 154, for the differences between the Stoic Seneca and Cynicism (referring to the same text).

excesses, and a practical ethical idealism.'[72] One should therefore beware of equating Cynicism and Stoicism.[73]

In the light of this, the very wide range of authors referred to by some as 'Cynic' becomes rather problematic. It *may* be justified to cite Epictetus on Cynics, Dio, the Cynic epistles, Demonax and Diogenes almost indiscriminately even though such texts display a wide variety of underlying presuppositions, and each reflects a rather different form of 'Cynicism'.[74] It is even more problematic if authors such as Musonius Rufus, Seneca, or Epictetus outside 3.22 are cited as evidence of the 'Cynic' background when these writers are usually regarded as Stoic rather than Cynic. There is, for example, no evidence that Epictetus or Seneca explicitly adopted the role of a Cynic wandering preacher. It is also not entirely clear when it is justifiable to cite the evidence of Dio.[75]

Downing is certainly aware of these difficulties and has sought to answer some of the problems raised.[76] For example, he defends the use of a very wide range of sources in general terms by claiming that 'first-century Cynicism [was] a movement of

[72] Malherbe, 'Self-Definition among Epicureans and Cynics', in B. F. Meyer & E. P. Sanders (eds), *Jewish and Christian Self-Definition Vol. 3: Self-Definition in the Greco-Roman World* (Philadelphia: Fortress, 1982) 46–59, p. 49. For the importance of Cynic asceticism as the distinguishing mark of the Cynic, see too Downing, *Cynics and Christian Origins*, 36; Vaage, *Galilean Upstarts*, 13f.

[73] And hence one should perhaps avoid terms like 'Cynic-Stoic' in the present discussion.

[74] For the considerable variety within the Cynic 'movement', see Malherbe, 'Self-Definition'; also his introduction to his *The Cynic Epistles* (Missoula: Scholars Press, 1977) 1; D. B. Dudley, *A History of Cynicism* (London: Methuen, 1937) 37; W. A. Meeks, *The Moral World of the First Christians* (London: SPCK, 1987) 53. Cf. too H. W. Attridge, 'The Philosophical Critique of Religion under the Empire', *ANRW* II.16.1, 45–78, p. 56: amongst Cynics there was 'little, if any, doctrinal concern, and hence little consistency in their attitude toward religious belief and observation'.

[75] It would appear that Orations 6, 8, 9, 10 reflect the time of Dio's vagrant life in the style of a Cynic preacher: cf. Dudley, *History*, 151.

[76] See further my 'Cynic Q?', 353f., from which this section is partly adapted. Vaage accuses me at this point of being 'quite mistaken in asserting that [he, i.e. Vaage] questions "whether there is really as great a variety within genuine Cynicism as Malherbe claims"' ('Q and Cynicism', 204 = *Galilean Upstarts*, 12, referring to my 'Cynic Q?', 353 n. 18). In fact, Vaage misreads my footnote which says that he does not discuss this *other* issue of who and what can legitimately be taken as 'Cynic', and *only* deals with the question of 'whether there is really as great a variety within genuine Cynicism as Malherbe claims'.

considerable diversity but still exhibiting a family resemblance'.[77] However, Cynics shared a great deal in common with a broad cross-section of their society. Hence it may be that if Cynics and Stoics can be found to be saying similar things, this is not so indicative of a distinctively Cynic outlook, but rather a reflection of the fact that Cynics shared quite a lot with their con- temporaries. Thus when Downing addresses the problem again in some detail,[78] and concludes that he will accept as Cynic certainly all the views of a self-styled Cynic as well as those of others which are 'akin' to those explicitly labelled as Cynic, there are a number of questions begged. All the views or utterances of a self-styled Cynic are not necessarily quintessentially 'Cynic' 'views'. They may simply reflect commonplaces of the day shared by many people. So too taking the views of others which are adjudged to be 'akin' to those of Cynics as also 'Cynic' is somewhat suspect since this presupposes the idea of a fixed body of distinctively Cynic views. In fact, the kinship may simply reflect the fact that the Cynics' sayings are not so distinctive after all. To put it crudely, if an Epictetus sounds like a Diogenes, has one already prejudged the issue by putting things this way round? Could it be that it is Diogenes who sounds like a more Stoic Epictetus?

We must also remember that Cynics were not renowned for their 'views', to say the least. As I have noted earlier, there was doubt about whether Cynics were really to be regarded as philosophers at all: cf. Diogenes Laertius' recording of the doubts whether 'Cynicism is really a philosophy and not, as some maintain, just a way of life' (6.103). Thus Cynics took the 'short cut' to happiness by by-passing philosophy. Hence the notion of specifically Cynic 'ideas' is rather a strange one. One should not perhaps expect to find too many specific 'ideas' of Cynics when all the stress was on practical living. The notion of a Cynic philosophy was despised by the Cynics themselves.[79]

---

[77] 'Cynics', 584f.

[78] *Cynics and Christian Origins*, 26–56.

[79] The point is made in passing by Betz, 'Jesus and the Cynics', 459, in relation to Vaage's work seeking to show that Q's language of the kingdom, or love of enemies, is close to Cynic 'ideas': 'he [Vaage] does not seem to notice that both love of the enemy and kingdom of God involve ideas and doctrines, not only ethical action.' Downing, *Cynics and Christian Origins*, 35f., argues for the literary pretensions of some Cynics. Nevertheless, this was not necessarily to set out a Cynic set of ideas. This perhaps comes more in Epictetus' picture of the ideal Cynic in 3.22 — but is Epictetus himself a Cynic?!

4.5. Genre[80]

Further problems may arise in claims made by others about the genre of Q. Vaage and Mack do not really discuss the question of genre explicitly, but the issue does seem to arise at a number of points in the work of Downing. His 1988 *Biblica* article (to which my own 1989 'A Cynic Q?' was largely a response) was entitled (in part) 'A Genre for Q: The "Lives" of Cynic Philosophers'. In this, the claim seems to be made that Q can be seen *generically* as a 'life' of a Cynic philosopher; what seems to be implied is that there is a reasonably well-defined, or at least identifiable, genre of 'the life of a Cynic philosopher' and that Q shows sufficient similarities with this genre to be ascribed to the same genre.

It is however extremely doubtful whether one can identify such a specific genre. There were certainly 'lives' of philosophers produced in antiquity; moreover, many of these took the form of collections of sayings or anecdotes about the subject of the work (cf. Lucian's *Life of Demonax*). However, it is not at all clear that when the subject of a 'life' was a *Cynic* 'philosopher', then the presentation was significantly different from that of other 'lives' so that one can appropriately distinguish a '*Cynic* life' as a separable genre.[81] In one sense it may be appropriate to see Q in generic terms as a 'life', a βίος, especially if one defines βίος sufficiently broadly.[82] But it is quite another matter to go one stage further and argue that a *Cynic* 'life' is a generically distinct entity.

Downing's argument is mostly at the level of a discussion of the contents of Q, and the nature of the individual elements or units which go to make up Q. Certainly this is an important and vital part of any determination of genre: a text is made up, at least at one level, of the sum of its parts and a text does not exist independently of its constituent parts. Nevertheless, most would agree that the genre of a text concerns aspects of the text in question which involve more than just a consideration of its individual parts. Genre concerns a text considered as a totality, as a whole. Thus the ways in which the individual parts of the text

---

[80] For a fuller discussion, see my 'Cynic Q?', 359–64.

[81] Cf. the list of chreia collections in Kloppenborg, *Formation*, 340f., including, for example, the life of Bion in Diogenes Laertius 4.47–51.

[82] As is done by Burridge, *What are the Gospels*, and see also Downing's recent article 'A Genre for Q', esp. pp. 5–16, arguing that on Burridge's definition of a 'life', or biography, Q can fit the bill very well.

are combined to form the finished product determine the genre quite as much as the individual elements.[83]

For the most part, the evidence for a 'Cynic life' as a generic parallel to Q is taken from Diogenes Laertius' *Lives of the Cynic Philosophers* in his Book 6, and Lucian's *Life of Demonax*. I shall consider the question of the contents of the individual elements of Q shortly. But at this point it may be worth noting some important differences between the way in which the Q material is structured into larger units and the Cynic 'lives'. One difference seems to lie in the level of structuring which Q exhibits. Diogenes Laertius' collection of chreiai about the Cynics he writes about is extremely unstructured. There is little clear evidence of design in the arrangement of the (mostly) unrelated chreiai which appear one after the other. Downing claims that the same is true of Q.[84] This however does not seem to do justice to Q at all. It is true that the structure of Q as a whole may be difficult to determine, but it is on any showing clearly the case that long sub-sections of Q are quite tightly structured with close interrelationships. Thus the Sermon in Q 6:20–49 contains very similar material focusing on ethical teaching, and perhaps structured via an inclusio involving 6:20–23 and 6:47–49 (cf. p. 143 above). The sayings on cares (Q 12:22–31) form a tightly structured sequence on a common theme, as do the woes (Q 11:39–52) and the eschatological teaching of Q 17:22–37. All this is very far from the very loose and un-structured arrangement of the material in much of the Cynic lives. The Cynic chreiai are considerably shorter than the relatively long discourses of Q's Jesus inveighing against the Pharisee/lawyers, warning of the day of the Son of Man, or spelling out the ethos of his followers in relation to their attitudes to others or their life-style. In seeking to refute this, Downing can rightly refer to the problem of trying to make links between the

---

[83] Downing's insistence (in a number of places) on considering genre solely on the basis of the presence of individual elements taken in isolation in a text (cf. especially his earlier 'Contemporary Analogies to the Gospels and Acts: "Genres" or "Motifs"?', in C. M. Tuckett (ed.), *Synoptic Studies* (Sheffield: JSOT Press, 1984) 51–64; cf. too *Cynics and Christian Origins*, 99f.) is in my view rightly criticised by Burridge, *What are the Gospels?*, 94f.

[84] Cf. his 'Quite like Q'. 200; *Cynics and Christian Origins*, 120: 'once the account in Q or in Laertius has got under way there is no obvious overall structure, though there does seem in both to be some piecemeal arrangement by theme or by catchword or by both'.

larger units.[85] He also argues that some of the Cynic material may be thematically related and arranged. Nevertheless, the links concerned seem to be far more tenuous than those which bind the individual sayings within each Q section together. Clearly such a judgement is somewhat subjective, and some level of (fairly basic) organisation has been claimed in, for example, Diogenes Laertius 6.[86] Nevertheless, the fact remains that the organisation of the material in Q seems to be significantly different from that in other Cynic collections —, so much so that it becomes correspondingly harder to see a *generic* similarity between them. Kloppenborg says:

> When seen in the context of chriae collections, Q ranks with the most highly organised and structured of them. . . . Q is very far from being a 'random collection of sayings' and is erroneously regarded as a pure sedimentation of oral tradition. It is, on the contrary, a carefully constructed composition which employs literary techniques characteristic of ancient sayings collections. In fact, in terms of its internal structure, it ranks somewhat higher than works such as *Demonax* and the Diogenes chriae, and closer in level of organisation (though not in type of organisation) to *'Abot*.[87]

Even this more nuanced view seems to force the evidence somewhat. Kloppenborg gives no real examples of organising principles in the material about Diogenes or Demonax which come near the (at times) tightly structured arrangement in Q. Nor is there much comparable in *m. 'Abot*. It is hard to envisage how anyone hearing or reading the series of brief, loosely appended chreiai about Diogenes in Diogenes Laertius 6 and the series of woes in Q 11:37–52, or the mission discourse in Q 10:2–16, would conceive of these as coming from documents of the same genre, or at least in terms of anything more specific than a very 'broad' genre (cf. p. 105 above). In terms of an abstract, modern idea of 'chreia collections', Q could (just) be seen as belonging within such a genre and hence not *sui generis* (this is

---

[85] *Cynics and Christian Origins*, 121, referring to the problem of linking the story of the healing of the centurion's servant and the material on John the Baptist in Q 7, though scholars such as Jacobson would see a broad structuring unity even at this level: cf. his *First Gospel*, ch. 5, where he argues that the whole section Q 3–7 is concerned with John and Jesus and their interrelationship.

[86] See Kloppenborg, *Formation*, 310f., for a discussion; also Downing, *Cynics and Christian Origins*, 121.

[87] Kloppenborg, *Formation*, 323f.

basically Kloppenborg's thesis). But in terms of audience reaction, Q and the Cynic lives do not seem close enough for contemporary hearers/readers to have been immediately struck by their literary or generic similarities.

It may also be worth noting the fact here that the categorising of Q as a 'chreia collection' may also tell against the theory of Vaage and Mack that 'Q^1' is to be seen as Cynic. It is true that the Cynic Lives can appropriately be regarded as chreia collections. But according to Kloppenborg's analysis, the chreiai in Q characterise 'Q^2', rather than 'Q^1', indeed they serve to distinguish the alleged layers.[88] It is thus rather odd, to say the least, to have a generic similarity between the Cynic material and Q^2, whilst asserting that the primary link between Q and Cynic traditions is at the level of Q^1. This problem can be alleviated in part by assigning some chreiai to Q^1 rather than to Q^2.[89] However, this distinction in forms used in the two alleged layers was a part of the argument for distinguishing the layers in the first place; hence the transfer of chreiai to Q^1 undermines a further support in the argument for the existence of the strata themselves.

Further differences between Q and the Cynic lives emerge when one notes the notorious lack of any real 'biographical' (in the modern sense) information in Q. Diogenes Laertius starts most of his lives with a small note giving some biographical information about the subject of his life.[90] Laertius also ends each life by listing all the books each person had written and (sometimes) telling how they died. All this has no parallel in Q: there is no 'biographical' information about Jesus or John at the start of the Q material, and, notoriously, Q gives no account of the death of Jesus (or of John).[91]

---

[88] Cf. Kloppenborg, *Formation*, 168, 306–16, 322–5.

[89] Kloppenborg lists Q 3:7–9; 7:1–10, 18–23, 24–26; 11:14–15, 17–18a, 16 + 29 as chreiai in Q^2 (*Formation*, 168). Of these 7:24–26; 11:14–20 (taken as a whole) are assigned by Vaage to Q^1 (*Galilean Upstarts*, 10).

[90] Cf. his introduction to the life of Antisthenes: 'Antisthenes, the son of Antisthenes, was an Athenian. It was said, however, that he was not of pure Attic blood . . . His mother was supposed to have been a Thracian' (6.1); or on Diogenes: 'Diogenes was a native of Sinope, son of Hicesius, a banker' (6.20). Lucian's *Demonax* is similar: 'He was a Cypriot by birth and not of common stock as regards civic rank and property' (with then further details about his education) (*Demonax* 3).

[91] Downing points out that some of the smaller lives in Laertius do not mention the philosopher's death ('Quite like Q', 203; *Cynics and Christian Origins*, 122). But most of these are so short as to be no real parallel to Q: the

In terms of the structure and arrangement of the texts, there are thus significant differences between Q and the Cynic lives. At one level the contents also differ in that some important elements of the Cynic lives do not reappear in Q. Thus it seems hard to see a *generic* similarity between Q and specifically *Cynic* lives. As already noted, it may be that the category of a 'life', βίος, is sufficiently broad to include Q. The possibility then that Q might be similar to Cynic lives would have to depend on a consideration of the contents of Q. But the category of 'Cynic Life' itself does not seem sufficiently close to Q (if it indeed is identifiable as a generic class at all) to be comparable at many levels.

4.6. *Contents*

What though of the contents of Q? It is here that most is claimed by Downing, Vaage, Mack and others in asserting that the similarities between Q and the Cynic material are sufficiently extensive and significant to make it appropriate to talk of a 'Cynic Q'. As we saw when looking at the problem of genre in general, individual words and sayings are often ambiguous on their own. So too there is no doubt that some element of similarity can be shown between Q and Cynic materials.[92] So the question arises how far this is a real similarity to the extent that the Q sayings should be interpreted in a Cynic fashion and how far any similarity is only superficial.

Yet however one judges any positive parallels which might exist, one may note here a number of negative points of non-agreement, i.e. features which are present — some would say highly characteristic — in one side of the alleged pairing but absent from the other. This applies to both Q and Cynicism.

On the side of Cynicism, one characteristic feature of Cynics was their 'shamelessness' (ἀναίδεια), the anti-social behaviour that led to deliberately provocative challenges to conventional society by doing such things as breaking wind or defecating in

---

'life' of Onesicritus has no real chreiai about him at all (Diogenes Laertius 6.84), the life of Monimus (6.82–83) has only one, that of Mendemus (6.102) also only has one saying to attribute to him. These are then scarcely conceivable as self-contained literary units comparable to Q. For the lack of any 'biographical' detail as an important difference between Q and the Cynic material, cf. too Betz, 'Jesus and the Cynics', 473.

[92] Cf. the very existence of the works of Vaage, Downing, Mack and others.

public.[93] Of this there is nothing comparable in Q (or the rest of the gospel tradition).[94] Similarly the 'boldness' (παρρησία) of Cynics was renowned, above all in their readiness to stand up to rulers of the day and speak their mind. Again Q has nothing directly comparable: the nearest is perhaps Q's Jesus inveighing against others in, say, the woes of Q 11 — but this is rarely face-to-face (at least in Q: the bulk of the controversy stories in the gospels are in Mark).[95] Downing points out that features such as this are not always present in Cynic traditions.[96] Nevertheless, the absence of such features does not help the theory that a first-century group of people *not* showing such characteristics in their behaviour would have been regarded by others as Cynics.

Conversely, on the side of Q, there is an interest in physical healing and in eschatology which is foreign to Cynicism. I remain unpersuaded by Vaage's suggestion that the ἀσθενεῖς of Q 10:9 are simply the morally 'weak',[97] and the reference here does seem to show a positive interest in the removal of physical illness. Such an interest is also attested in the reply of Jesus to the Baptist in Q 7:22, in the Beelzebul controversy, and in the healing of the centurion's servant. Similarly the stress on eschatology (cf. below) is hard to parallel elsewhere in Cynic traditions.[98]

So too at a more superficial level in one way, the 'heroes of the day' in the two traditions are different. In Q there is no reference to people like Diogenes, Socrates, Heracles or any of the classic 'heroes' of Cynicism; rather, the figures to whom appeal is made are the *prophets*. (However, in Q¹, from which the prophetic references are mostly excised as part of 'Q²', the sole figure of the past who is mentioned in Solomon (Q 12:27) and there negatively

---

[93] Cf. Downing, *Cynics and Christians Origins*, 50f.

[94] Though Cynics may have varied in this respect: Cf. Downing, ibid.; Kloppenborg, *Formation*, 313 (on Demonax).

[95] Perhaps the nearest parallel to Cynic παρρησία in the gospels is Jesus' retort (though again *in*direct) to Herod in Luke 13:31–33: but this is not Q!

[96] In *Cynics and Christian Origins*, 46–50, he takes a number of such catchwords and shows that they do not occur in many Cynic texts; yet it is a matter not just of the words themselves but also of what they refer to.

[97] So Vaage, *Galilean Upstarts*, 33. See p. 148 n. 30 above.

[98] Sato, 'Prophetie oder Weisheit?', 400. *Pace* Downing, *Cynics and Christian Origins*, 124. There may well be an idea of a post-mortem judgement by some Cynics; but this is unlike the eschatology as I tried to outline it in ch. 5 above. On the references to the 'kingdom' in Q, see ch. 5 above.

— possibly even via a critique which could be seen as 'Cynic' in some sense.)[99]

What then of the positive parallels which may exist between Q and Cynicism? There is no space here to undertake a full comparison of all the parallels adduced by Vaage, Downing and others. To try to discuss all such parallels would require a separate monograph in its own right. I have sought to provide some kind of comparison elsewhere, as have others.[1] For a fuller account of some possible parallels the reader is therefore referred to these other discussions. I have argued elsewhere that some of the parallels claimed turn out to be not very close at all. For example, Downing suggests as a possible parallel that 'John [the Baptist] expects an acceptance of a humiliating public start to discipleship, as does Diogenes in a number of stories'.[2] But the Cynic stories adduced as parallels here, of Diogenes offering his head to be struck (Diogenes Laertius 6.21), or giving a would-be follower a tunny to carry (Diogenes Laertius 6.36), bear only the most superficial of resemblances to John's baptism. It is not apparent why John's baptism should be regarded as a 'humiliating' public start. Further, the Cynics did not have a *common* 'visual act' which symbolises the start of the life of a Cynic (unless it be taking the cloak, the staff and the wallet, but in that case the parallel in Q is *not* John's baptism). Diogenes' acts are simply one-off incidents.

Downing might well wish to counter all this by saying that the parallel is a very weak one,[3] but showing that one individual

---

[99] Cf. the implied negative judgement on Solomon 'in all his glory'. But the negative critique is remarkably muted by Cynic standards!

[1] See my 'Cynic Q?', 364–75. In more general terms, see Horsley, *Sociology*, 47; Betz, 'Jesus and the Cynics', 471–75; also Witherington, *Jesus the Sage*, 123–43. Witherington's analysis is slightly different from my own in that he focuses on the question of whether Jesus was a Cynic, and hence ranges more widely than the Q material. (So also the briefer treatments of Horsley and Betz.) Witherington also perhaps talks too readily of direct influence of one figure on another (Jesus on Dio, or Musonius, or vice versa) without considering the possibility that both might reflect common concerns but without a direct (literary?) relation between them. Cf. Vaage's strictures on confusing parallels with derivation, which are perhaps appropriate to Witherington's analysis here.

[2] 'Quite like Q', 205.

[3] He does not mention it in what is effectively his rewriting of his 'Quite like Q' article in his chapter on Q in his *Cynics and Christian Origins*, cf. pp. 124f. for the equivalent place.

possible parallel is weak does not destroy the whole case.[4] There is thus always the danger of one person claiming that the strength of his/her argument has been missed by another critic who has side-stepped the most important possible connections which are being claimed. Yet the problem of space in the present volume remains!

Thus, whilst fully aware of the dangers of a selective approach, I focus here on the life-style and apparent dress of (at least some of) the Q Christians, as evidenced by the mission charge (Q 10:2–11) and perhaps in the sayings about cares (Q 12:22–31). It is here that the parallel between the Q disciples and Cynics has been seen as the strongest: this was the point at which Theissen adduced the parallel, as we have seen. Further, the focus on life-style would be an entirely appropriate way to identify something that is quintessentially Cynic as we have also seen: for Cynics the supremely important thing was not philosophising or having ideas, but living out the Cynic life in practice. Similarly, Downing concedes (at times) that there might be some differences in nuance between what was said by Christians and what was said by Cynics: but what would have been all important would have been how people *appeared* to others. The Christians would have looked like Cynics, and perhaps intended to look like Cynics and sound like Cynics, despite any possible differences.[5] So too, Vaage clearly sees the mission charge as a key text in his argument.[6]

Now it is true that in terms of visual public appearance, there is at one level a degree of similarity between the Cynics and any Q disciples who followed the instructions of the mission charge to the letter. Both appear to have discarded conventional garb and

---

[4] In his more recent 'Genre of Q', Downing takes me to task for what he takes to be unjustified criticism of his case by claiming that his parallels are too 'general' (p. 22 n. 58), whilst I myself am equally guilty of making sweeping generalisations and assumptions about the nature of Q as governed by eschatology. He says that the generality 'as such is no drawback, if these similarities are real, and numerous . . .' The point is that if the similarity is too general, it ceases to be 'real' enough to be significant. 'Reality' — sadly — in this context has to be a relative, not an absolute, concept. On my own 'assumptions' about the nature of Q, see below.

[5] For possible differences between Cynics and Christians, see his 'Cynics', 584, 588, but his later articles and studies play down any differences almost to vanishing point (at least for those Christians where the parallels are strong). The importance of 'audience reaction' is frequently mentioned by Downing: cf. my 'Cynic Q?', 351 n. 9, for references.

[6] It occupies pride of place as the first analysis undertaken from which the rest follow logically.

adopted a visual appearance of extreme poverty. However, when one looks at the texts in detail, the parallel may not have the significance which others see here. Many have pointed out that the *distinguishing marks* of the Cynic were the πήρα, the staff and the cloak.[7] However, for the Q missionaries, *no* πήρα and *no* staff are allowed. Thus even at the level of visible outward appearance to others, the Q missionaries must have looked rather *un*like Cynic preachers. Further, the fact that the Cynic πήρα was in part a begging 'bowl' (as well a repository for food) would mean that the Q missionaries, with no πήρα, would be very visibly different from Cynic preachers in their behaviour as it impinged on others, as well as in their dress: they were *not* to be like beggars from the general public. Thus, Theissen comments:

> The prohibition of bag and staff was probably intended to avoid the least shadow of an impression that the Christian missionaries were these beggars [i.e. Cynic preachers], or were like them.[8]

Both Downing and Vaage have responded to this by claiming that the staff, cloak and wallet were by no means essential to characterise the Cynic.[9] Vaage says that the stereotyped picture of the Cynic is just a stereotype and it is easy to find exceptions. Thus Diogenes only takes a staff late in life according to Diogenes Laertius 6.23, and Teles advocates dispensing with a πήρα (Teles 44H).[10] Other instances can be adduced of Cynics advocating extreme asceticism.[11] Nevertheless the exceptional nature of the texts adduced can count against the theory as well. The absence of the πήρα (for which only the Teles text provides a *possible* counter example, though see n. 11 above) is highly unusual for a

[7] There are a large number of references in the Cynic Epistles where taking up the cloak and the wallet (and sometimes the staff) is clearly a reference to adopting the Cynic way of life: cf. *Crates* 16, 23, 33; *Diogenes* 7, 15, 19, 26, 30, 34, 38, 46. Cf. too Diogenes Laertius 6.13, 23 and many others.

[8] Theissen, *Social Reality*, 47 (= *Studien*, 93 = 'Wanderradikalismus', 259). For other similar views, see Horsley, *Sociology*, 47; H. C. Kee, *Christian Origins in Sociological Perspective* (London: SCM, 1980) 58; further references in Vaage, *Galilean Upstarts*, 150 n. 15; Downing, *Cynics and Christian Origins*, 32f.

[9] Downing, *Cynics and Christian Origins*, 33f.; Vaage, *Galilean Upstarts*, 26f.

[10] However, the wallet here may be the wallet in which the rich man accumulates wealth, and not necessarily the Cynic begging bowl and/or repository for food.

[11] Cf. Diogenes Laertius 6.37 on Diogenes getting rid of his cup for drinking to show his total independence of material goods; and from the Cynic epistles, cf. *Anacharsis* 5, or *Socrates* 6, on going barefoot (cf. the Q instructions not to wear sandals).

Cynic; the texts noted in n. 7 above imply clearly that the 'normal' Cynic garb *was* to carry the πήρα and wear the cloak: the evidently standard nature of the terminology seems to make this clear. Further, whilst the wallet and the cloak are almost always mentioned together in these texts, the staff is sometimes omitted: hence the reference to Diogenes not having a staff may not be so significant. Thus, the Q commands do serve to distinguish in part the Q disciples from the stereotypical Cynic — and precisely because it is the stereotype, the instructions might serve to make the distinction in the minds of any who accepted the stereotype.

On the other hand, one must also remember the difficulties of positing *any* Cynic presence in the milieu which is usually ascribed to Q (cf. above on date and provenance, and the problems of positing the existence of any Cynics in small towns or villages of first-century Galilee). In my earlier 'Cynic Q?' article, I simply cited the remarks of Theissen and Kee noted above and left things there. I have since become more persuaded that perhaps the alleged parallel has no significance at all. If, in fact, there were no other Cynics in the situation of the Q disciples, then it is unlikely that anyone seeing the Q disciples would have had in mind the Cynic stereotype. Thus the absence of a wallet would have rung no bells at all. Robinson also points out that, unlike the Cynic texts which almost always mention the 'cloak' in this context, Q has no mention of a 'cloak' here.[12] If the Q instructions were intending clearly to demarcate the Q disciples from the archetypal Cynic by banning the wallet, one would also expect a similar instruction to ban the 'cloak' (τρίβων).[13] Given all the problems of seeing any Cynic presence at all in the setting of Q, and the striking lack of any reference to important parts of what seems to have been the standard terminology associated with Cynic dress and the Cynic way of life, it is hard to see any relationship between the Q instructions and Cynicism as envisaged by Downing and others.

[12] Robinson, 'Cynic Hypothesis', 260. He also refers to the fact that when a 'staff' is mentioned in the Cynic texts (he confines attention primarily to the Cynic epistles), a different Greek word is generally used (βακτήρια or a similar cognate) from that which appears in the Q mission instructions ('ράβδος). I am perhaps slightly less persuaded by this, since it is not clear that the language was so technical that synonyms would not have served as well.

[13] Robinson points out ('Cynic Hypothesis', 261 n. 56) that Q 6:29 envisages a person wearing ἱμάτιον and a χιτών, whereas Cynics were expected to replace both with a τρίβων: cf. *Ps.Diogenes* 30.

A similar ethos to that of the mission charge is also possibly reflected in the cares tradition (Q 12:22–31) where the Q disciples are exhorted not to worry about material things, like the birds and the lilies. The statement of Dio is often noted as an important parallel here:[14]

> Do you not see the beasts there and the birds, how much freer from sorrow they live than human beings and how much more happily also, how much healthier and stronger they are, now each of them lives the longest life possible, although they have neither hands nor human intelligence. But to counterbalance these and other limitations, they have one very great blessing — they own no property. (Dio 10.16.)

However, there are also important differences in the background and presuppositions of such sentiments. Above all there is a radical difference in the underlying ethos. With Cynics, the ethos is to give up one's possessions and live a life of austerity and physical deprivation in the belief that that life as such will provide true and lasting happiness and fulfilment. Moreover the ideal for the Cynic is a life of self-sufficiency (αὐτάρκεια) and independence from the rest of society. In Q the ethos is radically different: it is to encourage *not* independence, but dependence — upon God. There is thus a significant difference between Q 12:22ff. and Dio 10 in that the latter is advocating radical independence and self-sufficiency.[15] Further, for the Cynic the life of poverty *was* itself happiness and the means by which one attained one's goal of fulfilment.[16] By contrast, in the Q tradition, as I have tried to show earlier, there is no question of austerity or asceticism itself being welcomed. This is the point at which we started the present discussion of Q and Cynicism: Christians in Q are called to give up their security, their old family ties, etc. and to join the Christian cause; but it is promised that God knows the needs of His children before they ask and will supply those needs

---

[14] Cf. Vaage, *Galilean Upstarts*, 62; Downing, *Cynics and Christian Origins*, 137.

[15] Cf. too Witherington, *Jesus the Sage*, 124, 134; also K. Berger & C. Colpe, *Religionsgeschichtliches Textbuch zum Neuen Testament* (Göttingen: Vandenhoeck & Ruprecht, 1987) 102. (This text from Dio is one of the very *few* Cynic texts they cite in seeking parallels to the Q tradition from non-Jewish contemporary literature. The paucity of Cynic parallels, and the great diversity of other parallels cited in Berger and Colpe's collection, is also noted by Robinson, 'Cynic Hypothesis', 251f.)

[16] Cf. Downing, *Cynics and Christian Origins*, 31f.

plentifully,[17] and the Q disciples clearly regard the failure of their audience to respond positively and provide them with food and shelter as persecution in some sense. Further, the aim of the life-style chosen does not appear to be to commend the life-style of poverty as such, or of having a minimum level of need, as in Cynicism. What is at stake in Q is the preaching of the imminent arrival of the eschatological kingdom of God. As we saw above, it is the eschatological element which dominates the section in Q on cares in Q 12:22ff. (at least in its present form). So too it is the preaching of the kingdom that dominates the message of the missionaries in Q 10:2ff. (cf. v. 9).[18] There is little, if anything, comparable in Cynicism to correspond to this stress on eschatology. Thus the Cynic analogy provides no deep similarity to the ethos of the Q Christians.

Conclusion

If then it is this stress on eschatology that dominates the Q preaching, then it would seem most likely that the strange wandering existence apparently adopted by some Q Christians should be seen in the same light. Rather than being a demonstration of Cynic virtues of freedom from possessions, the life-style demonstrates, in a kind of prophetic symbolic 'sign'

---

[17] Cf. Q 12:30; also the beatitudes, especially the second and third beatitudes which promise an end to hunger and sorrow (Q 6:21). It is for this reason (partly) that I would interpret the first beatitude, which promises the kingdom to the 'poor', as primarily a future hope holding out the promise of an end to 'poverty' and suffering. See p. 141 n. 9 above. The same would also be shown if (as I tried to argue earlier) the prophecy of Isa 61 lies behind the Q version of the beatitudes. (Isa 61 is certainly echoed in Q 7:22.) The good news for the poor in the terms of reference of Isa 61 is certainly not that poverty itself is good news! For this at the level of Q too, see also J. M. Robinson, 'The Jesus of Q as Liberation Theologian', in Piper (ed.), *The Gospel Behind the Gospels*, 259–74. My interpretation is thus totally contrary to Vaage (see especially *Galilean Upstarts*, 56f.) who interprets the 'kingdom' as virtually the life of poverty itself, and all that changes is one's perception of the poverty. See the discussion of some of the references to the kingdom in Q in ch. 5 above.

[18] See pp. 148–52 above. When Downing criticises me ('Genre', 24) for offering 'generalisations' on the interpretation of Q which are as broad and as questionable (by implication more so!) as those I criticise him for, by claiming a pan-eschatological interpretation of Q, and asserts in part that 'it is not obvious from the text of Q', I would answer that it is precisely the text of Q and the references to the kingdom in 10:9 and 12:31 which *do* determine the interpretation here.

analogous to prophetic actions in the OT, the total trust and confidence in God who is about to inaugurate the kingdom; indeed it may be that the life-style is intended to display the way of life that is appropriate in the kingdom.[19] Mealand has pointed to the paradisal elements in some of this teaching, and has suggested that what may be in view is a return to the primeval conditions of Paradise which, in a standard Jewish *Endzeit-Urzeit* correlation, was believed to be prepared for the world by God in the End-time.[20]

The strange life-style is thus to be seen as part of a realised eschatology in Q:[21] the trust and confidence in God as the one who will provide for all His children's needs is lived out in practice by this group of itinerant preachers who put their trust in God to do precisely what He has promised. Clearly though, at least in the post-Easter situation, these preachers did not find universal acceptance. And the material support, believed to come ultimately from God but presumably to be mediated through human agencies, failed to materialise when the mission was rejected and experienced hostility. Thus, a life of itinerant joy became a life of homeless hardship. It is perhaps this mixture in the life of discipleship that the Q tradition reflects. It is however far removed from anything very like Cynicism as we know it in terms of either its theory or practice.

---

[19] D. L. Mealand, *Poverty and Expectation in the Gospels* (London: SPCK, 1980) 87.

[20] Mealand, ibid.

[21] Whether this is Q or Jesus is perhaps immaterial. In many respects it is clear that this model of discipleship provides a strong degree of continuity between Jesus and the later church: cf. Kuhn, 'Nachfolge', *passim.*

12

<hr>

The Gentile Mission and the Law

The situation of hostility which appears to exist between the Q Christians and their Jewish contemporaries raises two important issues. First, if the hostility was felt (at least on the Christian side) to be so strong, had a situation developed whereby Q Christians had gone, or felt driven, outside the confines of the Jewish people to propagate their message? Had the Q community started actively to proselytise among Gentiles?

The second question could be seen as in one sense not unrelated to the first: if Q Christians felt alienated from their Jewish contemporaries, how far did they question their own Jewishness? This latter question will occupy us in more general terms in the last chapter. Here I will focus on one particular aspect of Jewishness, namely obedience to the Torah. Our knowledge of first-century Christianity shows that the issue of Law observance was a pressing one for many parts of the Christian movement. What then, if anything, can be discerned about the attitude of Q to the Law? In this chapter, I shall therefore look at the two issues of the Gentiles, and the Law, in Q before going on to a more general consideration of the attitude of Q to Israel in the final chapter.

1. The Gentile Mission in Q

The question of Q's attitude to a possible Gentile mission has been frequently debated in recent studies of Q.[1] Opinions have varied widely. Some have argued that Q presupposes and welcomes the Gentile mission;[2] others have claimed that Q

<hr>

[1] See the very full summary of the history of scholarship on this issue in U. Wegner, *Der Hauptmann von Kafarnaum (Mt 7,28a; 8,5–10.13 par Lk 7,1–10). Ein Beitrag zur Q-Forschung* (WUNT 2.14; Tübingen: Mohr, 1985) 305–27.

[2] So Manson, *Sayings*, 20; Lührmann, *Redaktion*, 58, 86f.; Zeller, 'Logion', 93; Laufen, *Doppelüberlieferungen*, 192–4, 237–43; Uro, *Sheep*, 210–23.

rejected the idea of such a mission, or was unconcerned by the issue.[3] Others still have claimed that Q presupposes the existence of the Gentile mission, but that Q's primary concern is to address the Jewish people and that it uses the fact of the success of Christian appeals to Gentiles as part of its message to Jews.[4] Others too, have argued that Q's attitude to Gentiles developed over the course of time.[5]

The data has been reviewed many times in the discussion and hence need not be repeated here in minute detail. It is clear that the evidence is inconclusive and ambiguous. On the one hand, those who believe that Q welcomed the Gentile mission refer to several texts in Q which seem to reflect a very positive attitude to Gentiles.[6] We have noted some of these in passing already in our discussion of Q's polemic against 'this generation'. At several points, Q refers to various Gentiles in a very positive way, by contrast with the negative attitude to 'this generation'. Thus the Queen of the South and the Ninevites are held up as examples of people who responded positively to the wisdom of Solomon and the preaching of Jonah, by contrast with this generation which has failed to repent even though 'something greater' is present (Q 11:31f.). In Q 10:13–15 and 13:28f. the view is more forward-looking: it is predicted that Gentiles will fare better than, and indeed possibly replace, Jews in the eschatological kingdom. The story of the healing of the centurion's servant in Q 7:1–10 holds

[3] Cf., with varying nuances, Steck, *Geschick*, 287f.; Hoffmann, *Studien*, 292f.; Schulz, *Q*, 244f.; 410ff.; Wegner, *Hauptmann*, 327–34.

[4] See P. D. Meyer, 'The Gentile Mission in Q', *JBL* 89 (1970) 405–17, = chap. 2 of his *Community of Q*, 7–28; cf. also Jacobson, *First Gospel*, 110, 256.

[5] Cf. Zeller, 'Logion', 92f. Polag also sees a greater openness to Gentiles reflected in his second postulated redactional stage as compared to the first, where the focus is much more on the polemic against Israel (cf. his *Christologie*, 90–3, 168). Within Kloppenborg's influential three-stage model, any attitude by Q to the Gentile mission as such is not generally an issue, though in his theory, the final ('Q³') stage represents a powerful attempt to reintegrate Q within Torah-obedient Judaism; but whether this has any implications in relation to attitudes to Gentiles is not discussed.

[6] Manson's phrase is often cited: Q 'shows a friendly attitude towards Gentiles' (*Sayings*, 20). Manson's claim is that Q displays such an attitude 'more than any other of the synoptic sources'. Thus: 'The Roman centurion, whose faith could not be paralleled in Israel; the people of Tyre and Sidon; the men of Nineveh, who were readier to repent than the Chosen People; and the Queen of the Sheba, who was more eager for the wisdom of Solomon than the Jewish contemporaries of Jesus for the Kingdom of God — these are all Q characters: and to Q belongs the statement that people from all the ends of the earth will find their way into the Kingdom' (ibid.).

the Gentile centurion up as an example of one who has shown 'faith', and whose faith apparently exceeds anything that Q's Jesus has found elsewhere in Israel.

[EXCURSUS. In an important and stimulating recent essay, Catchpole has argued that in Q 7:1–10 the centurion is not necessarily a Gentile and that the story does not intend to draw any contrast between Gentile faith and Jewish faith. Rather, the centurion is ethnically neutral;[7] no reserve by Jesus is intended in Jesus' first response to the centurion's messengers;[8] the discussion about the 'worthiness' of the centurion need not be based on his non-Jewishness in the face of a Jew, but is better explained in Christological terms as his unworthiness as a human being in the face of one who is κύριος;[9] and Jesus' concluding observation about not finding such faith 'in Israel' need be no different to Matt 9:33, which 'simply declares that what has just happened (in Israel, of course) is greater in kind than anything which has previously happened (also in Israel, of course)'.[10]

Some parts of the total argument are however more persuasive than others. Catchpole's discussion about the LkR nature of Luke's extra verses in Luke 7:3–6a, 7a seems to me fully convincing.[11] So too he makes a powerful, and to my mind convincing, case for the Q version of Jesus' initial response in Matt 8:7 being quite neutral in relation to any Jew/Gentile sensitivities.[12] So too the man's response can very appropriately be explained in terms of 'Christological' factors rather than any ethnic differentiation (though see p. 216 above).

[7] *Quest*, 292f. The whole essay appears in *Quest*, 280–308.

[8] Catchpole takes Jesus' reply in Matt 8:7 as the Q version, the more extensive Lukan version in Luke 7:3–6a being LkR. The words in Matt 8:7 (ἐγὼ ἐλθὼν θεραπεύσω αὐτόν) are sometimes taken as a negative question reflecting scruples about Jewish purity laws forbidding a Jew to enter a Gentile house, or about Jesus' limiting of his ministry to Jews (cf. Luz, *Matthäus II*, 14, for the first; Wegner, *Hauptmann*, 380, for the second). Catchpole argues that no sensitivity about Jew/Gentile distinctions need be reflected at all: the response of Jesus to come is quite normal (cf. Mark 5:24), any scruples about Jew/Gentile distinctions are not explicit (contrast Mark 7:27f.), and the ἐγώ could be MattR (cf. Matt 10:16; 12:28; 23:34 and the Lukan parallels: see Catchpole, *Quest*, 291f.)

[9] *Quest*, 298–304.

[10] *Quest*, 307.

[11] *Quest*, 293–8, contra e.g. Wegner, *Hauptmann*, who argues that the expansion is due in part to a pre-Lukan Sondergut version of the story on which Luke depends.

[12] See n. 8 above.

Nevertheless it is hard to evade completely the notion that the man is a Gentile, *and* that this is referred to at the end of the story. It is true that ἑκατοντάρχης can be used in the LXX and in Josephus to refer to Jews.[13] Yet few of the references given by Catchpole suggest that a first-century reader would have thought that the Q account was referring to a Jewish person. The LXX references all refer to the distant past of Israel's history, as do most of the references in Josephus (*Ant.* 6.40; 7.233, 368; 9.143, 148, 151, 156, 188). The one reference in Josephus to the contemporary situation (*War* 2.578) clearly implies that 'centurions' were basically not a very 'Jewish' institution. In the situation of the prelude to the outbreak of the war with Rome, Josephus realises that if the Jews are to be successful in their fight, they would have to be organised in a similarly disciplined way: hence he (Josephus) set about organising the army by (among other things) appointing centurions to match the Roman organisation.[14]

In any case it seems most likely that both Matthew and Luke, as the earliest 'interpreters' of Q, both interpreted the story as referring to a Gentile. The clear parallel between this centurion and the non-Jewish Cornelius of Acts 12 at the level of Luke's understanding is universally recognised. And Matthew interprets the story here by appending the saying Q 13:28f. (= Matt 8:11f.) with the threat of Jews (the 'sons of the kingdom') being replaced by Gentiles in the kingdom,[15] clearly implying that the Jew/Gentile distinction is in (at least his) mind.

So too the reference to 'Israel' in v. 9 seems hard to explain if no Jew/Gentile distinction has ever been in view. Matt 9:33 may

[13] See the references in Catchpole, *Quest*, 293.

[14] 'He [Josephus] understood that the Romans owed their invincible strength above all to discipline and military training . . . he observed that their discipline was due to the number of their officers, and he therefore divided his army on Roman lines and increased the number of his company commanders. He instituted various ranks of soldiers and set over them decurions and centurions . . .' (*War* 2.577f.).

[15] *Pace* Davies-Allison, *Matthew II*, 27f.; also Catchpole, *Quest*, 306, who would refer this to diaspora Jews replacing others. But if there is any idea of 'replacement' here, then it is hard to see diaspora Jews as only allowed 'in' because of the failure of other Jews. Part of Allison's argument is that such a negative statement about all Jews is scarcely credible. Perhaps though the statement is less a 'straight' prediction of what is going to happen, but more a warning of what might happen if nothing is done, and hence a plea to others to ensure that it does not materialise: cf. p. 165 above on eschatology in general.

not be quite so close a parallel as it concludes a section where Matthew's Jesus has been teaching and working with Israel; the Pharisees (the speakers in Matt 9:33) are, for Matthew, Israel's leaders, and the verse thus summarises both Jesus' activity in this part of the gospel and the reaction it has provoked. But the whole section is governed by an Israel consciousness and this may be reflected in the ἐν τῷ Ἰσραήλ of Matt 9:33. There is however no clear equivalent rationale for Q 7:9 within Q unless the story itself suggests an Israel consciousness; and this only seems to be available if the centurion is thought of as a non-Jew, thus contrasting with the situation amongst Jews, i.e. ἐν τῷ Ἰσραήλ.

I would certainly agree with Catchpole that the situation in Q about the expected fate of 'the Jews' is by no means a clear black-and-white one, and that 'Israel' (in the sense of all Jews) has not been written off entirely (cf. ch. 6, the discussion there of the meaning of 'this generation' and the significance of the polemic against this generation). So too, as will be made clear in the rest of this section, I do not believe that this story in Q functions as a warrant for a full-blown Gentile mission, or even necessarily for the presence of any Gentiles within Q's ranks in any substantial numbers. Nevertheless, the way in which this centurion functions in the story *is* similar to the way in which other Gentiles function elsewhere in Q, viz., to act as the means whereby a rebuke against a Jewish audience can be mounted.][16]

Other texts are often thought to be relevant here. The image of the 'harvest' in Q 10:2 may refer to the judgement of Gentiles (cf. Joel 3:13–14; Isa 27:11; Hos 6:11) and hence the call to send labourers to the harvest may imply the existence of a Gentile mission.[17] Similarly the parable of the Great Supper could be interpreted as a warning that after the Jewish failure to respond to Jesus, the mission will be sent out to the Gentiles.[18] And the parable of the mustard seed, with its concluding reference to the

---

[16] Cf. *Quest*, 283, referring to Q 10:13–15; 11:31f. See also Kloppenborg, *Formation*, 120. (Catchpole sets up his own essay as an alternative to Kloppenborg; but, in fact, Kloppenborg's interpretation may not be so different: for Kloppenborg, the 'development of the healing story into an apology for Gentile inclusion occurred already in the oral stage. Its reception into Q is to be seen in the context of Q's polemic against Israel's lack of recognition of the authority of Jesus and his message'.)

[17] Lührmann, *Redaktion*, 60.

[18] Lührmann, *Redaktion*, 87; Uro, *Sheep*, 219f.

great tree acting as home for all the birds of the air, could be an allusion to the incoming of Gentiles into the kingdom.[19] Others too have referred to the very negative nature of the polemic against Israel in Q as evidence for the existence of the Gentile mission being embraced positively by Q Christians. Lührmann, for example, argues that all hope for Israel has now been surrendered and hence the mission has turned to non-Jews.[20]

The problem of Q's attitude to the Gentile mission is also bedevilled by uncertainty regarding one or two key texts in Matthew or Luke alone which might have been part of Q. For example, some have argued that Matt 10:5–6 might have been in Q, in which case Q would betray a very negative attitude to the Gentile mission.[21] Others have argued that Luke 10:8b ('eat whatever is set before you') was in Q; and this instruction only really seems to make sense in the context of a Gentile missionary situation where Jewish food laws are not presupposed.[22] The question of the origin of Matt 10:5f. and Luke 10:8b cannot be discussed in detail here. Although Schürmann has argued strongly for the inclusion of Matt 10:5f. in Q, he has convinced few and most have rejected his theory.[23] Hence it would probably be dangerous to build anything in terms of a postulated Q attitude on the basis of this one unit appearing in Matthew alone.[24] The question of Luke

---

[19] Laufen, *Doppelüberlieferungen*, 192f.; Uro, *Sheep*, 218f.

[20] Lührmann, *Redaktion*, 47, 88; cf. too Kloppenborg, Formation, 148, 167. See too p. 196 n. 5 above.

[21] H. Schürmann, 'Mt 10,5b-6 und die Vorgeschichte des synoptischen Aussendungsberichtes', *Traditionsgeschichtliche Untersuchungen* (Düsseldorf: Patmos, 1968) 137–49; cf. too Davies & Allison, *Matthew II*, 164; Catchpole, *Quest*, 165–71.

[22] See Laufen, *Doppelüberlieferungen*, 219f., 288, 292; Uro, *Sheep*, 67–70.

[23] Cf. the critiques of Hoffmann, *Studien*, 258–61; Laufen, *Doppelüberlieferungen*, 237–43. Catchpole's argument in support of such a theory is based largely on the tension which the verse creates within Matthew's gospel as a whole. (Unlike Schürmann, he ascribes only v. 5b to Q, attributing v. 6 to MattR: for Schürmann, both verses are Q.) But this simply restates the problem rather than solving it, at least for Matthew: if the half verse is a pre-Matthean tradition which Matthew positively disagrees with, why is it still retained in his gospel?

[24] Catchpole also argues that the 'narrow and particularist' presuppositions of Matt 10:5b fit with other material in Q (*Quest*, 170). This *may* be so (in which case the verse would not add much to our understanding of Q in this respect). But the rest of Q is perhaps more ambiguous, and it would then probably be dangerous to allow a verse, whose existence in Q is itself disputed, to determine the interpretation of the ambiguous parts of the unquestionably Q material.

10:8b is more debated and problematic. Some have taken the half-verse as due to LkR, Hoffmann in particular arguing that Luke's redactional aim is to locate the mission in the 'town' and to smooth out some of the discrepancies in the source material.[25] Uro has shown that Hoffmann's analysis is not fully convincing:[26] Luke's text is in fact not particularly smooth and v. 8b still jars somewhat after v. 8a. Uro himself inclines to the view that v. 8b was in Q, since Luke himself would not create a text *de novo* which seemed to imply Jesus sanctioning a Gentile mission, and moreover one in which the Jewish food laws were in effect abrogated (cf. Acts 10, 15). This seems however unconvincing. Wherever Luke 10:8b comes from originally, it evidently was approved of sufficiently by Luke to be retained here. We cannot drive too much of a wedge between Luke 10:8b and Luke's own views: Luke cannot be too un-Lukan! Since the evidence is ambiguous, it would probably be too dangerous to place any weight on this part-verse in the present discussion and use it in any way as part of an argument about Q's attitude to a Gentile mission. At the most, we can only say that the verse is consistent with a positive attitude to such a mission, if the latter can be established from elsewhere in Q. We therefore turn to the other evidence reviewed earlier.

Many have pointed out that a great deal of this evidence is wholly inconclusive in the present context. A 'friendly attitude to Gentiles' is certainly present in the Q texts cited. However, as others have observed, the Gentiles mentioned are generally not people who are present for Q: rather, the reference is to the past (as in Q 11:31f.) or to the future (cf. Q 10:13–15; 13:28f.).[27] The story of the centurion's servant in Q 7:1–10 does (probably: cf. above) refer to a Gentile reacting positively to Jesus in Jesus' present (and hence by implication is almost certainly seen as paradigmatic for Q's present); nevertheless there is nothing in the story to suggest that the centurion in Q is anything other than an exceptional case. Nothing indicates that the centurion stands at the head of a long line of other Gentiles who are responding positively, either to Q's Jesus or to later Q Christians.[28] So too we had reason earlier to question the view that the polemic against 'this generation' was so fierce that it could only be explained by

---

[25] See Hoffmann, *Studien*, 276–81; also Schulz, *Q*, 407.
[26] See Uro, *Sheep*, 68f.
[27] Hoffmann, *Studien*, 293; Wegner, *Hauptmann*, 327.
[28] Cf. Hoffmann, *Studien*, ibid.

the theory that Q had surrendered all hope for Israel. I argued in ch. 6 above that 'this generation' does not necessarily comprise all Israel, and that the polemic is so strong precisely because the Christian group is seeking to intensify the appeal to its Jewish audience to change. And indeed I tried to show that in some instances in Q, a ray of light shows through the polemic giving a hint of hope for the audience (see p. 205 above on Q 13:35b).

Other texts may well be indecisive in the present discussion. The reference to the harvest in Q 10:2 is probably not conclusive since the image can be used of judgement directed to Israel as well as Gentiles.[29] The parables of the mustard seed and the Great Supper are also not clearly positive in relation to a Gentile mission. If the image in the former, of the birds nesting in the great tree, is meant to refer to Gentiles coming into the kingdom, one could still argue that this is part of the eschatological future, and not a feature of present reality. So too the imagery in the parable of the Great Supper is notoriously ambiguous. If one disregards the features in Matthew and Luke which are almost universally accepted as redactional, i.e. the burning of the 'city of those murderers' in Matt 22:7 and the double mission of the servants in Luke 14:22f., then there is no clear indication in the story that the first guests represent the Jews and that those summoned in from the streets are Gentiles. The two groups could just as easily represent Jewish leaders and other Jewish people, or 'pious' and 'sinners'.[30] We could perhaps read a Jew/Gentile distinction into the imagery if we knew of its presence in the wider context already, and in fact the wider context in Q (assuming that the Lukan order of Q material reflects the Q order reasonably accurately) is probably one of warnings to Israel with accompanying threats that Gentiles will replace Jews in the kingdom (cf. Q 13.28f.; 13:34f., which are the Q passages which immediately precede the parable in Luke).[31] However, it is still

---

[29] Hoffmann, *Studien*, 292; Meyer, 'Gentile Mission', 417; Wegner, *Hauptmann*, 328, points out that Q lacks what texts like Isa 27:11 and Joel 3:13 contain, viz. an explicit reference to Gentiles in the immediate context.

[30] Cf. the survey in Dupont, 'Parabole des invités', 676–8, for a survey of different possible interpretations of the parable.

[31] Cf. Uro, *Sheep*, 219f.; Kloppenborg, 'Jesus and the Parables of Jesus in Q', in Piper (ed.), *The Gospel Behind the Gospels*, 275–319, p. 292, refers to Q 13:28f. and 13:34f. as suggesting an 'allegorical' interpretation of the parables. I take it that this implies that the rejected guests are intended to be Jews and the new guests Gentiles.

unclear whether this is intended to imply a set of positive instructions about a Gentile mission. The parable functions primarily as a warning to the listeners not to be like the first guests who refuse to respond. Thus, even if the second group of guests brought in to replace the original guests are thought of as Gentiles, the parable is primarily about those who are refusing to respond, rather than about their possible replacements.[32] This interpretation would thus be in line with Meyer's theory that Q uses the Gentile mission as part of its plea to Israel to repent, but without necessarily engaging in such missionary activity directly (cf. n. 4 above).

If then much of the evidence for a Gentile mission being presupposed by Q is ambiguous, can we go to the other extreme and say that Q opposed such a mission? Some have referred in this context to Q's attitude to the Jewish Law, claiming that the conservative position in relation to the Law reflected in Q must exclude the possibility of Q's being positive about any Gentile mission.[33] This argument is however probably equally inconclusive. We shall see shortly that Q does indeed have a strict attitude to the Law. Q's Jesus does not wantonly break the Law, and Q Christians are exhorted by Q's Jesus not to break the Law themselves (cf. Q 11:42d; 16:17). Nevertheless, this issue is probably something of a red herring in the present context.

When thinking about 'the' Gentile mission, one cannot simply correlate a positive attitude to such a mission with a critical attitude to the Jewish Law and vice versa. It is quite clear from the Pauline letters that debates were engendered by the Christian mission reaching out to Gentiles with problems then being raised about the requirements of the Law which Gentile converts were expected to observe. Yet it is equally clear that in those debates, the issue is not simply one of a pro-Gentile, anti-Law party versus an anti-Gentile, pro-Law party. The debate for Paul concerns the question whether Gentile converts are expected to obey one specific command in the Law, namely that of circumcision. But there is nothing to suggest that for Paul Gentile converts are free

[32] Similar to this is the interpretation of Weder, *Gleichnisse*, 189f. (at least at the level of Jesus): the parable is not about drawing distinctions between two groups of people; rather, *all* are in the position of those who are invited, and all are exhorted by the parable to respond.

[33] See Schulz, *Q*, 401f.: 'Diese Q-Gemeinde kannte keine Völkermission vor dem nahen Ende, weil nirgendwo in Q die Kulttora grundsätzlich und bewußt abrogiert wird' (also pp. 244, 306); Wegner, *Hauptmann*, 332.

from all obligations to the whole of the Law. Gentiles are still expected to obey some parts of the Law (e.g. the love command and parts of the Decalogue: cf. Rom 13), even if it is notoriously difficult to work out how and where Paul distinguished between different parts of the Law. Further, there is no evidence to suggest that, in the Judaising debates in which Paul was involved, anyone ever objected to the whole principle of a Gentile mission *per se*. The point of dispute was the precise circumstances under which a Gentile could/should become a Christian. The question of whether a Gentile could become a Christian at all was universally accepted, as far as we can tell.[34] Thus, when Schulz and Wegner talk of a 'gesetzfreie Heidenmission',[35] and appear to assume that this is the only form of Gentile mission we can conceive, the issue is being put in far too black-and-white terms. No Gentile mission in early Christianity was entirely 'gesetzfrei', not even Paul's. Thus an appeal to Q's rigorist attitude to the Law cannot necessarily determine Q's attitude to any missionary activity directed to Gentiles.

There is however one other factor which is not often brought into the discussion of Q and the Gentile mission and which may take us a little further. This concerns the presence in Q of slighting references to Gentiles in Matt 5:47 and Q 12:30.[36] In these text, 'Gentiles' appear as apparently the 'natural' group to mention when the writer wants to refer to people who are 'obviously' beyond the pale, disapproved of, outside any in-group, and clearly distinguished from 'us'. In Matt 5:47 it is a question of people who 'clearly' behave in a way that is regarded as second-rate in only reciprocating good to those from whom they expect to receive back similar favours themselves. And in Q 12:30 it is a question of people getting their priorities wrong. The tone in both cases is not overtly polemical: the teaching is addressed to those 'inside' the 'community' and is not a piece of violent invective against Gentiles themselves. Yet the very fact that the sayings are so *un*polemical may be revealing: for they seem to betray a mentality for which 'Gentiles' are not included in 'our'

[34] See Uro, *Sheep*, 215.

[35] Schulz, *Q*, 306; Wegner, *Hauptmann*, 332.

[36] It is almost universally accepted that Matthew has preserved the Q version more accurately than Luke in referring in slighting terms here to 'Gentiles' in Matt 5:47, where Luke has the more general 'sinners': see p. 202 n. 20 above. The reference to Gentiles in Q 12:30 occurs in both Matthew and Luke and hence is secure as the wording of Q.

community. They are not 'one of us'. There is a clear 'us/them' mentality emerging here and 'they' are apparently described as 'Gentiles', almost without thinking.

This makes it very hard to conceive of Gentiles forming anything more than a tiny minority in the group of Christians responsible for Q. And it is correspondingly hard to believe that Q Christians were actively engaged in any positive mission to Gentiles. Moreover, the fact that the references to Gentiles are so un-polemical also makes it unlikely that Q had undertaken a Gentile mission which had ended in failure: otherwise, one would expect more invective similar to Q's harsh words against 'this generation'. It is also hard to conceive of Q Christians undergoing a significant change in their attitude to Gentiles, as if the outlook implied in Matt 5:47 and Q 12:30 represented an early view (or the view of a 'Q¹')[37] and Q Christians later became more open to Gentiles. For then the problem remains why these unflattering references to Gentiles were allowed to remain in Q at all. A changed attitude to Gentiles in a later stage, or edition, of Q might more naturally have led to some redactional modification of texts that would surely have been somewhat embarrassing to a community containing Gentiles.[38] The fact that the references are left unaltered and unmodified suggests that no great change in outlook is identifiable in this respect. The presence of the story of the centurion's servant in Q 7:1–10 suggests that Q is aware of the existence of Gentiles who have responded positively to Jesus and perhaps to the Jesus movement after Easter. But no more than awareness seems to be shown. The most likely situation thus seems to be one similar to that postulated by Meyer and others (cf. n. 4 above): Q is aware of a Gentile mission, but not actively engaged in it. Any references to Gentile conversions, or Gentile participation in the blessings of the kingdom, are not so much a reflection of the missionary activity of Q Christians but are used as part of Q's

[37] Both verses are, of course, in 'Q¹' according to Kloppenborg's model.

[38] Such editorial modifications may be present in Luke, who changes the 'Gentiles' of Matt 5:47 to 'sinners', and who qualifies the 'Gentiles' of Q 12:30 as the 'Gentiles of the world' (Luke 12:30: τοῦ κόσμου is not in Matthew), perhaps to distinguish 'worldly Gentiles' from Gentile Christians (cf. Goulder, *Luke*, 541). The presence of these references in Matthew does, of course, remain a problem on any showing, there being an almost unbearable tension between texts such as these (cf. too Matt 10:5; 15:24) and the apparently thoroughly positive reference to the mission to the Gentiles in the post-resurrection era (Matt 28:19f.).

polemical arsenal to address a Jewish audience by intensifying the appeal to other Jews.

2. Q and the Law

2.1. Q 16:16–18

An obvious starting-point for any discussion about the theme of the Law in Q is the saying in Q 16:17. There is widespread agreement that this saying stems from Q, though the precise reconstruction of the Q wording is debated.[39] The interpretation of the saying at the levels of both MattR and LkR has given rise to enormous debate. Insofar as there is scholarly agreement about anything in relation to this verse, most would probably agree that the final clause in Matthew's version ἕως ἄν πάντα γένηται (v. 18d) is due to MattR.[40] Moreover, it seems most plausible that the purpose of this addition by Matthew is to modify the force of the saying which comes to him from his tradition. The tradition says that the Law remains in force until 'heaven and earth pass away',[41] and Matthew interprets this temporal clause by his second ἕως clause in v. 18d. The implication may be that, for Matthew, in some sense 'all is accomplished' (whether in the coming of Jesus or in the death

[39] Pace Luz, *Matthew 1–7*, 258; M. Klinghardt, *Gesetz und Volk Gottes. Das lukanische Verständnis des Gesetzes nach Herkunft, Funktion und seinem Ort in der Geschichte des Urchristentums* (WUNT 2.32; Tübingen: Mohr, 1988) 18. See Kosch, *Tora*, 159–63 and the discussion below. Kloppenborg, *Q Parallels*, 180, simply says that 'most authors' agree in ascribing the verse to Q.

[40] See G. Barth, 'Matthew's Understanding of the Law', in Bornkamm, Barth and Held, *Tradition and Interpretation in Matthew*, 66; Strecker, *Weg*, 143; J. P. Meier, *Law and History in Matthew's Gospel* (AnB 71; Rome: Biblical Institute Press, 1976) 58; Guelich, *Sermon*, 145; Davies & Allison, *Matthew II*, 494. U. Luz, 'Die Erfüllung des Gesetzes bei Matthäus', *ZThK* 75 (1978) 398–435, pp. 416f., is unusual in ascribing v. 18d to Matthew's tradition (on the basis of an alleged stereotyped form of an Amen saying as isolated by K. Berger), and v. 18b to MattR. This, however, ignores the possibility that Matthew may have reordered the saying when adding to it. Luz himself admits in his later commentary that the saying with v. 18d could scarcely have existed in isolation, whereas with v. 18b it could: see *Matthew 1–7*, 258, where he indicates a more agnostic position: 'I consider the problem unsolvable.'

[41] There is debate as to whether this means 'never', or whether it is meant to be a genuinely temporal reference to the apocalyptic consummation of this age. Majority opinion is probably in favour of the latter view: cf. the literature cited in Guelich, *Sermon*, 144; Luz, *Matthew 1–7*, 265f.

and resurrection of Jesus); thus the conditions of the temporal clause have now been met, and hence in the new age of the Christian Church, one iota or keraia of the Law might fall, as indeed the following antitheses suggest.[42] Matthew's use of Q is thus to qualify very radically a statement which Matthew himself may have understood as implying that the Law would remain valid for at least the whole of the present era.

The meaning of Luke 16:17 at the level of LkR is much debated. Elsewhere in the Lukan writings, it would seem that the Law was not regarded as permanently valid for the Christian, and the issue of whether the Christian should obey the detailed commands of the Law does not seem to have been a very pressing one for Luke.[43] Some have argued that the form of the saying in Luke 16:17 should be interpreted along the lines of the formally similar saying in Luke 18:25 ('It is easier for a camel to go through the eye of a needle than for a rich man to enter the kingdom of God'). To say that 'it is easier for x than y' does not necessarily mean that x is totally impossible, but only that it is something that will happen only with great difficulty.[44]

Nevertheless, it is hard to see such an interpretation of the saying being the correct one at the level of Luke's source. The precise wording of the source here is not absolutely certain, though most would argue that Luke's version is more likely to be original: for example, Luke's use of εὐκοπώτερον is not easily

---

[42] Needless to say, such an interpretation is much disputed, but see Meier, *Law*, 63f.; Guelich, *Sermon*, 148f., with further references; also, in a slightly more nuanced form, C. E. Carlston, 'The Things that Defile (Mark vii.14) and the Law in Matthew and Mark', *NTS* 15 (1968) 75–95, pp. 78f.

[43] The issue is much debated in contemporary Lukan study: see the survey of opinion in K. Salo, *Luke's Treatment of the Law. A Redaction-Critical Investigation* (Helsinki: Suomaleinen Tiedeakatemia, 1991) 13–23. For the view above, see S. G. Wilson, *Luke and the Law* (SNTSMS 50; Cambridge University Press, 1983); also R. Banks, *Jesus and the Law in the Synoptic Tradition* (SNTSMS 28; Cambridge University Press, 1975); C. L. Blomberg, 'The Law in Luke–Acts', *JSNT* 22 (1984) 53–80. This is, of course, not to deny that Luke regards it as theologically important to show that Christianity is in a line of continuity with Judaism: hence his portrait of Paul in Acts as the Law-abiding Jew *par excellence*. But this may be more of an apologetic ploy to show Christianity as a religion of antiquity, rather than to press observance of the Jewish Law on the Christian Church.

[44] See Wilson, *Law*, 44f., and Salo, *Luke's Treatment*, 144f., for a full discussion of this verse with further references. Cf. Banks, *Jesus and the Law*, 215: 'a rhetorical figure which merely emphasises how hard it is for the Law to pass away'; also Guelich, *Sermon*, 165.

explicable as LkR.[45] Almost certainly the Q saying is asserting the abiding validity of the Law in the present.[46] Thus P. D. Meyer comments aptly: 'Q's saying, in contrast to Matthew's revision, is not concerned with the future possibility of the Law becoming void but with the present impossibility of its being void.'[47] Such an idea is not really that of either Matthew or Luke and hence we are probably justified in seeing a distinctive feature of Q emerging here.

The probable context of the saying within Q is also revealing. Most would agree that the saying about the Law comes from a small sub-section in Q containing at least the verses Luke 16:16–18 with their Matthean parallels.[48] The problem of identifying any common thread running through the whole of the material in Luke 16 at the level of LkR is well known and hence many have suggested that Luke has simply repeated a block of sayings which in part comes to him from his tradition. The possibility that these three sayings occurred together in Q is also supported by a

[45] See Laufen, *Doppelüberlieferungen*, 588 n. 84, for a full list of bibliographical references of those supporting Lukan originality here; also Kosch, *Tora*, 161; Catchpole, *Quest*, 236. Some have pointed to the clumsy nature of Matthew's two ἕως clauses and argued that it cannot be the case that both ἕως clauses are due to MattR, so that at least one ἕως clause must have been part of Matthew's source here. Hence either Q contained one such ἕως clause and thus Luke's εὐκοπώτερον form of the saying is due to LkR, or Matthew and Luke had access to different forms of the saying in their traditions. (Cf. Schulz, *Q*, 114; Meier, *Law*, 59f., for Matthew as more original; Guelich, *Sermon*, 143f., for two independent versions.) However, Matthew may have wished to modify the force of the Q saying by adding v. 18d and he prepared for this by changing the form of the 'heaven and earth passing away' clause into a temporal clause in v. 18b. The slight clumsiness may then be due to Matthew's redactional activity modifying the Q saying in two stages.

[46] Cf. also Strecker, *Weg*, 144; Carlston, 'Things that Defile', 78; Marshall, *Luke*, 630; Merklein, *Gottesherrschaft*, 92f.; Laufen, *Doppelüberlieferungen*, 354; Kloppenborg, 'Nomos and Ethos', 45f.; Kosch, *Tora*, 434; Catchpole, *Quest*, 236. The same is the view of those who would see Luke's version as redactional. Thus, for example, Meier too, who claims that Matthew's version (without v. 18d) is more original, agrees that the saying in Q is asserting the abiding validity of the Law (*Law*, 59). In this context, therefore, the precise reconstruction of the Q wording may not be critical.

[47] Meyer, *Community of Q*, 67.

[48] For what follows, see my *Revival*, 153f., with further references, especially the earlier discussion of H. Schürmann, '"Wer daher eines dieser geringsten Gebote auflöst . . ." Wo fand Matthäus das Logion Mt 5,19?', in *Traditionsgeschichtliche Untersuchungen zu den synoptischen Evangelien* (Düsseldorf: Patmos, 1968) 126–36; also Laufen, *Doppelüberlieferungen*, 352–4; Kloppenborg, 'Nomos and Ethos', 43–5; Kosch, *Tora*, 427–44; Catchpole, *Quest*, 232–8.

consideration of the Matthean contexts of the sayings. Matt 5:17 looks suspiciously like Matthew's rewriting of the saying in Luke 16:16. (Matthew's close parallel to Luke 16:16 comes elsewhere in Matt 11:12f.; however, the relocation can be adequately explained as due to MattR, bringing together sayings about John the Baptist, whereas the converse change is very difficult to explain as due to LkR.)[49] Matthew also has a parallel to the divorce saying of Luke 16:18 in Matt 5:32. The close proximity of the parallels to Luke 16:16, 17, 18 within Matt 5, in vv. 17, 18, 32, thus adds additional weight to the argument that these three verses belonged together within Q.

Within this slightly wider Q context, the saying in Q 16:17 gains added force. The preceding saying in Q 16:16 raises far more problems than can be dealt with here. It is however almost universally agreed that the more original form of the saying is represented in one half by Luke 16:16a (Matt 11:13 is probably MattR with its inversion of 'Law' and 'prophets' and its use of the verb to 'prophesy'). The more original form of the other half of the saying may be represented in Matt 11:12 (Luke 16:16b clearly owes a lot to LkR: cf. the use of πᾶς and εὐαγγελίζεται).[50] The version in Q thus probably said that 'the Law and the prophets were until John'. Quite apart from the problem of the relative position of John, the saying states that in some sense at least the era of the Law is ended. The following saying in Q 16:17 clearly has the effect of modifying this considerably, or at least of guarding against one particular interpretation. Whatever Q 16:16 implies, it must not, according to this interpretation, be taken as suggesting that the Law is no longer to be applied. A new era may in one sense have superseded that of the Law and the prophets; but the Law is still to be obeyed. It looks very much as if the second saying is a reaction against the first.[51] The positioning of Q 16:17 in Q thus probably represents the redactional activity of at least one stage of the Q tradition, imposing its own interpretation and modification of the saying in Q 16:16.

---

[49] Cf. Davies & Allison, *Matthew II*, 253; Kloppenborg, 'Nomos and Ethos', 44.

[50] See p. 136 above.

[51] For a similar view, cf. Polag, *Christologie*, 79; also Laufen, *Doppelüber-lieferungen*, 355; Kloppenborg, 'Nomos and Ethos', 45. H. Schürmann, 'Zeugnis', 170f., would see Q 16:16 as modifying and clarifying Q 16:17 in Q. But the fact that the saying about the eternal validity of the Law comes second in both Luke and Matthew, and hence almost certainly in Q as well, suggests that v. 17 is intended to qualify v. 16 and not vice versa: see Merklein, *Gottesherrschaft*, 92f.; Kosch, *Tora*, 434.

The saying which follows in Q, Q 16:18, is again notoriously difficult to interpret. The apparent total ban on divorce in this saying is certainly open to very different interpretations. According to some, it represents a radical attack on the written Law of Deut 24:1 itself.[52] According to others, no such attack is intended: being stricter than the Law requires does not constitute a fundamental attack on the Law itself.[53] If this is a radical attack on the Law, then one would have to ascribe the verse to a later stage of the Q redaction, modifying again the strict nomism of the preceding saying. On the other hand, the verse could be seen as an example of how the general saying of Luke 16:17 is to be put into practice by the Q community. The Law is to be obeyed, and obeyed even more rigorously than by some Jews, with no appeals to any 'let-out' clauses such as the divorce regulations. In favour of this last interpretation, one could appeal to Qumran texts such as the Damascus Document and the Temple Scroll which appear to suggest that at least some members of the Qumran sect regarded divorce as wrong, though without in any way making any radical attack on the Law itself.[54] If this latter interpretation is adopted, then the three Q verses considered in this section present a reasonably coherent and consistent viewpoint. With the

---

[52] Cf. Wilson, *Law*, 46f.

[53] Sanders, *Jesus*, 256, followed by Salo, *Luke's Treatment*, 148. But I am unpersuaded by Salo's other suggestion that Luke may have thought that Jesus' teaching on divorce here was very radical in relation to the Law, wanted to hide this from his readers as far as possible, but felt that he could not expunge the tradition completely and hence included this one verse on the topic (pp. 146f.). Any constraints on Luke's editorial activity do not seem to have prevented him from excising unwanted material elsewhere in the tradition.

[54] See Fitzmyer, *Luke*, 1121, with reference to CD 4.20–5.1; 11QTemple 57.17–19. Klinghardt's suggestion (*Gesetz*, 83–96) is that the saying is to be interpreted in relation to purity regulations, in particular the demand of the Law that priests should not marry, or remarry, anyone other than a virgin (cf. Lev 21:7, 13f.; Ezek 44:22); the saying might then represent the application of priestly regulations to all people, as appears to have happened with the Pharisees and with other groups. The argument is suggestive, especially in the light of the possible links with Pharisees elsewhere in Q (see below). However, the interpretation of this verse seems unpersuasive. The focus here is specifically on marrying divorcees, not on marrying anyone with sexual experience (e.g. widows), as in the priestly regulations. The text from *PseudPhoc* 205 ('Do not add marriage to marriage'), adduced by Klinghardt as illustrating the possibility of such a view being widespread, is not clearly rejecting divorce: it might just as easily be a reference to polygamy. On Klinghardt's interpretation here, see Salo, *Luke's Treatment*, 148 n. 104.

arrival of John and Jesus a new era has dawned, but this is not one where the Law loses any of its validity. The demands of the Law still apply for the Christian. Such an attitude to the Law emerges from other parts of the Q material as we shall see.

2.2. *Tithing: Q 11:42*

Q 11:39–52 contains the series of woes against scribes and/or Pharisees, some of which we have already considered in detail. In Matt 23, all the sayings are directed against the 'scribes and Pharisees', apparently viewed as an undifferentiated group. This stereotyped address is almost certainly due to MattR.[55] In Luke 11, and perhaps also in Q, the sayings are divided into two groups, one set of sayings directed against Pharisees, the other against νομικοί/γραμματεῖς.[56] In all the woes, there are at times quite marked differences in the wording of the Matthean and Lukan versions, though in general terms the existence, and the general meaning, of the Q version is not in doubt. I start with the saying about tithing in Q 11:42.

Some differences between Matthew and Luke's versions are relatively easy to explain; others are less important in the present discussion. As we have already seen, Matthew's address, 'scribes and Pharisees', is probably MattR, so that the Lukan version is probably more original in having the saying directed against 'Pharisees' alone. Matthew's reference to 'the weightier matters of the Law' may also be MattR.[57] The difference between whether 'justice' is accompanied by 'mercy and faith' (Matthew) or 'love of God' (Luke) probably need not concern us here.[58] In either case, Jesus is contrasting the tithing practices of the Pharisees with more fundamental principles which evidently should have precedence.

The final clause of the saying clearly changes the accent. Whether Matthew's ἀφεῖναι or Luke's παρεῖναι is more original here again need not concern us at this point. What is important is that the final clause ('these things you ought to have done

---

[55] So Haenchen, 'Matthäus 23', 49; Schulz, *Q*, 96; Garland, *Matthew 23*, 41, and many others.

[56] For this division already in Q, see Kosch, *Tora*, 92, with further references.

[57] So Barth, 'Law', 80; Schulz, *Q*, 100; Sato, *Q und Prophetie*, 227; Kosch, *Tora*, 113f., who also gives further literature.

[58] Luke is regarded as secondary by Schulz, *Q*, 100f.; Barth, 'Law', 80; Strecker, *Weg*, 136; Kosch, *Tora*, 114–6; Catchpole, *Quest*, 264f.

without neglecting the others') looks very much like a secondary comment by a later editor seeking to correct any 'misunderstandings' which the rest of the saying might imply. Without the final part, the logion could easily be taken as suggesting that tithing is unimportant and to be regarded as an optional extra. The final clause makes it clear that this is not the case. Tithing must still be undertaken and any appeals to great principles such as justice, etc. must not undermine in any way the actual practice of tithing. Thus many have seen Q 11:42c as a redactional addition in Q, reasserting the principle of tithing.[59] At the level of this Q redaction, it would appear that the editor wants to insist on the importance of this particular legal practice for the Christian community. It is not the case that for Q, some reassessment of the Jewish Law is in mind here, as if the ceremonial law were being made subservient to the ethical law.[60] This may be the case in Q's tradition (i.e. without the final part of the saying). The effect of the Q redaction is to go in the opposite direction and to assert that the ceremonial aspect of the Law is on a par with the rest.[61]

---

[59] See Hoffmann, *Studien*, 170; Schenk, *Synopse*, 76; Polag, *Christologie*, 80; Merklein, *Gottesherrschaft*, 83; Zeller, *Kommentar*, 69; Kloppenborg, 'Nomos and Ethos', 42f.; Kosch, *Tora*, 114, 131, 144. Older interpretations which excised this clause from Luke and regarded it as an interpolation from Matthew (cf. Garland, *Matthew 23*, 139f., for details) have clearly missed the facet of Q's ideas about the Law being discussed here and have too readily ignored the complex tradition-history which lies between Jesus and our finished Gospels. (The fact that the final clause is missing from some western manuscripts of Luke is easily explained as due to Marcionite infuence.)

Catchpole, *Quest*, 265, 272, argues that the present form of the woe displays a balance and a clarity, with a chiastic structure, which makes it hard to drive a traditio-critical wedge through its centre. However, if the whole of the final clause is seen as secondary, the negative first half (i.e. the woe alone) has its own integrity. Catchpole's complaint — that by itself the first half would be 'unclear, because it might be attacking the practice of careful tithing as well as failure to practise the fundamental covenant obligations . . .' (p. 265) — may be precisely the reason why the addition was felt to be necessary.

[60] So Schulz, *Q*, 103; also Schürmann, 'Zeugnis', 174f., who speaks of 'eine Gruppe gesetzestreuer Judenchristen, die aber dem pharisäischen Legalismus gegenüber die ethische Seite der Tora, besonders das Liebesgebot, akzentuieren'.

[61] Kloppenborg, 'Nomos and Ethos', 42, argues that 'Q' does not support the practice of tithing at all but simply ridicules Pharisaic practice, since the practice described corresponds in no way with any legal rules we know. (For a similar interpretation of the woes as ridiculing, or lampooning, the Pharisees, see Vaage, *Galilean Upstarts*, 66–86.) However, *pace* Kloppenborg, it is not clear

What precisely is the practice being commended here in Q? Unfortunately certainty is not possible since Matthew and Luke disagree in their wordings. In Matthew the (scribes and) Pharisees are accused of tithing 'mint, dill and cummin'; in Luke it is 'mint, rue and every herb'. Rules about tithing were of particular concern to the Pharisees, as far as we can tell (cf. below). The OT decreed that farm and garden produce, especially 'corn, wine and oil' (often mentioned in this context) should be tithed; and we know that later rabbis had lengthy discussions about what was and was not liable to tithing. As in all such instances, we can never be certain whether the decisions recorded in later times applied in first-century Judaism. However, according to the later rabbis, dill and cummin were required to be tithed (*m. Ma'aserot* 4:5; *m. Demai* 2:1). Mint is not mentioned in this context. Rue is explicitly excluded as liable to tithe (*m. Shebi'it* 9:1), and it is regarded as certain that not 'every herb' was tithed. Thus the Matthean version gives three items which probably were tithed (the position of mint being uncertain);[62] the Lukan version gives at least two items which were not tithed.

Almost without exception, commentators have accepted the Matthean version as more original, because it fits our knowledge of Judaism better.[63] This may be the case, though we cannot be certain. Saying anything about the Pharisees with confidence is notoriously difficult, but it would appear that the Pharisees of the pre-70 era were above all concerned with food, tithing, and purity laws, and they took enormous care to ensure that the Law was kept (see ch. 13 below). Moreover, they were evidently prepared at times to take upon themselves more demands than the Law

---

that the practice of tithing mint, etc. does not reflect the practice of the Pharisees: see the discussion below here. In any case it is not quite clear from Kloppenborg's discussion whether his claim about 'Q' concerns the tradition before or after 11:42c was added. Kloppenborg argues that 11:42c is a very late, i.e. post 'Q²', addition. We shall discuss the relative age of the postulated addition later. Certainly with the full verse, it is hard to see the saying as ridiculing tithing; and even without the last part of the verse, it is by no means clear that the saying should be interpreted this way.

[62] Part of Kloppenborg's argument that the Matthean text (which he takes to be Q) cannot reflect current practice concerns the late date of the evidence. The late date must, of course, be conceded; but the total absence of any other data either way makes it precarious to deduce (as Kloppenborg seems to do) that these regulations were *not* in force in the earlier period.

[63] Cf. Schulz, *Q*, 100; Garland, *Matthew 23*, 137; Fitzmyer, *Luke*, 948, and many others.

strictly required. If the Pharisee's prayer recorded in Luke 18:12
reflects anything at all of Pharisaic practice, it suggests that at
least some Pharisees paid more in tithes than was strictly
necessary. Jeremias suggests that the Pharisee of Luke 18 was
paying tithes on his corn, wine and oil to cover the possibility that ·
the person from whom he had bought them had not paid full
tithes already.[64] But it could equally well be the case that some
Pharisees decided to pay tithes on more things than were strictly
required by the Law. If this is the case, the Lukan version of the
saying in Q 11:42c might make more sense than its parallel in
Matthew. Indeed, if the Lukan version is more original, then the
force of the saying becomes all the greater: the comment is not
just about those who keep the Law but about those who
voluntarily do more than the Law requires.[65] But either way, the
practice which is implicitly questioned in the opening part of the
saying, but reaffirmed with the final (editorial) clause, is the
practice of a law of special concern to Pharisees.[66] The Q
community is thus expected to continue the practice of tithing as
practised by the Pharisees (though whether this is intended to
stay within the current rules, or to go beyond them in works of
supererogation, is not quite clear).

2.3. Purity: Q 11:39–41

Apparently very near the saying about tithing in Q is the saying
about purity (Q 11:39–41). Unfortunately the precise Q wording
is probably irrecoverable as the evangelists have worked over the
tradition independently.[67] Further it is not clear where (if at all)
the saying shifts from being a statement about purification
practices to being a metaphor about the moral state of a person.
Clearly both Matthew and Luke regard the saying as ultimately
metaphorical, referring to people rather than cups. This may well
be right at the level of Q too (and indeed of Jesus, if the saying
goes back to Jesus). It is however worth noting that the saying
does not condemn the practice of purity rites in any way.[68] It is

---

[64] Jeremias, *Parables*, 140.

[65] This though is rather different from Kloppenborg's suggestion that the
woe is deliberately ridiculing and mocking Pharisaic practice by describing
what is *not* done: rather, it may be referring to, and criticising, what *is* done.

[66] So Schulz, *Q*, 101; Garland, *Matthew 23*, 140.

[67] Schulz, *Q*, 96f.; Kosch, *Tora*, 105–14.

[68] Schulz, *Q*, 98f.; also S. Westerholm, *Jesus and Scribal Authority* (Lund:
Gleerup, 1978) 89.

true that there is no explicit affirmation of such rites (as in Q 11:42c) but the accent lies elsewhere.

It is also worth noting that the saying has force only if the practice referred to in the opening statement, 'you cleanse the outside of the cup', corresponds with the current practice of those addressed. Neusner has sought to show that such practice can be identified fairly precisely.[69] *M. Kelim* 25:1 states that the outside of the cup and the inside are separate for the purposes of purity considerations. Hence if one part becomes unclean it does not affect the other. Neusner examines the discussion of *m. Berakot* 8:2 in *y. Berakot* 8:2 and concludes that the practice implied in this gospel saying reflects the views of Shammaite Pharisees. Hillelites thought that the inner part of the cup was always decisive: the outer part was always held to be unclean. Thus the outer part had no effect on the inner part. The school of Shammai disagreed, holding that the two parts were independent, and hence one can cleanse the outside of the cup first. The force of the metaphor depends on the practice described, i.e. first cleansing the outside of the cup, being generally accepted by the listeners.[70] Hence the saying would have force primarily for those who are putting Shammaite beliefs into practice. Neusner accepts that the thrust of the gospel saying is at the metaphorical level of people, not utensils, but his analysis makes some striking observations about the *Sitz im Leben* in which such a saying would have force.[71]

[69] J. Neusner, '"First cleanse the inside". "Halakhic" Background of a Controversy Saying', *NTS* 22 (1976) 486–95.

[70] This is effectively denied by Kloppenborg, 'Nomos and Ethos', 39, who argues in part that cleansing only the outside of a cup would have been impossible since cleansing would have been by total immersion in a *mikveh* pool: hence the woe is reducing the distinction between outside and inside to 'an absurd caricature' and ridicule. But whatever practice is envisaged, the logic is not as Kloppenborg implies, since the argument would then have to be that one cannot cleanse the outside without automatically cleansing the inside as well. But in the text as we have it, the distinction between the outside and the inside is assumed, at least for cups; and what is criticised is a *failure* to cleanse the inside (whether of cups or people) while cleaning the outside, not doing so by default.

[71] For the view that the saying presupposes Shammaite practice, see also A. Finkel, *The Pharisees and the Teacher of Nazareth* (Leiden: Brill, 1964) 141, though Finkel argues on the basis of *m. Berakot* 8:2 alone. Neusner's argument has been criticised by H. Maccoby, 'The Washing of Cups', *JSNT* 14 (1982) 3–15. Maccoby argues that, contrary to Neusner, the saying is nothing to do with ritual purification at all. The saying is referring to simple hygienic cleaning

2.4. Sabbath: Q 14:5

Another Q tradition which is relevant for the present discussion
is the saying about rescuing someone from a pit on the sabbath
(Q 14:5). This is not always regarded as a genuine part of Q,
though the substantial agreement between Matthew and Luke
here makes it highly likely that a saying of this nature did form
part of Q.[72] Once again the precise Q wording is uncertain and
the situation is complicated by some doubt about the precise
Lukan text at this point. In particular there is textual doubt about
who/what has actually fallen into a pit, with various manuscript
support for 'son', 'ox', 'ass' or almost any combination of these
three. I have examined this tradition elsewhere and so will not
repeat the same analysis again.[73] The conclusion of that
discussion was that the most primitive form of the saying is one
which referred to a 'son' who had fallen into a pit on the sabbath.
Matthew's reference to a 'sheep' is probably MattR and the
additional references to animals in Luke 14:5 may be due to
assimilation to, or influence from, the similar story in Luke 13:15.

---

and is metaphorical throughout: the 'cup' is a metaphor for the person of the
Pharisee. However, it is not then clear what 'cleaning the outside' refers to.
Presumably it is something to do with the Pharisees' practice of worrying about
their physical bodies, and, if Neusner is right (cf. below), then a crucial part of
this would have concerned ritual purification. In any case it is hard to take the
whole saying as wholly metaphorical, since one would expect some of the verbs
and pronouns to slip into the second person: cf. Garland, *Matthew 23*, 145f.
Neusner's (and Finkel's) interpretation does have the merit of locating the
saying, which is addressed to Pharisees, within the broad contours of Pharisaic
piety.

[72] It is not mentioned by Lührmann or Hoffmann in their monographs, nor
is it included by Neirynck and Van Segbroek in the list of passages assigned to
Q in their *New Testament Vocabulary* (Leuven University Press & Peeters, 1984)
5. Schulz, *Q*, 41, explicitly denies that this is a part of Q, partly on the basis of
the difference in wording between Matthew and Luke, partly on the grounds
that the view of the sabbath law implied here — that the Law can be broken to
help other people — is inconsistent with the attitude to the Law elsewhere in
Q. But if the analysis offered here is correct, then this verse fits very well with a
(strict Jewish) casuistic interpretation of the Law. Those who would ascribe the
verse to Q include Bussmann, Schmid, Schürmann: see Polag, *Fragmenta Q*,
72f.; Kloppenborg, *Q Parallels*, 160; also now F. Neirynck, 'Luke 14,1–6. Lukan
Composition and Q Saying', in C. Bussmann & W. Radl (eds.), *Der Treue Gottes
Trauen* (FS G. Schneider; Freiburg: Herder, 1991) = *Evangelica II*, 183–204;
Kosch, *Tora*, 200–6.

[73] See my *Revival*, 98f.

Part of the problem raised by the tradition here is to know the precise legal background, and again the limited nature of our knowledge of first-century Judaism becomes a critical factor. As far as we can tell, it would not have been regarded as a legitimate breach of the sabbath law to rescue an animal which had fallen into a pit, but it would have been regarded as legitimate to rescue a person in such a situation. The Q saying refers to the example of a human being, rather than an animal, falling into a pit as providing a precedent for working on the sabbath. It thus appears to reflect very precisely the interpretation of the sabbath law by contemporary Jews in a way that other strands of the gospel tradition do not.[74] (Mark's gospel is notorious for having Jesus justify his behaviour in a way that no Jew would accept;[75] so too Matthew's adaptations of the Q tradition fail to satisfy Jewish sensibilities, since no Jew apparently accepted that one could rescue a sheep from a pit on the sabbath.)[76]

Q 14:5 appears at first sight to be an isolated saying in Q. There is no clear evidence of the context in Q in which the saying occurred.[77] Nevertheless it is clear that the saying must have been part of a wider context. It cannot have existed in isolation. It clearly acts as the first half of an *a minori ad maius* argument; and the argument cannot really have been anything other than an attempt to justify Jesus' working on the sabbath.[78] The point to notice here is that such an argument would have real force in a Jewish context in a way that defences by Jesus in other strands of the gospel tradition do not (cf. above). Jesus is here appealing to an example which the Jews themselves would accept as a legitimate breach of the sabbath law. It may well be that such an appeal would not have convinced Jesus' opponents about the

[74] This applies, of course, to the reference to the 'son' in the text, but not the 'ox'!

[75] See C. G. Montefiore, *The Synoptic Gospels I* (London: Macmillan, 1927) 81f., on the saying in Mark 3:4 (the Markan context in which Matthew's version of the Q saying is placed): Jesus 'seems to evade the argument by a counter argument, which, however ingenious, is not really to the point'.

[76] See Strecker, *Weg*, 19.

[77] Both Neirynck and Kosch argue strongly against the theory that Luke 14:1–6 itself may have been a Q story omitted (bar v. 5) by Matthew.

[78] Kosch, *Tora*, 207–10, argues that the saying has nothing to do with legal discussions at all: it simply refers to actual concrete practice and is quite un-interested in the problem of sabbath law observance. This seems unpersuasive: it is hard to conceive of the saying originating in a setting which is not in some way concerned explicitly with the question of sabbath observance.

legitimacy of some of the specific actions of Jesus on the sabbath recorded in the gospels: after all, rescuing a man from a pit was a matter of saving his life and the principle of working to save life on the sabbath was accepted by all; the problem with Jesus' actions on the sabbath as recorded in the gospels is that they are not actions which necessarily save physical life.[79] We do not have the second half of the argument in Q, and hence we do not know precisely what action of Jesus on the sabbath is here being defended. However, the force of the saying is clear. Jesus is shown as not acting wantonly. If he does break the sabbath law, he does so by appealing to accepted and legally defined exceptions to the Law. The Jesus of Q thus operates on the sabbath within the Law as defined by later tradition to a far greater extent than the Jesus of Mark or the Jesus of Matthew.

2.5. *Other Evidence from Q*

Other Q texts may provide some subsidiary evidence to supplement the picture which has emerged so far. In particular, the versions of the double love command in Matt 22:34–40 and Luke 10:25–28 may be relevant here. I have argued elsewhere for the existence of the Q source at this point in the tradition.[80] The extensive agreements between Matthew and Luke against Mark, many of which are hard to explain as redactional, are most easily accounted for by the existence of a version of this story in Q as well as in Mark.[81] The one point worth noting here is that in Q

---

[79] However, the appeal to the principle of saving life on the sabbath (cf. Mark 3:4), if it does go back to Jesus, could be seen as an attempt to re-evaluate what constitutes 'saving life': Jesus' miracles of healing on the sabbath illustrate the 'healing' effect of his gospel which strikes at a deeper level than only the physical.

[80] *Revival*, 125ff.; see also R. H. Fuller, 'The Double Commandment of Love: a Test Case for the Criteria of Authenticity', in Fuller (ed.), *Essays on the Love Commandment* (Philadelphia: Fortress, 1978) 41–56; K. Kertelge, 'Das Doppelgebot der Liebe im Markusevangelium', in *A Cause de l'Evangile* (FS J. Dupont; Paris: Cerf, 1985) 303–32, pp. 307–10; J. Lambrecht, 'The Great Commandment Pericope and Q', in Piper (ed.), *The Gospel Behind the Gospels*, 73–96.

[81] The most important are the common description of the man who speaks with Jesus as a νομικός (if that is indeed the correct reading in Matt 22:35), the reference to the man 'testing' Jesus, the address of Jesus as 'teacher', and the use of the phrase 'in the Law'. To these can be added the common omission of the monotheistic confession of Deut 6:4 (cf. Mark 12:29), and the critique of

the question about the great commandment is apparently a hostile one (Luke 10:25 ἐκπειράζων; Matt 22:35 πειράζων) . The question is put by a νομικός, which links with the second half of the series of woes in Luke 11 par Matthew 23 where the final three woes are directed against the νομικοί. It is of course notoriously difficult to identify precisely the νομικοί and the φαρισαῖοι in the Gospels, and to see what links if any it is justifiable to draw between either group and the later rabbis. J. Bowker has suggested that there was probably a steady increase in overlap between the two groups during the second-temple period.[82] It would not be unreasonable to see the Q community as also envisaging some connection between the two. It is true that the Q

---

sacrifice in Mark 12:32f. (Lambrecht, 'Great Commandment', 79–81, notes a few more common omissions.)

The most powerful case against such a theory has been mounted by J. Kiilunen, *Das Doppelgebot der Liebe in synoptischer Sicht* (Helsinki: Suomaleinen Tiedeakatemia, 1989). See too F. Neirynck, 'The Minor Agreements and Q', in Piper (ed.), *The Gospel Behind the Gospels*, 49–72, pp. 61–4. Both argue that the agreements can be explained as independent redaction by Matthew and Luke. However, not all Kiilunen's arguments are persuasive. For example, the reference to the νομικός in Matthew (perhaps the hardest feature to explain as redactional) is said by Kiilunen (pp. 37f.) to be due to Matthew's concentration on the theme of the νόμος; yet the fact remains that the word occurs only here in Matthew, and is not at all easy to ascribe to MattR, given Matthew's clear predeliction for the word γραμματεύς. νομικός may also not be very characteristic of Luke, since Luke uses γραμματεύς in Acts, and never introduces νομικός in a Markan context. Kiilunen's attempt to distinguish between a singular and plural use of γραμματεύς in Luke, whereby a singular 'scribe' means only a town clerk (cf. Acts 19:35: see Kiilunen, pp. 54–6; cf. too Neirynck, 'Minor Agreements', 63, and 'Luke 14,1–6', 190–3), seems to me to be somewhat artificial: if the singular noun meant one thing, it is hard to see why the plural would have been interpreted differently by either Luke or his readers. I am not persuaded either that Luke's ἐκπειράζων can easily be seen as LkR. *Pace* Kiilunen (pp. 59f., also Neirynck, 'Minor Agreements', 64), the context in Luke is not really a very hostile one, and antagonism *to Jesus* can only be read into Luke 10:29a with some difficulty.

(The possibility that νομικός is not part of Matthew's text should probably be rejected. The manuscript evidence for omitting the word [f¹ e syrˢⁱⁿ] is very weak and would not be considered seriously were it not for the difficulty of explaining the word in Matthew. Presence in a source, rather than either a redactional creation or a later scribal addition, seems a more satisfactory explanation.)

[82] J. Bowker, *Jesus and the Pharisees* (Cambridge University Press, 1973) 21–3; cf. also Hengel, *Charismatic Leader*, 56; Westerholm, *Jesus and Scribal Authority*, 26. Others would argue that 'Pharisees' and 'scribes' are almost synonymous: cf. Sanders, *Jesus*, 198.

woes distinguish between the two groups, but the fact that the woes (probably) occur together in Q suggests that for Q the two groups are not unrelated. Thus the pericope of the great commandment shows that the Jesus of Q is facing and dealing with some suspicion on the part of scribes/lawyers and/or Pharisees over the question of the Law. The detailed reply of Jesus in Q (apart from the actual double love command itself) is probably irrecoverable. Matt 22:40 almost certainly represents MattR of Mark, and Luke's version has been strongly redacted to link up with the following parable of the Good Samaritan.[83]

Further hostility in relation to scribes and/or Pharisees is also evidenced in the remaining Q woes which we have not considered in detail here. However, it is worth noting that all the remaining woes (with the possible exception of Q 11:46) concern the behaviour of the Pharisees or lawyers: what is attacked is their love of publicity, their inner 'impurity', their guilt in inflicting violence on the prophets, and so on.[84] Q 11:46 may be the exception in that the lawyers are criticised for 'loading' people with 'burdens hard to bear'. (Presumably the reference is to the detailed prescriptions of the interpretation of the Law.) Yet the real critique is that the lawyers have failed to help other people with their burdens. The burdens themselves are not really questioned in principle.

2.6. *Strata within Q?*

The Q material considered so far shows a deep concern that the Law should be maintained; it is aware that Jesus could be seen as antinomian, and Q appears to represent a strong movement to 'rejudaise' Jesus. But what stage in the development of the Q tradition does such a concern reflect? I argued above that the presence of Q 11:42c and the positioning of Q 16:17 after 16:16 represents editorial activity. But is this editorial work that of the 'final' Q editor, or of a pre-redactional stage in the tradition? Rather diverse answers have been given to this question in past studies. Thus, for example, two contrasting views are represented by the works of Kosch and Kloppenborg. Kosch argues that this

---

[83] Fuller, 'Double Commandment', 42f.; Fitzmyer, *Luke*, 881; Kiilunen, *Doppelgebot*, 68f.

[84] Cf. Manson, *Sayings*, 99, says of the first three woes in Luke 11: 'These three woes are all concerned with character and conduct. There is in them no polemic against Pharisaism as such.'

editorial activity reflects a relatively early stage in the development of the tradition: the texts are somewhat isolated within Q and do not really characterise the rest of the Q material — indeed they are somewhat at variance with other potentially Torah-critical parts of Q (e.g. 11:41; 10:7a); moreover, Q 11:42c and 16:17 only modify individual sayings (i.e. Q 11:42ab and 16:16 respectively), and they do not seem to be redactionally qualifying the larger speech complexes in Q. Thus Kosch argues that these few editorial elements reflect an early stage in Q's tradition history.[85] By contrast, Kloppenborg argues that these elements reflect a very late stage in the development of the tradition. He sees close links between 11:42c and 16:17 on the one hand and the temptation narrative on the other, where Jesus is shown supremely as the one who is obedient to scripture. He argues (as indeed do many) that the temptation narrative is a late-comer into Q, post-dating almost all of the rest of Q. Hence the editorial notes in Q 11:42c and 16:17 are also to be assigned to this very late stage in the development of Q, i.e. to the postulated 'Q³' stage.[86]

Of the two theories, Kosch's is perhaps more likely on literary grounds. The fact that the editorial modifications (in Q 11:42c; 16:17) come within larger units suggests that these modifications have not been added after these units had already been formed.[87] Yet in a more deep-seated way, Kosch and Kloppenborg are not so far removed from each other. Despite their differences, both agree that the concerns of these Torah-centred verses or part-verses do not characterise other major parts of Q: hence for Kosch they are pre-redactional; for Kloppenborg they are effectively 'post-redactional', since for most who follow Kloppenborg's model, prime interest is often focused on the 'Q²' redactional stage which dominates so much of the Q material. I would however question whether it is right to relegate the sentiments expressed in verses like Q 11:42c and 16:17 to the sidelines of Q quite so much.

Kloppenborg is undoubtedly correct to refer to the link between these verses and the temptation narrative. It is however by no means so obvious that the temptation narrative is a late-

---

[85] Kosch, *Tora*, 166, 458f., 462. Kosch is strongly influenced by Schürmann's general theory of the development of the tradition.

[86] Kloppenborg, 'Nomon and Ethos', passim, esp. pp. 46f.

[87] The situation is similar to the problem of the precise position of Q 7:27 in the tradition history of Q: see p. 133 above.

comer into Q. I have argued this in detail elsewhere and will not
repeat all the details of that discussion here.[88] In part the
argument is somewhat circular in the present context since the
issue is precisely how far the dominant theme of the temptation
narrative, showing Jesus as obedient to scripture, really is in line
with the rest of Q. However, it should also be noted that several
other features of the temptation narrative do show close links
with other parts of Q. Thus the implied critique of concern for
food and material goods in the first temptation[89] fits well with
the similar sentiments expressed in the cares tradition (Q 12:22–
31) and the sayings on prayer (Q 11:2–4, 9–13), at least as I have
tried to interpret them (see pp. 149–55 above). So too the
reference to Jesus here as Son of God, often thought to be
anomalous in relation to the rest of Q where 'Son of God' is not
the most common Christological category, again fits well with the
Q 11 + Q 12 passages where Jesus' followers are exhorted to
address God as Father (11:2) and assured that their Father knows
their needs and will supply them (12:30; cf. 11:13). Hence the
Devil's opening gambit 'If you are the Son of God . . .' may, for Q,
not be intending to distinguish Jesus from others in a
Christological way, but rather to show what true divine sonship
really entails, and hence provide a paradigm for the Christian
who is a son/daughter of the one who is to be addressed as
Father.[90]

In the second temptation, the refusal of Jesus to perform a
stupendous miracle, solely for its own sake,[91] coheres closely with
the Sign of Jonah passage (Q 11:29–32: cf. pp. 256–66 above). In
both Jesus refuses to act in any way that will compel the audience
to accept his claims. The only 'sign' that will be given is the sign of
Jonah, and for Q that refers to the present activity of Jesus'
preaching and all the inherent ambiguity in the claims made

---

[88] See my 'Temptation Narrative'.

[89] The three temptations differ in order in Matthew and Luke (though both
agree in their ordering of the first). I am following the widely held view that
Matthew has preserved the Q ordering whilst Luke has inverted the second
and third temptations in order to have the scene with Jesus on the pinnacle of
the temple in Jerusalem as the climax of the pericope as a whole. Cf. Schulz, *Q*,
177; Fitzmyer, *Luke*, 165, 507; Davies & Allison, *Matthew I*, 364. For a full
discussion, see H. Mahnke, *Die Versuchungsgeschichte im Rahmen der synoptischen
Evangelien* (Frankfurt: Lang, 1978) 170–82.

[90] For more details, see my 'Temptation Narrative', 494–8.

[91] See my 'Temptation Narrative', 498f., for a consideration of other possible
interpretations of the temptation.

thereby. Further evidence of such ambiguity is shown elsewhere in Q. For example, Q 7:22f. makes it clear that, although Jesus is fulfilling the Isaianic prophecies in his miracles (Q 7:22), it is still possible to take offence at Jesus (Q 7:23). Similarly, the twin parables of the mustard seed and the leaven (Q 13:18–21) appear to reflect an awareness that the present is characterised by unseen, minute, hidden realities, and the parable seeks to give reassurance that the future with all its glory is assured. So too, we have seen that the main emphasis in large parts of the eschatological teaching of Q's Jesus is to arouse eschatological awareness in a situation where people appear to think that the present life is quite normal and will carry on without interruption (cf. p. 295 above). The present is thus for Q evidently not clear and transparent for the reality which the Q Christians evidently believe to be underlying or imminent. Such an awareness runs through the whole of Q and hence the second temptation coheres with this very closely.

The third temptation is not so clearly of a piece with the rest of Q, and yet it may cohere just as well. The story line concerns the true object of worship; indeed the story is told in such a way that any monotheistic hearer/reader would agree that there is no real option: if a rival for worship appears alongside God, then God must always be the 'winner'. Yet for later texts of Q, there are perhaps more insidious rivals to God which are present. This may be implied in Q 16:13, where money ('mammon') appears as a potential rival to God for the object of service. This in turn links with the material in the mission charge and on cares, where the hearers are encouraged to put all concern for material goods and money on one side. The temptation also concerns the 'kingdoms' of the world, which then contrasts powerfully with the stress in the rest of Q on the other 'kingdom' spoken of by Jesus, the kingdom of God. And the first beatitude (which may have followed immediately after the temptation narrative in Q) speaks of the kingdom of God being associated with the poor (Q 6:20), so that God and the poor belong together inextricably in a way that excludes all concern for riches and mammon.

There is thus a close connection between several of the key themes of the temptation narrative and the rest of Q. In terms of its form, the temptation narrative is certainly somewhat unlike other parts of Q, with its pattern of dialogue between Jesus, who only speaks to cite scripture here, and a mythical demonic figure.

On the other hand, the temptation narrative is clearly one of the introductory pericopes to Q, and introductory pericopes are often equally dissimilar to the rest of the text they introduce. The Johannine prologue with its explicit Logos Christology is in many respects unlike the rest of John's gospel (where there is no explicit Logos Christology). Similarly the Markan prologue, whether it be Mark 1:1–13 or 1:1–15, is unlike the succeeding narrative and also contains an encounter with Satan — yet many have seen these opening verses in the gospel serving to set out in theological terms what will be described in more 'historical', and less picturesque, language in the subsequent narrative. The Q temptation narrative may act in precisely the same way. Thus the concern for material goods, the desire for certainty via authenticating signs, and the tendency to set up rivals to God, are all shown here to be demonic in origin. Even though, or perhaps precisely because, some may not have seen similar issues in such terms, the temptation narrative seeks to show unequivocally the nature of the issues involved as being a threat to the sovereignty of God Himself.

So far, however, we have not considered the importance of Jesus' being obedient to scripture. Clearly this is a vital part of the temptation narrative.[92] Clearly too, as Kloppenborg observes, it serves to unite the temptation narrative with the vv. 11:42c and 16:17. But is this then evidence of a very late, and not very widespread (in Q), concern on the part of a Q[3] editor? The observations offered above hopefully go some way to showing that the temptation narrative is not so unlike, and dissimilar to, the rest of Q that it must be ascribed to a tertiary, late redaction. But equally it must be noted that Q 11:42c and 16:17 are not so isolated within Q. These two verses or part-verses are perhaps the clearest instances of redactional modifications of an earlier tradition (i.e. 11:42ab and 16:16 respectively). But the concerns of these two verses are present elsewhere in Q too. If, as I tried to argue earlier, Luke 14:5/Matt 12:11 is part of Q, then this too shows Jesus as working within the presuppositions of Jewish legal argumentation. If Luke 10:25–28 belonged to Q (at least in part), as I also argued above, then this too shows Jesus, in a story in the form of

---

[92] Cf. Mahnke, *Versuchungsgeschichte*, 198; Kloppenborg, *Formation*, 258; Luz, *Matthew 1–7*, 186: 'The connecting thought among all three temptations is not polemic against a certain (mis)understanding of Jesus' sonship with God but the obedience of Jesus to the word of God.'

a *Streitgespräch* (often thought to characterise only the temptation narrative in Q), meeting some kind of hostile challenge (cf. the reference to the man 'testing' Jesus) by referring to the words of scripture itself.

There are too a number of other places in Q where Jesus refers to scripture, at least implicitly, to bolster his message. Further, Catchpole has pointed out that several of these occur in what would normally be regarded as redactional passages (or for Kloppenborg, 'Q²').[93] Thus the accusation against Capernaum in Q 10:14 echoes the taunt against the king of Babylon in Isa 14:13, 15. The final dismissal of the would-be seekers after Jesus in Q 13:26f. echoes Ps 6:9. The lament over Jerusalem in Q 13:34f. finishes with a clear allusion to Ps 118:26. The end of the parable of the mustard seed, with its reference to the great tree, clearly echoes the ideas of Ezek 17 and/or Dan 4. The warning of internecine strife (Q 12:51–53) echoes Mic 7:6.[94] Moreover passages like Q 10:14; 13:26f; and 13:34f. are clearly integral parts of that layer in Q which is dominated with polemical language against 'this generation', and ideas of Wisdom and the rejection of the prophets which we considered in ch. 6. They are clearly then part of the stratum which elsewhere I have assigned to Q's redaction. There seems therefore no very good reason for denying that the passages such as the temptation narrative and the redactional additions in 11:42c and 16:17 belong at that stage as well. Thus the 'editorial' additions can be perfectly adequately explained as additions at the stage of the (single) Q redaction which I have postulated up to now. It seems therefore unnecessary, and inappropriate, to ascribe this material either to an early, or a very late, stage unrelated to the rest of Q.[95]

---

[93] Catchpole, *Quest*, 231f.

[94] A very full list of possible OT citations or allusions in Q is given by R. Hodgson, 'On the Gattung of Q: A Dialogue with J. M. Robinson', *Biblica* 66 (1985) 73–95, pp. 77–84, though I am not persuaded that all of them are necessarily Q (e.g. Luke 9:61) or genuine OT allusions (Q 10:5 cf. 1 Sam 25:6?; Q 10:7 cf. Lev 19:13 or Deut 24:14f.?; Q 10:21, 24 cf. Isa 29:14 or Isa 6:9f.?; Q 11:42 cf. Mic 6:8?). Certainly, many of the allusions are *so* allusive that it seems precarious to talk, as Hodgson does, of Q possibly being itself, or taking over, a 'testimony' collection.

[95] I remain unpersuaded, *pace* Kosch, *Tora*, 467, that verses like Q 10:7a: 11:41 are critical of the Torah. Evidently they *could* be read as implicitly questioning aspects of the Law in another context — but there is no clear evidence that such a context is provided by Q!

2.7. Q 9:60

Perhaps the one saying in Q that would tell against the picture outlined above would be the saying recorded in Q 9:60 'Let the dead bury their dead', apparently playing loose with the most fundamental filial duty and probably even the commandment in the Decalogue to honour one's father and mother.[96] Yet whatever the saying may imply, one can note that no legal presuppositions or consequences are either raised or drawn out in the present Q context. The saying is not overtly about Torah observance: it is about discipleship and the commitment to Jesus which overrides everything else. Clearly far-reaching implications can be drawn (as modern scholarship testifies!). Perhaps all one can say is that Q neither draws any such consequences, nor gives any hint that such issues are at stake.

Conclusion

The Q material we have considered exhibits a strongly 'conservative' attitude to the Law. Tendencies in the tradition which might be interpreted in a way that would challenge the authority of the Law are firmly countered (the only possible exception to this being in Q 9:60). Further, there is some strong concern to uphold the Pharisaic interpretation of the Law. However, coupled with this is an intense hostility to non-Christian Pharisees and/or non-Christian scribes/lawyers. Does such a picture have any further implications for where the community which preserved this Q material, and for which its sentiments were presumably congenial, might be placed on a first-century 'map'? It is this broader question which I shall seek to address in the final chapter.

---

[96] This is about the only instance in the whole of the gospel tradition where Sanders, in his discussion of Jesus (rather than Q) and the Law, concedes that Jesus may have challenged the Law: see his *Jesus*, 252–5. The unparalleled attitude to filial obligation here is also emphasised by Hengel, *Charismatic Leader*.

13

———————

Q and Israel

Much of the material discussed in this book has concerned, either implicitly or explicitly, the problem of the relationship in Q between the Christian movement and the Jewish people. In this chapter therefore I shall try to draw some of the various threads together to see if a coherent and consistent picture emerges for the way in which the Q Christians regarded themselves in relation to Judaism. Further, I shall try to see if the evidence reviewed so far can be used to make any more precise suggestions about the *Sitz im Leben* of the group of people who preserved Q, and for whom its sentiments were presumably congenial.

In the discussion of Q and the Law (ch. 12 above), I argued that Q shows a somewhat conservative attitude to the Jewish Law. There is certainly nothing which explicitly questions observance of the Law in any way; and there are one or two hints that Q was at least aware of tendencies that might give rise to such questioning, and was concerned to nip such tendencies in the bud quite firmly (cf. Q 11:42c; 16:17; 4:1–13). The horizons of Q Christians seem thus to be firmly fixed within the bounds of Torah-observance.

A similar picture emerged from our discussion of the attitude to Gentiles and any possible Gentile mission in Q. Q seems to show awareness of the existence of a Gentile mission, or at least of the presence of (perhaps isolated) Gentiles within the sphere of salvation offered by the Christian message. But there seems to be no awareness at all of any problems that such a mission might create in relation to the Law, in particular of the question of how far Gentile Christians are expected to obey the Jewish Law.[1] Rather, I argued above that the existence of Gentile Christians seemed only to have been appealed to by Q as part of its continuing passionate plea to the Jewish people to respond positively to the Christian message. Any 'missionary' activity in Q seems

---

[1] Unless perhaps Luke 10:8b belonged to Q: cf. p. 399 above.

confined to Judaism. So too this view is reinforced by Q's passing references to Gentiles in Q 12:30; Matt 5:47. Such language clearly implies an 'us and them', or 'in-group/out-group' mentality. But the way in which the 'out-group', or 'them', can be referred to quite casually as 'Gentiles' (alongside tax-collectors in Matt 5:47) suggests that the Q Christians regarded themselves primarily as Jewish and (at least part of) Israel.

Such an attitude is consistent too with what I argued above in relation to Q's polemic against Israel. At one level, this polemic is extremely fierce and unrelenting. As we have seen, such ferocity has led some scholars to claim that the Q Christians had given up all hope for the 'conversion' of their Jewish contemporaries and had consigned all Israel mentally to judgement. However, I argued above that such a theory was not fully convincing. Rather, the aim of the Q Christians was to change Israel, to make their Jewish contemporaries aware of the disaster that was threatening them if they did not 'repent'. Hence the aim of the polemic was not to gloat ghoulishly over a catastrophe that was inevitably coming, but to arouse others in order to save them, perhaps too looking forward to possible success (cf. above on 13:35).[2]

How then can we best summarise Q's attitude to Israel/Judaism? How did Q Christians regard themselves in relation to their Jewish contemporaries? How much separation had occurred — at both the social and the ideological level?

Such questions raise enormous conceptual problems. Further, the answers to them are heavily dependent on who is giving the answers. Clearly, any group of Christians within early Christianity must have appeared, both to themselves and outsiders, as in some sense a group distinct from their Jewish neighbours in concrete social terms and also in terms of elements of their ideology. At the social level, any form of group meeting would have served to accentuate the distinctiveness of the group; and in terms of ideology, the positive attitude to the person of Jesus and his teaching must have marked off the Christian group from others.

---

[2] The situation I am positing is, of course, also different from that suggested by those who would see a number of different layers within Q reflecting different levels of alienation of the Q Christians from their Jewish contemporaries (cf. Schürmann, 'Redekomposition'; Horn, 'Christentum'; also perhaps Jacobson, *First Gospel*). As I argued in ch. 9 above, even the overtly most polemical passages in Q (Q 11:49–51; 13:28f.; 13:34f.) may be seeking to intensify the appeal to their addressees from with*in* the same community, rather than reflecting increasing separation between two 'communities'.

On the other hand, any Christian group would also display elements of continuity: at the ideological level Christianity has never cut its roots from Judaism;[3] and at the social level the fact that Christians and non-Christian Jews lived alongside each other inevitably entailed a degree of social overlap and relationship. Further, the very existence of hostility reflects an element of social identity between the two groups. From the Jewish side, the 'persecution' of the Christian movement can only really be seen as stemming from a belief that the Christians constituted a threat from within to Judaism's self-identity.[4] If Christianity had been perceived as a religion quite separate from Judaism, then Jews would presumably have ignored it completely. Moreover, it is likely that the extreme nature of the hostility indicates (almost paradoxically) the closeness of the relationship between the two groups.[5] Thus the existence of the (at times) very harsh and fierce polemic in Q against non-Christian Jews, and the belief that Jews are 'persecuting' the Christians,[6] probably indicates a large measure of social and ideological overlap between the Christian group and their non–Christian neighbours.

What is perhaps striking in Q is the way in which, from the Christian side, there seems to be a conscious effort being made to minimise the social rupture which the existence of the Christian claims has engendered. This is the thrust of two important essays by Catchpole,[7] and the following discussion is much indebted to Catchpole's pioneering work here, even if one or two details of his argument may perhaps be questioned. Catchpole starts by referring to the Great Sermon in Q, in particular the opening beatitudes. The key position of the Sermon in Q, providing the first extended block of Jesus' teaching, and the relative position of the beatitudes themselves right at the start of this block, gives these beatitudes programmatic significance for Q. I argued above

[3] With the exception, of course, of Marcion!

[4] See E. P. Sanders, *Paul, the Law and the Jewish People* (Philadelphia: Fortress, 1983) 192, on Paul's treatment at the hands of Jewish authorities. Also A. E. Harvey, 'Forty Strokes Save One: Social Aspects of Judaising and Apostasy', in A. E. Harvey (ed.), *Alternative Approaches to New Testament Study* (London: SPCK, 1985) 79–96.

[5] See, from the side of a sociologist on conflict theory, Coser, *Social Conflict*, 67–85: 'The closer the relationship, the more intense the conflict' (p. 67).

[6] Though see ch. 9 above for discussion of the question how much active, or physical, persecution was actually involved.

[7] Catchpole, *Quest*, ch. 3 'The Inaugural Discourse' (pp. 79–134), and ch. 4 'Reproof and Reconciliation' (pp. 135–50).

that probably all three opening beatitudes in their Q form reflect the language of Isa 61,[8] a text which was clearly of great importance for Q (cf. Q 7:22).[9] Catchpole also refers to the fact that the beatitude form itself may be significant in the light of the frequency with which this form is used in relation to the covenant and the blessings flowing from the covenant relationship.[10] Further, this concern for the 'poor'[11] reflects a constant and consistent element within the covenant relationship inaugurated by God between Himself and His people: God is one who cares for the poor and Israel too has a constant obligation to do the same.[12] Thus the claim of Q 6:20f. that the 'poor' will receive final (eschatological)[13] blessing is simply a reiteration of the fundamental belief of the Jewish people about the nature of God. As Catchpole says,

> The self-awareness of the people of God is concerned, and the concentration on the poor reflects the conviction that the God of the covenant's concern for the marginalised and vulnerable on the fringes of his people (humanly speaking), for those who found themselves at the wrong end of the socio-economic spectrum, for those who shared the defencelessness of the orphan and the widow, for those who tend to be deprived of justice and victimised by the rich and powerful — for these persons the God of the covenant's concern remains unchanged.[14]

This conclusion could probably be strengthened if it were accepted that Luke 4:16ff. belonged to Q. I have tried to argue earlier that the quotation of Isa 61 (with the line from Isa 58:6) was indeed pre-Lukan and came to Luke from Q.[15] In the earlier discussion I concentrated on the Christological significance of the citation, arguing that Jesus is portrayed here as an eschatological prophetic figure (rather than as a royal messianic figure). However, just as significant may be the ideas that this

---

[8] See pp. 223–6 above.

[9] Especially too if Luke 4:16ff. belonged to Q: see pp. 226–37 above.

[10] *Quest*, 86f., referring to Deut 33:29; Ps 33:12; 84:12; 144:15; 146:5; Isa 30:18; 56:2, etc.

[11] The 'mourners' and the 'hungry' are probably the *same* group of people: see p. 226 above.

[12] For God as the protector of the poor: 2 Sam 22:28; Ps 35:10; 72:2, 4, 12; Isa 26:6; 49:13, etc. In the Law, cf. Exod 22:25–27; 23:10–11; Lev 19:9–10; Deut 15:7–11, as well as the tirades of the prophets (Isaiah, Amos, etc.)

[13] See p. 141 above.

[14] *Quest*, 86f.

[15] See pp. 226–37 above.

citation evokes in relation to a theology of Jubilee, and it is to this that we shall now turn briefly.

Many have in fact argued that implicit in this composite citation of Isa 61 + 58 in Luke 4 is the idea of the Jubilee.[16] The 11QMelch scroll from Qumran has now shown clearly how the ideas and the vocabulary of the Jubilee legislation could be, and were, used to refer to the eschatological hopes for salvation and/ or judgement for the people.[17] In Luke 4 the stress on ἄφεσις which links the two parts of the citation (from Isa 61 and Isa 58) together serves to emphasise the Jubilee ideas in the Isa 61 text itself.[18] Nevertheless, despite the strong hint of Jubilee ideas in the citation of Luke 4:18f. itself, a number of scholars have expressed doubts as to whether such ideas should be seen as significant in relation to the whole of Lukan theology, since Luke himself does not appear to develop this specific aspect significantly elsewhere even if the social concern expressed in the Jubilee legislation is clearly of importance for Luke. Thus, Turner writes:

> It would be hazardous on the basis of this evidence even to begin to speak of a *Lucan* jubilee theology — far more so to make this a *central* motif in Luke's soteriology, as R. B. Sloan does, for Luke nowhere uses the distinctive jubilee vocabulary ... and nowhere else develops unambiguously jubilee concepts. Nevertheless Strobel is probably right to suggest that for his programmatic speech of Jesus Luke *chose to use a source derived from a community amongst whom jubilee hopes were important.*[19]

If, as I argued earlier, Luke 4:18f. and its use of Isa 61 derives from Q, then perhaps the 'source derived from a community amongst whom jubilee hopes were important' could be Q!

Catchpole has in fact shown that the influence of ideas from Isa 61 are far more deep-seated in Q's Great Sermon than simply

---

[16] R. B. Sloan, *The Favorable Year of the Lord. A Study of Jubilary Theology in the Gospel of Luke* (Austin, TX: Scholars, 1977), and many others: see the survey in Schreck, 'Nazareth Pericope', 450–4; Koet, *Five Studies*, 31f.

[17] D. Seccombe, *Possessions and the Poor in Luke–Acts* (Linz: Plöchl, 1982) 55.

[18] Koet, *Five Studies*, 31. ἄφεσις is used for דרור in Lev 25:10 and Isa 61:1 (and for the יובל), also for the שמטה of Deut 15.

[19] M. Turner, 'Jesus and the Spirit in Lucan Perspective', *TynBull* 32 (1981) 3–42, p. 21 (my italics at the end). Cf. too Tannehill, *Narrative Unity*, 68: 'While it seems clear that Isa 61:1–2 develops themes from the Jubilee year, it is not so clear that the author of Luke–Acts was aware of the connection between this passage and the law of Jubilee.'

the presence of direct verbal allusions might suggest. For example, we have seen that Q 6:30 exhorts people to give to those who borrow and not even to demand the loan back: where a loan is asked for a gift is to be given.[20] The language used may also be significant. The Greek verb used is δανίζω, the same verb that is used in the legislation for the Sabbath year in Deut 15 LXX.[21] Now the Sabbath year legislation is part of the background which feeds into the Jubilee law itself in Lev 25.[22] Thus, implicit in the idea of the 'year of the Lord's favour' of Isa 61:2 as the time of Jubilee may be the idea too of the release of all debts and an implicit refusal to allow debts (via lending) to arise at all. The exhortation in Q 6:30 is thus to put into practice the conditions of the Jubilee, announced at the start of the Sermon. The command thus 'spells out the didactic implications of the kerygma, proclaimed so simply but so majestically in the beatitudes'.[23]

There may also be a further allusion to Jubilee ideas in Q 6:37 and the language of 'releasing'. Luke's four-fold exhortation here (do not judge, do not condemn, release, give) may well represent the more original Q version, and Matthew's shorter version, referring to judging alone, may be due to MattR: although the longer Lukan version is often regarded as LkR,[24] the image of folding a garment to hold grain (Luke 6:38b) looks to be peculiarly Palestinian and unlikely to have been created by Luke himself.[25] If then the Lukan version does in fact reflect the Q wording, it may be that the exhortation to 'release' (ἀπολύετε) is an intentional echo of the exhortation in Isa 58:6 to 'loose' (λῦε) the bonds of wickedness and to undo (διάλυε) the bands of the yoke: these commands immediately precede the exhortation to let the oppressed go free, which is the extra line inserted into the Isa 61 citation in Luke 4.[26] If this parallel were accepted, it would

---

[20] See pp. 305–6 above.

[21] Catchpole, *Quest*, 113.

[22] Though Koet, *Five Studies*, 31f., warns against running the two together.

[23] Catchpole, *Quest*, 113. It is worth noting that Luke himself seems unaware of this link. Luke does not place Q 6:30 in relation to lending but to a robbery situation: cf. p. 305 above. Luke does repeat the lending idea in 6:34, but the motivation is quite different: in Luke it is part of the attack on the Hellenistic reciprocity ethic.

[24] Schulz, *Q*, 146; Fitzmyer, *Luke*, 641, and others.

[25] Schürmann, *Lukasevangelium*, 362f.; Catchpole, *Quest*, 121f.

[26] See R. Albertz, 'Die "Antrittspredigt" Jesu im Lukasevangelium auf ihrem alttestamentlichen Hintergrund', *ZNW* 74 (1983) 182–206, p. 203.

further strengthen the case that ideas from Isa 61, and perhaps ideas associated with the specific composite citation of Isa 61 + 58 in Luke 4:18f., underlie the ethical demands in the Q Sermon.

More significant for the present context may be Catchpole's analysis of the material in Q 6:31ff. Catchpole has argued (to my mind convincingly) that underlying the ethical demands here is the command to 'love your neighbour as yourself' of Lev 19:18.[27] What is dominant here is the exhortation to 'love' (Q 6:32 picking up the previous teaching given under the general rubric of 'love your enemies' in 6:27). In the rhetorical questions of Q 6:32f. the clear implication is that there is a community consciousness; but also that community is clearly Israel. Those addressed see themselves as an 'in group'; and the 'out group', from whom the addressees naturally distinguish themselves, are 'Gentiles'.[28] What is in mind is thus a national self-consciousness, and the 'nation' concerned is precisely Israel herself. Catchpole also refers to the key position of the Golden Rule in Q 6:31 which sets up the self and the self's wishes as the chief criterion by which to judge ethical action. These three elements — love, Israel, self — all come together in the key text Lev 19:18 ('you shall love your neighbour as yourself'), where the 'neighbour' is clearly primarily one's fellow Israelite. Thus, Catchpole concludes that in this Q sequence,

> the persecuted ones are thus addressed along the lines of the ancient text, interpreted strictly in its own terms. Of any pre-occupation with defining, still less with redefining, the neighbour, there is not the slightest trace. The community to which the editor and his audience belong is therefore not so much a Christian church as Israel. . . . Every effort is made therefore to be faithful simultaneously to the confession of Jesus and the command of Moses.[29]

Some of the consequences of this for concrete social relationships are then spelt out in the following section in Q 6:36–38. Q 6:36 should probably be taken as a heading for what follows,

---

[27] *Quest*, 115.

[28] For Matt 5:47 as Q, see p. 202 n. 20 above.

[29] *Quest*, 115f. Catchpole's analysis, which argues that the whole of Q 6:31ff. is virtually a commentary on Lev 19:18, I find more convincing than that of Kosch, who argues that Jesus' sayings and the OT are simply running in parallel. (See Kosch, *Tora*, 386–426.)

rather than as a summary of what precedes;[30] and further, the language of 'mercy' (οἰκτίρμων) again evokes the idea of the covenant relationship between Yahweh and His people.[31] The exhortation to imitate God in respect of this capacity of showing 'mercy' is widely attested in later Jewish texts.[32] What this means in practice is spelt out in what follows in Q. There is first (probably) the double command expressed in both negative and positive terms: do not judge or condemn; rather, forgive and give generously. If one is justified in seeing the longer form, with the positive counterparts to the negative commands not to judge, as part of Q (cf. p. 430 above), then the emphasis should probably be taken as falling on the second half of this example of antithetic parallelism. This may be also confirmed by the stress on the final element (to give) which is engendered by the expansion via the image of the grain in the folded garment (6:38b). Thus, the stress in Q seems to lie on the positive side of the double saying, and this in turn expounds further the exhortation to show mercy (6:36). Thus, the Q unit exhorts its hearers to show the same mercy that is characteristic of the God of Israel and to do this by exercising compassion, forgiveness and generosity to others.[33] Further, these exhortations develop the earlier appeals to give generously (6:30), to forgive by refusing to answer evil with evil (6:29) and above all to love one's enemies rather than let hate overrule the relationship.

According to Catchpole, these rather general exhortations are then given more concrete application in the sayings that follow concerning reasoning and reproof, especially in the saying about the mote and the beam in Q 6:41f. Here too, Catchpole's other essay becomes relevant in some further evidence on the basis of other non-Christian Jewish texts for the pattern of teaching to be found in a number of Q sayings. The often-noted parallel to the mote-beam saying in *b. Arak* 16b suggests that the context for the saying is to be located in a situation of reproof and correction of one party by another. Now reproof implies an attempt to reconcile, to overcome divisions that arise, to nullify enmity and

[30] Schürmann, *Lukasevangelium*, 359. Hence contra Piper, *Wisdom*, 36ff. who takes 6:37 as the heading. The section may be much more theocentric than Piper allows.

[31] *Quest*, 117. Cf. Exod 34:6; Deut 4:31; Ps 103:8; 111:4, etc.

[32] *Targ Jerus.* on Lev 22:28, cited in SB II, 159: 'As our Father is merciful in heaven, so you should be merciful on earth.' Marshall, *Luke*, 265; Davies & Allison, *Matthew I*, 561. Cf. Lev 19:2 for the general idea in relation to 'holiness'.

[33] Catchpole, *Quest*, 117f.

discord, and to create community. Thus the saying about the mote and the beam should probably be seen in conjunction with other sayings in Q about the importance of forgiveness and reconciliation, especially Q 17:3f. (on the importance of un-limited forgiveness, even if there is no repentance on the part of the offender)[34] and 12:58f.(on the need for reconciliation). There is enough significant overlap between Q 17:3f. and 6:41f., as well as possibly 12:58f., to show that importance of the theme of personal reconciliation for the Q Christians in their environment. Catchpole also points to the common use of the term ἀδελφός in Q 17:3 and 6:41, and refers to the fact that probably underlying all these passages is the command of Lev 19:17 (in the immediate context of the love command in Lev

---

[34] I am however less persuaded by Catchpole's further argument in his second essay that the Q sequence in Q 17:3f. also contained Matt 18:16a + 17 between Q 17:3 (= Matt 18:15) and Q 17:4 (= Matt 18:21f.). Catchpole argues that the reference to repeated repentance in Luke 17:4b is probably LkR (there is no Matthean parallel, the reference to repeated repentance is somewhat bizarre if followed by yet more repeated sinning, and repentance is a strong Lukan theme) and the resulting transition from 17:3 to 17:4ac is too abrupt without some intervening stage such as Matt 18:16a, 17. This is also supported with reference to an alleged stereotyped pattern of similar texts dealing with reproof and reconciliation in 1QS 5–6, CD 9 and *T. Gad* 6, which also suggest some kind of interim process as envisaged by Matt 18.

However, the parallels do not demand that something like Matt 18:16a–17 must have intervened between Q 17:3 and 17:4. The passage in *T. Gad* 6 does not have any reference to an extended rebuke by a wider body, and the transition from forgiveness after repentance to unlimited forgiveness even after no repentance (*T. Gad* 6:3, 7) is only marginally less abrupt than that between Q 17:3 and the probable Q version of 17:4.

More difficulties come in Catchpole's understanding of Matt 18:17 which he seeks to interpret as in line with other Q texts. Catchpole concedes that some break of relationships (e.g. table fellowship) may be implied, but claims that there is still an inbuilt extremely positive element: for Catchpole, the saying does not refer to excommunication, but simply to the *attitude* of the reprover ('let him be *to you* . . .'). The recalcitrant offender is to be regarded as 'a Gentile and a tax-collector'. But Q 6:32f. has made clear that these are people who only adopt a reciprocity ethic, who only love/do good to those who do the same to them. As such they are not to be imitated. For Q, therefore, the demand is for something different: unlike Gentiles who only love those who love them, the Q Christians must exercise love, mercy and forgiveness to those who offend.

This seems to confuse the offender (who is to be 'to you like a Gentile or tax-collector') between being subject and object. The verse seems to envisage the offender as solely the object to be treated. Yet Catchpole's interpretation seems to demand that he be a (negative) example for the *subject* treating the other: he is to be a negative example to the hearer of how not to behave *to* others. Further, the confusion of subject and object makes for an extremely

19:18) to ensure that one does not 'hate' one's 'brother', but instead one should 'rebuke' one's neighbour. The context and parallelism here makes it quite clear that 'brother' means fellow-Israelite.[35] Thus the community consciousness behind these sayings is exclusively and precisely Jewish: the community addressed is not a Christian 'church' separate from Judaism, but Israel itself in its totality. Thus what Q pleads for in all these instances is that forgiveness, love and compassion be shown to one's 'brother', i.e. one's fellow-Israelite. The horizon is entirely intra-Jewish; but equally it is no less than fully Jewish. As we saw above, there is a sense in which Jews are threatened with final and definitive rejection (cf. Q 12:10): yet perhaps this is only a threat of what might happen if nothing is done, and the assumption seems to be throughout Q that the appeal to Jews must be maintained continually. Despite the hostility experienced, attempts must be made to heal the rifts in the community. Forgiveness and reconciliation must be attempted before it is too late.

If the above argument is correct, then it suggests that the divisions between the Christians behind Q and the Jewish community were not that deep. Certainly there was hostility, though the very existence of hostility itself indicates a — possibly considerable — degree of positive overlap between the two groups as well as the negative difference which becomes overt in the hostility. At least from the Christian side, it would appear that any split was still not that severe at the social level. It would seem that the Q Christians had not given up hope for Israel; and they did not think of themselves as a separate community. Obviously at one level there is separation: those who support the Christian cause are distinguished from those who do not — the non-Christians are not Christians! But in terms of the self-understanding of the Q Christians, the important social divisions

---

compressed, and somewhat forced, understanding of the verse. The offender is to be treated like a Gentile, i.e. an undesirable; in particular, *his* attitude of only loving his friends is to be avoided, so that you are to be different, and hence you are to treat him as a desirable and *not* undesirable. The logic seems tortuous at best! It seems easiest to take the verse at its face value as implying far more of a fixed boundary consciousness than is evident elsewhere in Q. Given the fact that the transition from Q 17:3 to Q 17:4 is not impossible (and not so different from *T. Gad* 6), there seems to be no good reason to try to force Matt 18:17 into a Q mould which it will only fit with some considerable difficulty.

[35] *Quest*, 145.

appear to be primarily those separating Israel as a whole from Gentiles, and the Q Christians are, at least in their own estimation, within that boundary alongside their fellow Jews.

Further, we hear nothing in Q suggesting boundary creation by separate social or cultic practices. It is not clear if John the Baptist's rite of baptism is to be repeated by the later (i.e. later than John the Baptist) Q Christians (though it would in one way be surprising if it was not). Yet it is not spelt out how much significance this has in relation to boundary formation in sociological terms. It *may* be significant that there is no reference at all to the Eucharist in Q. Q's Jesus does not institute a new cultic act, which clearly in some way would serve to separate Christians from those who do not belong to the group and thus who do not share in the cult.[36] Any argument from silence is obviously fraught with danger, especially when, as in the case of Q, one is trying to discern a Christian group's self-understanding in such an indirect way, viz., by looking only at the traditions *about Jesus* which they have preserved, and moreover only those to which we have access via Matthew and Luke. Nevertheless, it may not be entirely without significance that the tradition about Jesus' institution of the Eucharist was not one preserved in Q (or at least the form of Q to which we now have access, albeit indirectly). There is thus no indication that Q Christians are being encouraged to separate themselves from the social and religious life of their Jewish neighbours. Indeed, the evidence reviewed in the last chapter suggests that, in relation to tithing practices and Torah-observance in general, the opposite is the case. There is thus little evidence of a specifically Christian community consciousness or social self-awareness. In terms of nomenclature used by others, the Christians of Q are striving to be 'Christian Jews', not 'Jewish Christians'.[37] In other words, the

[36] For the social significance of the Eucharist in this context, as reinforcing boundary formations, see W. A. Meeks, *The First Urban Christians* (New Haven & London: Yale University Press, 1983) ch. 5.

[37] By 'Christian Jews', I mean Christian supporters who still maintained their place within Jewish religious and social society (if indeed one can distinguish between the two!); by 'Jewish Christians', I mean those who had, whether by choice or by outside pressure, made the move of setting up a 'community' (at least in some sense) separate from their Jewish contemporaries, even though maintaining the highest level of continuity with their Jewish roots. (As noted above, no Christians before Marcion ever cut themselves off from their Jewishness entirely.) For this terminology, see J. L. Martyn, 'Glimpses into the History of the Johannine Community', in M. de Jonge (ed.), *L'Evangile de Jean.*

Q supporters are 'Christian'[38] sympathisers striving to stay within the boundaries of Judaism and with no apparent awareness yet that those boundaries might be too restrictive to contain both themselves and their Jewish contemporaries.

Whether others in the contemporary situation would have seen things in the same way is another matter. We have already seen that many have argued that Q Christians were facing intense persecution, perhaps being excluded from social gatherings. If that were the case, it would imply that perhaps the non-Christian contemporaries of the Q Christians would have regarded them *not* as 'Christian Jews', but precisely as 'Jewish Christians', i.e. a group whose distinctiveness from their contemporaries had reached a sufficiently clear form that they should be seen as constituting a separate social, and perhaps even in some sense 'religious', entity. In fact, I argued above that even the so-called persecution passages in Q may reflect a rather less violent situation than is often thought, and that the main reaction from Jewish contemporaries may rather have been one of sullen apathy rather than physical violence (see ch. 9 above). In that case, then even from the non-Christian side, there may have been not very much awareness of the Christian group as socially, or 'religiously', very distinct. Clearly there were differences. But on neither side does there seem to be any evidence that the differences between Christians and others have created hardened — or even hardening — social barriers.

To use more sociological jargon, what I am arguing is that the Christian group reflected in Q may have been more of a 'reform movement' working within Israel than a 'sect' separated from its Jewish contemporaries by a rigid line of demarcation. I am fully aware of all the dangers of using the language of 'sect' in the present context.[39] The word itself is used in a variety of different ways by different sociologists, by NT scholars seeking to exploit sociological insights for NT studies, as well as being used in a non-

---

Sources, rédaction, théologie (BETL 44; Gembloux & Leuven: Duculot & Leuven University Press) 149–75, pp. 160, 164. The distinction is often used in relation to Johannine studies to distinguish possible groups of Christian sympathisers/ supporters reflected in the fourth gospel. I am grateful to my colleague Dr Martin de Boer for drawing my attention to this.

[38] See p. 107 above for the use of this term. I think that denial of the term to the Q followers of Jesus is simply counter-productive.

[39] Cf. the valuable discussion of B. Holmberg, *Sociology and the New Testament* (Minneapolis: Fortress, 1990) 77–117.

technical sense in several contexts. So too there is an acute danger in applying the word to an early Christian group in relation to an alleged parent body of 'Judaism': the 'sect' terminology as used by e.g. Troeltsch was part of a distinction between a 'sect' and a 'church'; hence here the 'church' would presumably have to be 'Judaism', though we now realise all too clearly how variegated and non-unitary first-century Judaism was. There is no space here to enter into the debate of how one might, or should, seek to define a 'sect'. Nor am I competent to do so. All I am doing here is to identify in very general terms a distinction between a 'reform movement', working within a parent group, and a 'sect', which sees itself as in some real sense separate from the parent group, with its own clearly defined boundaries which distinguish it clearly and visibly from the parent.[40] And all I am claiming is that the group of Christians reflected in Q do not yet seem to have reached that state of self-conscious 'sectarian' differentiation from their neighbours.[41]

In this Q then perhaps represents a stage prior to that of Matthew. For Matthew, a 'sectarian' (at least in a fairly loose sense) model of the Christian community in relation to its Jewish neighbours is more defensible. The precise nature of the split between Christians and Jews by the time of Matthew is much debated,[42] though it is clear that the lines between the two groups have solidified very considerably. It is dubious how far Matthew holds out any hope for Israel. Some individuals may still be the object of the Christian mission.[43] But the main thrust of large parts of Matthew seems profoundly pessimistic about any

---

[40] I am *not* therefore concerned with other alleged characteristics of a 'sect', e.g. egalitarianism or anticlericalism, or its attitude to the 'world'. In the present context, the 'world' could be highly ambiguous: is it the Jewish world, or the world of the Roman Empire?

[41] For the distinction, and the terminology used here (i.e. 'sect' vs. 'reform movement'), cf. F. B. Watson, *Paul, Judaism and the Gentiles* (SNTSMS 56; Cambridge University Press, 1986) 38–40; P. F. Esler, *Community and Gospel in Luke–Acts* (SNTSMS 57; Cambridge University Press, 1987) 47–53. Both deal with other parts of the NT (Paul and Luke respectively), and both argue that in each case the move from reform movement to 'sect' *has* already taken place.

[42] Cf. the essays of Stanton, 'Synagogue and Church', and 'The Gospel of Matthew and Judaism', *Gospel for a New People*, 113–45, 146–68 respectively; also Luz, *Matthew 1–7*, 87–90.

[43] Much depends on how one interprets the phrase πάντα τὰ ἔθνη in Matt 28:19: cf. Stanton, *Gospel for a New People*, 137f., for a discussion of the issues involved.

rapprochement between Christians and Jews. Matthew's redactional addition to the parable of the wicked husbandmen in Matt 21:43 clearly interprets the parable in national terms ('the kingdom of God will be taken from you and given to another ἔθνος'); and the well-known (and almost certainly redactional) verses in Matt 22:7 (the king of the parable of the Great Supper burning up the city of the guests who have not responded to the invitation to the meal) and Matt 27:25 ('his blood be on us and on our children') seem to underline the guilt and definitive rejection of the Jewish people by God. So too, the well-known Matthean habit of referring to Jewish institutions as 'their' or 'your' synagogue/scribes has indicated to many scholars that the Matthean community is sharply distinguishing itself at the social level by having rival institutions alongside those of the Jewish community.[44] On any showing there is clearly an element of self-awareness on the part of Matthean Christians distinguishing themselves from, and partly distancing themselves from, their Jewish neighbours.

Such a self-awareness does not appear to be present in Q. Clearly there are tensions. Clearly there are differences. But the aim of the Q Christians is to seek to bridge those differences, to stay within the broad Jewish community of which they are a part, and not to separate off into a separate conventicle or 'sectarian' ghetto. Can we though be any more precise about where this group of Christians might be placed on any first-century reference grid of Palestinian Judaism? In a final section of this chapter I offer one possible suggestion to seek to answer such a question.

Q and the Pharisees

In the discussion of Q and the Law, I sought to show that Q's Jesus displays an extremely 'conservative' attitude to the Law. Q portrays Jesus as one who is thoroughly obedient to the Law right at the start in the temptation narrative; and at a few points, I argued that the Q editor intervenes in the tradition to ensure that Jesus' teaching is not (mis)interpreted as implying that observance of the Law is dispensable (cf. above on Q 11:42c and 16:17). Further, I claimed the Law concerned is sometimes those

---

[44] For 'their synagogues', see Matt 4:23; 9:35; 10:17; 12:9; 13:54; cf. 23:34 ('your'); for 'their scribes', see Matt 7:29, and Matt 13:52; 23:34 makes it clear that for Matthew there are Christian scribes as well.

parts of the Law of particular concern to the Pharisees (cf. on tithing and purity — though, of course, the whole Law was of concern to the Pharisees). Alongside this is the fact that the woes in Q 11 single out the Pharisees and lawyers as (a) particular group(s) for a very pointed polemical attack. This is the one section in Q where a particular group within the broad Jewish audience is explicitly and (for us) unambiguously mentioned.[45] But we may also note the fact that John the Baptist's preaching in Q may have been addressed to Pharisees (see p. 116 above); similarly Luke 10:25–28, if part of Q (see pp. 416–7 above), shows Jesus reacting to a hostile 'lawyer', and for Q, the series of woes makes clear that lawyers and Pharisees are closely related, if not identical; and if Luke 7:29f. belonged to Q (cf. Matt 21:32 and see p. 116 above), the Pharisees are again mentioned as an explicit group in opposition to John. There is thus a certain amount of indirect evidence, additional to the woes of Q 11, to suggest that Pharisees may have been particularly in mind as the target of quite a lot of the polemic in Q.[46]

Now I noted above that polemic and conflict are sometimes the more intense the closer the 'warring' factions are.[47] This suggests that it may be worthwhile to consider the possibility that the Q Christians and the Pharisees, as well as being quite antagonistic to each other, may have been quite close to each other at the same time. In order to develop this further, we need to know a little more about the Pharisees themselves.

---

[45] The point is also noted by Theissen, *Gospels in Context*, 227–34 (= *Lokalkolorit*, 238–45), though he does not develop the idea in the same way as here: he deduces from the mention of the Pharisees that perhaps Pharisees are the main opponents for Q, and seeks to deduce limits for the dating of Q (see p. 101 above).

[46] This in turn suggests that there is no need necessarily to drive too much of a wedge between earlier woes (directed to Pharisees) and later polemic (directed more widely). In any case, the anti-Pharisaic language is retained by the final editor as apparently material that is still regarded as relevant for the final version of Q! On the other hand, we should perhaps not make the polemic in Q too uniform and it may be that there are different groups in mind at different points in Q. Cf. my earlier discussion in ch. 9 above, where at a number of points I argued that some of the polemical language only makes sense if directed against people who already have had some kind of commitment to the Christian cause (cf. Q 6:46; 12:9). But whether such a *Sitz im Leben* will explain all the polemic in Q is not at all certain.

[47] Cf. p. 427 n. 5 above and the reference to Coser; also Stanton, *Gospel for a New People*, 98–106.

Sadly our knowledge of first-century Pharisaism is notoriously sketchy. If anything we have become even more aware in recent years just how sketchy our knowledge is: paradoxically we know how little we know![48] In recent study, the pioneering work has been done by J. Neusner, whose theories on the pre-70 Pharisees are well-known.[49] Neusner has tried to distinguish within the vast body of later rabbinic texts the material which can be traced back to the earliest (i.e. pre-70 CE) period. His criterion is mainly to focus on traditions which are explicitly ascribed to a group, or to a known Pharisaic figure, of the pre-70 era as evidence of pre-70 Pharisaism, as well as looking at laws which logically must be pre-70 (because they are presupposed later). When this is done, Neusner argues that the vast bulk of legal matters discussed by the Pharisees in this period seem to have been issues concerned with purity laws and tithing. This contrasts quite forcibly with the evidence we have (e.g. from Josephus) of Pharisees in earlier periods, when it seems that Pharisees were extremely active and influential in the politics of their day.[50] Thus Neusner argues that, during the first half of the first century, the Pharisees withdrew from public life and the sphere of public influence very considerably. Perhaps under the influence of Hillel, Pharisees changed from a 'political party into a table fellowship sect',[51] aiming in part too, to live their lives in a state of purity prescribed for priests in the temple. Thus the era of Pharisaic dominance only arises after the events of 70 CE.

Many aspects of Neusner's claims about the Pharisees have been radically questioned by Sanders.[52] Sanders has questioned whether the Pharisees were as uninfluential as Neusner believes; he has also disputed Neusner's claim that Pharisees were concerned above all with issues of purity and tithing, or that they were seeking to maintain a level of purity prescribed for priests. Some of Sanders' critique is persuasive. On the issue of the (quite widespread) view that Pharisees were seeking to keep themselves

---

[48] I have discussed the whole question of our knowledge of the Pharisees in my 'Les Pharisiens avant 70 et le Nouveau Testament', in D. Marguerat (ed.), *Juifs et Chrétiens au premier siècle: La déchirure* (Geneva: Labor et Fides, 1995, forthcoming). For more details in what follows, see my article.

[49] See especially his *The Rabbinic Traditions about the Pharisees before 70* (Leiden: Brill, 1971).

[50] For example, under John Hyrcanus, Alexander Jannaeus or Salome Alexandra: see Josephus, *Ant.* 13.288–300, 399–411; *War* 1.107–114.

[51] *Rabbinic Tradition*, 305.

[52] *Jewish Law*, esp. ch. III.

in a state of priestly purity, Sanders has I believe made a convincing case to the contrary. Many of the debates do not concern specifically priestly issues (e.g. the law on impurity caused by creeping things [Lev 11:32–39]);[53] other debates, e.g. on corpse impurity, hardly ever presuppose that Pharisees tried to avoid such impurity completely.[54] It seems clear that Pharisees tried to maintain a level of purity higher than that of many of their contemporaries; but it was also clearly lower than that prescribed for priests.[55]

However, other aspects of Sanders' critique are less persuasive. Neusner's theory that Pharisees were above all interested in purity and tithing matters has been questioned by Sanders for relying too heavily on the traditions which contain a specific name ascribed to them and for ignoring the vast bulk of anonymous laws which must have been common ground to the Pharisees and others.[56] Sanders may well be justified in one way in that there was no doubt a lot of common ground between Pharisees and other Jews. After all the Pharisees were themselves Jews! Nevertheless the fact remains that it was these issues which later traditions ascribed to named figures of the past and therefore (perhaps) highlighted in this way. Thus, as Dunn says,

> Despite Sanders, it must be significant that such a high percentage of the attributed traditions focus on one main aspect of practical piety. It strongly suggests that these rulings were sensitive matters or matters of dispute among the predecessors of the rabbis, so that relevant rulings were remembered by the post-70 dominant party by their attribution to leading figures of the past or as part of the houses' disputes.[57]

[53] Sanders, *Jewish Law*, 163.

[54] *Jewish Law*, 155. At one point in the Mishnah (*Dem* 2:3) a view is attributed to R. Judah that a *haber* (?= Pharisee?) should not incur impurity from a corpse; but it is then explicitly stated that this was not the view shared by anyone else. The duty of a Jew to make appropriate arrangements for the burial of a member of his/her own family was taken very seriously. Thus the acquisition of corpse impurity through touching a corpse would have occurred regularly. There is no indication in our sources that Pharisees tried to avoid incurring such impurity when required.

[55] Cf. *m. Hag.* 2:7, and my discussion of this in the article mentioned above (n. 46 above).

[56] Cf. Sanders, *Jesus and Judaism*, 388 n. 59.

[57] J. D. G. Dunn, 'Pharisees, Sinners, and Jesus', in Dunn, *Jesus, Paul and the Law* (London: SPCK, 1990) 61–88, p. 64.

Thus, it does seem appropriate to see concerns for purity and tithing as an important — if not exclusive — concern of the Pharisees in this early period.

The problem of the importance and influence of the Pharisees during the period is also debated. As we have already noted, Neusner has argued that the Pharisees under the leadership of Hillel retreated significantly from public life in the first half of the first century CE. Sanders has again questioned such a claim, referring to the appearance of Pharisees at various points in the history of the period as active during armed revolts and rebellions (cf. Saddok the Pharisee mentioned alongside Judas in the revolt of 6 CE by Josephus, *Ant.* 18.4).[58] Nevertheless, it remains striking that Josephus never mentions explicitly the presence of individual Pharisees during the period 6–66 CE in his whole account of this period.[59] There is thus a silence on Josephus' part covering the best part of sixty years: over half a century. Sanders himself warns against the danger of generalising too readily in relation to a group like the Pharisees over a long period.[60] Thus the disappearance from sight of Pharisees during the period 6–66 CE remains striking. The 'few rebellious acts in 20 and 4 BCE and 6 CE' scarcely seem enough to warrant the conclusion that 'they were present, that they continued teaching, *(and) that they had influence*' (cf. above: my stress) throughout the whole 120 year period from 63 BCE to 66 CE and certainly does *not* show that they were

[58] Cf. Sanders' comment: 'The disappearance of the Pharisees from the history of the period 63 BCE to 66 CE, except for a few rebellious acts in 20 and 4 BCE and 6 CE, cannot be entirely accidental. The few outbursts show that they were present, that they continued teaching that they had influence, and that sometimes they could raise, or help raise, a mob. These outbursts count against Neusner's view that the Pharisees withdrew from public life.' See his *Judaism: Practice and Belief 63 BCE – 66 CE* (London: SCM, 1992) 402.

[59] Unless he himself is the exception. However, there are now serious doubts about whether Josephus means (in his *Life* 12) to suggests that he himself actually became a Pharisee: see the very full study of S. Mason, *Flavius Josephus on the Pharisees* (Leiden: Brill, 1991).

[60] 'It makes no more sense to say that the Pharisees were hypocritical and legalistic during the two hundred years or so of their history than it would to say that Christians were charitable and always loved their enemies during an equivalent period in their history. One gains no historical understanding by using such terms as "hypocrisy" and "charitableness" to cover the actual practice of a sizable group over a long period.' (*Judaism,* 401.) But what applies to 'hypocrisy' and 'charity' over a two hundred year period probably applies equally well to political involvement and influence over a sixty year period.

influential during the period around the start of the Christian movement.

On the other hand, we have to note too a number of generalising summaries by Josephus which testify to the great popularity of the Pharisees among the general population at this period. For example:

> They [= the Pharisees] are extremely influential among the townsfolk; and all prayers and sacred rites of divine worship are performed according to their exposition. This is the great tribute that the inhabitants of the cities, by practising the highest ideals both in their way of living and in their discourse, have paid to the excellence of the Pharisees. (*Ant.* 18.15)

> They [= the Sadducees] accomplish practically nothing, however. For whenever they assume some office, though they submit unwillingly and perforce, yet submit they do to the formulas of the Pharisees, since otherwise the masses would not tolerate them (*Ant.* 18.17).

So too, whatever the precise interpretation of Josephus' account in his *Life* 12, it evidently made sense for him to suggest that he followed the Pharisaic way of life as either the dominant one, or as the one which it was politically most astute to be seen to follow. Further, if, as Mason has argued persuasively in his recent monograph (n. 57 above), Josephus himself was *not* sympathetic to the Pharisees, then the notes about their widespread popularity become all the more striking and give a greater impression of historical accuracy, working as they would then do against Josephus' own *Tendenz*.[61]

The evidence thus seems to point in two opposite directions simultaneously. The Pharisees appear on the one hand as a small group in the first part of the first century, lacking any high political profile and only interested in a rather restricted sphere of interest; on the other hand, they are presented as enjoying very considerable popular support. One way out of this dilemma may be to note that Josephus' own interests may well have coloured things here. Josephus' interest is primarily in the governing classes, and it is these

---

[61] Hence I would disagree with the views of Neusner and others, that the very positive picture of the Pharisees, especially in the *Antiquities*, is due to Josephus' own pro-Pharisaic bias. On this, see the discussion in my article (n. 46 above).

whom he usually mentions explicitly. Others are generally ignored.[62] Josephus' silence about specific activity of Pharisees may thus be due simply to the fact that Pharisees were not politically influential in this period. To this extent Neusner would seem to be correct: at least at the level of the *de facto* situation, the Pharisees' status and ability to exercise political power and influence differed in the first half of the first century from what it had been in the earlier period under Hyrcanus, Salome Alexandra and (though to a lesser extent) under Herod.

Nevertheless, such a diminution in Pharisaic influence may not have been entirely to the liking of the Pharisees themselves. In this respect Neusner's theories may be more questionable. Neusner argues that the Pharisees consciously withdrew from public life to become a small purity sect (cf. above). However, against this must be set the apparent popularity of the Pharisees with the people according to Josephus; and the fact that such popularity may not be in line with Josephus' own *Tendenz* suggests that Josephus may be relied upon at this point. A rather more consistent picture emerges if one follows Saldarini's picture of the Pharisees in relation to their social situation. He argues persuasively that the Pharisees were a 'retainer class' throughout the period. They were not amongst the governing classes; they did not necessarily have a great deal of political power, certainly in the pre-70 era. However, that does not mean that they surrendered all hope of getting such power and influence during the period. The fact that they did not actually have much influence (as implied by Josephus' silence) should not necessarily be taken (with Neusner) as a willing acceptance of the situation and the result of a conscious decision to withdraw from public life. Rather, they more likely constituted a group that continually jockeyed for power and tried to gain power, though with varying degrees of success at different periods in history.[63]

[62] 'Only when individuals or groups gained ruling power or became important for the rulers does Josephus give them extensive treatment. He does not give a full description of the aristocracy, much less of the people, nor does he talk about bureaucrats, scribes, priests (other than chief priests) or local leaders as separate classes or groups. From the viewpoint of the governing class, which is the viewpoint Josephus takes, the Pharisees and many other Jewish groups and classes are unimportant, minor forces on the social scene and so they are neglected, except when they have major political effect.' (A. J. Saldarini, *Pharisees, Scribes and Sadducees in Palestinian Society* [Edinburgh: T. & T. Clark, 1989] 84.)

[63] Cf. Saldarini, *Pharisees*, 281.

How then does the evidence of the NT, and especially the evidence of the gospels and Q, appear when set against this background? In one way the pictures converge well. In general terms, the Pharisees do not appear in the NT as politically powerful figures. Gamaliel in Acts 5 has some influence; but no other Pharisees appear in positions of political leadership. They are (notoriously) absent from the accounts of Jesus' trial and only appear on stage during the pre-passion ministry of Jesus.

Yet in relation to that ministry, the Pharisees are often very significant figures. They appear as the leading sparring partners with Jesus on a number of occasions during the legal disputes. They question Jesus and argue with him and appear to provide one of the leading opposition groups to Jesus. Yet what is so striking (and indeed what others have observed in the past) is the degree of similarity between Jesus and the Pharisees in the gospels. Indeed at times this is almost explicit. In Mark 2:18 Jesus' disciples are asked why they are not fasting in the way that the disciples of John and the Pharisees fast. The implication seems to be that they should be doing the same as the Pharisees (and others). Similarly in Mark 7:2, Jesus' disciples are asked why they do not follow the custom of the Pharisees in washing their hands before eating.[64] Again the assumption seems to be that Jesus and his disciples were expected to obey Pharisaic rules. And we have seen how the Q sayings about purity and tithing (Q 11:39–41 and Q 11:42) portray Jesus as criticising some Pharisees but without ever questioning the fundamental importance of the Pharisaic practice of tithing itself or their concern for purity. All this suggests that the debate between the Jesus movement and the Pharisees is in part one that is being conducted on the basis of a large number of common presuppositions. Thus, on the basis of this evidence, R. A. Wild has suggested that Jesus himself was closely connected with the Pharisaic movement.[65]

Wild's argument is persuasive in several ways. The suggestion that Jesus had close links with the Pharisees has been made by others before, though not quite via this kind of argument, which

---

[64] Mark says this is also the custom of 'all the Jews'. As is recognised in all the commentaries, this is clearly wrong, since handwashing was only required of priests at this period. However, it may have been an obligation taken on themselves voluntarily by the Pharisees.

[65] R. A. Wild, 'The Encounter between Pharisaic and Christian Judaism: Some Early Gospel Evidence', *NovT* 27 (1985) 105–24.

is in many respects convincing.[66] However, the details of his argument may need more careful nuancing. In particular, the evidence from Mark may be rather different from the evidence of Q, and the Jesus of Mark comes over as much more polemical in relation to the Law and Pharisaic observance than Wild allows. The saying in Mark 7:15, for example, is particularly striking in this respect. At what stage the saying was attached to the hand-washing debate is not clear. Many would argue that the (almost certainly) redactional nature of v. 14 suggests that the connection between v. 15 and what precedes is due to MkR.[67] In any case it is hard to eliminate completely all elements of polemic from the saying. Wild follows the suggestion of many others that the form of antithetical parallelism in v. 15 should not be taken as an absolute negation of the first half of the saying. 'It is not A but B' should be taken as implying that B is more important than A, but that A is not excluded.[68] Nevertheless, even if the saying originally was not to do with all the food laws of Leviticus,[69] it is still placing concerns about external purity at a lower level than concern for 'inner purity'.[70] There is certainly nothing in Mark 7:15 corresponding to the injunction in Q 11:42c. Thus, whilst Wild is justified in pointing to the fact that the debate in Mark 7:1, 2, 5 presupposes that Jesus' disciples are apparently being expected to observe specifically Pharisaic mores (in particular here the practice of ritual hand-washing which all agree was not required of all Jews at this period), the Jesus of Mark 7 comes over as rather more opposed to such discipline.

Similarly the tradition in Mark 2:15–17 perhaps implies that the scribes of the Pharisees expect Jesus to observe strict rules of table fellowship by not eating with 'tax-collectors and sinners'. Yet Mark's Jesus refuses to go along with such demands and rejects them completely. The question of fasting in Mark 2:18 is

[66] See the survey in Sanders, *Jesus and Judaism*, 291f. More often a link between Jesus and the Pharisees is postulated by ascribing many of the references to the Pharisees as Jesus' opponents in the gospels to later Christian editing.

[67] Cf. my *Revival*, 105.

[68] Wild, 'Encounter', 119, appealing to Westerholm, *Jesus and Scribal Authority*, 83.

[69] Clearly the interpretation of the saying depends very heavily on the context in which it is placed: see especially J. D. G. Dunn, 'Jesus and Ritual Purity: a Study of the Tradition History of Mk 7,15', in *A Cause de l'Evangile* (FS J. Dupont; Paris: Cerf, 1985) 251–76.

[70] Carlston, 'Things that Defile', 95.

perhaps more complicated, in that Jesus' reply seems to involve a temporal distinction between the present (when no fasting is appropriate: v. 19) and the future (when fasting will be reintroduced: v. 20). Yet the overall thrust of the story is clear: fasting is in principle now abrogated.

Against all this background the material in Q stands out in even sharper relief. The Jesus of Q appears to be much less overtly polemical in this sense. As we have seen, the accusations of Q's Jesus against his 'opponents' never question the validity of the practice or the rules of the Pharisees at all. Purity laws are affirmed, but ('simply'?) extended to cover inner as well as outer purity. Tithing is explicitly affirmed in what may be a conscious intervention by the Q editor. Wild may be right in suggesting that originally Jesus' disciples had close links with the Pharisaic movement (though our concern here is not to recover the historical Jesus). Such a picture emerges from both the Markan and Q material examined. However, it is only in Q that Jesus himself emerges as one who affirms these links positively. In Mark, and perhaps in Mark's tradition, we see Jesus distancing himself from the Pharisaic viewpoint. It would thus appear that the community which preserved the Q material may also have preserved positive links with the Pharisaic movement in a way that most other primitive Christian groups about which we have any evidence did not. Further, the possible connection of some of the sayings considered with views of Shammaite Pharisees would tie in well with Neusner's further theories about the dominant position of Shammaite Pharisaism in the pre-70 era.[71] However, one cannot say any more than this.

A lot of this evidence might then fit together if Q emanated from a Christian community in close touch with Pharisaism, experiencing some hostile suspicion from non-Christian Pharisees.[72] Yet the very existence of the hostility may reflect the closeness of the relationship. If my earlier analysis of the status and influence of the Pharisees is correct, then the question arises

---

[71] Neusner, *Rabbinic Traditions II*, 1–5. See pp. 412–3 above on the woe on purity.

[72] A similar claim has been made by Hodgson, 'Gattung', with a similar methodology to that offered here, but appealing to different Q texts. Hodgson does not go so far as to suggest that the Q community claimed to be Pharisees, but he does suggest that the Q community should be seen within a context of (hostile) Pharisaic Judaism. Hodgson also starts from the belief that the Pharisees were concerned above all with issues of table fellowship

all the more sharply why the Pharisees were at all interested in the new Christian movement. The lack of influence by the Pharisees presumably meant that they could not, and probably did not, try to convince the ordinary masses that they should follow them. The *'am ha'aretz* could be dismissed, ignored, pitied, loved, but one presumes not attacked virulently. Certainly we do not hear of large-scale 'persecution' of fellow Jews by Pharisees in this period! Why then should the new Christian movement have apparently provoked reaction and opposition from the Pharisees? Why did the Pharisees take any notice at all of the early Christians? And conversely, why did the Christians (and/or Jesus) take any notice of the Pharisees? The gospel picture in general might be simply a reflection of the post-70 era, when all agree that Pharisaic Judaism came to the fore and became the dominant force within Judaism. However, the tradition of controversies with Pharisees looks to be too deeply embedded in the gospel tradition for that. It is there clearly in Q, which I argued is pre-70. It is clearly evident in the strong opposition provided by the one 'convert' from Pharisaism to Christianity we know of in the pre-70 period, i.e. Paul; and Theissen has shown that strong Pharisaic opposition to the Christian movement can certainly be evidenced in the period up to c. 55 CE.[73]

In fact there must have been quite a lot in common between the Pharisaic movement and the new Christian movement. Both could be classified as 'reform groups' or 'renewal movements' within Judaism. If the tradition is Matt 23:15 has any vestige of reality in it, the Pharisees may have sought to proselytise a little. And the evidence I reviewed above suggests that they were continually jockeying for power during this period (though with varying degrees of success). The Christian movement too sought to expand and influence others. The common links implied in the woes in Q 11:39–42 suggest that the two movements, or at least the Q Christians and the Pharisees they encountered, shared a considerable degree of overlap. The very fact that two were interested in each other, as well as evidently coming into conflict

---

and tithing, basing himself on the work of Neusner, and he argues that the same concerns are reflected in Q texts such as Q 4:4; 10:7; 11:42; 13:29; 17:26f (see especially 'Gattung', 88–90). However, apart from Q 11:42 (discussed above), I am not convinced that these texts are really to do with issues of table fellowship.

[73] Though see pp. 101–2 above for the question of whether we can distinguish between a pre-55 and a post-55 situation so easily in this respect.

with each other, suggests that the two groups may have overlapped. Thus, the Christian group may have been claiming to be a genuine part of the Pharisaic movement. If it were not, the group would probably have been ignored by the non-Christian Pharisees. It is then possible that Q may provide us with some further evidence of followers of Jesus with some close sympathies with those of non-Christian Pharisees. We know from elsewhere that some Pharisees became Christians: at least one evidently rejected his Pharisaism strongly (cf. Paul in Phil 3:5–8); some seem to have maintained their allegiance to the Pharisaic movement when becoming Christians (cf. Acts 15:5). Perhaps in Q we see a group of Christians whose sympathies are with the latter group in one way,[74] though the hostility which has arisen in such a social grouping has already led to some tension.[75]

The separation of Christian communities from their Jewish neighbours, in terms of both ideologies and social ties, was a long and complex one.[76] In Q we see perhaps a relatively early stage in that history. Certainly it is earlier than Matthew. So too it seems that, in Q, the desire on the Christian side is *not* to separate. Perhaps too even on the non-Christian side, the desire is for the same end: hostility, even 'persecution', presupposes a *joint* purpose and an awareness of solidarity, the 'persecution' itself

---

[74] Whether we can go further and identify the groups concerned, as is suggested by Theissen, seems to me uncertain. The Q Christians were, as far as we can tell, based in Galilee (cf. p. 102 above); the Christian Pharisees of Acts 15 are in Jerusalem. So too the question of how far the Q Christians might relate to the Pauline mission is unclear. Theissen suggested that the 'wandering radicals' reflected in the gospel tradition might be behind some of the problems encountered by Paul in Corinth: cf. his 'Legitimation and Subsistence: An Essay in the Sociology of Early Christian Missionaries', in *The Social Setting of Pauline Christianity* (ET Edinburgh: T. & T. Clark, 1982) 27–67. However, it is unlikely that this can relate directly to the Q-'group' I have sought to analyse here, if only because of geographical considerations: the Q group I have sited in Galilee, far from Paul in Corinth. For further doubts about whether Q as such lies behind the troubles in Corinth, see my '1 Corinthians and Q' (even though it seems likely that interpretation of Jesus traditions was an important factor in the debates in Corinth). Nevertheless it is not impossible that the Christian group reflected in Q was part of a broader movement within early Christianity.

[75] However, I argued in ch. 9 above that the 'tension' may not yet have led to any violent, full-scale physical 'persecution' of Christians. The situation may have been much more officially 'low key' and more at the level of informal suspicion and social tension.

[76] See J. D. G. Dunn, *The Parting of the Ways* (London: SCM, 1991).

being one means to try to reunite into a whole again what is perceived as threatening to fracture and disintegrate.

Perhaps it is the tragedy of subsequent history that the efforts of the Q Christians in this respect, and also of their Jewish contemporaries, were ultimately frustrated.

Bibliography

Achtemeier, P. J., 'The Lucan Perspective on the Miracles of Jesus', *JBL* 94 (1975) 547–62.

Albertz, R., 'Die "Antrittspredigt" Jesu im Lukasevangelium auf ihrem alttestamentlichen Hintergrund', *ZNW* 74 (1983) 182–206.

Allison, D. C., 'Matt. 23:39 = Luke 13:35b as a Conditional Prophecy', *JSNT* 18 (1983) 75–84.

Attridge, H. W., 'The Philosophical Critique of Religion under the Empire', *ANRW* II.16.1, 45–78.

Bammel, E., 'Das Ende von Q', in *Verborum Veritas* (FS G. Stählin; Wuppertal: Brockhaus, 1970) 39–50.

Banks, R., *Jesus and the Law in the Synoptic Tradition* (SNTSMS 28; Cambridge University Press, 1975).

Barr, J., *The Semantics of Biblical Language* (London: SCM, 1961).

Barrett, C. K., *The Holy Spirit in the Gospel Tradition* (London: SPCK, 1947).

Barth, G., 'Matthew's Understanding of the Law', in Bornkamm, Barth and Held, *Tradition and Interpretation in Matthew*.

Bauer, W., *Orthodoxy and Heresy in Earliest Christianity* (ET Philadelphia & London: Fortress & SCM, 1971).

Bayer, H. F., *Jesus' Predictions of Vindication and Resurrection* (WUNT 2.20; Tübingen: Mohr, 1986).

Beardslee, W. A., 'Uses of the Proverb in the Synoptic Gospels', *Int* 24 (1970) 61–73.

Berger, K., *Formgeschichte des Neuen Testaments* (Heidelberg: Quelle und Meyer, 1984).

Berger, K. & Colpe, C., *Religionsgeschichtliches Textbuch zum Neuen Testament* (Göttingen: Vandenhoeck & Ruprecht, 1987).

Bertram, G., στενός κτλ, *TWNT* VII, 604–8.

Betz, H. D., *Essays on the Sermon on the Mount* (ET Philadelphia: Fortress, 1985).

Betz, H. D., 'Jesus and the Cynics: Survey and Analysis of a Hypothesis', *JR* 74 (1994) 453–75.

Billerbeck, M., 'Greek Cynicism in Imperial Rome', in *Die Kyniker in der modernen Forschung* (Amsterdam: B. R. Grüner, 1991) 147–66.

Black, M., *An Aramaic Approach to the Gospels and Acts* (Oxford University Press, 1967³).

— 'The Use of Rhetorical Terminology in Papias on Mark and Matthew', *JSNT* 37 (1989) 31–41.

Blomberg, C. L., 'The Law in Luke–Acts', *JSNT* 22 (1984) 53–80.

Boring, M. E., 'The Unforgivable Sin Logion Mk III 28–29/Matt XII 31–32/Lk XII 10. Formal Analysis and History of the Tradition', *NovT* 18 (1976) 258–79.

— *Sayings of the Risen Jesus. Christian Prophecy in the Synoptic Tradition* (SNTSMS 46; Cambridge University Press, 1982).

Bornkamm, G., Barth, G. & Held, H. J., *Tradition and Interpretation in Matthew* (ET London: SCM, 1963).

Bowker, J., *Jesus and the Pharisees* (Cambridge University Press, 1973).

Bultmann, R., *The History of the Synoptic Tradition* (ET Oxford: Blackwell, 1963).

— *The Theology of the New Testament I* (ET London: SCM, 1952).

Burridge, R. A., *What are the Gospels?* (SNTSMS 70; Cambridge University Press, 1992).

Bussby, F., 'Is Q an Aramaic Document?', *ExpT* 65 (1954) 272–5.

Busse, U., *Die Wunder des Propheten Jesus. Die Rezeption, Komposition und Interpretation der Wundertradition im Evangelium des Lukas* (FzB 24; Stuttgart: Katholisches Bibelwerk, 1977).

— *Das Nazareth-Manifest Jesu* (SBS 91; Stuttgart: Katholisches Bibelwerk, 1978).

Bussmann, W., *Synoptische Studien* (Halle: Buchhandlung des Waisenhauses, 1929).

Butler, B. C., *The Originality of St Matthew* (Cambridge University Press, 1951).

Cadbury, H. J., 'Dust and Garments', in F. J. Foakes Jackson & K. Lake (eds), *The Beginnings of Christianity. The Acts of the Apostles V* (London: Macmillan, 1933) 269–77.

Caird, G.B., *Jesus and the Jewish Nation* (London: Athlone Press, 1965).

Cameron, P. S., *Violence and the Kingdom. The Interpretation of Matthew 11:12* (Frankfurt: P. Lang, 1984).

Cameron, R., 'What did you come out to see? Characterisations of John and Jesus in the Gospels', *Semeia* 49 (1990) 35–69.

Caragounis, C., *The Son of Man* (WUNT 2.38; Tübingen: Mohr, 1986).

Carlston, C. E., 'The Things that Defile (Mark vii.14) and the Law in Matthew and Mark', *NTS* 15 (1968) 75–95.

— 'Wisdom and Eschatology in Q', in Delobel (ed.), *LOGIA*, 101–19.

Carlston, C. E. & Norlin, D., 'Once More — Statistics and Q', *HTR* 64 (1971) 59–78.

Carroll, J. T., *Responses to the End of History. Eschatology and Situation in Luke–Acts* (SBLDS 92; Atlanta: Scholars, 1988).

Casey, P. M., *Son of Man* (London: SPCK, 1979).

— 'The Jackals and the Son of Man (Matt.8.20/Luke 9.58)', *JSNT* 23 (1985) 3–22.

— 'General, Generic and Indefinite: the Use of the Term "Son of Man" in Aramaic Sources and in the Teaching of Jesus', *JSNT* 29 (1987) 21–56.

Catchpole, D. R., 'The Son of Man's Search for Faith (Luke xviii 8b)', *NovT* 19 (1977) 81–104.

— 'The Ravens, the Lilies and the Q Hypothesis', *SNTU* A/6–7 (1981–82) 77–87.

— 'The Angelic Son of Man in Luke 12:8', *NovT* 24 (1982) 255–65.

— 'Q and "The Friend at Midnight"', *JTS* 34 (1983) 407–24.

— 'The Law and Prophets in Q', in *Tradition and Interpretation in the New Testament* (FS E. E. Ellis; Tübingen: Mohr, 1987) 95–109.

— 'Q, Prayer and the Kingdom: A Rejoinder', *JTS* 40 (1989) 377–88.

— *The Quest for Q* (Edinburgh: T. & T. Clark, 1993).

— 'The Anointed One in Nazareth', in M. C. de Boer (ed.), *From Jesus to John* (FS M. de Jonge; Sheffield Academic Press, 1993) 231–51.

Charlesworth, J. H. (ed.), *Old Testament Pseudepigrapha* 2 vols (London: Darton, Longman & Todd, 1983 & 1985).

Chilton, B. D., *God in Strength: Jesus' Announcement of the Kingdom* (Freistadt: Plöchl, 1979).

Christ, F., *Jesus Sophia: die Sophia Christologie bei den Synoptikern* (Zürich: TVZ, 1970).

Collins, A. Y., 'The Origin of the Designation of Jesus as "Son of Man"', *HTR* 80 (1987) 391–407.

Collins, A. Y., 'The Son of Man Sayings in the Sayings Source', in M. P. Horgan & P. J. Kopelski (eds), *To Touch the Text* (FS J. A. Fitzmyer; New York: Crossroad, 1989) 369–89.

Collins, J. J., *The Apocalyptic Imagination* (New York: Crossroads, 1984).

— 'Apocalyptic Literature', in R. A. Kraft & G. W. E. Nickelsburg (eds), *Early Judaism and Its Modern Interpreters* (Philadelphia: Fortress, 1986) 345–69.

— 'The Son of Man in First Century Judaism', *NTS* 38 (1992) 448–66.

Colpe, C., ὁ υἱὸς τοῦ ἀνθρώπου, *TWNT* VIII, 403–81.

Conzelmann, H., *The Theology of St Luke* (ET London: Faber, 1960).

Coser, L., *The Functions of Social Conflict* (London: Routledge & Kegan Paul, 1956).

Cotter, W. J., 'The Parable of the Children in the Market Place, Q (Lk) 7:31–35: An Examination of the Parable's Image and Significance', *NovT* 29 (1987) 289–304.

Crenshaw, J. L., 'Wisdom in the OT', *Interpreter's Dictionary of the Bible* Supplementary Volume (Nashville: Abingdon, 1976) 952–6.

— 'Method in Determining Wisdom Influence upon "Historical" Literature', *JBL* 88 (1969) 129–42.

— 'Prolegomena', in J. L. Crenshaw (ed.), *Studies in Ancient Israelite Wisdom* (New York: KTAV, 1976) 1–45.

Crossan, J. D., *In Fragments: The Aphorisms of Jesus* (San Francisco: Harper & Row, 1983).

— *The Historical Jesus. The Life of a Mediterranean Jewish Peasant* (Edinburgh: T. & T. Clark, 1991).

Cullmann, O., *The Christology of the New Testament* (ET London: SCM, 1959).

Dahl, N. A., 'Eschatology and History in Light of the Qumran Texts', in *The Crucified Messiah* (ET Minneapolis: Augsburg, 1974) 129–45.

— 'The Parables of Growth', in *Jesus in the Memory of the Early Church* (Minneapolis: Augsburg, 1976) 141–66.

Davies, W. D., *The Setting of the Sermon on the Mount* (Cambridge University Press, 1966).

Davies, W. D. & Allison, D. C., *The Gospel according to Saint Matthew* (Edinburgh: T. & T. Clark, vol. I 1988; vol. II 1991).

Delobel, J., 'La rédaction de Lc IV,14–16a et le Bericht vom Anfang', in Neirynck (ed.), *L'Evangile de Luc*, 113–33.

Delobel, J. (ed.), *LOGIA. Les Paroles de Jésus — The Sayings of Jesus* (BETL 59; Leuven University Press & Peeters, 1982).

Denaux, A., 'Der Spruch von den zwei Wegen im Rahmen des Epilogs der Bergpredigt', in Delobel (ed.), *LOGIA*, 305–35.

— 'The Q-Logion Mt 11,27/Lk 10,22 and the Gospel of John', in Denaux (ed.), *John and the Synoptics*, 163–99.

— (ed.), *John and the Synoptics* (BETL 101; Leuven University Press & Peeters, 1992).

Devisch, M., 'Le document Q, source de Matthieu, problématique actuelle', in M. Didier (ed.), *L'Evangile selon Matthieu. Rédaction et théologie* (BETL 29; Gembloux: Duculot, 1972) 71–97.

— 'Le relation entre l'évangile de Marc et le document Q', in M. Sabbe (ed.), *L'Evangile selon Marc. Tradition et Rédaction* (BETL 34; Leuven University Press, 1974) 59–91.

Dibelius, M., *From Tradition to Gospel* (ET New York: Scribner's, 1935).

Didier, M. (ed.), *L'Evangile selon Matthieu. Rédaction et théologie* (BETL 29; Gembloux: Duculot, 1972) 71–97.

Dömer, M., *Das Heil Gottes. Studien zur Theologie des lukanischen Doppelwerkes* (BBB 51; Köln-Bonn: P. Hanstein, 1978).

Donfried, K. P., 'The Allegory of the Ten Virgins (Matt 25:1–13) as a Summary of Matthean Theology', *JBL* 93 (1974) 415–28.

Downing, F. G., 'Towards the Rehabilitation of Q', *NTS* 11 (1965) 169–81.

— 'Redaction Criticism: Josephus' Antiquities and the Synoptic Problem', *JSNT* 8 (1980) 46–66; 9 (1980) 29–48.

— 'Contemporary Analogies to the Gospels and Acts: "Genres" or "Motifs"?', in Tuckett (ed.), *Synoptic Studies*, 51–64.

— 'Cynics and Christians', *NTS* 30 (1984) 584–93.

— 'The Social Contexts of Jesus the Teacher: Construction or Reconstruction', *NTS* 33 (1987) 439–51.

— *Jesus and the Threat of Freedom* (London: SCM, 1987).

— 'Compositional Conventions and the Synoptic Problem', *JBL* 107 (1988) 69–85.

— *Christ and the Cynics: Jesus and Other Radical Preachers in First-Century Tradition* (Sheffield Academic Press, 1988).

— 'Quite Like Q. A Genre for "Q": The "Lives" of Cynic Philosophers', *Biblica* 69 (1988) 196–225.

— *Cynics and Christian Origins* (Edinburgh: T. & T. Clark, 1992).

— 'A Paradigm Perplex: Luke, Matthew and Mark', *NTS* 38 (1992) 15–36.

Downing, F. G., 'A Genre for Q and a Socio-Cultural Context for Q: Comparing Sets of Similarities with Sets of Differences', *JSNT* 55 (1994) 3–26.

Dudley, D. B., *A History of Cynicism* (London: Methuen, 1937).

Dungan, D. L., 'Mark — The Abridgement of Matthew and Luke', *Jesus and Man's Hope I* (Pittsburgh Theological Seminary, 1970) 51–97.

— (ed.), *The Interrelations of the Gospels* (BETL 95; Leuven University Press & Peeters, 1990).

Dunn, J. D. G., *Baptism in the Holy Spirit* (London: SCM, 1970).

— *Jesus and the Spirit* (London: SCM, 1975).

— *Unity and Diversity in the New Testament* (London: SCM, 1977).

— *Christology in the Making* (London: SCM, 1980).

— 'Jesus and Ritual Purity: a Study of the Tradition History of Mk 7,15', in *A Cause de l'Evangile* (FS J. Dupont; Paris: Cerf, 1985) 251–76.

— 'Pharisees, Sinners, and Jesus', in Dunn, *Jesus, Paul and the Law* (London: SPCK, 1990) 61–88.

— *The Partings of the Ways* (London: SCM, 1991).

Dupont, J., *Les Béatitudes I–III* (Paris: Gabalda, 1969).

— 'La parabole des invités au festin dans le ministère de Jésus', *Etudes*, 667–705.

— 'La Parabole des Talents ou des Mines (Mt 25,14–30; Lc 19,12–27)', *Etudes*, 744–60.

— *Etudes sur les Evangiles Synoptiques* (BETL 70; Leuven University Press & Peeters, 1985).

Edwards, R. A., 'The Eschatological Correlative as a Gattung in the New Testament', *ZNW* 60 (1969) 9–20.

— *The Sign of Jonah in the Teaching of the Evangelists and Q* (London: SCM, 1971).

— *A Theology of Q. Eschatology, Prophecy and Wisdom* (Philadelphia: Fortress, 1976).

Eichhorn, J. G., *Über die drey ersten Evangelien. Einige Bemerkungen zu ihrer künftigen kritischen Behandlung* (Leipzig: Weidmann, 1794).

— *Einleitung in das Neue Testament* (5 Bde.; Leipzig: Weidmann, 1804–27).

Elliott, J. H., *A Home for the Homeless. A Sociological Exegesis of 1 Peter* (London: SCM, 1981).

— 'Social-Scientific Criticism of the New Testament: More on Methods and Models', *Semeia* 35 (1986) 1–33.

Ellis, E. E., 'Gospel Criticism', in P. Stuhlmacher (ed.), *Das Evangelium und die Evangelien* (WUNT 28; Tübingen: Mohr, 1983) 27–54.

Ernst, J., *Johannes der Täufer* (BZNW 53; Berlin: de Gruyter, 1989).

Esler, P. F., *Community and Gospel in Luke–Acts* (SNTSMS 57; Cambridge University Press, 1987).

Farmer, W. R., *The Synoptic Problem* (London: Macmillan, 1964).

— 'A Fresh Approach to Q', in J. Neusner (ed.), *Christianity, Judaism and Other Greco-Roman Cults. Studies for Morton Smith at Sixty. Part One* (Leiden: Brill, 1975) 39–50.

— 'A Response to Joseph Fitzmyer's Defense of the Two Document Hypothesis', in Farmer (ed.), *New Synoptic Studies* (Macon: Mercer University Press, 1983) 501–23.

— 'The Two Gospel Hypothesis', in Dungan (ed.), *Interrelations*, 125–56.

— *The Gospel of Jesus: The Pastoral Relevance of the Synoptic Problem* (Louisville: Westminster John Knox, 1994).

Farrer, A., 'On Dispensing with Q', in D. E. Nineham (ed.), *Studies in the Gospels. Essays in Memory of R. H. Lightfoot* (Oxford: Blackwell, 1967) 55–88.

Finkel, A., *The Pharisees and the Teacher of Nazareth* (Leiden: Brill, 1964).

Fitzmyer, J. A., 'The Priority of Mark and the "Q" Source in Luke', in *Jesus and Man's Hope I* (Pittsburgh Theological Seminary, 1970) 131–170.

— *The Gospel according to Luke I–IX* (New York: Doubleday, 1981).

— *To Advance the Gospel: New Testament Studies* (New York: Crossroad, 1981).

Fleddermann, H., 'The Cross and Discipleship in Q', *SBL 1988 Seminar Papers* (Atlanta: Scholars, 1988) 472–82.

Focant, C. (ed.), *The Synoptic Gospels. Source Criticism and the New Literary Criticism* (BETL 110; Leuven University Press & Peeters, 1993).

Foerster, W., ἔχιδνα, *TWNT* II, 815.

Fowler, A., *Kinds of Literature: An Introduction to the Theory of Genres and Modes* (Oxford University Press, 1982).

Friedrichsen, T. A., 'The Matthew–Luke Agreements against Mark', in Neirynck (ed.), *L'Evangile de Luc*, 335–92.

Fuller, R. H., *The Formation of New Testament Christology* (London: Lutterworth, 1965).

Fuller, R. H., 'The Double Commandment of Love: A Test Case for the Criteria of Authenticity', in Fuller (ed.), *Essays on the Love Commandment* (Philadelphia: Fortress, 1978) 41–56.

Funk, R., 'Beyond Criticism in Quest of Literacy: The Parable of the Leaven', *Int* 25 (1971) 149–70.

Garland, D. E., *The Intention of Matthew 23* (NovTSupp 52; Leiden: Brill, 1979).

Goulder, M. D., *Midrash and Lection in Matthew* (London: SPCK, 1974).

— 'On Putting Q to the Test', *NTS* 24 (1978) 218–234.

— 'Some Observations on Professor Farmer's "Certain Results . . ."', in Tuckett (ed.), *Synoptic Studies*, 99–104.

— 'The Order of a Crank', in Tuckett (ed.), *Synoptic Studies*, 111–30.

— *Luke — A New Paradigm* (JSNTSS 20; Sheffield Academic Press, 1989).

— 'Luke's Knowledge of Matthew', in G. Strecker (ed.), *Minor Agreements* (GTA 50; Göttingen: Vandenhoeck & Ruprecht, 1993) 143–62.

— 'Luke's Compositional Origins', *NTS* 39 (1993) 150–2.

Goulet-Cazé, M.-O., 'Le cynisme à l'époque impériale', *ANRW* II.36.4, 2720–2823.

Grässer, E., *Das Problem der Parusieverzögerung in den synoptischen Evangelien und in der Apostelgeschichte* (BZNW 22; Berlin: de Gruyter, 1969).

Green, H. B., 'The Credibility of Luke's Transformation of Matthew', in Tuckett (ed.), *Synoptic Studies*, 131–56.

— 'Matthew 12.22–50 and Parallels: An Alternative to Matthean Conflation', in Tuckett (ed.), *Synoptic Studies*, 157–76.

Grundmann, W., 'Weisheit im Horizont des Reiches Gottes' in R. Schnackenburg, J. Ernst, J. Wanke (eds), *Die Kirche des Anfangs* (FS H. Schürmann; Freiburg: Herder, 1978) 175–99.

Guelich, R. A., *The Sermon on the Mount* (Waco: Word, 1982).

Guenther, H. O., 'The Sayings Gospel Q and the Quest for Aramaic Sources: Rethinking Christian Origins', *Semeia* 55 (1992) 41–76.

Gundry, R. H., *Matthew: A Commentary on His Literary and Theological Art* (Grand Rapids: Eerdmans, 1982).

— 'Matthean Foreign Bodies in Agreements of Luke with Matthew against Mark', in Van Segbroek et al (eds), *The Four Gospels 1992*, 1467–95.

Haenchen, E., 'Matthäus 23', *ZThK* 48 (1951) 38–63.

Hahn, F., *Christologishe Hoheitstitel* (FRLANT 83; Göttingen: Vandenhoeck & Ruprecht, 1963).

— 'Das Gleichnis von der Einladung zum Festmahl', in *Verborum Veritas* (FS G. Stählin; Wuppertal: Brockhaus, 1970) 51–82.

Hamerton-Kelly, R. G., *Pre-existence, Wisdom and the Son of Man* (SNTSMS 21; Cambridge University Press, 1973).

Hare, D. R. A., *The Theme of Jewish Persecution of Christians in the Gospel according to St Matthew* (SNTSMS 6; Cambridge University Press, 1967).

— *The Son of Man Tradition* (Minneapolis: Fortress, 1990).

Harnack, A., *The Sayings of Jesus* (ET London: Williams & Norgate, 1908).

Hartin, P. J., *James and the Q Sayings of Jesus* (JSNTSS 47; Sheffield Academic Press, 1991).

Harvey, A. E., 'Forty Strokes Save One: Social Aspects of Judaizing and Apostasy', in A. E. Harvey (ed.), *Alternative Approaches to New Testament Study* (London: SPCK, 1985) 79–96.

Havener, I., *Q: The Sayings of Jesus* (Wilmington: Glazier, 1987).

Hawkins, J. C., 'Probabilities as to the so-called Double Tradition of St. Matthew and St. Luke', in W. Sanday (ed.), *Studies in the Synoptic Problem* (Oxford: Clarendon, 1911) 95–138.

Hengel, M., 'Proseuche und Synagoge: Jüdische Gemeinde, Gotteshaus und Gottesdienst in der Diaspora und in Palestina' in G. Jeremias, H. W. Kuhn, H. Stegemann (eds), *Tradition und Glaube* (FS K. G. Kuhn; Göttingen: Vandenhoeck & Ruprecht, 1971) 157–84.

— *Judaism and Hellenism* (ET London: SCM, 1974).

— *The Charismatic Leader and His Followers* (ET Edinburgh: T. & T. Clark, 1981).

— *Between Jesus and Paul* (ET London: SCM, 1983).

Hennecke, E. (ed.), *New Testament Apocrypha. Volume One* (London: SCM, 1963).

Hickling, C. J. A., 'The Plurality of "Q"', in Delobel (ed.), *LOGIA*, 425–9.

Higgins, A. J. B., *Jesus and the Son of Man* (Philadelphia: Fortress, 1964).

— *The Son of Man in the Teaching of Jesus* (SNTSMS 39; Cambridge University Press, 1980).

Hirsch, E. D., *Validity in Interpretation* (Yale University Press, 1967).

Hodgson, R., 'On the Gattung of Q: A Dialogue with J. M. Robinson', *Biblica* 66 (1985) 73–95.

Hoehner, H. W., *Herod Antipas* (SNTSMS 17; Cambridge University Press, 1972).

Hoffmann, P., 'Πάντες ἐργάται ἀδικίας. Redaktion und Tradition in Lk 13,22–30', *ZNW* 58 (1967) 188–214.

— *Studien zur Theologie der Logienquelle* (NTAbh 8; Münster: Aschendorff, 1972).

— Review of S. Schulz, *Q — Die Spruchquelle der Evangelisten*, in *BZ* 19 (1975) 104–15.

— 'Tradition und Situation. Zur "Verbindlichkeit" des Gebots der Feindesliebe in der synoptischen Überlieferung und in der gegenwärtigen Friedensdiskussion', in K. Kertelge (ed.), *Ethik im Neuen Testament* (Freiburg: Herder, 1984) 50–118.

— 'Die Sprüche vom Sorgen in der vorsynoptischen Überlieferung', in H. Hierdeis & H. S. Rosenbusch (eds), *Artikulation der Wirklichkeit* (FS S. Oppolzer; Frankfurt: Peter Lang, 1988) 73–94.

— 'Jesu "Verbot des Sorgens" und seine Nachgeschichte in der synoptischen Überlieferung', in D.-A. Koch, G. Sellin, A. Lindemann (eds), *Jesu Rede von Gott und ihre Nachgeschichte* (FS W. Marxsen; Gütersloh: G. Mohn, 1989) 110–41.

— 'Jesus versus Menschensohn', in L. Oberlinner & P. Fiedler (eds), *Salz der Erde–Licht der Welt* (FS A. Vögtle; Stuttgart: Katholisches Bibelwerk, 1991) 165–202.

— 'QR und der Menschensohn. Eine vorläufige Skizze', in Van Segbroek et al (eds), *The Four Gospels 1992*, 421–56; ET 'The Redaction of Q and the Son of Man: A Preliminary Sketch', in Piper (ed.), *The Gospel Behind the Gospels. Studies on Q*, 159–98.

Holmberg, B., *Sociology and the New Testament* (Minneapolis: Fortress, 1990).

Holtzmann, H. J., *Die synoptischen Evangelien. Ihr Ursprung und geschichtlicher Charakter* (Leipzig: Engelmann, 1863).

Honoré, A. T., 'A Statistical Study of the Synoptic Problem', *NovT* 10 (1968) 95–147.

Hooker, M. D., *The Son of Man in Mark* (London: SPCK, 1967).

— 'In His Own Image', in M. D. Hooker & S. G. Wilson (eds), *What About the New Testament? Essays in Honour of Christopher Evans* (London: SCM, 1975) 28–44.

Horbury, W., 'The Benediction on the *Minim* and Early Jewish-Christian Controversy', *JTS* 33 (1982) 19–61.

Horbury, W., 'The Messianic Associations of "the Son of Man"', *JTS* 36 (1985) 34–55.

Horn, F. W., 'Christentum und Judentum in der Logienquelle', *EvTh* 51 (1991) 344–64.

Horsley, R. A., 'Josephus and the Bandits', *JSJ* 10 (1979) 37–63.

— 'The Sicarii. Ancient Jewish Terrorists', *JR* 59 (1979) 435–58.

— 'The Zealots: Their Origin, Relationships and Importance in the Jewish Revolt', *NovT* 28 (1986) 159–92 .

— *Sociology and the Jesus Movement* (New York: Crossroad, 1989).

— 'Logoi Prophētōn? Reflections on the Genre of Q', in B. A. Pearson (ed.), *The Future of Early Christianity* (FS H. Koester; Minneapolis: Fortress, 1991) 195–209.

— 'Q and Jesus: Assumptions, Approaches and Analyses', *Semeia* 55 (1991) 175–209.

Horsley, R. A., and Hanson, J. S., *Bandits, Prophets, and Messiahs. Popular Movements in the Time of Jesus* (Minneapolis: Winson, 1985).

Hull, J. M., *Hellenistic Magic and the Synoptic Tradition* (London: SCM, 1974).

Hultgren, A. J., 'Paul's Pre-Christian Persecutions of the Church. Their Purpose, Locale and Nature', *JBL* 95 (1976) 97–111.

Jacobson, A. D., *Wisdom Christology in Q*, Ph.D. Dissertation, Claremont, 1978.

— 'The Literary Unity of Q', *JBL* 101 (1982) 365–89.

— 'The Literary Unity of Q. Lc 10,2–16 and Parallels as a Test Case', in Delobel (ed.), *LOGIA*, 419–23.

— *The First Gospel. An Introduction to Q* (Sonoma: Polebridge, 1992).

— 'Apocalyptic and the Synoptic Sayings Source Q', in Van Segbroek et al (eds), *The Four Gospels 1992*, 403–19.

Jeremias, J., Ἰωνᾶς, *TWNT* III, 410–3.

— *The Parables of Jesus* (ET London: SCM, 1963).

— *New Testament Theology* (ET London: SCM, 1971).

— *Die Sprache des Lukasevangeliums* (Göttingen: Vandenhoeck & Ruprecht, 1980).

Keck, L. E., 'Toward the Renewal of New Testament Christology' *NTS* 32 (1986) 362–77.

Kee, H. C., *Jesus in History* (New York: Harcourt, Brace & World, 1970).

— *Christian Origins in Sociological Perspective* (London: SCM, 1980).

— 'The Transformation of the Synagogue after 70 C.E.: Its Import for Early Christianity', *NTS* 36 (1990) 1–24.

Kee, H. C., 'The Changing Meaning of Synagogue: A Response to Richard Oster', *NTS* 40 (1994) 281–3.

Kelber, W., *The Oral and Written Gospel* (Philadelphia: Fortress, 1983).

Kermode, F., *The Genesis of Secrecy* (Cambridge, Mass.: Harvard University Press, 1979).

Kertelge, K., 'Das Doppelgebot der Liebe im Markusevangelium', in *A Cause de l'Evangile* (FS J. Dupont; Paris: Cerf, 1985) 303–32.

Kiilunen, J., *Das Doppelgebot der Liebe in synoptischer Sicht* (Helsinki: Suomalainen Tiedeakatemia, 1989).

Kilpatrick, G. D., 'The Disappearance of Q', *JTS* 42 (1941) 182–4.

Klinghardt, M., *Gesetz und Volk Gottes. Das lukanische Verständnis des Gesetzes nach Herkunft, Funktion und seinem Ort in der Geschichte des Urchristentums* (WUNT 2.32; Tübingen: Mohr, 1988).

Kloppenborg, J. S., 'Tradition and Redaction in the Synoptic Sayings Source', *CBQ* 46 (1984) 34–62.

— 'The Formation of Q and Antique Instructional Genres', *JBL* 105 (1986) 443–62.

— 'Blessing and Marginality: The "Persecution Beatitude" in Q, Thomas and Early Christianity', *Foundations and Facets Forum* 2 (1986) 36–56.

— *The Formation of Q* (Philadelphia: Fortress Press, 1987).

— 'Symbolic Eschatology and the Apocalypticism of Q', *HTR* 80 (1987) 287–306.

— *Q Parallels* (Sonoma: Polebridge, 1988).

— 'Nomos and Ethos in Q', in J. E. Goehring et al. (eds), *Gospel Origins and Christian Beginnings* (FS J. M. Robinson; Sonoma: Polebridge, 1990) 35–48.

— '"Easter Faith" and the Sayings Gospel Q', *Semeia* 49 (1990) 71–99.

— 'Jesus and the Parables of Jesus in Q', in Piper (ed.), *The Gospel Behind the Gospels*, 275–319.

Klostermann, E., *Das Matthäusevangelium* (Tübingen: Mohr, 1927).

Knibb, M. A., 'The Date of the Parables of Enoch: A Critical Review', *NTS* 25 (1979) 345–59.

Koch, K., *The Growth of the Biblical Tradition* (London: A. & C. Black, 1969).

Koester, H., 'GNOMAI DIAPHOROI: The Origin and Nature of Diversification in the History of Early Christianity', in Robinson & Koester, *Trajectories*, 114–57.

Koester, H., 'One Jesus and Four Primitive Gospels', in Robinson & Koester, *Trajectories*, 158–204.

— 'Apocryphal and Canonical Gospels', *HTR* 73 (1980) 105–30.

— *Ancient Christian Gospels* (London & Philadelphia: SCM & Trinity, 1990).

Koet, B. J., *Five Studies on Interpretation of Scripture in Luke–Acts* (Leuven University Press & Peeters, 1989).

Kollmann, B., 'Lk 12,35–38 — Ein Gleichnis der Logienquelle', *ZNW* 81 (1990) 254–61.

Kosch, D., *Die eschatologische Tora des Menschensohnes. Untersuchungen zur Rezeption der Stellung Jesu zur Tora in Q* (NTOA 12; Freiburg & Göttingen: Universitätsverlag & Vandenhoeck & Ruprecht, 1989).

— 'Q: Rekonstruktion und Interpretation', *FZPT* 36 (1989) 409–25.

Küchler, M., *Frühjüdische Weisheitstraditionen* (Freiburg & Göttingen: Universitetsverlag & Vandenhoeck & Ruprecht, 1979).

Kuhn, H.-W., 'Nachfolge nach Ostern', in D. Lührmann & G. Strecker (eds), *Kirche* (FS G. Bornkamm; Tübingen: Mohr, 1980) 105–32.

Kühschelm, R., *Jüngerverfolgung und Geschick Jesu* (Klosterneuburg: Österreichisches Katholisches Bibelwerk, 1983).

Kümmel, W .G., *Promise and Fulfilment* (ET London: SCM, 1957).

— *Introduction to the New Testament* (ET London: SCM, 1975).

Kürzinger, J., 'Die Aussage des Papias von Hierapolis zur literarischen Form des Markusevangeliums', *BZ* 21 (1977) 245–64.

Lambrecht, J., 'The Great Commandment Pericope and Q', in Piper (ed.), *The Gospel Behind the Gospels*, 73–96.

Lampe, G. W. H., 'The Lucan Portrait of Christ', *NTS* 2 (1956) 160–75.

Lang, F., πῦρ κτλ, *TWNT* VI, 927–53.

Laufen, R., *Die Doppelüberlieferungen der Logienquelle und des Markusevangeliums* (BBB 54; Bonn: Hanstein, 1980).

Légasse, S., 'L'oracle contre "cette génération" (Mt 23,34–36 par Lc 11,49–51) et la polémique judéo-chrétienne dans la Source des Logia', in Delobel (ed.), *LOGIA*, 237–56.

Lindars, B., 'The Apocalyptic Myth and the Death of Christ', *BJRL* 57 (1975) 366–87.

Lindars, B., *Jesus Son of Man* (London: SPCK, 1983).

Linnemann, E., *The Parables of Jesus: Introduction and Exposition* (ET London: SPCK, 1966).

— 'Jesus und der Täufer', Festschrift für Ernst Fuchs (Tübingen: Mohr, 1973) 219–36.

Lips, H. von, *Weisheitliche Traditionen im Neuen Testament* (WMANT 64; Neukirchen-Vluyn: Neukirchener, 1990).

Lührmann, D., *Die Redaktion der Logienquelle* (WMANT 33; Neukirchen-Vluyn: Neukirchener, 1969).

— 'Liebet eure Feinde (Lk 6,27–36/Mt 5,39–48)', *ZThK* 69 (1972) 412–38.

— 'Erwägungen zur Geschichte des Urchristentums', *EvTh* 32 (1972) 452–67.

— *Das Markusevangelium* (Tübingen: Mohr, 1987).

— 'The Gospel of Mark and the Sayings Collection Q', *JBL* 108 (1989) 51–71.

Luz, U., 'Die wiederentdeckte Logienquelle', *EvTh* 33 (1973) 527–33.

— 'Die Erfüllung des Gesetzes bei Matthäus', *ZThK* 75 (1978) 398–435.

— *Das Evangelium nach Matthäus I & II* (Zürich & Neukirchen-Vluyn: Benziger & Neukirchener, 1985 & 1990).

— *Matthew 1–7* (ET Edinburgh: T. & T. Clark, 1990).

Maccoby, H., 'The Washing of Cups', *JSNT* 14 (1982) 3–15.

Mack, B., *The Myth of Innocence* (Philadelphia: Fortress, 1988).

— *The Lost Gospel. The Book of Q and Christian Origins* (San Francisco: HarperCollins, 1993).

Mahnke, H., *Die Versuchungsgechichte im Rahmen der synoptischen Evangelien* (Frankfurt: Lang, 1978).

Malherbe, A. J., *The Cynic Epistles* (Missoula: Scholars Press, 1977).

— 'Pseudo-Heraclitus Epistle 4: The Divinisation of the Wise Man', *JAC* 21 (1978) 42–64.

— 'Self-Definition among Epicureans and Cynics', in B. F. Meyer & E. P. Sanders (eds), *Jewish and Christian Self-Definition Vol. 3: Self-Definition in the Greco-Roman World* (Philadelphia: Fortress, 1982) 46–59.

— *Social Aspects of Early Christianity* (Philadelphia: Fortress, 1983).

Manson, T. W., *The Sayings of Jesus* (London: SCM, 1949).

Marshall, I. H., *The Gospel of Luke* (Exeter: Paternoster, 1978).

Martyn, J. L., 'Glimpses into the History of the Johannine Community', in M. de Jonge (ed.), *L'Evangile de Jean. Sources, rédaction, théologie* (BETL 44; Gembloux & Leuven: Duculot & Leuven University Press) 149–75.

März, C. P., '"Feuer auf die Erde zu werfen, bin ich gekommen ..." Zum Verständnis und zur Entstehung von Lk 12,49', in *A Cause de l'Evangile* (FS J. Dupont; Paris: Cerf, 1985) 479–511.

— 'Lk 12,54b-56 par Mt 16,2b.3 und die Akoluthie der Redequelle', *SNTU* 11 (1986) 83–96.

— 'Zur Q-Rezeption in Lk 12,35 — 13,35 (14,1–24)', in Focant (ed.), *Synoptic Gospels*, 177–208.

Mason, S., *Flavius Josephus on the Pharisees* (Leiden: Brill, 1991).

Massaux, E., *Influence de l'Evangile de saint Matthieu sur la littérature chrétienne avant saint Irénée* (repr. BETL 75; Leuven University Press & Peeters, 1986).

McKenzie, J., 'Reflections on Wisdom', *JBL* 86 (1967) 1–9.

McNicol, A. J., 'The Composition of the Eschatological Discourse', in Dungan (ed.), *Interrelations*, 157–200.

Mealand, D. L., *Poverty and Expectation in the Gospels* (London: SPCK, 1980).

Meeks, W. A., *The First Urban Christians* (New Haven & London: Yale University Press, 1983).

— *The Moral World of the First Christians* (London: SPCK, 1987).

Meier, J. P., *Law and History in Matthew's Gospel* (AnB 71; Rome: Biblical Institute Press, 1976).

Meinertz, M., '"Dieses Geschlecht" im Neuen Testament', *BZ* 1 (1957) 283–9.

Menzies, R. P., *The Development of Early Christian Pneumatology with Special Reference to Luke–Acts* (JSNTSS 54; Sheffield Academic Press, 1991).

— 'Spirit and Power in Luke–Acts: A Response to Max Turner', *JSNT* 49 (1993) 11–20.

Merklein, H., *Die Gottesherrschaft als Handlungsprinzip. Untersuchung zur Ethik Jesu* (FzB 34; Würzburg: Echter, 1978).

— 'Die Umkehrpredigt bei Johannes dem Täufer und Jesus von Nazaret', *BZ* 25 (1981) 29–46, = *Studien zu Jesus und Paulus* (WUNT 43; Tübingen: Mohr, 1987) 109–26.

Meyer, P. D., *The Community of Q*, Ph.D. Dissertation, University of Iowa, 1967.

— 'The Gentile Mission in Q', *JBL* 89 (1970) 405–17.

Meyers, E., 'Synagogue', *Anchor Bible Dictionary* 6 (New York: Doubleday, 1992) 251–60.

Miller, R. J., 'The Rejection of the Prophets in Q', *JBL* 107 (1988) 225–40.

Morgenthaler, R., *Statistische Synopse* (Zürich: Gotthelf, 1971).

Moule, C. F. D., *An Idiom Book of New Testament Greek* (Cambridge University Press, 1968).

— *The Origin of Christology* (Cambridge University Press, 1977).

Neirynck, F., 'Q', *Interpreter's Dictionary of the Bible, Supplementary Volume* (Nashville: Abingdon, 1962) 715–6 .

— 'John and the Synoptics', in M. de Jonge (ed.), *L'Evangile de Jean. Sources, rédaction, théologie* (BETL 44; Gembloux & Leuven: Duculot & Leuven University Press) 73–106 (= *Evangelica I*, 365–400).

— 'The Symbol Q (= Quelle)', *ETL* 54 (1978) 119–25 (= *Evangelica I*, 683–90).

— *Jean et les Synoptiques* (BETL 49; Leuven University Press, 1979).

— *Evangelica I* (BETL 60; Leuven: University Press & Peeters, 1982).

— 'Recent Developments in the Study of Q' in Delobel (ed.), *LOGIA*, 29–75 (= *Evangelica II*, 409–63) .

— 'Ac 10,36–43 et l'Evangile', *ETL* 60 (1984) 109–17 (= *Evangelica II*, 227–36).

— 'ΤΙΣ ΕΣΤΙΝ Ο ΠΑΙΣΑΣ ΣΕ; Mt 26,68/Lk 22,64 (diff. Mk 14,65)', *ETL* 63 (1987) 5–47 (= *Evangelica II*, 95–138).

— (ed.), *L'Evangile de Luc. The Gospel of Luke* (BETL 32 rev. ed.; Leuven University Press & Peeters, 1989).

— 'Q^{Mt} and Q^{Lk} and the Reconstruction of Q', *ETL* 66 (1990) 385–90 (= *Evangelica II*, 475–80).

— 'Luke 14,1–6. Lukan Composition and Q Saying', in C. Bussmann & W. Radl (eds), *Der Treue Gottes Trauen* (FS G. Schneider; Freiburg: Herder, 1991), = *Evangelica II*, 183–204.

— *Evangelica II* (BETL 99; Leuven University Press & Peeters, 1991).

— 'Literary Criticism, Old and New', in Focant (ed.), *The Synoptic Gospels*, 11–38.

— 'The Minor Agreements and Q', in Piper (ed.), *The Gospel Behind the Gospels*, 49–72.

Neirynck, F. & Van Segbroek, F., *New Testament Vocabulary* (BETL 65; Leuven University Press & Peeters, 1984).

Bibliography

467

Nestle, E., 'Anise and Rue', *ExpT* 15 (1904) 528.

Neusner, J., *The Rabbinic Traditions about the Pharisees before 70* (Leiden: Brill, 1971).

— '"First cleanse the inside". "Halakhic" Background of a Controversy Saying', *NTS* 22 (1976) 486–95.

Nickelsburg, G. W. E., *Resurrection, Immortality and Eternal Life in Intertestamental Judaism* (London: Oxford University Press, 1972).

— 'The Apocalyptic Message of 1 En 92–105', *CBQ* 39 (1977) 309–28.

— 'Son of Man', *Anchor Bible Dictionary* 6 (New York: Doubleday, 1992) 137–50.

Norden, E., *Agnostos Theos* (Berlin: Teubner, 1913).

Ollrog, W. H., *Paulus und seine Mitarbeiter. Untersuchungen zu Theorie und Praxis der paulinischen Mission* (WMANT 50; Neukirchen-Vluyn: Neukirchener, 1979).

O'Neill, J. C., 'The Man from Heaven: *Sib.Or.* 5.256–259', *JSP* 9 (1991) 87–102.

Orchard, B., *Matthew, Luke & Mark* (Manchester: Koinonia, 1976).

Oster, R. E., 'Supposed Anachronism in Luke–Acts's Use of συναγωγή: A Rejoinder to H. C. Kee', *NTS* 39 (1993) 178–208.

Perrin, N., *What is Redaction Criticism?* (London: SPCK, 1969).

Piper, J., *Love Your Enemies, Jesus' Love Command in the Synoptic Tradition and the Early Christian Paraenesis* (SNTSMS 38; Cambridge University Press, 1979).

Piper, R. A., *Wisdom in the Q-Tradition* (SNTSMS 61; Cambridge University Press, 1989).

— (ed.), *The Gospel Behind the Gospels. Current Studies on Q* (NovTSupp 75; Leiden: Brill, 1994).

Pokorny, P., *The Genesis of Christology* (ET Edinburgh: T. & T. Clark, 1987).

Polag, A., *Die Christologie der Logienquelle* (WMANT 45; Neukirchen-Vluyn: Neukirchener, 1977).

— *Fragmenta Q* (Neukirchen-Vluyn: Neukirchener, 1982).

Rad, G. von, *Old Testament Theology Volume One* (ET Edinburgh: Oliver & Boyd, 1962).

— *Wisdom in Israel* (ET London: SCM, 1972).

Rengstorf, K. H., γελάω κτλ, *TWNT* I, 656–60.

Rese, M., *Alttestamentliche Motive in der Christologie des Lukas* (Gütersloh: Mohn, 1969).

Robinson, J. M., 'Die Hodayot Formel in Gebet und Hymnus des Frühchristentums', in *Apophoreta* (FS E. Haenchen, BZNW 30; Berlin: Töpelmann, 1964) 194–235.

— 'LOGOI SOPHON: On the Gattung of Q', ET in Robinson & Koester, *Trajectories*, 71–113.

— 'Jesus as Sophos and Sophia', in R. L. Wilken (ed.), *Aspects of Wisdom in Judaism and Early Christianity* (University of Notre Dame Press, 1975) 1–16.

— 'On Bridging the Gulf from Q to the Gospel of Thomas (or Vice Versa)', in C. W. Hedrick & R. Hodgson (eds) *Nag Hammadi, Gnosticism and Early Christianity* (Peabody, Mass.: Hendrickson, 1986) 127–75.

— 'The Q Trajectory: Between John and Matthew via Jesus', in B. A. Pearson (ed.), *The Future of Early Christianity* (FS H. Koester; Minneapolis: Fortress, 1991) 173–94.

— 'The Sayings Gospel Q', in Van Segbroek et al (eds), *The Four Gospels 1992*, 361–88.

— 'Die Logienquelle: Weisheit oder Prophetie?', *EvTh* 53 (1993) 367–89.

— 'The Jesus of Q as Liberation Theologian', in Piper (ed.), *The Gospel Behind the Gospels*, 259–74.

— 'The History-of-Religions Taxonomy of Q: The Cynic Hypothesis', in T. Schweer & S. Rink (eds), *Gnosisforschung und Religionsgeschichte* (FS K. Rudolph; Marburg: Diagonal, 1995) 249–65.

— 'Building Blocks in the Social History of Q', in H. Taussig & E. Castelli (eds), *Rethinking Christian Origins: A Festschrift in Honor of Burton L. Mack* (Philadelphia: Trinity Press International, forthcoming [1996]).

— '*Galilean Upstarts*: A Sot's Cynical Disciples', paper read at the 1994 SBL meeting, Chicago, forthcoming in a FS for Robert Funk, in *Forum*.

Rosché, T., 'The Words of the Jesus and the Future of the "Q" Hypothesis', *JBL* 79 (1960) 210–20.

Saldarini, A. J., *Pharisees, Scribes and Sadducees in Palestinian Society* (Edinburgh: T. & T. Clark, 1989).

Salo, K., *Luke's Treatment of the Law. A Redaction-Critical Investigation* (Helsinki: Suomalainen Tiedeakatemia, 1991).

Sanday, W. (ed.), *Oxford Studies in the Synoptic Problem* (Oxford: Clarendon, 1911).

Sanders, E. P., *Paul, the Law and the Jewish People* (Philadelphia: Fortress, 1983).

Sanders, E. P., *Jesus and Judaism* (London: SCM, 1985).
— *Jewish Law from Jesus to the Mishnah* (London: SCM, 1990).
— *Judaism: Practice and Belief 63 BCE–66 CE* (London: SCM, 1992).
Sanders, E. P. & Davies, M., *Studying the Synoptic Gospels* (London: SCM, 1989).
Sato, M., *Q und Prophetie* (WUNT 2.29; Tübingen: Mohr, 1988).
— 'Q: Prophetie oder Weisheit? Ein Gespräch mit J. M. Robinson', *EvTh* 53 (1993) 389–404.
— 'Wisdom Statements in the Sphere of Prophecy', in Piper (ed.), *The Gospel Behind the Gospels*, 139–58.
Sauer, J., 'Traditionsgeschichtliche Erwägungen zu den synoptischen und paulinischen Aussagen über Feindesliebe und Wiedervergeltungsverzicht', *ZNW* 76 (1985) 1–28.
Schenk, W., *Synopse zur Redenquelle der Evangelien* (Düsseldorf: Patmos, 1981).
— 'Die Verwünschung der Küstenorte Q 10,13–15: Zur Funktion der konkreten Ortsangaben und zur Lokalisierung von Q', in Focant (ed.), *The Synoptic Gospels*, 477–90.
Schleiermacher, F. , 'Über die Zeugnis des Papias von unseren beiden ersten Evangelien', *Theologische Studien und Kritiken* 5 (1832) 735–68.
Schlier, H., ἀρνέομαι, *TWNT* I, 468–71.
Schlosser, J., 'Le Logion de Mt 10,28 Par. Lc 12,4–5', in Van Segbroek et al (eds), *The Four Gospels 1992*, 621–31 .
Schmidt, D., 'The LXX Gattung "Prophetic Correlative"', *JBL* 96 (1977) 517–22.
Schmidt, T. E., *Hostility to Wealth in the Synoptic Gospels* (JSNTSS 15; Sheffield: JSOT Press, 1987).
Schmithals, W., *Einleitung in die drei ersten Evangelien* (Berlin & New York: de Gruyter, 1985).
Schneider, G., 'Das Vaterunser des Matthäus', in *A Cause de l'Evangile* (FS J. Dupont; Paris: Cerf, 1985) 57–90.
Schottroff, L. & Stegemann, W., *Jesus von Nazareth. Hoffnung der Armen* (Stuttgart: Kohlhammer, 1978).
Schrage, W., *The Ethics of the New Testament* (ET Edinburgh: T. & T. Clark, 1988).
Schreck, C. J., 'The Nazareth Pericope: Luke 4,16–30 in Recent Study', in Neirynck (ed.), *L'Evangile de Luc*, 399–471.
Schrenk, G., δική κτλ, *TWNT* II, 180–229.

Schulz, S., *Q — Die Spruchquelle der Evangelisten* (Zürich: TVZ, 1971).

Schürmann, H., 'Der "Bericht vom Anfang". Ein Rekonstruktionsversuch auf Grund von Lk 4,14–16' in *StEv* 2 (*TU* 87; Berlin, 1964), 242–58.

— 'Zur Traditionsgeschichte der Nazareth-Perikope Lk 4,16–30', in *Mélanges Bibliques* (FS B. Rigaux; Gembloux: Duculot, 1970) 187–205.

— '"Wer daher eines dieser geringsten Gebote auflöst . . ." Wo fand Matthäus das Logion Mt 5,19?', in *Traditionsgeschichtliche Untersuchungen zu den synoptischen Evangelien* (Düsseldorf: Patmos, 1968) 126–36.

— 'Mt 10,5b-6 und die Vorgeschichte des synoptischen Aussendungsberichtes', *Traditionsgeschichtliche Untersuchungen zu den synoptischen Evangelien* (Düsseldorf: Patmos, 1968) 137–49.

— 'Protolukanische Spracheigentümlichkeiten?' in *Traditionsgeschichtliche Untersuchungen zu den synoptischen Evangelien* (Düsseldorf: Patmos, 1968) 209–27.

— *Das Lukasevangelium I* (Freiburg: Herder, 1969).

— 'Das Zeugnis der Redenquelle für die Basileia-Verkündigung Jesu', in Delobel (ed.), *LOGIA*, 121–200 .

— 'Beobachtungen zum Menschensohn-Titel in der Redequelle', in *Jesus und der Menschensohn* (FS A. Vögtle; Freiburg: Herder, 1975) 124–47.

— 'Die Redekomposition wider "dieses Geschlecht" und seine Führung in der Redenquelle (vgl. Mt 23,1–39 par Lk 11,37–54). Bestand - Akolouthie - Kompositionsformen', *SNTU* A/11 (1986) 33–81.

— 'Zum Komposition der Redenquelle. Beobachtungen an der lukanischen Q-Vorlage', in C. Bussmann & W. Radl (eds), *Der Treue Gottes Trauen* (FS G. Schneider; Freiburg: Herder, 1991) 325–42.

Schweizer, E., πνεῦμα κτλ, *TWNT* VI, 387–453.

— 'Formgeschichtliches zu den Seligpreisungen Jesu', *NTS* 19 (1973) 121–6.

Scobie, C. H. H., *John the Baptist* (London: SCM, 1964).

Scott, R. B. Y., 'The Study of the Wisdom Literature', *Int* 24 (1970) 20–45.

Seccombe, D., *Possessions and the Poor in Luke–Acts* (Linz: Plöchl, 1982).

Seeley, D., 'Blessings and Boundaries: Interpretations of Jesus' Death in Q', *Semeia* 55 (1991) 131–46.

Seeley, D., 'Jesus' Death in Q', *NTS* 38 (1992) 222–34.

Sevenich-Bax, E., *Israels Konfrontation mit den letzten Boten der Weisheit* (MThA 21; Altenberge: Oros, 1993).

Sloan, R. B., *The Favorable Year of the Lord. A Study of Jubilary Theology in the Gospel of Luke* (Austin, TX: Scholars, 1977).

Smith, J. Z., *Drudgery Divine: On the Comparison of Early Chistianity and the Religions of Late Antiquity* (London & Chicago: School of Oriental and African Studies & Chicago University Press, 1990).

Smith, M., 'Zealots and Sicarii: Their Origin and Relations', *HTR* 64 (1971) 1–19.

Soarez Prabhu, G. M., *The Formula Quotations in the Infancy Narrative of Matthew* (AnB 63; Rome: Biblical Institute Press, 1976).

Stählin, G., ὀργή (NT), *TWNT* V, 419–48.

Stanesby, D., *Science, Reason and Religion* (London & New York: Routledge, 1988).

Stanton, G. N., 'On the Christology of Q', in B. Lindars & S. S. Smalley (eds), *Christ and Spirit in the New Testament* (FS C. F. D. Moule; Cambridge University Press, 1973) 27–42.

— 'Aspects of Early Christian–Jewish Polemic and Apologetic', *NTS* 31 (1985) 377–92.

— *A Gospel for a New People. Studies in Matthew* (Edinburgh: T. & T. Clark, 1992).

Steck, O. H., *Israel und das gewaltsame Geschick der Propheten* (WMANT 23; Neukirchen-Vluyn: Neukirchener, 1967).

Stegemann, W., 'Wanderradikalismus im Urchristentum? Historische und theologische Auseinandersetzung mit einer interessanten These', in W. Schottroff & W. Stegemann, *Der Gott der kleinen Leute* (München: Chr. Kaiser, 1979) 94–120.

Stoldt, H. H., *History and Criticism of the Marcan Hypothesis* (ET Edinburgh: T. & T. Clark, 1980).

Strecker, G., *Der Weg der Gerechtigkeit* (FRLANT 82; Göttingen: Vandenhoeck & Ruprecht, 1962).

— 'Die Makarismen der Bergpredigt', *NTS* 17 (1971) 255–75.

— 'Die Antithesen der Bergpredigt', *ZNW* 69 (1978) 36–72.

Streeter, B. H., 'St Mark's Knowledge and Use of Q', in Sanday (ed.), *Oxford Studies*, 165–84.

— 'The Literary Evolution of the Gospels', in Sanday (ed.), *Oxford Studies*, 210–27.

— *The Four Gospels* (London: Macmillan, 1924).

Stuhlmacher, P., *Das paulinische Evangelium* (FRLANT 95; Göttingen: Vandenhoeck & Ruprecht, 1968).

Suggs, M. J., *Wisdom, Christology and Law in Matthew's Gospel* (Cambridge: Harvard University Press, 1970).

Tannehill, R. C., 'The Mission of Jesus according to Luke iv 16–30', in W. Eltester (ed.), *Jesus in Nazareth* (BZNW 40; Berlin: de Gruyter, 1972) 51–75.

— *The Sword of His Mouth* (Missoula: Scholars, 1975).

— *The Narrative Unity of Luke–Acts* (Philadelphia: Fortress, 1986).

Taylor, V., 'The Order of Q', *JTS* 4 (1953) 27–31.

— 'The Original Order of Q', in A. J. B. Higgins (ed.), *New Testament Essays. Studies in Memory of T. W. Manson* (Manchester University Press, 1959) 95–118.

Theissen, G., 'Wanderradikalismus. Literatursoziologische Aspekte der Überlieferung von Worten Jesu im Urchristentum', *ZThK* 70 (1973) 245–71 (= *Studien*, 79–105).

— '"Wir haben alles verlassen" (Mc. X.28). Nachfolge und soziale Entwurzelung in der jüdisch-palästinischen Gesellschaft des 1.Jahrhunderts n.Ch.', *NovT* 19 (1977) 161–96 (= *Studien*, 106–41).

— *The First Followers of Jesus. A Sociological Analysis of the Earliest Christianity* (ET London: SCM, 1978).

— *Studien zur Soziologie des Urchristentums* (WUNT 19; Tübingen: Mohr, 1979).

— *The Social Setting of Pauline Christianity* (ET Edinburgh: T. & T. Clark, 1982).

— *Lokalkolorit und Zeitgeschichte in den Evangelien* (NTOA 8; Göttingen & Freiburg: Vandenhoeck & Ruprecht & Universitätsverlag, 1989). ET *The Gospels in Context: Social and Political History in the Synoptic Tradition* (Edinburgh: T. & T. Clark, 1992).

— *Social Reality and the Early Christians* (Edinburgh: T. & T. Clark, 1993).

Tödt, H. E., *Der Menschensohn in der synoptishen Überlieferung* (Gütersloh: Gerd Mohn, 1959); ET *The Son of Man in the Synoptic Tradition* (London: SCM, 1965).

Tuckett, C. M., 'Luke 4, Isaiah and Q', in Delobel (ed.), *LOGIA*, 343–354.

— *The Revival of the Griesbach Hypothesis* (SNTSMS 44; Cambridge University Press, 1983).

— '1 Corinthians and Q', *JBL* 102 (1983) 607–19.

— 'The Beatitudes: A Source-Critical Study', *NovT* 25 (1983) 193–207.

Tuckett, C. M., 'On the Relationship between Matthew and Luke', *NTS* 30 (1984) 130–42.

— (ed.), *Synoptic Studies. The Ampleforth Conferences of 1982 and 1983* (JSNTSS 7; Sheffield: JSOT Press, 1984).

— *Nag Hammadi and the Gospel Tradition* (Edinburgh: T. & T. Clark, 1986).

— 'Deuteronomy 21,23 and Paul's Conversion', in A. Vanhoye (ed.), *L'Apôtre Paul. Personnalité, Style et Conception du Ministère* (BETL 73; Leuven University Press & Peeters, 1986) 345–50.

— *Reading the New Testament* (London: SPCK, 1987).

— 'Thomas and the Synoptics', *NovT* 30 (1988) 132–57 .

— 'A Cynic Q?', *Biblica* 70 (1989) 349–76.

— 'Q, Prayer and the Kingdom', *JTS* 40 (1989) 367–76.

— 'Synoptic Tradition in the Didache', in J. M. Sevrin (ed.), *The New Testament in Early Christianity* (BETL 86; Leuven University Press & Peeters, 1989) 197–230.

— 'Response to the Two Gospel Hypothesis', in Dungan (ed.), *Interrelations*, 47–62.

— 'Q and Thomas: Evidence of a Primitive "Wisdom Gospel"?', *ETL* 67 (1991) 346–60.

— 'On the Stratification of Q', *Semeia* 55 (1991) 213–22.

— 'The Temptation Narrative in Q', in Van Segbroek et al (eds), *The Four Gospels 1992*, 479–507.

— 'The Minor Agreements and Textual Criticism', in G. Strecker (ed.), *Minor Agreements* (GTA 50; Göttingen: Vandenhoeck & Ruprecht, 1993) 119–43.

— 'The Son of Man in Q', in M. C. de Boer (ed.), *From Jesus to John* (FS M. de Jonge; Sheffield Academic Press, 1993) 196–215.

— 'Mark and Q', in Focant (ed.), *Synoptic Gospels*, 149–76.

— 'Les Pharisiens avant 70 et le Nouveau Testament', in D. Marguerat (ed.), *Juifs et Chrétiens au premier siècle: La déchirure* (Geneva: Labor et Fides, 1996, forthcoming).

Turner, M., 'Jesus and the Spirit in Lucan Perspective', *TynBull* 32 (1981) 3–42.

— 'The Spirit and the Power of Jesus' Miracles in the Lucan Conception', *NovT* 33 (1991) 124–52.

— 'The Spirit of Prophecy and the Power of Authoritative Preaching in Luke–Acts: A Question of Origins', *NTS* 38 (1992) 66–88.

Turner, N., *Grammatical Insights into the New Testament* (Edinburgh: T. & T. Clark, 1965).

— 'Q in Recent Thought', *ExpT* 80 (1969) 324–8.

Unnik, W. C. van, 'Die Motivierung der Feindesliebe in Lukas VI 32–35', *NovT* 8 (1966) 288–300.

Uro, R., *Sheep among the Wolves: A Study of the Mission Instructions of Q* (Helsinki: Suomalainen Tiedeakatemia, 1987).

Vaage, L. E., *Q: The Ethos and Ethics of an Itinerant Radicalism* (Ph.D. Dissertation, Claremont, 1987).

— 'The Son of Man Sayings in Q', *Semeia* 55 (1991) 103–29.

— 'Q and Cynicism: On Comparison and Social Identity', in Piper (ed.), *The Gospel Behind the Gospels*, 199–229.

— *Galilean Upstarts. Jesus' First Followers according to Q* (Valley Forge: Trinity International Press, 1994).

Vaage, L. E. & Kloppenborg, J. S., 'Early Christianity, Q and Jesus: The Sayings Gospel and Method in the Study of Christian Origins', *Semeia* 55 (1991) 1–14.

Van Segbroek, F., Tuckett, C. M., Van Belle, G. & Verheyden, J. (eds.), *The Four Gospels 1992* (BETL 100; FS for F. Neirynck; Leuven University Press & Peeters, 1992).

Vassiliadis, P., 'The Nature and Extent of the Q-Document', *NovT* 20 (1978) 49–73.

— 'Did Q Exist?', Ἐκκλησία καὶ Θεολογία 1 (1980) 287–328.

Vermes, G., *Jesus the Jew* (London: Collins, 1973).

Vielhauer, Ph., 'Gottesreich und Menschensohn in der Verkündigung Jesu', *Aufsätze zum Neuen Testament* (München: Kaiser, 1965) 55–91 .

— 'Jesus und der Menschensohn', *Aufsätze zum Neuen Testament* (München: Kaiser, 1965) 92–140.

Vögtle, A., 'Der Spruch vom Jonaszeichen', in *Synoptische Studien* (FS A. Wikenhauser; München: Karl Zink, 1953) 230–77.

— 'Die Einladung zum großen Gastmahl und zum königlichen Hochzeitsmahl', *Das Evangelium und die Evangelien* (Düsseldorf: Patmos, 1971) 171–218.

— 'Bezeugt die Logienquelle die authentische Redeweise Jesu vom "Menschensohn"?', in Delobel (ed.), *LOGIA*, 77–99.

Walker, R., *Die Heilsgeschichte im ersten Evangelium* (FRLANT 91; Göttingen: Vandenhoeck & Ruprecht, 1967).

Walker, W. O., 'The State of the Synoptic Question', *Perkins Journal* 40 (1987) 14–19.

Walker, W. O., 'Nazareth: A Clue to Synoptic Relationships?' in E. P. Sanders (ed.), *Jesus, the Gospel and the Church* (FS W. R. Farmer; Macon: Mercer University Press, 1987) 105–18.

Wanke, J., 'Kommentarworte: Älteste Kommentierungen von Herrenworte', *BZ* 24 (1980) 208–33.

Watson, F. B., *Paul, Judaism and the Gentiles* (SNTSMS 56; Cambridge University Press, 1986).

Webb, R. L., *John the Baptizer and Prophet* (JSNTSS 62; Sheffield Academic Press, 1991).

Weder, H., *Die Gleichnisse Jesu als Metaphern* (FRLANT 120; Göttingen: Vandenhoeck & Ruprecht, 1984).

Wegner, U., *Der Hauptmann von Kafarnaum (Mt 7,28a; 8,5–10.13 par Lk 7,1–10). Ein Beitrag zur Q-Forschung* (WUNT 2.14; Tübingen: Mohr, 1985).

Weisse, C. H., *Die evangelische Geschichte, kritisch und philosophisch bearbeitet* (Leipzig: Breitkopf und Hartel, 1838).

— *Die Evangelienfrage in ihrem gegenwärtigen Stadium* (Leipzig: Breitkopf und Hartel, 1856).

Wellek, R. & Warren, A., *Theory of Literature* (Harmondsworth: Penguin, 1973).

Wellhausen, J., *Einleitung in die drei ersten Evangelien* (Berlin: Reimer, 1905, 1911[2]).

Wenham, J. W., *Redating Matthew, Mark & Luke* (London: Hodder & Stoughton, 1991).

Wernle, P., *Die synoptische Frage* (Leipzig & Tübingen: Mohr, 1899).

Westerholm, S., *Jesus and Scribal Authority* (Lund: Gleerup, 1978).

Wild, R. A., 'The Encounter between Pharisaic and Christian Judaism: Some Early Gospel Evidence', *NovT* 27 (1985) 105–24.

Wilson, S. G., *Luke and the Law* (SNTSMS 50; Cambridge University Press, 1983).

Wink, W., *John the Baptist in the Gospel Tradition* (SNTSMS 7; Cambridge University Press, 1968).

Witherington, B., *Jesus the Sage. The Pilgrimage of Wisdom* (Edinburgh: T. & T. Clark, 1994).

Woude, A. S. van der & de Jonge, M., '11QMelchizedek and the New Testament', *NTS* 12 (1966) 301–26.

Zeitlin, S., 'Zealots and Sicarii', *JBL* 82 (1961) 395–9.

Zeller, D., 'Das Logion Mt 8,11f/Lk 13,28f und das Motiv der Völkerwallfahrt', *BZ* 15 (1971) 222–37; 16 (1972) 84–93.

Zeller, D., 'Der Zusammenhang der Eschatologie in der Logienquelle', in P. Fiedler & D. Zeller (eds.), *Gegenwart und kommendes Reich* (FS A. Vögtle; Stuttgart: Katholisches Bibelwerk, 1977) 67–77.

— 'Die Bildlogik des Gleichnisses Mt 11:16/Lk 7:31', *ZNW* 68 (1977) 252–7.

— *Die weisheitliche Mahnsprüche bei den Synoptikern* (FzB 17; Würzburg: Echter, 1977).

— 'Die Versuchung Jesu in der Logienquelle', *TTZ* 89 (1980) 61–73.

— 'Redaktionsprozesse und wechselnder "Sitz im Leben" beim Q-Material', in Delobel (ed.), *LOGIA*, 395–409.

— Kommentar zur Logienquelle (Stuttgart: Katholisches Bibelwerk, 1984).

— 'Entrückung zur Ankunft als Menschensohn (Lk 13,34f.; 11,29f.)' in *A Cause de l'Evangile* (FS J. Dupont; Paris: Cerf, 1985) 513–30.

— 'Eine weisheitliche Grundschrift in der Logienquelle?', in Van Segbroek et al (eds), *The Four Gospels 1992*, 389–401.

Index of Modern Authors

Index of References

(More extended treatment of Q passages are denoted by page references in italics.)